Teaching Students with Special Needs in Inclusive Settings

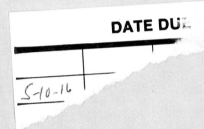

Teaching Students with Special Needs in Inclusive Settings

Tom E. C. Smith
UNIVERSITY OF ARKANSAS AT LITTLE ROCK

Edward A. Polloway
LYNCHBURG COLLEGE

James R. Patton
UNIVERSITY OF TEXAS

Carol A. Dowdy
UNIVERSITY OF ALABAMA AT BIRMINGHAM

ALLYN AND BACON
Boston London Toronto Sydney Tokyo Singapore

Senior editor: Ray Short
Production editor: Deborah Brown
Editorial assistant: Christine M. Shaw
Cover administrator: Linda Knowles
Composition buyer: Linda Cox
Manufacturing buyer: Louise Richardson
Marketing representative: Ellen Mann
Editorial-production service: P. M. Gordon Associates
Text designer: Rita Naughton
Cover designer: Susan Paradise

Library of Congress Cataloging-in-Publication Data

Teaching students with special needs in inclusive settings / Tom E. C.
    Smith ... [et al.].
        p.   cm.
    Includes index and bibliographical references.
    ISBN 0–205–14653–8 (hardcover)
    1. Mainstreaming in education.   2. Special education.
3. Classroom management.   I. Smith, Tom E. C.
LC3965.T43   1995
371.9'046—dc20   94–34735
                                                          CIP

Printed in the United States of America

10 9 8 7 6 5 4 3 2 1   99 98 97 96 95 94

For Bonnie, Jake, and Alex
Carolyn and Lyndsay
Joy and Kimi
Jim, Cameron, and Meredith

Contents

Chapter 3   Inclusion Models   64

Chapter 4   Teaching Students with Learning Disabilities   96

Chapter 9   Communication Disorders   **248**

Chapter 10   Teaching Students Who Are Gifted   **286**

Chapter 11 Teaching Students at Risk 318

Chapter 12 Classroom Organization and Management 348

Preface

Services for students with disabilities have evolved significantly over the past two decades. Before the passage of federal legislation in the mid-1970s, few students with disabilities were provided services in public schools. For those students who were in public special education programs, services were most often provided in segregated classrooms with limited or no opportunities for interaction with nondisabled students. With the mandate to provide a free appropriate public education in the least restrictive environment for all school-age students with disabilities came a significant improvement in services for these students. The result was the rapid growth in special education programs and the resource room as the service model of choice. This educational model allowed most students with disabilities opportunities to interact with their nondisabled peers, at least on a limited basis.

The normalization movement continued to press for more integrated services for students with disabilities in public school programs. As a result, many consumers of special education services, as well as many professionals, began to believe that the dichotomous educational system, one for nondisabled students and one for those with disabilities, was not the best way of meeting the needs of students. Rather than pulling students with disabilities out of general education classrooms and providing specialized instruction in resource rooms, advocates of inclusion proposed that all students with disabilities, including those with severe problems, should be educated in general educational programs.

The authors of this textbook agree with many of the tenets of the inclusion movement. The fact that many students with disabilities can achieve successfully in general education classroom settings has been shown through many research projects. Despite these findings, we strongly believe that in order for the inclusion movement to be as successful as possible, general education faculty and staff must be trained in meeting the diverse needs of students with disabilities. Special education teachers must also be trained in the inclusion model in order to provide appropriate services to students in general education classrooms. In addition to the inclusion movement having a positive impact on many students with disabilities, another critical reason for our supporting this movement is the belief that all students who need special interventions will more likely receive them in inclusive schools. Students will no longer have to meet the restrictive criteria for eligibility for special education services in order to receive special attention. In the current system, many of these students who fail to meet eligibility criteria for special education services are denied appropriate educational programs.

It is our strong opinion that students with disabilities and other special needs must be provided with appropriate education programs, not on the basis of clinical classification or overriding philosophy, but on the basis of their individual educational needs. By providing programs based on the individual strengths and weaknesses of students, as well as their long-term goals and objectives, our educational system will better serve its students. Thus, while we support the inclusion movement, we still believe that individual student needs should drive educational programs.

The textbook is organized into fifteen chapters, with each of the major categorical disability groups addressed in individual chapters. Although we do not think that categorical classification is necessary to provide appropriate services, the reality is that many schools and educators will continue to use a categorical model to identify which students are in need of special education. Therefore, the categorical orientation is included in this book to help prepare teachers, both general and special education, to meet the needs of all students in their schools.

In addition to chapters on separate disability categories, chapters on students who are gifted and those who are at risk are also included to provide information that will be needed in order to meet the needs of all students in inclusive settings. Separate chapters on behavior management, elementary curricula, secondary curricula, and working with families are also included to provide teachers with a sound background of practical applications that can be used effectively in inclusive classrooms.

A special feature of the text is the series of boxes that are found in each chapter. These boxes present practical, easy-to-use suggestions for providing services to students with disabilities. Each chapter has a box on inclusion, which provides suggestions for promoting the inclusion of students, a box on technology, and a box on multicultural issues, which presents information useful in meeting the multicultural needs of students in our schools. In addition to these three types of boxes, a fourth box presents information unique to the content of the particular chapter. The thematic boxes are designated with particular icons.

Terms that are set in **boldface** in the text can be found in the Glossary section at the end of the book.

 represents inclusion boxes,

 designates technology boxes, and

 is used for multicultural boxes,

 depicts boxes unique to each chapter.

Acknowledgments

We would like to gratefully acknowledge numerous individuals who were instrumental in the development of this text. At the top of our list are all the members of our families who were supportive during the textbook development. Also, the editorial and production staff at Allyn & Bacon—in particular, Ray Short and his assistant, Christine Shaw, and Deborah Brown—deserve a strong note of appreciation. Ellen Mann, marketing, and Susan Finkelstein of P. M. Gordon Associates also deserve a strong "thank you." And finally, we would like to thank all those who provided professional reviews of the manuscript: Darryl Bauer, Marshall University; Joan Forsgren-White, Utah State University; Gayle L. Nash, Eastern Michigan University; William E. Davis, University of Maine at Orono; Karen N. Janssen, Eastern Kentucky University; Patricia A. Connard, The Ohio State University; and F. Richard Olenchak, The University of Alabama. Their reviews made the textbook significantly better.

TECS, EAP, JRP, CAD

Teaching Students with Special Needs in Inclusive Settings

CHAPTER 1

Inclusive Education:
An Introduction

Introduction

The public education system in the United States is unique among many industrial countries. It attempts to provide 12 years of equal educational opportunity to all children at the expense of taxpayers. In doing so, it does not simply cater to students who are from wealthy homes or who have special talents and gifts in academic endeavors, or even to just those students who are considered "typical" in their learning abilities and behaviors. Rather, the public education system serves many different kinds of children, ranging from students who learn easily to those who have difficulty; from those with appropriate behaviors to those with behavior problems; from those with normal physical and sensory skills to those with deficits in these areas; from those who successfully achieve through their public school years to those who drop out of school; and from those who are from the majority culture to those from minority cultures.

Including all students in a free public education system is a philosophical position based on the United States Constitution. The movement to establish a free educational system, the Common School Movement, was led by Horace Mann in the mid-nineteenth century (Smith, 1990). The purpose of providing equal educational opportunity was an educated citizenry to ensure democracy, a concept advocated as early as Colonial times by Thomas Jefferson, who supported public education for poor children as well as those with family resources (Stainback, Stainback, Courtnage, & Jaben, 1985).

As a result of providing education for all children, teachers in today's public schools must provide instruction and other educational services to meet the needs of a very diverse student population. They must develop ways to serve as many students as possible in general education environments (Smith & Smith, 1989). Traditionally, the focus in teacher education programs for classroom teachers has been on teaching students who do not have learning or behavior problems. However, the reality is that today's teachers must be prepared to teach all kinds of students, including those who present special needs in classrooms. Teachers do not have the luxury of teaching only students who learn easily and behave in a manner the teachers deem appropriate based on their own cultural standards; they must be prepared to deal effectively with all kinds of students.

Although the tenets of public education for all children were in place by the beginning of the twentieth century, it took several major changes to create a system that enables children from some groups to access the educational system. Initially, girls were excluded from publicly supported schools. Many of our founding fathers thought that education was primarily important for males. Girls were considered potential mothers and wives, with little need for formal education. The result was a system that excluded many girls from the educational system. By the early twentieth century, this barrier had been removed in most instances and girls were afforded access to public schools.

Although students from minority cultures were provided free education in the early 1900s, their right to equal access to schools was not provided until the latter 1950s and 1960s. Prior to the United States Supreme Court ruling in the *Brown v. Board of Education, Topeka, Kansas* case in 1954, minority children were educated in "separate but equal" schools. The ruling in the *Brown* case stated that children could not be denied access to any public schools on the basis of race. This decision basically ended any legal support for separate but equal schools for different cultural groups, thus legally dismantling segregated public education (McCarthy & Cambron-McCabe, 1987).

The final group of students to seek and gain equal access to public education were those classified as disabled. Students with **disabilities** were traditionally denied access to public education programs. Prior to federal legislation that was passed in the mid-1970s, many schools simply told parents of students with disabilities that the school did not have programs for their children. The only recourses available for most parents were private educational programs or programs specifically designed for "handi-capped" students. In many cases, parents paid for these educational programs out of their own resources.

In some schools, students with **physical disabilities** or **mental retardation** were provided services, but these services were nearly always in self-contained, isolated class-rooms. These students rarely interacted with nondisabled students, and their teach-ers did not routinely come into contact with other teachers in the school. The programs that did exist, in addition to being isolating, were also very small. The result was that only a very few students could be served.

The reasons for these limited, segregated services are many; however, they were primarily the result of an evolving public education system that attempted to provide a free education for all children. Between 1850 and 1975 the public education system in this country evolved into one where compulsory education was enacted. In try-ing to meet the needs of as many students as possible, the school system addressed the needs of the most homogeneous group of students. Students who did not exhibit sim-ilar learning needs and capabilities, based on chronological age, or who disrupted the educational system for the majority of students, were simply excluded entirely or seg-regated into special classes. The result was the development of a **dual system** of edu-cation, one for the majority of students, and one for those with disabilities and other special needs (Knoll & Meyer, 1987).

Since the mid-1970s, services to students with disabilities have changed dramati-cally. Not only are more appropriate services provided by schools, they are frequently provided in **resource rooms** and general education classrooms by collaborating spe-cial education and classroom teachers (Baum & Duffelmeyer, 1989–1990). Many different activities occurred to reach this point, including parental advocacy, legisla-tion, and litigation. These factors will be discussed later in the chapter. As stated by Madeline Will, when she was Assistant Secretary for the Office of Special Education and Rehabilitative Services, U.S. Department of Education,

> It is important that the nation's schools prepare all students to identify, analyze, and resolve problems as they arise; to increase their ability to respond and cope in a flexible manner with change; to develop character, which serves as the firm basis for sound judgment and

considered decision making; and to enter the community as informed and educated citizens who are capable of living and working as independent and productive adults. (Will, 1984, p. 413)

Students with Special Needs

Many students do not fit the mold of the "typical" student. These include those with identified disabilities, those who are classified as gifted and talented, and those who are **"at risk"** for developing problems. It has been estimated that slightly over 11% of school-age children, or approximately 4.9 million students, are classified as disabled (U.S. Department of Education, 1993). Another 10% to 20% experience learning and behavior problems but not significantly enough to be classified as disabled (Will, 1984). Still another group of students who require special attention are those at risk for developing problems. These students include those who are potential dropouts (Cosden, 1990), those from minority cultures, those who speak English only as a second language, students from low-income homes, and those who abuse drugs or alcohol. Students who become pregnant, those from single-parent homes (Johnson, Pugach, & Devlin, 1990), and students considered "socially maladjusted" are also at risk for developing problems (Nelson, Rutherford, Center, & Walker, 1991). Adding all these students together, plus those students who obviously need assistance but do not fit into any distinct group, results in a total group that approximates half of all students in public schools. Although many of these students do not fit into the specific classification as "disabled" and are therefore not eligible for special education services, school personnel cannot afford to ignore the special problems of these students (Cosden, 1990; Greer, 1991; Hill, 1991).

The diversity among students in public schools represents the "norm" rather than the exception (Johnson et al., 1990). If our public schools are to be effective, school personnel must address the needs of each of these groups. They must be able to identify and help develop and implement programs. A first step for classroom teachers is to understand the types of students they need to serve.

Students with Disabilities

One of the largest groups of students with special needs in the public school system, and the most visible, is those formally classified as disabled. Students with disabilities are defined as those who exhibit one of several specific conditions that result in their need for special education and related services to facilitate academic, social, and emotional development. General disability categories include cognitive deficits, processing deficits, emotional and behavioral problems, physical disorders, sensory problems, and health-related disorders.

Within the general areas are many different specific disabilities that can affect the success of students in school. Most states and local school districts adhere to the specific disability categories included in federal mandating legislation. These include

♦ Mental retardation
♦ Learning disabilities

- ◆ Serious emotional disturbance
- ◆ Visual impairment
- ◆ Hearing impairment
- ◆ Speech impairment
- ◆ Other health impairment
- ◆ Orthopedic impairment
- ◆ Traumatic brain injury
- ◆ Autism

Table 1.1 reveals the number of students in each disability category receiving special education services in public schools.

School personnel need to be aware that many different types of students are found in these ten categories. For example, the broad disability area **"other health impaired"** includes students with cardiac problems, asthma, and sickle cell anemia, to name a very few. Even the category of learning disabilities is comprised of an extremely heterogeneous group of students. The fact that disability categories are comprised of different types of students makes simple conclusions about certain "types" of students impossible.

TABLE 1.1   **Disability of Students Ages 6–21 Served under IDEA, Part B and Chapter 1 of ESEA (SOP): Number and Percentage, School Year 1991–1992**

Disability	IDEA, Part B		Chapter 1 (SOP)		Total	
	Number	Percent[a]	Number	Percent[a]	Number	Percent[a]
Specific learning disabilities	2,218,948	51.3	30,047	16.6	2,248,995	49.9
Speech or language impairments	990,016	22.9	10,655	5.9	1,000,671	22.2
Mental retardation	500,986	11.6	53,261	29.3	554,247	12.3
Serious emotional disturbance	363,877	8.4	36,793	20.2	400,670	8.9
Multiple disabilities	80,655	1.9	17,747	9.8	98,402	2.2
Hearing impairments	43,690	1.0	17,073	9.4	60,763	1.3
Orthopedic impairments	46,222	1.1	5,468	3.0	51,690	1.1
Other health impairments	56,401	1.3	2,479	1.4	58,880	1.3
Visual impairments	18,296	0.4	5,873	3.2	24,169	0.5
Deaf-blindness	773	0.0	650	0.4	1,423	0.0
Autism	3,555	0.0	1,653	0.9	5,208	0.1
Traumatic brain injury	285	0.0	45	0.0	330	0.0
All disabilities	4,323,704	100.0	181,744	100.0	4,505,448	100.0

[a]Percentages sum within columns.
Source: 15th Annual Report to Congress on the Implementation of IDEA (1993), Washington, DC: U.S. Department of Education, p. 5.

Another problem in learning about the disabilities experienced by students in schools is that students who need special assistance do not all fit neatly into some of the categories. Also, some definitions of disability are very different from, and often much broader than, the one used by the U.S. Department of Education. For example, the **Americans with Disabilities Act (ADA)** defines disabilities in a much broader fashion, thereby expanding the group of students who might be included in a disability category. Although school personnel must adhere to the requirements and criteria established by the U.S. Department of Education, they must remember that many students who are not eligible for classification as disabled still need assistance if they are to succeed in educational programs.

The majority of students with disabilities experience mild disabilities and are included in general education classrooms for at least a portion of each school day. A smaller number of students, with more severe disabilities, are more likely educated in segregated, special education environments. However, even some of these students with more severe disabilities may also be included in general education classrooms part of the time (Hamre-Nietupski et al., 1989; Thousand & Villa, 1990; York & Vandercook, 1991). Most classroom teachers will be directly involved in educating students with disabilities. The following section provides information on each of the major disability categories recognized in most school districts.

Cognitive Deficits.   Students who experience **cognitive deficits** are generally classified as having mental retardation. In general, these students experience general problems with learning, memory, problem solving, adaptive behavior, and social skills (Epstein, Polloway, Patton, & Foley, 1986; Beirne-Smith, Patton, & Ittenbach, 1994). Students with mental retardation are usually identified through intelligence tests and measures of adaptive behavior. By definition, these individuals score less than 70 on intelligence (IQ) tests and have concurrent deficits in adaptive behavior (American Association on Mental Retardation, 1992). During the 1991–1992 school year, more than 500,000 students in grades K–12 were classified as having mental retardation (U.S. Department of Education, 1993).

Processing Deficits.   Students with **processing problems** are generally classified as having **learning disabilities.** Although the category is difficult to define (Swanson, 1991; Kavale, Forness, & Lorsbach, 1991; Stanovich, 1991), in general, the achievement of students with learning disabilities is not commensurate with their abilities. They have average to above average intellectual abilities but below average achievement in one or more areas (Swanson, 1991). Unlike students with mental retardation who perform below average in all areas, students with learning disabilities frequently do well in some tasks and poorly in others. While the cause of learning disabilities is unclear, the assumption, although controversial, is that there is a neurological dysfunction that causes the learning disability (Hynd, Marshall, & Gonzalez, 1991).

Students with learning disabilities have only been served in special education programs since the 1970s. Prior to that time, a few students classified as minimally brain injured or minimally brain damaged may have been provided special education services, but the number of students in this group was very small. The growth of this category primarily occurred during the 1980s. Currently, learning disabilities are the predominant type of disability found among public school students; approximately 2.2 million students were classified as having a learning disability during the 1991–1992 school year (U.S. Department of Education, 1993).

Emotional and Behavior Problems.   Students with emotional and behavior problems are those whose inappropriate behaviors or emotions result in disruptions for themselves or others in their environment. Although not as controversial as the learning disability category, this entire category of disabilities is controversial, beginning with terminology and definition (Kauffman & Wong, 1991; Peacock Hill Working Group, 1991). The federal government uses the term ***serious emotional disturbance*** as the label for this group of students. The Council for Children with Behavior Disorders (CCBD), a division of the Council for Exceptional Children (CEC), the leading special education professional organization, uses the term *emotional behavior disorders* (EBD) to identify the group. CCBD believes that this label is a more appropriate identifier for students exhibiting these problems. There are several reasons why CCBD favors the term *emotional behavior disorders,* including these (Huntze, 1985):

- ◆ It does not indicate a specific cause.
- ◆ It does not suggest a particular intervention approach.
- ◆ It better reflects students served in special education classrooms.
- ◆ It is less stigmatizing than the label "seriously emotionally disturbed."

Still another problem with the label used is that the terms *seriously emotionally disturbed* and *emotional behavior disordered* are primarily used by educators. Mental health professionals, such as psychologists, psychiatrists, and others who work with these children, use a completely different set of labels to identify them.

Sensory Problems.   Some students have problems with sensory skills, their visual or auditory abilities. Since the majority of information provided by teachers is presented orally or visually, deficits in sensory skills can result in significant problems. **Visual impairment** includes two subcategories—**blind** and **low vision.** Students who are classified as blind are unable to read using print, regardless how much the print is enlarged. Those with low vision experience vision problems but are able to read print when it is enlarged by various degrees. Children who must learn to read using Braille create more problems for classroom teachers than those with low vision. Many low-vision students are capable of success in general education classrooms as long as materials are enlarged for them. Braille students, on the other hand, require more extensive intervention services and specialists to teach Braille skills.

Students who experience hearing problems are also divided into two groups. **Deaf** students are those who have a hearing loss of 90 decibels or more: those classified as **hard of hearing** have decibel losses between 26 and 89. Most hard-of-hearing students can be accommodated in general education classes with the assistance of amplification devices to facilitate hearing. These students do not need to use an alternative communication method, such as sign language. Deaf students, however, may require sign language or another alternative communication mode and may require the presence of a sign language interpreter in order to be successfully included in general education classrooms.

Physical Problems.   Some students have intact sensory, processing, and cognitive skills, but have problems with their physical abilities. Physical problems experienced by some students include **cerebral palsy, spina bifida, muscular dystrophy,** respiratory problems, polio, amputation, and other problems that result in physical problems of mobility and arm and hand use. For students who manifest these kinds of problems, the primary consideration is physical accessibility and accommodations for problems with writing and manipulation. Commonsense accommodations can be used effectively with many of these students in general education classrooms. Approximately 1.1% of all students receiving special education services are classified as physically disabled (U.S. Department of Education, 1993).

Health Problems.   Problems related to health can also result in difficulties in school. Federal legislation refers to these students as **"other health impaired."** Students classified as other health impaired present a variety of conditions, including

- ◆ Acquired immune deficiency syndrome (AIDS)
- ◆ Diabetes
- ◆ Cystic fibrosis
- ◆ Asthma
- ◆ Sickle cell anemia
- ◆ Hemophilia
- ◆ Cardiac problems
- ◆ Arthritis
- ◆ Cancer
- ◆ Epilepsy

Approximately 1.3% of students in special education suffer from health problems (U.S. Department of Education, 1993).

The extent of special services for students with health problems will vary significantly, depending on the exact nature of the problems. For many students with health problems, stamina and maintaining sufficient good health to remain in school are the primary concerns. Therefore, teachers must provide accommodations that enable this group of students to stay in class as much as possible. Another primary concern for teachers when dealing with students who are experiencing health problems is monitoring. Teachers need to be aware of the side effects of medication, symptoms suggesting changes in health conditions, and specific actions to take in time of medical crises.

Traumatic Brain Injury.   **Traumatic brain injury (TBI)** is one of two disability categories recognized by the U.S. Department of Education in 1990. TBI can be defined as

> an insult to the brain, not of a degenerative or congenital nature but caused by an external physical force, that may produce a diminished or altered state of consciousness, which results in impairment of cognitive abilities or physical functioning. It can also result in the

disturbance of behavioral or emotional functioning. These impairments may be either temporary or permanent and cause partial or total functional disability or psychosocial maladjustment. (Savage, 1988, p. 2)

Although TBI has been newly classified as a disability that results in eligibility for special education services under Public Law 94–142, students with TBI have likely been previously served in special education programs under different categories, such as mental retardation, learning disabilities, or emotional problems. The specific category children with TBI were served under was determined by the manifested characteristics. For example, if a student with TBI manifested cognitive deficits resulting in meeting the criteria for services in the category of mental retardation, the student was served under this category. Students with TBI that resulted in processing disorders were served as learning disabled, and those with behavior problems were likely served as emotionally disturbed.

Autism.   **Autism** was also recognized as a disabling condition by the U.S. Department of Education in 1990. Autism can be described as a lifelong and severely incapacitating disability that manifests itself within the first three years of a child's life (Knoblock, 1982). Although the degree of autism and specific characteristics differ among children, typical characteristics include

- Abnormal ways of relating to people, objects, and events
- Unusually high or low activity levels
- Insistence that the environment and routine remain unchanged
- Little imaginative play; use of toys and objects in an unconventional manner
- Severe impairment of social interaction development
- Repetitive movements such as rocking and spinning, head banging, and hand twisting

(National Information Center for Children and Youth with Handicaps [NICHY], 1990, p. 1)

Children with autism have traditionally been excluded from general education classroom programs. However, when a highly structured classroom environment can be maintained, these students frequently do well in these settings (NICHY, 1990). When placed in general education classroom settings, children with autism have a tendency to model the appropriate behaviors of their chronological age peers, rather than the inappropriate behaviors they may observe when isolated in a self-contained classroom that only contains children with autism.

Students Classified as Gifted and Talented

In addition to some students having disabilities that result in impaired learning or behaviors, some students differ from their peers by having above-average intelligence and learning abilities. These students, classified as **gifted and talented,** were traditionally defined and identified using intelligence quotient test scores (IQ scores). IQ scores of 120, 130, 140, or higher were used as the primary criterion for identifying students as gifted and talented. Current definitions used to identify gifted and talented children are much broader. Although no one definition is accepted by all groups, most focus on students who are capable of making significant contributions to society in a variety of areas, including academic endeavors, creativity, mechanical skills, motor skills, and skills in the fine arts.

Students "at Risk" for School Problems

Some students who do not fit into a specific disability category or have an above average capacity to achieve also present problems for the educational system. These students, classified as being "at risk," manifest characteristics that could easily lead to learning and behavior problems (Cosden, 1990; Greer, 1991; Heward & Orlansky, 1992; Johnson et al., 1990). Students considered at risk include

◆ Potential dropouts
◆ Drug and alcohol abusers
◆ Students from minority cultures
◆ Students from low-income homes
◆ Teenagers who become pregnant
◆ Students who speak English as a second language

These students may present unique problems for teachers who attempt to meet their educational needs in general education classrooms. Since students in the at-risk group

Poverty in the United States remains a major problem in our society and increases the risk factor for children having problems.

are not eligible for special education services, classroom teachers bear the primary responsibility for their educational programs, which need to be modified to meet their needs.

Current Services for Students with Special Needs

Most students with special needs receive the majority of their education in general education classrooms from classroom teachers. For students who are gifted or at risk, this is routine. Students in these two groups have always remained in general education classes for most of their instruction. However, students with disabilities were historically served in segregated special education classrooms; they rarely interacted with nondisabled students and classroom teachers.

The process of including these students into general education classrooms has been called **mainstreaming, or inclusion.** Inclusion can be defined as the physical, sociological, and instructional inclusion of students with special needs into general education classrooms for the majority of the school day. Inclusion is more than merely physically locating students with special needs in classrooms with their chronological age peers: it requires that they be included with all aspects of the classroom and their educational needs met through services provided within the general education classroom.

Actions Leading to Inclusion of Students with Disabilities

Students with disabilities were traditionally taught in special classrooms or special, separate schools by special education teachers. During the years 1950 to 1970, the self-contained classroom became the primary setting for serving students with disabilities. This service model resulted in general education teachers and students rarely interacting with students in self-contained settings, thus adding to the isolation of students with disabilities. This segregated service approach gave way to mainstreaming students with disabilities into general education classrooms either full-time or for part of each school day. The process of mainstreaming did not just happen but came about as a result of several factors. These included the civil rights movement, federal and state legislation, litigation, and actions by advocacy groups.

The Civil Rights Movement.   Prior to the 1950s, students from minority racial groups were educated in "separate but equal" schools. Most towns had separate schools for African-American children and separate schools for white children. Often, Mexican-American and Asian children were educated in the "white" schools. The civil rights movement to eliminate discrimination based on racial differences emerged as a social force in the 1950s. This movement culminated in the 1960s with the dismantling of schools segregated on the basis of race. State and federal court cases and legislation mandated equal access to all schools by children from all backgrounds.

Parents of students with disabilities watched the civil rights movement achieve success. They soon realized that they could model the actions of civil rights groups and gain better services for their children. Using legislation, litigation, and advocacy,

Guidelines and Teaching Strategies

A number of general guidelines and possible teaching strategies can be gleaned from the discussion in this chapter. These are offered as vehicles to help teachers meet the special classroom needs of language-different students.

1. Avoid negative statements about the child's language or dialect, exercising particular caution in front of large groups. Rather than saying, "I don't understand you" or "You're not saying that right," offer a statement such as, "Could you say that in a different way to help me understand?"
2. Reinforce oral and written language production as it occurs naturally throughout the day. A first goal in working with language-different pupils is to maintain and subsequently increase their language output. Reinforcing desired productions will help ensure that this goal is reached.
3. During any formal language instruction period, work with five or fewer pupils so each has several chances to make an oral response. Working with a small group allows group members to see each other and permits the teacher to physically prompt and reinforce each student.
4. Set specific goals and objectives for language development just as you would for other instructional areas.
5. Reduce tension during language instruction by moving to a less formal part of the room. Arrange as relaxed an environment as possible so that pupils feel free to make oral and written contributions in the new language they are learning.
6. Encourage the learners to produce longer and more complex utterances. Develop and maintain systematic records showing each pupil's growth in language.
7. During language instruction encourage Standard and non-Standard English speakers to talk about language differences and to compare different language forms.
8. Involve people from the linguistically different community in the total school program as much as possible so these persons can share language experiences.

Source: Polloway, E. A., & Smith, T. E. C. (1992). *Language instruction for students with disabilities* (2nd ed.) (pp. 83–84). Denver, CO: Love Publishing. Used with permission.

they sought to gain equal opportunities for their children who had been denied access to public education solely on the basis of having a disability.

Legislation.   Probably the one factor that was most responsible for the inclusion of students with disabilities into general education classrooms was legislation, which was often enacted in response to litigation. Parents of students with disabilities noted that the civil rights legislation passed in the 1960s helped break down segregation barriers in schools. Therefore, they advocated for legislation that would have the same result for their children. In advocating for appropriate legislation, parents also noted that funds needed to be provided and teachers appropriately trained to meet the needs of students with disabilities.

The most important legislation to help students with disabilities access general education programs was Public Law 94–142, which was passed in 1975 and implemented in 1978. However, prior to the passage of this legislation, several other legislative acts helped pave the way. These included (Smith, Price, & Marsh, 1986)

1. *Public Law 83–531* (1954)   Provided funds for research in mental retardation. This was the first federal legislation that targeted mental retardation.
2. *Public Law 89–10* (1964)   Provided funds for educating disadvantaged students. Students with disabilities were often included in these programs.
3. *Public Law 89–313* (1965)   Provided funds for children in hospitals and institutions. It still provides a funding source for children educated in these settings.
4. *Public Law 91–230* (1969)   Consolidated federal programs for students with disabilities; recognized learning disabilities as a disability. This was the key to the rapid expansion of services for students classified as having a learning disability.
5. *Public Law 92–424* (1972)   Required that 10% of Head Start funds go to children with disabilities. The result was that many children with disabilities were included in Head Start programs.
6. *Section 504 of the Rehabilitation Act of 1973.*   This legislation was a civil rights statute for persons with disabilities. It applied to various entities that received federal funds, and prohibited discrimination based on the presence of a disability.
7. *Public Law 93–380* (1973)   Forerunner of PL 94–142; required services for students with disabilities. Many of the provisions of PL 93–380 were later incorporated in PL 94–142.

Public Law 94–142, the Education for All Handicapped Children Act (EHA), was the legislation that literally opened the doors of public schools and general education classrooms to students with disabilities. In fact, the basic intent of PL 94–142 was to provide equal educational opportunity for students with disabilities (Berres & Knoblock, 1987). The legislation required schools to seek out and implement appropriate educational services for all students with disabilities, regardless of the severity. Public Law 94–142 has many components that require schools to provide appropriate, individualized services to students with disabilities, and actively involve parents in the educational process. For general education teachers, the most important part of the legislation is the requirement that students with disabilities must be educated with their nondisabled peers as much as possible.

In the 1990 reauthorization of PL 94–142, the name of the legislation was changed from the Education for All Handicapped Children Act to the **Individuals**

with Disabilities Education Act (IDEA). There are many key components of PL 94–142. Table 1.2 briefly summarizes these key components and gives implications for general education classroom teachers.

Child Find   Public Law 94–142 requires schools to seek out students with disabilities. In order to meet this mandate, schools have conducted a number of activities, including the dissemination of child find posters, commercial and public television commercials, newspaper articles, and other widespread public relations campaigns. The first priority for services was for students with disabilities who had not received any services. Prior to passing PL 94–142, Congress noted that approximately 1 million school-age students with disabilities had been completely denied all public educational services.

Nondiscriminatory Assessment   Before students can be classified as disabled and determined to be eligible for special education services, they must be administered a comprehensive evaluation. The evaluation must not discriminate against students from minority cultural groups. The requirement for **nondiscriminatory assessment** resulted from evidence that certain norm-referenced, standardized tests are inherently discriminatory toward students from minority racial and low socioeconomic groups. Studies on this topic have revealed that many commonly used, norm-referenced tests place students from minority backgrounds at a distinct disadvantage because of their different cultural experiences (Smith et al., 1986). Teachers and other school personnel must be extremely cautious when interpreting standardized test scores for their students. The scores may not reflect an accurate estimate of the student's abilities.

TABLE 1.2   **Key Components of PL 94–142**

Provisions	Description
Least restrictive environment	Children are educated with nondisabled children as much as possible.
Individualized education program	All children served in special education must have an individualized education program (IEP).
Due process rights	Disabled children and their parents must be involved in decisions about special education.
Due process hearing	Parents and schools can request an impartial hearing if there is a conflict over special education services.
Nondiscriminatory assessment	Students must be given a comprehensive assessment that is nondiscriminatory in nature.
Related services	Schools must provide related services, such as physical therapy, counseling, and transportation, if needed.
Free appropriate public education	The primary requirement of PL 94–142 is the provision of a free, appropriate public education to all school-age children with disabilities.

Individualized Education Program (IEP)   A key component of PL 94–142 is the requirement that all students with disabilities have an **individualized education program (IEP).** The IEP, based on information collected during the comprehensive assessment, is developed by a group of individuals knowledgeable about the student. At a minimum, this group must include

- The child's teacher
- A representative of the school, other than the teacher, who is qualified to provide or supervise special education programs
- One or both parents of the child
- The child, where appropriate
- Other individuals at the discretion of the parent or school

Of this group of individuals, the parent's participation is critical. Although schools may proceed to develop and implement an IEP if a parent simply wishes not to attend, the absence of the parent leaves a great deal to be desired when developing a program that is appropriate for an individual student.

Least Restrictive Environment   A critical element in PL 94–142 is the **least-restrictive-environment** requirement. Educating students with disabilities in the least restrictive environment means that they should remain with their nondisabled chronological age peers as much as possible. Specifically, the law requires that students with disabilities remain with their nondisabled peers "to the maximum extent appropriate." The law further states that special classes, separate schooling, or other removal of students with disabilities from general educational settings should only happen when students with disabilities cannot be successful in general education classrooms, even with supplementary aids and services. The least restrictive environment obviously results in the inclusion of students with disabilities into general education classrooms. Just exactly how much each student is included depends on the student's IEP. Some students are able to benefit from full-time inclusion, while others may require only minimal placement in general education classrooms. Public Law 94–142 requires schools to provide a continuum of placement options for students, with the IEP determining the most appropriate placement.

For the majority of students with disabilities and other special needs, placement in general education classrooms for at least a portion of each school day is the appropriate option. Students with more severe disabilities may be less likely to benefit from inclusion and will generally spend less time with their nondisabled peers.

Although the law requires, and has resulted in, more inclusion of students with disabilities, there is still debate concerning how much inclusion is ideal. Wang and Birch (1984) note that "The spotlight must be turned to increasing the capabilities of the regular school environment to meet the needs of individual students, rather than instituting mere cosmetic changes in the placement of students" (p. 393). It is likely that this debate will continue for the next several years, since many professionals as well as parents disagree on this issue.

The implementation of the least-restrictive-environment concept is what has resulted in classroom teachers becoming involved with students with special needs.

Now, general education teachers and special education teachers must share in the responsibility for education. This shared responsibility requires close communication among all teachers involved with specific students (Marsh, Price, & Smith, 1983; Podemski et al., 1984; Smith et al., 1986).

Due-Process Safeguards.   Providing **due-process safeguards** to students with disabilities and their parents is another requirement of PL 94–142. Prior to this legislation, school personnel often made unilateral decisions about a student's education, including placement and specific components of the educational program; parents had little input and little recourse if they disagreed with the school. Due-process safeguards provided by PL 94–142 make parents and schools equal partners in the educational process. Parents must be notified and give their consent if schools want to assess a student or change the student's educational program.

When the school and parents do not agree on the educational program, either party can request a due-process hearing. A due-process hearing is an administrative appeals process in which parents and schools present evidence and testimony to an impartial hearing officer who decides on the appropriateness of an educational program. The decision of the hearing officer is final and must be implemented unless it is appealed to state or federal court (Smith, 1983; Smith et al., 1986). Table 1.3 provides a brief description of the due-process safeguards provided by PL 94–142.

TABLE 1.3   **Due-Process Requirements of PL 94–142**

Requirement	Explanation	Reference
Opportunity to examine records	Parents have a right to inspect and review all educational records.	Sec. 121a.502
Independent evaluation	Parents have a right to obtain an independent evaluation of their child at their expense or the school's expense. The school pays only if it agrees to the evaluation or is required by a hearing officer.	Sec. 121a.503
Prior notice; parental consent	Schools must provide written notice to parents before the school initiates or changes the identification, evaluation, or placement of a child. Consent must be obtained before conducting the evaluation and before initial placement.	Sec. 121a.504
Contents of notice	Parental notice must provide a description of the proposed actions in the written native language of the home. If the communication is not written, oral notification must be given. The notice must be understandable to the parents.	Sec. 121a.505
Impartial due-process hearing	A parent or school may initiate a due-process hearing if there is a dispute over the identification, evaluation, or placement of the child.	Sec. 121a.506

Source: Final regulations, P.L. 94–142 (1977).*Federal Register.* Washington, DC: U.S. Government Printing Office. *42* (163).

In 1990, PL 94–142 was reauthorized by Congress. The reauthorization was named the Individuals with Disabilities Education Act (IDEA). IDEA reauthorized the major components of PL 94–142 and made several significant changes. The law (1) required schools to actively plan for a student's transition from school to post-school environments, (2) replaced the word *handicapped* from the original law with the word *disabled,* and (3) added traumatic brain injury (TBI) and autism as separate handicapping categories covered by the law.

Litigation.   In addition to legislation, litigation has played a major role in the development of current services to students with disabilities. Beginning with the *Brown* case and continuing for the next several decades, litigation helped "radicalize" the way students with disabilities are served in public schools (Prasse, 1986). Important litigation has focused on numerous issues, including (1) the right to education for students with disabilities, (2) nonbiased assessment for students, (3) procedural safeguards for students with disabilities, (4) the right to an extended school year at public expense for some students, (5) related services for students, and (6) the interpretation by the U.S. Supreme Court of the intent of Congress in PL 94–142 (Prasse, 1986; Prasse & Reschly, 1986; Smith, 1990; Turnbull, 1986). Several landmark court cases from the 1970s and 1980s helped shape the current special education services.

Brown v. Board of Education   As previously noted, the civil rights movement in the 1950s and 1960s served as a blueprint for parents who advocated for equal opportunities for their children with disabilities. The landmark civil rights court case, *Brown v. Board of Education,* initiated the dismantling of racially segregated public education. As a result, it provided a legal precedent for dismantling segregated public education based on disabilities. The Brown case, therefore, even though it did not focus on students with disabilities, was a very important case for special education (Stainback et al., 1985).

PARC v. Pennsylvania   In the early 1970s, the Pennsylvania Association for Retarded Citizens represented a group of parents of students with mental retardation and filed a legal suit against the state of Pennsylvania because children with mental retardation were denied access to public education. The case resulted in a consent decree in which the state of Pennsylvania agreed to provide educational programs for students with mental retardation. Additionally, the state agreed to seek out these students and provide educational programs in general education environments whenever possible (Smith et al., 1986; Smith, 1990).

Mills v. District of Columbia (1974)   About the same time as the PARC case, a group of parents in Washington, DC, filed suit against the public school system, requesting that schools provide access to public schools for their children with mental retardation. The court ruled in favor of the parents, expanding the ruling to include all students with disabilities. Furthermore, the *Mills* court refused to allow schools to claim fiscal inability as an excuse for not providing appropriate services to this group of students (Podemski et al., 1984). This ruling has been used as precedent in cases where limited financial resources were the stated reason for limited services.

Comparison of IDEA, Section 504, and the ADA

	The IDEA	Section 504	The ADA
Mission	To provide a free, appropriate public education (FAPE) in the least restrictive environment.	To provide persons with disabilities, to the maximum extent possible, the opportunity to be fully integrated into mainstream American life.	To provide all persons with disabilities broader coverage than Section 504 in all aspects of discrimination law.
Scope	Applies to public schools.	Applies to any program or activity that is receiving federal financial assistance.	Applies to public or private employment, transportation, accommodations, and telecommunications, regardless of whether federal funding is received.
Coverage	Only those who are educationally disabled, in that they require special education services, ages 3–21 years.	All qualified persons with disabilities regardless of whether special education services are required in public elementary, secondary, or postsecondary settings.	All qualified persons with disabilities, and qualified nondisabled persons related to or associated with a person with a disability.
Disability Defined	A listing of disabilities is provided in the act, including specific learning disabilities.	No listing of disabilities provided, but inclusionary criteria of any physical or mental impairment that substantially limits one or more life activities, having a record of such an impairment, or being regarded as having an impairment.	No listing of disabilities provided. Same criteria as found in Section 504. HIV status and contagious and noncontagious diseases recently included.
Identification Process	Responsibility of school district to identify through "Child Find" and evaluate at no expense to parent or individual.	Responsibility of individual with the disability to self-identify and to provide documentation. Cost of the evaluation must be assumed by the individual, not the institution.	Same as Section 504.

	The IDEA	Section 504	The ADA
Service Delivery	Special education services and auxiliary aids must be mandated by Child Study Team and stipulated by the Individual Education Program.	Services, auxiliary aids, and academic adjustments may be provided in the general education setting. Arranged for by the special education coordinator or disabled student services provider.	Services, auxiliary aids, and accommodations arranged for by the ADA coordinator. Requires that accommodations do not pose an "undue hardship" to employers.
Funding	Federal funds are conditional to compliance with IDEA regulations.	No authorization for funding attached to this civil rights statute.	Same as Section 504.
Enforcement Agency	Office of Special Education and Rehabilitative Services in U.S. Department of Education.	The Office for Civil Rights (OCR) in the U.S. Department of Education.	Primarily the U.S. Department of Justice, in conjunction with the Equal Employment Opportunity Commission and Federal Communications Commission. May overlap with OCR.
Remedies	Reimbursement by district of school-related expenses is available to parents of children with disabilities to ensure a FAPE.	A private individual may sue a recipient of federal financial assistance to ensure compliance with Section 504.	Same as Section 504 with monetary damages up to $50,000 for the first violation. Attorney fees and litigation expenses are also recoverable.

Source: Adapted from *Handicapped Requirements Handbook*, January 1993, Washington, DC: Author. Thompson Publishing Group. Adapted with permission.

Rowley v. Henry Hudson School District   In 1984, the United States Supreme Court ruled on its first case related to PL 94–142. The case dealt with a school providing a student with a hearing impairment with a sign language interpreter. The Henry Hudson School District in New York had provided the services of a sign language interpreter for the student for one school year, but refused to provide the service in a subsequent year because the student was doing well. The due-process hearing officer, federal district court, and federal appellate court ruled in favor of the parents, requiring the school to provide the interpreter. In these rulings, it was stated that the sign language interpreter was required to maximize the student's educational achievement. However, the U.S. Supreme Court reversed all previous rulings and stated that a sign language interpreter was not required. In making the ruling, the Court for the first time interpreted the congressional intent of PL 94–142. It stated that Congress never intended for schools to "maximize" the educational progress of students with disabilities, but simply to make available to these students an appropriate educational program (Turnbull, 1986).

Although many disability advocates were upset by the ruling, after further consideration, most agreed with the fairness of the decision. In reality, the public education system in the United States does not maximize the achievement ability of most students. What it does is to provide a sound, free education for all students. The very nature of public education being for the masses means it cannot provide the best possible programs; it simply provides good programs. Therefore, schools are required to make a free appropriate education accessible to students with special needs—not the best program, but one that meets the unique needs of each student.

In addition to these cases, several additional cases have resulted in important decisions in some "gray" areas. Table 1.4 summarizes some of these cases.

Parental Advocacy.   The third primary force that facilitated the passage of PL 94–142 and its amendments was parental advocacy. Parental advocacy was not only a separate force that encouraged schools to integrate students with disabilities; it was directly involved with the legislation and litigation forces that were directed toward breaking down barriers for these students. Without parental advocacy, Congress would not have passed PL 94–142. Also, parental advocacy was directly responsible for litigation that forced many schools to include students with disabilities in general education classrooms. "While professional and legislative advocates approached the issue of integration from a theoretical or political perspective, parents confronted the issue from a very personal one" (Berres & Knoblock, 1987, p. 3). The result was a

TABLE 1.4 **Additional Court Cases**

Diana v. State Board of Education, 1970	Parents of Spanish-speaking students filed litigation challenging the placement of their children in classes for EMR children. Ruling resulted in requirements to implement nondiscriminatory assessment methods, including testing students in their native language.
Larry P. v. Riles, 1977	Parents of African-American children filed suit challenging inappropriate placements of their children in EMR classes. Ruling required schools to stop using standardized IQ test to place children in EMR classes and to reduce the disproportionate number of African-American children in EMR classes. Also required schools to retest every African-American student in EMR classes.
Armstrong v. Kline, 1979	Parents challenged the state of Pennsylvania's rule against supporting students beyond the traditional 180-day school year. Ruling found that some students with disabilities might need extended school year to prevent significant regression. For these children, schools are responsible to provide such summer programming.
Honig v. Doe, 1988	The issue in this case dealt with school expulsion. Parents contended that children with disabilities should not be expelled without due process. Court ruled that students cannot be expelled if the inappropriate behavior is related to the disability.

powerful coalition of forces that targeted discriminatory practices which excluded students with disabilities from public education.

Parental advocacy could not have focused as sharply on the inclusion issue without the framework of advocacy groups. The power of such organizations is what frequently results in changes in educational systems (Berres & Knoblock, 1987). The National Association for Retarded Citizens (NARC), formed in 1950, played a major role in getting local school districts, state education agencies, and the federal government to require the inclusion of students with disabilities in general education classroom opportunities. Following the lead of the NARC, other groups, such as the Association for Children with Learning Disabilities (ACLD), continued to pressure schools to provide appropriate educational services in the least restrictive setting.

Reasons for Supporting Inclusion of Students with Disabilities

The current trend in serving students with disabilities is to provide appropriate services in inclusive settings with nondisabled students as much as possible. Although inclusion has been in place for most of the 1980s, the practice continues to be debated (Stainback et al., 1985). Some professionals continue to believe that students with disabilities are best served in self-contained classrooms by teachers specifically trained to meet their educational needs; others advocate their placement in general education classrooms. Also, some parents of students with disabilities prefer self-contained placement to protect their children from ridicule and rejection by nondisabled peers.

There are many reasons why the focus of services for students with disabilities moved from segregated, self-contained programs to inclusive settings. These include efficacy studies that investigated segregated programs, opportunities for interaction between students with disabilities and students without disabilities (Roberts, Pratt, & Leach, 1991); improved opportunities for social interaction; and improved academic performance for mainstreamed students (Stevens & Slavin, 1991). Although no significant research has conclusively provided justification to serve students through inclusive programs, much of the work that has been done indicates that students do as well or better in integrated settings than in segregated environments.

Efficacy Studies

Prior to PL 94–142, special education for students with disabilities was primarily delivered in separate, special education classrooms. With this model, special education teachers rarely interacted with general education teachers, and students with disabilities had only limited contact with students who were not disabled. In the late 1960s and early 1970s, several articles questioned the practice of segregated special education (Smith, Price, & Marsh, 1986). These reports were classified as "efficacy studies" and had a major impact on the mainstreaming movement.

Probably the most damaging report on the practice of separate special education programs was published by Dunn (1968). In this position paper Dunn concluded that students with mental retardation who were educated in segregated, special classes achieved no better than their peers who remained in general education classrooms. In a later article, Dunn (1973) came to the following conclusions regarding separate classes for students with disabilities:

- ◆ Students with mild mental retardation, as a group, do as well academically in general education classrooms as they do in special classrooms.
- ◆ Regardless of placement, students with mental retardation do not work up to their mental capacity.
- ◆ Students with mental retardation in segregated special education classes do not achieve better then their peers placed full-time in general education classrooms.
- ◆ The higher the intellectual functioning of the students with mental retardation, the less they like special class placement and the lower their self-concepts.

These conclusions made professionals and parents ask: "If special classes do not improve the chances for students with disabilities to do better academically than they would in regular classrooms, why segregate them from their age peers?"

Similar Methodologies

In addition to students with disabilities in special classes performing no better than their peers in general education classrooms, there also appear to be no major differences in the methods used to teach students with disabilities and other students. Instructional methodologies are generally the same for all students. Although instruction should be individualized to meet the needs of each student, "the development of behavioral objectives, curricular-based assessment procedures, task analysis, the arrangement of antecedents and consequences, and open education/discovery learning methods" are basically the same for all students (Stainback & Stainback, 1984, p. 103).

Even classroom teachers acknowledge the common instructional methodologies for different students. In a survey of 197 elementary and secondary classroom teachers, the majority of both groups indicated that they would not alter instruction significantly due to the inclusion of students with disabilities in their classes. Rather than altering instructional methodologies based on clinical labels of students, teachers should individualize instructional approaches on learning characteristics. Research has found that students from different special education categories actually learn from similar instructional approaches (Smith et al., 1986; Smith et al., 1993).

Interaction between Students with and without Disabilities

One of the principal reasons for inclusion is to provide opportunities for interaction between students with disabilities and those without disabilities (Roberts et al., 1991). Students have a tendency to imitate the behaviors of other students in their environments. Therefore, students with disabilities who are only able to interact with other disabled students will likely imitate whatever inappropriate behaviors are exhibited. Being able to model the behaviors of nondisabled students in general education class-

Characteristics of Individuals with Mild Disabilities and Technology-Based Applications

Student Characteristic	Technologies and Applications
Deficits in basic academic subjects and skills	Drill-and-practice software, integrated learning systems, hypermedia
Need for repeated practice and review	Drill-and-practice software, integrated learning systems, teacher tool software, hypermedia
Memory deficits	Personal productivity tools
Short attention span	Gamelike software activities, simulations, instruction supported or delivered by videodiscs
Inefficient learning strategies	Problem-solving software, personal productivity tools
Lack of background knowledge	Content-area software, videodisc macrocontexts, hypermedia
Lack of higher-order skills	Writing tools, simulation and problem-solving software, instruction supported and delivered by videodiscs, content-area software, electronic networks, personal productivity tools
Motivational deficits	All technology-based applications

Source: Okolo, C. M. (1993).Computers and individuals with mild disabilities. In J. D. Lindsey, (Ed.), *Computers and exceptional individuals* (p. 113). Austin, TX: Pro-Ed.

rooms is considered a major advantage of inclusion. Roberts et al. (1991) conducted a study to determine the social behaviors of students with disabilities in classroom and playground settings. The study investigated the types of interactions among students, the individuals involved in interactions, and the quality of the interactions. Results of the study included the following:

1. Disabled and nondisabled students displayed minimal levels of disruptive behaviors in both settings.
2. Amounts of interactions with peers and adults did not differ between students with disabilities and those without disabilities.
3. Students with disabilities interacted approximately 50% of the time on the playground, and their interactions did not differ significantly with their nondisabled peers.

A major conclusion of the study was that including the students with disabilities in classrooms and playground settings promoted their interaction and social acceptance by nondisabled students.

One of the principal reasons for inclusion is to provide opportunities for interaction between students with and without disabilities.

In another study, Ray (1986) investigated the social position of students with disabilities included in general education classrooms. The social interaction of 60 students with mild disabilities was evaluated. Results indicated that although the students with disabilities were considered less socially acceptable by their teachers and nondisabled peers, their social interactions were the same as their nondisabled classmates. These results suggest that including students with disabilities in general education classrooms does not have a negative impact on their social interactions.

Often, students with disabilities and those without disabilities do not have the skills to interact with each other. Students may be placed in classroom situations together without a great deal of preparation. Putnam, Rynders, Johnson, and Johnson (1989) found that with collaborative skill instruction, both students with disabilities and their "typical" peers were much more successful in interacting than a control group of students who were not provided the instruction. Therefore, although interaction among students is a primary purpose for inclusion, school personnel must provide instruction to facilitate the process.

Improved Academic Performance

Although not a primary reason for including students with disabilities, it is hoped that placement in general education classrooms will enhance the academic performances of these students. The efficacy studies previously cited indicated that segregating students did not result in improved academic performance. Many students with disabilities actually performed no better in specialized settings than their peers in general education classes. Some studies have actually shown improved academic performances of included students with disabilities.

Stevens and Slavin (1991) analyzed studies that compared students with and without disabilities in achievement when cooperative learning was used in the classroom. The cooperative learning involved collaboration among students in the learning process. They concluded: "When cooperative learning instructional processes include individual accountability and group rewards, they are likely to have a positive effect on the achievement of students both with and without disabilities" (p. 279).

There is little doubt that students with disabilities included in general education classrooms can be successful. The key is for both classroom and special education teachers to work together to restructure the classroom environment, and for school administrators to support the intervention (Wade & Gargiulo, 1989–1990). Continuing to break down the artificial barriers that exist between general education and special education systems with collaboration, sharing expertise, and sharing resources is necessary for the achievement of successful inclusion (Bauwens, Hourcade, & Friend, 1989; Stainback et al., 1985). Although collaboration among school personnel is not new, it has not always been used optimally between general education and special education personnel. The inclusion of students with disabilities in general education classrooms requires optimal collaboration (Idol & West, 1991).

Classroom Teachers and Students with Disabilities

Classroom teachers play a vital role in the education of students with disabilities. Sharing responsibility among classroom teachers, special education teachers, and other specialists, such as reading teachers, is the key to providing effective educational programs for all students. Prior to the inclusion of students with disabilities into general education classrooms, the role of classroom teachers with these students was primarily limited to referring students for special programs. This frequently resulted in these students being totally excluded from general education classroom programs.

As a result of the inclusion movement, classroom teachers have had to become significantly more involved in the education of all students, including those with disabilities. In order to effectively provide educational services for all students, classroom teachers must be able to perform many different skills, such as

◆ Acting as a team member on assessment and IEP committees
◆ Advocating for children with disabilities when they are in general education classrooms and in special programs
◆ Counseling and interacting with parents of students with disabilities
◆ Individualizing instruction for students with disabilities
◆ Understanding and abiding by due-process procedures required by federal and state regulations
◆ Being innovative in providing equal educational opportunities for all students, including those with disabilities

In general, the classroom teacher controls the educational programs for all students in the classroom, including students with disabilities. Students with disabilities, students at risk for developing problems, and those classified as gifted and talented are all taught by classroom teachers. The attitude of the teacher toward students and the general climate the teacher establishes in the classroom have a major impact on the success of all students, particularly those with disabilities.

Attitudes of Teachers

Attitudes can be defined as predispositions toward behavior. Attitudes are learned, and appear to be affected by the amount of knowledge and contact a person has regarding a particular issue or group (Smith et al., 1986). An individual's attitude about something will affect that person's behaviors. For example, if a teacher has a negative attitude toward bilingual education and believes that students who have a primary language other than English should not be in regular classrooms, that teacher will behave differently toward those students than will a teacher who believes these students should be in regular classrooms.

The way teachers' attitudes affect their behaviors toward certain groups of students has been the subject of numerous studies. In general, these studies have concluded that there is a direct relationship between teachers' attitudes and their behaviors. Some of the consequences that can result when teachers have negative attitudes toward a particular group of students include (1) unfair grading practices, (2) unfair assignments, (3) inappropriate behavior consequences, (4) inappropriate modeling opportunities for other students, and (5) lowered self-concepts among those students rejected.

Another important way attitudes affect students with disabilities is the impact they have on the tone of the classroom. Classroom teachers have a major impact on students with disabilities by setting the tone of the classroom. Teachers establish and enforce classroom rules, develop grading practices, use various reinforcement strategies, and set homework and other expectations for students. Some variables that are controlled by teachers that have a major impact on classroom tone and students include:

1. *Definition of a "Good" Student.*   Teachers like some students better than others. This may be determined by the values held by a teacher relative to what constitutes a "good" student.
2. *Classroom Rules.*   It is possible for all students to obey classroom rules, and teachers must enforce rules. Classroom rules are a part of the total set of expectations established by the teacher that play an important role in the success of students. Depending on the classroom rules, some students with disabilities have an easy or difficult time being successful.
3. *Student–Teacher Interactions.*   Teachers vary a great deal in the amount of time and extent they interact with students. Some teachers have a very interactive style; others prefer to remain "apart" from their students. Some students with disabilities may need a great deal of teacher interaction to make them feel secure in the classroom.

4. *Student–Student Interaction.*   Interaction with peers is as important for some students as interaction with adults. For students with disabilities, acceptance by their peers may be critical for their success in general education classrooms; they need the support of their peers. Teachers who create an environment that encourages positive interactions among students may make it more likely that students with disabilities will be successful in their classrooms than teachers who limit such interactions.

The primary function of teachers, both general education and special, is to teach. Good teaching has been described in many different ways. Researchers have attempted to determine good teaching based on student outcomes, parental opinions, peers, supervisor ratings, and self-evaluations. One way to gauge good teaching is to ask those who are taught. A 15-year-old student with learning disabilities was asked just this question and provided twenty good teaching tips. Although the student was describing good teaching qualities for special education teachers, the same twenty suggestions are also critical for classroom teachers when dealing with students with disabilities (Gallegos & Gallegos, 1990):

1. To be more understanding.
2. To be more involved with the students.
3. I feel that some teachers will not pay attention.
4. I think that teachers should look at the students a little better than what they do.
5. Teachers should put students where they belong and where they can handle it at that level.
6. My math teacher watches me constantly.
7. I think that the teacher should be helpful in and out of the classroom.
8. Some teachers like my math teacher don't give students a chance to talk about what they need.
9. I don't think that teachers should do things that bother or disturb and also do things that make us uncomfortable.
10. Don't believe every test score that you see.
11. Students shouldn't have to answer every single question after a chapter.
12. Teachers should be patient with the students.
13. The teachers shouldn't pick a teacher's pet.
14. The teachers should come well dressed to school instead of old clothing.
15. Teachers shouldn't give students homework that they can't finish in a classroom.
16. The teachers should be more appreciative to students when they do a good job. They need that kind of help.
17. The teachers should let students do what they want to do. Like get a drink and use the pot.
18. Teachers shouldn't touch opposite sex students. That makes students feel uncomfortable.
19. I don't like some teachers that hit students.
20. Some students should be rewarded for the good they do. (p. 15)

Current Issues in Serving Students with Disabilities

There are numerous issues that currently impact on services to students with disabilities. Several of these issues are not new, but have been debated for several years. However, they continue to be discussed, and future actions related to these issues will have a great impact on students with disabilities.

Regular Education Initiative (REI) and Inclusion

In the 1980s, the **regular education initiative (REI)** was proposed. The REI, which has evolved into inclusion of students with disabilities in general education, acknowledges the dichotomous nature of our public education system, namely general education and special education. Proponents of inclusion advocate for the dismantling of this artificial barrier, which separates education for different kinds of students. Although proposed by special education professionals, the idea has resulted in a division in opinions. Some special education professionals suggest that inclusion is inappropriate and that it will actually eliminate appropriate educational programs for students with disabilities. Others continue to push for full implementation of the inclusion concept.

General education teachers and administrators are also divided over inclusion. The obvious question asked by this group is: "How can we serve students with significant problems along with all of the other students currently in classes?" Inclusion is complex and cannot be implemented without a great deal of planning. Also, significant support services will have to be put in place to assist general education classroom teachers in implementing the process.

Education Reform

Fueled by the critical reports issued in the early 1980s, many education reforms have been proposed for public education. The reports, highlighted by *A Nation at Risk* issued by the National Commission on Education (1983), were highly critical of the current public education system.

Responses to the reports have been numerous. Politicians and professionals have proposed numerous "fixes" for the system, including more math and science courses, tougher graduation requirements, extending the school day and year, and reforming teacher education programs. Special educators and many other professionals serving students with disabilities have expressed many concerns about the proposed changes. These individuals are concerned that many of the so-called reforms will make it even more difficult for students with disabilities to receive appropriate educational services.

For example, students who are at risk for dropping out of school will now find it more difficult to complete the necessary requirements for a high school diploma. They may therefore choose to drop out rather than deal with a system that appears to be making it more difficult for them to succeed. Also, students who are intellectually

Inclusion Checklist for Your School

____ 1. Do we genuinely start from the premise that each child belongs in the classroom he or she would otherwise attend if not disabled (or do we cluster children with disabilities into special groups, classrooms, or schools)?

____ 2. Do we individualize the instructional program for all the children whether or not they are disabled and provide the resources that each child needs to explore individual interests in the school environment (or do we tend to provide the same sorts of services for most children who share the same diagnostic label)?

____ 3. Are we fully committed to maintenance of a caring community that fosters mutual respect and support among staff, parents, and students in which we honestly believe that nondisabled children can benefit from friendships with disabled children and disabled children can benefit from friendships with nondisabled children (or do our practices tacitly tolerate children teasing or isolating some as outcasts)?

____ 4. Have our general educators and special educators integrated their efforts and their resources so that they work together as integral parts of a unified team (or are they isolated in separate rooms or departments with separate supervisors and budgets)?

____ 5. Does our administration create a work climate in which staff are supported as they provide assistance to each other (or are teachers afraid of being presumed to be incompetent if they seek peer collaboration in working with students)?

____ 6. Do we actively encourage the full participation of children with disabilities in the life of our school, including co-curricular and extracurricular activities (or do they participate only in the academic portion of the school day)?

____ 7. Are we prepared to alter support systems for students as their needs change through the school year so that they can achieve, experience successes, and feel that they genuinely belong in their school and classes (or do we sometimes provide such limited services to them that the children are set up to fail)?

____ 8. Do we make parents of children with disabilities fully a part of our school community so they also can experience a sense of belonging (or do we give them a separate PTA and different newsletters)?

____ 9. Do we give children with disabilities just as much of the full school curriculum as they can master and modify it as necessary so that they can share elements of these experiences with their classmates (or do we have a separate curriculum for children with disabilities)?

____ 10. Have we included children with disabilities supportively in as many as possible of the same testing and evaluation experiences as their nondisabled classmates

▼

(or do we exclude them from these opportunities while assuming that they cannot benefit from the experiences)?

This checklist may help school personnel in evaluating whether their practices are consistent with the best intentions of the inclusion movement. Rate your school with a + for each item where the main statement best describes your school and a 0 for each item where the parenthetical statement better describes your school. Each item marked 0 could serve as the basis for discussion among the staff. Is this an area in which the staff sees need for further development? Viewed in this context, an inclusive school would not be characterized by a particular set of practices as much as by the commitment of its staff to continually develop its capacity to accommodate the full range of individual differences among its learners.

Source: Rogers, J. (1993). *Research Bulletin.* Washington, D.C.: Phi Delta Kappa, Center for Evaluation, Development, and Research. Used with permission.

capable of doing well in school, but have significant reading deficits, may find it more difficult to successfully complete the added course requirements implemented in many schools. Although the reforms implemented were done so with the best of intentions for all students, many may adversely affect the success of students with disabilities.

Summary

- The public school system in the United States attempts to provide 12 years of equal educational opportunity to all its citizens.

- Today's student population is very diverse, including those students with a variety of disabilities.

- The 1950s and 1960s were the decades when students from minority cultures won their right to equal educational opportunities.

- Many students in today's schools have unique special needs.

- A sizable percentage of students are at risk for developing problems do present learning or behavior problems, or may be classified as having a disability.

- The largest group of students with special needs in the public school system is those formally classified as disabled.

- Although there are 10 recognized categories of disabilities in schools, many students do not fit neatly into a specific category.

- Mental retardation, learning disabilities, and emotional and behavior disorders make up the majority of student disabilities.

- Students that are at risk for developing problems, and those considered gifted and talented, also require special attention from school personnel.

◆ Services for students with disabilities have evolved significantly over the past 20 years.

◆ Current services for students with disabilities focus on inclusion, including students in general education classroom situations as much as possible.

◆ The civil rights movement, legislation, and litigation all helped shape the current service system for students with disabilities.

◆ Public Law 94–142, now the Individuals with Disabilities Education Act (IDEA), provides the framework for services to students with disabilities in school settings.

◆ IDEA requires that students with disabilities be educated in the least restrictive environment, using an individualized education program (IEP).

◆ Recently there has been a movement in special education away from categories to more generic interventions based on students' needs rather than clinical labels.

◆ General education teachers play a very critical role in providing services to students with disabilities.

◆ The attitudes of classroom teachers are extremely important in the quality of services rendered to students with disabilities.

References

Abrahamse, A., Morrison, P., & Waite, L. (1988). *Beyond stereotypes: who becomes a single teenage mother.* Santa Monica, CA: Rand Corporation.

American Association on Mental Retardation. (1992). *Mental retardation: Definition, classification, and systems of supports* (9th ed.). Washington, DC: Author.

Baum, D. D., & Duffelmeyer, S. D. (1989–1990). The regular education initiative: Is it developing roots? *National Forum of Special Education Journal, 1,* 4–11.

Bauwens, J., Hourcade, J. J., & Friend, M. (1989). Cooperative teaching: A model for general and special education integration. *Remedial and Special Education, 10,* 17–22.

Beirne-Smith, M., Patton, J. R., & Ittenbach, R. (1994). *Mental retardation* (4th ed.). Columbus, OH: Merrill.

Berres, M. S., & Knoblock, P. (1987). Introduction and perspective. In M. S. Berres & P. Knoblock (Eds.), *Program models for mainstreaming* (pp. 1–18), Austin, TX: Pro-Ed.

Cosden, M. A. (1990). Expanding the role of special education. *Teaching Exceptional Children, 22,* 4–6.

Dunn, L. M. (1968). Special education for the mildly retarded—Is much of it justifiable? *Exceptional Children, 35,* 5–22.

Dunn, L. M. (1973). *Exceptional children in the schools: Special education in transition.* New York: Holt, Rinehart & Winston.

Epstein, M. H., Polloway, E. A., Patton, J. R., & Foley, R. (1986). Mild retardation: Student characteristics and services. *Education and Training in Mental Retardation, 24,* 7–16.

Gallegos, A. Y., & Gallegos, M. L. (1990). A student's perspective on good teaching: Michael. *Intervention in School and Clinic, 26,* 14–15.

Greer, J. V. (1991). At-risk students in the fast lanes: Let them through. *Exceptional Children, 57,* 390–391.

Hamre-Nietupski, S., Ayres, B., Nietupski, J., Savage, M., Mitchell, B., & Bramman, H. (1989). Enhancing integration of students with severe disabilities through curricular infusion: A general/special educator partnership. *Education and Training in Mental Retardation, 24,* 78–88.

Heward, W. L., & Orlansky, M. D. (1992). *Exceptional children: An introductory survey of special education* (4th ed.). New York: Merrill.

Hill, D. (1991). Tasting failure: Thoughts of an at-risk learner. *Phi Delta Kappan, 73,* 308–310.

Huntze, S. L. (1985). A position paper of The Council for Children with Behavior Disorders. *Behavioral Disorders, 10,* 167–174.

Hynd, G. W., Marshall, R., & Gonzalez, J. (1991). Learning disabilities and presumed central nervous system dysfunction. *Learning Disability Quarterly, 14,* 283–295.

Idol, L., & West, F. (1991). Educational collaboration: A catalyst for effective schooling. *Intervention in School and Clinic, 27,* 70–78.

Johnson, J. L. (1988). The challenge of substance abuse. *Teaching Exceptional Children, 20,* 29–31.

Johnson, L. J., Pugach, M. C., & Devlin, S. (1990). Professional collaboration. *Teaching Exceptional Children, 22,* 9–11.

Kauffman, J. M., & Wong, L. H. (1991). Effective teachers of students with behavioral disorders: Are generic teaching skills enough? *Behavioral Disorders, 16,* 225–237.

Kavale, K. A., Forness, S. R., & Lorsbach, T. C. (1991). Definition for definitions of learning disabilities. *Learning Disability Quarterly, 14,* 257–267.

Knoblock, P. (1982). *Teaching and mainstreaming autistic children.* Denver, CO: Love Publishing.

Knoll, J. A., & Meyer, L. H. (1987). Integrated schooling and educational quality: Principles and effective practices. In M. S. Berres & P. Knoblock (Eds.), *Program models for mainstreaming* (pp. 41–59). Austin, TX: Pro-Ed.

McCarthy, M. M., & Cambron-McCabe, N. H. (1987). *Public school law: Teachers' and students' rights* (2nd ed.). Boston: Allyn & Bacon.

Marsh, G. E., Price, B. J., & Smith, T. E. C. (1983). *Teaching mildly handicapped children.* St. Louis: Mosby.

National Center for Education Statistics. (1990). *The condition of education, 1990 edition.* Washington, DC: U.S. Department of Education.

National Commission on Education. (1983). *A nation at risk.* Washington, DC: U.S. Government Printing Office.

National Information Center for Children and Youth with Handicaps. (1990). *Children with autism.* Washington, DC: Author.

Nelson, C. M., Rutherford, R. B., Center, D. B., & Walker, H. M. (1991). *Exceptional Children, 57,* 406–413.

Okolo, C. M. (1992). Computers and individuals with mild disabilities. In J. D. Lindsey (Ed.), *Computers and Exceptional Individuals*. (pp. 109–127). Austin, TX: Pro-Ed.

Peacock Hill Working Group. (1991). Problems and promises in special education and related services for children and youth with emotional or behavioral disorders. *Behavioral Disorders, 16,* 299–313.

Podemski, R. S., Price, B. J., Smith, T. E. C., & Marsh, G. E. (1984). *Comprehensive administration of special education.* Rockville, MD: Aspen Systems.

Polloway, E. A., & Smith, T. E. C. (1992). *Teaching language to students with disabilities* (2nd ed.). Denver: Love Publishing.

Prasse, D. P. (1986). Litigation and special education: An introduction. *Exceptional Children, 52,* 311–312.

Prasse, D. P., & Reschly, D. J. (1986). Larry P.: A case of segregation, testing, or program efficacy? *Exceptional Children, 52,* 333–345.

Putnam, J. W., Rynders, J. E., Johnson, R.T., & Johnson, D. W. (1989). Collaborative skill instruction for promoting positive interactions between mentally handicapped and non-handicapped children. *Exceptional Children, 55,* 550–557.

Ray, B. M. (1986). Measuring the social position of the mainstreamed handicapped child. *Exceptional Children, 52,* 57–62.

Roberts, C., Pratt, C., & Leach, D. (1991). Classroom and playground interaction of students with and without disabilities. *Exceptional Children, 57,* 212–224.

Rogers, J. (1993). *Research Bulletin.* Washington, DC: Phi Delta Kappa Center for Evaluation, Development, and Research.

Savage, R. C. (1988). Introduction to educational issues for students who have suffered traumatic brain injury. In R. C. Savage & G. F. Wolcott (Eds.), *An educator's manual: What educators need to know about students with traumatic brain injury.* Southborough, MA: National Head Injury Foundation.

Smith, G., & Smith, D. (1989). Schoolwide study skills program: The key to mainstreaming. *Teaching Exceptional Children, 21,* 20–23.

Smith, T. E. C. (1983). Status of due process hearings. *Exceptional Children, 48,* 232–236.

Smith, T. E. C. (1990). *Introduction to education* (2nd ed.). St. Paul, MN: West Publishing.

Smith, T. E. C., Finn, D. M., & Dowdy, C. A. (1993). *Teaching students with mild disabilities.* Ft. Worth, TX: Harcourt Brace Jovanovich.

Smith, T. E. C., Price, B. J., & Marsh, G. E. (1986). *Mildly handicapped children and adults.* St. Paul, MN: West Publishing.

Stainback, W., & Stainback, S. (1984). A rationale for the merger of special and regular education. *Exceptional Children, 51,* 102–111.

Stainback, W., Stainback, S., Courtnage, L., & Jaben, T. (1985). Facilitating mainstreaming by modifying the mainstream. *Exceptional Children, 52,* 144–152.

Stanovich, K. E. (1991). Conceptual and empirical problems with discrepancy definitions of reading disability. *Learning Disability Quarterly, 14,* 269–280.

Stevens, R. J., & Slavin, R. E. (1991). When cooperative learning improves the achievement of students with mild disabilities: A response to Tateyama-Sniezek. *Exceptional Children, 57,* 276–280.

Swanson, H. L. (1991). Operational definitions and learning disabilities: An overview. *Learning Disability Quarterly, 14,* 242–255.

Thousand, J. S., & Villa, R. A. (1990). Strategies for educating learners with severe disabilities within their local home schools and communities. *Focus on Exceptional Children, 23,* 1–24.

Turnbull, H. R. (1986). Appropriate education and *Rowley. Exceptional Children, 52,* 347–352.

Wade, P., & Gargiulo, R. M. (1989–1990). *National Forum of Special Education Journal, 1,* 59–65.

Wang, M. C., & Birch, J. W. (1984). Effective special education in regular classes. *Exceptional Children, 50,* 391–398.

Will, M. C. (1984). Educating children with learning problems: A shared responsibility. *Exceptional Children, 52,* 411–415.

Wilson, L. R. (1985). Large-scale learning disability identification: The reprieve of a concept. *Exceptional Children, 52,* 44–51.

York, J., & Vandercook, T. (1991). Designing an integrated program for learners with severe disabilities. *Teaching Exceptional Children, 23,* 22–28.

CHAPTER 2

Referral, Assessment, and Individualized Education Programs

Introduction

Educational programs for students with disabilities can best be understood when attention is paid to the process by which a student is considered as a candidate for special services. This process is governed by the Education for All Handicapped Children Act (PL 94–142) and its successor, the Individuals with Disabilities Education Act (PL 101–476) as well as by regulations in each respective state. This chapter reviews key concepts in referral, assessment and the development and implementation of individualized education programs (IEPs)—three key components of this overall process.

Let us begin with a broad context for these procedures. Three concepts are worthy of note. *First,* it is important to realize that all educational procedures must be consistent with the due process clause under the Constitution, which ensures that no person will be deprived of legal rights or privileges without appropriate established procedures being followed. Relative to special education, the implications of the due process clause have resulted in the following considerations:

1. Parents or guardians must receive written notification (in their native language) before evaluative efforts can begin.
2. Special education programs must be reviewed at least on an annual basis.
3. Parents have a right to question educational program decisions in an impartial hearing.
4. A student has the right to be granted a surrogate parent if circumstances make this necessary.

The critical element for teachers is to ensure the establishment of an open and fair process for initially determining whether to provide special education services to a student and subsequently deciding what form they will take. Ultimately, the best interests of the student should guide decisions and practice.

A *second* consideration is to appreciate the overall flow pattern for the referral/assessment/IEP process. Guidelines for procedures vary from state to state. One example of state timelines is presented in Figure 2.1. As can be seen in the figure, the process includes referral to a child study team, review by that team, possible subsequent referral to the central office (i.e., the special education office), assessment procedures, and then an eligibility decision. The development of an IEP would then follow.

A *third* general concern has to do with the key players in the process. Participants include special and general education teachers, administrative staff, ancillary personnel (e.g., school psychologists, speech-language therapists, school social workers), parents, and the student. Involving many people should not be an issue of compliance or mere happenstance. Beyond the obvious fact that many people should have a vested interest in the educational program for a student, the unique element is that their involvement should be focused on a team approach. Thus, the key decisions to

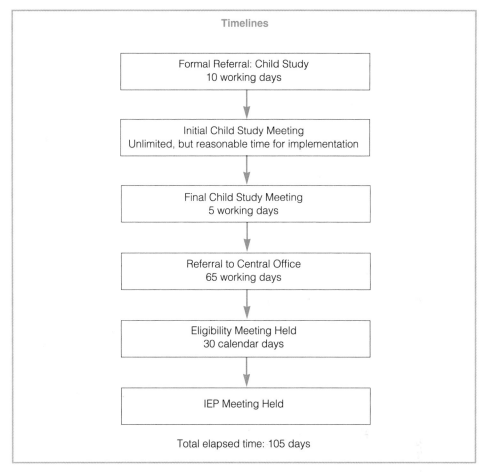

Figure 2.1   **Referral to Special Education**

be made about a child are to be made by a team representative of various disciplines and/or relationships with the student. As McLoughlin and Lewis (1990) noted, teams are charged with making decisions concerning eligibility for special services, design of the IEP, evaluation of IEPs, and reevaluation of eligibility. Further, teams are significantly involved in the prereferral process described here within the context of the work of child study teams.

Child Study and Referral

The child study and referral process can be considered the initial component of a collaborative model between professionals. Included within this process are initial contacts and collaboration between general and special education teachers followed by

40

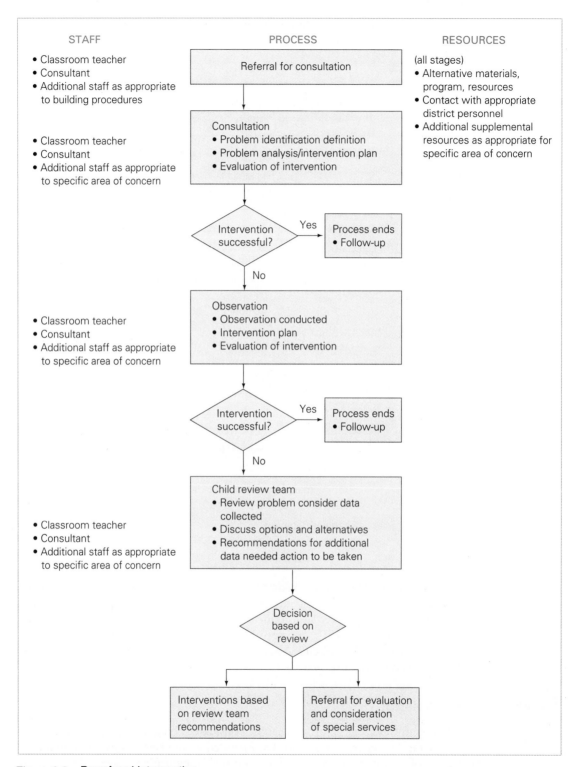

Figure 2.2　**Prereferral Intervention**
Source: From "Implementing a prereferral intervention system: Part I, The model" by J. L. Graden, A. Casey, & S. L. Christenson, *Exceptional Children, 51,* p. 380. Copyright 1985 by The Council for Exceptional Children. Reprinted with permission.

prereferral interventions (i.e., interventions to be attempted in the general education classroom prior to formal referral for evaluation for special education). Figure 2.2 outlines a series of procedures that provide a broad conceptualization for this process. The figure provides a framework for the discussion that follows.

The child study and **referral process** ordinarily begins with concerns voiced by a classroom teacher about the performance or progress of a student. Other referral sources could be parents, end-of-year reviews of student progress, or an external service provider. At this juncture a group of building personnel review available information and attempt to generate suggestions for improvement relative to the student's difficulties. Depending upon geographical area, this team may be referred to as a screening committee, a **child study committee,** or a teacher assistance team (Chalfant, Pysh, & Moultrie, 1979). The team's task is to attempt to assist the teacher in modifying instruction or to determine if a referral for comprehensive special education evaluation is warranted. If a specific area of difficulty can be identified, evaluative information from screening tests will often be included as part of the data set to be reviewed for decision making.

To illustrate the process of referral, Table 2.1 provides summary data on the bases for common special education referrals. Note that in this data set, reported by Lloyd, Kauffman, Landrun, and Roe (1991), academic problems predominated as a basis

TABLE 2.1 **Percentage of Referrals**

Reason	Percentage
General academic problems	35
Reading problems	31
Attention problems	23
Writing problems	15
Arithmetic problems	12
Language problems	12
Sensory problems	11
Nonspecific behavioral problems	9
Aggressive, disruptive, delinquent	7
Immaturity, inadequacy	6
Peer–adult relationships	6
Overactivity	5
Emotional problems	5
Noncompliance	4
Anxious, fearful, withdrawn	2
Depression	1

Source: Adapted from Lloyd, J. W., Kauffman, J. M., Landrum, T. J., & Roe, D. L. (1991). Why do teachers refer pupils for special education? An analysis of referral records. *Exceptionnel, 2,* p. 119. Used with permission.

for referral. The data offer a glimpse into the kinds of difficulties with which a child study team must deal in order to meet the needs of students who are struggling in the classroom.

Given this backdrop of referral patterns, it is illustrative to consider typical educational intervention strategies that may be employed. Interventions include, for example, remedial techniques, grouping or instructional program placement, peer tutoring, and management strategies. Table 2.2, taken from Brown, Gable, Hendrickson, and Algozzine (1991), provides an analysis of the type of prereferral intervention strategies that were recommended across age levels in the school programs studied in this research. The specific ratings for each of the strategies is identified for grades from kindergarten/first grade to senior high school. Figure 2.3 provides a sample form that may be used for decision making at an initial child study meeting. It provides a structure for defining the problems(s) and identifying when instructional strategies and/or assessment procedures should be implemented.

The purpose of child study or teacher assistance teams is to review concerns and design prereferral interventions rather than to pass cases on for comprehensive special education evaluation. This process appears to be both *effective* in helping teachers and students and *efficient* in generally forwarding referrals of only those students needing specialized services. In one study, Chalfant and Pysh (1989) reported that only 21% of the students reviewed by child study teams resulted in referral for a comprehensive evaluation.

Because the vast majority of students who are disabled are referred during the elementary years, the process is often less visible at the secondary level. However, since the demands of the middle school and high school settings are more complex, it is

TABLE 2.2 **Frequency of Use of Prereferral Intervention Strategies by Grade Level**

Intervention Strategy	K–1 (Mean[a])	2–3 (Mean)	4–6 (Mean)	Junior High (Mean)	Senior High (Mean)
Individualized instruction	3.69	3.31	3.18	2.84	2.62
Behavior management	3.77	3.60	3.48	3.00	2.72
Small group teaching	3.71	3.37	3.22	2.40	2.06
Modify curriculum	3.35	3.00	2.66	2.44	2.12
Modify classroom	3.11	2.80	2.63	2.63	2.18
Consult/collaborate	3.77	3.71	3.70	3.53	3.31
Parent conferences	3.89	3.66	3.72	3.27	2.80
Peer tutoring	2.49	2.66	2.72	2.36	2.22
Parent volunteers	2.35	2.43	1.82	1.16	1.20
Cooperative learning	2.40	2.37	2.30	1.97	1.74

[a]Arithmetical averages based on a five-point scale.
Source: Adapted from Brown, J., Gable, R. A., Hendrickson, J. M., & Algozzine, B. (1991). Preferential intervention practices of regular classroom teachers: Implications for regular and special education preparation. *Teacher Education and Special Education, 14*, p. 194.

Student _____

Date of Referral to Child Study _____

Date of Child Study Meeting _____

Referral Source _____

Grade _____   CA _____ / _____
                                         year   month

Initial Child Study Minutes

Definition of Problem:

Recommended Strategies:

Recommended Screening Testing:

Child Study Members Present:

_____ principal and/or child study chairman   _____ speech/language therapist
_____ special education teacher(s)   _____ reading specialist
_____ classroom teacher(s)   _____ guidance counselor(s)
_____ referring teacher/source   _____ other (specify) _____

Tentative Date for Subsequent Child Study Review _____

Figure 2.3   **Initial Child Study Meeting Form**

critical that the process of child study and referral be retained as an integral part of school activities at these levels as well.

Increasingly, the expectation in the schools will be that students with disabilities will be retained in general education classes as much as possible. Consequently, the classroom teacher can anticipate that multiple steps may precede formal referral for evaluation. In concluding this section, it is illustrative to consider the five steps that Henry and Flynt (1990) propose as constituting prereferral activities.

1. The general education teacher who suspects a disability should screen the student by considering varied sources of information (e.g., prior and current performance indicators).
2. The teacher should follow confirmation of previous learning problems with anecdotal observation.
3. The teacher should conference with the parents and, as appropriate, the student to establish the nature of the problem and discuss the situation at home.

4. The teacher should develop strategies and methods for classroom and home.
5. The student would then be referred to a preassessment team made up of fellow educators who will propose strategies the teacher may use to help the student in the classroom (i.e., teacher assistance team).

Assessment

Assessment is a multifaceted process. It is best viewed as a generic term that refers to the gathering and analysis of information used to make instructional, administrative, and guidance decisions concerning individual students (Wallace, Larsen, & Elksnin, 1992). Assessment relative to special education is often considered within the context of eligibility decisions. However, assessment includes evaluative efforts associated with initial screening, program design and instructional decision making, in addition to eligibility for services.

An important initial distinction to make is between assessment and testing. As Polloway and Jones-Wilson (1992) noted, a useful differentiation can be made by first defining *testing* as the presentation of tasks or questions to a student within an organized context in order to obtain a score. In this sense, testing would only be considered one aspect of *assessment,* which looks at the global evaluative results and the implications of performance. Furthermore, assessment is concerned with qualitative as well as quantitative components of performance on related tasks both formally and informally observed within and outside a given testing setting. Although testing often unfortunately becomes an end in itself in the schools (Wallace et al., 1992), assessment seeks to capture a more complete picture of the student through the determination of current functioning levels. Forming this picture is essential to effective educational planning and instruction.

Data from assessment should be central to instructional decision making. Polloway and Patton (1993) suggest the term *assessment-based instruction* to affirm the idea that sound instruction should be preceded by an appropriate analysis of learning-related behaviors as well as an evaluation of the learning environment and student future need. Dowdy and Smith (1991) use the term ***future-based assessment*** to place particular importance on the latter concern. Its focus is on the role of assessment in planning for the student's future.

Formal Assessment

Formal assessment instruments are generally available commercially. They typically contain detailed guidelines for administration, scoring and interpretation as well as statistical data regarding validity, reliability, and standardization procedures. They are most often ***norm-referenced***—that is, the tests provide quantitative information comparing the performance of an individual student to others in her norm group (determined, for example, by age, grade, and/or gender). Test results are usually reported in the form of test quotients, percentiles, and age or grade equivalents. These tools are most useful early in an assessment procedure, when relatively little is known of a student's strengths and weaknesses, and thus they may help to identify areas in which

Guidelines for Teacher Behavior during Staffings

- ◆ Be prepared. Have all of your information organized for your brief presentation.

- ◆ Be concise. Speak only to the current issue. Do not meander or wander off the topic.

- ◆ Be honest. Report exactly what you know and don't know. Don't make up information you don't have.

- ◆ Have a written summary prepared. Be able to disseminate a statement of the student's progress to committee members. This will help keep you and them on-task.

- ◆ Don't make statements that go beyond your objective data about the student's progress. If it is necessary to offer an opinion, make sure the committee knows it is just that and not necessarily a fact.

- ◆ Encourage comments from others, especially parents and the student (if present).

Source: Westling, D. L., & Koorland, M. A. (1989). *The special educator's handbook* (p. 47). Boston: Allyn & Bacon. Used with permission.

informal assessment can begin. The ability to compare the student to her age and grade peers is also an advantage in making eligibility and placement decisions and fulfilling related administrative requirements.

Formal tests serve two primary functions: surveying ability in an instructional domain and diagnosing difficulties. Survey tests are usually administered to obtain a global score or level of functioning. Numerous tests are used to serve this purpose. Two common examples of survey tests that may be used as part of the special education assessment process are the *Peabody Individual Achievement Test–Revised* (Markwardt, 1989) and the *Wide Range Achievement Test–Revised* (Jastak & Wilkinson, 1984).

Diagnostic tests attempt to obtain more specific information about strengths and weaknesses. Two examples of formal diagnostic tests that are often used for instructional program development are the *Key Math–Revised* (Connolly, 1988) and the *Gray Oral Reading Test–Revised* (GORT–2) (Wiederholt & Bryant, 1986).

Formal tests provide quantitative and sometimes qualitative data based on student performance in the testing situation. However, a key principle is that these tests can only endeavor to obtain a measure of a student's best performance in a contrived situation versus truly representing a student's typical performance under natural conditions.

Formal testing constitutes one important part of the assessment process.

Professionals can make more informed decisions about the use of formal instruments if they study the instrument and become familiar with its features, benefits, and possible liabilities. One way to do this is to consult one or more of the several excellent resources on tests. Two particularly apt sources are the *Buros Mental Measurements Yearbook* (Conoley & Kramer, 1989) and *Tests in Print* (1989). Both are periodically revised and updated.

Informal Assessment

Informal assessments are usually more loosely structured than formal instruments and are more closely tied to teaching.

Such tools are typically devised by teachers to determine what skills or knowledge a child possesses. Their key advantage should be the direct application of assessment data to instructional programs. By incorporating assessment results into the teaching program and by monitoring student responses each day, teachers can achieve reliable measurements that reveal patterns of fluctuation in performance.

Criterion-referenced testing (**CRT**) compares a student's performance with a criterion of mastery for a specific task, disregarding an emphasis on his relative standing in a group. This form of informal assessment can be especially useful when documentation of progress is needed for accountability because the acquisition of skills can be clearly demonstrated. As Wallace et al. (1992) stressed, CRTs are quite popular because they focus attention on specific skills in the curriculum, provide measures of progress toward mastery, and assist teachers in designing instructional strategies. Traditionally, most criterion-referenced tests have been produced by teachers, but more recently publishers have begun to produce assessment tools of this type.

One important and popular form of criterion-referenced assessment is curriculum-based assessment, which, unlike norm-referenced tools, uses the actual curriculum as the standard and thus provides a basis for evaluating and modifying the curriculum for an individual student (McLoughlin & Lewis, 1990). This type of assessment can serve many purposes: identification, eligibility, instructional grouping, program planning, progress monitoring, and program evaluation (Hasbrouck & Tindal, 1992; Marston & Magnusson, 1985). Curriculum-based assessment can assist in focusing attention on changes in academic behavior within the context of the curriculum being used, thus enhancing the relationship between assessment and teaching (Deno & Fuchs, 1987). Because curriculum-based assessment encourages reliance on methods keyed to the curriculum and administered by classroom teachers, it is also more ecologically valid than norm-referenced testing (Fuchs & Fuchs, 1986).

According to Fuchs, Fuchs, and Hamlett (1990), there are four ways in which curriculum-based measures can be used to improve instructional programs. The *first* is to determine whether the student's actual rate of progress is higher than expected. The goal is increased when this is found to be the case. The *second* use comes when assessing the need to modify a program. A "line of best fit" is drawn through the scores of the student. The steepness of the line or the position of scores in relation to the line determines whether a modification in the program is deemed to be necessary. The *third* use essentially serves as a vehicle for comparing instructional methods. Here the results of different instructional methods the teacher uses are graphed and compared. The one that yields the best results stands out and is chosen over the others. *Fourth,* to modify and improve programs, the student's actual responses to CBM test items are analyzed before considering any of the other three procedures.

Curriculum-based measures can be developed through systematic analysis of a given curriculum, selection of specific items, and construction of assessment formats (e.g., questions, cloze activities, worksheets). Idol, Nevin, and Paolucci-Whitcomb (1986) suggested developing three different forms of the same instrument which can be used on alternate days of testing. Although manuals and other resources for developing curriculum-based instruments exist, they serve primarily as guides because instruments used in the classroom should reflect the curriculum being followed in that venue.

Ecological Assessment

Educational assessment has increasingly begun to reflect a trend toward an appreciation of the ecology of the student. Consequently, data obtained on an individual are now more frequently being subjected to an analysis of how these data relate to the child's functioning in the various environments in which he lives and learns. Although a full discussion of ecological assessment is beyond the scope of this chapter, the following discussion highlights some basic considerations.

Clearly the key focus of ecological assessment is to place the evaluation process within the context of the student's environment. In so doing, the process takes on a central element of *functionality;* that is, the concern becomes how well the student functions in his current environment or the one into which he will be moving. By shifting more toward a focus on functionality, the emphasis of programs can then shift away from correcting deficits and more toward determining how to build strengths and interests.

An emphasis on ecological assessment necessarily results in a broadening of the assessment process. Additionally, it offers professionals a way of validating findings. We conclude this discussion with some strategies adapted from Luckasson et al. (1992) for adding validity to the process being followed:

- ◆ Conduct a subsequent administration of a second instrument by another professional so that results can be averaged or jointly considered.
- ◆ Review case histories of the student.
- ◆ Interview key persons in the student's life.
- ◆ Observe the student in his natural environments (e.g., classroom, home).
- ◆ Interview the student directly or interact with her in a play or other social or less formal setting for assessment.

Issues of Bias in Assessment

The importance of assuring fair and equitable assessment procedures clearly was emphasized in PL 94–142. This basic assumption of the law stated that assessment procedures must be established to

assure that testing and evaluation materials and procedures utilized for the purposes of evaluation and placement of handicapped children will be selected and administered so as not to be racially or culturally discriminatory. Such material or procedures shall be provided and administered in the child's native language or mode of communication, unless it is clearly not feasible to do so, and no single procedure shall be the sole criterion for determining an appropriate educational program for a child.

As Zucker and Polloway (1987) noted, this regulation within PL 94–142 stemmed directly from court cases that served as legal precursors for this federal legislation. For example, these cases related to the use of IQ in the placement of minority children into classes for students with mental retardation (e.g., *Larry P. v. Riles,* 1972; *Diana v. State Board of Education,* 1970) and "tracking systems" in the public schools (e.g., *Hobson v. Hansen,* 1967). The decision in *Hobson v. Hansen* was that tests standardized on a white middle-class population were used to effectively classify students by socioeconomic status rather than by ability.

As a consequence of this legal challenge, and consistent with best educational practice, multifactorial assessment is necessary in any consideration of eligibility and evaluation for special education. When a child to be evaluated does not differ from the norm culturally or in any other significant manner that would preclude the use of traditional tests, evaluation is relatively straightforward. When the child differs, however, other modified approaches must be considered (Zucker & Polloway, 1987). As Wallace et al. (1992) stressed,

> it is clear that bias in the evaluation of students, particularly those from a minority background, can and will significantly affect the educational opportunities afforded these youngsters. To minimize the effects of bias in the evaluation, it is absolutely essential that every [professional]... be aware of the various ways in which bias is exhibited and take steps to minimize its effects when making educational decisions. (p. 473)

These authors stressed that many sources of possible bias can be found in the assessment process, ranging from administrative practices such as proximity to student and physical contact, to gender of tester and testee, to cultural and ethnic prejudice, to linguistic variance.

A special concern has to do with the accurate assessment of individuals who experience specific sensory or motor disabilities. For example, individuals who are hearing impaired may require a nonverbal test, whereas persons who are visually impaired require measures that do not rely on object manipulation and do not include cards or pictures (Reschly, 1987). An individual with a severe motor impairment may have limited voluntary responses and may need to respond via an eye scan or blink. Students who have multiple disabilities compound the challenges faced by the person with responsibility for the assessment task. Browder and Snell (1988) noted that some individuals simply lack "test behaviors." For example, they may refuse to stay seated for an assessment session or may exhibit interfering self-stimulatory behavior (e.g., hand flapping, rocking). Further, test results should not be unduly affected by disabilities in receptive or expressive language capabilities. Such disabilities may cause the test to be a measure of the problem itself rather than a valid assessment of level of functioning. Considered collectively, these problem areas can make traditional testing procedures not feasible, inadvertently resulting in discriminatory practices (Browder & Snell, 1988; Luckasson et al., 1992).

Bailey and Harbin (1980) noted that nondiscriminatory evaluation requires that data be gathered by an interdisciplinary team in a nondiscriminatory fashion, with an awareness of how bias could enter the decision-making process, and with the knowledge of how to control it. This general admonition serves as a backdrop to specific cautions concerning assessment procedures. To account for issues of cultural difference as well as other concerns that may arise in ensuring appropriate assessment procedures, the following principles, adapted from Grossman (1983), Turnbull and Wheat (1983), and Luckasson et al. (1992), provide governing procedures:

- ◆ The assessment process should be initiated only when sufficient cause is documented.
- ◆ Parents must consent to the assessment and have the right to participate in, and appeal, any determinations made and any program decisions that follow from assessment.
- ◆ Assessments are to be undertaken only by fully qualified professionals.

Guidelines for Assessment of Culturally Diverse Learners

To achieve a nonbiased, functional approach to assessment of culturally diverse learners, it is recommended that educators:

1. Focus attention on classroom and school learning environments and away from perspectives that have little validity within school environments (e.g., medical- and mental-health-based models).
2. Attend to the predisposing factors that characterize the learner, teacher, administrator, and other school personnel (e.g., culture, expectations, tolerance levels, learning and reinforcement history, family conditions).
3. Focus on observable student and teacher behaviors and the context in which they occur.
4. Attend to the conditions under which behaviors are observed, taught, or required.
5. Establish specific, measurable, instructionally based standards for acceptable academic and social behaviors.
6. Develop and implement prereferral intervention procedures that force an assessment of the student's current learning environment before referral and certification are considered, and provide a means of documenting the effects of each prereferral attempt.
7. Acknowledge and apply instructional procedures that have been shown to be effective and efficient.
8. Focus evaluation practices on assessment of the instructional process (i.e., teaching behaviors, instructional organization, and instructional support).
9. Avoid placing the responsibility for learning or performance failure on the student.
10. Encourage teacher trainers and others in higher education to take functional assessment perspectives that focus on children at risk for academic and/or behavioral difficulties.
11. Stimulate a realignment of professionals (e.g., psychologists, administrators) toward a functional assessment perspective.

Source: Sugai, G., & Maheady, L. (1988). Cultural diversity and individual assessment for behavior disorders. *Teaching Exceptional Children, 21*, pp. 28–31.

♦ Assessment procedures must be adjusted to account for specific disabilities in hearing, vision, health, or motor impairment.
♦ Assessments should be modified to accommodate individuals whose culture and/or language differs from the population upon whom the instruments were standardized.

♦ Conclusions and recommendations should be made on the basis of multiple sources of data, including input from people directly acquainted with the person (e.g., parents) and direct observations of the student.

♦ Periodic reassessments must be made (at least every three years) to reevaluate previous judgments and to consider necessary programming changes.

As Polloway and Jones-Wilson (1992) noted, the cautions that must be considered in assessment can generally be summarized into one key point: Assessment efforts must be clearly undertaken for the express purpose of providing information that will lead to effective programming. Thus, the utility of the results is measured by how closely they ultimately relate to effective instruction.

Role of the Classroom Teacher

The preceding discussion on assessment has outlined the process followed in special education as well as highlighting key considerations. Although much of this information is critical to all professionals involved in the process of evaluating students with disabilities, the question remains: What are the concerns that specifically apply to the classroom teacher? The following list summarizes aspects with particular relevance for the general education professional.

1. Ask questions about the assessment process. Special education teachers and school psychologists should be committed to clarifying the nature of the assessments used and the interpretation of the results.
2. Seek help as needed in conveying information to parents. Speece and Mandell (1980) noted that support in conferences with parents was a high priority for classroom teachers but unfortunately was rarely provided by special educators.
3. Provide input into the process. Formal test data should not be allowed to contradict observations in the classroom about a student's ability, achievement, and learning patterns. A valid diagnostic picture should accommodate multiple sources of data.
4. Observe assessment procedures. If time and facilities are available (e.g., a one-way mirror), an opportunity to observe the testing process can not only be educational but also enhance your ability to have input into decision making.
5. Consider issues of possible bias. Since formal assessments are often administered by an individual relatively unknown to the child (e.g., a psychologist), inadvertent bias factors between examiner and examinee may be more likely to creep into the results. Work with other staff to ensure that an unbiased process is effected.
6. See assessment as possibly exploratory as well as possibly confirming. Too often, after a student is not judged eligible for special services, there is resentment toward the assessment process. However, if the process is to be functional and useful, then the key commitment should be to eliciting useful information to help the student, not solely effecting the eligibility decision.

Individualized Education Programs (IEPs)

The results of assessment should be translated into educational plans for instructional goals. The individualized education program (IEP) is an annual description of services planned for students with disabilities. The IEP is a direct requirement under PL 94–142, and now IDEA, which mandates that all students with disabilities receive a free and appropriate public education, and which acknowledges that they need both a unique and a specially designed instructional program.

The intent of the requirement that an IEP be written on each student identified as disabled was that the focus of intervention needed to be placed on individual needs. The primary intent of the IEP was based on the notion that student needs should drive the educational program rather than preexisting program design determining the student's program (Harvey, 1978). The IEP itself was to be developed by a team comprised of teachers, a school administrator, the parents, and, where appropriate, the student. Following an analysis of relevant diagnostic data, the multidisciplinary team writes an IEP reflecting the student's educational needs.

Although IEPs may serve varied purposes, Polloway and Patton (1993) indicate that three are most prominent. First, IEPs can provide instructional *direction*. Well-written goal setting can help to remedy an approach to instruction that consists of pulling together isolated or marginally related exercises. Second, IEPs can function as the basis of *evaluation;* annual goals then serve as standards against which to judge student progress and teacher effectiveness and efficiency. Third, IEPs can improve *communication* among members of the team. IEPs should facilitate planning and program implementation among staff members, teachers, and parents, and, as appropriate, between teachers and students.

A frequently discussed issue has been the functionality and value of the IEP. Unfortunately, the IEP is often developed more for compliance than for guiding instruction (Smith & Simpson, 1989). Dudley-Marling (1985) surveyed teachers regarding the usefulness of IEPs and found that most agreed that IEPs had general utility but indicated that IEPs were not used in the planning of instruction. This concern was underscored by the fact that the IEP was not often accessible. Similar findings on teachers' views of the lack of the instructional relevance of IEPs have been reported elsewhere (Margolis & Truesdell, 1987; Morgan & Rhode, 1983).

Functionality has been further investigated in studies on the congruence between the needs of students and IEP goals (e.g., Epstein, Patton, Polloway, & Foley, 1992; Lynch & Beare, 1990; Smith, 1990a; Smith & Simpson, 1989), and between specific assessment data and instructional goals (Fiedler & Knight, 1986). These studies collectively failed to find a clear relationship between student needs and IEP goals. Lynch and Beare (1990) extended this analysis to the observation of classroom lessons and found low correspondence between the instruction being provided and students' needs, annual goals, and short-term objectives.

When the examination of IEPs has focused on the nature of the goals written, some interesting observations have emerged. For the most part, researchers have reported an overemphasis on academic remediation goals and a relative paucity of goals for behavioral and social skill development (e.g., Lynch & Beare, 1990; McCormick & Fisher, 1983; Smith & Simpson, 1989) except for students with behavioral disorders (e.g., Smith, 1990a; Epstein et al., 1992; McBride & Forgnone, 1985). Further areas such as career development, transitional planning, and functional life skills preparation are noticeably missing from the IEPs of many students with learning disabilities, mild mental retardation, or behavioral disorders (e.g., Epstein, Polloway, Patton, & Foley, 1989; Epstein et al., 1992; McBride & Forgnone, 1985; Polloway, Patton, Epstein, Acquah, Decker, & Carse, in press). If the IEPs analyzed in these studies accurately reflect classroom practice, it would appear that students are not being provided a comprehensive curriculum (i.e., transition-oriented, tied to integration, and sensitive to long-term needs; see Polloway, Patton, Epstein, & Smith, 1989).

Finally, analyses of IEPs by Epstein et al. (1992), McBride and Forgnone (1985), Smith (1990a), and Smith and Simpson (1989) raise a number of questions about not only the type but also the quantity of goals being written. These studies highlight the question of whether the comprehensive needs of students with learning and behavioral problems are being adequately addressed when so few (3 or 4) annual goals are written.

The generally pessimistic research on the validity and utility of IEPs had led to a questioning of their contribution to the development of appropriate programs. Smith

Parental involvement in the development of the individualized education program is both a legal requirement as well as an important aspect in the design of appropriate school programs.

(1990b) suggested that the existing research indicates only minimal compliance with the process and thus a failure to achieve "specially designed instruction." If IEPs have only limited functionality, logically some action for a mandate for either strengthening the guidelines or deleting the requirement must be entertained (Epstein et al., 1992). Despite research that the IEP has not successfully fulfilled its mission, little has been done to respond to the dilemma and correct the situation (Smith, 1990b).

How then, in response to these dilemmas, should teachers approach the task of formulating and using individualized education programs? It is critical that the task of IEP writing and implementation, rather than being burdensome or irrelevant, should serve as a catalyst for enhancing the education of the individual child (Turnbull, Strickland, & Hammer, 1978). For the IEP concept to achieve functionality, teachers must move beyond seeing IEPs as paperwork and must view them as symbols of specially tailored programs in areas of instructional need. For this to occur, teachers need to use the plan as a basis for subsequent teaching decisions. Only in this way can annual goals, which should serve as the basis for determining short-term objectives, eventually be reflected in ongoing instructional planning. The discussion that follows illustrates the principles underlying the development of IEPs.

Components

There are eight required components in the IEP: present level of performance, annual instructional goals, short-term objectives, statement of special services to be provided, description of integration into general education programs consistent with the least restrictive alternative, schedules for initiation and evaluation of objectives, and the signed consent/documentation.

Positive goals provide an appropriate direction for instruction. Additionally, for students over the age of 16 (and on occasion at earlier ages), a related component under the IDEA is the designation of needed transition services (i.e., an individualized transition plan). Once issues of types of services have been resolved, the three components that are key to instruction remain: levels of performance, annual goals, and short-term objectives. These three are reflected in the sample IEP in Figure 2.4.

Levels of performance provide a summary of assessment data on a student's current functioning, which is to serve as the basis for the establishment of annual goals. Therefore, the information should include data for each priority area in which instructional support is needed. Depending on the individual student, for example, consideration might be given to reading, math, and other academic skills, written and oral communication skills, vocational talents and needs, behavioral patterns, self-help skills, and motor skills.

Performance levels can be provided in various forms such as formal and informal assessment data, behavioral descriptions, and specific abilities delineated by checklists or skill sequences. Functional summary statements of an individual's strengths and weaknesses draw on information from a variety of sources rather than relying on any one form of description. Test scores in math, for example, might be combined with a description of how the child performed on a curriculum-based measure such as a computational checklist. In general, the phrasing used to define levels of performance

Computerized IEPs—Point and Counterpoint?

In an article entitled "Individualized Education Programs (IEPs) in Special Education—From Intent to Acquiescence," in the September 1990 issue of *Exceptional Children*, Steven W. Smith examines the norms and standards originally intended (circa 1975) for IEPs by Public Law 94–142 and contrasts them with the reality of present-day (circa 1990) IEP design and implementation factors. In his writing, Smith acknowledges that computerized IEPs help streamline the administrative areas of IEP production. However, Smith also argues—quite strongly—that the use of computerized IEPs appears to produce documents inferior to handwritten IEPs! You be the judge.

Numerous computer-managed instructional systems (CMI), or educational management systems that use computer software to manage the [individualized education program (IEP)], have been designed to relieve the burden of paperwork and cost created by the [Education for All Handicapped Children Act's (EAHCA] mandate. . . .

Even though the issues of cost and time can be managed effectively by computer-assisted IEPs, as reported in the literature, the issue of a quality IEP is infrequently mentioned. . . . [The literature that focuses on finding effective computer-assisted systems to manage the IEP process and accompanying documentation] is important to analyze because its research focus has shifted from the original spirit and intent of the EAHCA [i.e., from IEP quality issues emphasizing factors such as multidisciplinary assessment, comprehensive educational planning, and parental involvement] to concerns about reducing the cost and time necessary to complete IEPs (minimal compliance) by computer assistance. The emphasis on being able to complete the IEP process and document in less time with less cost thereby fostering more favorable teacher attitudes toward the IEP is viable; however, the reason for the shift from developing quality IEPs to aiding the completion of the document remains conjecture.

Thus the focus [on finding effective computer-assisted systems to manage the IEP process] is one of the most curious stages of IEP research, not only because of the current acceptance of the IEP (despite its skeptical past), but because of the potential sentiment that a "quick fix" using technology can accomplish what other recommendations for improving IEPs have not. Perhaps the IEP's evolution toward a technocratic solution is special education's last effort to arrive at a state-of-the-art document. The IEP, as managed by computers, would now be generated by technicians, using formulas and following rules, rather than using the intended individualized or personalized problem solving to provide an appropriate education. Use of technology to formulate IEPs represents a response to the failure of special education practice to conceptually embrace the concept of what we know about IEPs versus what we do. Thus, efforts now are undertaken to ensure minimal compliance, the very nature of which the EAHCA was intended to preclude.

Sparse mention of quality [in the computerized IEP literature] leads to questions regarding IEPs generated by computers. Have the heal-all powers of technological assistance generated this phase of IEP research? . . . [Are] the obstacles to exemplary compliance [found in much of the IEP research literature] making quality IEPs

▼

a non-issue"? Has exemplary compliance of the IEP become subordinate to the realities of time, effort, and money? Although answers to these questions are conjecture, one [computer managed instruction] effect on the IEP is clear—the IEP and its mission to provide individualized education within the spirit and intent of EAHCA has become a waning concern. Little if any suggestions are found [in the literature addressing using computer-assisted systems] for implementing IEPs toward the law's original intent of quality programming based on the values of an appropriate education. (Smith, 1990b, pp. 10–11)

Source: Gardner, J. E., & Edyburn, D. L. (1993). Teaching applications with exceptional individuals. In J. D. Lindsey (Ed.), *Computers and exceptional individuals* (p. 279). Austin, TX: Pro-Ed. Used with permission.

should be positive and describe things the child *can do* as opposed to being negatively stated. For example, the same information is conveyed by the two following statements but the former demonstrates the more positive approach: "The student can identify 50% of times tables facts" versus "The student does not know half of the facts." Appropriately written performance levels provide breadth and specificity of data in order to generate relevant and appropriate annual goals.

The second, central IEP instructional component is ***annual goals.*** Each student's goals should be individually determined to meet unique needs and abilities. Since it is obviously impossible to predict the precise amount of progress a student will make in a year, goals should be reasonable projections of what the student will accomplish. In order to develop reasonable expectations, teachers can consider a number of variables, including the chronological age of the child, the expected rate of learning and past and current learning profiles.

Annual goals should be measurable, positive, student-oriented, and relevant (Polloway and Patton, 1993). *Measurable* goals provide a basis for evaluation. Statements should use terms that denote action and can therefore be operationally defined (e.g., pronounce, write), rather than vague, general language that confounds evaluation and observer agreement (e.g., know, understand). *Positive* goals provide an appropriate direction for instruction. Avoiding negative goals creates an atmosphere that is helpful in communicating with parents as well as in charting student progress. Goals should also be *oriented to the student.* Developing students' skills is the intent, and the only measure of effectiveness should be what is learned, rather than what is taught. Finally, goals must be *relevant* to the individual's actual needs. Unfortunately, as noted earlier, research indicates that goals on IEPs frequently do not meet this criterion.

Annual goals should subsequently be broken down into *short-term objectives*, detailed in a logical and sequential series to provide a general plan for instructional focus. The objectives should move a student from the student's current level of performance through a sequence of objectives toward the relevant annual goal.

Short-term objectives can be derived only after goals are written. They should be based on a task analysis process, with skill sequences and checklists providing a foundation for dividing an annual goal into its logical major components. The four criteria to be applied to annual goals are even more appropriately applied to short-term

Peabody Individual Achievement Test		Peabody Picture Vocabulary Test–Form A		Durrell Analysis of Reading Difficulty	
general info.	4.0	CA	11-2	word analysis	3-M
total test	3.5	receptive vocabulary age	8-11	date	5/94
date	5/94	date	5/94		

Tommy's ability to answer comrehension questions after silent reading was good on the second-grade level.

Annual Goal #1:   Tommy will be able to answer comprehension questions with 90 percent accuracy after listening to a passage on the 4th-grade level.

		Dates	
Objectives	Evaluation	Begun	Completed
1. will answer comprehension question with 90 percent accuracy after listening to a mid-3rd grade level passage	mid-third grade level passage high third		
2. will answer comprehension question with 90 percent accuracy after listening to a high-3rd grade level passage	high third grade level passage		
3. will answer comprehension question with 90 percent accuracy after listening to a mid-4th grade level passage	mid-fourth grade level passage		

Annual Goal #2:   Tommy will be able to pronounce and spell short, long, and variant vowel pattern one syllable words with 80 percent accuracy.

1. will pronounce and spell short vowel pattern words with 80 percent accuracy	phonics checklist		
2. will pronounce and spell long vowel pattern words with 80 percent accuracy	phonics checklist		
3. will pronounce and spell r-controlled vowel pattern words with 80 percent accuracy	phonics checklist		

Figure 2.4   **Sample IEP**
Source: Adapted from Polloway, E. A., & Smith, J. E. (1982). *Teaching language skills to exceptional learners* (pp. 111–113). Denver: Love Publishing.

objectives. Since the objectives are more precise, the measurable criterion should be enhanced through the inclusion of a criterion for mastery. Table 2.3 presents a series of annual goal/short-term objective clusters.

Numerous computer software programs provide sequenced goal objective clusters. Although the benefit of reduced paperwork and time to generate objectives can be substantial, teachers must be careful to ensure that a student's curriculum and hence his IEP remains consistent with his individual needs.

Role of Classroom Teacher

Although IEPs have always been intended to be jointly developed by all those involved in the student's educational program, in practice it has often largely fallen to special education teachers to develop them. Consequently, apparent abuses of the system have been common. Instances of general education classroom teachers asking if they were "allowed to see the IEP" or of parents being asked to copy over the IEP so they "would be involved in its 'writing'" (Turnbull & Turnbull, 1986) have been too common.

TABLE 2.3 Goal-Objective Clusters

Goal 1 SWBAT[a] correctly use capitalization and punctuation in sentences with 90% accuracy.

Objective 1: SWBAT begin the first word of each sentence with a capital letter with 90% accuracy.

Objective 2: SWBAT capitalize the pronoun "I" and the names of other persons with 90% accuracy.

Objective 3: SWBAT capitalize these proper nouns—the name of the school, streets, cities, state, months of the year, and days of the week—with 90% accuracy.

Objective 4: SWBAT place a period at the end of all sentences that make a statement with 90% accuracy.

Objective 5: SWBAT place a question mark at the end of sentences that ask a question with 90% accuracy.

Goal 2 SWBAT write a well-organized paragraph of four sentences showing appropriate punctuation and sentence structure.

Objective 1: Given 10 sentences incorrectly punctuated, SWBAT make corrections with 95% accuracy.

Objective 2: Given 10 sentences containing structural errors, SWBAT make corrections with 95% accuracy.

Objective 3: SWBAT write a well-organized paragraph of three sentences showing appropriate punctuation and sentence structure.

Objective 4: SWBAT write a well-organized paragraph of four sentences showing appropriate punctuation and sentence structure.

Goal 3 When a list of 50 words is presented orally, SWBAT correctly identify all the sounds of initial consonants with 100% accuracy.

Objective 1: When a list of 25 pairs of consonant sounds is presented orally, SWBAT correctly indicate, by raising his hand, those pairs of sounds that are the same 100% of the time.

Objective 2: When presented with a set of cards, each one containing a different consonant letter, SWBAT correctly choose each time the card displaying the same letter as the initial consonant sound of words presented orally.

---

[a]SWBAT = Student will be able to. . .

Guidelines for Preparing for Future IEPs

- ◆ At least one month before IEPs are to be developed, begin gathering and synthesizing student progress data.

- ◆ Adminster formal and informal tests, collect work samples, bring performance charts up to date.

- ◆ Prepare an informal draft of future goals and objectives.

- ◆ Consider alternative placements and, if possible, allow the student to spend brief periods of time in these settings.

- ◆ Work with parents in advance by helping them develop a list of information to share.

- ◆ Plan for the possibility of more than one meeting in order to allow airing of all the views of the group members.

- ◆ Try to include the student in the IEP process. Ask the student to list three good things about school, three things he or she would like to change, and three things he or she would like to learn.

Source: Westling, D. L., & Koorland, M. A. (1989). *The special educator's handbook* (p. 45). Boston: Allyn & Bacon. Used with permission.

Ideally, the classroom teacher should be involved in the IEP meeting. However, whether or not this occurs, an efficient means for input to be provided into its development should be developed (e.g., a pre-IEP informal meeting) or the consequence may be that the document does not reflect the student's needs in the integrated classroom. Furthermore, the IEP itself should be readily available as a reference tool throughout the year. In particular, the goal/objective clusters should be kept in proximity if the IEP is to influence the provision of instructional programs.

If IEPs are to be truly functional, annual goals and short-term objectives ultimately should be reflected in instructional plans in the classroom. Clearly, though, short-term objectives are not intended to convey weekly plans, let alone daily plans. However, if the IEP represents key concerns for an individual student within the academic year, teachers should refer to the document periodically in order to ensure that instruction is consistent with the long-term needs of the student. When significant variance is noted, this discrepancy may become the basis for a correction in course in terms of instruction or perhaps a rationale for a change in the goals and/or objectives of the IEP.

In concluding their discussion on IEPs, Epstein et al. (1992) indicated that teachers must not lose sight of the spirit of individualization that should guide the IEP process. Teachers need to view the documents not just as a process of legal compliance but rather as the assurance that students' individual needs will be met. Unless acceptance of the rationale and spirit for the IEP as originally intended in PL 94–142 is confirmed, the concept is likely to be perceived more as a necessary bookkeeping activity than as the basis for assuring a specially designed educational program for students who are disabled.

Summary

◆ All procedures associated with special education programs must be consistent with due process requirements.

◆ Each state provides timelines that govern the referral/assessment/IEP process.

◆ Prereferral intervention is a process of assisting students in the general education classroom prior to any referral for full assessment.

◆ Child study or teacher assistance committees are responsible for helping teachers modify instruction for a student experiencing learning difficulties.

◆ Child study teams who have been trained in their work can be both effective in assisting teachers and efficient in limiting referrals.

◆ Assessment includes testing but is a broader concept that is tied to the development of educational interventions.

◆ Formal assessment is based on the administration of commercial instruments, typically for survey or diagnostic purposes.

◆ Informal assessment includes a variety of tools that can enhance a teacher's knowledge of students' learning needs.

◆ Curriculum-based measures are tied to the class curriculum and assess a student within this context.

◆ Ecological assessment places the evaluative data obtained within the context of a student's environment, thus rendering it more functional.

◆ The control of bias in assessment is not only essential to accurate and fair evaluation but also a legal requirement.

◆ Classroom teachers may not administer formal assessments but nevertheless are important members of any assessment process and should be informed about the assessment process.

References

Bailey, D. B., & Harbin, G. L. (1980). Nondiscriminatory evaluation. *Exceptional Children, 46*, 590–596.

Browder, D., & Snell, M. E. (1988). Assessment of individuals with severe disabilities. In M. E. Snell (Ed.), *Severe disabilities*. Columbus, OH: Merrill.

Brown, J., Gable, R. A., Hendrickson, J. M., & Algozzine, B. (1991). Prereferral intervention practices of regular classroom teachers: Implications for regular and special education preparation. *Teacher Education and Special Education, 14,* 192–197.

Chalfant, J. C., & Pysh, M. V. (1989). Teacher assistance teams: Five descriptive studies on 96 teams. *Remedial and Special Education, 10*(6), 49–58.

Chalfant, J. C., Pysh, M. V., & Moultrie, R. (1979). Teacher assistance teams: A model for within-building problem solving. *Learning Disability Quarterly, 2*(3), 85–96.

Connolly, A. J. (1988). *Keymath—Revised: A diagnostic inventory of essential mathematics.* Circle Pines, MN: American Guidance Service.

Conoley, J. C., & Kramer, J. J. (1989). *Tenth mental measurements yearbook.* Lincoln, NE: Buros Institute.

Deno, S. L., & Fuchs, L. S. (1987). Developing curriculum-based measurement systems for data-based special education problem-solving. *Focus on Exceptional Children, 19*(8), 1–16.

Diana v. State Board of Education, C-70-37 R.F.P. (N.D., California, Jan. 7, 1970, and June 18, 1972).

Dowdy, C. A., & Smith, T. E. C. (1991). Future-based assessment and intervention. *Intervention in School and Clinic, 27,* 101–106.

Dudley-Marling, C. (1985). Perceptions of the usefulness of the IEP by teachers of learning disabled and emotionally disturbed children. *Psychology in the Schools, 22,* 65–67.

Epstein, M. H., Patton, J. R., Polloway, E. A., & Foley, R. (1992). Educational services for students with behavior disorders: A review of individualized education programs. *Teacher Education and Special Education, 15,* 41–48.

Epstein, M. H., Polloway, E. A., Patton, J. R., & Foley, R. (1989). Mild retardation: Student characteristics and services. *Education and Training in Mental Retardation, 24,* 7–16.

Fiedler, J. R., & Knight, R. R. (1986). Congruence between assessed needs and IEP goals of identified behaviorally disabled students. *Behavioral Disorders, 12,* 22–27.

Fuchs, L. S., & Fuchs, D. (1986). Effects of systematic formative evaluation: A meta-analysis. *Exceptional Children, 53,* 199–208.

Fuchs, L. S., Fuchs., D., & Hamlett, C. L. (1990). Curriculum-based measurement: A standardized, long-term goal approach to monitoring student progress. *Academic Therapy, 25,* 615–632.

Gardner, J. E., & Edyburn, D. L. (1993). Teaching applications with exceptional individuals. In J. D. Lindsey (Ed.), *Computers and Exceptional Individuals* (pp. 264–286). Austin, TX: Pro-Ed.

Graden, J. L., Casey, A., & Christenson, S. L. (1985). Implementing a prereferral intervention system: Part I, The model. *Exceptional Children, 51,* 377–384.

Grossman, H. J. (1983). *Classification in mental retardation.* Washington, DC: American Association on Mental Deficiency.

Harvey, J. (1978, May). *What's happening in personnel preparation at BEH.* Paper presented at the 58th Annual CEC Convention, Kansas City, MO.

Hasbrouck, J. E., & Tindal G. (1992). Curriculum-based oral reading fluency norms for students in grades 2 through 5. *Teaching Exceptional Children, 24*(3), 41–44.

Henry, N. A., & Flynt, E. S. (1990). Rethinking special education referral: A procedural model. *Intervention in School and Clinic, 26,* 22–24.

Hobson v. Hansen, 269 F. Supp. 401 (D.D.C.), 1967.

Idol, L., Nevin, A., & Paolucci-Whitcomb, P. (1986). *Collaborative consultation.* Rockville, MD: Aspen Systems.

Jastak, S. R., & Wilkinson, G. S. (1984). *The wide range achievement test—Revised.* Wilmington, DE: Jastak Associates.

Larry P. v. Riles, C-71-2270 (RFP, District Court for Northern California 1972.

Lloyd, J. W., Kauffman, J. M., Landrum, T. J., & Roe, D. L. (1991). Why do teachers refer pupils for special education? An analysis of referral records. *Exceptionality, 2,* 115–126.

Luckasson, R., Coulter, D., Polloway, E. A., Reiss, S., Schalock, R., Snell, M., Spitalnik, D., & Stark, J. (1992). *Mental retardation: Definition, classification and systems of supports.* Washington, DC: American Association of Mental Retardation.

Lynch, E. C., & Beare, P. L. (1990). The quality of IEP objectives and their relevance to instruction for students with mental retardation and behavioral disorders. *Remedial and Special Education, 11*(2), 48–55.

McBride, J. W., & Forgnone, C. (1985). Emphasis of instruction provided LD, EH, and EMR students in categorical and cross-categorical programming. *Journal of Research and Development in Education, 18*(4), 50–54.

McCormick, P. K., & Fisher, M. D. (1983). *An analysis of individualized education program goals selected for learning disabled students* (ERIC Document Reproduction Service No. 160–801). Washington, DC.

McLoughlin, J. A., & Lewis, R. B. (1990). *Assessing special students* (3rd ed.). Columbus, OH: Merrill.

Margolis, H., & Truesdell, L. A. (1987). Do special education teachers use IEPs to guide instruction? *The Urban Review, 19,* 151–159.

Markwardt, F. C. (1989). *Peabody individual achievement test—Revised.* Circle Pines, MN: American Guidance Service.

Marston, D., & Magnusson, D. (1985). Implementing curriculum-based measurement in special and regular education settings. *Exceptional Children, 52,* 266–276.

Morgan, D. P., & Rhode, G. (1983). Teachers' attitudes toward IEPs: A two year follow-up. *Exceptional Children, 50,* 64–67.

Polloway, E. A., & Jones-Wilson, L. (1992). Principles of assessment and instruction. In E. A. Polloway & T. E. C. Smith (Eds.), *Language instruction for students with disabilities* (pp. 87-120). Denver, CO: Love Publishing.

Polloway, E. A., & Patton, J. R. (1993). *Strategies for teaching learners with special needs* (5th ed.). Columbus, OH: Merrill/Macmillan.

Polloway, E. A., Patton, J. R., Epstein, M. H., Acquah, T., Decker, T. W., & Carse, C. (in press). *Characteristics and services in learning disabilities: A report on elementary programs* (ERIC Document Reproduction Service). Washington, DC.

Polloway, E. A., Patton, J. R., Epstein, M. H., & Smith, T. E. C. (1989). Comprehensive curriculum for students with mild handicaps. *Focus on Exceptional Children, 21*(8), 1–12.

Polloway, E. A., Patton, J. R., Payne, J. S., & Payne, R. A. (1989). *Strategies for teaching learners with special needs* (5th ed). Columbus, OH: Merrill.

Polloway, E. A., & Smith, J. E. (1982). *Teaching language skills to exceptional learners.* Denver, CO: Love Publishing.

Public Law 94–142 (1975). *Federal Register, 42,* 42474–42518.

Public Law 101-476 (1990). *Federal Register, 54,* 35210–35271.

Reschly, D. J. (1987). *Adaptive behavior.* Tallahassee, FL: Florida Department of Education.

Smith, S. W. (1990a). A comparison of individualized education programs (IEPs) of students with behavioral disorders and learning disabilities. *Journal of Special Education, 24,* 85–100.

Smith, S. W. (1990b). Individualized education programs (IEPs) in special education: From intent to acquiescence. *Exceptional Children, 57,* 6–14.

Smith, S. W., & Simpson, R. L. (1989). An analysis of individualized education programs (IEPs) for students with behavior disorders. *Behavioral Disorders, 14,* 107–116.

Speece, D., & Mandell, C. (1980). Resource room support services for regular classroom teachers. *Learning Disability Quarterly, 3*(1), 49–53.

Sugai, G., & Maheady, L. (1988). Cultural diversity and individual assessment for behavior disorders. *Teaching Exceptional Children, 21,* 28–31.

Tests in Print (1989). Austin, TX: Pro-Ed.

Turnbull, A. P., Strickland, B., & Hammer, S. E. (1978). IEPs: Presenting guidelines for development and implementation. *Journal of Learning Disabilities, 11,* 40–46.

Turnbull, A. P., & Turnbull, H. R. (1986). *Families, professionals, and exceptionality: A special partnership.* Columbus, OH: Merrill.

Turnbull, H. R., & Wheat, M. J. (1983). Legal responses to classification. In J. L. Matson, & J. A. Mulick (Eds.), *Handbook of mental retardation* (pp. 157–169). New York: Pergamon.

Wallace, G., Larsen, S. C., & Elksnin, L. K. (1992). *Educational assessment of learning problems.* Boston: Allyn & Bacon.

Westling, D. L., & Koorland, M. A. (1989). *The special educator's handbook.* Boston: Allyn & Bacon.

Wiederholt, J. L., & Bryant, B. (1986). *Gray oral reading test—Revised.* Austin, TX: Pro-Ed.

Zucker, S. H., & Polloway, E. A. (1987). Issues in identification and assessment in mental retardation. *Education and Training in Mental Retardation, 22,* 69–76.

CHAPTER 3

Inclusion Models

Introduction

The setting where students with disabilities should be provided educational and related services is a much-discussed, much-debated topic. In fact, the entire issue of where these students should be educated has "received more attention, undergone more modifications, and generated even more controversy than have decisions about how or what these students are taught" (Jenkins & Heinen, 1989, p. 516). The setting where students with disabilities are educated has a direct impact on who provides those services and the collaborations required to provide them (Smith, Finn, & Dowdy, 1993).

Although it is still debated, the preferred placement for students with disabilities has come full circle during the past two decades. First, students were served entirely in general education classes by classroom teachers. This gave way to providing services in special schools, then special classes, then resource rooms and general education classroom combinations (Jenkins & Heinen, 1989).

Currently, approximately 70% of all students with disabilities are included for a substantial portion of each school day in general education classrooms and taught by general education classroom teachers (Danielson & Bellamy, 1989). Including these students simply means that they spend at least a portion of each school day in classrooms with their age-appropriate peers. The inclusion of students with disabilities can be implemented in many different ways. Students can be placed in general education classrooms for a majority of the school day and "pulled out" periodically and provided instruction in resource settings by special education teachers. Another approach to inclusion is the *full* **inclusion** of students with disabilities in general education classrooms, with the concurrent dismantling of most special education programs. In this latter model, special education teachers may go into general education classrooms and work with students who are experiencing difficulties, as well as working directly with classroom teachers to develop and implement methods and materials that will meet the needs of many students. There is a continuum of inclusion options, and schools use the model that best suits their needs.

Regarding physical location, there are two general approaches to serving students with disabilities in public schools: (1) programs where students receive some form of special education programming in special education classrooms by special education teachers, and (2) programs where the needs of students with disabilities are provided totally within general education environments, either by classroom teachers or by a team of classroom and special education teachers. The specific placement of students with disabilities falls along a continuum of options. This **continuum of services** model provides a range of placement options from institutional to full-time placement in general education classrooms. In the early 1970s, Deno (1970) presented a continuum of services model with seven options. Figure 3.1 presents this model. Deno's model and similar versions of continuum models do not depict the infinite number of options that are possible between each stage. Therefore, although

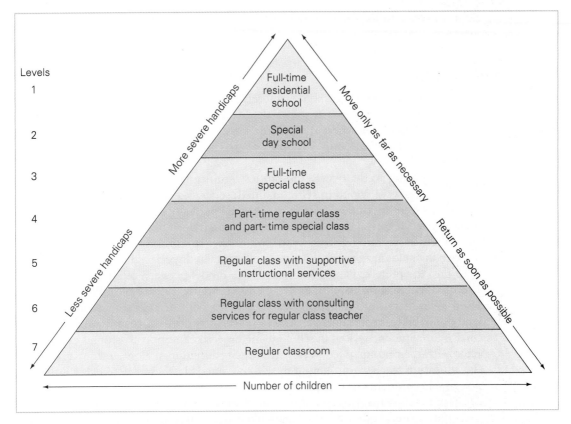

Figure 3.1 Cascade of Special Education Services
Source: From "Special education as developmental capital" by E. Deno, *Exceptional Children, 37,* 1970, 235. Copyright 1970 by The Council for Exceptional Children; and from "A framework for considering some issues in special education" by M. C. Reynolds, *Exceptional Children, 28,* 1962, 368. Copyright 1962 by The Council for Exceptional Children. Reprinted by permission.

Deno's model notes seven different placement possibilities, in reality there are an unlimited number of combinations of placement options for students with special needs (Smith et al., 1993).

Programs Where Students Receive Intervention in Special Education Settings

Traditionally, over the past 25 years, students with disabilities have received their educational programs in specialized classrooms. These settings could be **self-contained, special classes** or **resource rooms.** Serving students with disabilities in special programs was based on the presumption "that students with learning problems cannot be effectively taught in regular education programs even with a variety of support" (Will, 1986, p. 412). The only logical solution, therefore, to providing appropriate educational programs for these students was to remove them from the general education environment and have their educational programs provided by specialists trained specifically to meet their problems.

Special Class Approach

In the special class approach, students receive the majority of their programming from a special education teacher in a special education classroom. This differs from the resource room model, where the student spends a large portion of the school day in general education classrooms and only goes to the special education room for special assistance.

Historically, students with disabilities significant enough to warrant attention from teachers were served in self-contained, separate classrooms. Teachers in these classrooms were specifically trained to serve the population of students in the classes, usually on a categorical basis: that is, teachers were trained to teach students with mental retardation, learning disabilities, or some other specific disability group.

Serving students with disabilities in self-contained special education classes developed into the preferred and dominant service model between 1950 and 1970 (Idol, 1983; Podemski, Price, Smith, & Marsh, 1984; Smith, 1990; Smith, Price, & Marsh, 1986). Teachers were trained to teach students with disabilities, usually only one kind of disability, in all subject areas. However, the primary focus was on a functional curriculum. Students placed in self-contained special education classrooms rarely interacted with their nondisabled peers, often even eating lunch alone. Likewise, the special education teacher who taught in self-contained classes interacted very little with nondisabled students or classroom teachers. The self-contained classroom was thus isolating for students with disabilities and their teachers.

Many general education teachers liked the self-contained special class model because they did not have to deal with students who differed from their view of "typical" children. The role of classroom teachers in the self-contained model was extremely limited. As previously noted, students with disabilities in self-contained programs rarely interacted with general education teachers or their nondisabled peers. The classroom teacher might have indirect contacts with students who were disabled but rarely had to provide instructional services to this group. The primary role of general education teachers in the self-contained model was to refer students for the program. This primarily occurred in lower elementary grades, where the majority of students with disabilities are identified.

Currently, self-contained classrooms are used much less frequently than integrated settings to serve students with disabilities (Danielson & Bellamy, 1989). During the late 1960s and early 1970s, parents and professionals began questioning the efficacy of this model (Smith et al., 1986). With the passage of PL 94–142 and the requirement to serve students with disabilities in the least restrictive environment, the special class model was doomed as the preferred service model for the majority of students with disabilities (Blackman, 1989). In the 1990–1991 school year, only 25.1% of all students with disabilities were served in separate classes, compared to nearly 100% of students with disabilities prior to PL 94–142 (U.S. Department of Education, 1993). The movement away from special class programs has not been without dissent. Advocates for special classes have noted several advantages to serving students with disabilities in this type of setting. These include (Cegelka & Prehm, 1982)

- ◆ The special class teacher has added flexibility to schedule activities in the classroom.
- ◆ The development of friendships among peers is facilitated by small group instruction.
- ◆ It is more likely that parents will form stronger bonds and stronger advocacy potential.
- ◆ Groups with similar learning levels can be easily formed.
- ◆ In self-contained classes, the special education teacher assumes the role of total responsibility for the students.

Regardless of these stated advantages, the model has had many critics. The movement away from self-contained classrooms to integrated settings was sparked by several factors. These included, as noted in Chapter 1, efficacy studies, the civil rights movement (Brady, McDougall, & Dennis, 1989), and parent advocacy (Smith et al., 1986).

Still another reason for the demise of the popularity of the self-contained classroom was the growing philosophy of **"normalization"** (Brady et al., 1989). Normalization can be defined as "the creation of as normal as possible a learning and social environment for the exceptional child and adult" (Kirk & Gallagher, 1989, p. 14). Special classes, which segregate students with disabilities from their nondisabled age peers, cannot be considered a "normal" school placement. One way to implement the philosophy was through inclusion, which resulted in the widespread reduction of special classes.

One final reason for the demise of the self-contained special class model was a growing awareness of the diversity of students with disabilities (Morgan, 1985; Smith et al., 1986). Although the special class was the predominant model, the majority of students with disabilities served in special education were those with mild mental retardation. As exceptional populations, such as students with learning disabilities and emotional problems and those at risk for school failure, became recognized and were added to other disability groups—such as those with mental retardation, visual impairments, hearing impairments, and physical problems—the number of students needing special education grew significantly. The feasibility of serving all of these students in isolated, special classes became less attractive.

Resource Room Model

The passage of PL 94–142 in 1975 resulted in significant changes in the way students with special needs were served. A key requirement of the law was the requirement to educate students with disabilities in the least restrictive environment. The least-restrictive-environment mandate requires schools to place students with disabilities with their nondisabled peers as much as possible. Regulations implementing the law require that schools ensure "that to the maximum extent appropriate, children

Resolution No. 4 on Inclusion

A Resolution on Inclusion was adopted. Below are excerpts of the text:

WHEREAS, the U.S. Congress has enacted laws in recent years, such as the Individuals with Disabilities Education Act (IDEA), the Rehabilitation Act, The Developmental Disabilities Act, and the Americans with Disabilities Act (ADA), whose purposes and policies increase freedom of association for people with mental retardation and other disabilities through elimination of segregation in schools, work places and choice of residence and lifestyles; and

WHEREAS, The mission of The Arc states: "The Arc is committed to securing for all people with mental retardation the opportunity to choose and realize their goals of where and how they learn, live, work and play"; and

WHEREAS, It is essential for Arc chapters to provide leadership and to set a positive example in their activities, programs and services consistent with the spirit and intent of the federal laws identified above and the mission of The Arc: now, therefore be it

RESOLVED that The Arc and all its member chapters will:

1) Model a strong belief and commitment to the implementation of full membership and participation for all people with mental retardation by providing activities, programs and services that model best practices and positive approaches for including people with mental retardation in every aspect of community life; and

2) Communicate a strong belief and commitment to the implementation of full membership and participation for people with mental retardation in all publications, business and networking with other associations and agencies; and

3) Actively advocate at the federal, state and local levels for the systematic redirection of public policies and funding of services, supports, and benefits for people with mental retardation as necessary to reinforce their efforts to achieve full integration and inclusion in society consistent with the spirit and intent of the Individuals with Disabilities Act, the Rehabilitation Act, The Developmental Disabilities Act, the Americans with Disabilities Act, and the mission of The Arc.

Source: In Touch. Newsletter of the Association for Retarded Citizens–California. October 13, 1993. Los Angeles, CA.

with disabilities, including children in public or private institutions or other care facilities, are educated with children who are not disabled" (*Federal Register,* August 23, 1977, p. 42497). The regulations further state that "special classes, separate schooling or other removal of children with disabilities from the general educational environment occurs only when the nature or severity of the disability is such that education in regular classes with the use of supplementary aids and services cannot be achieved satisfactorily" (p. 42497). The result was the application of the continuum of services model for integration.

The primary service delivery option used for most students with disabilities is the resource room model (Smith et al., 1986; U.S. Department of Education, 1993). The resource room is a special education classroom. However, unlike the self-contained special class, the resource room is where students go only for special instruction. For the majority of the school day, most students attend general education classrooms; the classroom teacher becomes the lead teacher for these students. This means that students in resource rooms spend a large part of each school day with their nondisabled, chronological age peers, and are in resource rooms only for special assistance in deficit areas (Smith et al., 1993).

Prior to the passage of PL 94–142, the resource room model was used in some school districts but was not widespread. As a result of PL 94–142 requiring the inclusion of students with disabilities, the resource room has become the leading placement option for students with disabilities. The 14th Annual Report to Congress shows that 35% of all students with disabilities, more than 1.6 million, received special education services in resource rooms during the 1990–1991 school year (U.S. Department of Education, 1993).

Although the resource room model can be implemented in different ways, there are several similarities in all resource rooms (Marsh & Price, 1980):

1. The student divides the day between the resource room and the classroom.
2. Resource room scheduling is usually done so that only small groups of students are in the resource room at any one time.
3. Instruction is almost totally individualized and centers around the objectives and goals of the IEP for each child.
4. The focus of instruction may include remediation of student's basic skills or assistance in passing regular class subjects, an approach termed accommodation.
5. The teacher should be a certified special educator with experience and training in management of a resource room.
6. Successful resource room programs require extensive interaction and cooperation between the special education program and the general education classes of the building (Smith et al., 1986, p. 141).

Advantages of the Resource Room Model.   There are several obvious advantages of the resource room model over self-contained, special classes. The most important one is that students with disabilities have an opportunity to interact with their chronological age peers (York, Vandercook, MacDonald, Heise-Neff, &Caughey, 1992). In the special class model, students are isolated from these peers; they rarely have an opportunity to interact with them and model their behaviors. This is extremely important. Students have a tendency to model their peers. Therefore, students who only have the opportunity to interact with other students who are disabled may not have access to nondisabled role models. This can result in students modeling inappropriate behaviors and poor study habits rather than the behaviors that are desired. Opportunities for social interactions are enhanced in the resource room model (Jenkins, Odom, & Speltz, 1989).

Including students with disabilities can also have a positive impact on nondisabled students. Students in general education classrooms have a more positive opinion of students with disabilities placed in their classes than they do of students with disabilities who are placed in full-time special classes (York et al., 1992). Bak, Cooper, Dobroth, and Siperstein (1987) studied the expectations of nondisabled students about two groups of students with disabilities, those in general education classes and those in special classes. The results of the study revealed that the nondisabled students considered students in resource rooms/general education classroom placements as being more capable than those placed full time in special education settings. These results suggest that "children are sensitive to the differences between peers who attend different educational placements from their regular classrooms" (Bak et al., 1987, p. 154). In another study that investigated the outcomes of including students with severe disabilities in general education classes in a middle school, nearly 90% of the nondisabled students thought that the inclusion should be continued in the future (York et al., 1992).

Another important advantage of the resource model is that students with disabilities are able to receive instruction from several teachers (Cegelka & Prehm, 1982). In self-contained, special class settings, only special education teachers provide instruction to students. Students do not get to take advantage of different teachers with diverse expertise. Although this may not have a negative effect on elementary aged students, where the majority of instruction focuses on basic skill development, as students get older and are enrolled in content classes, they need to have the opportunity to be taught by teachers who are experts in particular content areas.

In the resource room, students with disabilities are able to receive intensive instruction in areas where they are having difficulties and remain in general education classrooms for socialization activities and instruction in specific subject areas. The resource room enables students to receive instruction in basic skills areas twice, in the general education room with their chronological age peers and in the resource room in a one-on-one or small group setting (Rich & Ross, 1989).

A caution when using the resource room model (or any other model that includes students with disabilities in general education classrooms for instructional activities) is that simply placing students in these classrooms does not guarantee academic gains. Mere physical proximity with their nondisabled peers does not result in improved academic development for students with disabilities (Jenkins et al., 1989; Jenkins, Speltz, & Odom, 1985). In addition to the type of placement, instructional activities, attitudes of the teacher and classmates, and appropriateness of the placement all play an important role in the success of students with disabilities.

Disadvantages of the Resource Room Model. Despite the numerous advantages of the resource room model, this approach does not offer the ultimate answer to the

Factors Complicating IEPs for Children from Diverse Cultural Backgrounds

- *Lack of assessment personnel.* There is a lack of skilled personnel who can test children in their native language and who are qualified to interpret performance in light of children's linguistic and cultural characteristics. As a result, modifications in assessment procedures, for example, the introduction of an interpreter into the testing environment, often have significant effects upon standardization.

- *Inadequate procedures.* Assessment instruments and procedures are inadequate for the purpose of identifying handicapping conditions among culturally diverse children. Inadequacies of such instruments and procedures are often not considered when reaching decisions related to school problems and educational programming.

- *Lack of trained personnel.* Many culturally diverse handicapped children cannot be provided an appropriate education due to the lack of special education personnel who are uniquely trained to serve this population. Of particular concern is the lack of personnel who can provide instruction in a child's native language (Ortiz & Yates, 1981).

- *Limited knowledge base.* Research in the area of special education for culturally diverse handicapped children is almost nonexistent. The evidence that is available is basically deductive or generalized from studies in bilingual education, special education, or general theories of learning. Yet, without legitimate data and knowledge specific to this population, efforts to provide appropriate services will continue to be based upon assumptions and intuitions.

- *Lack of instructional materials.* Few materials are specifically designed for handicapped children from linguistically and culturally diverse backgrounds. Instructional personnel usually adapt materials or create their own—a difficult task, given the absence of a theoretical basis for modification, adaptation, or creation.

- *Bilingual education.* There is growing concern that bilingual education has become an alternative to special education placement. Education personnel who make placement decisions may hope that, by putting a child in a class with a teacher who speaks the child's native language, a remedy for the child's handicapping condition will emerge. However, bilingual educators often find that they do not have the necessary training to determine whether a child is handicapped or to provide educational interventions to help exceptional children. Further, bilingual teachers are unable to prevent the inappropriate placement of exceptional children in their classes.

Source: Podemski, R. S., Price, B. J., Smith T. E. C., & Marsh, G. E. *Comprehensive administration of special education* (pp. 117–118) Rockville, MD: Aspen Systems.

complex question of appropriate placement for all students with disabilities (Rich & Ross, 1991). One major disadvantage is scheduling students for placement in general education classes. In a major study of a large school district, Zigmond and Sansone (1986) found that many students classified as having mild disabilities spent very little time in general education classrooms. A detailed analysis of the schedules of 844 elementary students with mild disabilities revealed that only 14.5% of their scheduled time was spent in general education programs. A further finding was that the majority of time spent by these students in general education classes was in special subjects, such as art and music. Only 3% to 7% of the students' time was scheduled for academic classes, such as reading and math.

A key purpose for including students with disabilities in general educational settings is the opportunity for socialization between students with disabilities and their nondisabled peers. Although generally positive, opportunities for social integration between students with disabilities and their nondisabled peers can result in negative consequences (Ray, 1985).

Role of Special Education Personnel.   A key role of special education personnel in the resource room model is to collaborate with classroom teachers to deliver appropriate programs to students with disabilities. Resource room teachers cannot simply focus on their students only when they are in the special education classroom. Close collaboration between the resource room teacher and the classroom teacher must occur to ensure that students receiving instruction in the special education room and general education classroom are not getting confused by contradictory methods, assignments, curricula, and so on. The special education teacher should take the lead in opening up lines of communication and facilitating collaborative efforts. Table 3.1 summarizes some of the skills necessary for cooperation. These skills are necessary for classroom teachers as well as special education teachers in order for the resource room model to be successful.

Role of Classroom Teachers.   Unlike in the special class model, classroom teachers have numerous roles in the resource room model. One primary role is referral. The majority of students with mild disabilities and other special needs are referred for services by classroom teachers. Students with mild mental retardation, learning disabilities, and mild behavior problems are likely placed in lower elementary classrooms before their problems become extensive enough to warrant a referral. Also, students with visual and hearing losses and physical or health problems may also be placed in lower elementary grades because the problems are not easily recognizable or have not yet resulted in significant learning or behavior difficulties. General education teachers are often the first persons in the schools to recognize that a student is experiencing problems that could require special education services.

Classroom teachers need to play a more important role than simply making special education referrals. One role is to implement interventions that can possibly ameliorate problems and thereby prevent students from having to get labeled and served in special education programs. Many states and local school districts actually require classroom teachers to implement, and document, intervention strategies attempted

TABLE 3.1 **Skills Necessary for Cooperation**

When working with another professional, you should

- Understand and respect each other's particular skills and roles.
- Preplan activities so both know what the other will do and when.
- Not argue in front of students, parents, or other teachers.
- Watch each other's activities carefully in order to complement strategies and tactics.
- Ask questions of each other about actions or techniques that are not clear following teaching or therapy sessions.
- Share useful materials or literature on your procedures.
- Formulate needs assessment for future activities.

When working with and supervising a paraprofessional, these guidelines should be helpful:

- Develop a daily schedule of activities.
- Demonstrate and verbally explain specific teaching tactics to be used for particular lessons and students.
- Take time to observe your aide's performance.
- Provide reinforcement and corrective feedback for specific actions.
- Evaluate your paraprofessional's performance in writing on a regular basis (at least monthly) and review the evaluation with him or her.
- Any documented weak areas should receive remedial attention by the supervising teacher. These efforts should also be documented.
- Do not criticize the paraprofessional, especially in front of the students. When criticism is necessary, make it constructive and private.
- Deal immediately with any problems that may arise.
- Be sure that the paraprofessional is fully informed about every aspect of classroom activity. Maintain full communication.
- Be open to suggestions from your paraprofessional.
- Inform your paraprofessional about your expectations of him or her.

Source: Adapted from Westling, D. L., & Koorland, M. A. (1988). *The special educator's handbook.* (p. 204). Boston: Allyn & Bacon. Used with permission.

prior to a formal referral (Jenkins & Leicester, 1992). Henry and Flynt (1990) suggest several steps that can be taken prior to the formal referral of students for services in special education programs. These include (1) screening the entire class to determine the beginning of any problems; (2) preparing detailed records on students identified during the screening phase; (3) calling a parent conference; and (4) implementing prereferral strategies.

Prereferral Interventions   The obvious purpose of prereferral actions is to reduce the number of students formally referred for special education programs. Pianta (1990) described several reasons supporting prereferral activities. These include the continued growing special education population, controversy concerning eligibility rules and procedures (Pianta, 1990), and confusing and nebulous definitions of several disabilities. Hopefully, many students are able to benefit enough from the prereferral interventions to avoid being placed in the special education system. Pugach and Johnson (1989a) suggest several additional reasons to require prereferral interventions:

◆ Acknowledgement of the complex, expensive, and time-consuming process required by PL 94–142 to make special education programs accessible for students with disabilities

◆ A redistribution of special education resources away from efforts on students who do not need intensive interventions to more immediate problem solving and more interactions with general education personnel

◆ An effort to deal effectively with learning and behavior problems exhibited by some students in general education classrooms without having to label students with inappropriate terms. If prereferral interventions are to be successful, special education personnel and general education classroom teachers must alter their views of special services. All school personnel must adopt a special education model that focuses on prevention rather than remediation (Pianta, 1990)

Specialized Instruction   An even more expanded role for classroom teachers in the resource room model requires them to develop and implement **specialized instruction** for students with disabilities (Jenkins & Leicester, 1992). When students with disabilities remain in general education classses for all or the majority of the school day, the classroom teacher assumes the primary role for the education of these children rather than transferring this problem to special education teachers (Pugach & Johnson, 1989a). This requires classroom teachers to be very involved in the education of students with disabilities.

When designing instruction for students with disabilities in general education classrooms, teamwork among classroom teachers, special education teachers, parents, and support personnel is critical. In order for the IEP team to develop an appropriate, functional program, all parties must participate and work together. Other principles that must be utilized include (York & Vandercook, 1991):

1. *Inclusion.*   If the inclusion of students with disabilities in general education classes is to be successful, students must truly be "included" members of the class. This means that students need to be involved in all classroom activities, not simply physically placed in the classroom.

2. *Individualization.*   Educational programs for students must be truly individualized. Students with similar clinical labels may not benefit from the same interventions. Each student's strengths and weaknesses must be taken into consideration and incorporated into the educational program.

3. *Flexibility.*   IEPs should be flexible; they must be considered working documents that should be followed but that can be modified if necessary. Completing an IEP form and filing it away until the end of the year is not utilizing the IEP as it should be or as federal regulations intended it to be used.

Classroom teachers must assume a significant role in educating students with disabilities who are included in their classrooms. Although they need to be able to work closely with special education teachers, they must be prepared to take the lead in providing appropriate educational programs to all their students.

Programs Where Students Receive Education in General Education Classrooms

Just as full-time special class placement of students with disabilities began to receive criticisms in the early 1970s, resulting in the development of the resource room model, resource room programs have begun to be criticized. As stated by Madeline Will (1986), then assistant secretary of education, "Although well intentioned, this so-called 'pull-out' approach to the educational difficulties of students with learning problems has failed in many instances to meet the educational needs of these students and has created, however unwittingly, barriers to their successful education" (p. 412).

The result has been a call for dismantling the dual educational system, general and special, in favor of a unified system that attempts to meet the educational needs of all students (Reynolds, Wang, & Walberg, 1987). Rather than spending a great deal of time and effort identifying students with specific problems, and therefore determining that they are "eligible" for special education services, proponents of moving to a single educational system suggest that efforts be expended on providing appropriate services to all students. In the early 1980s, this model was actually advocated by Renzulli and Reis (1985) for students classified as gifted and talented. Their model, called schoolwide enrichment, afforded gifted programming services to all students without the students having to meet restrictive eligibility criteria.

Regular Education Initiative (REI) and Inclusion

The model for including students with special needs fully in general education programs was originally called the Regular Education Initiative (REI). More recently, the term *inclusion* has been used to identify this program model. Inclusion can be defined as "the movement advocating that the general education system assume unequivocal, primary responsibility for all students in our public schools—including identified disabled students as well as those students who have special needs of some type" (Davis, 1989, p. 440). The inclusion movement had its beginnings in the early 1980s, when various professionals began questioning the purposes for maintaining a dual educational system (Stainback & Stainback, 1984; Wang & Birch, 1984; Will, 1986).

Proponents of inclusion have noted numerous advantages to serving students with disabilities in general education environments. These include (Huefner, 1988):

1. *Reduction of Stigma.*   Serving students with disabilities in general education classrooms reduces the chances of stigma associated with students who have to leave the classroom for special services.
2. *Better Understanding across Disciplines.*   Inclusion encourages special education teachers and classroom teachers to work together. This reduces the mystique of "special education" and facilitates collaboration among professionals.
3. *On-the-Job Training for General Educators in Special Education Skills.*   Individualization and other special interventions, such as task analysis, behavior

management, and curricular adaption can be learned by classroom teachers, with special education teachers serving as role models.

4. *Reduction of Mislabeling of Nondisabled Students.*   Serving all students in general education classrooms, including those with special needs, reduces the requirement for labeling and therefore the possibility of mislabeling.

5. *Spillover Benefits to All Students.*   Nondisabled students are able to benefit from interactions with their peers who experience various learning and behavior problems.

6. *Suitability of the Model to Needs of Secondary School Students.*   Serving students with special needs in general education classes enhances the likelihood of adaptions to instruction and content in various content courses.

7. *Prospect for Master Teacher Staffing in Special Education.*   Inclusion, which can be implemented using the consultation/collaboration model, encourages the chances for developing a master teacher professional who can meet the needs of a divergent student population. This not only benefits students with identified learning needs; it also benefits those who are at risk for developing learning and behavior problems.

In general, advocates of inclusion note that general education classrooms can be appropriate learning environments for many students with disabilities and students at risk for developing problems (Brady & Taylor, 1989). They argue several points, including these:

◆ The current dual system of education has numerous problems, making it difficult to provide appropriate education to many students, some identified as disabled and others who have special needs.

◆ The current dual education system is cost-ineffective in that it maintains duplications.

◆ Merely having access to general education programs is not sufficient to guarantee equal educational opportunity for students with disabilities and those at risk for developing disabilities.

◆ The current dual system of education is discriminatory and programmatically ineffective (Davis, 1989).

Advocates for inclusion suggest that implementation of the model will result in fewer students being identified with negative, often self-fulfilling labels and the quicker identification of learning problems in all students (Wang & Birch, 1984). Stainback and Stainback (1984) provide a series of reasons to support the notion that the needs of students with disabilities does not, in itself, warrant the maintenance of a dual system of education, one general and one special. These reasons include the following:

1. *"Special" and "Regular" Students.*   The current dual system of general and special education assumes that there are two distinct types of children, special and regular. In reality, all students display a variety of characteristics along a

Microcomputer Applications

Type of Use	Description	Features	Cautions
Drill and Practice	Reinforces previously learned information and provides student with practice	• Many students need extra practice • The more sophisticated programs include graphics, animation, and sound • Best used as adjunct to ongoing program	• Can be overused • Does not teach new concepts • Best to have students work independently • Avoid software that draws attention to students who make an incorrect response
Tutorial	Presents new or previously presented material, then assesses the student's understanding of the information	• Additional instruction for those who need more time to grasp concepts • Best used as adjunct to ongoing instruction	• Not the most effective way of presenting new information to special learners • Best to have students work independently
Simulation	Allows students to experience vicariously real-life events which are not easily shown in a traditional setting	• Powerful • Can provide more concrete examples of abstract concepts • Realistic • Very useful with students with limited experimental backgrounds • Require participation • Suitable for cooperative arrangements	• Problems can arise if students do not possess prerequisite knowledge and/or skills • Readability may be too high • May have too many rules • Best to use after some introduction and exposure to the topic • Students may need help in generalizing computer-displayed events to real world

Source: Adapted from Serna, L. A., & Patton, J. R. (1989). Science. In G. A. Robinson, J. R. Patton, E. A. Polloway, & L. R. Sargent, (Eds.), *Best Practices in Mild Mental Retardation* (p. 197). Reston, VA: Division on Mental Retardation, CEC. Used with permission.

continuum; there simply is no way to divide all students into two groups. All students exhibit strengths and weaknesses that make them unique.

2. *Individualized Services.* There is no single group of children who can benefit from individualized educational programming. The dual system of special and general education adopts the notion that students with disabilities require individual education, whereas other students do not. In fact, some research suggests that students with diverse characteristics do not benefit from different instructional techniques. If future research concludes that individualized

instruction does indeed result in improved education, then all students should be afforded the opportunity.

3. *Instructional Methods.* Contrary to many beliefs, there are not special teaching methods that are only effective with students who have disabilities. Good, basic instructional programs can be effective for all students.

4. *Classification.* A dual system of education, general and special, requires extensive, time-consuming, and costly efforts to determine which system students fit and, in the case of those students determined to be eligible for special education, which disability category they fit. Unfortunately, classification often is unreliable, results in stigma, and does not lead to better educational programming.

5. *Competition and Duplication.* Perpetuating the general and special systems has resulted in competition between professionals as well as a duplication of efforts. If our educational system is to improve, all educators must work together, sharing expertise, effective methods, and educational goals.

6. *Eligibility by Category.* The dual system results in extensive effort being spent on determining who is eligible for special services. The programs for students are often based not on their specific needs, but on which category they are placed in. Placements and even curricular options are often restricted on the basis of clinical classification. For example, students classified as having mental retardation may be placed in work-study programs without having the opportunity to participate in regular vocational education.

7. *"Deviant" Label.* A major negative result of the dual system is the requirement to place "deviant" labels on students. In order to determine that a student is eligible for the special system, a clinical label must be attached. Few if any would argue that clinical labels result in positive reactions. The routine reaction to the labels "mental retardation," "emotionally disturbed," and even "learning disabled" is that the labels mean that the student is not capable of doing something as well as other students. Table 3.2 summarizes some of the primary differences between a dual system and a unified system of education.

There are several overriding premises concerning the inclusion movement. These include the fact that all educators, including general education and special education teachers, school assessment personnel, and administrators, must work together to use all available means for ensuring that every child achieves success in school (Wang & Birch, 1984; Wang & Walberg, 1988). This sharing of the responsibility for the success of every child helps in breaking down the artificial barriers that have separated special education and programs for at-risk students from general education.

Another major premise of inclusion is that all educational programs, including special education, remedial programs, and other enrichment activities, should occur in the general education environment as much as possible. Students should not have to be singled out and removed from the classroom to receive appropriate educational programming, except in extreme cases (Wang & Birch, 1984; Wang & Walberg, 1988).

TABLE 3.2   **Comparison of Dual and Unified Systems**

Concern	Dual System	Unified System
1. Student characteristics	Dichotomizes students into special and regular	Recognizes continuum among all students of intellectual, physical, and psychological characteristics
2. Individualization	Stresses individualization for students labeled special	Stresses individualization for all students
3. Instructional strategies	Seeks to use special strategies for special students	Selects from range of available strategies according to each student's learning needs
4. Type of educational services	Eligibility generally based on category affiliation	Eligibility based on each student's individual learning needs
5. Diagnostics	Large expenditures on identification of categorical affiliation	Emphasis on identifying the specific instructional needs of all students
6. Professional relationships	Establishes artificial barriers among educators that promote competition and alienation	Promotes cooperation through sharing resources, expertise, and advocacy responsibilities
7. Curriculum	Options available to each student are limited by categorical affiliation	All options available to every student as needed
8. Focus	Student must fit regular education program or be referred to special education	General education program is adjusted to meet all students' needs

Source: From "A rationale for the merger of special and regular education" by W. Stainback and S. Stainback, *Exceptional Children, 51,* p. 107. Copyright 1984 by The Council for Exceptional Children. Reprinted with permission.

Obviously, the **restructuring** of the current educational system and the inclusion movement will impact on all school personnel. In particular, classroom teachers and special education personnel will be affected. The implementation of inclusion will undoubtedly require general education to "develop its capabilities for accommodating a broad continuum of instructional practices and services" (Wang & Walberg, 1988, p. 129).

Although proponents of inclusion have articulated numerous reasons to support the model, there are many opponents to its implementation. Opponents of inclusion oppose a quick movement to the full inclusion of all students with disabilities in general education classes, and the concomitant dismantling of special education classes. They believe that there has not been sufficient research into the effects of inclusion to abandon currently existing special education programs. These opponents argue that if inclusion "is adopted too quickly on a widespread basis, it could bring serious harm to the very students it is designed to help" (Davis, 1989, p. 441).

Inclusion is primarily a special education movement. In fact, very few general educators have been involved in its conceptualization. To underline this point, Lieberman (1985) noted that the movement is like "a wedding in which we, as special educators, have forgotten to invite the bride (regular educators)" (p. 513).

If inclusion is to be embraced by the majority of educators to the point that it can be implemented successfully, then several factors must occur. First, general education professionals must become involved in the conceptualization and implementation of the inclusion movement, including training in how it should be implemented. Although both advocates and opponents of inclusion routinely discuss the impact that inclusion will have on school principals, classroom teachers, and other school staff, there has not been a concerted effort to involve these individuals in its design and implementation (Davis, 1989). This is imperative if inclusion is to be successful (Smith et al., 1993).

Still another group of individuals who should be involved in planning for inclusion is consumers. Parents of students with special needs, as well as students who will benefit from services, should be included in planning efforts (Davis, 1989). Since inclusion most directly impacts on the students with disabilities and their parents, they should be extensively involved in planning this initiative.

If inclusion is ever to be implemented successfully, it must be recognized for what it is—an attempt to improve the entire educational system to meet the many diverse needs of students (Davis, 1989). As previously discussed, the student population in the United States is not homogeneous; rather, it is a very heterogeneous group. Students literally come in all shapes, sizes, and capacities. Inclusion is an approach to restructuring the entire educational system to better meet the needs of all students, not just those who meet the specific eligibility criteria as disabled.

Advantages of Inclusion.   Students have been shown to interact more with their nondisabled peers when fully included in general education classrooms (Wang & Birch, 1984). Since many students with disabilities, especially those with mild disabilities, are capable of independent or semi-independent living as adults, they need to have experiences interacting with their nondisabled peers. Adults with disabilities who are successful must deal with a nondisabled adult world. Experiencing interactions during the school years will help prepare students for this "real-world" environment.

The interactions between students with disabilities and their teachers also appears to be influenced by full-time inclusion in general education classrooms. Wang and Birch (1984) found that students served in resource rooms interacted less than their peers who were included full-time in general education classes. Again, to be prepared for postschool environments, these individuals need as much experience as possible interacting with individuals who do not have disabilities.

Specific advantages of inclusion, therefore, appear to be increased interactions between students with disabilities and their age-appropriate peers and teachers. Still other advantages include

◆ Less stigma than being pulled out of the classroom to receive instruction in the special education classroom

Serving students with disabilities in general education classrooms reduces stigma associated with being pulled out for resource rooms.

- Increased levels of self-esteem
- Avoidance of the problems often associated with identification and eligibility determination of students for special education
- Closer interactions among all school personnel in working with all students
- The dismantling of the artificial dual system of education currently provided in schools

Disadvantages of Inclusion.   Just as there are many supporters of inclusion and reasons for its implementation, there are also professionals and parents who decry the movement. Among the reasons they use to oppose inclusion are the following:

1. General educators have not been involved sufficiently and are therefore not likely to support the model.
2. General educators as well as special educators do not have the collaboration skills necessary to make inclusion successful.
3. There is limited empirical data to support the model. Therefore, full implementation should be put on hold until sound research supports the effort.
4. Full inclusion of students with disabilities into general education classsrooms will take away from students without disabilities and lessen their quality of education.
5. Current funding, teacher training, and teacher certification is based on separate educational systems.
6. Some students with disabilities do better when served in special education classes by special education teachers.

There are many pros and cons concerning the inclusion movement. Proponents of inclusion are convinced that the model is the most effective way to provide services to all students, including those with disabilities, those who are at risk for developing learning and behavior problems, and those who are traditionally served in general education classes. Likewise, opponents of inclusion strongly advocate not implementing the model without a great deal of further research and debate.

Role of Special Education Personnel.   Special education personnel become a much more integral component in the school with inclusion. In the current dual system, special education teachers only provide instructional programming to students identified as disabled and determined eligible for special education programs under state and federal guidelines. In inclusive schools these teachers work with a variety of students, including students having difficulties but not identified specifically as having a disability. The special education teacher works much more closely with classroom teachers in the inclusion model.

Role of Classroom Teachers.   The role of classroom teachers also changes dramatically with inclusion. Their role has primarily been identification and referral, and possibly the provision of some instructional services to students with disabilities, but in the inclusive school they are fully responsible for all students, including those with identified disabilities. Special education support personnel are available to collaborate on educational programs for all students, but the primary responsibility is assumed by the classroom teacher.

Methods to Enhance Inclusion of Students with Disabilities

Teachers must develop strategies to facilitate the successful inclusion of students with disabilities in general education classrooms. Neither classroom teachers nor special education teachers want students with disabilities simply "dumped" into general education classes (Banks, 1992), and the successful inclusion of students does not normally happen without assistance. School personnel must work on effective methods to cooperate to provide appropriate programs to all students, not just those who typically do well in general education classrooms and those who are successful in special education programs. There are generally two methods to facilitate the inclusion of students with disabilities into general education classes. One method deals with facilitating the acceptance of these students by their peers, the other focuses on collaboration among educators who provide instructional programs.

Improving Acceptance of Students with Disabilities by Their Peers

Students with disabilities need to be included in general classroom environments in several ways. Not only do they need to be included physically and instructionally, they also need to be included socially. As a result, acceptance of students with disabilities by their nondisabled peers is very important. There are three general ways teachers can facilitate this acceptance: providing information, curricular infusion, and cooperative teaching efforts.

Providing Information.   A key technique to enhance inclusion is to provide information to nondisabled students about disabilities in general and about the specific disabilities that some of their peers may display. Teachers may want to use such techniques as bibliotherapy, where students read stories about children with disabilities, or they may want to provide information directly about disabilities. Often, teachers have a unit of study on a particular disability if they are aware that a student with that particular problem will be moving into the classroom. Providing information needs to occur at both the elementary and secondary levels. Teachers need to modify their activities to the age levels of their students.

Curricular Infusion.   Another method for enhancing the inclusion of students with disabilities is curricular infusion. **Curricular infusion** can be described as an ongoing component of the curriculum. "Emphasis is placed on expanding the general education curriculum to include reference to disabilities at appropriate points, not to alter the focus of the curriculum to disability-related issues" (Hamre-Nietupski et al., 1989, p. 78).

There are several advantages to curricular infusion over add-on activities about disabilities (Hamre-Nietupski et al., 1989):

1. Both general and special education personnel share in the inclusion activities and develop a partnership to promote inclusion.
2. Students without disabilities have the opportunity to develop an awareness of their peers with disabilities that is more natural than when special emphasis is given to talking about student differences.
3. When school personnel change, the curricular content that addresses disabilities remains intact.

Table 3.3 describes examples of infusion activities in junior high school settings.

Cooperative Teaching Efforts.   A primary method of enhancing inclusion of students with disabilities with their nondisabled peers is through collaborative skill instruction. Many students, both with and without disabilities, simply do not have the necessary skills to interact with each other. Therefore, instructional programs designed to teach collaborative skills may be necessary. Putnam, Rynders, Johnson, and Johnson (1989) studied the effectiveness of providing such training to a group of students with and without disabilities. In the study, students in heterogeneous groups (including disabled and nondisabled students) were instructed in specific collaborative skills, such as sharing materials and ideas, encouraging participation, and saying nice things to other individuals in the group. The results of the study revealed that, when compared to a control group of students who had not received skill instruction, the group receiving instruction demonstrated significantly improved interaction skills, such as looking at each other, talking to each other, and working together. In order

TABLE 3.3 **Seventh-Grade Science Infusion Activities**

Unit: Genetic/Environmental Influences on Development

A. Class discussion.
   1. Genetic and environmental causes of disabilities.
   2. Identification of similarities between disabled/nondisabled individuals.
   3. Past (segregated) versus present (integrated) educational model.
B. Teams debate segregated vs. integrated education.
   1. Four-person teams are formed.
   2. Teams visit integrated/segregated programs.
   3. Teams gather written information on integration/segregation.
   4. Guest speakers, one pro-integration, one pro-segregation, debate before the class.
   5. Teams debate before the class using previously gathered information.
C. Each student writes a position paper on integration/segregation.
D. All students visit students with severe disabilities to get to know them better.

Source: Hamre-Nietupski, S., Ayres, B., Nietupski, J., Savage, M., Mitchell, B., & Bramman, H. (1989). Enhancing integration of students with severe disabilities through curricular infusion: A general/special educator partnership. *Education and Training in Mental Retardation, 24,* p. 82. Used with permission.

for students with disabilities to be successfully included in general education classrooms, teachers must make a concerted effort both to facilitate their acceptance by other students and to provide appropriate instructional activities through collaboration with other school personnel.

Collaboration and Consultation

Classroom teachers and teachers who primarily teach students with disabilities must interact and work together on a routine basis. As previously noted, prior to the inclusion of students with disabilities into general education classrooms, there was little interaction between classroom and special education teachers. Special education teachers provided instruction to students with disabilities in separate classrooms and had little if anything to do with classroom teachers and students without disabilities. Likewise, in the segregated model, classroom teachers had minimal interactions with special education teachers and students who received services from these teachers. There was definitely a dichotomous service system, which was separated with philosophical as well as physical barriers.

The advent of including students with disabilities in general education classrooms changed all of that. Rather than rarely interacting, general and special education teachers were required to interact by PL 94–142 and the ensuing least-restrictive-environment. Without this interaction, the likelihood of inclusion being successful was extremely limited (York et al., 1992).

Regardless of which service delivery model is used—the resource room/pullout model or the full inclusion model—teachers whose primary focus is on nondisabled students and those who primarily serve students with disabilities must interact and collaborate. The degree of this interaction will influence the success or failure of individual students in educational programs.

The key to success is collaboration, which can be defined as sharing in the activities necessary to provide appropriate educational programs to students with disabilities. Using collaboration, all teachers and school support personnel work together in the planning and implementation phase of educational programming. There are several assumptions underlying collaboration in the schools (Idol & West, 1991):

1. Educational collaboration is not a new concept in schools.
2. Educational collaboration is not an end unto itself; rather, it is a catalytic process used in interactive relationships among individuals working toward a mutually defined, concrete vision or outcome (e.g., students who become well-adjusted and productive citizens).
3. Educational collaboration is an interact relationship first, then a technique or vehicle for change.
4. The foci and outcomes of educational collaboration are multiple, with student outcomes being only one important outcome—the others being adult and system/organizational outcomes.
5. Educational collaboration as an adult-to-adult interactive process can be expected to have an indirect impact on student outcomes; thus, the process of educational collaboration among adult team members typically yields changes in team member attitudes, skills, knowledge, and/or behaviors first, followed by changes in student and/or organizational outcomes.
6. Educational collaboration may be used as a team process for effective planning and decision making as well as problem solving: thus, it can be an effective tool for proactive strategic planning or reactive, but efficient, problem solving in any organizational structure in the school environment (p. 72).

Linked with collaboration are the consultation actions that need to occur. Collaboration and consultation are two approaches to help general education and special educational personnel work together to better serve all students, those with and those without disabilities, those classified as academically talented and those who are not, those who have no apparent problems and those who are at risk for developing problems—all students (Smith et al., 1993). The collaboration and consultation model can be described as "an interactive planning decision-making, or problem-solving, process, involving two or more team members" (Idol & West, 1991, p. 72). It is based on multidisciplinary actions that support classroom teachers as they provide instructional services to students with disabilities. This approach appears to hold "great potential" for a very diverse group of students in general education classes who are experiencing problems (Bauwens, Hourcade, & Friend, 1989). It is not limited to students identified as having a recognized disability under federal law, but facilitates appropriate educational services for all students.

There are two major components in the collaboration and consultation model. These include consultation, where special education teachers "consult" with other school personnel, and **collaboration,** where all educators collaborate in providing programs to students with disabilities. **Consultation** is the multidisciplinary planning aspect of the model; collaboration is the multidisciplinary cooperative teaching that results from the planning (Bauwens et al., 1989). The use of both terms has caused terminology problems that occasionally have resulted in misunderstandings.

Currently, *collaboration* and *consultation* are used together to describe the way interactions occur when providing services to students with disabilities in general education classes. This is due primarily to the fact that "effective contemporary consultation must incorporate true collaboration among multidisiplinary personnel" (Phillips & McCullough, 1990, p. 293). Accepting this premise that collaboration is an integral component of consultation reduces the likelihood for misunderstanding and confusion with the model.

There are several basic tenets in the collaboration and consultation model. These include (Phillips & McCullough, 1990)

1. Joint responsibility for problems (i.e., all professionals share responsibility and concern for all students)
2. Joint accountability and recognition for problem resolution

The consulting component of the collaboration and consultation model focuses on multi-disciplinary planning to meet the needs of students experiencing problems in general education classrooms.

3. The belief that pooling talents and resources is mutually advantageous, with the following benefits:
    a. Increased range of solutions generated
    b. Diversity of expertise and resources available to engage problems
    c. Superiority and originality of solutions generated
4. The belief that teacher or student problem resolution merits expenditure of time, energy, and resources
5. The belief that correlates of collaboration are important and desirable (i.e., group morale, group cohesion, increased knowledge of problem-solving processes, and specific alternative problem-solving processes and classroom interventions) (p. 295)

The consultation component of the collaboration/consultation model focuses on multidisciplinary planning to meet the needs of a student experiencing problems in a general education classroom. This is the decision-making portion of the model. Donaldson and Christiansen (1990) describe a process that can be used in the decision-making activities. Making decisions about a student involves determining when the student experiences problems, the types of problems experienced, and the options available to help the student succeed in the general education classroom.

A problem that often occurs in the consultation and collaboration model is parity among general and special educators involved in a student's program (Pugach & Johnson, 1989b). Too often, it may be easy for the special education teacher to assume the role of "specialist," whereas in reality, all parties involved in the collaborative effort must be viewed as equally capable of helping students with disabilities (Pugach & Johnson, 1989b). Special educators and classroom teachers must be true collaborators (Graden, 1989). Success in developing an atmosphere of parity requires all parties to enter into the collaboration/consultation model with a mindset that all team members share equal responsibility for students, and have unique and important contributions to make to the process (Tindal & Taylor-Pendergast, 1989).

When implemented properly, peer collaboration can have a positive impact on teachers' abilities to accommodate students with disabilities. In a study completed by Johnson and Pugach (1991), it was demonstrated that peer collaboration can improve teachers' abilities to deal with school-based problems. With the movement to integrate students with disabilities into general education classrooms growing, and the realization that many students can be considered as having special needs or at risk for developing special needs, the importance of the collaboration and consultation model becomes apparent.

Job Description Written by a Graduate of the Resource/Consulting Teacher Program

The Role of a Resource/Consulting Teacher

Julie Keller

As a resource/consulting teacher, I would provide services to children having mild academic and behavioral problems in two ways:

1. working directly with the child in the resource room;
2. helping the child indirectly by working with his/her teacher, parents, and peers.

The direct services that I would provide would include:

1. testing the child in the curricular material used in the classroom to find appropriate placement;
2. giving the child daily, direct instruction in that material so that the child will be able to make an easier transition back to the classroom;
3. taking and charting daily measures of the child's performance to see if skills are being mastered;
4. basing instructional decisions on the data charted from these daily measures.

The indirect services that I would provide would include:

1. consulting with the general classroom teacher to
   - help assess and place children using the curricular materials used in the classroom;
   - provide tests based on the classroom curriculum and give instruction on how to develop and use them;
   - assist in modifying the classroom curriculum, when necessary, to meet the needs of the child;
   - show how to take daily measures of a child's academic and social behavior;
   - help implement reinforcement contingencies for behavior management in the classroom;
2. establishing parent groups for discussion of and help with issues of concern to parents of mildly handicapped children;
3. training older peers, parent volunteers, and teacher aides to work with younger children as tutors so that they receive the individualized instruction they need;
4. offering inservice workshops for teachers that focus on special interest areas such as
   - constructing curriculum-based assessments;
   - using direct instruction techniques;

- implementing programs for child management;
- measuring daily performance data in a regular classroom.

Source: Idol, L. (1983). *Special educator's consultation handbook* (p. 194). Austin, TX: Pro-Ed. Used with permission.

Summary

- The setting where students with disabilities should be provided educational and related services is a much-discussed and much-debated topic.

- The preferred placement for students with disabilities has come full circle during the past two decades.

- Currently about 70% of all students with disabilities are served a substantial portion of each school day in general education classrooms.

- The preferred service model for students with disabilities between 1950 and 1970 was segregated classroom settings.

- In the self-contained model, special education teachers were trained to teach specific types of students, primarily based on clinical labels.

- Classroom teachers had a very limited role in special education in the self-contained classroom model.

- Many parents advocated for more inclusion of their students than was possible in the self-contained model.

- The least-restrictive-setting mandate of PL 94–142 was the impetus to the development of the resource room model.

- The resource room is currently the most widely used service option for students with disabilities in schools.

- Opportunities for social interaction with nondisabled students is a primary advantage of resource rooms over self-contained classrooms.

- There are several disadvantages of the resource room model, including the stigma associated with going to the resource room, and scheduling students in and out of general education classrooms.

◆ In the resource room model, the special education teacher not only provides direct instruction to students but also interacts with classroom teachers about specific students.

◆ The Regular Education Initiative (REI) and inclusion call for the dismantling of the current dual system of education, which includes general education and special education.

◆ Inclusion reduces stigma for students with disabilities, reduces mislabeling, has spillover benefits for all students, and breaks down the artifical barriers created by clinical labels.

◆ Students with disabilities and other students interact more freely and naturally in an inclusive setting.

◆ There are some disadvantages to inclusion, including the fact that general educators have not been involved in the movement and there is limited empirical data to support the model.

◆ There are numerous methods to enhance the chances of inclusion of students with disabilities, including collaborative skill instruction.

◆ The collaboration and consultation model requires a very close working relationship between classroom teachers and special education teachers.

◆ The roles of general education personnel and special education teachers change dramatically in the collaboration and consultation model.

References

Algozzine, B., Morsink, C. V., & Algozzine, K. M. (1988). What's happening in self-contained special education classrooms? *Exceptional Children, 55,* 259–265.

Bak, J. J., Cooper, E. M., Dobroth, K. M., & Siperstein, G. N. (1987). Special class placements as labels: Effects on children's attitudes toward learning handicapped peers. *Exceptional Children, 54,* 151–155.

Banks, J. (1992). A comment on "Teacher perceptions of the Regular Education Initiative." *Exceptional Children, 58,* 564.

Bauwens, J., Hourcade, J. J., & Friend, M. (1989). Cooperative teaching: A model for general and special education integration. *Rural and Special Education, 10,* 17–22.

Bender, W. N., & Ukeje, I. C. (1989). Instructional strategies in mainstream classrooms: Prediction of the strategies teachers select. *Rural and Special Education, 10,* 23–30.

Blackman, H. P. (1989). Special education placement: Is it what you know or where you live? *Exceptional Children, 55,* 459–462.

Brady, M. P., McDougall, D., & Dennis, H. F. (1989). The schools, the courts, and the integration of students with severe handicaps. *The Journal of Special Education, 23,* 43–55.

Brady, M. P., & Taylor, R. D. (1989). Instructional consequences in mainstreamed middle school classes: Reinforcement and corrections. *Rural and Special Education, 10,* 31–36.

Byrnes, M. (1990). The regular education initiative debate: A view from the field. *Exceptional Children, 56,* 345–349.

Cegelka, P. T., & Prehm, H. J. (1982). *Mental retardation: From categories to people.* Columbus, OH: Merrill.

Danielson, L. C., & Bellamy, G. T. (1989). State variation in placement of children with handicaps in segregated environments. *Exceptional Children, 55,* 448–455.

Davis, W. E. (1989). The regular education initiative debate: Its promises and problems. *Exceptional Children, 55,* 440–447.

Deno, E. (1970). Special education as development capital. *Exceptional Children, 37,* 231–237.

Donaldson, R., & Christiansen, J. (1990). Consultation and collaboration: A decision-making model. *Teaching Exceptional Children, 22,* 22–25.

Graden, J. L. (1989). Redefining "prereferral" intervention as intervention assistance: Collaboration between general and special education. *Exceptional Children, 56,* 227–231.

Hamre-Nietupski, S., Ayres, B., Nietupski, J., Savage, M., Mitchell, B., & Bramman, H. (1989). Enhancing integration of students with severe disabilities through curricular infusion: A general/special educator partnership. *Education and Training of the Mentally Retarded, 24,* 78–88.

Henry, N. A., & Flynt, E. S. (1990). Rethinking special education referral: A procedural model. *Intervention, 26,* 22–24.

Huefner, D. S. (1988). The consulting teacher model: Risks and opportunities. *Exceptional Children, 54,* 403–414.

Idol, L. (1983). *Special educator's consultation handbook.* Austin, TX: Pro-Ed.

Idol, L., & West, J. F. (1991). Educational collaboration: A catalyst for effective schooling. *Intervention, 27,* 70–78.

In Touch. Newsletter of the Association for Retarded Citizens—California, October 13, 1993. Los Angeles, CA.

Jenkins, J. R., & Heinen, A. (1989). Students' preferences for service delivery: Pull-out, in-class, or integrated. *Exceptional Children, 55,* 516–523.

Jenkins, J. R., & Leicester, N. (1992). Specialized instruction within general education: A case study of one elementary school. *Exceptional Children, 58,* 555–563.

Jenkins, J. R., Odom, S. L., & Speltz, M. L. (1989). Effects of social integration of preschool children with handicaps. *Exceptional Children, 55,* 420–427.

Jenkins, J. R., Speltz, M. L., & Odom, S. L. (1985). Integrating normal and handicapped preschoolers: Effects on child development and social interaction. *Exceptional Children, 52,* 7–17.

Johnson, L. J., & Pugach, M. C. (1991). Peer collaboration: Accommodating students with mild learning and behavior problems. *Exceptional Children, 57,* 454–461.

Kirk, S. A., & Gallagher, J. J. (1989). *Educating exceptional children* (5th ed.). Boston: Houghton-Mifflin.

Lieberman, L. M. (1985). Special education and regular education: A merger made in heaven? *Exceptional Children, 51,* 513–516.

McGill, N. B., & Robinson, L. (1989). Regular education teacher consultant. *Teaching Exceptional Children, 21,* 71–73.

Marsh, G. E., & Price, B. J. (1980). *Teaching adolescents with handicaps.* St. Louis: Mosby.

Morgan, S. R. (1985). Children in crisis: A team approach in the schools. Austin, TX: Pro-Ed.

Ortiz, A. A., & Yates, J. R. (1981). *Exceptional hispanics.* Austin, TX: Texas Education Agency.

Phillips, V., & McCullough, L. (1990). Consultation-based programming: Instituting the collaborative ethic in schools. *Exceptional Children, 56,* 291–304.

Pianta, R. C. (1990). Widening the debate on educational reform: Prevention as a viable alternative. *Exceptional Children, 56,* 306–313.

Podemski, R. S., Price, B. J., Smith, T. E. C., & Marsh, G. E. (1984). *Comprehensive administration of special education.* Rockville, MD: Aspen Systems.

Pugach, M. C., & Johnson, L. J. (1989a). Prereferral interventions: Progress, problems, and challenges. *Exceptional Children, 56,* 217–226.

Pugach, M. C., & Johnson, L. J. (1989b). The challenge of implementing collaboration between general and special education. *Exceptional Children, 56,* 232–235.

Putnam, J. W., Rynders, J. E., Johnson, R. T., & Johnson, D. W. (1989). Collaborative skill instruction for promoting positive interactions between mentally handicapped and non-handicapped children. *Exceptional Children, 55,* 550–557.

Ray, B. M. (1985). Measuring the social position of the mainstreamed handicapped child. *Exceptional Children, 52,* 57–62.

Renzulli, J. S., & Reis, S. M. (1985). *The schoolwide enrichment model: A comprehensive plan for educational excellence.* Mansfield Center, CT: Creative Learning Press.

Reynolds, M. C., Wang, M. C., & Walberg, H. J. (1987). The necessary restructuring of special and regular education. *Exceptional Children, 53,* 391–398.

Rich, H. L., & Ross, S. M. (1989). Students' time on learning tasks in special education. *Exceptional Children, 55,* 508–515.

Rich, H. L., & Ross, S. M. (1991). Regular class or resource room for students with disabilities? A direct response to "Rich and Ross, A Mixed Message." *Exceptional Children, 57,* 476–477.

Serna, L. A., & Patton, J. R. (1989). Science. In G. A. Robinson, J. R. Patton, E. A. Polloway, & L. R. Sargent(Eds.), *Best Practices in Mental Retardation.* Reston, VA: Division on Mental Retardation, CEC.

Smith, T. E. C. (1990). *Introduction to education* (2nd ed.). St. Paul, MN: West Publishing.

Smith, T. E. C., Finn, D. M., & Dowdy, C. A. (1993) *Teaching students with mild disabilities.* Ft. Worth, TX: Harcourt Brace Jovanovich.

Smith, T. E. C., Price, B. J., & Marsh, G. E. (1986). *Mildly handicapped children and adults.* St. Paul, MN: West Publishing.

Stainback, W., & Stainback, S. (1984). A rationale for the merger of special and regular education. *Exceptional Children, 51,* 102–111.

Tindal, G., Shinn, M. R., & Rodden-Nord, K. (1990). Contextually based school consultation: Influential variables. *Exceptional Children, 56,* 324–336.

Tindal, G. A., & Taylor-Pendergast, S. J. (1989). A taxonomy for objectively analyzing the consultation process. *Remedial and Special Education, 10,* 6–16.

U.S. Department of Education. (1977, August 23). *Federal Register.* Washington, DC: U.S. Government Printing Office.

U.S. Department of Education. (1993). *15th annual report to Congress on the implementation of IDEA.* Washington, DC: Author.

Wang, M. C., & Birch, J. W. (1984). Comparison of a full-time mainstreaming program and a resource room approach. *Exceptional Children, 51,* 33–40.

Wang, M. C., & Walberg, H. J. (1988). Four fallacies of segregationism. *Exceptional Children, 55,* 128–137.

Westling, D. L., & Koorland, M. A. (1988). *The special educator's handbook.* Boston: Allyn & Bacon.

Will, M. C. (1986). Educating children with learning problems: A shared responsibility. *Exceptional Children, 52,* 411–415.

York, J., & Vandercook, T. (1991). Designing an integrated program for learners with severe disabilities. *Teaching Exceptional Children, 23,* 22–28.

York, J., Vandercook, T., MacDonald, C., Heise-Neff, C., & Caughey, E. (1992). Feedback about integrating middle-school students with severe disabilities in general education classes. *Exceptional Children, 58,* 244–258.

Zigmond, N., & Sansone, J. (1986). Designing a program for the learning disabled adolescent. *Remedial and Special Education, 7,* 13–17.

CHAPTER 4

Teaching Students with Learning Disabilities

Introduction

Just as it is difficult to identify children with learning disabilities from their peers by looks, you cannot distinguish adults with learning disabilities from other adults. You may be surprised to find that many important and famous people have achieved significant accomplishments in spite of the existence of a severe learning disability. Adults with learning disabilities can be found in all professions. They may be teachers, lawyers, doctors, blue-collar workers, or politicians! Read the vignettes that follow and see if you can identify the names of the individuals with learning disabilities.

During his childhood, this young man was an outstanding athlete, achieving great success and satisfaction from sports. Unfortunately, he struggled in the classroom. He tried very hard, but he always seemed to fail academically. His biggest fear was being asked to stand up and read in front of his classmates. He was frequently teased about his class performance, and he described his school days as sheer torture. His only feelings of success were experienced on the playing field.

When he graduated from high school, he didn't consider going to college because he "wasn't a terrific student, and never got into books all that much." Even though he was an outstanding high-school pole vaulter, he did not get one scholarship during his senior year. He had already gone to work with his father when he was offered a $500 football scholarship from Graceland College. He didn't accept that offer; instead he trained in track and field. Several years later, he won a gold medal in the Olympics in the grueling decathlon event! In case you haven't guessed, this story is about Bruce Jenner.

This individual was still illiterate at age 12, but he could memorize anything! Spelling was always impossible for him, and as he said, "he had trouble with the A, B, and that other letter." He also was a failure at math. He finally made it through high school, but he failed his first year at West Point. He did graduate, with the help of tutors, one year late. His special talent was in fighting wars, and, during World War II, he was one of our most famous generals. Of course, this story is about George Patton.

Other famous people with learning disabilities include Leonardo da Vinci, Tom Cruise, Nelson Rockefeller, Winston Churchill, Woodrow Wilson, F. W. Woolworth, Walt Disney, Ernest Hemingway, Albert Einstein, George Bernard Shaw, and Thomas Edison (Harwell, 1989; Silver, 1984). Like these and others, individuals with learning disabilities are often misunderstood and teased early in life for their inadequacies in the classroom. To be successful in life, they must be creative and persistent. Adults with learning disabilities succeed by sheer determination to overcome their limitations and focus on their talents.

Perhaps the most difficult aspect of understanding and teaching students with learning disabilities is the fact that the disability is hidden. When students with obviously normal intelligence fail to finish their work, interrupt inappropriately, never seem to follow directions, and turn in sloppy, poorly organized assignments, it is natural to blame poor motivation, lack of effort—even an undesirable family life.

However, the lack of accomplishment and success in the classroom does have a cause; the students are not demonstrating these behaviors to upset or irritate their teachers. A learning disability is a cognitive disability; it is a disorder of thinking, reasoning, and language ability. Because the dysfunction is presumed to be in the central nervous system, the presence of the disability is not obvious. There is no prosthetic device to announce the disability (Harwell, 1989). The following letter from a parent of a child with a learning disability illustrates misunderstanding about this condition (Smith, 1979, pp. 13–14):

Dearest Joan,

I can't tell you how much I'm looking forward to your visit—it's been 8 years since the last one. I'm glad your family is growing well—I wish I could say the same.

Henry is almost 9, and I feel 90. You remember how sick he was as a baby when you were here last? Well, he kept that up for 2 years—colds, croup, ear-aches, bronchitis—never properly getting over one before he came down with another. It seemed like he never had time to just plain grow like other children. Bill was an angel—he did extra things with Rosie while I coped with Henry.

Once he walked, Henry always looked battered because he kept falling. I used to carry a silver 50-cent piece to press on his bumps to keep them from turning black and blue. He walked and talked at the normal age, like Rosie, but he was different. There was a pain deep inside me that just ached for this child—and it still does. Everything seemed so hard for Henry, though he was full of smiles and spark. *Too* much spark. He was everywhere and into everything—still is. I could lose him in a flash. One time I ran upstairs to get a clean pair of rubber pants, and, when I came down, the front door was open and Henry was in the middle of the street with a police car stopped and a policeman about to pick him up and look for the right house! Now he climbs way up high in trees and can't get down, and it terrifies me.

For 8 years, Joanie, I've lived with a pit-of-the-stomach fear that something will happen to him. It's a desperate feeling of "Oh my God—what will go wrong next?" I dread every time the phone rings. Bill's folks say, "A few good spankings will set him straight." Mother says I just need patience. Dad says, "What are you trying to do—turn him into a sissy? He's all boy." I'm trying everything I know how to do. I'm exhausted from trying. But when I take Henry out, people look at me askance and say, "Lady, *do* something about this child."

His nursery school teacher said I babied him because he couldn't button or zip, and his clothes were forever falling off. His kindergarten teacher said I should discipline him more because he was too lazy to learn his letters and numbers. His first grade teacher called one parent conference after another. I tried to help Henry sit still and learn his letters. At the same time, Rosie complained that I was *never that easy on her,* and she hassled Henry half to death, telling him, "Just *try,* Henry. You're not *trying!*" Bill and Rosie and the neighbors all told me I spoiled him, so I tried to be tougher. I took away the TV, which was the only thing he enjoyed, but he cried all the time and seemed more babyish than ever. I couldn't make him be more independent because he had so little to be independent *with!*

The pediatrician says not to worry, he's a "late bloomer." The eye doctor says he sees well. The Hearing Society gave some routine tests at school and tried to tell me he was deaf—and it took three ear specialists and an audiologist to prove that he wasn't. Now we've been sent to a psychiatrist who makes both Bill and me feel like the most inadequate parents in the world. He's asking us if our marriage is OK, and I sometimes wonder if it is! We've stopped going out or seeing friends. Henry is repeating second grade, and Bill has a session with him every night because he says I molly-coddle him. He shuts the door but I hear his voice getting louder and more impatient, then Henry crying and the books being slammed down on the table—and I wonder if our life will ever be good again.

I'm angry. Joanie, I hate the world for doing this to us. I wish we could just pick up Henry, get on a boat, and take him clear away from it all. Do you understand that we love this handsome little boy and we don't know what to do? He doesn't sit still and he can't do his school work. And yet he talks so intelligently (such a big vocabulary!), and he describes things wonderfully. He *is* intelligent. Do you know he's called "dumb-head," "retard," "spaz" by the other children! I don't know which of us is crying more—Henry or me. Bill is carrying so much responsibility at the office that I try not to burden him with too much of this.

It will be so good to have you to talk to, and I'll try to make your visit a good one. I promise.

Love,
Sue

Our understanding of learning disabilities and the services available to children and adults is improving. However, since the field is relatively new, there is little agreement on the terms and definitions that should be used (Deiner, 1993). Major differences in policies for defining the population and determining eligibility exist across the United States. Because of these inconsistencies, it is hard to get an accurate picture of the number of children with learning disabilities.

The American Academy of Pediatrics (1988) suggests that more than 1 out of 10 students in public schools have a disability and that, of these, half have a learning disability. The child-count figures calculated by the federal government indicate that more than 2.2 million children, ages 6–21, were classified as having, and received services for, learning disabilities during 1991–1992 (U.S. Department of Education, 1993). Gerber and Levine-Donnerstein (1989) and the U.S. Department of Education (1993) reported that the number of students classified as learning disabled (LD) has risen 183% since 1976–1977.

Learning Disabilities Defined

The initial studies of children later described as having learning disabilities were done by physicians interested in brain injury in children. Over the years, there has been much controversy and confusion, as more than 90 terms were introduced into the literature to describe these children (Deiner, 1993). The most common include *minimal brain dysfunction (MBD), brain damaged, central process dysfunction,* and *language delayed.* To add to the confusion, separate definitions were also offered to explain each term.

The term *specific learning disabilities* was coined in 1962 and first adopted publicly in 1963 at a meeting of parents and professionals. Kirk (1962) developed the generic term in an effort to unite the field, which was torn between theorists promoting the perceptual deficit theory and constituents of the speech and language theory (Bender, 1992). The term was received favorably because it did not have the negative connotations of the other terms and did describe the primary characteristic of the children.

Federal Definition

In 1968 the U.S. Office of Education formed the National Advisory Committee on Handicapped Children. The committee developed a definition of learning disabilities that would later be adopted into federal law in the Learning Disabilities Act of 1969. This definition was modified only slightly to be included in the most recent reference to learning disabilities in federal law, the 1977 *Federal Register*. This definition states:

> "Specific learning disability" means a disorder in one or more of the basic psychological processes involved in understanding or in using language, spoken or written, which may manifest itself in an imperfect ability to listen, think, speak, read, write, spell or to do mathematical calculations. The term includes such conditions as perceptual handicaps, brain injury, minimal brain dysfunction, dyslexia, and developmental aphasia. The term does not include children who have learning problems which are primarily the result of visual, hearing, or motor handicaps, of mental retardation, or emotional disturbance, or of environmental, cultural, or economic disadvantage. (p. 45083)

The National Joint Committee on Learning Disabilities Definition

Critics of the definition in the *Federal Register* (U.S. Department of Education, 1977) charge that major problems exist with the wording of the exclusion clause, the vagueness of terms such as *basic psychological processes*, and the confusing terms cited such as dyslexia, brain injury, and perceptual handicaps (Hammill, Leigh, McNutt, & Larsen, 1981). In 1981 a group of professionals representing various organizations concerned with the area of learning disabilities formed the National Joint Committee on Learning Disabilities (NJCLD) to study issues and attempt to resolve differences. Although it was a difficult task, over time the group developed an alternative definition. This definition reads:

> Learning Disabilities is a generic term that refers to a heterogeneous group of disorders manifested by significant difficulties in the acquisition and use of listening, speaking, reading, writing, reasoning, or mathematical abilities. These disorders are intrinsic to the individual and presumed to be due to central nervous system dysfunction. Even though a learning disability may occur concomitantly with other handicapping conditions (e.g., sensory impairment, mental retardation, social and emotional disturbance), or environmental influences (e.g., cultural differences, insufficient/inappropriate instruction, psychogenic factors), it is not the direct result of those conditions or influences. (Hammill et al., 1981, p. 336)

In 1988 this definition was slightly changed by the Committee to reflect current research that suggests that learning disabilities "may occur across a life span" and that "problems in self-regulatory behaviors, social perception, and social interaction may exist with learning disabilities but do not by themselves constitute a learning disability" (NJCLD, 1988, p. 1).

Although this definition has been endorsed by most professional organizations, it has not been written into federal law, so most states have continued to use a variation of the 1977 definition. There is still much variation across states. It is important to be familiar with the definition and criteria for identification currently used in your state.

Mercer, King-Sears, and Mercer (1990) surveyed the state departments of education regarding their definition and the criteria used for eligibility. They cited five components as the most commonly used and noted whether these components were being used more or less than an earlier survey (Mercer, Hughes, & Mercer, 1985) had suggested.

The most commonly cited component was *academic deficits*. This area had remained a constant over time, with over 96% of the states using this component in either the definition or the criteria for eligibility. The second most consistently used component was the *exclusion clause*. Use of this criterion had increased to 94% of the states using it. Also increasing in usage were the *discrepancy* and *processing components*. Ninety-two percent of the states used the processing component in the definition; however, only 27% used it in establishing eligibility. Although 64% used the *neurological component* in the definition, only 4% used it to establish eligibility.

Eligibility Criteria

Because of the vagueness of the definition and the difficulty of measuring nebulous constructs such as the processing component, the federal government specified stronger criteria to determine eligibility for placement in a learning disabilities classroom. After a national debate that lasted two years after PL 94–142 was passed in 1975, the federal regulations for definition and identification criteria for learning disabilities were published in the *Federal Register* (USDE, 1977). These are considered minimal standards, and states may require additional criteria. The criteria include the following:

- ◆ *Multidisciplinary Team*   A group of individuals is required to determine eligibility, including a classroom teacher, at least one individual qualified to perform diagnostic examinations of children, and a learning disabilities specialist.
- ◆ *Observation*   A student must be observed by at least one member of the team in the general education classroom. The purpose of the observation is to document the manifestation of the disability in the classroom.
- ◆ *Criteria for Determining a Disability*
  1. The team must determine the existence of a severe discrepancy between achievement and intellectual ability in one or more of the following areas: (a) reading skills, (b) reading comprehension, (c) mathematical calcula-

tions, (d) mathematical reasoning, (e) written expression, (f) oral expression, (g) listening comprehension.

2. The team may not identify a student as having a specific learning disability if the severe discrepancy between ability and achievement is primarily the result of (a) a visual, hearing, or motor handicap, (b) mental retardation, (c) emotional disturbance, or (d) economic disadvantage.

3. The team must document that appropriate learning opportunities have been provided.

◆ *Written Report*   A written report is required to provide information to document that each of the above criteria was met. It must be noted on the report whether all team members agree with the findings of the team (USOE, 1977, p. 65083).

A more straightforward definition is offered by Harwell (1989), who identifies an individual with a learning disability as one who

1. Can see
2. Can hear
3. Has general intelligence in the near-average, average, or above-average range
4. Has educational difficulties that do not stem from inadequate educational experience or cultural factors
5. Does not acquire and use information efficiently due to some impairment in perception, conceptualization, language, memory, attention, or motor control.

The *Federal Register* (USDE, 1977) focuses on the language, academic, and exclusion concepts and does *not* include the identification of the processes, such as attention and memory, involved in acquiring and using information. However, it is these characteristics and others that create the biggest barriers to success in the general education classroom and later in the work force. Teachers should be very familiar with the characteristics of learning disabilities and the impact they might have on functioning in a general education classroom. They should also understand that these characteristics are not manifested intentionally but occur as a result of a presumed central nervous system dysfunction.

Etiology of Learning Disabilities

Experts generally agree that learning is hindered in children with learning disabilities because there is a problem in how the brain processes information (American Academy of Pediatrics, 1988). In a pamphlet for parents, the Academy of Pediatrics describes the problem as

> similar to a distorted television picture caused by technical problems at the station. There is nothing wrong with the TV camera at the station or the TV set at home. Yet, the picture is not clear. Something in the internal workings of the TV station prevents it from presenting a good picture. There may be nothing wrong with the way the children take in

information. Their senses of sight and sound are fine. The problem occurs after the eyes or ears have done their job. . . . (p. 7)

Why this happens most frequently remains unknown. The literature suggests several causes that primarily center around genetic factors and trauma induced during prenatal, perinatal, and postnatal events (Bender, 1992). New areas of research include the environmental influences of substances such as lead and the possibility of a chemical imbalance in the brain (Mercer, 1992).

1. *Prenatal Causes*   Several teratogenic insults that may occur during pregnancy have been linked to learning problems. The most common include use of alcohol, cigarettes, and other drugs, such as cocaine and prescription and nonprescription drugs. Through the mother's exposure, the fetus is exposed to the toxins, causing malformations of the developing brain and central nervous system. Although significant amounts of overexposure to these drugs may cause serious problems, such as mental retardation, no safe levels have been identified.

2. *Perinatal Causes*   These traumas occur during the birth process. They may include prolonged labor, anoxia, prematurity, and injury from medical instruments such as forceps (Mercer, 1992). Although not all children with a traumatic birth are found to have learning problems later, a significant number of children with learning problems do have a history of complications during this period (Blackman, 1983).

3. *Postnatal Causes*   The primary accidents and diseases linked to learning problems are high fever, encephalitis, meningitis, stroke, and head trauma (Mercer, 1992). Head injury has become so common that it was included as a separate category of special education under the 1990 Individuals with Disabilities Education Act (IDEA).

4. *Genetic/Hereditary Influences*   The evidence of genetic causes of a learning disability is contradictory. Some studies have cited the large number of relatives with learning problems in children identified with learning disabilities; however, this research has been criticized as not controlling for environmental influences (Cole, 1980). Chromosomal abnormalities have also been linked to learning disabilities (Vogel & Motulsky, 1986). Research in this area continues to show promise.

Characteristics of Learning Disabilities

Learning disabilities are primarily described as a deficit in academic achievement (reading and mathematics) and/or language (written language, listening, or oral language). Because instruction and assessment in these areas generally begin in kindergarten and first grade, most children are not identified until their formal schooling begins, or during grades 1–3. However, since learning disabilities are presumed to be a central nervous system dysfunction, characteristics may be manifested throughout the lifespan (Mercer, 1992).

Characteristics in the Preschool Child

Identification and special education services for preschool children are very controversial. The National Joint Committee on Learning Disabilities (NJCLD) issued a paper in 1985 describing these issues and needs. The greatest complication in identifying preschool children is their tremendous differences in growth and maturation. The NJCLD report on the Preschool Child (1985) warns against prematurely labeling a young child as learning disabled.

Tests at the preschool level are primarily predictive (Mercer, 1991). No single procedure for identification has been adopted (Bender, 1992). Some early warning signs that may be used to identify at-risk preschool children have been identified by the American Academy of Pediatrics (1988). Although they caution that children mature at different rates, the following characteristics are recommended benchmarks:

1. *Language Delay*   Children should be putting sentences together by age 2 $1/2$.
2. *Difficulty with Speech*   A child's language should be understood more than 50% of the time by the age of 3.
3. *Coordination Problems*   By the age of 5, children should be tying shoes, buttoning clothes, hopping, and cutting.
4. *Short Attention Span*   Although attention span increases with age, between ages 3 and 5, children should be sitting and attending while being read a short story.

Intervention.   In addition to the controversy surrounding assessment and identification of learning disabilities in preschool children, much has been written for and against the effectiveness and cost-effectiveness of early intervention programs for these children. Bender (1992) summarizes research in this area by stating that early intervention for some preschool children with learning disabilities—particularly those from low socioeconomic minority groups—is effective.

Mercer (1992) provides an overview of the curriculum models primarily used in preschool programs for children with learning disabilities. These include developmental, cognitive, and behavioral models. The *developmental model* stresses provision of an enriched environment. The child is provided numerous experiences and opportunities for learning. Development is stimulated through language and story telling, field trips, and creative opportunities.

The ***cognitive model*** is based on Piaget's work. Stimulating the child's cognitive or thinking abilities is the primary focus. Activities are designed to improve memory, discrimination, language, concept formation, self-evaluation, problem solving, and comprehension. This is a new area of research and is experiencing great success.

Concepts from direct instruction and the theory of reinforcement form the basis for the ***behavioral model.*** Measurable goals are set for each student, behaviors are observed, and desirable behavior is reinforced. Direct instruction is provided to accomplish goals, and progress is charted to provide data to determine the next task for instruction.

Mercer (1992) recommends a program that combines features from each of the approaches. He suggests some structure, availability of free-choice activities, direct instruction in targeted areas, daily charting and feedback, developmental activities, and spontaneous learning experiences.

Characteristics in the Elementary School Child

During grades 2 through 6, the emergence of academic problems begins to be readily apparent, and the discrepancy between intellectual ability and academic achievement may be documented (Mercer, 1992). Figure 4.1 demonstrates the wide variety of problems that may be characteristic of individuals with learning disabilities.

Academic and Language Deficits.   During the elementary years the discrepancy between ability and achievement begins to emerge. The seven academic and language areas that may be affected by a learning disability are identified in the *Federal*

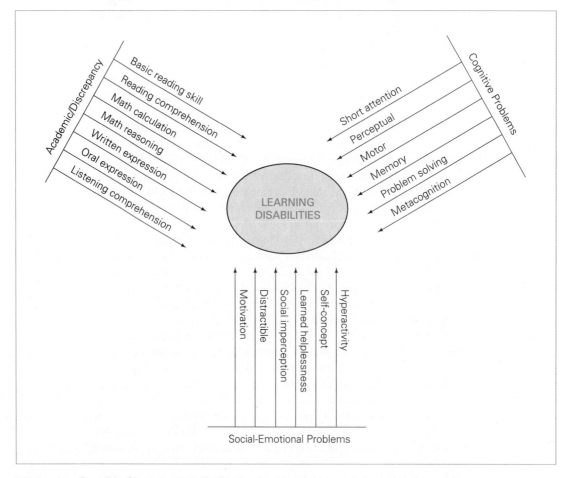

Figure 4.1   **Possible Characteristics Indicating the Variability within Learning Disabilities**
Source: Mercer, C. D. (1992). *Students with learning disabilities.* New York: Merrill. Used with permission.

Register (USDE, 1977). These include problems in *basic reading skills* and *reading comprehension*. Children with learning disabilities may struggle with oral reading tasks. They may read in a strained voice with poor phrasing, ignore punctuation, and grope for words like a much younger child. The oral reading problems cause tremendous embarrassment to these children. Carnine, Silbert, and Kameenui (1990) confirm that a student's self-image and feelings of confidence are greatly affected by reading experience. Deficits in reading skills can also lead to acting out behavior and poor motivation.

Some children with learning disabilities may be able to call the words correctly but not remember what they have read. Comprehension problems may include one or more of the following: (a) identifying the main idea, (b) recalling basic facts and events in a sequence, (c) making inferences or evaluating what has been read (Mercer, 1992).

Another major academic problem area is mathematics. Students with learning disabilities may have problems in *math calculations* or *math reasoning* (USDE, 1977). These disabilities may interfere with practical daily living tasks and lead to social and emotional problems (Mercer, 1992). Cawley and Miller (1989) suggest that children with learning disabilities may progress about one year in math for every two years in school.

During grades 2 through 6, academic problems begin to become very obvious.

Use an Acquisition Outline

For students who need help understanding how the *parts* of a lesson fit together to make a *whole,* Wood (1991) presented an approach teachers can easily use. It includes a step-by-step explanation by the teacher, who introduces topics one by one and returns to each one for review at regular intervals. While the teacher is presenting information, students use either a blank or partial outline and record relevant information. For example:

> Subject: English
> Topic: Romanticism
>
> I. Definition
>   A. Literary movement of the _____ century
>   B. Reacted against _____
>
> II. Characteristics
>   A. Interest in _____ rather than in society
>   B. Sympathy for the _____
> III. Gothic Elements
>   A. Grotesque—emphasis on _____
>   B. _____ —spiritual agony

Learning disabilities in the area of *written expression* are beginning to receive more recognition as a potentially serious problem. The three main areas of concern are handwriting, spelling, and written expression. The impact of written language problems increases with a student's age because so many school assignments require a written product. Smith (1981) suggests that to improve written communication skills, students must receive direct, concentrated instruction.

Language deficits are found in the areas of *oral expression* and *listening comprehension.* In using oral language to communicate, there is *spontaneous language,* where the individual initiates what is said, and, *demand language,* where another person asks a question or controls the circumstances in which the child must respond. Children with learning disabilities may have striking differences in these areas, being very effective with spontaneous language and having striking problems with demand language. In a situation where a parent or teacher has asked a question, the child may answer, "huh?," or respond quickly, "I don't know." Children may ask for the question to be repeated or not answer at all. Again, this is a confusing response and one in which the child is apt to be labeled as lazy or uncooperative (Silver, 1984).

Other common oral language problems include difficulty in retrieving words, with children often using a less appropriate word choice because the right word will not come to them (Bos & Vaughn, 1988). The response rate and sentence articulation of children with learning disabilities may be slower than their nondisabled peers (Ackerman, Dykman, & Gardner, 1990). They tend to use simpler, less mature language and confuse sequences in retelling a story (Merritt & Liles, 1987). These deficits in expressive language suggest possible difficulties in receptive language or listening as well.

One of the newest areas of concern and research for children with language-learning disabilities is the area of **pragmatics** or use of language in social-communication situations (Boucher, 1986). These children are sometimes unsuccessful in fully participating in conversation. They may need extra time to process incoming information, or they may not understand the meaning of the words or word sequences. Nonverbal language cues may be missed. They may not understand jokes; they may laugh inappropriately or at the wrong times. Group work is often difficult, as is giving or following directions. Language disabilities can contribute significantly to difficulties in other social situations as well (Boucher, 1986).

Social-Emotional Problems.   The literature suggests that to be socially accepted students should be cooperative, share, offer pleasant greetings, have positive interactions with peers, ask for and give information, and make conversation (Gresham, 1982). Some children with learning disabilities actually have a strength in the area of social skills. However, several characteristics of learning disabilities can create difficulties in the social and emotional areas.

The problems in *language, memory, problem solving, attention, hyperactivity,* and *distractibility* interfere with academic achievement and exacerbate feelings of frustration and failure (Coleman, 1985). Positive interactions and exchange of information often does not occur. Because of behavior and language differences, children with learning disabilities need more guidance and structure. Over time, this can create feelings of overdependency, and eventually *learned helplessness* occurs. Social deficits can even lead to school failure (Bryan, 1991).

Research suggests that children in elementary school exhibit an overall or globally low level of self-concept (Bender, 1987a). Over the years of failure, often being labeled dumb or lazy by other students and sometimes even teachers, the students with learning disabilities are left feeling inadequate and devalued (Silver, 1984). Signs of depression might be expressed through pervasive sadness and withdrawal or by turning their frustration into aggression and irritability.

Either way, the cycle of failure is continued until intervention takes place. One young man stated that the people at school kept telling him he was smart, but he knew they were just saying that because he couldn't read or do math like the other children. Children with learning disabilities are smart enough to know when they are being conned! Reinforcement should only be applied to a specific task that has been done well.

Intervention.   There is no longer debate regarding the desirability of children with disabilities being included to the greatest degree possible in the general education setting. The question is how to best prepare both the children with disabilities and nondisabled children for positive interactions. Changing a student's self-image, social ability, and social standing is difficult. Until recently, the research and focus of the literature in learning disabilities was primarily on the efficacy of treatments for the most obvious characteristic—academic deficits. The importance of social skills is just now being recognized and given the attention it deserves.

Intervention in the area of social standing and interaction can take two courses: The focus can be on changing the child or on changing the environment. Optimally both would receive attention. Good teaching techniques can lead to academic achievement and eventually to higher self-esteem. It is very important to create a positive learning environment with praise and encouragement for specific accomplishments. Set goals and be very explicit about expectations for academic work and behavior in the class. Monitor progress closely and provide frequent feedback (Mercer, 1992).

Students should be asked higher-level questions that require problem solving and reasoning. Opportunities need to be provided for students to generalize learned information across settings. The most effective learning environment is supportive but encourages independence. Students should be given responsibilities. They should be reinforced for making positive comments about themselves and about other students (Mercer, 1992).

A number of programs are available commercially; however, these are prepackaged and may not meet the specific needs of your students. There are many techniques that may be implemented successfully in either the general or special education classroom. Some of the specific teaching strategies for improving social competencies and building self-concept have been summarized by Lerner (1993). She suggests activities that fall into the following four areas:

1. *Body Image and Perception of Self*   Make a scrapbook to tell about each student. Have students make and solve puzzles about the body.
2. *Sensitivity*   Study pictures of faces, gestures, and films to determine the social meaning. Study voices to determine moods.
3. *Social Maturity*   Through role play and discussion of actual social acts and ethical dilemmas, give students situations and have them determine the consequences. Have students plan and organize weekend activities with friends.
4. *Learning Strategies and Social Skills Training*   Teach students strategies about how to stop and think before responding, to visualize the effects of their options, to visually or verbally rehearse the chosen response, and to monitor their own success.

The overall goal of social programs is to teach socially appropriate behavior and social skills that are self-generated and self-monitored. The cognitive problems of students with learning disabilities often make this type of decision making very difficult.

Cognitive Problems.   Cognitive abilities enable one to be aware, to think and reason, conceptualize, and be creative. Unfortunately, some of the characteristics of learning disabilities interfere with the cognitive process. Mercer (1992) cites cognitive deficits in children with learning disabilities as problems in *attention, perception, motor abilities, problem solving,* and *metacognition.*

Cultural and Linguistic Considerations Related to IEP Development

Selection of IEP Goals and Objectives

Considerations for IEP Development	Classroom Implications
IEP goals and objectives accommodate the student's current level of performance.	• At the student's instructional level • Instructional level based on student's cognitive level, not the language proficiency level • Focus on development of higher-level cognitive skills as well as basic skills
Goals and objectives are responsive to cultural and linguistic variables.	• Accommodates goals and expectations of the family • Is sensitive to culturally based response to the disability • Includes a language use plan • Addresses language development and ESL needs

Selection of Instructional Strategies

Considerations for IEP Development	Classroom Implications
Interventions provide adequate exposure to curriculum.	• Instruction in student's dominant language • Responsiveness to learning and communication styles • Sufficient practice to achieve mastery
IEP provides for curricular/ instructional accommodation of learning styles and locus of control.	• Accommodates perceptual style differences (e.g., visual vs. auditory) • Accommodates cognitive style differences (e.g., inductive vs. deductive) • Accommodates preferred style of participation (e.g., teacher vs. student-directed, small vs. large group) • Reduces feelings of learned helplessness
Selected strategies are likely to be effective for language minority students.	• Native language and ESL instruction • Teacher as facilitator of learning (vs. transmission) • Genuine dialogue with students • Contextualized instruction • Collaborative learning • Self-regulated learning • Learning-to-learn strategies
English as a second language (ESL) strategies are used.	• Modifications to address the student's disability • Use of current ESL approaches • Focus on meaningful communication

Strategies for literacy are included.	• Holistic approaches to literacy development • Language teaching that is integrated across the curriculum • Thematic literature units • Language experience approach • Journals

Source: Garcia, S. B., & Malkin, D. H. (1993). Toward defining programs and services for culturally and linguistically diverse learners in special education. *Teaching Exceptional Children, 26*, pp. 52–58. Used with permission.

Lerner (1993) likens the learning process to the way a computer functions with input stimuli, memory and the cognitive processing system, and output performance. In order to process information or learn from the environment, a new stimulus must enter the brain. Stimuli are primarily received by the auditory channel through listening and the visual channel through reading or receiving other visual input. Learning also takes place through touching, smelling, and tasting. Perceptual problems suggest that the mechanism being stimulated is somehow faulty and not receiving the stimulus as it is being presented. The problem may also be in the lack of sufficient attention to the stimulus.

Once the stimulus has entered the brain, the brain must decide the value of the information—whether it should be remembered or discarded. If it is to be remembered, the new information must be organized and connected to previously learned information. During this step, the process of judging and critical evaluation occurs. Long-term memory must be accessed for permanent storage. One problem with memory is the retrieval process. Students with learning disabilities often have unusual memory abilities in that they may remember something one day and not be able to recall it the next.

In order to demonstrate knowledge or thinking, a motoric output such as oral language, written language, or physical-motor response is required. Metacognition occurs when a student uses a variety of strategies, determines the most efficient strategy to use under different situations, and can evaluate the outcome to refine the strategy for future use. Developing these skills of cognition through special education intervention holds promise for improving the learning process for students with learning disabilities (Lerner, 1993).

Intervention.   Cognitive intervention has only recently received support from the learning disabilities professionals. Some very powerful techniques are being studied to improve learning. Some of the ideas are relatively simple and require only common sense. First, and most important, is being sure a child is paying attention to the stimulus being presented. This might be done by dimming the lights, calling for attention, or establishing eye contact. Without attention, learning will not take place.

Lerner (1993) suggests that teachers present new information in well-organized, meaningful chunks. As new information is presented for memory, it should be linked to previously learned, meaningful information. For example, to teach subtraction, the teacher would demonstrate the relationship to addition. Students should also be encouraged to rehearse new information and be given many opportunities for practice. These and other effective learning strategies are presented in Table 4.1.

Characteristics in the Adolescent

Adolescents with learning disabilities experience academic failure and evidence language and cognitive deficits similar to those described in the previous section. In fact, research suggests that, as these students progress through school, they fall progressively further behind academically (Deshler, Schumaker, & Lenz, 1984). In addition, school demands increase, and assignments require much more complex thinking and planning. Mercer (1992) cites the following new challenges that face adolescents with learning disabilities:

- Gaining information from lectures
- Gaining information from difficult, secondary texts with high readability levels
- Demonstrating knowledge through tests that require good test-taking and study skills
- Expressing knowledge through written responses
- Working independently with little feedback
- Demonstrating cognitive and thinking skills to organize information for a task and self-evaluation
- Interacting successfully with teachers and peers in group activities, following rules, asking for help, accepting criticism, resisting peer pressure, and maintaining a pleasant manner
- Demonstrating effort and motivation

These pressures are summarized by Deshler, Warner, Schumaker, and Alley (1983) as they state the following:

> The critical tasks and demands of the regular classroom in secondary schools are complex and diverse. They require of students a well-honed set of skills in the areas of critical listening, note taking, written expression, problem-solving, etc. In addition, students are expected to function independently of teacher or peer assistance and to compete with others. In short, for many LD adolescents, the often-referred-to shift from a skills emphasis at the elementary level to content emphasis in the secondary grades becomes a devastating reality. (pp. 257–258)

In addition to the major changes in the school environment, the adolescent with learning disabilities is experiencing the traumatic developmental changes typical of adolescence. Major changes occur in the physical, psychological and personality, and cognitive areas. The children are worried about their appearance. If adolescents do not approve of their own looks, the results are feelings of self-consciousness and inferiority.

Although problems generally continue in the social-emotional area throughout adolescence, the studies on self-concept suggest a possibility for improvement. Bender (1987b) found that adolescents learned to think of themselves differently in school and other situations. Although they may continue to feel badly about themselves rel-

TABLE 4.1 **Learning Strategies**

Self-Questioning

Students quietly ask themselves questions about the material. This process is also referred to as verbal mediation. The internal language, or covert speech, helps organize material and behavior. Camp and Bash (1981) suggest the following types of questions:

What is the problem? (or) What am I supposed to do?
What is my plan? (or) How can I do it?
Am I using my plan?
How did I do?

Verbal Rehearsal and Review

Students practice and review what they have learned. This self-rehearsal helps students remember. People forget when the brain trace, which is a physical record of memory, fades away. Recitation and review of material to be learned help the student remember.

Students observe the instructor's modeling of verbalization of a problem.
Students instruct themselves by verbalizing aloud or in a whisper.
Students verbalize silently.

Organization

To aid in recall, students figure out the main idea of the lesson and the supporting facts. The organization of the material has a great deal to do with how fast we can learn it and how well we can remember it. Already-existing memory units are called chunks, and through *chunking*, new material is reorganized into already-existing memory units. The more students can relate to what they already know, the better they will remember the new material.

Using Prior Knowledge

New material is linked to already-existing memory units. The more students can relate what they are learning to what they already know, the better they will remember.

Memory Strategies

If new material is anchored to old knowledge, students are more likely to remember it. For example, one student remembered the word *look* because it had two eyes in the middle. Some pupils can alphabetize only if they sing the "ABC" song. Some adults can remember people's names by using a mnemonic device that associates the name with a particular attribute of that individual, for example "blond Bill" or "green-sweater Gertrude."

Predicting and Monitoring

Students guess about what they will learn in the lesson and then check on whether their guesses were correct.

Advance Organizers

This technique establishes a mindset for the learner, relating new material to previously learned material. Students are told in advance about what they are going to learn. This sets the stage for learning and improves comprehension and the ability to recall what has been learned.

TABLE 4.1   **Learning Strategies** *(Continued)*

Cognitive Behavior Modification

This behavioral approach teaches students self-instruction, self-monitoring, and self-evaluation techniques (Meichenbaum, 1977). There are several steps:
>   The teacher models a behavior while giving an explanation.
>   The student performs the task while the teacher describes it.
>   The student talks the task through out loud.
>   The student whispers it to himself or herself.
>   The student performs the task with nonverbal self-cues.

Modeling

The teacher provides an example of appropriate cognitive behavior and problem-solving strategies. The teacher can talk through the cognitive processes being used.

Self-Monitoring

Students learn to monitor their own mistakes. They learn to check their own responses and become conscious of errors or answers that do not make sense. To reach this stage requires active involvement in the learning process to recognize incongruities.

Source: Lerner, Janet W., *Learning Disabilities: Theories, Diagnosis, and Teaching Strategies,* Sixth Edition. Copyright © 1993 by Houghton Mifflin Company. Used with permission.

ative to their school achievement, they may think more highly of themselves in areas unrelated to school. However, Bender (1992) noted that the years of failure take a toll on the students with learning disabilities and may lead to personality disorders, which can mean pervasive unhappiness. The low self-esteem and feelings of failure generally prohibit high motivation for schoolwork. Ness and Price (1990) report psychological problems including feelings of incompetence, inadequacy, frustration, and anger. They also describe shyness and excessive dependency in this population.

Generally, the cognitive deficits used to describe younger children with learning disabilities continue into adolescence. Characteristics that interfere with functioning include problems in attention and memory, poor problem-solving skills, and deficits in planning and organizing (Smith, Finn, & Dowdy, 1993). The combined cognitive and language deficits can interfere significantly with deciding how to act in the new social situations brought about by increased independence. With the advanced language skills of normal adolescents, these children may experience greater failure in communication and may suffer more rejection, which can have long-lasting effects (Polloway & Smith, 1992).

Intervention.   To help ameliorate the pervasive feelings of unhappiness, school environments must be structured to create successful experiences. One method is to involve students more in designing their educational experiences and monitoring their own success (Schunk, 1985). Motivation is also a key ingredient to successful high school programming. An excellent summary of the motivation research is provided by Brophy (1987). This information is included in Table 4.2.

TABLE 4.2 **Strategies for Motivating Students to Learn**

Research on student motivation to learn indicates promising principles suitable for application in classrooms, summarized here for quick reference.

Essential Preconditions

1. Supportive environment
2. Appropriate level of challenge/difficulty
3. Meaningful learning objectives
4. Moderation/optimal use

Motivating by Maintaining Success Expectations

5. Program for success
6. Teach goal setting, performance appraisal, and self-reinforcement
7. Help students to recognize links between effort and outcome
8. Provide remedial socialization

Motivating by Supplying Extrinsic Incentives

9. Offer rewards for good (or improved) performance
10. Structure appropriate competition
11. Call attention to the instrumental value of academic activities

Motivating by Capitalizing on Students' Intrinsic Motivation

12. Adapt tasks to students' interests
13. Include novelty/variety elements
14. Allow opportunities to make choices or autonomous decisions
15. Provide opportunities for students to respond actively
16. Provide immediate feedback to student responses
17. Allow students to create finished products
18. Include fantasy or simulation elements
19. Incorporate game-like features
20. Include higher-level objectives and divergent questions
21. Provide opportunities to interact with peers

Stimulating Student Motivation to Learn

22. Model interest in learning and motivation to learn
23. Communicate desirable expectations and attributions about students' motivation to learn
24. Minimize students' performance anxiety during learning activities
25. Project intensity
26. Project enthusiasm
27. Induce task interest or appreciation
28. Induce curiosity or suspense
29. Induce dissonance or cognitive conflict
30. Make abstract content more personal, concrete, or familiar
31. Induce students to generate their own motivation to learn
32. State learning objectives and provide advance organizers
33. Model task-related thinking and problem solving

Source: Brophy, J. (1987). "Synthesis of Research on Strategies for Motivating Students to Learn," *Educational Leadership,* 45, 2:45. Reprinted with permission of the Association for Supervision and Curriculum Development. Copyright 1987 by ASCD. All rights reserved.

Setting goals for instruction that are relevant to the futures of these students is critical (Dowdy & Smith, 1991). Smith et al. (1993) recommend specific content areas needed for students that should be addressed by the high school special education teacher. Since students with learning disabilities may go on to college or go directly into employment, the high school curriculum should prepare them for either future challenge as well as the ongoing challenges of high school. Areas that need to be addressed include

1. Preparation for high school content classes
2. Preparation for the high school graduation exam
3. Counseling for each day's crises (includes social skills training)
4. Preparation for independent living
5. Preparation for postsecondary training (including study skills)
6. Preparation for employment or military service

Characteristics in the Adult

Learning disabilities are manifested in childhood and often persist into adult life (Johnson & Blalock, 1987; White, 1992). The definition of learning disabilities adopted by the Rehabilitation Services Administration (1985) to describe adolescents and adults with learning disabilities cites the characteristics of this population as "attention, reasoning, processing, memory, communication, reading, writing, spelling, calculation, coordination, social competence, and emotional maturity" (p. 11).

Dowdy (1992) suggests that these behaviors impact on adults in their personal and work lives as significantly as they have interfered with school success. The primary areas of impact in adults are in vocational and social domains (White, 1992). Adults with learning disabilities are often reported as employed, but more often in part-time work or in jobs of lower status (deBettencourt, Zigmond, & Thornton, 1989). They also report less satisfaction with their personal lives (White, 1992).

Intervention. The primary adult agency which offers treatment or intervention to promote employment for adults with learning disabilities is the Rehabilitation Services Administration. An office of this vocational rehabilitation (VR) agency is located in every state, and VR counselors are trained to identify the characteristics which will limit employment for adults and adolescents with learning disabilities and to provide services to those who are eligible. For more information on these services see Dowdy, Smith, and Nowell (1992).

Efficacy of Intervention Approaches

Accepted Intervention Approaches

Over the years, much controversy and change in the recommended treatment procedures for individuals with learning disabilities have been seen. In the 1970s a huge debate existed between advocates for perceptual training of auditory and visual

Precautions for Computer Use and Maintenance

◆ Dust should be cleaned from ventilation slots in the equipment.

◆ Avoid shocks and vibration. Have printers placed on a table or stand separate from the computer.

◆ Any liquids should not be allowed near or on the computer. A spill could ruin internal electronic parts or, worse, cause an electrical fire.

◆ Extremes in temperature will damage the computer. Make sure there is adequate ventilation, heating, and cooling in the room.

◆ Be sure ventilation holes in the computer's cabinet are not blocked by placing objects on, under, or too close to the equipment.

◆ Use one electrical circuit for the computer only (not shared with other devices).

◆ Be sure to use a grounded receptacle. Do not defeat the ground feature of the male plug.

◆ Avoid static electricity during dry conditions. Place an antistatic mat in front of the equipment. A spark from your hand to the computer can erase data and ruin electronic components. Always touch a metal object before handling a diskette.

◆ Use a line filter to help regulate fluctuation in the electricity supply to the computer. These devices plug in between the power source and the computer's electrical power cord.

◆ Always cover the microcomputer when not in use.

◆ Keep connecting cables as short as possible and out of the way. Cables should not lie on the floor.

◆ If an electrical blackout occurs, unplug the computer components until after power is restored. This protects against surges in electricity to the equipment.

◆ Lightning, nearby motors, telephones, disk drives, fluorescent lamps, vacuum cleaners, and connected electrical plugs can cause interference that disrupts the operations of the computer and results in erratic behavior.

Source: Westling, D. L., & Koorland, M. A. (1989). *The special educator's handbook* (p. 92). Boston: Allyn & Bacon. Used with permission.

processes and direct instruction in the deficit academic area(s) (Engelmann & Carnin, 1982). A convincing article by Hammill and Larsen (1974) provided an analysis of research showing that perceptual training did little to improve basic academic skills. This triggered a move toward a skills approach in which direct instruction was implemented in the areas of academic deficit.

In the 1980s and 1990s, the field is evolving to include a focus on cognitive approaches. Students are being taught to analyze the demands of a task in order to solve the problem (Loper, 1980), they are being provided with strategies for learning (Deshler & Schumaker, 1986; Swanson, 1990), and they are being trained in techniques to monitor their own learning and behavior (Hallahan, Lloyd, Kneedler, & Marshall, 1982). In a review of various treatment approaches, Lloyd (1988) concludes that no one approach can be cited as the best. He does suggest that the the most effective ones are structured, goal-oriented, provide multiple opportunities for practice, include a strategy, are oriented for independence, comprehensive, and detailed.

More data-based research is needed to validate academic interventions for this population. A review of the literature found that only 4% of the articles published in the area of learning disabilities in the last ten years presented data on the efficacy of intervention models (Lessen, Dudzinski, Karsh, & Ackerman, 1989). Special education and general education teachers must continue to monitor the literature to make the best choices for teaching their students and to avoid treatment approaches that have not been supported by data-based research.

Controversial Intervention Approaches

Some interventions, often presented to the public through television or newsstand magazines, are controversial and are not validated as effective for students with learning disabilities. Educators may be asked for an opinion on one of these therapies by parents who are attempting to find solutions for their children's frustrating problems. A brief overview of these nontraditional approaches is provided. More extensive reviews are provided by Rooney (1991) and Silver (1987).

One of the most recent controversial therapies involves the prescription of tinted glasses as a cure for dyslexia. In this approach, scotopic sensitivity, proposed to interfere with learning, is treated by identifying a colored lens to reduce sensitivity. Rooney (1991) notes that the studies that support this treatment do not meet acceptable scientific standards and should be viewed with caution.

An older treatment theory is orthomolecular therapy involving vitamins, minerals, and diet. Proponents of this treatment claim that large doses of vitamins and minerals straighten out the biochemistry of the brain to reduce hyperactivity and to increase learning. Hair analysis and blood studies are used to determine the doses needed.

Feingold's Diet is another dietary treatment frequently cited. Feingold (1975) proposed that negative behaviors such as hyperactivity and limited learning were due to the body's reaction to unnatural substances such as food colorings, preservatives, and artificial dyes. His patients were asked to keep a comprehensive diary of their diet and to avoid harmful chemical substances. Other diets have centered around avoiding sugar and caffeine.

Another proponent of orthomolecular therapy suggests that the negative behaviors are the result of allergies to food and environmental substances (Silver, 1987). The research on the efficacy of these interventions is usually comprised of clinical studies without control groups. When control groups are used, the diets do not stand up to conclusive standards. Benefits have been noted for only a small percentage of children.

Vision therapy or training is another controversial treatment applied to individuals with a learning disability. This theory is based on the supposition that learning disabilities are the result of visual defects when the eyes do not work together and that these deficits can be cured by visual training. This has been a widespread practice supported primarily by groups of optometrists. The American Academy of Ophthalmology (1984) has issued a statement clearly stating that "no credible evidence exists to show that visual training, muscle exercises, perceptual, or hand/eye coordination exercises significantly affect a child's Specific Learning Disabilities"(p. 3).

Silver (1987) reviewed another controversial therapy involving the use of vestibular dysfunction medication to cure dyslexia. He noted that the relationship between dyslexia, the vestibular system, and the medication was not supported by research. Silver also warned that physicians often do not have adequate techniques to diagnose dyslexia consistently and are using doses of medication that are not recommended by the pharmaceutical companies.

Silver is also concerned about the widespread use of other medications such as Ritalin for learning and attention problems. He warns that prescriptions are often given based on the recommendations of parents or teachers alone without a comprehensive evaluation. Rooney (1991) states that the actual effectiveness of the medication is less an issue than the concerns that (1) the medication is prescribed without a thorough evaluation, (2) educational and behavioral treatments are not implemented in conjunction with the medication, and (3) there is insufficient monitoring of the

Classroom teachers are often the first to talk to parents about a child's learning problems.

effects of the medication. Monitoring these effects is a very important part of the role of classroom teachers.

Role of Classroom Teacher

Although parents are generally the first to become aware of at-risk characteristics such as hyperactivity and inattention in their young children, it is usually the classroom teacher who provides the first source of help. The general education teacher has the most experience with normal behavior and achievement. Because of this, the differences between the child with a learning disability and normally achieving children soon become evident. It is important to begin systematically recording teacher observations so that data will be available to make decisions regarding a referral for a special education evaluation and to show parents.

If the child ultimately is understood to have a learning disability, the work is just beginning for the classroom teacher. The first challenge is to be sure that the results of the diagnostic assessment are understood. Be aware of the child's strengths and challenges so that planning, and ultimately instruction, can accommodate the child's learning differences.

The next challenge is to be sure the children in the general education classroom and the child with the learning disability understand the disability and the need for special education. It can be pointed out that children who go to a learning disabilities teacher must "pass" an IQ test to get into the class! Primarily, children should be made aware that all people are different. Popp (1983) offers the following activities to sensitize children to individual differences:

1. Place two plants in front of the children and ask them to describe the ways they are alike and different.
2. Repeat the exercise with two children. Focus the discussion on the acceptance of differences and the fact that people do not like to be teased about their differences.
3. Have children draw or write about favorite foods and foods that they do not like. Older children may write about their own strengths and weaknesses. Determine the degree of agreement across the class. Focus on the fact that it is okay for people to be different.
4. Read the book *Is It Hard? Is It Easy?* (Green, 1960) to younger children.

Other teaching tips for general educators have been offered in Chapters 13 and 14 on accommodations for elementary and secondary classrooms and Chapter 12 on classroom management. In addition to those suggestions, the following list of recommended guidelines for teaching children and adolescents with learning disabilities have been compiled from work by Mercer (1992), Deiner (1993), and Bender (1992):

1. Be consistent in class rules and daily schedule of activities.
2. State rules and expectations clearly. Tell children what to do—not what *not* to do. For example, instead of saying, "Don't run in the halls," say "Walk in the halls."

Modifications for Students with Learning Disabilities

Program Modifications

- ◆ Alternative admission requirements
- ◆ Priority registration
- ◆ Special financial aid arrangements
- ◆ Special housing requests
- ◆ Substituting one course for another (e.g., foreign language or math)
- ◆ Part-time rather than full-time study

Instructional Modifications

- ◆ Taped textbooks
- ◆ Readers
- ◆ Note-taking modifications:
  Carbonless paper
  Note takers
  Tape recorder
  Laptop computer
- ◆ Testing modifications:
  Extended time
  Separate locations
  Different format
  Reader
  Oral exam (or taped answers to be transcribed later)
  Use of a word processor or typewriter
  Use of aids during the exam (calculator, dictionary, spell-checker, etc.)
  Alternative demonstration of mastery
- ◆ Auxiliary aids and equipment
- ◆ Adapting or modifying methods of instruction

Source: Brinckerhoff, L. C., Shaw, S. F., & McGuire, J. M. (1993). *Promoting postsecondary education for students with learning disabilities* (p. 223). Austin, TX: Pro-Ed. Used with permission.

3. Give advance organizers to prepare children for any changes in the day's events and to highlight the important points to be covered during instructional time.
4. Eliminate or reduce visual and auditory distractions when children need to concentrate. Help children focus on the important aspects of the task.
5. Give directions in clear, simple words. A long series of directions may need to be broken down and given one at time. Reinforcement may need to be provided as each step is completed.

6. Begin with simple activities focused on a single concept and build to more abstract ideas as the child appears ready. If problems occur, check for the presence of the prerequisite skills or knowledge of the vocabulary being used.
7. Use concrete objects or demonstrations when teaching a new concept. Relate new information to previously known concepts.
8. Teach the children strategies for remembering.
9. Present information visually, auditorially, and through demonstration to address each child's preferred learning style.
10. Use a variety of activities and experiences to teach or reinforce the same concept. Repetition can be provided without the boredom.
11. Use activities that are short or encourage movement. Some children may need to work standing up!
12. Incorporate problem-solving or other activities that involve the children. Use both higher-level and lower-level questions.
13. Always gain the student's attention before presenting important information.
14. Use cooperative instructional groupings and peer tutoring to vary modes of instruction.
15. Plan for success!

Summary

◆ A teacher would never stand over a child wearing a hearing aid and demand that he or she listen, or tell a blind child to look at the book and try harder to read! Yet a child with a specific learning disability in reading or listening—also caused by central nervous dysfunction or damage—is often subjected to this kind of abuse.

◆ A learning disability is a frequently misunderstood disability; teachers must try to determine whether the behavior that is of concern is a result of the disability or is a purposefully defiant behavior.

◆ Learning disabilities is a relatively young field with much controversy over the definition, etiology, and eligibility criteria.

◆ The most widely used criterion for identifying a learning disability is a severe discrepancy between ability and achievement that cannot be explained by another handicapping condition or lack of learning opportunity.

◆ Characteristics of learning disabilities are manifested across the lifespan.

◆ Learning disabilities are manifested in seven academic areas: Reading skills, reading comprehension, mathematical calculations, mathematical reasoning, written expression, oral expression, and listening comprehension.

◆ Other common characteristics of learning disabilities include social-emotional problems, perception, memory, problem solving, attention, hyperactivity, and distractibility.

◆ Children with learning disabilities are primarily educated in the general education classroom with accommodations; their special education needs are met by a learning disability specialist, using a variety of educational strategies.

◆ Adults with learning disabilities tend to have social and emotional problems and difficulty maintaining employment at their maximum potential.

◆ Caution must be used to avoid controversial nontraditional treatment approaches.

◆ The role of the classroom teacher includes implementing prereferral changes in the environment or instructional methods, referring the at-risk child, collaborating with parents and other professionals, and using teaching strategies delineated in this chapter and other sections of the text to facilitate success for their students with learning difficulties.

References

Ackerman, P. T., Dykman, R. A., & Gardner, M. Y. (1990). Counting rate, naming rate, phonological sensitivity, and memory span: Major factors in dyslexia. *Journal of Learning Disabilities, 23,* 325–327.

American Academy of Ophthalmology. (1984). Policy statement. *Learning disabilities, dyslexia, and vision.* San Francisco: Author.

American Academy of Pediatrics. (1988). *Learning disabilities and children: What parents need to know.* Elk Grove Village, IL: Author.

Bender, W. N. (1987a). Behavioral indicators of temperament and personality in the inactive learner. *Journal of Learning Disabilities, 20,* 301–305.

Bender, W. N. (1987b). Secondary personality and behavioral problems in adolescents with learning disabilities. *Journal of Learning Disabilities, 20,* 280–285.

Bender, W. N. (1992). *Learning disabilities: Characteristics, identification, and teaching strategies.* Needham Heights, MA: Allyn & Bacon.

Blackman, J. A. (1983). *Medical aspects of developmental disabilities in children birth to three: A resource of special-services providers in the educational setting.* Iowa City, IA: University of Iowa.

Bos, C. S., & Vaughn, S. (1988). *Strategies for teaching students with learning and behavior problems.* Boston: Allyn & Bacon.

Boucher, C. R. (1986). Pragmatics: The meaning of verbal language in learning disabled and nondisabled boys. *Learning Disability Quarterly, 9,* 285–295.

Brinckerhoff, L. C., Shaw, S. F., & McGuire, J. M. (1993). *Promoting postsecondary education for students with learning disabilities.* Austin, TX: Pro-Ed.

Brophy, J. (1987). Synthesis of research on strategies for motivating students to learn. *Education Leadership, 45*(2), 45.

Bryan, T. (1991). Social problems and learning disabilities. In B. Wong (Ed.), *Learning about learning disabilities* (pp. 195–231). San Diego: Academic Press.

Camp, B., & Bash, M. (1981). *Think aloud.* Champaign, IL: Research Press.

Carnine, D., Silbert J., & Kameenui, E. J. (1990). *Direct instruction reading* (2nd ed.). Columbus, OH: Merrill.

Cawley, J. F., & Miller, J. H. (1989). Cross-sectional comparisions of the mathematical performance of children with learning disabilities: Are we on the right track toward comprehensive programming? *Journal of Learning Disabilities, 23,* 250–254.

Coleman, J. M. (1985). Achievement level, social class, and the self-concepts of mildly handi-capped children. *Journal of Learning Disabilities, 18,* 26–30.

Cole, G. S. (1980). Evaluation of genetic explanations of reading and learning problems. *Journal of Special Education, 14,* 365–383.

deBettencourt, L. U., Zigmond, N., & Thornton, H. (1989). Follow-up of postsecondary-age rural learning disabled graduates and dropouts. *Exceptional Children, 56,* 40–49.

Deiner, P. L. (1993). *Resources for teaching children with diverse abilities.* Ft. Worth, TX: Harcourt Brace Jovanovich.

Deshler, D. D., Schumaker, J. B. (1986). Learning strategies: An instructional alternative for low-achieving adolescents. *Exceptional Children, 52*(6), 483–490.

Deshler, D. D., Schumaker, J. B., & Lenz, B. K. (1984). Academic and cognitive interventions for LD adolescents: Part I. *Journal of Learning Disabilities, 17,* 108–117.

Deshler, D. D., Warner, M. M., Schumaker, J. B., & Alley, G. R. (1983). The learning strategies intervention model: Key components and current status. In J. D. McKinney & L. Feagans (Eds.), *Current topics in learning disabilities* (Vol. 1) (pp. 77–89). Norwood, NJ: Ablex.

Dowdy, C.A. (1992). Identification of characteristics of specific learning disabilities as a critical component of the vocational rehabilitation process. *Journal of Rehabilitation, 58*(3), 51–54.

Dowdy, C. A., & Smith, T. E. C. (1991). Future-based assessment and intervention. *Intervention in School and Clinic, 27*(2), 101–106.

Dowdy, C. A., Smith, T. E. C., & Nowell, C. H. (1992). Learning disabilities and vocational rehabilitation. *Journal of Learning Disabilities, 25*(7), 442–447.

Engelmann, S., & Carnine, D. (1982). *Theory of instruction.* New York: Irvington.

Feingold, B. F. (1975). *Why your child is hyperactive.* New York: Random House.

Garcia, S. B., & Malkin, D. H. (1993). Toward defining programs and services for culturally and linguistically diverse learners in special education. *Teaching Exceptional Children, 26,* 52–58.

Gerber, M. M., & Levine-Donnerstein, D. (1989). Educating all children: Ten years later. *Exceptional Children, 56,* 17–27.

Green, M. (1960). *Is it hard? Is it easy?* New York: William R. Scott.

Gresham, F. M. (1982). Misguided mainstreaming: The case for social skills training with handicapped children. *Exceptional Children, 48*(5), 422–431.

Hallahan, D. P., Lloyd, J. W., Kneedler, R. D., & Marshall, K. J. (1982). A comparison of the effects of self- versus teacher-assessment of on-task behavior. *Behavior Therapy, 13,* 715–723.

Hammill, D. D., & Larsen, S. C. (1974). The effectiveness of psycholinguistic training. *Exceptional Children, 41,* 5–14.

Hammill, D. D., Leigh, J. E., McNutt, G., & Larsen, S. C. (1981). A new definition of learning disabilities. *Learning Disability Quarterly, 7,* 429–436.

Harwell, J. M. (1989). *Learning disabilities handbook.* West Nyack, NY: Center for Applied Research in Education.

Idol, L. (1987). Group story mapping: A comprehension strategy for both skilled and unskilled readers. *Journal of Learning Disabilities, 20,* 196–205.

Johnson, D. J., & Blalock, J. W. (1987). Summary of problems and needs. In D. J. Johnson & J. W. Blalock (Eds.), *Adults with learning disabilities: Clinical studies* (pp. 227–296). Orlando, FL: Grune & Stratton.

Kirk, S. A. (1962). *Educating exceptional children.* Boston: Houghton Mifflin.

Lerner, J. W. (1993). *Learning disabilities: Theories, diagnosis, and teaching strategies.* Boston: Houghton Mifflin.

Lessen, E., Dudzinski, M., Marsh, K., & Van Acker, R. (1989). A survey of ten years of academic intervention research and practice. *Learning Disabilities Focus, 4*(2), 106–122.

Lloyd, J. (1988). Academic instruction and cognitive techniques: The need for attack strategy training. *Exeptional Education Quarterly, 1,* 53–63.

Loper, A. B. (1980). Metacognitive development: Implications for cognitive training of exceptional children. *Exceptional Education Quarterly, 1,* 1–8.

Meichenbaum, D. (1977). *Cognitive behavior management.* New York: Plenum.

Mercer, C. D. (1992). *Students with learning disabilities.* New York: Merrill.

Mercer, C. D., Hughes, C., & Mercer, A. R. (1985). Learning disabilities definitions used by state education departments. *Learning Disabilities Quarterly, 8,* 45–55.

Mercer, C. D., King-Sears, P., & Mercer, A. R. (1990). Learning disabilities definitions and criteria used by state education departments. *Learning Disabilities Quarterly, 13,* 141–152.

Merritt, D. D., & Liles, B. Z. (1987). Story grammar ability in children with and without language disorder: A story generation, story retelling, and story comprehension. *Journal of Speech and Hearing Research, 30,* 539–552.

National Joint Committee on Learning Disabilities and the Preschool Child. (1985, February). *A position paper of the National Joint Committee on Learning Disabilities.* Baltimore, MD: The Orton Dyslexia Society.

National Joint Committee on Learning Disabilities. (1988). [Letter from NJCLD to member organizations].

Ness, J., & Price, L. A. (1990). Meeting the psychosocial needs of adolescents and adults with LD. *Intervention, 26,* 16–21.

Polloway, E. A., & Smith T. E. C. (1992). *Language instruction for students with disabilities.* Denver, CO: Love Publishing.

Popp, R. A. (1983, Winter). Learning about disabilities. *Teaching Exceptional Children,* 78–81.

Rehabilitation Services Administration. (1985). Program policy directive (RSA-PPD-85-7, March 5). Washington, DC: U.S. Government Printing Office.

Rooney, K. J. (1991). Controversial therapies: A review and critique. *Intervention in School and Clinic, 26*(3), 134–142.

Schunk, D. H. (1985). Participation in goal setting: Effects on self-efficacy and skills of learning disabled children. *The Journal of Special Education, 19,* 307–316.

Silver, L. B. (1984). *The misunderstood child: A guide for parents of learning disabled children.* New York: McGraw-Hill.

Silver, L. B. (1987). The "magic cure": A review of the current controversial approaches for treating learning disabilities. *Journal of Learning Disabilities, 18,* 66–70.

Smith, D. D. (1981). *Teaching the Learning Disabled.* Englewood Cliffs, NJ: Prentice-Hall.

Smith, S. L. (1979). *No easy answers: Teaching the learning disabled child.* Cambridge, MA: Winthrop.

Smith, T. E. C., Finn, D., & Dowdy, C. A. (1993). *Teaching students with mild disabilities.* Ft. Worth, TX: Harcourt Brace Jovanovich.

Swanson, H. L. (1990). Instruction derived from the strategy deficit model: Overview of principles and procedures. In T. Scruggs & B. Wong (Eds.), *Intervention research in learning disabilities* (pp. 34–65). New York: Springer-Verlag.

U.S. Department of Education (USDE). (1977). Assistance to states for education of handicapped children: Procedures for evaluating specific learning disabilities. *Federal Register, 42,* 65082–65085.

U.S. Department of Education. (1993). *15th annual report to Congress on the implementation of IDEA.* Washington, DC: U.S. Government Printing Office.

Vogel, F., & Motulsky, A. G. (1986). *Human genetics.* New York: Springer-Verlag.

Westling, D. L., & Koorland, M. A. (1989). *The special educator's handbook.* Boston: Allyn & Bacon.

White, W. J. (1992). The postschool adjustment of persons with learning disabilities: Current status and future projections. *Journal of Learning Disabilities, 25*(7), 448–456.

Wood, J. W. (1991). *Adapting instruction for mainstreamed and at-risk students* (2nd ed.). New York: Merrill.

CHAPTER 5

Teaching Students with Mental Retardation

Introduction

Mental retardation is a powerful term used to describe a level of functioning significantly below what is considered to be "average." It conjures up a variety of images ranging from a stereotypical photo of an adolescent with Down syndrome, to a young child living in poverty and provided with limited experience and stimulation in the home, to an adult striving to adjust to the demands of a complex society. Since it is a generic term representing a highly diverse group of individuals so labeled, all of the images and, at the same time, none of these images, can be assumed to be accurate ones. The following case example emphasizes this point.

Working Toward Integration: A Case Example

The phrase "persons who are retarded are more like us than different from us" has been central to efforts to normalize life experiences for individuals with mental retardation. Sometimes events dramatically underscore this point. An example on a college campus is a good illustration.

Several years ago, the Student Council for Exceptional Children (SCEC) invited about 20 adolescents and adults who were residents of a state institution for persons with mental retardation to a campus dance attended by many members of the college community. By all accounts, the evening went quite well. A highlight of the evening occurred when one zealous SCEC member asked one of the apparently more withdrawn adults to dance. He hesitated, somewhat surprised at the invitation. After coaxing and cajoling however, he agreed. After the song, the college student inquired: "Where do you live?" "Lynchburg" was the reply. "Oh, and where do you work?" "I work here at Lynchburg College," he indicated. Perhaps sensing that this might be a prime example of the college's commitment to hire people with disabilities, the student questioned further: "What do you do on campus, I've not seen you around?" "I'm the chair of the Anthropology Department," came the response.

In the public schools, the most recent national data base (for 1991–1992) indicates that 0.96% of the estimated student population (ages 6–17) is identified as mentally retarded (U.S. Department of Education, 1993). However, a closer look at these data reveal a substantial variance in prevalence from 2.52% in Alabama to 0.89% in Virginia to 0.37% in California. Even a naive observer would at once conclude that the concept is not operationalized in the same way across the states. For that matter, the term itself may be eschewed in many areas. Hence, *mentally disabled, mentally handicapped, educationally handicapped, developmentally delayed,* or *developmentally disabled* may be the preferred description in a given geographical area. The underlying message of this variance is a clear one: Being mentally retarded is potentially quite stigmatizing, and avoiding labels or using alternative labels as well as providing opportunities for integration with peers who are not disabled are means that must be considered in order to create a more "normalized" life for such persons.

Mental Retardation Defined

The concept of mental retardation has created some problems for professionals in the field in attempting to formulate definitions to govern practice. Mental retardation has been most often characterized by two dimensions: limited intellectual ability and difficulty in coping with the social demands of the environment. Thus, all individuals with mental retardation must, by definition, demonstrate some degree of impaired mental abilities, most often seen as reflected in an **intelligence quotient (IQ)** significantly below average, which necessarily relates to a **mental age (MA)** appreciably lower than the individual's chronological age (CA). In addition, they would necessarily also demonstrate less appropriate **adaptive skills,** such as mature social behavior or functional academic skills, when compared to their same-age peers. Particularly in the case of individuals with mild disabilities, this discrepancy in adaptation can be relatively subtle and certainly not apparent based on a casual interaction in a nonschool setting. Rather, this group of individuals may be challenged most dramatically by the school setting and thus between the ages of 6 and 21; their inability to cope may be most evident, for example, in problems with peer relationships, difficulty in compliance with adult-initiated directions, or academic challenges.

American Association on Mental Retardation (AAMR) Definitions (1973, 1983)

The American Association on Mental Retardation (AAMR) has charged itself with developing and revising the definition of mental retardation for decades. This organization's efforts have generally been well recognized, and their 1973 definition (Grossman, 1973) was incorporated into PL 94–142. Although its use by the various states in terms of educational regulations and practice has been uneven (Frankenberger & Harper, 1988), the 1973 definition and its successors (i.e., Grossman, 1977, 1983) have been considered the basis for diagnosis in the field.

The Grossman (1983) definition, representing some relatively minor changes from its 1973 predecessor, is as follows:

> Mental retardation refers to significantly subaverage general intellectual functioning resulting in or associated with concurrent impairments in adaptive behavior and manifested during the developmental period. (p. 11)

Three components are central to this definition; these are briefly discussed here.

Intellectual functioning is intended as a summative conceptualization of abilities, such as the capacity to learn, solve problems, accumulate knowledge, adapt to new situations, and think abstractly. Operationally, however, it has generally been reduced to performance on a test of intelligence. Significantly below average is then defined as an IQ of approximately 70 or below. The 1983 AAMR definition recommended using a flexible upper IQ range of 70 to 75 rather than an exact cutoff of 70.

It is worth considering the key aspects of an IQ score as it relates to this first criterion for diagnosis. Since an IQ of 100 is the mean score on such tests, a person receiving a score of 100 is considered to have an average level of cognitive functioning. Based on statistical analysis, approximately 2.3% of IQs would be expected to lie below 70 and a like percentage above 130. Thus, to limit the diagnosis of mental retardation to persons with IQs of 70 to 75 or below is to suggest that, hypothetically, about 3% to 5% of the tested population may have significantly subaverage general intellectual functioning. However, as the definition clearly states, low IQ scores alone are not sufficient for diagnosis. Hence, we must next consider adaptive behavior.

An individual's *adaptive behavior* is a function of the degree to which, and the efficiency with which, the individual meets "the standards of maturation, learning, personal independence, and/or social responsibility that are expected for his or her age level and cultural group" (Grossman, 1983, p. 11). Continuing with this concept, Grossman (1983) emphasizes the idea of coping:

> *Adaptive behavior* refers to the quality of everyday performance in coping with environmental demands. The quality of general adaptation is mediated by level of intelligence; thus, the two concepts overlap in meaning. It is evident, however, from consideration of the definition of adaptive behavior, with its stress on everyday coping, that adaptive behavior refers to what people do to take care of themselves and to relate to others in daily living rather than the abstract potential implied by intelligence.

Two major components of adaptive behavior are the level of skill development and the relationship of acquired skills to developmental and chronological age. Particularly important are the skills necessary to function independently in a range of situations and to maintain responsible social relationships (Coulter & Morrow, 1978).

The third component of the definition is the ***developmental period.*** It has typically been the period of time between conception and 18 years of age (i.e., typical time for high school completion). Below-average intellectual functioning and disabilities in adaptive behavior must appear during this period in order for an individual to be considered mentally retarded.

AAMR Definition (1992)

Recently the AAMR has again revised its definition in order to bring it into line with developments in the 1980s and 1990s and to reflect changes in current thinking about persons with mental retardation. Although this revised definition is too recent to have had an influence on practice, it is important to consider because of its possible effects in the future and its further clarification of the concept of mental retardation.

According to the AAMR (1992) (also illustrated in Table 5.1),

> Mental retardation refers to substantial limitations in present functioning. It is manifested by significantly subaverage intellectual functioning, existing concurrently with related limitations in two or more of the following applicable adaptive skill areas: communication, self-care, home living, social skills, community use, self-direction, health and safety, functional academics, leisure, and work. Mental retardation begins before age 18.

The AAMR (1992) provided a further context for the definition. Specifically, the committee indicated that the appropriate application of the definition required con-

TABLE 5.1   **Key Adaptive Skill Areas**

Communication	Self-direction
Self-care	Health and safety
Home living	Functional academics
Social skills	Leisure
Community use	Work

Source: American Association on Mental Retardation (1992). *Mental retardation: Definition, classification and systems of supports.* Washington, DC: Author.

sideration of four key assumptions. These are detailed in Table 5.2. Note that these elements are deemed essential to the use of the AAMR's 1992 definition.

Several themes inherent in the 1992 definition can be highlighted. It retains the focus of the earlier AAMR definitions on the two key dimensions of intelligence and adaptation as well as the modifier of age of onset. However, the conceptual basis varies from those earlier efforts. Based generally on the conceptualizations of mental retardation developed by Greenspan (e.g., 1978, 1990), the 1992 definition reflects a more *functional approach,* thus shifting focus to the individual's functioning within the community rather than just dealing with the psychometric/clinical aspects of the person (e.g., IQ scores, limited adaptive behavior evaluations). For a fuller appreciation, the reader should consult the delineations provided in the 1992 manual.

Although the other AAMR definitions (e.g., Grossman, 1973, 1983) have been relatively widely cited and implemented to varying degrees in practice (see Franken-

TABLE 5.2   **Four Assumptions Essential to the Application of the Definition of Mental Retardation**

The following four assumptions are *essential* to the application of the definition.

1. Valid assessment considers cultural and linguistic diversity, as well as differences in communication and behavioral factors.
2. The existence of limitations in adaptive skills occurs within the context of community environments typical of the individual's age peers and is indexed to the person's individualized needs for supports.
3. Specific adaptive limitations often coexist with strengths in other adaptive skills or other personal capabilities.
4. With appropriate supports over a sustained period, the life-functioning of the person with mental retardation will generally improve.

Source: American Association on Mental Retardation (1992). *Mental retardation: Definition, classification and systems of supports.* Washington, DC: Author.

berger & Harper, 1988), it remains to be seen if the 1992 definition will eventually become the basis for state and federal statutes for educational, psychological, medical, and legal practice.

Classification in Mental Retardation

Historically, classification in this field has been done by both etiology (i.e., causes) and level of severity. Whereas the former has limited applicability to nonmedical practice, the latter has been used by a range of disciplines, including education and psychology. The classification system cited most often in the professional literature is the system developed by the AAMR (Grossman, 1983). This system uses the terms *mild, moderate, severe,* and *profound,* which are summative judgments that are to be based on both intelligence and adaptive behavior assessment. Often, however, the emphasis has been on the former only, so IQ scores have unfortunately been equated with level of functioning.

Terms such as *educable* and *trainable* reflect an alternative system that has often been used in school environments. These terms remain in use today in many localities and are likely to be used for some time in the future. As a result, it will not be uncommon to hear students referred to as EMR (educable mentally retarded) and TMR (trainable mentally retarded); the references generally, but not exactly, correspond to the 1983 AAMR system's mild and moderate/severe retardation, respectively. However, these terms are inherently stereotypical and prejudicial, and consequently (and appropriately) have often been criticized.

One alternative in practice has been to classify mental retardation according to only two levels of functioning (i.e., mild and severe) and to avoid reliance on IQ scores in considerations of level of severity. From this perspective, it would be assumed that levels of severity have some useful meaning, but that this meaning cannot be usefully captured by ranges of IQ scores. Rather, consideration of level of adaptive skills is seen as the relevant yardstick for determining level of retardation.

An emphasis on only two levels of disability represents a distinction that has a history of at least informal usage. As MacMillan (1989) observed:

> In common parlance of the early 1970s, "mildly" retarded was frequently used to describe borderline and mild categories, and it was sometimes used synonymously with EMR. In essence, it became an unspecific term contrasted with "severely" retarded which was used to refer to profoundly, severely, and moderately retarded categories in a single term. (p. 4)

This practice of the 1970s has been more widespread in the 1980s and early 1990s. Four examples illustrate this trend. The Association for Persons with Severe Handicaps, a professional organization and advocacy group, has effectively deemphasized distinctive levels of disability through the use of the generic term *severe* to refer to individuals who traditionally may have been classified as having moderate to profound mental retardation. Second, profound mental retardation has increasingly been used in a more restricted fashion to refer to a population of quite low incidence. Third, the two concepts of educable and mild mental retardation often have been used virtually interchangeably in school settings and research. Finally, the effects of early intervention have had the beneficial byproduct of altering the traditional notion that individuals with Down syndrome will be functioning at a level of moderate mental retardation, because research indicates a much greater range through mild retardation and, in some cases, even above the IQ cutoff for mental retardation (see Rynders, Spiker, & Horrobin, 1978; Rynders & Horrobin, 1990).

The retention of two levels of disability fits well with Dever's (1990) model of defining mental retardation from an instructional perspective. He suggested that

> it is not IQ that determines level of retardation but, rather, the amount and intensity of instruction required to move a person out of the category of "retarded." Thus, persons with mild retardation are those who know a great deal about living in the community without supervision and who require some instruction that could be provided under relatively non-intensive conditions. On the other hand, persons with severe or profound retardation are those who have acquired very few of the skills that are required for living in the community unsupervised and who require an enormous amount of instruction that may have to be provided under very intense conditions. Persons whose IQ would [otherwise] place them into the "moderately retarded" category under administrative definitions may be categorized as "mildly" or "severely" retarded if their instructional needs warrant such classification. (p. 150)

Finally, an emerging alternative is the recently promulgated classification system of the AAMR (1992), which has particular merit for use in integrated school settings. According to the new AAMR system, classification would not be derived from levels of disability (which the AAMR has recommended for elimination from usage) but rather from needed *levels of support.* Thus, this system would classify the needs rather than the deficits of the individual. This classification system would entail the designation of whether the child or adolescent needed intermittent, limited, extensive, or pervasive levels of supports most prominently as related to the ten specific adaptive skills areas designated in the new definition. Of course, in a given area, an individual may also need no support to function successfully. These levels of support are described as follows:

Intermittent: Supports on an "as needed" basis. Characterized by episodic nature, person not always needing the support(s), or short-term supports needed during lifespan transitions (e.g., job loss or an acute medical crisis); may be high- or low-intensity when provided.

Limited: An intensity of supports that are consistent over time, are time-limited but not of an intermittent nature, and may require fewer staff and less cost than more intense levels of support (e.g., time-limited employment training or transitional supports during the school to adult provider period).

Extensive: Supports characterized by regular involvement (e.g., daily) in at least some environments (such as work or home); not time-limited (e.g., long-term support and long-term home living support).

Pervasive: Supports characterized by their constancy and high intensity; provided across environments, potential life-sustaining nature. Pervasive supports typically involve more staff and intrusiveness than extensive of time-limited supports (AAMR, 1992).

Characteristics of Mental Retardation

The following discussion focuses on representative characteristics of students with mental retardation. The descriptors provided are based on individuals who would generally be viewed as having mild mental retardation. However, attention is also given to some areas that are relevant for students with more severe disabilities. In addition, the discussion in the chapters on sensory disabilities and communication disorders, respectively, have particular validity for understanding the needs of this population as well. We begin with a discussion of the nature of the population with mild retardation.

Students with Mild Mental Retardation

The population of students with mild mental retardation has experienced substantial changes since the mid-1970s in terms of the nature of the students identified and served. These changes have significantly altered traditional presumptions about the characteristics of this group (Polloway & Smith, 1988). Reasons for population change have included definitional changes and sociopolitical factors that have brought about an overall decrease in prevalence in mild mental retardation programs.

Data provided by the federal government offer a general picture of the magnitude of the numerical decreases that have occurred in the number of students served in programs for students with mental retardation. For example, between the school years 1976–1977 and 1988–1989, in the years following the passage of PL 94–142, virtually all states and territories showed a decline in the number of children served in such school programs, with the overall national decrease well in excess of 30% (MacMillan, 1989; U.S. Department of Education, 1993). This numerical "cure" (Reschly, 1988) reflects both the declassification of many students previously described as most "adaptive" in educable mentally retarded programs and the restrictiveness in eligibility procedures for other subsequently referred children who might have been considered borderline cases (Mascari & Forgnone, 1982; Polloway, 1984). As a consequence, programs in those states where significant reductions in prevalence estimates have occurred were more likely to be serving a population that MacMillan and Borthwick (1980) initially described as "a more patently disabled group" (p. 155) and a population more likely to include individuals with multiple disabilities (Forness & Polloway, 1987).

Given the limited research attention focused on students identified as mildly mentally retarded in the 1970s and 1980s (Haywood, 1979; Prehm, 1985), few recent data are available on this population. This concern is particularly important because the significant population shift questions the validity of the rich experimental foundation developed in past decades (Gottlieb, 1982; MacMillan, 1989). Thus, the following discussion simply highlights some areas that provide a reasonable portrait of the characteristics of students with mental retardation.

Cognitive Development

An understanding of students with mental retardation can productively begin with a consideration of cognitive development. In the broad sense, *cognition* subsumes virtually all aspects of learning and thus also potentially summarizes a variety of types of deficits that may interfere with learning.

The cognitive psychologist Piaget (1970, 1971) provided a framework for viewing the development of children by portraying them as active participants in life experiences. Piaget's model is based on the assumption that both qualitative and quantitative differences are reflected in a child's thinking at different developmental stages. This concept of discontinuous cognitive development is clearly reflected in his four stages (approximate mental age equivalents are noted in parentheses): (1) sensorimotor intelligence (MA = 0–1½ or 2 years); (2) preoperational thought (MA = 2–7 years); (3) concrete operations (MA = 7–11 years); and (4) formal operations (MA = 11 or 12+ years).

Although Piaget did not directly apply his theory to persons with disabilities, the model nevertheless provides some guidance for the design of instructional programs. The following list is adapted from Polloway, Payne, Patton, and Payne (1985) and Enright (1977):

1. Encourage interaction between children and the environment, establishing a relationship and being responsive to their needs. Children learn about themselves as they relate to the people and objects around them.
2. Provide children with experiences that stimulate all of their senses. Multisensory approaches to teaching can help to facilitate meaningful learning.
3. Because the child may have difficulty organizing her world, the teacher should assist by arranging the environment to offer stimulation, thus providing for mediated learning.
4. Consistency in daily routine will help the child function in a seemingly chaotic world. Set cognitive goals and devise activities with a concept in mind. Action-oriented activities facilitate attainment of the goal.
5. Avoid teaching skills that the child cannot generalize to other areas, thus not wasting time teaching activities that do not help the child attain additional control over the environment.

Language Development

Another major focus for understanding the needs of students with mental retardation is the language domain. Polloway and Smith (1992) have noted that no other area is more frequently associated with disabilities. They stated that "language-related problems are frequently among the greatest hurdles individuals must overcome to be fully integrated into society" (p. 2). Students with disabilities may face a range of language problems. These can include delay in development as well as disorders that may be reflected in unusual communicative patterns. Additionally, differences based on dialect-related cultural factors may be present, requiring teachers to assist culturally different students in developing standard English skills while not attacking the richness presented by diversity.

Hallahan and Kauffman (1982), Ingalls (1978), and Polloway, Epstein, and Cullinan (1985) elucidated the following language characteristics that may be found in students with mental retardation when compared to their same-age peers. However, since these individuals commonly exhibit exceptions to these generalizations, specific strengths and weaknesses should be assessed.

- ◆ Speech defects are significantly more common (e.g., articulation disorders).
- ◆ Language representations tend to be more concrete.
- ◆ Advanced rules of grammar often are troublesome.
- ◆ The rate of language acquisition is likely to be much slower.
- ◆ Deficits are often found even relative to nondisabled peers of the same mental age.
- ◆ The prevalence and severity of language problems are related to the severity of mental retardation.

Although the full instructional implications of these possible language problems are beyond the scope of the chapter, it is sufficient to note that teachers need to create an environment that facilitates language development. Basing their discussion on the work of Dudley-Marling and Searle (1988), Polloway and Smith (1992, p. 214) discussed four guidelines for facilitating the creation of an environment that promotes appropriate language development in students who have disabilities.

Language development is one of the most critical educational areas for students who are identified with mental retardation.

1. *Establish a physical setting that encourages talking.* Teachers can encourage talking by developing group activities for students, arranging the physical environment so that groups of students can work together, and bringing to class objects and topics that elicit discussion.
2. *Provide opportunities for students to interact with language.* Teachers are well aware that students like to talk; talking among students does not have to be orchestrated. But teachers have to redirect the simple desire to talk into more formalized learning activities. Reporting on experiences and group learning from each other are ways to enhance learning through talking.
3. *Provide opportunities for students to use language for a variety of purposes and with different audiences.* Older students, peers, and younger students offer various audiences for language activities. Having a variety of audiences mirrors the reality of speaking to many different kinds of people in different situations. This opportunity is important because learning language solely for a specific population will not lead to functional language abilities.
4. *Encourage student speech.* Students need to have their behaviors reinforced; thus, their use of language should be reinforced. Assuming that students will use their language without appropriate reinforcement is frequently disproven. When experiencing language problems, students likely will avoid language and therefore avoid certain failures. Often, students with oral language problems withdraw from social situations to avoid failure (p. 214).

Learning Processes

Although research on learning processes in children with mental retardation has been less common in recent years, some educationally relevant generalizations can be culled from the literature. The discussions that follow target some representative areas.

Attention.   The concept of *attention* can be broken down into three components: *attention span,* the length of time on task; *focus,* the inhibition of distracting or incidental stimuli; and *selective attention,* the discrimination of important stimulus characteristics (Alabiso, 1977). The latter two components are clearly related; Hagen and Kail (1975) illustrated this point in describing attentional processes as "how the individual selects the important information and ignores the unimportant from the vast amount of input that is available to the individual at any given time" (p. 165).

Instructional tasks make at least four attentional demands on the learner: maintaining the level of arousal necessary to attend, scanning the field of possible stimuli to select those relevant to the task at hand, shifting attention rapidly to accommodate changes in the relevant stimuli, and maintaining attention over time (Mercer & Snell, 1977). A series of classic research studies in the 1960s and 1970s confirmed the attentional difficulties often found in children with mental retardation (e.g., Zeaman & House, 1963, 1979; Hagen & Huntsman, 1971; Hagen & Kail, 1975). The key implication that can be derived from the research in this area is in the *importance of training students to be aware of the importance of attention and to learn how to actively*

Nonverbal Communication

Much of what is communicated is not verbalized but is conveyed through facial expressions and body movements that are specific to each culture. It is important to understand the crosscultural variations in order to avoid misunderstandings and unintentional offenses.

- *Silence.* Some cultures are quite comfortable with long periods of silence whereas others consider it appropriate to speak before the other person has finished talking. Learn about the appropriate use of pauses or interruptions in your client's culture.
- *Distance.* Some cultures are comfortable with close body space, whereas others are more comfortable at greater distance. In general, Anglo Americans prefer to be about an arm's length away from another person whereas Hispanics prefer closer proximity and Asians prefer greater distance. Give your client the choice by inviting him or her to "have a seat wherever you like."
- *Eye Contact.* Some cultures advise their members to look people straight in the eye (Anglos) whereas others consider it disrespectful (blacks), or a sign of hostility or impoliteness (Asians, Native Americans). Observe the client when talking and listening to get cues regarding appropriate eye contact.
- *Emotional expressiveness* varies greatly from one culture to another. Some cultures value stoicism whereas others encourage open expressions of such emotions as pain, joy, and sorrow. Asian-Americans may smile or laugh to mask other emotions.
- *Body movements* take on different meaning depending on the culture. Some consider finger or foot pointing disrespectful (Asian), whereas others would consider vigorous handshaking as a sign of aggression (Native American) or a gesture of good will (Anglo American). Observe the client's interactions with others to determine what body gestures are acceptable and appropriate in his or her culture. When in doubt, ask.

Source: Randall-David, E. (1989). *Strategies for working with culturally diverse communities and clients.* Washington, DC: Office of Maternal and Child Health, U.S. Department of Health and Human Services.

monitor its occurrence in their own learning efforts (e.g., Connis, 1979; Howell, Rueda, & Rutherford, 1983; Polloway, Patton, Payne, & Payne, 1989).

Mediational Processes

Students find learning tasks simpler when they can activate strategies to assist in problem solving, retention, or recall. These strategies are described as "mediational" because they involve the use of specific techniques to mediate between the task stimulus and the required response. Common strategies may include verbal rehearsal and repetition, labeling, classification, association, and imagery (Patton & Polloway, 1990).

Educators have used a variety of simple mediation techniques for years. Some of the most common school academic strategies used include, "When two vowels go walking, the first one does the talking"; "Thirty days hath September. . ."; and "i before e, except after c. . . . "

Research generally has indicated that students with mental retardation have difficulty producing mediational strategies (Bray, 1979; Robinson & Robinson, 1976), perhaps because they tend to be "inactive learners" (Strichart & Gottlieb, 1983)—a common description also typically applied to students with learning disabilities (Torgesen, 1982).

One area greatly influenced by mediational processes is that of *memory,* a process commonly seen as a deficit area in students with mental retardation. In particular, the extant research on memory points to difficulties specifically as related to short-term recall whereas long-term memory is an area in which students who are retarded apparently exhibit skills comparable to those of their peers (Morrison & Polloway, 1994). The following strategies (adapted from Polloway, Patton, Epstein, & Smith, 1989) can be used to enhance mediation, in general, and to assist in memory as appropriate:

◆ Instruction should focus on mediation strategies such as rehearsal, labeling, and verbal associations.
◆ Students should be taught content in manageable units.
◆ Content to be learned and retained should be meaningful and relevant to the student.
◆ When learning mediational strategies, students should have the opportunity to practice them to proficiency, have an opportunity to apply them, and be given reviews to ensure maintenance.
◆ Students should be directly taught how to chunk and group content information.
◆ Visual imagery can be used to help provide a picture into which the verbal information can be set.
◆ Reinforcement should be provided when needed to develop motivation to learn.

Motivational Concerns

Performance considered on an individual and/or a group basis may often fail to be consistent with projections. One apparent reason for this discrepancy could be the presence or absence of the necessary achievement motivation, developed within the student's home or school setting. Thus, it is important to understand the learning processes of all students, and particularly those with mental retardation, within the context of their motivation to perform. Several key concepts related to motivation are worth considering.

Environmental Print

In addition to using sight word lists, teachers who work with students with mental retardation can use *environmental print*. Using print that students see in their everyday world is both enjoyable and relevant. Environmental print activities ensure students of early success, especially that *"I really* can *read"* feeling so important to building their confidence. There are several ways to incorporate environmental print into the curriculum.

◆ *Use environmental print for student-made books.*   One way to build student interest in reading is to let children create their own books. When students are not yet proficient at writing or are unable to read enough words to construct sentences, let them cut out words, symbols, and pictures they recognize from

Magazines, especially the advertisements and articles about famous people
Food containers and labels, like cereal boxes or soup cans
Newspapers, especially sections that include titles of movies, names of their city and state, numbers, or local landmarks.

Students can paste or glue their print onto stiff paper, laminate the pages if desired, then let teachers bind the pages with ribbon or with spiral binding.

◆ *Use environmental print for beginning writing.*   Teachers can use a structured approach when teaching students to read with environmental print. The steps can progress from

Simple recognition of words and numbers exactly as they appear in the student's environment (complete with colors, symbols, and mascots), then
Recognition of the words and numbers with accompanying symbols, but in regular text-style and size print, then
Recognition and writing the print without *the colors or symbols* in normal text-style, then
Student-generated writing that includes the print.

Individuals with mental retardation often exhibit an *external locus of control,* because they perceive the consequences of their behavior to be the result of forces beyond their control. This is similar to the concept of *learned helplessness,* the "psychological state that frequently results when events are uncontrollable" (Seligman, 1975, p. 9). Although it is developmentally appropriate for young children to reflect an external locus, most children naturally shift to an internal locus of control as they mature.

Because many students with mental retardation may have experienced failure early in their school careers, they are likely to develop an *expectancy of failure* (Logan & Rose, 1982; MacMillan, 1982). To escape failure, they may attempt to avoid failure-producing situations and consequently may have reduced personal aspirations and may establish lower goals for themselves (Zigler, 1973).

Failure can also lead to a learning style characterized by *outerdirectedness,* which manifests as a reliance on others for assistance in completing work and solving problems. Outerdirectedness may result from an individual's distrust of his own abilities, often as a function of past failure. Although all students may occasionally say, "I can't do this," or, "This is too hard," some continuously require or demand the assistance of teachers, aides, or fellow students (Patton & Polloway, 1990).

Balla and Zigler (1979) identified three determinants that influence the development of these motivational styles: level of cognitive development (that is, persons functioning at a low intellectual level are most likely to be imitative); attachment to adults (that is, a strong dependence predicts a greater degree of outerdirection); and degree of past success (that is, failure experiences are most significant in producing an external orientation).

A motivational perspective encourages consideration of observed differences between functioning level and expected performance as possible reflections of past experiences, not as a reflection of a specific disability per se. It can be concluded that much can be done to assist students to maximize skills and thus enhance adjustment and independence. An instructor's ability to find ways to develop children's positive mindset toward learning will determine learning progress. Providing an atmosphere based on success experiences can help to develop learning based on self-reliance, success motivation, and desire to exceed the minimum (Patton & Polloway, 1990).

Social and Behavioral Characteristics

Individuals with mental retardation have often been found to exhibit social, behavioral, and emotional difficulties to a greater extent than is reported within the general population (Balthazar and Stevens, 1975; Epstein, Polloway, Patton, & Foley, 1989; Korinek & Polloway, 1993; Szymanski, 1980). Reiss, Levitan, and McNally (1982) theorized that increased risk of emotional/behavior problems should be expected because these individuals often must face social adjustment problems with limited problem-solving skills. Behavior/social adjustment problems thus have frequently been factors in decisions to refer students for special education. The concept of social competence is critical to an understanding of mental retardation (St. Claire, 1989).

Greenspan (1990) proposed a model of social competence divided into two subconstructs. *Intellectual aspects* include practical and social intelligence. Practical intelligence refers to maintaining oneself as an independent person in managing the activities of daily life, whereas social intelligence focuses on being able to understand social expectations, evaluate others, and judge how to conduct oneself. The second subconstruct, *personality aspects,* focuses on style aspects of competence, including temperament and character.

Features of Effective Drill-and-Practice Software

What to Look for	What to Avoid	Rationale
Programs that provide high rates of responding relevant to the skill to be learned	Programs that take too much time to load and run or that contain too many activities unrelated to the skill to be learned	The more time students spend on task, the more they learn.
Programs in which graphics and animation support the skill or concept that is being practiced	Programs with graphics or animation that are unrelated to the program's instructional objective	While graphics and animation may facilitate student interest in an activity, they may also distract students, interfere with skill mastery, and reduce practice time.
Programs in which reinforcement is used sparingly and approximates the type of reinforcement schedule students encounter in the classroom	Programs that provide a reinforcing graphic or activity after every correct response	If students are reinforced too frequently for correct responses, they may no longer exhibit those responses when fewer or no reinforcers are offered. Furthermore, excessive time spent engaging in the reinforcing activities detracts from time to learn and interferes with the development of automaticity.
Programs in which reinforcement is clearly related to task completion or mastery	Programs in which the events that occur when students are incorrect (e.g., an explosion) are more reinforcing than the events that occur when the student is correct (e.g., a smiling face)	Some programs may actually encourage students to practice the incorrect response in order to view the event that they find more reinforcing.
Programs in which feedback helps students locate and correct their mistakes	Programs in which students are merely told if they are right or wrong or are told to "try again"	Without feedback that informs them of the correct answer after a reasonable number of attempts, students may become frustrated and make random guesses.
Programs that store information about student performance or progress that can be accessed by the teacher at a later time	Programs without record-keeping features	Students may encounter difficulties with the skills covered by a program that require teacher intervention. However, teachers often find it difficult to monitor students as they work at the computer. Access to records of student performance enables the teacher to determine if a program is benefiting a student and whether the student needs additional assistance.

Programs with options for controlling features such as speed of problem presentation, type of feedback, problem difficulty, and number of practice trials	Programs that must be used in the same way with every student	Options are cost-effective; they enable the same program to be used with a broad range of students. Furthermore, they permit teachers to provide more appropriately individualized instruction.

Source: Okolo, C. M. Computers and individuals with mild disabilities. In J. D. Lindsey (Ed.), *Computers and exceptional individuals* (p. 117). Austin, TX: Pro-Ed. Used with permission.

Sargent (1991) developed another important model of **social competence** derived in part from Greenspan's work. This includes the conceptual framework presented in Figure 5.1, which embraces three processes: *social affect* (appearance to others), *social skills* (specific behaviors that are central to interactions), and *social cognition* (inclusive of understanding and being able to respond appropriately to various social situations). Specific examples of these three processes are as follows (pp. 4–5):

◆ Social Affect
   1. Cheerfulness
   2. Enthusiasm
   3. Confidence
   4. Optimism
   5. Risk taking
   6. Independence
   7. Good posture
   8. Good grooming
   9. Sense of humor
   10. Affection
   11. Assertiveness
◆ Social Skills Categories
   1. Interaction initiative (e.g., starting a conversation)
   2. Interaction responses (e.g., responding to a complaint)
   3. Personal social behaviors (e.g., dealing with embarrassment)
   4. Setting specific skills and behaviors:
      a. School behavior
      b. Workplace behavior
      c. Public setting behavior
      d. Family setting behavior
◆ Social Cognition
   1. Role taking/empathy
   2. Social discrimination and inference
   3. Social understanding/comprehension

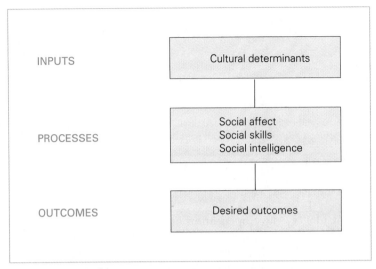

Figure 5.1   **Conceptual Framework of Social Competence**
Source: Sargent, L. R. (1989). Instructional competence to improve social competence. In G. Robinson, J. Patton, E. Polloway, & L. Sargent (Eds.), *Best practices in mild mental retardation* (p. 273). Reston, VA: CEC-MR.

    4. Understanding motives of others
    5. Moral and ethical judgments
    6. Referential communication
    7. Social problem solving

These attempts at model building represent positive developments for understanding social competence and, to some degree, mental retardation in general. Nevertheless, there have been relatively few recent studies of such problems. Polloway, Epstein, and Cullinan (1985), using the Behavior Problem Checklist (BPC) (Quay, 1977; Quay & Peterson, 1975, 1983), a rating scale of 55 specific problem areas, reported that students with retardation were more likely to exhibit behavior and emotional problems than were their peers. A total of 330 such comparisons were analyzed, with over 40% indicative of significantly more problems in the students identified as retarded. Overall, elementary pupils with mild mental retardation differed from their same gender peers on the most items, with a significant difference found for this group on 30 of 55 items for males and 36 of 55 items for females.

Comparative findings were particularly instructive in the area of self-concept. The general assumption has been that students with mental retardation would be expected to have lower levels of self-efficacy than their peers (Simeonsen, 1978). To the extent that any self-report instruments reflect items dealing with competence in specific skills (e.g., academic), it could be concluded that such self-appraisals would be accurate at least in that context. Findings from Polloway, Epstein, and Cullinan (1985) provide support for the existence of low self-concept as evaluated by teachers on items that encourage a focus on specific skill deficiencies.

To facilitate successful social interactions, social skills should be an explicit portion of the curriculum for many students with disabilities.

Research conducted with other methodologies has also confirmed the presence of social and behavior problems. For example, a study of elementary and secondary students with mild mental retardation (Polloway, Epstein, Patton, Cullinan, & Luebke, 1986) reported that, although over half of the students were rated by their teachers as popular or accepted, about one fourth were seen as either neglected or rejected. These findings complement studies reported by Gottlieb and colleagues. Gottlieb and Budoff (1973) reported that the more inappropriate that the behavior was, the more likely that the individual demonstrating the behavior would be rejected. Gottlieb, Semmel, and Veldman (1978) indicated that rejection results from the peers' perception of the inappropriate nature of overt behavior rather than academic incompetence, thus emphasizing a key social consideration in integration efforts and underscoring the need for instruction in social skills and social competence.

The general findings in the sociobehavioral domain reinforce the importance of instruction in social skills. It is apparent that students with mental retardation and related disabilities have unique educational needs that place them at risk for poor adult outcomes if appropriate interventions are not employed (Linden & Forness, 1986). Additionally, the success or failure of students with mental retardation in regular classes is often likely to be related to social competence. Gresham's (1982, 1984) reviews of integration led to the conclusion that children with disabilities interact infrequently and often negatively with their peers. Unfortunately, many students are

Purposes of Sex Education

Purposes of sex education for students who are mildly mentally retarded are as follows:

The student will

1. Understand and appreciate his or her own sexuality
2. Know basic male and female anatomy and male and female roles in the reproductive process
3. Understand that no one has the right to do something sexual to anyone else without permission
4. Understand the responsibilities of parenting
5. Understand that birth control methods should be used unless children can be provided for and are wanted
6. Understand his or her role in protecting personal health and the health of others
7. Know the resources available for persons who have been sexually abused or have contracted a sexually transmitted disease
8. Understand the social and sexual values of society.

Source: Sparks, S., & Caster, J. A. (1989). In G. Robinson, J. Patton, E. Polloway, and L. Sargent (Eds.), *Best practices in mild mental retardation* (p. 295). Reston, VA: CEC-MR. Used with permission.

placed in general education settings without attention to the necessary social skills to succeed and gain acceptance. As Sargent (1989) indicated, research that has highlighted social difficulties does not "urge abandonment of mainstreaming" but rather creates the "case for teaching social skills to pupils with disabilities for the purpose of enhancing their ability to benefit from integration" (p. 272). Thus a key implication is that systematic social skills instruction should be provided for students with mental retardation. This topic is discussed in further detail in Chapters 6 and 13.

Transition into Adulthood

Occupational success and community living skills are among the critical life adjustment variables that relate to successful transition into adulthood. The research on such variables does not provide much room for overconfidence with regard to students with mental retardation.

Polloway, Patton, Smith, and Roderique (1991) posed the question: "What happens when students who are mildly retarded get older?" They considered in particular the data that Edgar (1987, 1988, 1990; Affleck, Edgar, Levine, & Kortering,

1990) reported, indicating that students who went through special education programs have not fared well. Less than one half were either working or involved in training programs. Although few dropped out of school, this additional time in school had not been productive in terms of employment outcomes (Edgar, 1987). Only 21% were living independently 30 months after completion of secondary school, a figure that compares poorly to data on individuals without disabilities. The transition period can be seen as a time of "floundering" (Edgar, 1988); it is clearly more so for students who are mildly retarded. "Productive adulthood" was unfortunately an elusive goal for these students (Edgar, 1990). The challenge of productive adulthood is clearly demonstrated by Table 5.3, which identifies adult domains and relates them to Knowles' (1984) life problems areas.

In general the vast majority of adults with mental retardation can obtain and maintain gainful employment. Two critical factors, however, influence their success. First, postschool adjustment hinges on their ability to demonstrate personal and social behaviors appropriate to the workplace. Second, the quality of the transition programming provided will predict subsequent success. Such programs recognize that

TABLE 5.3   Demands of Adulthood

Adult Domains	Knowles' Domains	Examples
Vocational/education	Vocation and career	Being interviewed Getting along at work Changing jobs
Home and family	Home and family living	Dating Family planning Raising children Solving marital problems Financial planning
Recreation and leisure	Enjoyment of leisure	Choosing hobbies Buying equipment Planning recreational outing
Community involvement	Community living	Using community resources Voting Getting assistance
Emotional/physical health	Health	Exercising Treating medical emergencies Understanding children's diseases
Personal development	Personal development	Making decisions Dealing with conflict Establishing intimate relationships Understanding oneself

Source: Patton, J. R., Cronin, M. E., Polloway, E. A., Hutchison, D., & Robinson, G. A. (1989). Curricular considerations: A life skills orientation. In G. A. Robinson, J. R. Patton, E. A. Polloway, & L. Sargent (Eds.), *Best practices in mild mental retardation* (p. 27). Reston, VA: CEC-MR. Used with permission.

programming must reflect a top-down perspective that bases curriculum on the demands that await in the next environment in which the individual will live, work, socialize, and recreate.

Concluding Comments: Curricular Implications

A review of the characteristics of students with mental retardation highlights areas of need and also focuses attention on the curricular implications of inclusion. As special and general education teachers jointly develop and implement educational programs for these students, they should keep in mind that these students require a comprehensive, broad-based curriculum to meet their needs. The most effective programs for the students will provide appropriate academic instruction, adapted to facilitate learning. However, the curriculum cannot solely be academic in orientation, but rather should focus on concerns for social skills and the development of necessary transition skills in order to facilitate the students' success in general education classrooms and subsequent integration into community settings.

In making determinations relative to the curriculum, teachers will have to consider how responsive the general education classroom can be to the needs of students with mental retardation. Ultimately the goal of integration is not simply school inclusion but rather community or "life" inclusion; whichever curriculum achieves that purpose most effectively is the one that is likely to be most appropriate (Polloway et al., 1991). As Cassidy and Stanton (1959) suggested over three decades ago, the key question in evaluating the effectiveness of programs *is effective for what?* What is it that the schools are to impart to the students? Affleck et al. (1990) argued that although general education class placement is consistent with current philosophical and legal trends, educators must be cautious in designing programs that do not jeopardize our opportunity to secure the instructional intensity to meet skill needs while providing a curriculum that addresses the long-term needs of students. The challenge of inclusion for students with mental retardation is to ensure that the curriculum they pursue is responsive to their future.

Summary

- The concept of mental retardation is a powerful one that has variant meanings to both professionals and the lay public.

- The three central dimensions of the definition are lower intellectual functioning, deficits or limitations in adaptive skills, and an onset prior to age 18.

- The 1992 AAMR definition retains the three dimensions but also stresses the importance of four assumptions: cultural and linguistic diversity, an environmental context for adaptive skills, the strengths of individuals as well as their limitations, and the promise of improvement over time.

- Common practice in the field is to speak of two general levels of mental retardation, mild and severe.

◆ Emerging efforts in classification stress the levels of needed supports rather than levels of disability.

◆ Cognitive development for students with mental retardation can be enhanced by emphasizing active interaction with the environment and concrete experiences.

◆ To enhance language development, teachers should provide a facilitative environment, structure opportunities for communication, and encourage speech.

◆ Attention difficulties can be addressed by modifying instruction to highlight relevant stimuli and by training students to monitor their own attention.

◆ Teachers should teach not only content but also mediation strategies that facilitate learning. Examples include rehearsal, classification, and visual imagery.

◆ Memory problems respond to mediation strategies (as above) and to an emphasis on content that is meaningful and relevant.

◆ Many students with a history of failure have an external locus of control, which can be enhanced by an emphasis on success experiences and by reinforcement for independent work.

◆ Social competence is a critical component of instructional programs for students with mental retardation. Teaching social skills can have a positive effect on successful inclusion both in school and in the community.

◆ Educational programs must attend to transitional concerns so that students receive the appropriate training to prepare them for subsequent environments. The curriculum should thus have a "top-down" orientation.

References

Affleck, J. Q., Edgar, E., Levine, P., & Kortering, L. (1990). Post school status of students classified as mildly mentally retarded, learning disabled, or non-handicapped: Does it get better with time? *Education and Training in Mental Retardation, 25,* 315–324.

Alabiso, F. (1977). Inhibitory functions of attention in reducing hyperactive behavior. *American Journal of Mental Deficiency, 77,* 259–282.

American Association on Mental Retardation. (1992). *Mental retardation: Definition, classification and systems of support* (9th ed.). Washington, DC: Author.

Balla, D., & Zigler, E. (1979). Personality development in retarded persons. In N. R. Ellis (Ed.), *Handbook of mental deficiency: Psychological theory and research* (2nd ed.) pp. 143–168. Hillsdale, NJ: Lawrence Erlbaum.

Balthazar, E. E., & Stevens, H. A. (1975). *The emotionally disturbed, mentally retarded: A historical and contemporary perspective.* Englewood Cliffs, NJ: Prentice-Hall.

Bray, N. (1979). Strategy production in the retarded. In N. R. Ellis (Ed.), *Handbook of mental deficiency* (2nd ed.). Hillsdale, NJ: Lawrence Erlbaum.

Cassidy, V. M., & Stanton, J. E. (1959). An investigation of factors involved in the education placement of mentally retarded children: A study of differences between children in regular and special classes in Ohio. Columbus, OH: Ohio State University. (ERIC Document Reproduction Service No. ED 002752).

Connis, R. T. (1979). The effects of sequential pictorial cues, self-recording, and praise on the job task sequencing of retarded adults. *Journal of Applied Behavior Analysis, 12,* 355–361.

Coulter, W. A., & Morrow, H. W. (1978). *Adaptive behavior: Concepts and measurements.* New York: Grune & Stratton.

Cullinan, D., Epstein, M. H., Matson, J. L., & Rosemier, R. A. (in press). Behavior problems of mentally retarded and non-retarded adolescent pupils. *School Psychology Review.*

Dever, R. N. (1990). Defining mental retardation from an instructional perspective. *Mental Retardation, 28,* 147–153.

Dudley-Marling, C., & Searle, D. (1988). Enriching language learning environments for students with learning disabilities. *Journal of Learning Disabilities, 21,* 140–143.

Edgar, E. (1987). Secondary programs in special education: Are many of them justifiable? *Exceptional Children, 53,* 555–561.

Edgar, E. (1988). Employment as an outcome for mildly handicapped students: Current status and future directions. *Focus on Exceptional Children, 21*(1), 1–8.

Edgar, E. (1990, Winter). Is it time to change our view of the world? *Beyond Behavior,* 9–13.

Enright, D. B. (1977). *Cognition: An introductory guide to the theory of Jean Piaget for teachers of multiply handicapped children.* Watertown, MA: NE Regional Center for Services to Deaf-Blind Children.

Epstein, M. H., Polloway, E. A., Patton, J. R., & Foley, R. (1989). Mild retardation: Student characteristics and services. *Education and Training in Mental Retardation, 24,* 7–16.

Forness, S. R., & Polloway, E. A. (1987). Physical and psychiatric diagnoses of pupils with mild mental retardation currently being referred for related services. *Education and Training in Mental Retardation, 22,* 221–228.

Frankenberger, W., & Harper, J. (1988). States' definitions and procedures for identifying children with mental retardation: Comparison of 1981–82 and 1985–86 guidelines. *Mental Retardation, 26,* 133–136.

Gottlieb, J. (1982). Mainstreaming. *Education and Training of the Mentally Retarded, 17,* 79–82.

Gottlieb, J., & Budoff, M. (1973). Social acceptability of retarded children in non-graded schools differing in architecture. *American Journal of Mental Deficiency, 78,* 15–19.

Gottlieb, J., Semmel, M. I., & Veldman, D. J. (1978). Correlates of social status among mainstreamed mentally retarded children. *Journal of Educational Psychology, 70,* 396–405.

Greenspan, S. (1978). Social intelligence in the retarded. In N. R. Ellis (Ed.), *Handbook of mental deficiency: Psychological theory and research* (2nd ed.), (pp. 483–531). Hillsdale, NJ: Lawrence Erlbaum.

Greenspan, S. (1990, May). A redefinition of mental retardation based on a revised model of social competence. Paper presented at the annual meeting of the Academy on Mental Retardation. Washington, DC.

Gresham, F. M. (1982). Misguided mainstreaming: The case for social skills training with handicapped children. *Exceptional Children, 48,* 420–433.

Gresham, F. M. (1984). Social skills and self-efficacy for exceptional children. *Exceptional Children, 51,* 253–261.

Grossman, H. J. (1973). *Manual on terminology and classification in mental retardation.* Washington, DC: American Association on Mental Deficiency.

Grossman, H. J. (1977). *Manual on terminology and classification in mental retardation* (1977 rev.). Washington, DC: American Association on Mental Deficiency.

Grossman, H. J. (1983). *Classification in mental retardation.*Washington, DC: American Association on Mental Deficiency.

Hagen, J. W., & Huntsman, N. J. (1971). Selective attention in mental retardates. *Developmental Psychology, 5,* 151–160.

Hagen, J. W., & Kail, R. V. (1975). The role of attention in perceptual and cognitive development. In W. M. Cruickshank & D. P. Hallahan (Eds.), *Perceptual and learning disabilities in children: Vol. II. Research and Theory.* Syracuse, NY: University Press.

Hallahan, D. P., & Kauffman, J. M. (1982). *Exceptional children: Introduction to special education* (2nd ed.). Englewood Cliffs, NJ: Prentice-Hall.

Haywood, H. C. (1979). Editorial. What happened to mild and moderate mental retardation? *American Journal on Mental Deficiency, 83,* 429–431.

Howell, K. W., Rueda, R., & Rutherford, R. B. (1983). A procedure for teaching self-recording to moderately retarded students. *Psychology in the Schools, 20,* 202–209.

Ingalls, R. P. (1978). *Mental retardation: The changing outlook.* New York: Wiley.

Knowles, M. (1984). *The adult learner: A neglected species* (3rd ed.). Houston: Gulf Publishing.

Korinek, L., & Polloway, E. A. (1993). Social skills: Review and implications for instruction for students with mild mental retardation. In R. A. Gable & S. F. Warren (Eds.), *Advances in mental retardation and developmental disabilities* (Vol. 5, pp. 71–97). London: Jessica Kingsley.

Linden, B. E., & Forness, S. R. (1986). Post-school adjustment of mentally retarded persons with psychiatric disorders: A ten-year follow-up. *Education and Training of the Mentally Retarded, 21,* 157–164.

Logan, D. R., & Rose, E. (1982). Characteristics of the mildly mentally retarded. In P. T. Cegelka & H. J. Prehm (Eds.), *Mental retardation: From categories to people.* Columbus, OH: Merrill.

MacMillan, D. L. (1982). *Mental retardation in school and society* (2nd ed.). Boston: Little, Brown.

MacMillan, D. L. (1989). Mild mental retardation: Emerging issues. In G. Robinson, J. R. Patton, E. A. Polloway, & L. R. Sargent (Eds.), *Best practices in mild mental retardation* (pp. 1–20). Reston, VA: CEC-MR.

MacMillan, D. L., & Borthwick, S. (1980). The new educable mentally retarded population: Can they be mainstreamed? *Mental Retardation, 18,* 155–158.

Mascari, B. G. & Forgnone, C. (1982). A follow-up study of EMR students four years after dismissal from the program. *Education and Training of the Mentally Retarded, 17,* 288–292.

Mercer, C. D., & Snell, M. E. (1977). *Learning theory in mental retardation: Implications for teaching.* Columbus, OH: Merrill.

Morrison, G. M., & Polloway, E. A. (1994). Mental retardation. In G. Meyen & T. M. Skrtic (Eds.), *Exceptional children and youth: An introduction* (4th ed.). Denver, CO: Love Publishing.

Okolo, C. M. (1993). Computers and individuals with mild disabilities. In J. D. Lindsey (Ed.), *Computers and exceptional individuals* (pp. 111–124). Austin, TX: Pro-Ed.

Patton, J. R., Cronin, M. E., Polloway, E. A., Hutchison, D., & Robinson, G. A. (1989). Curricular considerations: A life skills orientation. In G. A. Robinson, J. R. Patton, E. A. Polloway, & L. Sargent (Eds.), *Best practices in mild mental retardation* (pp. 112–124). Reston, VA: CEC-MR.

Patton, J. R., & Polloway, E. A. (1990). Mild mental retardation. In N. G. Haring & L. McCormick (Eds.), *Exceptional children and youth* (5th ed.), (pp. 195–237). Columbus, OH: Merrill.

Piaget, J. (1970). Piaget's theory. In P. H. Mussen (Ed.), *Carmichael's manual of child psychology* (Vol. 1). New York: Wiley.

Piaget, J. (1971). *The language and thought of the child.* New York: World Publishing.

Polloway, E. A. (1984). The integration of mildly retarded students in the schools: A historical review. *Remedial and Special Education, 5*(4), 18–28.

Polloway E. A., Epstein, M. H., & Cullinan, D. (1985). Prevalence of behavior problems among educable mentally retarded students. *Education and Training of the Mentally Retarded, 20,* 3–13.

Polloway, E. A., Epstein, M. H., Patton, J. R., Cullinan, D., & Luebke, J. (1986). Demographic, social, and behavioral characteristics of students with educable mental retardation. *Education and Training of the Mentally Retarded, 21,* 27–34.

Polloway E. A., Patton, J. R., Epstein, M. H., & Smith, T. E. C. (1989). Comprehensive curriculum: Program design for students with mild handicaps. *Focus on Exceptional Children, 21*(8), 1–12.

Polloway, E. A., Patton, J. R., Payne, J. S., & Payne, R. A. (1989). *Strategies for teaching learners with special needs* (4th ed.). Columbus, OH: Merrill.

Polloway, E. A., Patton, J. R., Smith, J. D., & Roderique, T. (1991). Issues in program design for elementary students with mild retardation: Emphasis on curriculum development. *Education and Training in Mental Retardation, 26,* 142–150.

Polloway, E. A., Payne, J. S., Patton, J. R., & Payne, R. A. (1985). *Strategies for teaching retarded and other special needs learners.* Columbus, OH: Merrill.

Polloway, E. A., & Smith, J. D. (1988). Current status of the mild mental retardation construct: Identification, placement, and programs. In M. C. Wang, M. C. Reynolds, & H. J. Walberg (Eds.), *The handbook of special education: Research and practice* (Vol. II, pp. 1–22). Oxford, UK: Pergamon Press.

Polloway, E. A., & Smith, T. E. C. (1992). *Language instruction for students with disabilities.* Denver, CO: Love Publishing.

Prehm, H. H. (1985, January). Education and training of the mentally retarded: Mid-year report to the board of directors of CEC-MR. Unpublished manuscript.

Quay, H. C. (1977). Measuring dimensions of deviant behavior: The behavior problem checklist. *Journal of Abnormal Child Psychology, 5,* 277–289.

Quay, H. C. (1983). Classification. In H. C. Quay & J. S. Werry (Eds.), *Psychological disorders of childhood* (3rd ed.). New York: Wiley.

Quay, H. C., & Peterson, D. R. (1975). *Manual for the behavior problem checklist.* Champaign, IL: University of Illinois.

Randall-David, E. (1989). *Strategies for working with culturally diverse communities and clients.* Washington, DC: Office of Maternal and Child Health, U.S. Department of Health and Human Services.

Reiss, S., Levitan, G. W., & McNally, R. J. (1982). Emotionally disturbed, mentally retarded people: An underserved population. *American Psychologist, 37,* 361–367.

Reschly, D. (1988). Incorporating adaptive behavior deficits into instructional programs. In G. A. Robinson, J. R. Patton, E. A. Polloway, & L. R. Sargent (Eds.), *Best practices in mental disabilities* (Vol. 2, pp. 53–80). Des Moines, IA: Iowa State Department of Education.

Robinson, N. M., & Robinson, H. B. (1976). *The mentally retarded child* (2nd ed.). New York: McGraw-Hill.

Rynders, J. E., & Horrobin, M. J. (1990). Always trainable? New educable? Updating educational expectations concerning children with Down's syndrome. *American Journal of Mental Retardation, 95,* 77–83.

Rynders, J. E., Spiker, D., & Horrobin, J. M. (1978). Underestimating the educability of Down's syndrome children: Examination of methodological problems in recent literature. *American Journal of Mental Deficiency, 82,* 440–448.

Sargent, L. R. (1981, January). *Assessment documentation and programming for adaptive behavior: An Iowa task force report.* Des Moines, IA: State of Iowa, Department of Instruction.

Sargent, L. R. (1989). Instructional competence to improve social competence. In G. Robinson, J. Patton, E. Polloway, & L. Sargent (Eds.), *Best practices in mild mental retardation* (pp. 265–287). Reston, VA: CEC-MR.

Sargent, L. R. (1991). *Social skills for school and community.* Reston, VA: CEC-MR.

Seligman, M. E. P. (1975). *Helplessness: On depression, development, and death.* San Francisco: W. H. Freeman.

Simeonsen, R. J. (1978). Social competence. In J. Wortis (Ed.), *Mental retardation and developmental disabilities: An annual review* (Vol. X, pp. 130–171). New York: Brunner-Mazel.

Sparks, S., & Caster, J. A. (1989). In G. Robinson, J. Patton, E. Polloway, & L. Sargent (Eds.), *Best practices in mild mental retardation* (pp. 299–302). Reston, VA: Division on Mental Retardation, CEC.

St. Claire, L. (1989). A multidimensional model of mental retardation: Impairment, subnormal behavior, role failures, and socially constructed retardation. *American Journal of Mental Retardation, 94,* 88–96.

Strichart, S. S., & Gottlieb, J. (1983). Characteristics of mild mental retardation. In T. L. Miller & E. E. Davis (Eds.), *The mildly handicapped student* (pp. 37–65). New York: Grune & Stratton.

Szymanski, L. S. (1980). Psychiatric diagnosis of retarded persons. In L. S. Szymanski & P. E. Tanquay (Eds.), *Emotional disorders of mentally retarded persons: Assessment, treatment,* and *consultation* (pp. 61–81). Baltimore: University Park Press.

Torgesen, J. K. (1982). The learning disabled child as an inactive learner: Educational implications. *Topics in Learning and Learning Disabilities, 2*(1), 45–52.

U.S. Department of Education (1993). *15th annual report to Congress on the implementation of IDEA.* Washington, DC: U.S. Government Printing Office.

Widaman, MacMillan, Hemsley, Little, & Balow (1992).

Zeaman, D., & House B. J. (1963). The role of attention in retardate discrimination learning. In N. R. Ellis (Ed.), *Handbook of mental deficiency.* New York: McGraw-Hill.

Zeaman, D., & House, B. J. (1979). A review of attention theory. In N. R. Ellis (Ed.), *Handbook of mental deficiency.* New York: McGraw-Hill.

Zigler, H. (1973). Impact of institutional experience on behavior and development of retarded persons. *American Journal of Mental Deficiency, 28,* 1–11.

CHAPTER 6

Teaching Students with Emotional and Behavioral Disorders

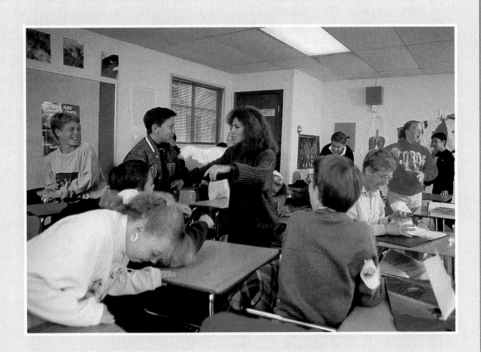

Introduction

Frank was a seven-year-old kindergartner who seemed to always be in trouble. On the very first day of school, he stole some crayons from one of his new classmates. When confronted with the fact that the crayons in his desk belonged to another student, Frank adamantly denied stealing them. Frank's behaviors have only gotten worse over the first six months of the school year. Ms. Walters, Frank's kindergarten teacher, uses a classroom management system that rewards students with checkmarks for appropriate behaviors. Students can redeem their checkmarks at the end of the week for various toys. Frank has never earned enough checkmarks to get a toy. Now he openly states that he doesn't care if he ever gets any checkmarks.

Frank's primary behavior difficulties revolve around his inability to leave his classmates alone. He is constantly pinching, pulling hair, or taking things from other students. Ms. Walters has Frank's chair separate from the other students in an attempt to prevent him from bothering them. Still, he gets out of his chair and manages to create disturbances regularly. Ms. Walters has sent Frank to the principal's office on numerous occasions. Each time he returns, his behavior is improved, but only for about half of the day. Then he returns to his old ways of causing problems for other students and Ms. Walters. Frank's schoolwork has begun to suffer as a result of his behavior problems. Whereas many of his classmates are beginning to read and can write their names, Frank still has difficulties associating sounds with letters and can only print his name in a very rudimentary form.

Ms. Walters has had four parent conferences about Frank. On each occasion, only Frank's mother came to the school. She indicates to Ms. Walters that she does not know what to do with Frank. There is no father figure in the home, and Frank has already gotten to the point where spankings don't seem to work. Ms. Walters and Frank's mother are both concerned that Frank's behavior will continue to get worse unless some solution is found. They are currently discussing whether to retain him in kindergarten for the next school year.

Although most children and youth are disruptive from time to time, the majority do not display behaviors that are sufficient to create serious problems in school. Most comply with classroom and school rules to the extent that they do not require extensive interventions. There are, however, some students whose behaviors and emotions result in significant problems. This may be due to the way school personnel deal with various student behaviors, or it may result even after several interventions have been tried. These students may exhibit behavior problems, or they may experience various levels of emotional disturbance. At any rate, students whose behaviors and emotions result in significant school problems, such as Frank in the preceding example, may require identification and intervention. At a minimum, they require classroom teachers to try different methods that could make a positive difference in the student's school success.

Although emotional and behavior problems may result in serious actions, such as suicides and depression, they have long been associated with acting out and disruptive behaviors in classrooms—in general, discipline problems. The primary problem faced by most teachers when dealing with students with emotional and behavior problems is classroom discipline.

Behavior problems are a major concern for professional educators (Elam, Rose, & Gallup, 1991). In a survey of general education classroom teachers, the behavior of students was cited as a primary reason for deciding to leave the teaching profession (Smith, 1990). Teachers noted that they had to spend too much time on student behavior problems and not enough on instruction. In a national study by Knitzer, Steinberg, and Fleisch (1990), it was found that 80% of all students identified as having emotional and behavior problems are educated in regular schools. Nearly 50% of these students spend some or all of their school day in general education classrooms with general education classroom teachers, not special education teachers.

Problems in Serving Students with Emotional and Behavioral Disorders

There are numerous problems in providing services to students with emotional and behavior problems. These problems include difficulties in defining emotional and behavioral disorders (E/BDs), difficulties in measuring behavior and emotions, diversity of behaviors among "normal" individuals, diversity of individuals with behavior and emotional problems, and difficulties identifying children with behavioral and emotional disorders.

Definition

One of the primary problems in providing services for students with emotional and behavior problems is defining the condition. Although there are numerous definitions related to this condition, most are vague and result in inaccurate interpretations. There are simply no easy ways to define and classify students based on disordered behavioral functioning (Wicks-Nelson & Israel, 1991). The behaviors and emotions expressed by individuals range across a very broad continuum. This makes it difficult to determine what is "normal" and what is aberrant. Difficulties in measuring behaviors and emotions, the differences among behavioral and emotional expectations across cultures, and the fact that the behaviors and emotions of most individuals vary from time to time make defining the disorder problematic (Rosenberg, Wilson, Maheady, & Sindelar, 1992).

Differing definitions lead to discrepancies in services provided by schools and mental health agencies. Currently, no national data show the number of students classified as emotionally disturbed/behaviorally disordered who receive mental health services; however, it is known that more than half of all school districts do not provide such services. Also, the majority of students who do receive mental health services from the state and local mental health agencies are not even classified as EBD by schools (Knitzer et al., 1990). This likely is the result of different definitions used by educators and mental health professionals.

Measurement

Unlike the field of mental retardation, the field of emotional and behavioral disorders does not have a single measurement device that can be used to identify and describe individuals with these types of disorders. Many definitions of mental retardation even refer to poor performance on IQ tests as a criterion for identification, and definitions of learning disabilities focus on poor performance in academic achievement, which is measured with achievement tests. In the area of emotional and behavioral disorders, "no single measure of social or emotional functioning is sufficiently reliable and valid to serve in the way that intelligence tests do in defining mental retardation or achievement tests do in defining learning disabilities" (Rosenberg et al., 1992, p. 5). The result is the reliance on rating scales and checklists as bases for identifying individuals as having emotional and behavior problems. This requires extensive use of subjective judgment on the part of individuals making the diagnoses, which may or may not prove valid.

Deviant Behavior of Normal Individuals

Another problem in serving students with emotional and behavior problems is the similarity between those students and other students who only occasionally exhibit inappropriate or deviant behaviors. It is difficult to accurately distinguish between individuals who require interventions and those who are simply behaving in "normal" inappropriate ways. All children, from time to time, display temper tantrums, crying outbursts, and aggressive behaviors; they are occasionally defiant to their parents and experience poor self-confidence, low self-esteem, and depression. But the majority of children who display these characteristics are not classified as having a disability. They are "just being boys" or "just being kids."

The fact that nondisabled children display some of the same characteristics as students classified as having emotional and behavior problems compounds difficulties associated with providing services to this group of students. Behaviors of all individuals are along a continuum ranging from very acceptable to very unacceptable; all students fall somewhere along this continuum. When behaviors become deviant enough to warrant labeling a student is difficult to determine. Also, students move along the continuum. On some days, their behaviors may place them in the very acceptable range, whereas on others, they may display severe behavior problems.

Diversity of Theoretical Explanations of Behavioral Disorders

There are several theoretical explanations of emotional and behavioral disorders and resulting intervention strategies. Unfortunately, these different explanations only add to the confusion about how to serve the population. The primary theoretical expla-

Using Technology to Record Behaviors

The following technological devices can make data/behavior recording easy:

Wrist Counter or Golf Counter.   Teachers can use a wrist counter or golf counter to keep a cumulative frequency count of specific behaviors. These devices are inexpensive and easy to manipulate; however, they may be difficult to find.

Grocery Counter.   A cumulative frequency count can also be kept by a grocery counter. These devices are readily available and easy to use. Another advantage is that they can be used to count behaviors that occur in high frequencies because of their four-digit design.

Index Card.   Probably the simplest, least expensive, and most readily available, index cards provide a good way to record data. All teachers have to do is carry around cards for each child that data is being collected on, and make a tally mark when a specific behavior occurs. Index cards make it easy to collect data on more than one child at a time.

Beads-in-a-Pocket.   Teachers can keep beads, or similar objects, in one pocket and transfer them to another pocket when a particular behavior occurs. This approach is obviously simple, inexpensive, and readily available. A drawback to this approach is the possibility of confusion about which pocket is which.

Printing Calculator.   Teachers can use a printing calculator to record specific behaviors that occur. Each type of behavior can have a number code, such as 1 for getting out of seat and 2 for talking out loud. After a recording period, teachers note on the tape the frequency of each type of behavior.

Source: Koorland, M. A., Monda, L. E., & Vail, C. O. (1988). Recording behavior with ease. *Teaching Exceptional Children, 21,* 59–60. Used with permission.

nations include (1) the **biophysical approach,** (2) **psychodynamic explanation,** (3) the **behavioral model,** (4) **cognitive-behavioral explanations,** (5) **sociological explanations,** and (6) the **ecological model.** These will be further discussed later in the chapter. The different theoretical models only add to the difficulties in serving students with emotional and behavior problems.

Identification

Whereas the identification of individuals suffering from severe emotional and behavior problems is relatively easy due to their overt aberrations, the identification of persons experiencing mild emotional and behavior problems is extremely difficult (Wicks-

How to Work with an Interpreter

1. Meet regularly with the interpreter in order to keep communications open and facilitate an understanding of the goals and purpose of the interview or counseling session. Certainly you should meet with the interpreter before meeting with the client.

2. Encourage the interpreter to meet with the client before the interview to find out about the client's educational level and his or her attitudes toward health and health care. This information can aid the interpreter in the depth and type of information and explanation that will be needed.

3. Speak in short units of speech, not long, involved sentences or paragraphs. Avoid long, complex discussions of several topics in a single interview.

4. Avoid technical terminology, abbreviations, and professional jargon.

5. Avoid colloquialisms, abstractions, idiomatic expressions, slang, similes, and metaphors.

6. Encourage the interpreter to translate the client's own words as much as possible rather than paraphrasing or "polishing" them into professional jargon. This gives a better sense of the client's concept of what is going on, his or her emotional state, and other important information.

7. Encourage the interpreter to refrain from inserting his or her own ideas or interpretations, or from omitting information.

8. To check on the client's understanding and the accuracy of the translation, ask the client to repeat instructions or whatever has been communicated in his or her own words, with the translator facilitating.

9. During the interaction, look at and speak directly to the client, not the interpreter.

10. Listen to clients and watch their nonverbal communication. Often you can learn a lot regarding the affective aspects of a client's response by observing facial expressions, voice intonations, and body movements.

11. Be patient. An interpreted interview takes longer. Careful interpretation often requires that the interpreter use long explanatory phrases.

Source: Randall-David, E. (1989). *Strategies for working with culturally diverse communities and clients.* Washington, DC: Office of Maternal and Child Health, U.S. Department of Health and Human Services.

Nelson & Israel, 1991). As noted previously, there is no diagnostic instrument such as the intelligence test that gives a good estimate of the child's emotional and behavioral functioning levels. Although there are instruments that rate behaviors and help determine the presence of emotional and behavior problems, they are far from scientific (Smith, Finn, & Dowdy, 1993). The result is that "judgments are always required to determine whether or not behavior is 'abnormal'" (Wicks-Nelson & Israel, 1991, p. 2).

The identification process frequently requires teachers and other professionals to determine if sociocultural and developmental age norms have been violated (Wicks-Nelson & Israel, 1991). The degree to which behaviors violate normative standards is a leading factor in identification (Grosenick, George, George, & Lewis, 1991). A major problem is that sociocultural norms differ significantly from one culture to another. Since classroom teachers and administrators are the two groups who refer most students for services in the emotional disturbance/behavioral disorder category, their understanding of normative behaviors among various cultures is very important. What may be considered deviant behavior in one culture may actually be the "norm" in another.

Because the identification process is so complex, emotional and behavioral disorders is the one disability category provided under IDEA that is significantly under-utilized (Zabel, 1991). During the 1991–1992 school year, the number of students receiving services in this category was approximately 400,000, or 9% of all students being served in special education programs. Although this number represents a 48% increase over the number of students served in 1976–1977, it still suggests that many students with emotional and behavior problems are not being served properly (U.S. Department of Education, 1993). When comparing the number of children served to the epidemiological estimates that 10% of the child population experiences emotional problems serious enough to warrant intervention, it becomes apparent that schools are serving between 10% and 30% of students who may need services (Knitzer et al., 1990).

Also, the students who need services may not be the ones who receive them. It appears that only students who exhibit the most severe characteristics associated with the emotionally disturbed/behaviorally disordered category are identified and receive services (Zabel, 1991). This results in numerous students who experience mild emotional and behavior problems being denied services.

Lack of Collaboration between Schools and Mental Health Agencies

A major problem in providing appropriate services to students with emotional and behavior problems is the lack of collaboration between schools and mental health agencies. Although students with emotional problems need the services of a wide array of professionals, there have been few efforts to encourage different agencies to work together to pool resources for this group of children. The result has been services that are fragmented and uncoordinated (Stroul & Friedman, 1986).

In 1984, the National Institute of Mental Health (NIMH) began funding its **Child and Adolescent Service System Program (CASSP).** The CASSP initiative has attempted to create systems of care for children and adolescents who experience emotional problems (Stroul & Friedman, 1986). Unfortunately, although more than half of all states have a CASSP system in place, the level of collaboration between mental health agencies and local schools is still limited.

Definition of Emotional Disturbance/ Behavioral Disorders

Regardless of the problems encountered, students with emotional and behavioral disorders must be identified and placed in appropriate educational settings (Smith, Finn, & Dowdy, 1993). A critical prerequisite for this to occur is an acceptable definition. Although there is no one definition accepted by all parties, the one used by the federal government for its category *seriously emotionally disturbed* (SED) is adopted in most state departments of education. The current federal definition for seriously emotionally disturbed is the following:

(i) The term means a condition exhibiting one or more of the following characteristics over a long period of time and to a marked extent, which adversely affects educational performance:
  (A) An inability to learn which cannot be explained by intellectual, sensory, or health factors;
  (B) An inability to build or maintain satisfactory relationships with peers and teachers;
  (C) Inappropriate types of behavior or feelings under normal circumstances;
  (D) A general pervasive mood of unhappiness or depression; or
  (E) A tendency to develop physical symptoms or fears associated with personal or school problems.
(ii) The term includes children who are schizophrenic or autistic.[1] The term does not include children who are socially maladjusted unless it is determined that they are seriously emotionally disturbed. (*Federal Register, 42* (163), 42478)

Although this definition is used in most states and local education agencies, it leaves a lot to be desired. In general, the definition is vague and may leave the reader wondering just what a child with serious emotional disturbance is like. A broad interpretation of the definition results in many more children being served in this category than when the definition is interpreted strictly. As evidenced by the underserved nature of this disability category, it appears that most states and local school districts interpret the definition strictly and serve far fewer children in the category than prevalence estimates would project as needing services.

Another problem is that most agencies other than schools that provide services to children and adolescents with emotional problems use the definition and classification system found in the ***Diagnostic and Statistical Manual of Mental Disorders (DSM–IV).*** This manual, published by the American Psychiatric Association (1994), uses a definition and classification system totally different from the one used in public schools. This only adds to confusion and results in fragmented services, where some children are considered disabled under one system but not eligible for services in another system.

---

[1] Autism has since been removed from this definition and placed in a separate category.

Children who experience emotional and behavioral disorders are made up of a very heterogeneous group.

Classification

Children who experience emotional and behavioral disorders make up an extremely heterogeneous population. Just as different levels of mental retardation have resulted in professionals' subcategorizing the group into smaller, more homogeneous subgroups, attempts have been made to classify students with emotional and behavior problems into more homogeneous subgroups. A system to classify individuals with a specific type of disability is simply a way to systematically group or categorize individuals (Wicks-Nelson & Israel, 1991). Several different classification systems are used to group individuals with emotional and behavioral disorders.

One classification system focuses on the clinical elements found in the field of emotional and behavior problems. The predominantly used reference for a clinical classification system is the DSM-IV (American Psychiatric Association, 1994). This manual is used by medical and psychological professionals much more than by educators. It categorizes individuals into several different clinical subtypes, such as developmental disorders, organic mental disorders, and schizophrenia. Although educators rarely use the DSM-IV classification system, they need to be aware of it because of the occasional need to interact with professionals from the field of mental health. Table 6.1 lists the major groups of disorders and some examples within each category.

The classification schemes used by teachers and other educators are more associated with functional behaviors and the resulting necessary school interventions. An

TABLE 6.1   **Major Components of DSM-IV**

Disorders usually first evident in infancy, childhood, or adolescence
Organic mental syndromes and disorders
Psychoactive substance use disorders
Schizophrenia
Delusional disorder
Psychotic disorders not elsewhere classified
Mood disorders
Anxiety disorders
Somatoform disorders
Dissociative disorders
Sexual disorders
Sleep disorders
Facitious disorders
Impulse control disorders not elsewhere classified
Adjustment disorders
Psychological factors affecting physical condition
Personality disorders

Source: American Psychiatric Association. *Diagnostic and statistical manual of mental disorders* (4th ed.).
Washington, DC: Author.

example of a classification system used in schools was developed by Quay and Peterson (1987). In their revised manual for a behavior checklist they described six major subgroups of children with emotional and behavior disorders:

Conduct Disorder   Individuals are classified as having a conduct disorder if they seek attention, are disruptive, and act out. This category includes behaving aggressively toward others.

Socialized Aggression   Students in this group are likely to join a "subcultural group," a group of peers who are openly disrespectful to their peers, teachers, and parents. Delinquency, truancy, and other "gang" behaviors are common among this group.

Attention Problems—Immaturity   This group of individuals can be characterized as having attention deficits, being easily distractible, and having poor concentration. Many students in this group are impulsive and may act without thinking about the consequences.

Anxiety/Withdrawal   Students classified in the anxiety/withdrawal group are self-conscious, reticent, and unsure of themselves. Their self-concepts are generally very low, causing them to simply "retreat" from the immediate activities. They are also anxious and frequently depressed.

Psychotic Behavior   This subgroup of students displays more bizarre behaviors than others. They may hallucinate, may deal in a fantasy world, and may even talk in gibberish.

Motor Excess   Students with motor excess are hyperactive. They have difficulties sitting still, listening to another individual, and keeping their attention focused. Often these students are also hypertalkative.

Children with autism at one time were included in the federal definition of serious emotional disturbance (Smith et al., 1993). Since these children frequently displayed behaviors that were considered extremely atypical, it was thought that they were experiencing emotional problems. However, over the past decade, professionals and advocates have come to acknowledge that autism is not an emotional problem but has an organic base. The result has been the removal of autism from the SED category. In the 1990 amendments to PL 94–142, autism was made a separate disability category.

Classification becomes less important when school personnel utilize a functional assessment/intervention model. This approach, which will be described in more detail later, places an emphasis on the determination of the environmental stimuli that result in inappropriate behaviors. Once these stimuli are identified and altered, the inappropriate behaviors may decrease or disappear (Foster-Johnson & Dunlap, 1993). In such instances, the specific classification of a student becomes moot.

Causes of Emotional and Behavior Problems

In most instances, the specific etiological factors associated with a particular student's emotional or behavior problems are unknown. There are, however, a host of factors that can contribute to an individual's emotional and behavior problems. These can primarily be dichotomized into biological and environmental factors.

Biological Factors

There is growing evidence that biology plays a critical role in a person's emotional development. Behavioral and emotional health appear to be influenced by genetic, neurological, or biochemical factors—singly, or in combination. For example, individuals whose parents have experienced significant psychological problems, such as schizophrenia, are at an increased risk for developing the condition (Smith, Price, & Marsh, 1986). Also, exposure to drug and alcohol abuse in utero has been shown to have a negative impact on the behaviors and emotions of children (Bauer, 1991). Although biological factors are obvious contributors to emotional and behavior problems, it is only rarely that a specific link can be made between a biological factor and emotional or behavior problems (Hallahan & Kauffman, 1991).

Environmental Factors

There has probably been more research into environmental factors that contribute to emotional and behavior problems than into biological ones. Although it cannot be concluded that environmental factors are the leading causes of emotional and behavior problems, the number of environmental factors that can have a significant impact on an individual's emotional and behavioral status is overwhelming. The environmental category includes the broad areas of family, school, and society.

Family. An individual's family has an extremely critical impact on growth and development, not only physical but also emotional. The interactions that occur between parents and children help mold the child's opinions, behaviors, and emotions. One factor that has been linked to emotional problems is child abuse. In a literature review on the topic, Morgan (1987) reported the following:

- Abused children exhibit poor impulse control and poor self-concepts, and are frequently angry.
- Prolonged, severe abuse could lead to fantasy aggression.
- Children suffering sexual abuse have a high rate of emotional problems.
- Children who experience incest may experience significant emotional problems.

The relationship between a parent and child is critical for the child's emotional development. Fear of abuse and rejection from parents has a major impact on healthy mental development.

School. Although some children are already experiencing emotional and behavior problems before they enter school, others actually develop these problems during their school years. The pressures and interactions that are present in school may contribute to the development or expansion of a student's problems (Hallahan & Kauffman, 1991). The school is an extremely critical part of a child's life. It is in the school that the student develops peer relationships and relationships with teachers. The success a student has in school, both academically and socially, plays a vital role in the student's emotional health.

In schools, teachers play an important role in the emotional and behavioral status of children. It is very possible for teachers to aggravate an emotional or behavior problem "if a teacher who is unskilled in managing the classroom or insensitive to students' individual differences creates an environment where aggression, frustration, or withdrawal are common responses to the environment or teacher" (Smith & Luckasson, 1992, p. 315). Teachers can also exacerbate an emotional or behavior problem by reinforcing inappropriate behaviors and ignoring appropriate behaviors, putting a great deal of pressure on the student to perform above ability levels, or adding to the student's poor self-concept by focusing on negative characteristics rather than positive traits.

Society. Societal problems can also impact on an individual's emotional and behavioral status. For example, an impoverished environment, including poor nutrition, a disrupted family, and a sense of frustration and hopelessness may lead to aggressive, acting-out behaviors (Smith & Luckasson, 1992). Too often, children are products of their physical and emotional environments. Children who are constantly reminded that problems are dealt with through physical or verbal assaults will likely model these behaviors. Children who are disciplined with physical interventions are more likely to use physical avenues to solve their problems.

For children growing up in seemingly hopeless situations, there are limited rewards for exhibiting appropriate behaviors and following societal rules. In the minds of many of these children and youth, the only way to get ahead is through crime, gang membership, and other inappropriate ways. In these situations, the society is the underlying factor that results in emotional and behavior problems.

Prevalence of Students with Emotional and Behavioral Disorders

As a result of the difficulty in defining and identifying emotional and behavioral disorders, the range of estimating the prevalence of the disorder is great (Knitzer et al., 1990). Obviously, when you use a broad definition that includes many mild behavioral deviations the result is a much larger prevalence estimate than when a stricter definition is used. The U.S. Department of Education estimates that 2% of students are emotionally disturbed (National Center for Education Statistics, 1991). This contrasts rather sharply with the 10% estimated by Bauer (1981), who was the author of the original definition modified for PL 94–142, the 22% estimated by Cotler (1986), and the 14% to 20% estimated by Brandenburg, Friedman, and Silver (1990) as having moderate to severe behavioral disorders. Although a specific prevalence rate has not been established, the 2% rate used by the federal government is generally considered too low (Center, 1985; Center & Eden, 1989–1990; Center & Obringer, 1987). The specific number will depend on the definition used and the interpretation of the definition by individuals who classify students.

Among students classified as having emotional and behavioral disorders, the majority are males. Some studies have revealed that as many as 10 times more boys than girls are found in special classes for students with behavior disorders (Rosenberg et al., 1992; Smith et al., 1986).

As previously noted, students with emotional and behavioral disorders are in the only group of students under PL 94–142 that are significantly underserved. Currently, less than 1.0% of the school-age population is being served as seriously emotionally disturbed, the federal label for students with emotional and behavioral disorders (Knitzer et al., 1990; U.S. Department of Education, 1990).

There are numerous likely explanations for this underrepresentation of students in the emotional and behavior disordered category, including (Center & Eden, 1989–1990)

- Misplacement of students with emotional and behavioral disorders in classes for students with learning disabilities
- Low per-pupil expenditures, resulting in too few teacher units
- Reluctance in using the "SED" label
- Overlooking depression as a type of SED
- Overlooking withdrawal as a type of SED

In addition to these reasons, it is likely that some schools do not identify students as emotionally and behaviorally disordered because they do not employ sufficient teacher units to adequately serve students in this category without adding additional teachers (Center & Eden, 1989–1990).

Characteristics of Students with Emotional and Behavioral Disorders

Students with emotional and behavior problems exhibit a wide range of characteristics. These characteristics range in type as well as intensity. The wide variability of behaviors and emotions experienced by all individuals results in a wide range of characteristics associated with individuals with emotional and behavior problems (Bullock, Zagar, Donahue, & Pelton, 1985).

Aggressive/Acting-Out Behaviors

A common characteristic of students with emotional and behavioral disorders is acting-out behaviors, commonly referred to as *conduct disorders*. Indeed, students' acting-out behaviors frequently result in their being referred for special education programs as emotionally disturbed. In a study of 145 school districts,

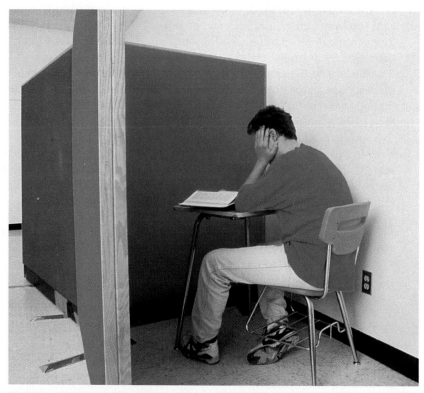

Children with emotional and behavioral disorders are usually unpopular among their peers and teachers.

Grosenick et al. (1991) found that the severity of the student's behavior is the leading characteristic associated with placement decisions for these students.

Aggressive and acting-out behaviors include verbal aggression, physical aggression, antisocial behaviors, disruptive behaviors, defiance to authority figures (including teachers), and negativism (Safran & Safran, 1987). Pullis (1991) investigated the prevalence of these types of behaviors in students classified as seriously emotionally disturbed in a sample of 224 students in 40 classrooms. The Behavior Problem Checklist revealed that 63% of the students experienced serious aggressive and acting-out problems.

Social Deficits

Students with emotional and behavioral disorders frequently display social deficits (Smith & Luckasson, 1992). These students are usually unpopular among their peers and teachers. Hallahan and Kauffman (1991) noted that students who are physically and verbally aggressive, and who are in constant conflict with authority figures, "are actively rejected, not just neglected, by their peers" (p. 189).

Although competence in social skills has always been important for students with emotional and behavior problems, its importance increased after schools started educating many of these students in general education settings (Smith et al., 1993). Unfortunately, research has indicated that the inclusion effort for many of these students fails, not because of academic deficits, but because of social problems (Nelson, 1988).

Irresponsibility

Irresponsibility is also common among students with emotional and behavior problems. Students with emotional and behavior problems rarely accept responsibility for their own actions. Rather, they deny they did anything wrong, and when confronted with evidence blame other students. As with social skills, irresponsibility became a more critical characteristic following the movement to include these students into general education classrooms for part of their instructional programs (Smith et al., 1993).

Hyperactivity/Distractibility

Hyperactivity and distractibility are often displayed by students who experience emotional and behavior problems. Hyperactivity can be simply defined as above-average motor activity levels. Frequently, it includes excessive verbal as well as physical activity.

Distractibility in students results in their having a very difficult time attending to classroom activities. This has an obvious negative effect on academic success. Students who are easily distractible may also become involved in activities that can disrupt the class. As a result of not attending to the teacher or learning activity, they are "available" to engage in activities that could impair other students' ability to attend to appropriate activities.

Lying, Cheating, Stealing

Although they are not considered major characteristics, lying, cheating, and stealing are behaviors that are common among students classified as having emotional and behavior problems. These characteristics, often found in varying degrees in children not classified as E/BD, may prevent successful inclusion of these students into general education settings. Although research has found that there is a correlation among these behaviors and aggressiveness (Rosenberg et al., 1992), there are also methods that can reduce these characteristics.

Academic Deficits

Although not commonly thought of as a problem for students with emotional and behavior problems, below-average academic performance is frequently a characteristic of these students (Bullock, 1992). Knitzer et al. (1990) stated that "only 30% function at or above grade level, with deficits increasing as the students get older" (p. xii).

Poor academic performance, which is a result of emotional and behavior problems, may also reinforce those problems. Students need to be successful. Consistently receiving poor grades in academic work can only lower their self-concepts. If students come to class with poor self-concepts, failure in academic work will only reinforce those self-concepts. Once a student has a poor self-concept, it impairs the confidence necessary to experience success. This vicious cycle must be broken if students with emotional and behavior problems are able to experience success in general class settings.

Depression

Students with emotional and behavior problems often experience depression. Although depression has frequently been overlooked as a problem for educators, recently school personnel have begun to take an interest in the disorder and its resulting school problems (Maag & Forness, 1991). Reasons for the recent increased interest in depression include (Wicks-Nelson & Israel, 1991)

- Developments in identification and treatment of depression in adults
- Developments in diagnostic practices
- New perspectives on developmental depression that has created an interest in depression in young children

Depression can be described generally as an unhappy mood. All individuals are depressed from time to time. However, for the most part, individuals come out of their depression after only a short episode that does not significantly affect the person's life. As a clinical problem, depression can have significant implications for students.

Anxiety

Anxiety is also a common characteristic among students with emotional and behavioral disorders. Anxiety can be defined as "a complex pattern of three types of reactions to a perceived threat: motor responses, physiological responses, and subjective responses" (Wicks-Nelson & Israel, 1991, p. 109). Examples of these reactions include avoidance, trembling, crying, increased heart rate, perspiration, breathlessness, and thoughts of danger. All of us have experienced anxiety from time to time, usually only to realize that it was unnecessary. Students with emotional and behavioral disorders experience frequent periods of anxiety.

Education of Students with Emotional and Behavior Problems

As noted, students with emotional and behavior problems represent the most underserved special population in special education. With fewer than 1% of all students classified as having this disorder, compared to prevalence estimates that top 10%, it is apparent that many students who could benefit from special programs are not served.

Regardless of the numbers of students who remain unidentified and unserved, thousands of students do receive specialized intervention services from classroom teachers, special education teachers, and specialists (Polloway & Smith, 1992). Although many of these students are formally classified as disabled, many others display behavior problems, but not to the degree necessary for a formal referral and diagnosis.

A major national study, completed in 1990, investigated educational services for students with emotional and behavioral problems. The study was published under the title of *At the Schoolhouse Door* (Knitzer et al., 1990). The following are examples of findings from the study:

- ◆ Over 80% of students classified as E/BD are educated in general education schools.
- ◆ Approximately 50% of students classified as E/BD are educated for at least a portion of each school day in general education classrooms by general education classroom teachers.
- ◆ There is limited or no mental health presence in most special education programs for E/BD students.
- ◆ Children and adolescents with E/BD get limited transition services.
- ◆ Parents of students with E/BD often encounter great difficulties in securing appropriate educational programs for their children.
- ◆ School-based mental health services are beginning in many schools across the country.
- ◆ Social skills training is nearly nonexistent in many schools.
- ◆ Efforts to include families more in students' programs is increasing.

Although not all negative, this study reveals significant gaps in educational services for students with E/BD. However, the study also suggests that improvements are being made in many school districts in the area of providing appropriate services to this large group of students.

Several specific steps must occur when educating students with E/BD. These begin with the important action of making an appropriate referral for services, followed up by providing appropriate services.

Intervention Approaches

Students with emotional and behavioral disorders are likely included in general education classrooms for at least a portion of each school day. The 15th Annual Report to Congress reported that nearly 46% of all students classified as seriously emotionally disturbed were served in general education classrooms or a combination of general classroom/resource room settings (U.S. Department of Education, 1993). Taking into consideration the prevalence rate of emotional and behavior problems, classroom teachers have to deal more with these students than any other disability group, except those with learning disabilities. In addition to these students, teachers also have to deal with students who display similar characteristics, but to a lesser degree.

Because many students with emotional and behavior problems are included in general education classrooms, teachers and special education teachers need to collaborate in developing and implementing intervention programs. Without this collaboration, appropriate interventions will be very difficult to provide. Consistency in behavior management and other intervention strategies among teachers and family members is critical. If students receive feedback from the special education teacher that significantly differs from the feedback received from the classroom teacher, confusion often results.

There are many different ways teachers can help students improve their behavior, from preventive measures to direct confrontation with the students. Chapter 12 will provide extensive information about ways to implement classroom management techniques into an educational system. A critical component in working with students with emotional and behavioral problems is the level of collaboration among the variety of professionals involved in providing services to this group of students. Very definitely, mental health professionals should be involved with services to these students, and in some cases, personnel from the juvenile justice system, child welfare system, and social work agencies should collaborate. Without a close working relationship among the many groups who may be involved in serving children and adolescents with E/BD, services will always be fragmented and disorganized.

There are numerous theoretical approaches that focus on educating students with emotional and behavior problems. However, no single approach works with all students in this classification. Still, some professionals advocate the adoption of a particular model when working with students with E/BD. There are five basic models that have been espoused for students with emotional and behavior problems. These are the (1) psychoanalytic approach, (2) psychoeducational approach, (3) humanistic model, (4) ecological approach, and (5) behavioral model. Table 6.2 summarizes these five models. The key is to ensure that whatever approach is used meets the needs of a particular student; individualization is critical.

Preventive Discipline

Probably the most effective means of working with students who display emotional and behavior problems is preventive in nature. If inappropriate behaviors can be prevented, then disruptions are minimal, and the student can attend to the learning task at hand. Preventive discipline can be described as "the teacher's realization that disci-

TABLE 6.2 **Theoretical Approaches to Educating Students with Emotional and Behavior Problems**

	Psychoanalytic Approach	Psychoeducational Approach	Humanistic Approach	Ecological Approach	Behavioral Approach
The problem	A pathological imbalance among the dynamic parts of the mind (id, superego, ego)	Involves both underlying psychiatric disorders and the readily observable misbehavior and underachievement of the child	Belief that the child is out of touch with his or her own feelings and can't find fulfillment in traditional educational settings	Belief that the child interacts poorly with the environment; child and environment affect each other reciprocally and negatively	Belief that the child has learned inappropriate responses and failed to learn appropriate ones
Purpose of educational practices	Use of psychoanalytic principles to help uncover underlying mental pathology	Concern for unconscious motivation/underlying conflicts *and* academic achievement/ positive surface behavior	Emphasis on enhancing child's self-direction, self-evaluation, and emotional involvement in learning	Attempts to alter entire social system so that it will support desirable behavior in child when intervention is withdrawn	Manipulates child's immediate environment and the consequences of behavior
Characteristics of teaching methods	Reliance on individual psychotherapy for child and parents; little emphasis on academic achievement; highly permissive atmosphere	Emphasis on meeting individual needs of the child; reliance on projects and creative arts	Use of nontraditional educational settings in which the teacher serves as resource and catalyst rather than as director of activities; nonauthoritarian, open, affective, personal atmosphere	Involves all aspects of a child's life, including classroom, family, neighborhood, and community, in teaching the child useful life and educational skills	Involves measurement of responses and subsequent analyses of behaviors to change them; emphasis on reward for appropriate behavior

Source: Hallahan, D. P., & Kaufman, J. M. (1991). *Exceptional children* (5th ed.) (p. 197). Englewood Cliffs, NJ: Prentice-Hall. Used with permission.

pline begins with a positive attitude that nurtures students' learning of personal, social, and academic skills" (Sabatino, 1987, p. 8). Rather than responding to inappropriate behaviors, adherents to positive discipline rely on interacting with students in a positive manner that removes the need for inappropriate behaviors.

Sabatino (1987) describes 10 components to a preventive discipline program:

1. Inform pupils of what is expected of them.
2. Establish a positive learning climate.
3. Provide a meaningful learning experience.
4. Avoid threats.
5. Demonstrate fairness.
6. Build and exhibit self-confidence.
7. Recognize positive student attributes.
8. Time the recognition of student attributes.

How to Deal with Fights between Students

- In a firm, strong voice, order (don't ask) the students to stop at once.
- If they don't respond, try again and send for or call another adult.
- If they stop, send them in separate directions, i.e., one to one corner of a room, the other to another corner. In some cases one can be sent to one classroom and the second to another, provided that procedure is approved by the other personnel involved.
- Direct the students to start working on some task. What they are working on is not as important as being engaged in something besides fighting.
- After things have settled down, talk to the students individually and apply the appropriate school rules.
- You may want to have the students involved write an essay about how each could have avoided the fight and what to do about similar situations in the future.

Source: Westling, D. L., & Koorland, M. A. (1989). *The special educator's handbook* (p. 147). Boston: Allyn & Bacon. Used with permission.

    9. Use positive modeling.
  10. Structure the curriculum and classroom environment.

Teacher behavior can greatly facilitate preventive discipline. As previously noted, teachers have to be consistent in meting out discipline. They must not treat inappropriate behaviors from one student differently than they treat misbehavior from other students. Teachers must also apply consequences systematically. Disciplining a student for an inappropriate behavior one time and ignoring the same behavior another time will only cause the student to be confused over expectations.

Classroom structure also has an impact on students' behaviors. Classroom structure is more than the simple arrangement of desks, it includes (Stainback, Stainback, & Froyen, 1987)

- *Physical Arrangement and Traffic Rules*   Teachers need to be able to see the entire classroom at all times, and they need to establish traffic patterns that limit opportunities for students to get into trouble with other students and objects.
- *Time Management*   Teachers need to ensure that students are on-task with constructive activities most of the time to prevent opportunities for misconduct. They should also be prepared for specific activities each day.
- *Assignments*   Assignments should be meaningful and not "busy work." Teachers should also ensure that assignments are clear, understandable, and within the capability of the students.

◆ *Grouping Practices*   Teachers should group students to avoid behavior problems. Some students simply do not need to sit near each other.
◆ *Classroom Atmosphere*   Teachers establish the classroom atmosphere with all of their actions. The atmosphere lets students know that they are respected and that the teacher is supportive of their learning efforts.

Chapter 12 will present extensive information regarding strategies that can be used to manage classroom behaviors. To reveal the diversity of approaches, Table 6.3 shows the percentage of behavior interventions used in 145 school districts included in a study completed by Grosenick et al. (1991).

Social Skills Instruction

As previously noted, students with emotional and behavioral disorders frequently display deficits in social skills (Knitzer, 1990; Rosenberg et al., 1992). Although many schools do not offer extensive opportunities for students to learn appropriate social skills (Knitzer et al., 1990), research has shown that such instruction can be extremely beneficial. Social skills are probably best learned naturally, from observing others

TABLE 6.3   **Percentage of Behavior Interventions Used in Districtwide BD Programs**

Type of Intervention	Not at All Used	Used in Some Classrooms/ Caseloads	Used in Most or All Classrooms/ Caseloads
Behavioral/Cognitive Strategies			
Positive reinforcement	0	5	95
Social skills training	1	18	81
Environmental management	9	23	68
Modeling	4	7	89
Self-control strategies	2	12	86
Time out	4	27	69
Generalization training	16	43	41
Use of aversives	33	40	27
Psychological Interventions			
Counseling	1	24	75
Peer group processes	5	34	61
Managing surface behaviors	0	11	89
Life space interviewing	38	31	31
Psychotherapy	49	30	21
Medication	31	55	14
Reactive Strategies			
Crisis management	0.7	21	78
Physical restraint	25	52	23
Suspension/expulsion	10	56	34

Source: Grosenick, J. K., George, N. L., George, M. P., & Lewis, T. J. (1991). Pubic school services for behaviorally disordered students: Program practices in the 1980s. *Behavior Disorders, 16,* 92. Used with permission.

Self-Monitoring with Countoons

Of all the disabilities that students bring with them to regular classrooms, emotional/behavioral disorders are perhaps the most difficult for teachers to deal with successfully. Students with emotional disturbance have traditionally been problematic for teachers because they often demonstrate behaviors that are annoying, disruptive, aggressive, and sometimes dangerous. These students may also challenge teachers' and administrators' authority, and the management of their behavior can be a stressful and exhausting task. Quite often, teachers express the hope that their students will some day begin to effectively manage their own behavior, relying less and less on the external control of authority figures in their lives.

One way of encouraging students to begin the process of developing and exercising self-control of their disruptive behavior is to teach them some *techniques for self-monitoring* and, if possible, to tie their performance in to a system of positive reinforcement. There are several strategies for self-monitoring, but one of the most effective is that described by Kaplan (1991). Kaplan uses a *countoon,* which is a three-frame cartoon. The first frame describes what the student must do, the second frame describes how the behavior will be measured and recorded, and the third frame represents what will happen to the student in terms of positive reinforcement.

Source: Kaplan, J. S. (1991). *Beyond behavior modification: A cognitive-behavioral approach to behavior management in the school.* Austin, TX: Pro-Ed. Used with permission.

who display appropriate skills, but there are times when a more formal instructional effort must be made.

When using a formal instructional process to teach social skills, a first step is to determine the level of social competence present in a student. Assessing social skills usually requires the use of informed judgments of persons who interact regularly with the individual student (Smith et al., 1993). Many different checklists are available to assist in assessing social competence. In addition to checklists, self-monitoring charts and sociometric measures may be used (Smith et al., 1993).

Following the assessment process, an instructional approach to teach deficiencies in social skills must be developed. There are numerous different methods to teach social skills, including modeling, direct instruction, prompting, and positive practice. There is no one particular approach that works more effectively than others; teachers must simply determine the method that will work best with a particular student. Table 6.4 summarizes the predominant methods for teaching social skills.

Functional Assessment

Using functional assessment to help develop effective intervention programs for students with emotional and behavior problems requires school personnel and family

TABLE 6.4 Summary Descriptions of Tactics to Teach Social Skills

Instructional Strategy	Description	Advantages	Disadvantages
Modeling	Exposing target student to display prosocial behavior.	Easy to implement.	Not sufficient if used alone.
Strategic placement	Placing target student in situations with other students who display prosocial behaviors.	Employs peers as change agents. Facilitates generalization. Is cost effective.	Research data inconclusive when used alone.
Instruction	Telling students how and why they should behave a certain way, and/or giving rules for behavior.	Overemphasizes norms/expectations.	Not sufficient if used alone.
Correspondence training	Students are positively reinforced for accurate reports regarding their behavior.	Facilitates maintenance and generalization of training. Is cost effective.	Very little documentation of effectiveness.
Rehearsal and practice	Structured practice of specific prosocial behavior.	Enhances skill acquisition.	Not sufficient to change behavior if used alone.
Positive reinforcement or shaping	Prosocial behaviors or approximations are followed by a reward or favorable event.	Strong research support for effectiveness.	Maintenance after treatment termination is not predictable.
Prompting and coaching	Providing students with additional stimuli/prompts that elicit the prosocial behavior.	Particularly effective after acquisition to enhance transfer to natural settings.	Maintenance after treatment termination is not predictable.
Positive practice	A consequence strategy in which student repeatedly practices correct behavior.	May produce immediate increases in prosocial behavior.	Long-term effectiveness not documented. Less restrictive approaches should be used first.
Multimethod training packages	Multicomponent instructional package that incorporates several behavioral techniques.	Greater treatment strength, and durability. Applicable to a wide range of children and settings.	

Source: Carter, J., & Sugai, G. (1989). Social skills curriculum analysis. *Teaching Exceptional Children, 22,* 38. Used with permission.

members to determine the context of the inappropriate behaviors. This method is based on the assumption that behaviors occur not only because of the consequence that follows, but also because of the circumstances in which they occur. Behavior simply does not occur in a vacuum, but is a function of ongoing, surrounding events (Cooper, Peck, Wacker, & Millard, 1993; Foster-Johnson & Dunlap, 1993).

When using a functional assessment approach, the first step is to determine the circumstances present that could be related to inappropriate behaviors. After determining these circumstances, hypothesis statements are created that attempt to describe the relationship between the behaviors and circumstances. Based on these hypothesis statements, possible intervention strategies are developed.

Medication and Students with Emotional and Behavior Problems

Many students with emotional and behavior problems experience difficulties in maintaining their attention and controlling their behavior levels. Although many students with attention deficits and hyperactivity do not have emotional and behavior problems, many do. For students experiencing these problems, "medication is the most frequently used (and perhaps overused) intervention" (Ellenwood & Felt, 1989, p. 16). Many different kinds of medication have been found to be effective with students' behavior problems (Forness & Kavale, 1988):

- Stimulants
- Tranquilizers
- Anticonvulsants
- Antidepressants
- Mood-altering drugs

The use of medication to help manage students with emotional and behavior problems is controversial and has been investigated extensively. Findings include the following:

1. Medication can result in increased attention of students.
2. Medication may result in reduced aggressive behaviors.
3. Various side effects can result from medical interventions.
4. The use of medication with children experiencing emotional and behavior problems should only be done with close monitoring and supervision (Smith, Finn, & Dowdy, 1993).

When medication is used to help students who are experiencing emotional and behavior problems, the primary role of the teacher is to monitor the child. Teachers need to be aware of the medication the student is taking and any possible side effects of the medication. The teacher should be asked for information on a regular basis by the parents or the student's physician to ensure that negative side effects are not beginning to appear. If the level or kind of medication is changed, the teacher needs to be informed immediately and given all new information about possible negative consequences that could result.

Role of Classroom Teachers

As previously noted, classroom teachers become involved with students with emotional and behavioral problems early. They are usually the ones who make the initial referral for this group of students (Polloway & Smith, 1992). Unless the problem exhibited by the student is severe, it will likely go unnoticed until the beginning of school. In addition to referring students, classroom teachers must be directly involved in implementing the student's individualized education program (IEP) because the majority of students in this category receive at least a portion of their educational program in general education classrooms. This, combined with the large number of students who from time to time display inappropriate behaviors but who are not identified as having emotional and behavior problems, means that classroom teachers must deal with behavior problems much of the time.

Kauffman and Wong (1991) point out that "effective teaching of behaviorally disordered students may require skills, attitudes, and beliefs different from those of teachers who work effectively with more ordinary students" (p. 226). However, there is no single characteristic that will guarantee success for teachers dealing with students who are experiencing emotional and behavior problems.

Summary

- Most children and youth are disruptive from time to time, but most do not require interventions. Some students' emotional or behavior problems are severe enough to warrant interventions.

- School discipline continues to rank highly on annual surveys about concerns of the educational system.

- There are many problems in serving students with emotional and behavior problems, including inconsistent definitions, numerous agencies involved, and limited measurement devices.

- Cultural and socioeconomic factors may create difficulties in identifying students with emotional and behavior problems.

- Definitions for emotional disturbance and behavioral disorders are generally vague.

- There is limited consistency in classifying persons with emotional and behavior problems.

- Emotional problems can be caused by biological or environmental factors.

- Family members and school personnel may help cause emotional and behavior problems.

- The prevalence of students with emotional and behavior problems ranges from a low of 1% or 2% to a high of 30%.

- Students with emotional and behavior problems are significantly underserved in schools.

- Although no one specific intervention method works with students with emotional and behavior problems, there are several theoretical orientations to serving this group.

◆ Preventive discipline is an important method to try to keep behavior problems from occurring.

◆ Although this treatment is highly controversial, many students with emotional and behavior problems receive medication in an attempt to control their behaviors.

References

American Psychiatric Association. (1987). *Diagnostic and statistical manual of mental disorders* (4th ed.). Washington, DC: Author.

Brandenburg, N. A., Friedman, R. M., & Silver, S. E. (1990). The epidemiology of childhood psychiatric disorders: Prevalence findings from recent studies. *Journal of the American Association of Child and Adolescent Psychiatry, 29,* 76–83.

Bullock, L. (1992). *Exceptionalities in children and youth.* Boston: Allyn & Bacon.

Bullock, L. M., Zagar, E. L., Donahue, C. A., & Pelton, G. B. (1985). Teachers' perceptions of behaviorally disordered students in a variety of settings. *Exceptional Children, 52,* 123–130.

Center, D. B. (1985). PL 94–142 as applied to DSM III diagnosis: A book review. *Behavioral Disorders, 10,* 305–306.

Center, D. B., & Eden, A. (1989–1990). A search for variables affecting under-identification of students with behavior disorders: II. *National Forum of Special Education Journal, 1,* 12–18.

Center, D. B., & Obringer, J. (1987). A search for variables affecting underidentification of behaviorally disordered students. *Behavioral Disorders, 12,* 169–174.

Cooper, L. J., Peck, S., Wacker, D. P., & Millard, T. (1993). Functional assessment for a student with a mild mental disability and persistent behavior problems. *Teaching Exceptional Children, 25,* 56–57.

Cotler, S. (1986). Epidemiology and outcome. In J. M. Reisman (Ed.), *Behavior disorders in infants, children, and adolescents* (pp. 196–211). New York: Random House.

Elam, S. M., Rose, L. C., & Gallup, A. M. (1991). The 23rd annual Gallup poll of the public's attitudes toward the public schools. *Phi Delta Kappan, 73,* 41–55.

Ellenwood, A. E., & Felt, D. (1989). Attention-deficit/hyperactivity disorder: Management and intervention approaches for the classroom teacher. *LD Forum, 15,* 15–17.

Forness, S. R., & Kavale, K. A. (1988). Planning for the needs of children with serious emotional disturbance: The National Mental Health and Special Education Coalition. *Behavior Disorders, 13,* 127–133.

Foster-Johnson, L., & Dunlap, G. (1993). Using functional assessment to develop effective, individualized interventions for challenging behaviors. *Teaching Exceptional Children, 56,* 44–52.

Grosenick, J. K., George, N. L., George, M. P., & Lewis, T. J. (1991). Public school services for behaviorally disordered students: Program practices in the 1980s. *Behavioral Disorders, 16,* 87–96.

Hallahan, D. P., & Kauffman, J. M. (1991). *Exceptional children.* Englewood Cliffs, NJ: Prentice-Hall.

Kaplan, J. S. (1991). *Beyond behavior modification: A cognitive-behavioral approach to behavior management in the school.* Austin, TX: Pro-Ed.

Kauffman, J. M., & Wong, K. L. H. (1991). Effective teachers of students with behavioral disorders: Are generic teaching skills enough? *Behavioral Disorders, 16,* 225–237.

Knitzer, J., Steinberg, Z., & Fleisch, B. (1990). *At the schoolhouse door.* New York: Bank Street College of Education.

Koorland, M. A., Monda, L. E., & Vail, C. O. (1988). Recording behavior with ease. *Teaching Exceptional Children, 21,* 59–60.

Maag, J. W., & Forness, S. R. (1991). Depression in children and adolescents: Identification, assessment, and treatment. *Focus on Exceptional Children, 24,* 1–19.

Morgan, S. R. (1987). *Abuse and neglect of handicapped children.* Boston: College Hill.

National Center for Education Statistics. (1991). *The condition of education, 1991 edition.* Washington, DC: Author.

Nelson, C. M. (1988). Social skill training for handicapped students. *Teaching Exceptional Children, 20,* 19–23.

Norby, J. M., Thurlow, M. L., Christenson, S. L., & Ysseldyke, J. E. (1990). *The challenge of complex school problems.* Austin, TX: Pro-Ed.

Polloway, E. A., & Smith, T. E. C. (1992). *Language instruction for students with disabilities.* Denver, CO: Love Publishing.

Pullis, M. (1991). Practical considerations of excluding conduct disordered students: An empirical analysis. *Behavioral Disorders, 17,* 9–22.

Quay, H., & Peterson, D. (1987). *Revised behavior problem checklist.* Coral Gables, FL: University of Miami.

Randall-David, E. (1989). *Strategies for working with culturally diverse communities and clients.* Washington, DC: Office of Maternal and Child Health, U.S. Department of Health and Human Services.

Ritter, D. R. (1989). Teachers' perceptions of problem behaviors in general and special education. *Exceptional Children, 55,* 559–564.

Rosenberg, M. S., Wilson, R., Maheady, L., & Sindelar, P. (1992). *Educating students with behavior disorders.* Boston: Allyn & Bacon.

Sabatino, D. A. (1987). Preventive discipline as a practice in special education. *Teaching Exceptional Children, 19,* 8–11.

Safran, J. S., & Safran, S. P. (1987). Teachers' judgments of problem behaviors. *Exceptional Children, 54,* 240–244.

Smith, D. D., & Luckasson, R. (1992). *Introduction to special education.* Boston: Allyn & Bacon.

Smith, T. E. C. (1990). *Introduction to education* (2nd ed.). St. Paul, MN: West Publishing.

Smith, T. E. C., & Dowdy, C. A. (1992). Future-based assessment for students with mental retardation. *Education and Training in Mental Retardation, 27,* 23–31.

Smith, T. E. C., Finn, D. M., & Dowdy, C. A. (1993). *Teaching students with mild disabilities.* Ft. Worth, TX: Harcourt Brace Jovanovich.

Smith, T. E. C., Price, B. J., & Marsh, G. E. (1986). *Mildly handicapped children and adults.* St. Paul, MN: West Publishing.Stainback, W., Stainback, S., & Froyen, L. (1987). Structuring the classroom to prevent disruptive behaviors. *Teaching Exceptional Children, 19,* 12–16.

Stroul, B. A., & Friedman, R. M. (1986). *A system of care for severely emotionally disturbed children and youth.* Washington, DC: CASSP Technical Assistance Center.

U.S. Department of Education (1993). *15th Annual Report to Congress on the Implementation of IDEA.* Washington, DC: Author.

Westling, D. L., & Koorland, M. A. (1988). *The special educator's handbook.* Boston: Allyn & Bacon.

Wicks-Nelson, R., & Israel, A. C. (1991). *Behavior disorders of childhood.* Englewood Cliffs, NJ: Prentice-Hall.

Zabel, R. K. (1991). Problems and promises in special education and related services for children and youth with emotional or behavioral disorders. *Behavioral Disorders, 16,* 299–313.

CHAPTER 7

Teaching Students with Sensory Impairments

Foundational Information

This chapter covers material related to the hearing and visual problems that some students placed in general education classrooms possess. The goal is to provide teachers with basic information about these impairments and offer specific recommendations for accommodating the needs of these students in a variety of instructional settings. Although this chapter provides much useful information related to teaching students who have hearing and visual problems, more detailed and comprehensive material is available elsewhere (Bess, 1988; Martin, 1987; Ross, Brackett, & Maxon, 1991).

Although there is some debate regarding the best setting in which to provide appropriate services to students with sensory impairments, many students with these conditions are likely to be placed in general education settings. This occurs because most are capable of handling the academic and social demands of these settings. However, for these students to receive an appropriate education, a variety of accommodative activities may be needed. These can range from minor seating adjustments to the use of sophisticated equipment for communicating or listening. Having students with these types of impairments may also necessitate that additional personnel (e.g., an interpreter) be present.

As suggested, in addressing the educational needs of these students, accommodations are likely to be required. To achieve this end, teachers must have accurate information about how to modify their classrooms and adapt instruction to meet student needs. In addition, teachers need to understand the psychosocial aspects of these types of disabilities. Ultimately, teachers must feel comfortable and confident that they can address the range of needs these students present.

The underlying assumption is that many students, even with their special needs, can be successful in general education settings. However, this can be achieved only when general education environments are receptive to these students and display certain accommodative features.

Sensory impairments are considered low incidence, since there are not large numbers of these students in the school population. The number of students (ages 6 to 21) with hearing or visual impairments who were officially identified and provided with special education and/or related services nationally for the school year 1991–1992 is reported in Table 7.1. As can be seen, these are not large numbers when one considers the total number of students in this age range. Furthermore, these groups represent a very small percentage of all students who are disabled.

However, having only one of these students in a classroom may seem overwhelming, as he or she may require a variety of modifications in the way a classroom is managed and certain instructional practices are implemented.

TABLE 7.1   **Students Aged 6 to 21 Served under IDEA, Part B, in 1991–1992**

Disability Area	Number of Students	Percentage of Total Number of Students Identified as Disabled
Hearing impairments	43,690	1.00
Visual impairments	18,296	0.40

Source: U.S. Department of Education (1993). *15th annual report to Congress on the implementation of IDEA.* Washington, DC: Office of Special Education Programs, Department of Education.

Common Themes across the Disability Areas

Certain factors have a significant effect on the nature of the impairments discussed in this and the next chapter and on how students deal with their specific conditions. The three factors that seem to have the most bearing on many different types of disabilities are severity, visibility, and age at acquisition (Heward & Orlansky, 1992). These factors are important to understand because they provide a general index of the needs students will have and an explanation for how certain students handle their lives.

Severity   The severity of the impairment suggests the extent of involvement of a condition. For students with sensory impairments, severity relates closely to communication ability and experiential background. Students with more severe sensory impairments are likely to use different methods of communication and assistive techniques for mobility. In addition, they probably will have had a more limited array of experiences upon which to relate new information.

Visibility   When a disability is visually apparent, it brings unwanted attention. Unfortunately, this attention focuses on the perceived negative features of an individual. For many students, this attention causes them to feel devalued. As a result, it becomes very important that these students learn to handle their feelings and be able to deal with the insensitive actions of others.

Age at Acquisition   Obviously, the age at which students acquire a disability has a profound effect on certain skills and abilities (e.g., language acquisition or concept development). Age also affects how students handle their condition and how educational personnel should address the condition. From a psychosocial perspective, if a condition is acquired through injury, time may be needed for a student to progress through the adjustment process before other interventions are meaningful.

Students with hearing and visual conditions represent a heterogeneous group. There are many different types of specific impairments resulting in different presenting problems and different ways of handling them. For this reason, it is crucial that teachers be prepared in a range of areas to work with students with these types of disabilities.

Some general suggestions of what teachers can do to enhance the students' acceptance of others and to maximize the chances of their succeeding in general education settings are listed here.

- ◆ Create learning environments that are supportive and nurturing, yet challenging and directed at developing independence.
- ◆ Strive to make students feel good about themselves and the work they are doing.
- ◆ Focus on student strengths, as these can often be overlooked with students who have pronounced disabilities.
- ◆ Create a classroom environment where students with special needs are accepted as valid members of the classroom community and recognized as contributing members of the class.
- ◆ Be available to students when they need to talk—teachers are likely to be among the most important people in the lives of these students.
- ◆ Be sensitive to the needs of families—a child who has a hearing or visual problem is stressful on parents and siblings.

The remainder of the chapter is divided into two major sections: hearing impairments and visual impairments. Each section provides basic information as well as general recommendations and specific suggestions for working with students with these conditions who are placed in general education classrooms.

Hearing Impairment

Hearing impairment is a hidden disability—at least to most people on first encounter with a person who is hearing impaired. An unknowing observer typically cannot tell from looking at physical features alone that a person is hearing impaired However, in any context where communicative skills are needed, hearing limitations become evident.

Students with a hearing disability pose a variety of challenges to the general classroom teacher. Although their numbers are increasing, relatively few students with profound hearing loss (deafness) are educated in general education settings. However, when these students are in general education classes, they need major accommodations (e.g., an interpreter).

The number of students who have some degree of hearing loss (i.e., mild to severe) is more noteworthy, because these students can function in general education settings more easily when certain accommodations are provided. For this to happen, it is critical for teachers to understand the nature of hearing impairments and to know how to address the needs associated with these conditions.

The importance of language acquisition and usage on the development of cognitive abilities and achievement in academic subject areas is unassailable. Hearing loss, even in milder forms, greatly affects language ability. This then leads to problems in academic areas, particularly in language-related subjects such as reading and written expression.

General education teachers, who have students with various types of hearing impairments in their classrooms, must be exposed to information that will facilitate the management of these students. Specifically, teachers need to know (a) the basic principles of the hearing process and hearing loss, (b) the indicators that a student might have a hearing impairment, (c) the typical educationally relevant characteristics of students with hearing loss, and (d) accommodative techniques for meeting the needs of students with hearing loss. Due to the lack of preservice exposure to these topics, school systems need to design appropriate inservice training. Maxon (1990) suggests the development of an "individualized in-service plan" to guide this endeavor.

Basic Concepts

This section provides an overview of basic information required to understand hearing impairments. Teachers benefit from having a working knowledge of this information by being able to teach more effectively and to communicate with other professionals and families.

Terminology.   A number of different terms are associated with hearing loss. As a result, there can be some confusion about what the terms actually mean. Three terms frequently encountered in print and in professional conversation are *hearing impairment, deafness,* and *hard of hearing.* Brief definitions of these terms, adapted from Ross, Brackett, and Maxon (1991) are provided next. Some school systems do use other terminology, such as *auditorily impaired.*

   ◆ *Hearing impairment* is a generic term that encompasses the entire range of hearing loss.
   ◆ *Deafness* refers to profound hearing loss such that the primary means of communication and speech/language development is visually based.
   ◆ *Hard of hearing* refers to significant hearing loss such that the primary means of communication is auditory based. Intervention techniques capitalize on the use of a person's residual hearing, with or without amplification.

There are more students who are hard of hearing than those who are deaf. Most students with hearing impairment whom general education teachers encounter have some residual hearing (Heward & Orlansky, 1992); however, as mentioned earlier, some students who are deaf are receiving their education in these settings as well. According to data compiled by the U.S. Department of Education (1993), 26.85% of students classified as hearing impaired are placed in general education full-time. Another 19.7% spend a greater part of their day in general education classrooms.

   An interesting point noted by Ross et al. (1991) is that students who are hard of hearing have more in common with normal-hearing peers than they do with children who are deaf. This observation is based on the fact that interaction and instruction can occur more easily when some residual hearing is available. It also underscores the notion that these students can be successful in general education classes.

Most students with hearing loss have some residual hearing but may still need to use augmentative communication.

Dimensions of Hearing Loss. Hearing loss can be categorized in four major ways. The two most frequently cited types of hearing loss are **conductive** and **sensorineural.** A third type, called mixed, refers to a condition where both conductive and sensorineural loss are present. A fourth type of hearing impairment relates to the processing stage in the hearing process and involves disorders occurring in the brain stem or hearing centers of the brain (i.e., central auditory processing). Table 7.2 provides information on these different types of hearing loss.

Another dimension of hearing loss that can have a significant impact on a student's ability to benefit from instruction is whether there is loss in one ear (unilateral) or in both ears (bilateral). With bilateral loss, the degree of loss in the different ears may vary as well. Students with unilateral loss may have difficulty localizing where sounds are originating and listening in settings that are noisy (Heward & Orlansky, 1992).

Formal Assessment. The assessment of hearing ability requires the use of various audiological techniques. The most common method of evaluating one's hearing is the use of **pure-tone audiometry,** in which sounds of different frequencies are presented at increasing levels of intensity. Bone conduction hearing can also be assessed to determine if there are problems in the sensorineural portion of the hearing mechanism.

TABLE 7.2   Information on Different Types of Hearing Loss

Type of Hearing Loss	Nature of Problem	Possible Causes	Structures Potentially Affected
Conductive	• Interruption in transmission of sound from outer ear to inner ear • Hearing loss can range from mild to severe • Loss is often temporary	• Ear infection (particularly middle ear infections) • Congenital abnormalities • Childhood diseases • Physical injuries • Foreign objects or wax buildup	• Pinna • Ear canal • Tympanic membrane • Bones of middle ear
Sensorineural	• Damage or problems with the cochleas (sensory) or auditory nerve (neural) • Hearing loss ranges from moderate to profound • Loss is usually permanent	• Genetic factors • Intrauterine problems (e.g., viral infections, ototoxic drugs) • Childhood diseases (e.g., measles, mumps, chicken pox, influenza) • Perinatal and postnatal insults (e.g., trauma, anoxia, loud noise, toxic substances)	• Sensory hair cells in the cochlea • Nerve
Mixed	• Evidence of both conductive and sensorineural loss	• Same as above	• Same as above
Central Auditory Processing	• Difficulty in understanding information arriving to brain • Certain types of brain dysfunction • Difficulty interpreting the meaning of sounds	• Often unknown etiology • Genetic	• Pathways to the brain • Hearing and processing centers of brain

The effect of a hearing loss on a student's ability to understand speech is a primary educational concern. Table 7.3 provides a breakdown of the levels of hearing loss. In addition, it also presents a general indication of the impact that a given decibel loss, across a number of frequency ranges, has on an individual.

Indicators of Possible Hearing Problems.   The disability of some students with varying degrees of hearing loss go undetected in school settings. As a result, it is extremely important for teachers to be aware of signs that a student may be experiencing hearing problems. Certain behaviors that may suggest that a student has a hearing impairment are presented here. Since these behaviors may also be associated with other concerns, they should be considered indicators warranting further investigation rather than conclusive proof that a hearing impairment exists.

Teachers should take notice and possibly refer a student for a comprehensive audiological evaluation if the student:

TABLE 7.3 **Ranges and Categories of Hearing Loss as a Function of dB Hearing Loss**

Up to 25 dB	Normal hearing: some experts believe the upper limit must only be 15 dB.
26 to 40 dB	Mild hearing loss: difficulty hearing faint or distant speech; some recent research suggests that even mild loss may cause subtle language delay.
41 to 55 dB	Moderate hearing loss: delayed speech and language acquisition; difficulty in producing certain speech sounds correctly; difficulty following conversation.
56 to 70 dB	Moderately severe hearing loss: can understand only amplified or shouted speech.
71 to 90 dB	Severe hearing loss: difficulty understanding even loud and amplified speech. Significant difficulty in learning and producing intelligible oral language.
91+ dB	Profound hearing loss: typically described as deaf; hearing does not play a major role in learning, producing, and understanding spoken speech and language.

Source: Hegde, M. N. (1991). *Introduction to communication disorders.* Austin, TX: Pro-Ed. Used with permission.

- Turns head to position an ear in the direction of the the speaker
- Asks for information to be repeated frequently
- Uses a loud voice when speaking
- Does not respond when spoken to
- Gives incorrect answers to questions
- Has frequent colds, earaches, or infections
- Appears inattentive and daydreams
- Has difficulty following directions
- Is distracted easily by visual or auditory stimuli
- Misarticulates certain speech sounds or omits certain consonant sounds
- Withdraws from classroom activities that involve listening
- Has a confused expression on face
- Has a restricted vocabulary

As recommended earlier, if one or more of these characteristics is observed, a referral should be considered to confirm or refute a suspected hearing problem. Not doing so could result in a student continuing to struggle with the communicative demands of school.

Related Factors of Educational Significance.   In addition to the type of hearing impairment and the extent of the loss as indicated in Table 7.3, three additional factors contribute significantly to the impact a hearing impairment has on academic performance.

The educational needs of students who develop language before acquiring a profound hearing loss are likely to be very different from the needs of those whose impairment is congenital or who lose their hearing in the first years of life. For the prelingual child, intervention is focused on the acquisition of language and the development of basic communication skills. This process is demanding and takes time.

The background experiences that students bring to a learning situation greatly affect what they get out of corresponding instruction. Many students with hearing impairment have had more restricted interactions with their environments due to their limited hearing abilities. For this reason, teachers need to be aware that these students may not have the same types of backgrounds that their classmates have had and should try to provide as many opportunities as possible to enrich their backgrounds.

A concept used to describe the relationship between a sound stimulus to which a student should attend (signal) and the competing extraneous sounds in the environment (noise) is the signal-to-noise ratio. It is extremely important that classroom situations provide a strong signal-to-noise ratio (i.e., the originating sound is loud and clear, as well as free from other distracting sounds) for students who can use their residual hearing.

Educationally Relevant Characteristics. The observed characteristics of students who have significant hearing loss fall into four categories: psychological, communication, academic, and social-emotional. These areas have been selected because of their meaningfulness to instructional settings. Specific characteristics related to each of these general categories are listed in Table 7.4.

TABLE 7.4   **Possible Characteristics of Students with Hearing Impairments**

Area of Functioning	Possible Effects
Intellectual/cognitive	• Intellectual ability range similar to hearing peers • Problems with certain conceptualizations
Speech/language	• Poor speech production (e.g., unintelligibility) • Tested vocabulary limited • Problems with language usage and comprehension, particularly abstract topics • Voice quality problems
Social/emotional/ behavioral	• Less socially mature • Difficulty making friends • Withdrawn behavior—feelings of being an outsider • Possible maladjustment problems • May resent having to wear a hearing aid or use other amplification devices • May be dependent on teacher assistance
Academic	• Achievement levels significantly below those of their hearing peers • Reading ability is most significantly affected • Spelling problems • Written language production is limited • Discrepancy between capabilities and performance in many academic areas

Educational Accommodations for Hearing-Impaired Students

As has been stressed throughout this chapter, the general education setting can be an appropriate setting for most students who are hard of hearing and for many students who are deaf. However, this statement is only true if the specific needs of these students are taken into consideration.

The following sections provide recommendations for accommodating these students in general education classrooms. A series of specific suggestions are listed at the end of each section. Both general recommendations and specific suggestions are clustered under three major areas: classroom management considerations, instructional accommodations, and social-emotional interventions.

Classroom Management Considerations.   The effective management of a classroom is critical to maximizing the potential for learning. This important topic is covered in detail in Chapter 12. Attention to certain dimensions of classroom management (see Figure 12.1) can facilitate the integration of students with various degrees of hearing impairment into general education settings.

Standard Operating Procedures   This dimension refers to the rules, regulations, and procedures that operate in a classroom. Students who have hearing impairments must be subject to the same requirements as other students. Some procedures may have to be modified due to the special needs of some students. For instance, students may be allowed to leave their seats to get the attention of a student who cannot hear a verbally initiated communication.

Teachers should always confirm that students understand the rules and procedures developed for the classroom. Teachers may also want to establish a buddy system (i.e., a peer support system). With such a system, a student with normal hearing is assigned to assist the student with a hearing impairment. Assistance can be given if there is a fire drill or in helping the student take notes during class sessions that are delivered in a lecture format.

Physical Dimensions   The major consideration related to the physical dimensions of the classroom relates to seating. Teachers need to ensure that students are seated to maximize the use of their residual hearing or to have an unobstructed view of their interpreter. Since information presented visually is extremely helpful to these students, they need to be positioned to take advantage of all visual cues.

Preinstructional Considerations   Teachers must also pay attention to various features that are intricately related to instruction. These include a range of activities about which decisions must be made and action taken prior to the presentation of actual instructional lessons. Specific suggestions related to grouping, lesson planning, materials acquisition and adaptation, and homework systems can be found here and in Chapter 13. Below are some specific suggestions:

- Seat students near the teacher or source of orally presented information.
- Seat students so they can take advantage of their residual hearing, avoid being

distracted either visually or auditorily, and follow different speakers during class discussions.

- ◆ Seat students who use interpreters so that they can easily see their interpreter, the teacher, and any visual aids that are used.
- ◆ Allow students to move about the classroom to position themselves for participation in ongoing events.
- ◆ Let students use swivel chairs.
- ◆ Reduce distracting and competing noise by modifying the classroom environment (e.g., carpeting on walls, corkboard on walls).
- ◆ Ensure that adequate lighting is available.
- ◆ Provide visual reminders indicating the amount of time left for an activity or until the end of class.
- ◆ Use cooperative learning arrangements to facilitate student involvement with hearing peers.
- ◆ Include a section of the lesson plan for special provisions for students with hearing impairments.
- ◆ Acquire and/or develop visually oriented materials to augment orally presented topics—use overhead projection systems when appropriate.
- ◆ Use homework-assignment books to guarantee that students understand their assignments.

Students with hearing loss should be seated near the front of the class, where oral information is presented.

Instructional Accommodations.   All basic elements of effective instructional practice will benefit students with hearing impairment. However, certain specific ideas will enhance their learning experiences.

Communication   Perhaps the most challenging aspect of teaching students whose hearing is affected is making sure that (a) they participate in the communicative activities (i.e., teacher to student, student to teacher, student to student) that are occurring in the classroom and (b) they are able to handle the reading and writing demands of the class.

Students who have profound hearing loss must rely on alternative methods of communication such as sign language or speech reading. Because these students typically become facile with standard forms of English, they can have significant problems in the areas of reading and writing. Sign language does not follow the grammatical conventions of English.

When students using some form of manual communication, usually **American Sign Language (ASL),** are in general education, teachers are not required to learn this language. However, teachers should make an effort to know some of the more common signs and to be able to finger spell the letters of the alphabet as well as the numbers one to ten.

If students can only communicate using sign language, an interpreter will most likely be present. Teachers should know some basic information about the role and functions of interpreter. Table 7.5 provides some general information about interpreters.

Teachers should be conscious of how well they are communicating with their students. The teacher's speech, location, and movement in the classroom can affect the facility with which a student with a hearing impairment can follow a discussion or lecture. The proper use of assistive equipment (e.g., amplification devices) can also make a difference. This topic is covered in a subsequent section.

Delivery of Instruction   This dimension requires that teachers utilize a host of recommended practices that allow students to learn more effectively and efficiently. One suggestion already mentioned, the use of visually oriented material, is especially valuable for students with hearing problems. Below are some specific suggestions:

- Make sure students are attending.
- Provide short, clear instructions.
- Speak clearly and normally—do not exaggerate the pronunciation of words.
- Keep your face visible to students.
- Avoid frequent movement around the classroom, turning your back on students while talking, and standing in front of a bright light source.
- Use gestures and facial expressions.
- Trim beards and moustaches if such facial hair interferes with the visibility of those who speech read.
- Maintain eye contact with the student, not the interpreter when present.
- Check with students to confirm whether they are understanding what is being discussed or presented.

Using Sign Language and Drama with Young Children

- *Use signs along with speech.*
  The combined use of spoken language and sign language is a technique that has proved to be successful with many children, including those who have autism, hearing impairments, or delayed speech development. Teachers can also create gestures for young children if signs are too abstract.

- *Create characters with signs.*
  Hand shapes can be used to represent the main features of a person or animal. In much the same way as people use their hands to make shadow figures of animals, sign language can represent recognizable features such as ears, a nose, or the tail of a pig. Gestures could be used to describe a person's characteristics, like a witch's long nose or fingernails. In dramatic play, students can let their signs and gestures represent costumes and their voices create the characters' personalities.

- *Change signs into puppets.*
  When children let their hands portray more than one character or object, it is possible for them to control movements and voices and to develop sequential stories. For example, if one hand is the bird's nest and the other is the bird, children can portray the bird flying to its nest, sitting on its eggs, talking to babies, or finding food.

- *Use sign language to illustrate concepts.*
  Combining sign language and dramatic activities allows students to see role models of the concepts in action (for example, the teacher portraying an animal or person who has to follow location directions such as *above, below, around,* and *in*). After the teacher has demonstrated the concept in the context of a scene, students can take turns elaborating and creating other situations in which the same concept can be depicted.

Source: Brown, V. (1988). Integrating drama and sign language. *Teaching Exceptional Children, 21* (1), 4–8. Used with permission.

- Encourage students to request clarification and to ask questions.
- Identify other speakers by name so that students can more easily follow a discussion among more than one speaker.
- Repeat the comments of other students who speak.
- Paraphrase or summarize discussions at the end of a class session.
- Write information when necessary.
- Have students take responsibility for making themselves understood.
- Provide students with advanced organizers such as outlines of lectures and copies of overhead transparencies used.

TABLE 7.5 **Interpreters in Education Settings**

General guidelines

- Include the interpreter as a member of the IEP team in terms of the communication needs of the student.
- Request an interpreter (i.e., do not let parents interpret for their children) for certain important situations (e.g., transition planning meetings).
- Supervise the interpreter if this person is involved with additional classroom tasks.
- Meet with the interpreter regularly to discuss the needs of the student and review ongoing communication patterns.
- Evaluate the effectiveness of interpreters.

Specific suggestions

- Allow the interpreter to be positioned so that the student can easily see both the teacher (or media) and the interpreter.
- Prepare the interpreter for the topic(s) that will be covered and the class format that will be followed.
- Provide copies of all visual materials (e.g., overhead transparencies) before class begins.
- Be sensitive to the "time-lag" factor associated with interpreting—the few-word delay that the interpreter lags behind the spoken message, used to ensure the student's understanding of the communication.
- Program breaks in lecturing if at all possible.
- Limit the teacher's movement so that the student can see the interpreter and teacher without difficulty.
- Check student understanding regularly—ensure that the student does not fake understanding.

- ◆ Preview new vocabulary and concepts prior to their presentation during a lecture.
- ◆ Use the demonstration-guided practice-independent practice paradigm as often as possible (see Polloway & Patton, 1993, for a comprehensive discussion of this paradigm).
- ◆ Utilize a variety of instructional formats, including demonstrations, experiments, and other visually oriented activities.
- ◆ Emphasize the main points covered in a lecture both verbally and visually .
- ◆ Use copious amounts of visual aids (e.g., overhead transparencies, slides, diagrams, charts, multimedia) to explain material.
- ◆ Provide summaries, outlines, or scripts of videotapes, videodiscs, or films.
- ◆ Let students use microcomputers to word process and to check their spelling and grammar.

Social-Emotional Interventions.   Classrooms are very complex social systems. In addition to the ongoing development of scholastic abilities and academic support skills, personal development is also occurring. Students need to learn how to get along with their peers and authority figures while they learn how to deal with their beliefs and emotions. Teachers are encouraged to help students develop a realistic sense of their abilities (i.e., strengths and weaknesses), become more responsible and independent, interact appropriately with their peers, and enhance their self-concept and sense of belonging (Ross et al., 1991). Below are some specific suggestions:

- Create a positive, supportive, and nurturing classroom environment.
- Encourage class involvement through active participation in classroom activities and interaction in small groups.
- Let students know that you are available if they are experiencing problems and need to talk.
- Help the students with normal hearing understand the nature of hearing impairment and what they can do to assist.
- Practice appropriate interactive skills.
- Encourage and assist students to get involved in extracurricular participation.
- Develop problem-solving abilities.
- Help students develop realistic expectations.
- Prepare students for dealing with the demands of life and adulthood.

Specialized Equipment

Students with hearing impairments placed in general education classrooms often use various types of devices to help them to maximize their communicative abilities. It is important for teachers to have a working knowledge of these systems so that they can ensure that the student is benefitting from the equipment.

The two systems described in this section are assistive listening devices—hearing aids and FM systems. **Cochlear implants,** prosthetic devices, are designed to replace defective cochlear structures. This technology is discussed elsewhere in this chapter.

Hearing Aids. Hearing aids are battery-powered electronic devices that act as amplifiers. Shimon (1992) describes how they work:

> A hearing aid is a small device that picks up sound with a microphone, amplifies and filters it, and then conveys that sound into your ear canal through a loudspeaker, also called a receiver. The amplifiers in the hearing aid make sound louder. The filters selectively choose which pitches in the incoming sound will be emphasized. (p. 96)

It should be noted that, although there are some differences in the hearing aids available on the market, they generally work in the manner just described.

Types of Hearing Aids Four types of hearing aids typically are used today: the in-the-ear (ITE) type (which is the most commonly used), the in-the-canal (ITC) type, the behind-the-ear (BTE) type, and the eyeglass type (Shimon, 1992).

Features Certain features that are common to all hearing aids are a microphone, volume controls, and batteries/battery compartments. Other features such as user-operated switches (e.g., on/off switches) and earmolds are found on some devices.

Digitally controlled hearing aids are now available. A key feature of such devices is that certain performance characteristics can be programmed into digital memory by hearing aid dispensers. This is attractive because it is possible to attain more accurate settings for individual users.

To assist students in maximizing the use of their hearing aids, teachers should

◆ Know what type of hearing aid a student uses
◆ Understand how the device works: on/off switch, battery function (e.g., selection, lifespan, insertion), volume controls
◆ Be able to determine whether a hearing aid is working properly
◆ Help students keep their hearing aids functioning properly (e.g., daily cleaning, appropriate storage)
◆ Make sure students avoid getting their aids wet, dropping/jarring them, spraying hairspray on them, and exposing them to extreme heat (Shimon, 1992)
◆ Keep spare batteries on hand

FM Systems. This type of system is useful with individuals who use auditory systems for acquiring information. An FM system works in the following way:

> An FM (frequency modulated) system is a wireless amplification system in which a speech signal is transmitted from a microphone via FM radio signals to an FM receiver. The microphone is worn by the teacher . . . and the receiver is worn by the student. (Madell, 1990)

Components Although there are a number of different FM systems on the market, they all have three major components: transmitter, receiver, and coupling system. The transmitter or microphone picks up the speech signal and sends it to a monaural or binaural receiver. The coupling device transmits the signal from the FM receiver to the child's ear or hearing aid.

For these systems to be effective, teachers should

◆ Ensure that the system is functioning properly
◆ Be sure that they turn the transmitter off when not engaged in instructional activities
◆ Perform daily troubleshooting of all components of the system (Brackett, 1990)
◆ Make sure background noises are minimized

The information discussed in this section on hearing impairment should provide teachers with a beginning understanding of how to meet the needs of students with hearing loss who are placed in general education classes. We strongly recommend that teachers consult with a hearing specialist to determine the best possible accommodations that provide an appropriate educational environment for students with hearing problems.

Visual Impairment

Students with visual impairment also pose unique challenges to teachers in general education. Although there are not large numbers of students whose vision creates learning-related problems (see Table 7.1), having one such student in a classroom may require a host of accommodations.

Vision plays a critical role in the development of concepts, the understanding of spatial relations, and using printed material. Therefore, these areas are significantly affected when a vision problem exists. Teachers can use standard instructional practices

Cochlear Implants

A cochlear implant consists of a set of electronic devices, some parts of which are surgically placed in the ear to assist individuals with profound sensorineural hearing loss. In essence, sound is converted into electrical impulses that are transmitted directly to the auditory nerve by virtue of this technology. Even though very few students have implants, their use is increasing.

A few points should be noted regarding cochlear implants. First, only certain students with profound hearing loss are candidates for this technology. Second, normal hearing is not restored by this surgical procedure, although various sound sensations are enhanced and interpreted by the brain.

A student with an implant is likely to experience major difficulties in hearing within a general education classroom. Teachers should

- Minimize noise levels in the classroom
- Arrange seating so that the student is close to the teacher or speaker and the implanted side of the head faces the sound source
- Know how to connect an FM system into the speech processor of the implant
- Understand the different features of the speech processor unit (e.g., on/off switch, sensitivity controls, battery level)
- Secure the speech processor on the student and keep cords from getting exposed
- Keep unit from getting wet
- Minimize the chances that a student may receive some type of head injury.

with some modifications with students who have some usable vision. With students who have very little or no vision available, teachers will need to implement alternative techniques to provide effective educational programs.

General education classes are appropriate settings for many students with visual impairments. However, teachers who will be working with these students need to understand the nature of a particular student's vision problem and to be able to utilize appropriate accommodative tactics. To accomplish this, teachers need to know the basic information related to four categories suggested in the previous section on hearing impairment: (a) fundamental concepts of vision and visual impairment, (b) signs of possible visual problems, (c) typical characteristics of students with visual problems, and (d) specific accommodative techniques for meeting student needs.

Basic Concepts

This section will define the terminology used to describe vision and visual problems, identify different types of vision problems, discuss how vision is assessed, and highlight the major educationally relevant characteristics associated with vision problems.

Terminology. As was the case with hearing impairment, a number of different terms are associated with this concept. A certain amount of confusion also exists regarding the exact meaning of visual terminology. The most frequently used terms, with accompanying definitions, that general education teachers will encounter are

- *Visual impairment,* a generic term that includes a wide range of individuals who display visual problems.
- *Blindness,* a term that has different meanings depending upon context, resulting in some professional confusion. Legal blindness refers to a person's visual acuity and field of vision. It is defined as a visual acuity of 20/200 or less in the person's better eye after correction, or a field of vision of 20° or less.

   An educational definition of blindness implies that a student must use braille (a system of raised dots that the student reads tactilely) or aural methods (Hallahan & Kauffman, 1991).
- *Low vision,* a term that implies that the individual possesses some functional vision that can be used for gaining information through written means with or without the assistance of optical, nonoptical, or electronic devices.

Students with low vision are very capable of handling the demands of most classroom settings. However, they will need some modifications to perform successfully. Students who are blind (i.e., have very little or no available vision) will need major accommodations to be successful in general education settings.

Types of Vision Problems. Visual problems can be categorized in a number of ways. One such system is depicted in Table 7.6. Specific visual problems and accompanying descriptions of them are provided. The most common type of vision problem found in students involves problems in refraction (e.g., myopia, hyperopia, astigmatism). Less severe cases are addressed through the use of corrective glasses or lenses. The major problem that teachers face in this situation is getting students to wear their glasses at the appropriate times. Other conditions highlighted in Table 7.6 represent visual problems with much more significant implications for the classroom.

A very important factor related to the type of visual problem a student displays is the time at which the problem developed. Critical differences exist between students who are born with a significant vision loss (congenital) and those who acquire an impairment later in life (adventitious). Heward and Orlansky (1992) describe this distinction.

> A child who has been blind since birth naturally has quite a different perception of the world than does a child who lost her vision at age 12. The first child has a background of learning through hearing, touch, and the other nonvisual senses, whereas the second child has a background of visual experiences on which to draw. (p. 335)

Children who are born with vision but lose it within the early developmental years will not benefit from their visual experiences and will function much like those children who are congenitally blind.

Formal Assessment. Students are screened for vision problems in schools, and, when problems are suspected, a more in-depth evaluation is conducted. The typical eye

TABLE 7.6 **Types of Visual Impairments**

Type	Definition
Disorders of the eye	
Myopia	Nearsightedness; condition allows focus on objects close but not at a distance.
Hyperopia	Farsightedness; condition allows focus on objects at a distance but not close.
Astigmatism	An eye disorder that produces images on the retina that are not equally in focus.
Disorders of the eye muscles	
Strabismus	Improper alignment of the two eyes causes two images being received by the brain, with the possible result of one eye becoming nonfunctional.
Nystagmus	Rapid, involuntary movements of the eye that interfere with bringing objects into focus.
Disorders of the cornea, iris, and lens	
Glaucoma	Fluid in the eye is restricted, causing pressure to build up and damage the retina.
Aniridia	Undeveloped iris, due to lack of pigment (albinism), results in extreme sensitivity to light.
Cataract	A cloudy film over the lens of the eye.
Disorders of the retina	
Diabetic retinopathy	Changes in the eye's blood vessels are caused by diabetes.
Macular degeneration	Damage to a small area near the center of the retina results in restricted fine central vision and difficulties in reading and writing.
Retinopathy of prematurity (ROP)	Excess oxygen to infants causes retinal damage; was called retrolental fibroplasia.
Retinal detachment	Detachment of the retina interrupts transmission of visual information to the brain.
Retinitis pigmentosa	Genetic eye disease leads progressively to blindness; night blindness is the first symptom.
Retinoblastoma	Tumor.
Optic nerve	
Atrophy	Reduced function of the optic nerve.

Source: Smith, D. D., & Luckasson, R. (1992). *Introduction to special education: Teaching in an age of challenge.* Boston: Allyn & Bacon. Used with permission.

examination is conducted to assess two basic dimensions: visual acuity and field of vision. Visual acuity is most often evaluated by the use of a **Snellen chart.** As Smith and Luckasson (1992) note, two versions of this chart are available: the traditional version using alphabetic letters of different sizes, and the other version using the letter "E" presented in different spatial arrangements and sizes.

Three different types of professionals may be involved directly or indirectly in varying aspects of the assessment process. A brief description of these specialists is provided below:

- **Ophthalmologist**—medical doctor specializing in eye disorders
- **Optometrist**—professional who evaluates vision and can prescribe corrective lenses
- **Optician**—person who makes corrective lenses

Indicators of Possible Visual Problems   It is important for teachers to be able to recognize potential vision problems in students who may have no history of such problems. A list of potential signs that, if noticed, should alert teachers to a possible vision problem is provided in Figure 7.1. If a teacher notices one or more of these characteristics, it may be appropriate to initiate a referral to determine whether a visual problem is present.

Characteristics.   The most educationally relevant characteristic of students who have visual impairments is the extent of their visual efficiency. However, visual impairment can affect other areas as well. Four areas of educational importance are the psycho-

Behavior

- Rubs eyes excessively
- Shuts or covers one eye, tilts head, or thrusts head forward
- Has difficulty in reading or in other work requiring close use of the eyes
- Blinks more than usual or is irritable when doing close work
- Holds books close to eyes
- Is unable to see distant things clearly
- Squints eyelids together or frowns

Appearance

- Crossed eyes
- Red-rimmed, encrusted, or swollen eyelids
- Inflamed or watery eyes
- Recurring styes

Complaints

- Eyes itch, burn, or feel scratchy
- Cannot see well
- Dizziness, headaches, or nausea following close eye work
- Blurred or double vision

Figure 7.1   **Symptoms of Possible Vision Problems**
Source: Hallahan, D. P., & Kauffman, J. M. (1991). *Exceptional children: Introduction to special education* (5th ed.). Boston: Allyn & Bacon. Used with permission.

logical, communication, academic, and social-emotional domains. Select characteristics related to these areas are listed in Table 7.7.

Educational Accommodations for Visually Impaired Students

As is the case for many students with special needs who receive their education in general classrooms, certain accommodations will enhance the quality of the programs for students with visual problems. This section recommends ways to address the needs of these students. As in the section on hearing impairment, a list of specific suggestions is offered at the end of each subsection. The following recommendations are organized according to four categories: general considerations, classroom management considerations, instructional accommodations, and social-emotional interventions.

General Considerations. The most important recommendation that can be given is for teachers to find out as much as possible about a student with a visual impairment from parents, former teachers, or vision specialists. By doing so, the teacher can expedite the acquisition of important information.

Similar to the need to learn about the equipment and techniques used by students who are hearing impaired, teachers should understand the technology and practices of these students. If a student is using a brailler or compressed speech tape player, the teacher should learn how these work.

TABLE 7.7 Possible Characteristics of Students with Visual Impairments

Area of Functioning	Possible Effects
Intellectual/cognitive	• Intellectual abilities similar to those of sighted peers • Concept development can depend on tactile experiences (i.e., synthetic and analytic touch) • Unable to use sight to assist in the development of integrated concepts • Unable to use visual imagery
Speech/language	• Relatively unimpaired in language abilities (blind)
Social/emotional/behavioral	• May display repetitive, stereotyped movements (e.g., rocking or rubbing eyes) • Socially immature • Withdrawn • Dependent • Unable to use nonverbal cues
Mobility	• Distinct disadvantage in using spatial information • Visual imagery and memory problems have functional implications
Academic	• Generally behind sighted peers

What to Do If You Meet a Person with a Visual Impairment

1. Identify yourself.
2. Ask the person if any assistance is needed.
3. Let the person with a visual impairment take your arm if a sighted guide is desired.
4. Place the person's hand on the back of a chair if the person wants to sit down.
5. Read the menu to a person with a visual impairment if the person does not have enough vision to read the print.
6. Orient the person's plate using a clock system (top of plate is 12 o'clock).
7. Always announce you are leaving a room when departing.
8. Never rearrange a room without reorienting the person with a visual impairment.
9. Never play with a dog guide when the dog is in harness and is "working."
10. Use terms such as "see"; watch"; and "look" with persons with visual impairments just as you would with sighted individuals.

Below are some specific accommodation suggestions:

- ◆ Ask whether a student needs assistance, if the student seems to be disoriented.
- ◆ Use words and terms that relate to sight such as "see you later"—students with visual impairments are not offended by such usage.
- ◆ Ensure that the student with a visual impairment understands the nature of her or his visual problem.
- ◆ Include students with visual impairments in all activities that occur in the class.

If students are to be socially accepted in general education classes, it will be necessary to teach the nondisabled classmates about visual impairment. Sensitizing students to the nature of visual impairment requires creating an environment where students can ask questions about the condition and answers can be given.

Classroom Management Considerations. A variety of classroom management tactics can be helpful to students who have vision problems. Classroom management is a multifaceted concept that includes a number of components that apply to all students, as discussed in Chapter 12. However, when students with vision problems are present, special attention needs to be given to three of the dimensions.

Standard Operating Procedures The same set of standards of expected behavior should be applied to students who have visual problems. However, certain procedures related to movement within the classroom may need to be modified. For instance, students with visual limitations may need freedom of movement to achieve visual advantage to maximize their involvement in ongoing activities or understanding of what is being discussed.

Physical Dimensions   Attention to selected aspects of the physical characteristics of the classroom is essential for safety and instructional reasons. Students with visual problems need to know the physical layout of the classroom so that they can navigate through it without harming themselves.

Seating is extremely important for students who are able to use their existing vision. Factors such as placement of the student's desk, lighting, glare, and distractions can contribute to the accommodative dimensions of a classroom.

Preinstructional Considerations   Adaptation of certain teaching-related events that should be made prior to actual instruction are often needed. Teachers will need to adapt class session schedules to allow extra time for students who use large-print or braille materials, as it takes longer for students to use these materials.

It may also be necessary to consider adaptations to test taking procedures. This might involve preparing an enlarged version of the test, allowing extra time to take the test, or arranging for someone to read the test to the student.

Some students may need special instruction in select study skills areas such as note taking, organizational skills, time management, and keyboarding. These become increasingly important as students move up to middle and high school.

Below are some specific accommodation suggestions:

- Assign a classmate to assist students who may need help with mobility in emergency situations.
- Teach students in the class the proper techniques of being a sighted guide.
- Contact staff members of upcoming field-trip sites to inform them that a student with a visual problem will be part of the visiting group.
- Inform students with visual problems when entering or leaving a room so that they are aware of your presence or absence.
- Practice movement patterns that are expected of all students.
- Orient students to the physical layout and other distinguishing features of the classroom.
- Maintain consistency in the placement of furniture, equipment, and instructional materials—remove all dangerous obstacles.
- Keep doors to cabinets, carts, and closets closed.
- Assist students in getting into unfamiliar desks, chairs, or other furniture.
- Eliminate all auditory distractions that may be present.
- Seat students to maximize their usable vision and listening skills—often a position in the front and center part of the room is advantageous.
- Seat students so that they are not looking into a source of light or bothered by glare from reflected surfaces.
- Ensure that proper lighting is available.

- ◆ Create extra space for students who may be using a piece of equipment (e.g., brailler, notebook computer) that will require extra space.
- ◆ Include a section of the lesson plan for special notes for accommodating students with visual problems in the lesson.

Instructional Accommodations

Teacher-Related Activities   As teachers are the principal agents in delivering effective instruction, they should be aware of certain techniques that will ensure success with students who have visual problems. A primary consideration is how to convey visually laden material to those who cannot use this material.

It is essential that teachers find ways to convey all visual material when students' vision does not allow them to engage this material. This will require some forethought and advanced planning to identify graphic material needing elaboration. As an example, a graphic depiction of the circulatory system in a life science book will necessitate that the teacher find alternative ways to convey the information being displayed in a two-dimensional illustration. Three-dimensional models or illustrations whose features have been raised to highlight important points might be employed to address this need.

Materials and Equipment   Using special materials and equipment is highly appropriate and necessary with students who have visual impairments. Some materials that seemingly are good ideas for certain students (e.g., large-print materials) must be considered in light of the individual needs of students. With this in mind, teachers are reminded to consult with vision specialists in selecting appropriate types of materials and equipment.

Many materials that are found in general education classrooms may pose problems for students who have problems with their vision. For instance, low-contrast materials and books that are printed on glossy paper can be very difficult for some students to use.

Although large-print materials seem like a good idea, they may be used inappropriately. Barraga and Erin (1992) recommend that these materials be used only as a last resort. They believe that large-print materials should be utilized only after other techniques (e.g., optical devices or reduction of the reading distance) have been tried.

Teachers also may want to use concrete materials (i.e., realia—realistic representations of actual items). However, it is important to note that concrete representations of large real-life objects may not be helpful with young students who are not able to understand the abstraction being presented.

Various optical, nonoptical, and electronic devices are also available for classroom use. These devices help students by enlarging existing printed images. If these types of devices are recommended for certain students, teachers will need to learn about them to ensure that they are used properly and to recognize when there is a problem. Teachers should practice the use of various optical and electronic devices with students after consultation with a vision specialist.

Some students with more severe visual limitations may use braille (a system of

Enhancing Inclusion of Students with Visual Impairments

◆ *Find out about who is available to help you.(Also, learn what their titles mean and what they do.)*
One very important person who typically works with students with visual impairments is the *itinerant teacher*. Itinerant teachers move from school to school working with individual students, and usually translate students' classwork into braille. Students may also receive training from an *orientation and mobility instructor*, who will teach them to move independently.

◆ *Learn how to adapt and modify materials and instruction. (The changes you make might also help other students.)*
Teachers face a wide variety of students with diverse abilities, styles of learning, and cultural and linguistic systems, as well as disparate economic situations, family structures, and value systems. The good news about the variety in the classroom is that teachers' efforts at individualizing instruction and materials for students with the greatest difference may result in adaptations that will benefit all students.

◆ *Learn as much as you can, and encourage the professionals you work with to do the same.*
One of the key ingredients for successful inclusion of students with disabilities is adequate education and support of the professionals who work with students who have disabilities.

◆ *Find out about training that may be available and ask to go.*
Often inservice training will be provided by your local school district, a regional service center or co-op, a nearby university, or a regional or national conference. Get your name on the mailing list of organizations whose focus is on visual impairments.

◆ *Suggest that others become informed, especially students,* who may have access to programs like the "Kids on the Block" puppet shows that teach about disabilities. Use your local library and bookstores to find print material that you can read and share.

◆ *Call parents and ask questions when you don't understand* terminology, equipment, or the reasons for prescribed practices. Then, keep an open mind.

◆ *Teach other students to assist in social as well as academic settings.*
Most young children are able and willing to help students with disabilities as they adjust to their new situation in a general classroom. Students can offer assistance at lunch, on the playground, and in fine arts classes, where there is less structure and routine.

Source: Viadero, D. (1989, November). Side by side. *Teacher Magazine Reader* (pp. 1–5). New York: Allyn & Bacon. Used with permission.

raised dots that represent letters, numbers, and contractions) as their primary means of dealing with written material. They may use instructional materials that are printed in braille and may also take notes using it. It is now possible through the use of computers for a student to write in braille and to have it converted to standard print. The reverse process is available as well. If a student uses this system of communication, the teacher should consult with a vision specialist to understand how it works.

Below are some specific accommodation suggestions:

- Call students by name and speak directly to them.
- Take breaks at regular intervals to minimize fatigue in listening or using a brailler or optic device.
- Ensure that students are seated properly so that they can see you if vision is available and hear you clearly.
- Vary the type of instruction used and include lessons that incorporate hands-on activities, cooperative learning, or the use of real-life materials.
- Use high-contrast materials whether this be on paper or on the chalkboard— dry erase boards may be preferable.
- Avoid using materials with glossy surfaces or any type of dittoed material.
- Use large-print materials only after other methods have been attempted and proven unsuccessful.
- Use various types of environmental connectors (e.g., ropes or railing) and other adaptations with students with visual problems when participating in physical education or recreational activities (Barraga & Erin, 1992).
- Avoid using written materials that are too crowded.

Social-Emotional Interventions   Although the literature is mixed on whether students with visual impairments are less well-adjusted than their sighted peers (Hallahan & Kauffman, 1991), many students with visual problems will benefit from attention to their social and emotional development. Social skill instruction may be particularly useful for these students. However, because we learn most of our social skills through observing others and imitating their behaviors, it is more difficult to teach these skills to students who are not able to see.

Concern about emotional development is warranted for all students, including those with visual problems. Teachers should make sure that students know that they are available to talk about a student's concerns. A system can be developed whereby a student who has a visual impairment can signal the need to chat with the teacher. Being accessible and letting students know that someone is concerned about their social-emotional needs is extremely important.

Below are some specific accommodation suggestions:

- Encourage students with visual problems to become independent learners and able to manage their own behaviors.
- Create opportunities for students to manipulate their own environment (Mangold & Roessing, 1982).
- Reinforce students for their efforts.

◆ Help students develop a healthy self-concept.
◆ Provide special instruction to help students acquire social skills needed to perform appropriately in classroom and social situations.
◆ Teach students how to communicate nonverbally (i.e., use of hands, etc.).
◆ Work with students to eliminate inappropriate mannerisms that some students with visual impairments display.

Summary

◆ Many students with sensory deficits are educated in general education classrooms.

◆ In order for students with sensory impairments to receive an appropriate education, various accommodations must be made.

◆ Students with hearing and visual problems represent a very heterogeneous group.

◆ Most students with hearing problems have some residual hearing ability.

◆ The description *hearing impairment* includes individuals with deafness and those who are hard of hearing.

◆ The extent of a hearing loss on a student's ability to understand speech is a primary concern of teachers.

◆ An audiogram graphically represents the results of an audiometric evaluation.

◆ Several factors should cue teachers in on a possible hearing loss in a particular student.

◆ Teachers in general education classrooms must implement a variety of accommodations for students with hearing impairments.

◆ The location where students with hearing losses are seated is critical for these students.

◆ The most challenging aspect of teaching students with hearing problems is making sure that they participate in the communicative activities that are occurring in the classroom.

◆ Specialized equipment, such as hearing aids and cochlear implants, may be necessary to ensure the success of students with hearing losses.

◆ Vision plays a critical role in the development of concepts such as understanding the spatial relations of the environment.

◆ Teachers must use a variety of accommodations for students with visual disabilities.

◆ Most students with visual disabilities have some residual or low vision.

◆ Refractive errors are the most common form of visual disability.

◆ Visual problems may be congenital, present at birth, or occur later in life.

◆ Ophthalmologists are medical doctors who specialize in visual problems.

◆ The most educationally relevant characteristic of students who have visual impairments is the extent of their visual efficiency.

◆ It is critical that students with visual impairments be socially accepted in their general education classrooms.

◆ Tests may need to be adapted when evaluating students with visual disabilities.

◆ Specialized materials may need to be used when working with students with visual problems.

◆ Using large-print and non-glare materials may be sufficient accommodation for many students with visual disabilities.

◆ A very small number of students require instruction in braille.

◆ Specialists to teach braille and develop braille materials may be needed in order to successfully integrate students with visual disabilities in general education classrooms.

References

Barraga, N. C., & Erin, J. N. (1992). *Visual handicaps & learning* (3rd ed.). Austin, TX: Pro-Ed.

Bess, R. H. (1988). *Hearing impairment in children*. Parkton, MD: York Press.

Brackett, D. (1990). Communication management of the mainstreamed hearing-impaired student. In M. Ross (Ed.), *Hearing-impaired children in the mainstream* (pp. 119–130). Parkton, MD: York Press.

Brown, V. (1988). Integrating drama and sign language. *Teaching Exceptional Children, 21,* 4–8.

Cochlear Corporation. (1992). *Issues and answers.* Englewood, CO: Author.

Hallahan, D. P., & Kauffman, J. M. (1991). *Exceptional children: Introduction to special education* (5th ed.). Boston: Allyn & Bacon.

Hardman, M. L., Drew, C. J., Egan, M. W., & Wolf, B. (1993). *Human exceptionality: Society, school, and family* (4th ed.). Boston: Allyn & Bacon.

Hegde, M. N. (1991). *Introduction to communicative disorders.* Austin, TX: Pro-Ed.

Heward, W. L., & Orlansky, M. D. (1992). *Exceptional children: An introductory survey of special education.* New York: Macmillan.

Madell, J. R. (1990). Managing classroom amplification. In M. Ross (Ed.), *Hearing-impaired children in the mainstream* (pp. 95–118). Parkton, MD: York Press.

Mangold, S. S., & Roessing, L. J. (1982). Instructional needs of students with low vision. In S. S. Mangold (Ed.), *A teacher's guide to the special educational needs of blind and visually handicapped children.* New York: American Foundation for the Blind.

Martin, F. N. (Ed.). (1987). *Hearing disorders in children: Pediatric audiology* (pp. 210–229). Boston: Allyn & Bacon.

Maxon, A. B. (1990). Implementing an in-service training program. In M. Ross (Ed.), *Hearing-impaired children in the mainstream* (pp. 257–274). Parkton, MD: York Press.

Maxon, A. B., & Brackett, D. (1987). The hearing-impaired child in regular schools. *Seminars in Speech and Language, 8,* 393–413.

Oyer, H. J., Crowe, B., & Haas, W. H. (1987). *Speech, language, & hearing disorders: A guide for the teacher*. Boston: Allyn & Bacon.

Perkins, W. H., & Kent, R. D. (1986). *Functional anatomy of speech, language, and hearing: A primer*. Boston: Allyn & Bacon.

Polloway, E. A., & Patton, J. R. (1993). *Strategies for teaching learners with special needs*. Columbus, OH: Merrill.

Ross, M., Brackett, D., & Maxon, A. B. (1991). *Assessment and management of mainstreamed hearing-impaired children: Principles and practices*. Austin, TX: Pro-Ed.

Schneiderman, C. R. (1984). *Basic anatomy and physiology in speech and hearing*. Boston: Allyn & Bacon.

Shimon, D. A. (1992). *Coping with hearing loss and hearing aids*. San Diego: Singular Publishing.

Smith, D. D., & Luckasson, R. (1992). *Introduction to special education: Teaching in an age of challenge*. Boston: Allyn & Bacon.

U.S. Department of Education. (1993). *15th annual report to Congress on the implementation of the Individuals with Disabilities Education Act*. Washington, DC: Office of Special Education Programs, Department of Education.

Viadero, D. (1989, November). Side by side. *Teacher Magazine Reader* (pp. 1–5). New York: Allyn & Bacon.

CHAPTER 8

Teaching Students with Physical Disabilities or Health Conditions

Case Study: Charles

The following is an excerpt of the Tucker and Colson (1992) case study involving traumatic brain injury (TBI):

> Charles is a sixth grader who wants to play football, wrestle, and waterski. He can't. His doctor preempted contact sports because he might reinjure his head. He was in a coma for 2 months last year after a car hit him.
>
> Charles is luckier than many who have similar injuries. He's back in school in his regular class. His seizures have stopped, and he's off medication to control them. His blurred vision is returning to normal. He still gets angry with peers who ask about his accident. He doesn't remember it, and he doesn't want them to mention it. What's the best way to turn Charles's friends into his allies as he continues recovery from his serious head injury?...
>
> ...Charles look[s] the same as he did before [his] accident, but [he] ha[s] more difficulty concentrating and focusing [his] attention now. It's hard for [him] to remember how to do things [he] knew well before [his] accident. [He is] finding it difficult to learn new skills, too. It's hard to organize stimuli and information, and [he] can't think of alternative solutions to a problem. [He is] easily frustrated, tire[s] easily, and [is] often irritable. ...Charles's exaggeration and overestimation of his abilities infuriates his classmates. [He] know[s] something is wrong, but [he doesn't] associate it with [his] head injury. [His] friends don't understand. Charles's friends tease him, and say they think he's retarded. ...
>
> ...Charles [is] not technically learning disabled, but [his] behavior seems similar. ...Charles was an average student who loved sports, especially football. [He] would have been considered learning disabled prior to [his] accident.
>
> ...[Charles] and other students with TBI can be most effectively served in schools if their complex needs are recognized and understood. Careful examination of the student's strengths and weaknesses can then be matched with services the school can provide. Realistic goals can be determined. It's important to maintain frequent, ongoing communication among school staff to monitor the student's performance and changing needs.
>
> The benefits of enlightened intervention will be measured by students' ability to accept realistic expectations for themselves and to function despite difficulties....

Foundational Information

This chapter addresses the needs of students with physical or health conditions who receive their education in general education settings. The goal, just like that of the preceding chapter, is to provide teachers with basic information about select conditions and offer specific recommendations for working effectively with these students.

Given that students with physical conditions are capable of handling the academic and social demands of general education classrooms, they are likely to be placed in these settings. Teachers need to have an accurate understanding of the various conditions that students have as well as a sensitivity to their psychosocial needs.

Physical and health impairments are also low-incidence conditions. That is, there are not large numbers of these students in the school population. The number of students (ages 6 to 21) with physical and health disabilities and provided with special education and/or related services for the school year 1991–1992 is reported in Table 8.1. It should be noted that, although the number of students formally identified is low, the actual number of students with various types of physical or health problems in school is higher. Other students are served under Section 504 mandates, or their conditions are not serious enough to warrant special services. However, they still require certain accommodative actions to address their educational needs.

As discussed in the previous chapter, three variables regarding impairment (severity, visibility, and age at acquisition) can have a major effect on a person's development and behavior. These factors are important to understand because they can help teachers better recognize student needs.

Just like students with other disabling conditions, those with physical or health impairments display a vast array of characteristics and presenting problems. This means that their presence in general education classrooms creates challenges to the teacher in terms of addressing their specific needs. For this reason, we feel it is important to restate the general suggestions offered in the previous chapter, as they apply equally to students with physical or health conditions.

- Create learning environments that are supportive and nurturing, yet challenging and directed at developing independence.
- Strive to make students feel good about themselves and the work they are doing.
- Focus on student strengths, as these can often be overlooked in students who have pronounced disabilities.
- Create a classroom environment where students with special needs are socially accepted and recognized as contributing members of the class.
- Be available to students when they need to talk—you are likely to be one of the most important people in the lives of these students.
- Be sensitive to the needs of families—a child who has a physical or health condition is stressful on parents and siblings.

Basic Concepts

Physical and health impairments represent a wide range of mostly chronic conditions that significantly affect the lives of people. Although there are many different types of

TABLE 8.1 **Students Age 6 to 21 Served Under IDEA, Part B: 1991–1992**

Disability Area	Number of Students	Percentage of Total Number of Students Identified as Disabled
Orthopedic impairments	46,222	1.1
Other health impairments	56,401	1.3

Source: U.S. Department of Education (1993). *15th Annual Report to Congress on the Implementation of IDEA.* Washington, DC: Office of Special Education Programs, Department of Education.

conditions that students may have, some are more frequently found in classrooms. As Heward and Orlansky (1992) note, "it is important for teachers . . . to understand how a particular condition may affect a child's learning, development, and behavior" (p. 376).

Nature of Physical and Health Impairments

As can be seen in Table 8.1, given the total number of students in school, the number of students with these conditions receiving some form of special education is not large. As noted earlier, some students who have various types of physical or health problems are not accounted for in these figures.

Different terminology is used to describe individuals with physical or health problems. The terms used in the Individuals with Disabilities Education Act are "orthopedically impaired" and "other health impaired" but other terms are used regularly in various states and provinces. The two terms used in this chapter, physical disability and health impairment, can be defined as follows:

- *Physical disability* refers to a condition that affects the structure or functioning of an individual's body;
- *Health impairment* refers to a condition in which the body's physical well-being is affected, requiring some form of ongoing medical attention (Smith & Luckasson, 1992).

Many different systems have been offered for categorizing physical and health impairments, all of which are based on arbitrarily selected distinctions. The taxonomy used in this chapter, as shown in Table 8.2, is organized into the following six categorical groupings of conditions: **neurological impairments, musculoskeletal disorders, chronic health conditions,** congenital disorders/malformations, accidents/trauma, and temporary conditions. The table is not an exhaustive listing of all possible conditions, but it does include representative examples of conditions associated with each category.

Educational Significance of Physical and Health Impairments

Teachers need to be aware that physical and health conditions can affect students' educations in a number of ways. First, students may miss a significant amount of school due to illness or hospitalizations. Second, it is possible that those students who have had an impairment for a substantial period of time will have limited experiential backgrounds due to restricted exposure to everyday events. Third, students who have more recently acquired an impairment will have to adjust to their new circumstances—a process that requires time. Fourth, certain physical or health conditions can have debilitating effects on learning. For instance, a traumatic brain injury often affects a student's cognitive abilities. Fifth, students may need help in improving their self-esteem due to negative feelings that result from their disability. Finally, various adaptive techniques and equipment may be needed to address the specific needs of these students.

TABLE 8.2 **Taxonomy of Physical Health Conditions**

Category	Specific Condition
Neurological impairments	Attention deficit disorder
	Cerebral palsy
	Multiple sclerosis
	Spina bifida
	Spinal cord injury
Musculoskeletal disorders	Juvenile rheumatoid arthritis
	Limb deficiency
	Muscular dystrophy
	Osteogensis imperfecta
	Scoliosis
Chronic health conditions	Allergies/asthma
	Cancer
	Cystic fibrosis
	Diabetes
	Headaches
	Hemophilia
	Hepatitis
	HIV/AIDS
	Kidney diseases
	Rheumatic fever
	Seizure disorders
	Sickle cell anemia
	Substance abuse
	Venereal diseases
Congenital disorders/malformations	Cleft lip/palate
	Congenital heart disease
	Cranial-facial abnormalities
	Cytomegalovirus (CMV)
	Drug exposure
	Fetal alcohol syndrome
	Hip dislocation
Accidents—trauma	Burns
	Child abuse
	Traumatic brain injury
Temporary conditions	Infectious diseases
	Limb injuries

Selected Physical and Health Impairments

The conditions selected, which are presented alphabetically, represent ones that teachers are more likely to encounter in their classrooms sometime during their teaching careers.

Asthma

Asthma is a relatively common condition affecting approximately three million children and youth under the age of 15 (American Academy of Allergy & Immunology, 1991). It is characterized by repetitive episodes of coughing, shortness of breath, and wheezing. The wheezing is caused by narrowing of the small air passages, which results from irritation of the bronchial mucous membranes. This irritation can be caused by allergic (pollen, molds, animal dander) or nonallergic (viral infections, air pollutants) triggers. All asthma attacks should be taken seriously, as they can be life-threatening for some children.

Medications are used to prevent attacks and to treat them when they occur. It is extremely important that teachers ensure that students take prescribed medication when scheduled without making a major event out of this activity. As with all medications, certain side effects should be expected. Some of the more common side effects include headaches, hand tremors, stomachaches, lethargy, and reduced ability to concentrate. Teachers should be able to recognize these side effects and understand how they may affect a student's performance and in-class behavior.

The list of potential **allergens** is extensive. Some potential classroom substances that may cause allergic reactions are: chalk dust, animal dander, fur, molds, pollens from plants, soap, clay, certain types of dyes contained in paint, various types of chemicals, and certain foods (e.g., chocolate). Knowledge of what a student is allergic to allows teachers to take appropriate preventive action.

Children with asthma need medication to prevent and treat asthma attacks.

Certain environmental and instructional adaptations may be necessary for students who have asthma. For example, carpets may need to be removed from the classroom, animals may not be appropriate, and dry eraser boards may need to be used in place of chalkboards. Moreover, forethought must be given to materials to be used in various science or art activities.

Some specific suggestions involving children who have asthma are as follows:

◆ Know the signs and symptoms of respiratory distress.
◆ Ensure that students have proper medications and that they are taken at the appropriate times.
◆ Allow students to rest when needed, as they are prone to tire more easily.
◆ Eliminate any known allergens found in the classroom.
◆ Determine what types of physical limitations might have to be invoked (e.g., restriction of certain physical activity, as such activity can induce attacks), but otherwise encourage students to play games and participate in activities.
◆ Recognize the side effects of prescribed medication.
◆ Remain calm if an attack occurs.
◆ Allow the student to participate in nonstressful activity until an episode subsides.
◆ Introduce a vaporizer or dehumidifier to the classroom when recommended by the student's physician.
◆ Work on the student's self-image.
◆ Sensitize other students in the class to the nature of allergic reactions.
◆ Develop an effective system for helping the student keep up with schoolwork, as frequent absences may occur.

Attention Deficit/Hyperactivity Disorder

This condition could be addressed in more than one of the chapters of this book. However, according the U.S. Department of Education, students identified as having an attention deficit/hyperactivity disorder can be classified under the category of "other health impaired." Advocacy groups have argued that this condition be recognized as a separate disabling condition under IDEA.

Attention deficit/hyperactivity disorder (ADHD) can be characterized as a condition that disrupts a student's ability to attend. It can be manifested in difficulty selectively attending to the important aspects of a stimulus situation or being able to sustain attention over time. The condition is usually associated with three "hallmark features": inattention, impulsivity, and hyperactivity (McBurnett, Lahey, & Pfiffner, in press). The educational implication of this condition is that students may encounter significant academic, behavior, and social problems due to their inability to attend.

A sense of the problems students who are ADHD present in classroom situations can be gleaned from the criteria used to define this disorder in the *Diagnostic and Statistical Manual of Mental Disorders* (DSM-IV) (American Psychiatric Association, 1993) depicted in Table 8.3. Table 8.3 illustrates a number of important features associated with this condition:

- Four codes or types of attentional disorders are possible: predominantly inattentive, hyperactive-impulsive, combined, and not otherwise specified.
- Onset must be prior to 7 years of age.
- The characteristics must persist for at least 6 months.
- Problems must be noticed in more than one setting.
- The problem must cause serious difficulties in functioning.

Accommodations for addressing the needs of students with ADHD fall under four general areas: environmental management tactics (i.e., group, physical, behavioral, and instructional management), student-controlled strategies, collaborative techniques, and **pharmacological intervention** (Dowdy et al., in press). However, we are only beginning to validate what might be recommended practice with this group (Fiore, Becker, & Nero, 1993).

Many students who have been diagnosed as having ADHD may be taking medication. The medications prescribed, such as Ritalin, are meant to control activity levels, thereby helping students attend to tasks better. The teacher's responsibility is to guarantee that the students take their medication and to monitor the side effects. Some of the more common side effects of this type of medication that teachers may notice are appetite loss, headaches, stomachaches, lethargy, motor or vocal tics, irritability, nervousness, and sadness.

Some specific suggestions regarding children with ADHD are as follows:

- Make sure students understand all classroom rules and procedures.
- Consider carefully seating arrangements of students with ADHD to avoid distractions and to be in proximity to the teacher.
- Adhere to the principles of effective classroom management as covered in Chapter 12.
- Understand that certain behaviors, although not desirable, are not meant to be noncompliant—students may not be able to control their behaviors.
- Allow students who are hyperactive to have opportunities to be active.
- Refrain from implementing a behavior management system that is predicated mostly on the use of negative reinforcement (i.e., threats, etc.).
- Group students with ADHD wisely, taking into consideration the purpose of the group and other students who will be members of the group.
- Prepare students for all types of transitions that occur in the school day (in and out of the room, between activities, etc.).
- Plan lessons with the needs of students who have ADHD in mind.
- Teach students to manage their own behaviors—this includes **self-monitoring, self-evaluation, self-reinforcement,** and **self-instruction.**
- Maintain ongoing communication with the student's home by using daily report cards or other instruments to convey information.
- Use homework assignment books with these students.
- Collaborate with special education personnel to develop behavioral and instructional plans for dealing with attention problems.

TABLE 8.3   Criteria for Attention Deficit/Hyperactivity Disorder

A. Either (1) or (2):

(1) Inattention: At least six of the following symptoms of inattention have persisted for at least 6 months to a degree that is maladaptive and inconsistent with developmental level:

   (a) Often fails to give close attention to details or makes careless mistakes in schoolwork, work, or other activities
   (b) Often has difficulty sustaining attention in tasks or play activities
   (c) Often does not seem to listen to what is being said to him or her
   (d) Often does not follow through on instructions and fails to finish schoolwork, chores, or duties in the workplace (not due to oppositional behavior or failure to understand instructions)
   (e) Often has difficulties organizing tasks and activities
   (f) Often avoids or strongly dislikes tasks that require sustained mental effort (such as schoolwork or homework)
   (g) Often loses things necessary for tasks or activities (e.g., school assignments, pencils, books, tools, or toys)
   (h) Often is easily distracted by extraneous stimuli
   (i) Often is forgetful in daily activities;

(2) Hyperactivity-Impulsivity: At least six of the following symptoms of hyperactivity-impulsivity have persisted for at least six months to a degree that is maladaptive and inconsistent with developmental level:

   Hyperactivity:

   (a) Often fidgets with hands or feet or squirms in seat
   (b) Often leaves seat in classroom or in other situations in which remaining in seat is expected
   (c) Often runs about or climbs excessively in situations where it is inappropriate (in adolescents or adults, may be limited to subjective feelings of restlessness)
   (d) Often has difficulty playing or engaging in leisure activities quietly
   (e) Always is "on the go" or acts as if "driven by a motor"
   (f) Often talks excessively;

   Impulsivity:

   (g) Often bursts out answers to questions before the questions have been completed
   (h) Often has difficulty waiting in lines or awaiting turn in games or group situations
   (i) Often interrupts or intrudes on others (e.g., butts into other's conversations or games).

B. Some symptoms that caused impairment were present before age 7.

C. Some symptoms that cause impairment are present in two or more settings (e.g., at school, work, and at home).

D. There must be clear evidence of clinically significant impairment in social, academic, or occupational functioning.

E. Does not occur exclusively during the course of a pervasive developmental disorder, schizophrenia or other psychotic disorder, and is not better accounted for by mood disorder, anxiety disorder, dissociative disorder, or a personality disorder.

Source: American Psychiatric Association. (1993). *Diagnostic and statistical manual of mental disorders* (4th ed.). Washington, DC: Author. Used with permission.

Cancer (Childhood)

Pediatric cancer is a relatively rare condition, occurring in fewer than 1 in 600 children prior to the age of 15 years (Stehbens, 1988). Yet, for those who must deal with this condition, it is an extremely demanding and exhausting situation. Cancer refers to the abnormal growth of cells that eventually has deleterious effects on various organ systems.

Childhood cancers can be categorized into leukemias, lymphomas, brain and spinal cord tumors, and solid tumors. **Leukemia** (acute lymphoblastic leukemia [ALL]) is the most common pediatric cancer, comprising 30% to 40% of all cases. This particular type of cancer originates in the bone marrow—the location where blood cells are produced. In both adults and children, the actual cause of most cancers is unknown.

The survival rates for children with cancer is steadily climbing. As Stehbens (1988) chronicles, in 1960 only 1% of acute leukemia patients survived to 5 years after diagnosis; by 1976, this figure had increased to 55%.

As one can imagine, learning that a child has cancer can put much stress on the individual and his or her family. The specific reaction parents have upon learning of the diagnosis cannot be predicted; however, parents will experience feelings of shock, disbelief, and denial.

Treatment of cancer involves chemotherapy, radiation therapy, surgery, and in some cases transplantation (bone marrow). Unfortunately, chemotherapy and radiation therapy have some uncomfortable side effects, which, for some children, are the most difficult part of the disease (Zwartjes, Zwartjes, & Spilka, 1980). Side effects vary according to the therapy used and the site being treated; the most common ones are nausea, vomiting, diarrhea, hair loss, fatigue, weight gain or loss, swelling, weakness, mouth and dental complications, and an increased susceptibility to infections.

A number of educational issues are associated with students who have cancer. Teachers need to be prepared to deal with the student's emotional reactions to this condition, the student's missing significant amounts of school, and changes in academic performance. Reentry to school after initial treatments poses major problems for the student and the teachers because of a reluctance to resume schooling.

When in school, the student may behave differently than prior to being diagnosed, and these changes can affect academic performance. Students with cancer may have more difficulty concentrating, interact less often with their peers, and be less participative in class activities. As indicated earlier, the student undergoing treatments will look different than before and, as a result, may feel very self-conscious.

Teachers need to create a classroom environment that is accepting and supportive of the student with cancer. During those times when the student may be hospitalized or at home, teachers can encourage communication with classmates (Zwartjes et al., 1980). The following suggestions should assist teachers in accommodating the needs of these students:

- Express your concern about a student's condition to the parents/family.
- Learn about a student's illness from hospital personnel and parents.
- Inquire about the type of treatment and anticipated side effects.

My Best Self

Part of creating an atmosphere that encourages an appreciation of uniqueness is providing experiences for each child to have a chance to feel really good about who he or she is. A healthy self-concept is a necessary stepping stone toward positive understanding and acceptance of others who are different from ourselves. This activity is designed to give everyone's self-concept a chance to soar!

Ask the students to form groups of no more than four or five. Each student will have one blank self-sticking tag for each member of his group and a writing implement. Taking turns, each student will complete orally the following types of sentence stems (the teacher may add, delete, or change these as desired):

I am sad when...
I am happy when...
Things I do best are...
The best thing that ever happened to me...
When I grow up...
If I had three wishes they would be...
My idea of a perfect Saturday is...
I wish I were better at...
My favorite TV shows are...
If I had $1,000 I would...

While one group member responds to these sentence stems the others in the group write on one of the tags a minimum of three one- or two-word positive comments they think describe that individual. The comments *must* be positive; no negative statements will be accepted. When the one student finishes, the others in the group read what they have written about him/her and then place the tags on the person. After everyone has had a turn, each person should be wearing three or four tags with at least three positive comments written on each one. Allow some time for everyone in the class to mingle and talk and show off their "best self." Don't be surprised if some decide to wear their tags the rest of the day!

Adapted from an exercise by Edwina Epps, Teacher, Ford Greene Elementary

Source: Pasternak, M. G. (1979). *Helping kids learn multi-cultural concepts: A handbook of strategies* (p. 74). Champaign, IL: Research Press. Used with permission.

♦ Ask about the student's feelings regarding the illness.
♦ Determine how much time the student will probably miss from school.
♦ Find out if there are any special medical needs the student will have.
♦ Treat the student like any other student in the class—aside from required accommodations, do not show any favoritism to the student.

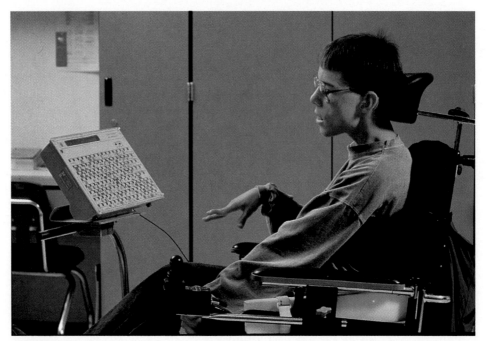

Technology has greatly enhanced the communication skills of students with muscular problems.

◆ Refer the student for any needed special education services.
◆ Prepare for a student's terminal illness and possible death.
◆ Encourage discussion and consideration of future events.
◆ Allow for exceptions to classroom rules and procedures when indicated (e.g., wearing a baseball cap to disguise hair loss from chemotherapy).
◆ Be available to talk with a student when the need arises.
◆ Share information about the student's condition and ongoing status with teachers of the student's siblings.

Cerebral Palsy

Cerebral palsy refers to a number of conditions with varying etiologies that produce a disability that is the result of muscular incoordination and weakness (Schleichkorn, 1993). A more formal definition has been developed by the National Information Center for Children and Youth with Handicaps (1991):

> A condition caused by damage to the brain, usually occurring before, during, or shortly after birth. "Cerebral" refers to the brain and "palsy" to a disorder of movement or posture. It is neither progressive or communicable. It is also not "curable" in the accepted sense, although education, therapy and applied technology can help persons with cerebral palsy lead productive lives. It is not a disease and should never be referred to as such. It can range from mild to severe. (p. 1)

According to Schleichkorn (1993), two out of every 1,000 live births in the United States will involve cerebral palsy. The cause of most cases of cerebral palsy is unknown. However, any number of events occurring before, during, or shortly after birth can cause cerebral palsy. Some suspected causes follow.

Prenatal   anoxia, maternal infection, metabolic disease, RH sensitization, teratogens (e.g., substance abuse)
Perinatal   asphyxia, trauma during delivery
Postnatal   head trauma, infections (e.g., meningitis), vascular problems, anoxia, tumors

The primary problems related to movement are not caused by dysfunctional muscles. It is the brain's ineffectiveness in controlling affected muscles that causes motoric limitations. Most students with cerebral palsy will also have various concomitant problems in speech, swallowing, vision, and hearing. Some students will also have mental retardation; however, it is important not to equate cerebral palsy with mental retardation.

Because cerebral palsy primarily affects muscle control, various systems have been developed to describe the differing movement characteristics and anatomical involvement. A brief description of each follows.

Motor Characteristics (Tver & Tver, 1991):

Spasticity   tense, inaccurate voluntary movement because of the involuntary contraction of the affected muscles when they are stretched
Athetosis   marked incoordination and almost constant motion of extremities e.g. much writhing movement that is not purposeful and difficult to control
Ataxia   uncoordinated movement and trouble with balance; gait characterized by lunges and lurches
Rigidity   continuous muscle tension and stiffness
Tremor   involuntary shaking and rhythmic motions
Atonia   lack of muscle tone; limpness and flaccidity

Limb Involvement or Topography (i.e., affected body areas):

Hemiplegia   (the most common type) one side of the body, upper and lower extremities included
Paraplegia   only legs
Quadriplegia   all four extremities
Diplegia   all four extremities are involved but legs are primarily involved with only slight involvement of arms

Due to advances in technology (e.g., augmentative communication) and instructional methodology (e.g., various accommodative procedures), it is now possible and desirable for students with severe forms of cerebral palsy to be placed in general education settings.

Students who have cerebral palsy will usually receive a variety of services including physical therapy to work on muscle movement, occupational therapy to work on

Movement Patterns and Types of Control Switches

Types of Control Switches	Movement Patterns
Rocking lever	Normal or abnormal upper-extremity patterns
Paddle switch	Head movement (through use of a mouthstick or headstick)
Tread switch	
Plate switch	
Wobble switch	Head, arm, or gross body movement; can be normal or abnormal
Leaf switch	Movement pattern used dependent on placement of switch
Flexit switch	
Air cushion pneumatic switch (pressure switch)	Head, arm, or leg movement dependent on switch placement
Touch switch	
Lever switch	Head movement
Joystick	Arm/hand movements
Wobble switch	

Source: Esposito, L., & Campbell, P. H. (1993). Computers and individuals with severe and physical disabilities. In J. D. Lindsey (Ed.), *Computers and exceptional individuals* (p. 163). Austin, TX: Pro-Ed. Used with permission.

daily living skills, and speech/language therapy to work on oral expression or teach the use of alternative communication systems. These students may use special orthotic devices such as braces or splints to assist them with various activities (e.g., range of motion). For instance, one of the most-used devices is the short leg brace, which aids in the prevention of the permanent shortening of the heel cords (Kurtz, 1992).

The major challenges facing the general education teacher who has a student with cerebral palsy in the classroom involve accessibility, communication, and social-emotional concerns. As some of these students use wheelchairs, teachers should ensure that the classroom environment is barrier-free.

Poor control of the musculature involved in speaking can have a significant effect on communication. Most of the time, getting used to the speech of the student will enhance the ease of understanding what is said. Sometimes it will be necessary to ask students to repeat their verbalizations to understand what is being communicated. There is nothing improper in asking the student to do so.

Many students who have cerebral palsy have to deal with the reality that their bodies look and act very differently from those of their peers. By the nature of their disability, these students may be excluded from conversations or other events that are part of everyday school life for the other students. This can result in feelings of inadequacy and isolation. Teachers should be ready to deal with any number of emotional reactions associated with having this condition. Some specific suggestions are as follows:

♦ Create a supportive classroom environment that encourages participation in every facet of the school day.

♦ Allow extra time for students to move from one location to another.

♦ Ask students to repeat verbalizations that may be hard to understand due to their speech patterns.

♦ Help develop a student's experiential background by providing many real-life activities.

♦ Learn the correct way for the student to sit upright in a chair or wheelchair and how to use any adaptive equipment (e.g., prone standers) that might be used.

♦ Understand the functions and components of a wheelchair and any special adaptive pieces that may accompany it.

♦ Consider the use of various augmentative communication techniques with students who have severe cerebral palsy (see Musselwhite, 1987).

♦ Encourage students to use computers that are equipped with expanded keyboards if necessary or other portable writing aids for taking notes or generating various written products.

♦ Consult physical and occupational therapists to understand correct positioning, posture, and other motor functioning areas.

Cystic Fibrosis

Cystic fibrosis is an inherited disease that affects the body's exocrine glands. In this disease, the glands secrete an abnormal amount of mucus throughout the body, most notably affecting the lungs and digestive tract. Abnormal amounts of sweat and saliva are also produced.

As mucus accumulates, a number of deleterious events emerge. In the lungs, the mucus blocks the bronchial tubes, leading to bacterial buildup and ultimately to respiratory infection. After many such infections, the lungs are significantly affected and weakened. The mucus buildup will also affect the pancreas by blocking certain enzymes from getting to the digestive tract. This results in foods being partially digested and later expelled from the body improperly as large noxious stools.

The tragedy of this disease is that it is terminal. On the average, children will live to their mid-teens before their bodies succumb to the stresses of this disease. The impact of the progressive deterioration caused by this condition on the individual child, on the family, and on other students in the class will be great. The ultimate death of the student also warrants careful preparation of all involved. A moving yet realistic account of the effects of this disease is described in the book *Alex: The Life of a Child* (Deford, 1983).

Teachers must make sure that students who have cystic fibrosis take special medication before they eat. It will also be important to understand that, as the disease progresses, the stamina and physical condition of the student will deteriorate. It is also crucial to appreciate the fact that the student will undergo rigorous and often painful therapies every day to dislodge mucus accumulations. Over time the disease and the treatments associated with it may cause emotional reactions in the student.

The following is a list of specific suggestions on dealing with students with cystic fibrosis:

- Prepare students in class for the realities of this disease (e.g., coughing, non-contagious sputum, gas).
- Learn how to clear a student's lungs and air passages, as such assistance may be needed after certain activities.
- Know the medications a student must take and be able to administer them (e.g., enzymes, vitamins).
- Consider certain restrictions on physical activities.
- Inquire about the therapies being used with the student.
- Support the implementation of special diets if needed.
- Provide opportunities for students to talk about their concerns, fears, and feelings.
- Ensure that the student is included in all class activities to whatever extent is possible.
- Prepare students for the eventual outcome of the disease by raising the topic of death and dying.

Diabetes (Juvenile Diabetes)

Diabetes, a metabolic disorder characterized by the inability to process sugar in a normal fashion, is caused by insufficient insulin production by the pancreas. Deiner (1993) cites the following symptoms that are frequently associated with the disease: "extreme thirst, frequent urination, constant hunger, loss of weight, itching, easy tiring, changes in vision, and slow healing of cuts and scratches" (p. 227).

The disease can be managed by attending to diet, exercise, and insulin supplementation. However, this condition can lead to serious complications such as blindness. The daily management routine typically involves an injection of insulin, which may be difficult to do with children who resist this uncomfortable event, and the testing of urine or blood.

Students who have diabetes may have school performance or concentration problems. Johnson (1988) notes that diabetes can affect cognitive functioning, particularly during or subsequent to hypoglycemic conditions. Other behaviors that are possible when a student is hypoglycemic include dizziness, trembling, or emotional reactions. When students have too much sugar in their bodies, symptomatic behaviors might be thirst, frequent urination, hunger, and drowsiness.

Below are some specific suggestion on dealing with diabetic students:

- Communicate regularly with the family to determine any special needs the student may have.
- Schedule snacks and lunch at the same time every day.
- Be prepared for a situation where the student needs to have sugar—hypo-glycemic conditions.
- Help the student deal with the disease.

Human Immunodeficiency Virus (HIV)

Human immunodeficiency virus attacks the body's immune system and leaves the individual vulnerable to opportunistic infections or cancers. In the later stages of the disease, when the immune system is in a very weakened state, the classification **Acquired Immune Deficiency Syndrome (AIDS)** is used. The number of cases of HIV and AIDS is growing nationally and internationally at alarming rates.

Two of the fastest-growing groups at risk for getting HIV are infants and teenagers. However, the actual number of students of school age who display symptoms are few. The incubation period for infants (i.e., the time between contracting HIV and developing symptoms) is approximately four years. Since this condition is terminal, these children will die before reaching school age. Adolescents are at great risk for contracting HIV; however, the incubation period for them is eight to ten years. Some students who are school age may be symptomatic as a result of blood transfusion of infected blood.

HIV is transmitted only through the exchange of semen and blood, or by breast-feeding. In adolescents and adults, transmission occurs primarily through sexual contact or by using contaminated needles. In infants, transmission occurs prenatally or during the delivery process from their HIV-infected mothers, although there is only a 30% risk of a mother infecting her child. As mentioned, other children can acquire HIV through HIV-contaminated blood transfusions, typically associated with hemophilia or surgery. The HIV virus cannot be spread through the air and does not survive for long in any environment outside the human body.

HIV involves a series of stages that can extend over the course of many years. When a person is first infected with HIV, there are no obvious signs of the disease, and testing will not show HIV infection (detection of antibodies) for 6 to 12 weeks after infection. At this point, a person is considered asymptomatic. The second stage, or symptomatic infection period, occurs when a person begins to show signs of a weakened immune system. The last stage in the progression of this disease (AIDS) involves the collapse of the immune system and is characterized by life-threatening infections and tumors (Colson & Colson, 1993).

The student who has HIV will most likely display an assortment of academic, behavior, and social-emotional problems. As mentioned, HIV affects the brain, resulting in cognitive, motor, and speech/language deficits. Emotional problems can arise from the terminal nature of the disease. Because of much misinformation, these students, as well as their families, can become socially isolated from friends, peers, and extended family.

Children with Developmental Delays Due to HIV

◆ *Kinds of Problems to Look for*
Children with HIV may be developmentally delayed at birth or may develop normally for a number of years, then begin to evidence delays at a later age. The deficits can follow episodes of high fever and may include gross and fine motor problems, inappropriate muscle tone, reduced flexibility and muscle strength, and loss of previously attained motor milestones. Cognitive impairments such as decreased intellectual levels, specific learning disabilities, mental retardation, visual or spatial deficits, and decreased alertness may also be present. In addition, both expressive and receptive language delays among children with HIV infection are common. There is also some evidence that children with HIV tend to develop emotional and behavioral problems, ranging from hyperactivity to lethargy.

◆ *Educators' Responsibilities*
Confidentiality of records must be maintained.
Frequent reevaluations should be conducted.
Procedures for placement changes should be streamlined because a student's health may change suddenly.
Only those with a "right to know" should be informed of the student's HIV status.
Training should be available to all school personnel.

Source: Seidel, J. F. (1992, September). Children with HIV-related developmental difficulties. *Phi Delta Kappan, 72,* 38–56. Used with permission.

If general education teachers have accurate, up-to-date information about HIV, then they can feel comfortable having a student with this condition in their classroom. It is equally important not to judge the behavior of parents who may have been responsible for infecting their children. More than likely, they too have the disease.

Some specific suggestions in dealing with students with HIV/AIDS are as follows:

◆ Follow the guidelines (universal precautions) developed by the Centers for Disease Control and the Food and Drug Administration for working with HIV-infected individuals (see Figure 8.1).
◆ Consult the student's parents and/or physician to determine if there are any special procedures that must be followed.
◆ Discuss HIV infection with the entire class, providing accurate information, dispelling myths, and answering any questions.
◆ Discuss with students in the class that the infected student's skills and abilities will change over time due to the condition.

The Centers for Disease Control and the Food and Drug Administration (1988) published guidelines designed to protect health care workers and to ensure the confidentiality of patients with HIV infection. These guidelines include the following information that is useful for classroom teachers.

- Blood should always be handled with latex or nonpermeable disposable gloves. The use of gloves is not necessary for feces, nasal secretions, sputum, sweat, saliva, tears, urine, and vomitus unless they are visibly tinged with blood. Handwashing is sufficient after handling material not containing blood.
- In all settings in which blood or bloody material is handled, gloves and a suitable receptable that closes tightly and is child-proof should be available. Although HIV does not survive well outside the body, all spillage of secretions should be cleaned up immediately with disinfectants. This is particularly important for cleaning up after a bloody nose or a large cut. Household bleach at a dilution of 1:10 should be used. Only objects that have come into contact with blood need to be cleaned with bleach.
- When intact skin is exposed to contaminated fluids, particularly blood, it should be washed with soap and water. Handwashing is sufficient for such activities as diaper change; toilet training; and clean-up of nasal secretions, stool, saliva, tears, or vomitus. If an open lesion or a mucous membrane appears to have been contaminated, AZT therapy should be considered.

Figure 8.1   **Universal Precautions for Prevention of HIV, Hepatitis B, and Other Blood-Borne Pathogens** ·
Source: Centers for Disease Control (1988). *AIDS Surveillance Report* (p. 7). Atlanta, GA: Author. Used with permission.

◆ Prepare for the fact that the student will die, especially if AIDS is present.
◆ Ensure that the student with HIV is included in all aspects of classroom activities.
◆ Be sensitive to the stress that a student's family is undergoing.

Infectious Diseases

Communicable diseases are common to settings such as school, where large numbers of individuals are in close contact with each other. Infections can be caused by bacteria, viruses, fungi, protozoa, or parasites. School-aged populations are most affected by bacterial and viral organisms, such as ear infections, chicken pox, conjunctivitis, and the flu. Although many of these infectious diseases are not chronic and therefore do not have long-term implications, others *are* chronic in nature. Teachers are advised to have a working knowledge of common infections to be able to prevent their transmission whenever possible. Here are some specific suggestions:

◆ Encourage students to wash their hands regularly throughout the day, as this is the single most effective tactic for minimizing the transmission of diseases.
◆ Have antibacterial soap available for students to use.
◆ Clean classroom surfaces (e.g., work areas) and classroom equipment daily.

- Collect trash in plastic bags.
- Wear gloves when dealing with body fluids (e.g., blood, mucus, vomit, and so forth).

Muscular Dystrophy

As Tver and Tver (1991) point out, muscular dystrophy is "an umbrella term used to indicate several inherited diseases of the muscles that cause progressive weakness and disability" (p. 160). The most common, and unfortunately the most serious, type is Duchenne dystrophy. This is a sex-linked disorder that affects males.

Duchenne dystrophy is a progressive disease characterized by a deterioration of the voluntary skeletal muscles in which fat cells and connective tissue replace muscle tissue. Individuals so affected ultimately lose their ability to walk, typically by age twelve, as well as the functional use of their arms and hands. Individuals will need to use a wheelchair and may not have enough strength in their arms to lift most objects. This muscle weakness will also lead to respiratory complications, which can result in major medical problems, necessitating invasive action (e.g., postural drainage techniques). This condition usually results in death by the teenage years.

Teachers will need to adapt their classrooms to accommodate the physical needs of students with this condition. Special equipment will be needed to assist many students in performing basic functions such as maintaining posture or mobility. If this is the case, teachers have to learn appropriate ways to move and position the student.

Following is a list of specific suggestions in dealing with students with muscular dystrophy:

- Be prepared to help the student deal with the loss of various functions.
- Involve the student in as many classroom activities as possible.
- Using assistive techniques that do not hurt the individual, help the student as needed in climbing stairs or in getting up from the floor.
- Understand the functions and components of wheelchairs.
- Monitor the administration of required medications.
- Monitor the amount of time the student is allowed to stand during the day.
- Be familiar with different types of braces (short leg, molded ankle-foot) students might use.
- Prepare other students in class for the realities of the disease.

Seizure Disorders

Seizures are not diseases but rather reactions to irregular periods of uncontrolled, abnormal electrical activity in the brain that can result from any number of causes. Epilepsy is an example of a seizure disorder.

There are different types of seizures, and their manifestations depend on which part of the brain is involved. Those in which seizure activity occurs throughout the entire cortex of the brain are referred to as generalized seizures (tonic-clonic, absence,

Pushing a Wheelchair

1. Over rough terrain or a raised area:
   a. Tilt the wheelchair by stepping down on tipping lever with foot as you pull down and back on hand grips.
   b. Continue to tilt chair back until it requires little or no effort to stabilize it.
   c. When the wheelchair is at the balance point, it can then be pushed over obstacles or terrain.
   d. Reverse the procedure and lower slowly. Make sure the wheelchair does not slam down or drop the last few inches.
2. Over curbs and steps:
   a. As you approach the curb or step, pause and tilt the wheelchair back to the balance point.
   b. When the wheelchair is stabilized, move toward curb until casters are on curb, and rear wheels come in contact with the curb.
   c. Move in close to the chair and lift the chair up by the handles. Roll the wheelchair up over the curb and push it forward.
   d. To go down, reverse the steps—back the wheelchair down off the curb without allowing it to drop down. Once rear wheels are down, step down on tipping lever and slowly lower casters.
3. Down a steep incline:
   a. Take the wheelchair down backward.
   b. The wheelchair can pick up speed too easily, and you can lose control if the wheelchair goes down first.
   c. Turn the chair around until your back is in the direction you plan to go.
   d. Walk backward, and move slowly down the ramp.
   e. Look backward occasionally to make sure you are staying on track and to avoid collisions.

myoclonic); those that are limited to a focal area on one side of the brain are referred to as partial seizures (complex partial). Brief descriptions of the different classifications of seizures are provided.

Generalized Tonic-Clonic Muscles become stiff (tonic phase), student loses consciousness and falls to floor, the body shakes violently as muscles alternately contract and relax for 2 to 5 minutes (clonic phase); ultimately the individual goes into a deep sleep, followed by natural sleep. During the contractions, the student may breathe heavily, salivate, and lose control of his or her bladder and bowels. This type of seizure may be preceded by an aura (an unusual sensory perception) that the individual may experience. The individual eventually wakes up, typically confused and disoriented, and may have a headache.

Absence   This is a less dramatic type of seizure characterized by momentary loss of consciousness that can vary in length from a few seconds up to 30 seconds. It can be recognized as a blank stare or eye fluttering and can occur several hundred of times a day. Stereotyped motor movements known as automatisms (e.g., tapping on a desk) are possible (Jan, Ziegler, & Erba, 1991). During these seizures individuals are unaware of what is going on around them and of anything they do during this time.

Complex Partial Seizure   This type of seizure is characterized by inappropriate or purposeless behaviors (e.g., being verbally abusive or walking around the room aimlessly) and may last for a few minutes. Students are unaware of events that occur during the seizure.

The impact of witnessing a convulsive seizure on those who are not familiar with such an event can be traumatic. Teachers need to prepare themselves as well as the entire class for the possible occurrence of a seizure. In addition, teachers need to know how to handle the classroom situation if a student experiences this type of seizure. This involves management of the person having the seizure and the other members of the class. Procedures for handling a tonic-clonic seizure that are recommended by the Epilepsy Foundation of America can be found in Figure 8.2.

Teachers must be vigilant in recognizing absence types of seizures because they are too often overlooked or misinterpreted as daydreaming or lack of interest. Because these seizures are momentary, it is easy to miss them. However, the student can begin to have serious academic problems as a result of the cumulative effects of loss of consciousness, especially if this type of seizure occurs on a very frequent and chronic basis.

Seizure disorders are usually treated through medication. In most cases, drugs are able to control the seizuring totally or to a great extent. However, in approximately 20% of the cases, medication will have no effect. Unfortunately, as has been pointed out before, these medications also have side effects of which teachers should be aware. Teachers should secure pertinent information about various medications from school health personnel or other medical sources.

Most of the time, teachers will know which students are prone to have seizures, as this knowledge will have been documented, and treatment will have been initiated. Nevertheless, a student can have a first seizure at any time. Whether it is a student with a history of seizures or one who is having a first seizure, teachers should observe the seizure and record various facets of what occurred. Figure 8.3 is an example of an observation format for doing this. The key to this system is to try to record information that relates to the time period before, during, and after the seizure.

In dealing with students experiencing seizures, the following specific suggestions should be used:

◆ Understand the patterns of a particular student's seizuring if this information is known.

◆ Sensitize other students in the class to the nature of the student's potential seizuring.

In a generalized tonic-clonic seizure, the person suddenly falls to the ground and has a convulsive seizure. It is essential to protect him or her from injury. Cradle the head or place something soft under it—a towel or your hand, for example. Remove all dangerous objects. A bystander can do nothing to prevent or terminate an attack. At the end of the episode, make sure the mouth is cleared of food and saliva by turning the person on his or her side to provide the best airway and allow secretions to drain. The person may be incontinent during a seizure. If the assisting person remains calm, the person will be reassured when he or she regains consciousness.

Breathing almost always resumes spontaneously after a convulsive seizure. Failure to resume breathing signals a complication of the seizure such as aspiration of food, heart attack, or severe head or neck injury. In these unusual circumstances, cardiopulmonary resuscitation must start immediately. If repeated seizures occur, or if a single seizure lasts longer than five minutes, the person should be taken to a medical facility immediately. Prolonged or repeated seizures may suggest *status epilepticus* (nonstop seizures), which requires emergency medical treatment. In summary, *first aid for generalized tonic-clonic seizures is similar to that for other convulsive seizures*.

- Prevent further injury. Place something soft under the head, loosen tight clothing, and clear the area of sharp or hard objects.
- Force no objects into the person's mouth.
- Do not restrain the person's movements unless they place him or her in danger.
- Turn the person on his or her side to open the airway and allow secretions to drain.
- Stay with the person until the seizure ends.
- Do not pour any liquids into the person's mouth or offer any food, drink, or medication until he or she is fully awake.
- Start cardiopulmonary resuscitation if the person does not resume breathing after the seizure.
- Let the person rest until he or she is fully awake.
- Be reassuring and supportive when consciousness returns.
- A convulsive seizure is not a medical emergency unless it lasts longer than five minutes or a second seizure occurs soon after the first. In this situation, the person should be taken to an emergency medical facility.

Figure 8.2 **Procedures for Handling Generalized Tonic-Clonic Seizures**
Source: Epilepsy Foundation of America (1992). *Seizure recognition and observation: A guide for allied health professionals.* Landover, MD: Author. Used with permission.

- ◆ Ensure that students are taking prescribed medications to control their seizures.
- ◆ Record the duration, frequency, and circumstances of all seizures.
- ◆ Ensure that the classroom environment is safe for a student who has convulsive seizures.

Spina Bifida

Spina bifida is a congenital condition characterized by a malformation of the vertebrae and spinal cord. It results from the bony spinal column failing to close completely

---

Student's Name _____John_____   Date of Seizure _____3/13/90_____

Time of Seizure _____about 9:00 a.m._____

Approximate Duration of Seizure _____2 minutes_____

Behavior before seizure
John appeared to be tired and complained of a headache. He was resting at his desk, putting his head down on his arms.

Initial seizure behavior
He let out a short cry. His whole body appeared to stiffen.

Behavior during seizure
John fell to the floor. His whole body, including his arms and legs, began to jerk violently. His eyes rolled upward and his eyelids were fluttering. John had lost consciousness and fallen to the floor. His facial skin was very pale and his lips were bluish. The seizure lasted about 2 minutes.

Behavior after seizure
John was very tired and wanted to rest. He complained that he had a severe headache.

Student reaction to seizure
John was quite upset and confused. He didn't seem to understand what had happened.

Peer reaction to seizure
At the time of the seizure, other children were not in the room. However, the children in the room should be made aware of the seizure, given an understanding of the behavior, and taught basic safety procedures. It was recommended that I call the local epilepsy foundation and the national Epilepsy Foundation of America (4351 Garden City Dr., Landover, MD 20785) for additional assistance.

Teacher comments
John was not injured. The school nurse assisted with the incident and the parents were notified. John's fears and concerns need to be addressed. I will begin by obtaining help from the local epilepsy foundation. The parents, school nurse, and guidance counselor will assist me in helping John address his concerns.

Figure 8.3   **Seizure Observation Form**
Source: Michael, R. J. (1992). Seizures: Teacher observations and record keeping. *Interventions in School and Clinic, 27,* 212. Used with permission.

during fetal development. This can result in an opening in the vertebral column, referred to as a **myelomeningocele,** sometimes exposing the spinal cord. Surgery to close the spinal opening is performed soon after birth.

Spina bifida is the most common cause of physical disability in children (Reigel, 1993). In mild cases, few problems exist, with perhaps some weakness noticeable in the affected area of the spine. However, no educational accommodations are likely to be needed. In more severe cases where the spinal cord has been exposed, school-age children may have a range of problems, including no sensation in parts of the body

Before Seizure Activity	During Seizure Activity	After Seizure Activity
What was the child doing prior to the seizure?	What was the level of consciousness during the seizure?	Did the child have:
Did the child appear to be ill or feverish?	Was the child's body rigid or limp?	A sense of drowsiness or confusion?
Was the child near flickering lights, such as a television or computer?	Were there any sudden jerking movements of the body or arms?	Any difficulty in regaining consciousness?
Had the child recently been napping?	Did the child appear to be sweaty, flushed, or pale?	Any weakness specific to one side of the body, arms, or legs?
Did the child sense anything different?	What were the child's eyes doing (i.e., rolled upward, turned to the left or right, eyelids fluttering, etc.)?	Any problems with vision?
sensations		Any recent changes in child's medication (i.e., dosage, type, etc.)?
smells	Were there any episodes of automatisms, (e.g., lip smacking, picking at clothes, fumbling, wandering around room, etc.)?	Was any injury sustained?
extreme fatigue		
drowsiness		
excitement		
headaches	Was there any evidence of twitching? Where did it begin? Did it progress to other parts of the body?	
verbalizations		
facial skin coloration		
staring		
excessive anxiety	Was there any occurrence of vomiting or incontinence?	
hyperventilation		
	Was there any evidence of cyanosis?	

Figure 8.4 **Guidelines for Seizure Observation**
Source: Michael, R. J. (1992). Seizures: Teacher observations and record keeping. *Interventions in School and Clinic, 27,* 213. Used with permission.

below the site of the spinal cord problem, no muscle control below this site (i.e., paralysis), spinal malformations, brittle bones due to poor circulation, and learning problems. Younger children also will not have control of their bowels or bladders. Other problems that can develop include seizures, obesity, visual deficits, and problems with joints such as the hip.

Most students with spina bifida function within the normal range of intelligence and should be placed in general education settings. Many students who have the myelomeningocele form of spina bifida will have learning disabilities. As a result, the suggestions offered in Chapter 4 will be useful with this group. Because of problems with mobility, these students will use various types of adaptive equipment including braces, walking aids, or wheelchairs. Like other students with physical or health conditions, these students may need help with their social-emotional needs. Some specific suggestions regarding this are as follows:

◆ Inquire about any acute medical needs the student may have.

◆ Learn about the various adaptive equipment a student may be using (see Baker & Rogosky-Grassi, 1993).

◆ Maintain an environment that assists the student who is using crutches by keeping floors from getting wet and removing loose floor coverings.

◆ Understand the use of a wheelchair as well as its major parts.

◆ Learn how to position these students to develop strength and to avoid sores from developing in parts of their bodies that bear their weight, or that result from pressure from orthotic devices they are using. They do not have sensation, and healing is complicated by poor circulation.

◆ Understand the process of **clean intermittent bladder catheterization (CIC),** as some students will be performing this process to become continent and avoid urinary tract infections—the process involves insertion of a clean catheter through the urethra and into the bladder, must be done four times a day, and can be done independently by most children by age 6.

◆ Be ready to deal with the occasional incontinence of students. Assure the student with spina bifida that this is not a problem and discuss this situation with other class members.

◆ Learn how to deal with the special circumstances associated with students who use wheelchairs and have seizures.

◆ Ensure the full participation of the student in all classroom activities.

◆ Help the student with spina bifida develop a healthy, positive self-concept.

◆ Notify parents if there are unusual changes in the student's behavior or personality or if the student has various physical complaints such as headaches or double vision—this may indicate a problem with increased pressure on the brain (Deiner, 1993).

Traumatic Brain Injury

Traumatic brain injury (TBI) is a condition characterized by some type of external insult to the brain resulting in "brain contusion, laceration, or compression or damage to the cerebral blood vessels" (Tver & Tver, 1991, p. 230). It can affect psychological/cognitive abilities, speech and language, physical functioning, and personal/social behaviors.

Traumatic brain injury can be caused by any number of events. The primary causes of head injury in children are motor vehicle accidents and abuse (Mira, Tucker, & Tyler, 1992). Other events such as bicycle accidents, sports injuries, or assaults account for some cases of TBI.

Information about the severity of a traumatic brain injury is important for teachers to know, as it can provide a sense of the expected long-term outcomes of a student. Although no standardized system has been developed to describe levels of severity, Mira et al. (1992) offer the following one, which is derived from a variety of sources:

Mild Signs of concussion or a blow resulting in some aftereffects, such as dizziness or loss of consciousness, for less than an hour; no skull fracture; majority of brain injuries are mild

Moderate Loss of consciousness for from 1 to 24 hours or evidence of a skull fracture; may develop secondary neurological problems such as swelling within the brain and subsequent complications; neurosurgery may be required

Severe Loss of consciousness for more than 24 hours, or evidence of contusion (actual bruising of brain tissue) or intracranial hematoma (bleeding within the brain); long-term medical care is likely; typical sequelae (consequences) include motor, language, and cognitive problems

The actual persisting effects of a traumatic brain injury on a given individual student will vary. Nevertheless, certain medical, sensory, cognitive, and behavioral sequelae are likely for students who have sustained moderate or severe injury. Some possible resultant characteristics of educational relevance are highlighted in Table 8.4.

TABLE 8.4 Persisting Features of Traumatic Brain Injury

Area of Functioning	Possible Effects
Physical/medical	• Reduced stamina & fatigue • Seizures (5%) • Headaches • Problems with regulation of various functions (e.g., growth, eating, body temperature)
Sensory	• Hearing problems (e.g., conductive and/or sensorineural loss) • Vision problems (e.g., blurred vision, visual field defects)
Cognitive	• Memory problems (e.g., storage & retrieval) • Attentional difficulties • Intellectual deficits • Reasoning and problem-solving difficulties
Language	• Word retrieval difficulties • Motor-speech problems (e.g., dysarthria) • Language comprehension deficits (e.g., difficulty listening) • Difficulty acquiring new vocabulary and learning new concepts • Socially inappropriate verbal behavior
Behavioral/emotional	• Problems in planning, organizing, and problem solving • Disinhibition • Overactivity • Impulsivity • Lack of self-direction • Helplessness or apathy • Inability to recognize one's injury

Source: Mira, M. P., Tucker, B. F., & Tyler, J. S. (1992). *Traumatic brain injury in children and adolescents: A sourcebook for teachers and other school personnel.* Austin, TX: Pro-Ed. Used with permission.

Intervention involves the efforts of professionals from many different disciplines, including teachers. As noted, the prognosis for recovery depends on many variables. Initially, it is "influenced by the type of injury and the rapidity and quality of medical and surgical care" (Bigge, 1991, p. 197). Later, it will be influenced by the nature of rehabilitative and educational intervention.

The reentry of students with TBI to school settings is particularly crucial and needs to be coordinated across a number of people. It should be noted that, in addition to the injury itself and its implications on functioning and potential learning, students probably will have missed a significant amount of schooling already. All of these factors can have a significant impact on educational performance.

Under the Individuals with Disabilities Education Act of 1990, TBI is a distinct category of disability, although some students may be provided services under Section 504. If they are identified under IDEA, they will have a written individual educational program (IEP); if served under Section 504, they will have an appropriate accommodation plan. Whatever plan is used, teachers will need to address the specific areas that have been identified as problematic. Table 8.5 is an adaptation of a list of target areas and suggested interventions that was originally developed by Mira et al. (1992).

Some specific suggestion on dealing with students with TBI are listed below:

- Prepare classmates for the reentry of a fellow student who has sustained a traumatic brain injury—it is important to deal with the changes in physical functioning and personality.
- Modify the classroom environment to ensure safety and to address any specific needs of the student.
- Minimize visual and auditory distractions that may interfere with attention to task.
- Be familiar with any special equipment that might be needed (e.g., augmentative communication devices).
- Be familiar with the type and administration procedures of any medications that might be prescribed.
- Consider special seating depending on needs.
- Ensure that students are attending to instructional activities—teach students to monitor their own attention behavior.
- Help students with memory problems by teaching them mnemonic strategies.
- Assist students who are having difficulty with organization.
- Break down learning tasks into substeps.
- Create many opportunities for the student to use problem-solving skills.
- Allow extra time for students to respond to questions, take tests, complete assignments, and move from one setting to another.
- Teach students requisite social skills appropriate for their age and needs.
- Implement behavior reduction techniques to eliminate inappropriate and undesirable behaviors.
- Help students to understand the nature of their injury.
- Provide information about academic, social, psychomotor progress to families on a regular basis. Describe the nature of the educational program.

TABLE 8.5   **Classroom Suggestions for Teaching Students with Traumatic Brain Injury**

- Receptive language
  Limit the amount of information presented at one time.
  Provide simple instructions for only one activity at a time.
  Have the student repeat instructions.
  Use concrete language.

- Expressive language
  Teach the student to rehearse silently before verbally replying.
  Teach the student to look for cues from listeners to ascertain that the student is being understood.
  Teach the student to directly ask if he or she is being understood.

- Maintaining attention
  Provide a study carrel or preferential seating.
  After giving instructions, check for proper attention and understanding by having the student repeat them.
  Teach the student to use self-regulating techniques to maintain attention (e.g., asking "Am I paying attention?" "What is the required task?").

- Impulsiveness
  Teach the student to mentally rehearse steps before beginning an activity.
  Reduce potential distractions.
  Frequently restate and reinforce rules.

- Memory
  Teach the student to use external aides such as notes, memos, daily schedule sheets, and assignment sheets.
  Use visual imagery, when possible, to supplement oral content.
  Teach visual imaging techniques for information presented.
  Provide repetition and frequent review of instruction materials.
  Provide immediate and frequent feedback to enable the student to interpret success or failure.

- Following directions
  Provide the student with both visual and auditory directions.
  Model tasks, whenever possible.
  Break multistep directions into small parts and list them so that the student can refer back when needed.

- Motor skills
  Allow the student to complete a project rather than turn in a written assignment.
  Have the student use a typewriter or a word processor to complete assignments.
  Allow extra time for completing tasks requiring fine-motor skills.
  Assign someone to take notes for the student during lectures.

Source: Adapted from: Mira, M. P., Tucker, B. F., & Tyler, J. S. (1992). *Traumatic brain injury: A sourcebook for teachers and other school personnel.* Austin, TX: Pro-Ed. Used with permission.

Other physical and health conditions exist, and general education teachers will encounter students who have them. Many of these other conditions, such as a student who has been severely burned or one who has cancer, will require teachers to obtain information about the condition as well as suggestions for accommodating the student in the classroom. Because so many conditions exist, only a few of them could be discussed in this chapter.

Teachers are encouraged to seek the assistance of school-based personnel who can provide useful information. Current and accurate information can be obtained from organizations that are associated with a specific condition (e.g., Cystic Fibrosis Foundation).

Summary

- ◆ Children with physical and health needs are entitled to an appropriate educational program as a result of IDEA.

- ◆ Physical and health impairments constitute low incidence disabilities.

- ◆ The severity, visibility, and age of acquisition impact on needs of children with physical and health impairments.

- ◆ Students with physical and health problems display a wide array of characteristics and needs.

- ◆ Students with physical problems qualify for special education under the *orthopedically impaired* category of IDEA.

- ◆ Students with health problems qualify for special education under the *other health impaired* categoy of IDEA.

- ◆ Asthma affects many children; teachers primarily need to be aware of medications to control asthma, side effects of medication, and the limitations of students with asthma.

- ◆ The survival rates for children with cancer have increased dramatically over the past 20 years.

- ◆ Teachers need to be prepared to deal with the emotional issues surrounding childhood cancer, including death issues.

- ◆ Children with cancer may miss a good deal of school; the school should make appropriate arrangements in these situations.

- ◆ Cerebral palsy is a condition that affects muscles and posture; it can be described by the way it affects movement or which limb is involved.

- ◆ Physical therapy is a critical component of treatment for children with cerebral palsy.

◆ Accessibility, communication, and social-emotional concerns are the primary areas that general educators must attend to.

◆ Cystic fibrosis is a terminal condition that affects the mucous membranes of the lungs.

◆ Juvenile diabetes results in children having to take insulin injections daily.

◆ Diet and exercise can help children manage their diabetes.

◆ Infants and teenagers are two of the fastest-growing groups to contract HIV.

◆ Teachers need to keep up to date with developments in HIV/AIDS prevention and treatment approaches.

◆ Teachers must know specific steps to take in case children have a generalized tonic-clonic seizure in their classrooms.

◆ Epilepsy is caused by abnormal activity in the brain that is the result of some brain damage or insult.

◆ Spina bifida is caused by a failure of the spinal column to close properly; this condition may result in paralysis of the lower extremities.

◆ Traumatic brain injury (TBI) is one of the newest categories recognized by IDEA as a disability category that results in special education services.

◆ Children with TBI exhibit a wide variety of characteristics, including emotional, learning, and behavior problems.

References

American Academy of Allergy and Immunology. (1991). *Stinging insect allergy*. Milwaukee, WI: Public Education Committee, American Academy of Allergy and Immunology.

American Academy of Allergy and Immunology. (n.d.). *Asthma and the school child (Tip #19)*. Milwaukee, WI: Author.

American Psychiatric Association. (1993). *Diagnostic and statistical manual of mental disorders (DSM-IV)*. Washington, DC: Author.

Baker, S. B., & Rogosky-Grassi, M. A. (1993). Access to school. In F. L. Rowlley-Kelly & D. H. Reigel (Eds.), *Teaching the students with spina bifida* (pp. 31–70). Baltimore, MD: Brookes Publishing.

Bigge, J. L. (1991). *Teaching individuals with physical and multiple disabilities* (3rd ed.). New York: Macmillan.

Centers for Disease Control. (1988). *AIDS surveillance report*. Atlanta, GA: Author.

Colson, S. E., & Colson, J. K. (1993). HIV/AIDS education for students with special needs. *Intervention in School and Clinic, 28*, 262–274.

Conlon, J. (1992). New threats to development: Alcohol, cocaine, and AIDS. In M. L. Batshaw & Y. M. Perrett (Eds.), *Children with disabilities: A medical primer* (3rd ed., pp. 111–136). Baltimore, MD: Brookes Publishing.

Deford, F. (1983). *Alex: The life of a child.* New York: New American Library.

Deiner, P. L. (1993). *Resources for teaching children with diverse abilities: Birth through eight.* Fort Worth, TX: Harcourt Brace Jovanovich.

Dowdy, C. A., Patton J. R., Smith, T., & Polloway, E. A. (in press). *Attention deficit disorders: Practical considerations.* Austin, TX: Pro-Ed.

Epilepsy Foundation of America. (1992). *Seizure recognition and observation: A guide for allied health professionals.* Landover, MD: Author.

Esposito, L., & Campbell, P. H. (1993). Computers and individuals with severe and physical disabilities. In J. D. Lindsey (Ed.), *Computers and exceptional individuals* (pp. 159–171). Austin, TX: Pro-Ed.

Fiore, T. A., Becker, E. A., & Nero, R. C. (1993). Educational interventions for students with attention deficit disorder. *Exceptional Children, 60,* 163–173.

Halsam, R. H. A., & Valletutti, P. J. (1985). *Medical problems in the classroom: The teacher's role in diagnosis and management.* Austin, TX: Pro-Ed.

Heward, W. L., & Orlansky, M. D. (1992). *Exceptional children: An introductory survey of special education* (4th ed.). New York: Macmillan.

Jan, J. E., Ziegler, R. G., & Erba, G. (1991). *Does your child have epilepsy?* (2nd ed.). Austin, TX: Pro-Ed.

Johnson, S. B. (1988). Diabetes melitus in childhood. In D. K. Rough (Ed.), *Handbook of pediatric psychology* (pp. 9–31). New York: Guilford Press.

Kurtz, L. (1992). Cerebral palsy. In M. L. Batshaw & Y. M. Perret (Eds.), *Children with disabilities: A medical primer* (3rd ed., pp. 441–469). Baltimore: Paul H. Brookes.

McDonald, E. T. (Ed.). (1987). *Treating cerebral palsy: For clinicians by clinicians.* Austin, TX: Pro-Ed.

Michael, R. J. (1992). Seizures: Teacher observations and record keeping. *Interventions in School and Clinic, 27,* 211–214.

Mira, M. P., Tucker, B. F., & Tyler, J. S. (1992). *Traumatic brain injury in children and adolescents: A sourcebook for teachers and other school personnel.* Austin, TX: Pro-Ed.

Musselwhite, C. R. (1987). Augmentative communication. In E. T. McDonald (Ed.), *Treating cerebral palsy: For clinicians by clinicians* (pp. 209–238). Austin, TX: Pro-Ed.

National Information Center for Children and Youth with Handicaps. (1991). *The education of children and youth with special needs: What do the laws say?* Washington, DC: Author.

Pasternak, M. G. (1979). *Helping kids learn multi-cultural concepts: A handbook of strategies.* Champaign, IL: Research Press.

Reigel, D. H. (1993). Spina bifida from infancy through the school years. In F. L. Rowley-Kelley & D. H. Reigel (Eds.), *Teaching the students with spina bifida.* Baltimore, MD: Brookes Publishing.

Rusk, H. (1977). *Rehabilitation medicine.* St. Louis: Mosby.

Schleichkorn, J. (1993). *Coping with cerebral palsy: Answers to questions parents often ask* (2nd ed.). Austin: TX: Pro-Ed.

Seidel, J. F. (1992). Children with HIV-related developmental difficulties. *Phi Delta Kappan, 72,* 38–56.

Smith, D. D., & Luckasson, R. (1992). *Introduction to special education: Teaching in an age of challenge.* Boston: Allyn & Bacon.

Stehbens, J. A. Childhood cancer. In D. K. Rough (Ed.), *Handbook of pediatric psychology* (pp. 135–161). New York: Guilford Press.

Taylor, J. M., & Taylor, W. S. (1989). *Communicable disease and young children in group settings.* Austin, TX: Pro-Ed.

Tver, D. F., & Tver, B. M. (1991). *Encyclopedia of mental and physical handicaps.* Austin, TX: Pro-Ed.

U.S. Department of Education. (1993). *15th annual report to Congress on the implementation of the Individuals with Disabilities Education Act.* Washington, DC: Office of Special Education Programs, Department of Education.

Zwartjes, G. M., Zwartjes, W. J., & Spilka, B. (1981). Students with cancer. *Today's Education, 70* (4), 20–23.

CHAPTER 9

Communication Disorders

KATHLEEN FAD

I got help for my speech from the time I was in kindergarten until third or fourth grade. Now my speech is as normal and anyone else's. When I get excited I still stutter and mispronounce words like anyone does.

A lot of what has happened to me is reflected in the way I am today. I have never been one to make a lot of friends. I have a lot of associates, but only one or two close friends. It was the same in kindergarten. It might be a habit from not having lots of friends then. I had one or two, maybe three friends who could understand me and who took the time to listen to me. They were what you'd call good active listeners who would try to understand me.

That time ties into today and the way I make speeches. Once you know how to do something, you enjoy doing it. I know people who were called dyslexic and now love to read. I will give a presentation in front of a crowd—no problem. I like to talk in public.

I can't remember any bad things about special ed or speech therapy. I thought I was the cream of the crop. I didn't feel bad at all. There were a lot of good, positive things. My teachers did things in an encouraging way. They really made the kids feel comfortable. I think they got better results that way. I liked my resource time and looked forward to it. I think that my experiences have helped me make some positive relationships. I am a lot more self-reliant.

Don Ayers
college student
Southwestern University

For most of us, the ability to communicate is a skill we take for granted. Our communication is effortless and frequent. In one day, we might share a story with family members, discuss problems with our coworkers, ask directions from a stranger on the street, and telephone an old friend. When we are able to communicate easily and effectively, it is natural to participate in both the commonplace activities required in daily living and the more enjoyable experiences that enrich our lives.

However, when our communication is impaired, absent, or qualitatively different, the simplest interactions may become difficult or even impossible. Moreover, because the communication skills that most of us use so fluently and easily almost always involve personal interactions with others, disorders in speech or language may also result in social problems. For children, these social problems are most likely to occur in school. School is a place not only to learn academics, but also to build positive relationships with teachers and enduring friendships with peers. When a student's communication disorder, however mild, limits his experiences, makes him feel different and inadequate, or undermines his confidence and self-esteem, the overall impact can be devastating.

Communication problems are often complex. There are many types of communication disorders, involving both speech and language. This chapter describes strategies that teachers can use with students who have communication disorders. Included are suggestions that will address specific communication disorders as well as associated problems in socialization and adjustment.

Definitions

Speech and **language** are interrelated skills, tools that we use to communicate. Heward and Orlansky (1992) define the related terms this way:

> *Communication* is the exchange of information and ideas. Communication involves encoding, transmitting, and decoding messages. It is an interactive process requiring at least two parties to play the roles of both sender and receiver. . . . *Language* is a system used by a group of people for giving meaning to sounds, words, gestures, and other symbols to enable communication with one another. . . . *Speech* is the actual behavior of producing a language code by making appropriate vocal sound patterns. Although it is not the only possible vehicle for expressing language (gestures, manual signing, pictures, and written symbols can also be used to convey ideas and intentions), speech is a most effective and efficient method. Speech is also one of the most complex and difficult human endeavors. (pp. 234–236)

Because various cultures develop and use language differently, the study of language is a complex topic. The **American Speech-Language-Hearing Association (ASHA)** (1982) included the following important considerations in its discussion of language: (a) language evolves within specific historical, social, and cultural contexts; (b) language is rule-governed behavior; (c) language learning and use are determined by the interaction of biological, cognitive, psychosocial, and environmental factors; and (d) effective use of language for communication requires a broad understanding of human interactions, including such associated factors as nonverbal cues, motivation, and sociocultural roles (p. 949).

Because language development and use are such complicated topics, determining what is *normal* and what is *disordered* communication is also difficult. According to Emerick and Haynes (1986), a communication difference is considered a disability when

♦ The transmission and/or perception of messages is faulty.
♦ The person is placed at an economic disadvantage.
♦ The person is placed at a learning disadvantage.
♦ The person is placed at a social disadvantage.
♦ There is a negative impact upon the person's emotional growth.
♦ The problem causes physical damage or endangers the health of the person (pp. 6–7).

In order to better understand communication disorders, it is helpful to be familiar with the dimensions of language and the terms used to describe the disorders.

Dimensions of Language

In its definition of communicative disorders, ASHA (1982) has described both *speech disorders* and *language disorders*. **Speech disorders** include impairments of *voice*, *articulation*, and *fluency*. **Language disorders** are impairments of comprehension or use of language, regardless of the symbol system used. A language disorder may involve the *form* of language, the *content* of language, or the *function* of language. Specific disorders of language form include **phonologic** and **morphologic impairments.** *Semantics* refers to the content of language, and *pragmatics* is the system controlling language function. Figure 9.1 contains the definitions of communication disorders as described by ASHA. The terms in this figure will be discussed in more detail later in the chapter. It is clear that the category of communication disorders is broad in scope

---

COMMUNICATIVE DISORDERS

A. A *speech disorder* is an impairment of voice, articulation of speech sounds, and/or fluency. These impairments are observed in the transmission and use of the oral symbol system.
  1. A *voice disorder* is defined as the absence or abnormal production of voice quality, pitch, loudness, resonance, and/or duration.
  2. An *articulation disorder* is defined as the abnormal production of speech sounds.
  3. A *fluency disorder* is defined as the abnormal flow of verbal expression, characterized by impaired rate and rhythm which may be accompanied by struggle behavior.
B. A *language disorder* is the impairment or deviant development of comprehension and/or use of a spoken, written, and/or other symbol system. The disorder may involve (1) the form of language (phonologic, morphologic, and syntactic systems), (2) the content of language (semantic system), and/or (3) the function of language in communication (pragmatic system) in any combination.
  1. Form of language
    a. *Phonology* is the sound system of a language and the linguistic rules that govern the sound combinations.
    b. *Morphology* is the linguistic rule system that governs the structure of words and the construction of word forms from the basic elements of meaning.
    c. *Syntax* is the linguistic rule governing the order and combination of words to form sentences, and the relationships among the elements within a sentence.
  2. Content of language
    a. *Semantics* is the psycholinguistic system that patterns the content of an utterance, intent, and meanings of words and sentences.
  3. Function of language
    a. *Pragmatics* is the sociolinguistic system that patterns the use of language in communication which may be expressed motorically, vocally, or verbally.

COMMUNICATIVE VARIATIONS

A. *Communicative difference/dialect* is a variation of a symbol system used by a group of individuals which reflects and is determined by shared regional, social, or cultural/ethnic factors. Variations or alterations in use of a symbol system may be indicative of primary language interferences. A regional, social, or cultural/ethnic variation of a symbol system should not be considered a disorder of speech or language.
B. *Augmentative communication* is a system used to supplement the communicative skills of individuals for whom speech is temporarily or permanently inadequate to meet communicative needs. Both prosthetic devices and/or nonprosthetic techniques may be designed for individual use as an augmentative communication system.

Figure 9.1 **Definitions of Communication Disorders from ASHA**
Source: American Speech-Language-Hearing Association. Definitions: Communicative Disorders and Variations, *ASHA, 24,* 949–950 (1982). Reprinted by permission of the American Speech-Language-Hearing Association.

and includes a wide variety of problems, some of which may overlap. It is not surprising that this group of disorders includes a large proportion of all students with disabilities.

Prevalence

Over 990,000 children and youth, about 3% of the school-age population, were classified as having speech or language impairments (SLI) during the 1991–1992 school year (U.S. Department of Education, 1993). These students have impairments in their ability to send or receive a message, to articulate clearly or fluently, or to comprehend the pragmatics of social interactions. Because many other students have other conditions as their primary disability but still receive speech-language services, the total number of students served by **speech-language pathologists** is about 5% of all school-age children. Students with communication disorders constitute about 22.9% of all students with disabilities. Recent years (1991–1992) have seen an increase in the number of students in this classification (U.S. Department of Education, 1993). Of the almost one million students identified as speech or language impaired, 93% (over 900,000) are 6 to 12 years of age (U.S. Department of Education, 1993). For this reason, most of the suggestions in this chapter focus on that age group, although many of the language development activities would also be useful with older students.

Placement Patterns

Placement patterns for students with disabilities usually vary by disability, according to students' individual needs. Usually, the milder the disability, the less restrictive the placement. Students with speech or language impairments are the most highly integrated of all students with disabilities. Since 1985, the large majority of students with SLI have been served in either regular classes or resource rooms. During the 1991–1992 school year, 78.9% of students with communication disorders were served in general education classroom placements and 13.9% were served in resource rooms (U.S. Department of Education, 1993). The small proportion served in separate classes most likely represents students with severe language delays and disabilities. For classroom teachers, having students with communication disorders in their classes is more the rule than the exception.

Because so many students with communication disorders are in general education, it is important that teachers be able to identify those students who may have speech or language problems, be familiar with common causes of communication disorders, know when problems are serious enough to require referral to other resources, and have some effective strategies for working with students in the general education environment.

Speech Disorders

This section of the chapter discusses speech disorders that include problems in *articulation, voice,* and *fluency.* The discussion includes (a) a description and definition, (b) a brief explanation of causes, and (c) information related to identifying problems serious enough to require a referral for possible assessment and/or remediation. Next, some suggestions will be presented for classroom teachers.

Disorders of Articulation

Disorders in articulation are the most common speech disorder (McReynolds, 1990). The ability to articulate clearly and correctly is a function of many variables, including a student's age and culture. Although some articulation errors are normal and acceptable at young ages, when students are older these same errors may be viewed as unacceptable and problematic. McReynolds (1990) has described the most common types of articulation errors: **distortions, substitutions, omissions, and additions.** (See Table 9.1.)

Causes of Problems in Articulation. Speech impairments can be either *organic* (i.e., having a physical cause) or *functional* (i.e., having no identifiable organic cause). Because disorders in articulation involve the quality of speech sounds, the child's environment must be considered. Many functional disorders may be related to the student's opportunities to learn appropriate and inappropriate speech patterns, including opportunities to practice appropriate speech and the absence or presence of good speech models in the environment. Many other functional articulation problems have causes that may be related to complex neurological or neuromuscular activities and might never be understood. Differences in speech can also be related to culture. These differences often do not constitute a speech disorder and will be discussed later in the chapter.

Organic articulation disorders are related to the physical abilities required in the process of producing speech sounds, which is a highly complex activity involving numerous neurological and muscular interactions. According to Oyer, Crowe, and

TABLE 9.1 The Four Kinds of Articulation Errors

Error Type	Definition	Example
Substitution	Replace one sound with another sound.	Standard: The ball is red Substitution: The ball is wed
Distortion	A sound in produced in an unfamiliar manner.	Standard: Give the pencil to Sally Distortion: Give the pencil to Sally (the /p/ is nasalized)
Omission	A sound is omitted in a word.	Standard: Play the piano Omission: P_ay the piano
Addition	An extra sound is inserted within a word.	Standard: I have a black horse Addition: I have a belack horse

Source: Reprinted with the permission of Macmillan Publishing Company from HUMAN COMMUNICATION DISORDERS, Third Edition, by George H. Shames and Elisabeth H. Wiig. Copyright © 1990 by Macmillan Publishing Company.

Haas (1987), organic causes of speech impairments may include problems such as cleft palate, dental malformations, or tumors. Other organic disorders (hearing loss, brain damage, or related neurological problems) may also result in disorders of speech. The severity of articulation disorders can vary widely, depending in part on the causes of the disorders.

When Articulation Errors Are a Serious Problem.   Because we know the developmental patterns for normal sound production, we are able to recognize those children who are significantly different from the norm. According to Sander (1972), the normal pattern of consonant sound production falls within relatively well-defined age limits. For example, children usually master the consonant *p* sound by age three, but may not produce a correct *s* sound consistently until age eight. Although young children between ages two and six often make articulation errors as their speech develops, similar errors in older students would indicate an articulation problem. At age three it might be normal for a child to say *wabbit* instead of *rabbit*. If a 12-year-old made the same error, it would be considered a problem, and the teacher might want to refer the student to a speech-language pathologist for evaluation. Figure 9.2 presents this pattern of normal development.

For a general education teacher, evaluating a student's articulation errors involves looking at the big picture, that is, how well the student is doing in class and whether the articulation disorder is interfering with either overall academic performance or social adjustment. Considering a few commonsense questions or situations may give some insight into whether the student has a serious problem and what, if anything, should be done about it.

- ◆ *Is the student's speech intelligible?*
  This may vary. Sometimes, the context of the student's speech will make it easier for listeners to understand her. Also, some errors are easier to understand than others. For example, omissions are usually more difficult to understand than distortions or substitutions.
- ◆ *Consider how many different errors the student makes.*
  If the errors are consistent, that is, the student repeats the same error rather than numerous different errors, he will be easier to understand. Peers and teachers will become familiar with his speech problems and he will have less of a problem relating to others. However, the problem should still be addressed so that the student's speech is intelligible to strangers.
- ◆ *Observe whether the articulation errors cause the student problems in socialization or adjustment.*
  If a student with articulation problems is ridiculed, excluded, or singled out because of her speech problem, then the teacher may want to refer her for a speech-language evaluation. Likewise, if a student is reluctant to speak in class, or seems self-conscious or embarrassed by her articulation errors, the general education teacher should seek an evaluation.
- ◆ *Consider whether the problems are due to physical problems. If they are, be sure that the student is referred to a physician.*

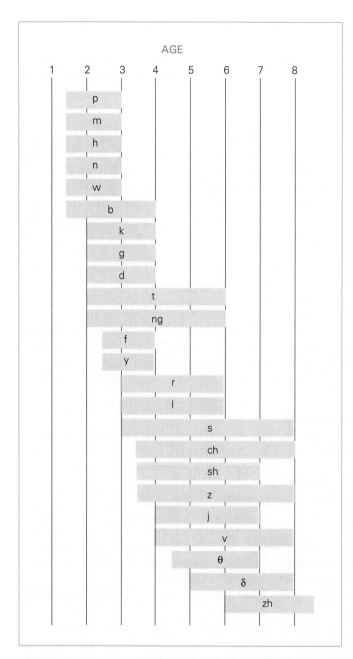

Figure 9.2 **Ages at Which 90% of All Children Typically Produce a Specific Sound Correctly.** Average estimates and upper age limits of customary consonant production. The solid bar corresponding to each sound starts at the median age of customary articulation; it stops at an age level at which 90% of all children are customarily producing the sound. The θ symbol stands for the breathed "th" sound, as in *bathroom,* and the ∂ symbol stands for the voiced "th" sound, as in *feather* (Smith and Luckasson, 1992, p. 168).
Source: Sander, E. K. (1972). When are speech sounds learned? *Journal of Speech and Hearing Disorders, 37,* 62. Reprinted by permission of the American Speech-Language-Hearing Association.

Some articulation problems are due to malformations of the mouth, jaw, or teeth. When the problems are structural, such as cleft lip or palate, many times they can be corrected surgically. Likewise, dental malocclusions (abnormal closures and fit of the teeth) can be corrected with orthodontic treatment.

Articulation problems can result in problems in
socialization or adjustment.

Voice Disorders

Voice disorders are abnormalities of speech related to volume, quality, or pitch. Voice
problems are not very common in children, and it is difficult to distinguish an unpleasant voice from one that would be considered disordered. People generally tolerate a
wide range of voices. Because our voices are related to our identities and are an integral part of who we are and how we are recognized, we usually allow for individual differences in voice. Voice disorders are not commonly thought of as either prevalent or
serious.

According to Heward and Orlansky (1992), there are two basic types of voice disorders, **phonation** and **resonance.** *Phonation* refers to the production of sounds by
the vocal folds. Humans have two vocal folds, which are located in the larynx and lie
side by side. When we speak, healthy vocal folds vibrate, coming together smoothly
along the length of their surfaces, separating, and then coming together again. These
movements are usually very rapid and are controlled by the air pressure coming from
the lungs. The rate of vibration controls the pitch of our voices (slow movements
result in a low pitch, and a faster rate results in a high pitch). If the vocal folds do not
meet and close together smoothly, the voice is likely to sound breathy, hoarse, husky,
or strained.

Disorders of *resonance* involve either too many sounds coming out through the air passages of the nose (hypernasality) or the opposite, too little resonance of the nasal passages (hyponasality). Hypernasality sounds like talking through one's nose or with a "twang," and hyponasality sounds like one has a cold or a stuffy nose. Because resonance is related to what happens to air that travels from the vocal folds into the throat, mouth, and nasal cavity, when there are abnormalities in any of these structures resonance problems can result.

Causes of Voice Disorders. Voice disorders can result from vocal abuse and misuse, trauma to the larynx from accidents or medical procedures, congenital malformations of the larynx, nodules, or tumors. Sometimes, voice disorders are related to other medical conditions, so when a student evidences a voice disorder, the speech-language pathologist will often refer him to an otolaryngologist (ear, nose, and throat doctor). Some examples of organic problems related to voice disorders include congenital anomalies of the larynx, Reye's syndrome, juvenile arthritis, psychiatric problems, or Tourette's syndrome. Because most of these conditions are relatively rare, it may be more likely that the student's voice disorder is a functional problem, perhaps resulting from learned speech patterns (Oyer, Crowe, & Haas, 1987).

When Voice Disorders Are a Serious Problem. A student who has a voice disorder should be observed over the course of several weeks, since many of the symptoms of voice disorders are similar to other temporary conditions such as colds, seasonal allergies, or minor respiratory infections (Oyer, Crowe, & Haas, 1987). One way to get a meaningful measure of the student's speech during this time is to tape record him several times during the observation period. The tape recordings will be helpful to the speech-language pathologist and will provide a basis for comparison. Again, our voices are part of our identity, and, quite often, differences in voice quality, volume, or pitch may be considered to be part of who we are, rather than a problem that requires correction. Teachers might ask themselves the following questions before referring a student for evaluation of a voice disorder:

- ◆ Is the student's voice having such an unpleasant effect on others that the student is excluded from activities?
- ◆ Is there a possibility that the voice disorder is related to another medical condition?
- ◆ Consider whether the voice quality might be related to a hearing loss.

Fluency Disorders

Fluency refers to the pattern of the rate and flow of a person's speech. Normal speech has a rhythm and timing that is regular and steady; however, normal speech patterns also include some interruptions in speech flow. We all sometimes stumble over sounds, repeat syllables or words, mix up speech sounds in words, speak too fast, or fill in pauses with "uh" or "you know." Often our dysfluencies of speech are related to stressful or demanding situations. When the interruptions in speech flow are so frequent or pervasive that a speaker cannot be understood, his efforts at speech are so intense that they are uncomfortable, or they draw undue attention, then the dysfluencies would be considered a problem (Hallahan & Kauffman, 1991).

Many young children, especially those between three and five, demonstrate dysfluencies in the course of normal speech development. Parents and teachers may become concerned about young children's fluency problems, but most of these dysfluencies of early childhood begin to disappear by age five. The most frequent type of fluency disorder is *stuttering,* which affects about 2% of school-age children, more often boys than girls (Smith & Luckasson, 1992).

Fluency problems usually consist of blocking, repeating, or prolonging sounds, syllables, words, or phrases. In **stuttering,** these interruptions are frequently obvious to both the speaker and the listener. Often, they are very disruptive to the act of speaking, much more so than are disorders of articulation or voice. When the speech dysfluencies occur, listeners may become very uncomfortable and try to finish the speaker's words, phrases, or sentences. This discomfort is exacerbated when a speaker's stuttering is accompanied by gestures, facial contortions, and/or physical movements. It is because stuttering is such a pronounced interruption of normal speech and also has a profound impact on listeners that the disorder receives a lot of attention, even though it is not as prevalent as other communication disorders (Hardman, Drew, Egan, & Wolf, 1990).

Causes of Fluency Disorders, Specifically Stuttering.   While there have been many suggested causes of stuttering over the years, the current thinking among professionals in the field of communication disorders is that there may be many different causes of the disorder. According to Van Riper and Emerick (1984), these theories include (a) the view that stuttering is related to emotional problems, (b) the idea that stuttering is the result of a person's biological makeup or of some neurological problem, and (c) the view that stuttering is a learned behavior. Although all of these theories have been considered, the one that seems to be most persistent is that stuttering is a learned behavior that results from normal dysfluencies evident in early speech development. There is also some interest in the role that heredity plays in the development of stuttering, largely because of the fact that male stutterers outnumber females by a ratio of four to one (Hardman, Drew, Egan, & Wolf, 1990).

There seems to be no doubt that the children who stutter are very vulnerable to the attitudes, responses, and comments of their teachers and peers. When considerable attention is focused on normal dysfluencies or when students begin to have negative feelings about themselves because of their stuttering, they may become even more anxious and their stuttering may get worse. Most students who stutter will require therapy by a speech-language clinician if they hope to avoid a lifelong problem that will affect their abilities to communicate, learn, work, and develop positive interpersonal relationships.

When Fluency Disorders Are a Serious Problem.   We know that many children outgrow their speech dysfluencies. However, classroom teachers should be sensitive to students' problems and be sure to refer children who stutter so that they receive speech therapy. Teachers may wish to consider the following when deciding whether speech dysfluencies are serious:

◆ *Is there a pattern of when the student is stuttering?*
Collect information about the student related to his stuttering. With careful observation, teachers may be able to determine if a student's stuttering occurs under specific conditions, that is, with certain individuals, in particular settings, or when in stressful situations.

◆ *Is the student experiencing social problems?*
Carefully monitor unstructured situations to determine the level of acceptance by peers. Much of the socialization that occurs in school takes place in the cafeteria, on the playground, in the halls, on the bus, and in other nonacademic settings. When students are not successfully relating to peers in these environments because of a stuttering problem, then the problem is likely to grow worse.

◆ *Is the student confident?*
Talk to the student to ascertain her level of confidence and self-esteem. One of the biggest problems facing a child who stutters is the interactive effect of the disorder. The more she stutters, the more likely she is to become anxious, fearful, or nervous when she speaks, so the more likely she is to stutter. Children in this cycle of behavior may be so self-conscious that they avoid situations where they are required to speak and become isolated from friends and teachers.

Classroom Accommodations for Speech Disorders

Build a Positive Classroom Climate. Regardless of the type of speech disorder that students in general education classes demonstrate, it is crucial that teachers make every effort to create a climate that is positive, accepting, and safe. The following key points are helpful to remember when dealing with children who have speech disorders.

◆ Don't think of or refer to students with speech disorders in terms of their behaviors ("students," not "stutterers").
◆ Work closely with the speech-language pathologist, follow her suggestions, and try to reinforce specific skills.
◆ Encourage the student.
◆ Be positive.
◆ Accept the child just as you would any other student in the class.
◆ Provide lots of opportunities for students to participate in oral group activities.
◆ Give students lots of chances to model and practice appropriate speech.
◆ Maintain eye contact when the student speaks.
◆ Be a good listener.
◆ Don't interrupt or finish the student's sentence for him.

◆ When appropriate, educate other students in the class about speech disorders and about acceptance and understanding.

◆ Reward the child just as you would reward any student.

Help Students Learn to Monitor Their Own Speech.   By using simple contract formats, teachers can help students focus on using the skills they learn in speech therapy. When students are aware of how to make sound correctly, they can then practice, monitor their own performance, and earn reinforcement from the teacher or parents whenever specific criteria are met.

Pair Students for Practice.   If students are going to master articulation skills, they will need to practice the skills taught by the speech-language pathologist. One way for students to practice specific sounds is to use practice exercises like those in *Hall's Articulation Remediation Training Sheets (HARTS)* (Butler-Hall, 1987). (See Figure 9.3.) With a partner, students can use short periods of down time like those between or before classes to work on their articulation. First, the student is trained in the speech therapy setting on a specific phoneme in a key word, for example the *ch* sound in *hatch*. After the student has reached 90% mastery of the sound in the key word, she then reads the key word and every other word on the skill sheet, in alternating sequence (*hatch, catch, hatch, witch, hatch, sandwich,* etc.). Each practice session should take no more than five minutes and provide students with practice that is simple and fun. Both of the partners should be reinforced for their participation. This practice format can also be used at home with parents.

Teach Students Affirmations and Self-Talk.   For students with speech disorders, especially stuttering, their confidence and attitudes are as important as their specific speech skills. Some research has supported the premise that we all talk to ourselves all of the time and that the more we talk to ourselves in certain ways the more we think about ourselves in those same ways. Although negative **self-talk** is common among individuals who have speech disorders, it is possible to change negative self-images to more positive ones.

Affirmations like those suggested by Daly (1991) can enable students to build their confidence. The goal of this positive self-talk is to replace the clients' old negative patterns, which might include statements like, "I could never do that" or "I can never talk on the phone without stuttering," with positive statements like "I am positive and confident. I know that I can handle any speaking situation by being in control of my speech" and "I enjoy saying my name clearly and smoothly when answering the telephone." Whenever a student slips back into a negative frame of mind, encourage him to mentally erase the negative ideas and immediately think of something positive. Students should also write their own affirmations in their own words, so that they remember them easily and are more likely to use them.

Modify Instruction and Materials.   The *Pre-Referral Intervention Manual (PRIM)* (McCarney & Wunderlich, 1988) presents numerous ways of intervening with stu-

Figure 9.3 **Sample Form for Articulation Practice**
Source: Butler-Hall, B. (1987). *Hall's articulation remediation training sheets (HARTS)*. Henderson, TX: Creations Publications. Used with permission.

dents who demonstrate speech errors. Some of the suggestions presented include the following:

◆ Set up a system of motivators to encourage students' efforts.
◆ Highlight material to identify key syllables and words in a passage.
◆ Give students practice listening so that they can learn to discriminate sounds.
◆ Tape-record the student's reading so that she can evaluate herself for omissions, additions, substitutions, or reversals.
◆ Reduce the emphasis on competition. Competitive activities may increase students' stress and result in even more speech errors.

Encourage Parents to Work with Their Children. There are many ways to structure practice activities so that students can work at home with their parents. One program is called "Weekday Speech Activities to Promote Carryover" (Figure 9.4). This series of activities is designed for the carryover phase of an articulation program. There are 36 worksheets for summer activities. They are designed to be an enjoyable approach to maintenance and generalization of sounds into everyday conversation. By completing the activities, students assume responsibility for correct production of sounds in environments other than the speech therapy room. It is suggested that students complete one activity per day, then have their parents discuss it with them and provide feedback and guidance.

Parents should be encouraged to work with their children to help develop communication skills.

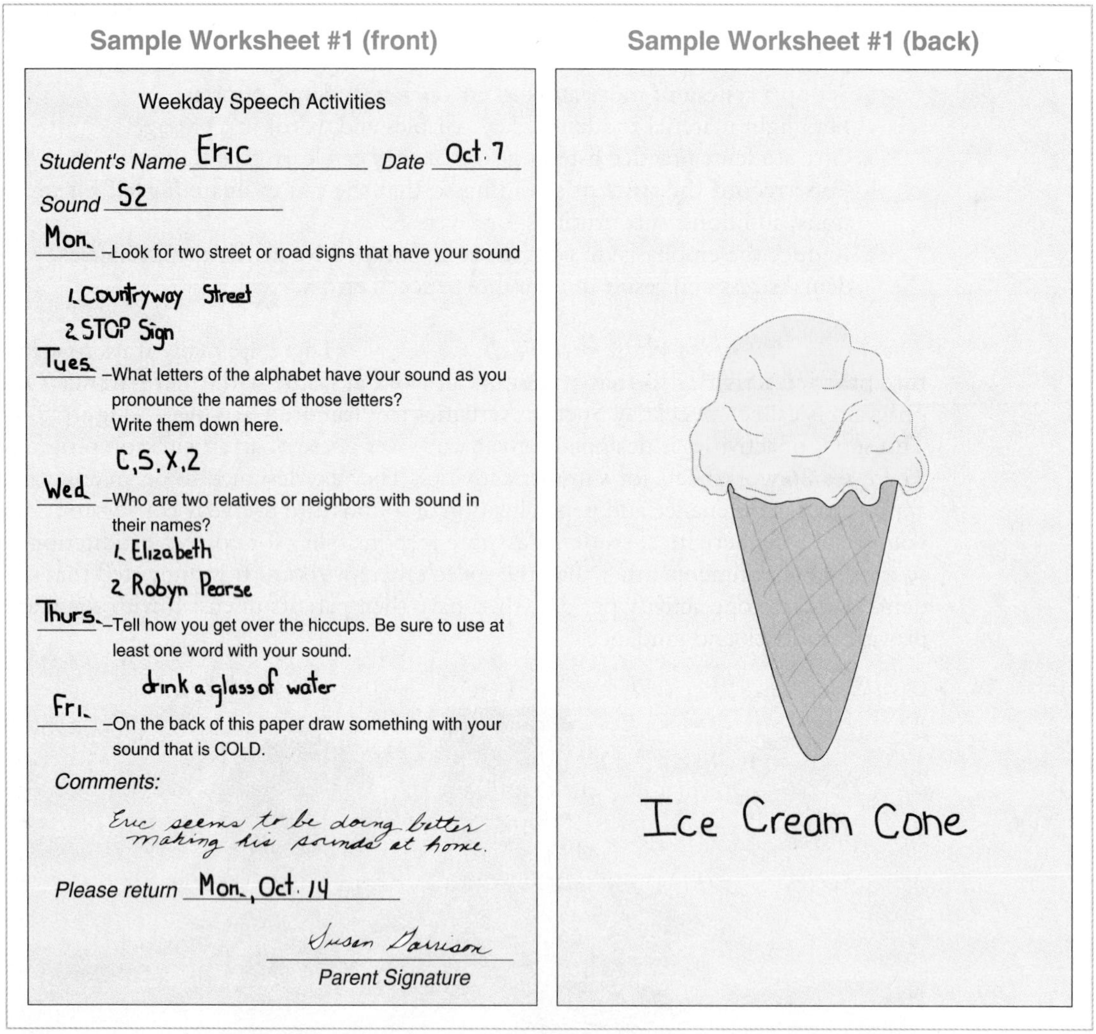

Sample Worksheet #1 (front)	Sample Worksheet #1 (back)

Weekday Speech Activities

Student's Name **Eric**   Date **Oct. 7**

Sound **S2**

Mon. —Look for two street or road signs that have your sound

1. Countryway Street
2. STOP Sign

Tues. —What letters of the alphabet have your sound as you pronounce the names of those letters? Write them down here.

C, S, X, Z

Wed —Who are two relatives or neighbors with sound in their names?

1. Elizabeth
2. Robyn Pearse

Thurs. —Tell how you get over the hiccups. Be sure to use at least one word with your sound.

drink a glass of water

Fri. —On the back of this paper draw something with your sound that is COLD.

Comments:

Eric seems to be doing better making his sounds at home.

Please return **Mon., Oct. 14**

Susan Garrison
Parent Signature

Ice Cream Cone

Figure 9.4   Speech Activities That Parents Can Use
Source: Fehling, R. H. (1993). *Weekday Speech Activities to Promote Carryover*. Austin, TX: Pro-Ed. Used with permission.

Teach Students Their Own Strategies.   Many of the speech problems that students demonstrate while young can be corrected and modified with therapy. While the therapy is going on, the teacher's focus should be on giving students strategies for successful learning. The strategies are little "tricks of the trade" that students can use to maximize their academic and social strengths. Some of the strategies also require accommodations on the part of the teacher in structuring situations and requirements.

- ◆ Teach them to relax with breathing exercises and/or imagery.
- ◆ Encourage them to participate in groups where responses do not have to be individually generated.
- ◆ Teach them to self-reinforce by recognizing when they are doing well and appreciating themselves.
- ◆ Let them practice skills with a friend in real situations so that they are not afraid or nervous when it's the "real thing."
- ◆ Let them tape-record their own speech and listen carefully for errors so that they can discriminate correct and incorrect sounds.
- ◆ Help them come up with strategies for dealing with specific people or situations that make them nervous (walking away, counting to 10 before they speak, deep breathing, etc.).

Language Disorders

Language is the system we use to communicate our thoughts and ideas to others. According to Lahey (1988), language is a code "whereby ideas about the world are expressed through a conventional system of arbitrary signals for communication" (p. 2). The interrelationships of what we hear, speak, read, and write become our format for sharing information.

For most of us, spoken language is the tool we use to communicate our ideas, but even the most articulate, fluent, pleasant speech would be useless without a language system that enables us to understand and be understood. Language is an integral component of students' abilities in reading, writing, and listening. Disorders of language may have a serious impact on academic performance. In recent years, the emphasis in the field of communication disorders has shifted away from remediation of speech problems to an increased focus on language disorders. Estimates today are that 50% to 80% of the children seen by speech-language pathologists have language disorders (Wiig, 1986).

More important for classroom teachers, however, is the fact that remediation of language disorders will often be as much their responsibility as it is the speech-language pathologist's. Although remediation of speech problems is provided primarily in a therapeutic setting and then supported and reinforced by the classroom teacher, teachers will often direct and manage overall language development.

We know that humans can communicate in several ways. Heward and Orlansky (1992) described a child's process for learning language this way: "A child may learn to identify a familiar object, for example, by hearing the spoken word *tree,* by seeing the printed word *tree,* by viewing the sign language gesture for *tree,* or by encountering a combination of these signals" (p. 235). We generally describe modes of communication as either *receptive language,* which involves receiving and decoding or interpreting language, or *expressive language,* which is the encoding or production of a message. Reading and listening are examples of **receptive language;** writing and speaking are forms of **expressive language.**

As with speech disorders, knowing the normal sequence of language development is important. Some children may be delayed in their development of language but

Teaching Listening Skills for Class Discussions

◆ Encourage active listening during directions.
You can do this in several ways:

1. Restate the directions in question form.
   "How many problems are you supposed to do?"
2. Ask a student to rephrase the direction.
   "Tell the class what page we need to read."
3. Write the key words from the direction on the board
   (not the entire direction; it discourages listening).

◆ Use listening buddies.
Students can rephrase information for each other in a cooperative structure. ("Turn to your partner and explain what the first step is.") Students could also quiz each other at regular intervals, either for test reviews or less formal checks for understanding.

◆ Encourage listening during lectures.
After stating the objectives for the lesson, one way to encourage good active listening is to make use of students' prior knowledge. Let students begin discussion of a topic with a brainstorming session. Brainstorming ideas is fun for students. Students can generate ideas and share information; teachers can acknowledge students' input and remind them of how much they already know.

◆ Arouse student curiosity.
There are numerous questioning strategies that arouse students' interest in various topics. At the beginning of a lesson, let students generate a list of questions about the topic. As the lesson progresses, return to the students' questions. Point out the ones that have been answered and, if there are still some questions unanswered at the end of the lesson, allow students to work independently or in cooperative groups to locate the information. Always try to encourage some higher-level *thinking questions* that call for creative, open-ended responses.

Source: Pruden, L. K. (1992). *Listen to learn.* Bedford, TX: GG Publishing. Used with permission.

still acquire skills in the same sequence as other children. Other children may acquire some age-appropriate language skills but have deficits in other specific skills areas. Table 9.2 briefly explains the normal developmental patterns of language development for children with language disorders and children without language disorders. Although they may refer to these general patterns of language development to judge

TABLE 9.2 Language Development for Children with Language Disorders and without Language Disorders

Language-Disordered Child			Normally Developing Child		
Age	Attainment	Example	Age	Attainment	Example
27 months	First words	*this, mama, bye bye, doggie*	13 months	First words	*here, mama, bye bye, kitty*
38 months	50-word vocabulary		17 months	50-word vocabulary	
40 months	First two-word combinations	*this doggie more apple this mama more play*	18 months	First two-word combinations	*more juice here ball more TV here kitty*
48 months	Later two-word combinations	*Mimi purse Daddy coat block chair dolly table*	22 months	Later two-word combinations	*Andy shoe Mommy ring cup floor keys chair*
52 months	Mean sentence length of 2.00 words		24 months	Mean sentence length of 2.00 words	
55 months	First appearance of -ing	*Mommy eating*		First appearance of -ing	*Andy sleeping*
63 months	Mean sentence length of 3.10 words		30 months	Mean sentence length 3.10 words	
66 months	First appearance of *is*	*The doggie's mad*		First appearance of *is*	*My car's gone!*
73 months	Mean sentence length of 4.10 words		37 months	Mean sentence length 4.10 words	
79 months	Mean sentence length of 4.50 words			First appearance of indirect requests	*Can I have some cookies?*
	First appearance of indirect requests	*Can I get the ball?*	40 months	Mean sentence length of 4.50 words	

Source: Leonard, L. (1990). Language disorders in preschool children. In G. H. Shames and E. H. Wiig (Eds.), *Human communication disorders: An introduction* (2nd ed., p. 242). New York: Macmillan. Reprinted with permission of Merrill, an imprint of Macmillan Publishing Company.

students' overall progress, teachers should not expect every child to follow this precise sequence on these exact timelines.

Dimensions of Language

Earlier in the chapter, terminology related to language disorders was introduced. We refer to the dimensions of language and their related impairments in terms of form, content, and function (or use). Students can demonstrate impairments in any or all of these areas of language.

Form.   **Form** describes the rule systems used in oral language. Three different rule systems are included when we discuss form: **phonology, morphology,** and **syntax.**

Phonology is the rule system that governs the individual and combined sounds of a language. Phonological rules vary from one language to another. For example, some of the guttural sounds heard in German are not used in English, and some of the vowel combinations of English are not found in Spanish.

Morphology refers to the rule system controlling the structure of words. Because the structures of words govern their meanings, comparative suffixes such as *-er* or *-est* and plural forms such as the *s* that changes *book* to *books* are important. Oyer, Crowe, and Haas (1987) provide an example of how morphemes (units of meaning) can change a basic word into similar words with many different meanings:

> The word "friend" is composed of one free morpheme that has meaning. One or more bound morphemes may be added, making "friend*ly*," "*un*friendly," "friend*less*," "friend-*liness*," "friend*ship*," and "friend*lier*." There are rules for combining morphemes into words that must be followed (e.g., "*dis*friend" is not an allowable word and thus has no meaning). (p. 61)

Syntax is the ordering of words in such a way that they can be understood. Syntax rules determine where words are placed in a sentence. Just like phonology, syntax rules vary from one language to another. Rules governing negatives, questions, tenses, and compound or simple sentences determine the meanings of word combinations. For example, the same words used in different combinations can mean very different things: *The boy hit the ball* is not the same as *The ball hit the boy.*

All of these rule systems affect how we use and understand language. Children's abilities to understand and correctly use all of these rules related to form develop sequentially as their language develops. Form is important not only in spoken language but in written language and in sign language systems, too.

Content.   *Content* refers to the intent and meaning of language and its rule system; *semantics* deals with the meaning of words and word combinations. Without specific words to label and describe objects or ideas, our language would have no meaning. When students fail to comprehend concrete and abstract meanings of words, inferences, or figurative phrases, it is difficult for them to understand more subtle uses of language such as jokes, puns, similes, proverbs, or sarcasm. As children mature, they are better able to differentiate meanings of similar words, classify by similarities, and understand abstract meanings of words.

Use.   When we use language in various social contexts, we follow another set of rules, *pragmatics.* The purpose and setting of our communication as well as the people with whom we are communicating determine the language we use. If children are to build and maintain successful relationships with others, it is important that they understand and effectively use skills appropriate to the context. For example, when children speak to adults, it is helpful if they use polite, respectful language; when they speak to their friends, they will most likely use less formal spoken language, demonstrate more relaxed body language, and take turns while talking (Owens, 1984).

Types and Causes of Language Disorders

Hallahan and Kauffman (1991) have described four basic categories of language disorders: absence of verbal language, qualitatively different language, delayed language development, and interrupted language development. Table 9.3 from Naremore (1980) summarizes these four categories and includes some suspected causes of each. For children who are not deaf, a complete absence of language would likely indicate severe emotional disturbance or severe mental retardation. Qualitatively different language is also associated with mental retardation and emotional disturbance. A good example of this type of problem is the echolalic speech of children with autism, who may repeat speech they hear in a singsong voice and fail to use their spoken language in a meaningful way. Delayed language occurs when a child develops language in the same sequence as other children, but at a slower rate. Causes of delayed language include mental retardation, hearing loss, or lack of stimulation or experiences. Sometimes language development is interrupted by illness or physical trauma. This type of language problem is increasingly common among children due to acquired brain

TABLE 9.3   Types of Language Disorders and Their Causes

Type	Commonly Suspected Causative Factors or Related Conditions
No verbal language	
Child does not show indications of understanding or spontaneously using language by age 3.	Congenital or early acquired deafness Gross brain damage or severe mental retardation Childhood psychosis
Qualitatively different language	
Child's language is different from that of nonhandicapped children at any stage of development—meaning and usefulness for communication are greatly lessened or lost.	Inability to understand auditory stimuli Childhood psychosis Learning disability Mental retardation Hearing loss
Delayed language development	
Language follows normal course of development, but lags seriously behind that of most children who are the same chronological age.	Mental retardation Experiential deprivation Lack of language stimulation Hearing loss
Interrupted language development	
Normal language development begins but is interrupted by illness, accident, or other trauma; language disorder is acquired.	Acquired hearing loss Brain injury due to oxygen deprivation, physical trauma, or infection

Source: Adapted from Naremore, R. C. (1980) Language disorders in children. In T. J. Hixon, L D. Shriberg, and J. H. Saxman (Eds.), *Introduction to Communication Disorders.* Englewood Cliffs, NJ: Prentice-Hall. Used with permission.

injury. In general education classrooms, teachers may encounter any or all of these types of language disorders at ranges from very mild to severe.

Indicators of Language Impairments

Some teachers may have an overall sense that a student is demonstrating language problems; others may not. Wiig and Semel (1984) have identified some indicators of language problems by grade levels:

Primary Grades:

◆ Problems in following verbal directions
◆ Difficulty with preacademic skills (recognizing sound differences)
◆ Phonics problems
◆ Poor word attack skills
◆ Difficulties with structural analysis
◆ Problems learning new material

Intermediate Grades:

◆ Word substitutions
◆ Inadequate language processing and production that affects reading comprehension and academic achievement

Middle and High School:

◆ Inability to understand abstract concepts
◆ Problems understanding multiple word meanings
◆ Difficulties connecting previously learned information to new material that must be learned independently
◆ Widening gap in achievement when compared to peers

In addition, Figure 9.5 presents a checklist of behaviors that may indicate either speech or language problems. Children who have language disorders sometimes develop patterns of interaction with peers, teachers, and family members that may result in behavior problems. The behavior problems might seem to have nothing to do with language problems but may in fact have developed in response to inabilities to read, spell, talk, or write effectively.

Classroom Accommodations for Language Disorders

Numerous strategies can be used in general education classrooms to improve students' language skills and remediate language deficits. The following section presents some ways of structuring learning situations and presenting information so that communication can be enhanced.

Teach Some Prerequisite Imitation Skills. (Nowacek & McShane, 1993)

◆ Show a picture (of a girl running) and say, "The girl is running."
◆ Ask the student to repeat a target phrase.

A Teacher's Checklist: Behaviors That *May* Indicate Communication Disorders

Speech

- Poor articulation
- Different voice quality
- Dysfluencies
- Slurred conversational speech

Language

- Has problems following oral directions
- Speech rambles; isn't able to express her ideas concisely
- Appears shy, withdrawn, never seems to talk or interact with others
- Asks questions that are off-topic
- Has a poor sense of humor
- Has poor comprehension of material read
- Doesn't plan ahead in pencil/paper activities
- Takes things literally
- Is not organized, appears messy
- Doesn't manage time well; has to be prodded to complete assignments

Figure 9.5   **Teacher's Checklist of Behaviors That *May* Indicate Communication Disorders**

- ◆ Positively reinforce correct responses.
- ◆ Present a variety of subject/verb combinations until the student correctly and consistently imitates them.

Increase Receptive Language in the Classroom.   Clary and Edwards (1992) suggest some specific activities to improve students' receptive language.

- ◆ *Give students practice following directions.*
  Begin with one simple direction and increase the length of the list of directions. Have the student perform a simple task in the classroom such as closing the door, turning around, and so on.
- ◆ *Have students pair up and practice descriptions.*
  Place two students at a table separated by a screen. Place identical objects in front of both students. Have one describe an object; the other must select the object being described. Reverse roles with a new set of objects
- ◆ *Let students work on categorizing.*
  Orally present a list of three words. Two should be related in some way. Ask a student to tell which two are related and why (e.g., horse, tree, dog).

Give Students Opportunities for Facilitative Play.   This type of interaction provides modeling for the students so that they can imitate and expand their own use of language. The following is an abbreviated sequence for facilitative play (Nowacek & McShane, 1993).

- ◆ The teacher models self-talk in a play activity. ("I'm making the cars go.")
- ◆ The teacher expands on the student's comments. ("Yes, the cars are going *fast*.")

◆ The teacher uses "buildups" and "breakdowns" by expanding on a student's ideas, breaking them down, then repeating them. ("Red car go? Yes, look at the red car. It's going fast on the road. It's going to win the race.")

Sometimes students who are reluctant to speak require encouragement. In addition to encouraging them with positive social interactions, teachers might also have to structure situations so that students must use language to meet some of their needs in the classroom. The strategies that follow should prompt students to use language when they otherwise might choose not to use it.

Elicit Language from Students.

◆ Have items out of reach so that the child has to ask for them.
◆ When a child asks for an item, give her the wrong item (she asks for a spoon and you give her a fork).
◆ Give a child an item that is hard to open so that he has to request assistance.
◆ When performing a task, do one step incorrectly (forget to put the milk in the blender with the pudding mix).
◆ Make items difficult to find.
◆ Give students an item that requires some assistance (an orange that needs peeling).

Often, the most effective techniques for language acquisition and use are those that will be easy for teachers to use and easy for students to generalize to everyday situations. Teachers can encourage generalization by naturalistic and situational strategies and real-life activities.

Use Naturalistic Techniques to Increase Language Use.

◆ Try *cloze* activities. ("What do you need? Oh, you need paint and a _____. That's right, you need paint and a brush.")
◆ Emphasize problem solving. ("You can't find your backpack? What should you do? Let's look on the hook. Is your coat there? What did we do to find your coat? That's right, we looked on the hook.")
◆ Use questioning techniques. ("Where are you going? That's right, you are going to lunch.")

Simulate Real-Life Activities to Increase Language Use.

◆ Let students simulate a newscast or commercial.
◆ Have students write and follow their own written directions to locations in and around the school.
◆ Play "social charades" by having students act out social situations and decide appropriate responses.
◆ Have one student teach an everyday skill to another (how to shoot a basket).
◆ Using real telephones, give students opportunities to call each other, giving, receiving, and recording messages.

Teachers should always try to have some fun with students. Using music and playing games are two ways language can be incorporated into enjoyable activities.

Use Music to Improve Language.

- Use songs that require students to request items (rhythm sticks or tambourines passed around a circle).
- Have picture symbols for common songs so that students can request the ones they like.
- Use props to raise interest and allow students to act out the story (during "Humpty Dumpty" the student falls off a large ball).
- Use common chants like "When You're Happy and You Know It" and let students choose the action (clap your hands).

Play Games That Require Receptive or Expressive Language.

- Do "Simon Says."
- Play "Musical Chairs" with words. (Pass a ball around a circle. When the teacher says a magic word, the student with the ball is out.)
- Use key words to identify and organize students. ("All of the boys with red hair stand up. Everyone who has a sister sit down.")
- Play "Twenty Questions." ("I'm thinking of a person." Students ask "yes" or "no" questions.)

Arrange Your Classroom for Effective Interactions.   For students who have either speech or language problems, the physical arrangement of the classroom can contribute to success. Some guidelines that may improve students' language development and use include the following (Breeding, Stone, & Riley, n.d.):

- Give instructions and important information when distractions are at their lowest.
- Use consistent-attention getting devices, either verbal, visual, or physical cues.
- Be specific when giving directions.
- Write directions on the chalkboard, flipchart, or overhead so that students can refer to them.
- Use students' names frequently when talking to them.
- Emphasize what you're saying by using gestures and facial expressions.
- Pair students up with buddies for modeling and support.
- Allow for conversation time in the classroom so that students can share information and ideas.
- Encourage students to use calendars to organize themselves and manage their time.

Use Challenging Games with Older Students.   Older students may require continued intervention to improve language skills. However, the activities chosen must be appropriate and not seem like "baby" games. Thomas and Carmack (1993) have collected ideas that could involve older students in enjoyable, interactive tasks.

◆ Read fables or stories with morals. Discuss outcomes and focus on the endings.

◆ Do "Explain That." Discuss common idioms and help students discover the connection between the literal and figurative meanings. (*She was on pins and needles.*)

◆ "Riddlemania" presents riddles to students and has them explain the humor.

◆ Have "Sense-Able Lessons." Bring objects to see, taste, hear, and smell, and compile a list of students' verbal comments (p. 155).

Modify Strategies So That Students Have Learning Tools.   When facilitating language development in older students, it is important to help them develop their own strategies to use in challenging situations (Thomas & Carmack, 1993). Requiring them to use higher-order thinking skills will both require and stimulate higher-level language.

◆ Pair students up to find word meanings. Use partners when working on categories such as synonyms or antonynms. Let students work together to master using a thesaurus.

◆ Teach students to categorize. Begin with concrete objects they relate to such as types of cars or names of foods, then move to more abstract concepts like feelings or ideas.

◆ Play reverse quiz games like "Jeopardy," in which students have to work backward to think of questions for answers (pp. 155–163).

Work Collaboratively with the Speech-Language Pathologist.   LINC (Language IN the Classroom) is a program modified and adapted for use in many school districts (Breeding, Stone, & Riley, n.d.). The philosophy behind the program is that language learning should occur in the child's most natural environment and in conjunction with other content being learned. The development of a student's language should relate to his world and should be a learning experience, not a teaching experience.

The purpose of the program is to strengthen the language system of those students in general education classrooms who need to develop coping and compensatory skills to survive academically. Another goal is to transfer language learned from the therapy setting to the classroom, thereby allowing children to learn to *communicate* as opposed to learning to *talk*. The teacher and the speech-language pathologist must both be present for the approach to be successful. The two professionals work together to plan unit lessons that develop language skills in students.

Hiller (1990) presented an example of how LINC works. His elementary school implemented classroom-based language instruction. At the beginning of the program, the speech-language pathologist visited each classroom for a specified amount of time each week (90 minutes) during the language arts period. The first 45 minutes were used for an oral language activity, often a cooking activity from the *Blooming Recipes* workbook (Tavzel, 1987). During the second 45 minutes, students did paragraph writing. For example, after preparing peanut butter on celery ("Bumps on a Log") students responded to these questions:

What was the name of the recipe we made?

Where did we do our preparing?

Who brought the peanut butter, celery, and raisins?

How did we make "Bumps on a Log"?

When did we eat "Bumps on a Log"?

Why do you think this recipe was called "Bumps on a Log"?

Responses were written on the board or on an overhead. Students copied the responses in paragraph format.

Teachers and speech-language pathologists later extended the activities to teaching language lessons on current topics, team-teaching critical thinking activities during science experiments, and team-planning and teaching social studies units. Reports from Hiller's and other schools using LINC programs described better collaboration among professionals, more accurate language referrals, and increased interest in speech-language activities among the entire staff.

Use Storytelling and Process Writing.   When children listen to and retell a story, they incorporate it into their oral language repertoire. McKamey (1991) has described a structure for allowing students to retell stories they had heard, tell stories from their own experience, and write down and illustrate their oral presentations. In process writing, students are instructed based on what they can already do. This and other whole- language experiences often allow students who have had negative language experiences to begin to succeed, to link written and spoken language, and to grow as communicators.

Language Differences Due to Culture

Children's patterns of speech and use of language reflect their culture and may be different from that of some of their peers. It is important not to mistake a language *difference* for a language disorder, but also it is important not to overlook a disorder in a student with language differences. Cultural variations in family structure, child-rearing practices, family perceptions and attitudes, and language and communication styles can all influence students' communication (Wayman, Lynch, & Hanson, 1990).

Relationship between Communication Style and Culture

Culture has a strong influence on the *style* of communication. Many areas of communication style can be impacted, including gender, status, and age roles; rules governing interruptions and turn-taking; use of humor; and how to greet or leave someone (Erickson, 1992). It is important that teachers be aware of the many manifestations of culture in nonverbal communication, as well. Differences in rules governing eye contact, the physical space between speakers, use of gestures and facial expression, and use of silence can cause dissonance between teachers and students of differing cultures.

A Southern Vowel Pronunciation

In some Southern dialects of English, words such as *pin* and *pen* are pronounced the same. Usually, both words are pronounced as *pin*. This pattern of pronunciation is also found in other words. List A gives words in which the *i* and *e* are pronounced the *same* in these dialects.

List A: *I* and *E* pronounced the same

1. *tin* and *ten*
2. *kin* and *Ken*
3. *Lin* and *Len*
4. *windy* and *Wendy*
5. *sinned* and *send*

Although *i* and *e* words in List A are pronounced the *same,* there are other words in which *i* and *e* are pronounced differently. List B gives word pairs in which the vowels are pronounced *differently.*

List B.   *I* and *E* pronounced differently

1. *lit* and *let*
2. *pick* and *peck*
3. *pig* and *peg*
4. *rip* and *rep*
5. *litter* and *letter*

Compare the word pairs in List A with those in List B. Is there a pattern that can explain why the words in List A are pronounced the *same* and why the words in List B are pronounced *differently?* To answer this question, you have to look at the sounds that are next to the vowels. Look at the sounds that come after the vowel. What sound is found next to the vowel in all of the examples given in List A?

Use your knowledge of the pronunciation pattern to pick the word pairs in List C that are pronounced the *same* (S) and those that are pronounced *differently* (D) in this Southern dialect.

List C: same or different?

_____ 1. *bit* and *bet*
_____ 2. *pit* and *pet*
_____ 3. *bin* and *Ben*
_____ 4. *Nick* and *neck*
_____ 5. *din* and *den*

How can you tell where *i* and *e* will be pronounced the same and where they will be pronounced differently?

Source: Adger, C. T., Wolfram, W., & Detwyler, J. (1993). Language differences. *Teaching Exceptional Children. 26,* 44–47. Used with permission.

Walker (1993) has described the effects that differences such as directness of a conversation, volume of voices used in conversations, and reliance of verbal (low context) versus nonverbal (high context) parts of communication affect attitudes toward

A child's cultural background has a strong influence on the *style* of communication.

the speaker. Teachers can respond to these and other cultural differences in several ways. These suggestions are adapted from Walker (1993) and should be helpful for teachers who want to enhance both overall achievement and communication skills with students who are culturally or linguistically different.

- ◆ Try to involve community resources, including churches and neighborhood organizations, in school activities.
- ◆ Make home visits.
- ◆ Allow flexible hours for conferences.
- ◆ Question your own assumptions about human behavior, values, biases, personal limitations, etc.
- ◆ Try to understand the world from the student's perspective.
- ◆ Ask yourself questions about an individual student's behavior in light of cultural values, motivation, and world views, and how these relate to his/her learning experiences.

Considerations in Assessment

Assessment in the area of communication disorders is often complicated, just as it is for students with learning disabilities. Because of the increasing numbers of students who are linguistically different and who require services in ESL (English as a Second Language) or who are Limited English Proficient (LEP), teachers should consult with personnel in special education, ESL, speech and language services, and/or bilingual education to obtain appropriate evaluation and programming services.

There are many considerations for assessment personnel who work with students having cultural and linguistic differences. The following suggestions have been adapted from Toliver-Weddington and Erickson (1992) and may be useful for classroom teachers who suspect that students may have communication disorders.

- When screening with tests, always select tests that have the most valid items for the skills to be assessed.
- Consider procedural modifications such as lengthening the time limit.
- Try to assess whether the minority child has had access to the information.
- Consider scoring the test in two ways, first as the manual indicates, then allowing credit for items that may be considered correct in the child's language system and/or experiences. (Record and report both ways and indicate the adjustments.)
- Focus on what the child does well rather than what he or she cannot do.

Because of the increasing number of students in public schools from cultural and/or linguistic minority groups, teachers are recognizing the need for information related to learning and communication styles as well as modifications to curriculum and instruction. Although many of these children will never be identified as having a communication disorder, teachers in general education must be aware that differences in language and culture may often impact a student's apparent proficiency in both oral and written communication.

Augmentative and Alternative Communications

The term *augmentative* describes techniques that supplement or enhance communication by complementing whatever vocal skills the individual already has (Harris & Vanderheiden, 1980). For some individuals (e.g., those who are severely neurologically impaired) these communication techniques are alternatives to speech. According to Shane and Sauer (1986), the term *alternative* applies when "the physical involvement of an individual is so extensive that the production of speech for communication purposes has been ruled out and an **alternative communication** system is required" (p. 2).

Communication techniques can be considered *aided* or *unaided*. Unaided techniques are those that do not require any physical object or entity in order to express information (e.g., speech, manual signs or gestures, facial communication). Aided communication techniques require some physical object or device to enable the individual to communicate (e.g., communication boards, charts, and mechanical/electrical devices). Because there are substantial numbers of individuals without speech due to mental retardation, traumatic brain injury, deafness, neurological disorders, or other causes, there has been increased demand for **augmentative** or alternative communication.

Students without spoken language may use a basic nonautomated **communication** board with no electronic parts. Typically, the board will contain common words, phrases, or numbers. The communication board can be arranged in either an alphabetic or nonalphabetic format (see Figure 9.6). Because they are easy to construct

Speech and Language Disorders and Types of Computer Applications

Disorder	Types of Applications
Articulation	Phonologic analysis, intelligibility analysis, drill-and-practice, and games
Voice	Biofeedback programs and client information
Fluency	Biofeedback and relaxation programs
Syntactic	Language sample analysis, drill and practice, games, and tutorials
Semantic	Language sample analysis and cognitive rehabilitation
Pragmatic	Problem solving and simulations
Hearing impairment	Visual feedback, sign language instruction with CAI, and telecommunication applications

Source: Cochran, P. S., & Bull, G. L. (1993). Computers and individuals with speech and language disorders. In J. D. Lindsey (Ed.), *Computers and exceptional individuals* (p. 146). Austin, TX: Pro-Ed. Used with permission.

and can be modified to fit the student's vocabulary, nonautomated communication boards are very useful in communicating with teachers, family members, and peers. There are some commercially available sets of symbols, including *The Picture Communication Symbols* (Mayer-Johnson, 1986) and *The Oakland Picture Dictionary* (Kirsten, 1981).

Electronic communication aids can encompass a wide variety of capabilities, from simple to complex. Often, a voice synthesizer is used to produce speech output, and written output is produced on printers or displays. Software that is increasingly more sophisticated can accommodate the many different needs of individuals who cannot produce spoken language. Following are some examples of communication aids with their key features (adapted from Shane & Sauer, 1986). Other examples are presented in the boxes on technology.

AllTalk:

◆ Human voice output communicator
◆ Can store anyone's voice as a message for any given location
◆ Completely user programmable
◆ User can design overlays to correspond to messages
◆ Voice programs can be stored on standard cassette player for later access

Light Talker:

◆ Microprocessor-based communication aid with synthesized speech output
◆ Operates with either *Express* or *Minspeak* firmware
◆ Fast, effective communication

me	you	we	are, is, am	fix	hold me	put away
my						
Pam / Karin	Mom	woman	be	forgot	hope	read
Judy / Red	Dad	man	believe	get	itches	see
Bob	boyfriend	baby	brush	give	like	sew
Sheila Ann	friends	boy	change clothes	go, walk	love	sit
Dennis Aide	doctor	girl	close	gossip	lying	sleep
foster parents	lawyer	O.T.	come	got	married	stop
him / her	social worker	P.T.	drink	hate	need	suppose
police	relative	speech therapist	eat	have	open	take
people	wife	husband	fall	help	pick up	talk/tell say/said
nobody	bitch	Hans Kasten 555-2083	divorce	cry	hide	kiss

Figure 9.6 Communication Board in Alphabetic and Nonalphabetic Formats
Source: Shane, H. C., & Sauer, M. (1986). *Augmentative and alternative communication.* Austin, TX: Pro-Ed. Used with permission.

SpeechPAC/Epson:

◆ Portable synthetic voice communicator
◆ Includes full-sized keyboard, built-in printer, LCD screen, and built-in micro-cassette drive for saving and loading programs
◆ User types messages on the keyboard
◆ Messages may be spoken or directed to the printer
◆ Can store up to 23,000 characters in memory, giving the user a completely customized voice output

Facilitated Communication

Facilitated communication is a process that has recently been used with individuals who have developmental disabilities, including autism. First introduced by Rosemary Crossley in Australia, facilitated communication usually involves having someone (a facilitator) support the arm or wrist of the person with autism, who then points to letters on a keyboard. The keyboard is often connected to a computer so that the individual's words can be displayed and/or printed (Kirk, Gallagher, & Anastasiow, 1993).

Much of the work done in facilitated communication has been carried out by Biklen (1990), who has reported great success with the procedure. At this time, results of research on the effectiveness of facilitated communication are mixed; some individuals have shown great promise, and others have not done as well.

Future Trends

Several forces are changing the field of communication disorders. First, general education teachers are likely to see more students with moderate to severe disabilities in their classrooms. The movement toward more inclusive environments for students will require classroom teachers to provide more instruction for these students. The case-loads of speech-language pathologists are continuing to grow, and there is an ever-increasing demand for services, especially in the area of language disorders. Although "pull-out" speech-language remediation will still be offered, many of the services will be delivered in an increasingly collaborative framework, with teachers and pathologists cooperating and sharing resources.

Another area of change is the expected continuation of technological advances. Some of the improved technology has already been described here; however, it is virtually impossible to keep up with the rapid improvements in this area. With continued improvements in technology, students with more severe communication disorders will have opportunities to interact with family members, teachers, and peers, perhaps participating in activities that would have seemed impossible ten years ago.

Author's note. The author would like to express her appreciation to Janice Maxwell, B.A., M.S. (SLP), for her assistance in providing much of the practical information that was presented in this chapter. Janice is an exemplary speech pathologist and a wonderful friend to teachers in general education.

First-Hand Account of Facilitated Communication

Autism: The Unknown World
Jesse Richard

Imagine going through part of your life as one kind of person and then one day your life changes. Before your eyes you are a new person. A person with new dreams and a new outlook on life. This is what happened to me.

Discrimination. Webster's dictionary defines it as, "To distinguish or differentiate between someone or something on the basis of race, sex, class, or religion; to act prejudicially." What does this mean to people with disabilities? Often times this means ridicule, harassment, weird looks from others who do not understand and disbelief in their abilities. Discrimination is not only damaging to those with disabilities, but their families as well. What can be done to help others understand? Providing information to them is only a small step. They must hear and see first-hand accounts of what a person with a disability must overcome each day of their life.

Once upon a time there was a boy who was born with autism. No one knew what this meant when they heard about this disease. His mother believed he could be somebody someday, but no one would listen. Then one day a lady came to his house and said, "I believe." Her name was Mary. She worked and worked with him to learn rules of life. Never did she give up on him. She was his teacher, his friend, and most importantly his advocate. She worked long hours to see him learn, but little did she know he was learning the most important thing in life. . . trust. A five-letter word to some, but something much more important to him. He would never be where he is today without Mary. She will forever be his friend no matter near or far. No one believed when she said what he could do. The story gets more exciting as his world begins to change. A lady from Australia comes to visit and said she believes. She brought with her a pocketful of dreams. He was opened the door to reality, the key was facilitated communication. The key to happiness. This key was a golden key that fit perfectly.

This boy is Jesse Richard. I was born with autism because God had a plan. A plan not revealed until only recently. A plan for my family and for me. For eighteen years I was labeled retarded, someone not able to speak and thought to have nothing to say. I did, but had no way to prove myself. So I almost gave up on myself, wondering what the plan was for me. To live with disability is a challenge every day, but to live is a challenge in itself. So I continued to live waiting for something to come my way. At last it arrived by plane across the sea and land to bring a new way to communicate.

Facilitated communicating is the way in which I communicate. Another person applying pressure on my wrist or hand allows me to concentrate on what I am doing instead of the other senses that bombard me all the time. I communicate using computers, hand-held computers, typewriters or anything that types. Some people are not sure if they believe that what I say is actually from my hand, because I have assistance on my hand. To accuse someone of not thinking for themselves is to rob them of their right to an independent life. As the saying goes, "Just because I can't speak doesn't mean I don't have anything to say."

Facilitation not only changed my life but my family as well. My mom and brother had learned to accept my disability for eighteen years. Now a miracle happens and all of a sudden I'm a new person. Imagine the overwhelming emotions; shock, disbelief, excitement and fear of the unknown. The unknown a frightening word because of all its uncertainties. The biggest challenge now is to learn who I am and to tell people about my experience, because it is something we must all remember. We must never give up. There is a plan for us all.

My next plan is to write to Donahue and be a guest speaker. After that meet the President and advocate for people with disabilities.

Source: Richard, J., Jackson, K., Ulrich, M., & Ulrich, A. (1993). *First hand: Personal accounts of breakthroughs in facilitated communication* (pp. 1–2). Madison, WI: DRI Press. Used with permission.

References

Adger, C. T., Wolfram, W., & Detwyler, J. (1993). Language differences. *Teaching Exceptional Children, 26,* 44–47.

American Speech-Language-Hearing Association. (1982). Definitions: Communicative Disorders and Variations, *ASHA, 24,* 949–950.

Biklen, D. (1990). Communication unbound: Autism and praxis. *Harvard Educational Review, 60*(3), 291–314.

Breeding, M., Stone, C., & Riley, K. (n.d.) *LINC: Language in the classroom.* Unpublished manuscript. Abilene Independent School District: Abilene, TX.

Butler-Hall, B. (1987). *Hall's articulation remediation training sheets (HARTS).* Henderson, TX: Creations Publications.

Clary, D. L., & Edwards, S. (1992). Spoken language. In E. A. Polloway, J. R. Patton, J. S. Payne, & R. A. Payne (Eds.), *Strategies for teaching learners with special needs* (4th ed., pp. 185–285). Columbus, OH: Merrill.

Cochran, P. S., & Bull, G. L. (1993). Computers and individuals with speech and language disorders. In J. D. Kindsey (Ed.), *Computers and exceptional individuals* (pp. 211–242). Austin, TX: Pro-Ed.

Communication Skill Builders. (1983). *Communication Skill Builders.* Tucson, AZ: Author.

Daly, D. A. (1991, April). *Multi-modal therapy for fluency clients: Strategies that work.* Paper presented at the Spring Convention of the Texas Speech-Language-Hearing Association, Houston, TX.

Emerick, L. L., & Haynes, W. O. (1986). *Diagnosis and evaluation in speech pathology* (3rd ed.). Englewood Cliffs, NJ: Prentice-Hall.

Erickson, J. G. (1992, April). *Communication disorders in multicultural populations.* Paper presented at the Texas Speech-Language-Hearing Association Annual Convention, San Antonio, TX.

Fehling, R. H. (1993). *Weekday speech activities to promote carryover.* Austin, TX: Pro-Ed.

Greene, M. C. L. (1986). *Disorders of voice.* Austin, TX: Pro-Ed.

Hallahan, D. P., & Kauffman, J. M. (1991). *Exceptional children. Introduction to special education* (5th ed.). Boston: Allyn & Bacon.

Hardman, M. L., Drew, C. J., Egan, M. W., & Wolf, B. (1990). *Human exceptionality. Society, school, and family* (3rd ed.). Boston: Allyn & Bacon.

Harris, D., & Vanderheiden, G. C. (1980). Augmentative communication techniques. In R. L. Schiefelbusch (Ed.), *Nonspeech language and communication: Analysis and intervention* (pp. 259–302). Austin, TX: Pro-Ed.

Heward W. L., & Orlansky, M. D. (1992). *Exceptional children. An introductory survey of special education* (4th ed.). New York: Macmillan.

Hiller, J. F. (1990) Setting up a classroom-based language instruction program: One clinician's experience. *Texas Journal of Audiology and Speech Pathology, 16*(2), 12–13.

Kirk, S. A., Gallagher, J. J., & Anastasiow, N. J. (1993). *Educating exceptional children* (7th ed.). Boston: Houghton Mifflin.

Kirsten, I. (1981). *The Oakland picture dictionary.* Wauconda, IL: Don Johnston.

Lahey, M. (1988). *Language disorders and language development.* New York: Macmillan.

Leonard, L. (1990). Language disorders in preschool children. In G. H. Shames & E. H. Wigg (Eds.), *Human communication disorders: An introduction* (2nd ed., pp. 210–247). Columbus, OH: Merrill.

McCarney, S. B., & Wunderlich, K. K. (1988). *The pre-referral intervention manual.* Columbia, MO: Hawthorne Educational Services.

McKamey, E. S. (1991). Storytelling for children with learning disabilities: A first-hand account. *Teaching Exceptional Children, 23,* 46–48.

McReynolds, L. (1990). Functional articulation disorders. In G. H. Shames & E. H. Wiig (Eds.), *Human communication disorders: An introduction* (2nd ed., pp. 139–182). Columbus, OH: Merrill.

Mayer-Johnson, R. (1986). *The picture communications symbols* (Book 1). Solana Beach, CA: Mayer-Johnson.

Naremore, R. C. (1980). Language disorders in children. In T. J. Hixon, L. D. Shriberg, & J. H. Saxman (Eds.), *Introduction to Communication Disorders* (pp. 111–132). Englewood Cliffs, NJ: Prentice-Hall.

Nowacek, E. J., & McShane, E. (1993). Spoken language. In E. A. Polloway & J. R. Patton (Eds.), *Strategies for teaching learners with special needs* (5th ed., pp. 183–205). Columbus, OH: Merrill.

Owens, R. E., Jr. (1984). *Language development: An introduction.* Columbus, OH: Merrill.

Oyer, H. J., Crowe, B., & Haas, W. H. (1987). *Speech, language, and hearing disorders: A guide for the teacher.* Boston: Little, Brown.

Pruden, L. K. (1992, November). *Classroom speech/language therapy—Are you ready?* Paper presented at the Crowley ISD Speech Hearing Conference, Crowley, TX.

Pruden, L. K. (1992). *Listen to learn.* Bedford, TX: GG Publishing.

Richard, J., Jackson, K., Ulrich, M., & Ulrich, A. (1993). *First hand: Personal accounts of breakthroughs in facilitated communicating.* Madison, WI: DRI Press.

Sander, E. K. (1972). When are speeech sounds learned? *Journal of Speech and Hearing Disorders, 37,* 62.

Shames, G. H., & Wiig, E. H. (1990). *Human communication disorders* (3rd ed.). New York: Macmillan.

Shane, H. C., & Sauer, M. (1986). *Augmentative and alternative communication.* Austin, TX: Pro-Ed.

Smith, D. D., & Luckasson, R. (1992). *Introduction to special education: Teaching in an age of challenge*. Boston: Allyn & Bacon.

Tavzel, C. S., & Staff of LinguiSystems. (1987). *Blooming recipes*. East Moline, IL: LinguiSystems.

Thomas, P. J., & Carmack, F. F. (1993). Language: The foundation of learning. In J. S. Choate (Ed.), *Successful mainstreaming: Proven ways to detect and correct special needs* (pp. 148–173). Boston: Allyn & Bacon.

Toliver-Weddington, G., & Erickson, J. G. (1992). Suggestions for using standardized tests with minority children. In J. G. Erickson (Ed.), *Communication disorders in multicultural populations* (1992, April). Paper presented at Texas Speech-Language-Hearing Association Annual Convention, San Antonio, TX.

U.S. Department of Education. (1993). *To assure the free appropriate public education of all children with disabilities. 15th annual report to Congress on the implementation of IDEA*. Washington, DC: U.S. Department of Education, Office of Special Education Programs, and U.S. Office of Special Education and Rehabilitative Services.

Van Riper, C., & Emerick, L. (1984). *Speech correction: An introduction to speech pathology and audiology* (7th ed.). Englewood Cliffs, NJ: Prentice-Hall.

Walker, B. (1993, January). *Multicultural issues in education: An introduction*. Paper presented at Cypress-Fairbanks Independent School District In-Service, Cypress, TX.

Wayman, K., Lynch, E., Hanson, M. (1990). Home-based early childhood services: Cultural sensitivity in a family systems approach. *Topics in Early Childhood Special Education, 10*(4), 65–66.

Wiig, E. H. (1986). Language disabilities in school-age children and youth. In G. H. Shames & E. H. Wiig (Eds.), *Human communication disorders* (2nd ed., pp. 331–383). Columbus, OH: Merrill.

Wiig, E. H., & Semel, E. (1984). *Language assessment and intervention for the learning disabled* (2nd ed.). Columbus, OH: Merrill.

CHAPTER 10

Teaching Students Who Are Gifted

Carmen

Carmen is truly an exceptional child and probably the most multitalented student I have had the opportunity to work with. Carmen was a student in my class for gifted/talented/creative students for six years, from the first to the sixth grade.

Learning came very easily for Carmen, and she excelled in all subjects. However, mathematics was her personal favorite. When she was in the fifth grade, she successfully completed prealgebra, and, when she was a sixth-grader, Carmen attended a seventh- and eighth-grade gifted mathematics class, where she received the highest grades in algebra. Carmen's writing skills were also well developed. Several of her essays and poems have already been published. When Carmen was a fourth-grader, she presented testimony to a NASA board defending and encouraging the junior astronaut program to continue. After completing her first year of junior high school, Carmen was awarded two out of five academic awards given to all seventh-grade students at her school. The awards were for outstanding achievement in science and mathematics. The latest information on Carmen tops everything else: As a tenth-grader, Carmen took the PSAT and recently received her scores. She received a perfect score!

Carmen is also musically talented. When Carmen was a second-grader, a music specialist who came to my room on a weekly basis informed me that Carmen should be encouraged to continue with her piano lessons because she demonstrated concert pianist abilities. When Carmen entered junior high school, she took up playing the clarinet in the band. At the end-of-the-year banquet, she received the top honor after being in the band for only one year.

Carmen is also psychomotorically talented. She is an accomplished gymnast, dances both the hula and ballet, has been a competitive ice skater (an unusual sport for someone from Hawaii), played soccer for two years on champion soccer teams, and was a walk-on for her junior high's cross-country track team.

Carmen is also artistically talented, demonstrates leadership abilities, has good social skills, and, wouldn't you know it, is simply beautiful.

Carmen's career goals have remained consistent for as long as I have known her. She wants to be either a dentist or an astronaut, but I have the feeling she can be both.

Children and youth such as Carmen who perform or have the potential to perform at levels significantly above those of other students have special needs as great as those of students whose disabilities demonstrably limit their performance. Equally important is the reality that these students are likely to spend most of their instructional day in general education settings. As a result, classroom teachers are well served if they have some basic information about giftedness and know some useful techniques for maximizing the educational experiences of these students.

Although most professionals in the area of gifted education argue that gifted students benefit more from a curricular focus different from that provided in typical general education settings, this chapter focuses on topics related to the inclusion of these students in general classrooms.

The rationale for including this chapter in this book is twofold: (a) many gifted, talented, or creative students spend a significant part of their school careers in general education settings and (b) many general education teachers are not prepared to deal with this population. Whether students with exceptional abilities should be taught in general education settings is debatable (see Maker, 1993); however, we must acknowledge that this is the setting in which most students will be placed.

Background Information

Students with exceptional abilities continue to be an underidentified, under-, and often inappropriately, served group. Unlike the situation for students with disabilities, no federal legislation exists that mandates appropriate education for these students. States and local school districts vary greatly in the type and quality of services provided—if indeed they are provided at all.

Students who could benefit from special programming are often not identified as a result of a number of factors, including ineffective assessment procedures. Teachers in general education may not be aware of various characteristics that suggest giftedness, particularly those associated with students who are culturally different.

For those students who are identified as gifted, a more common problem is the short amount of time allocated for special programming. In many schools, a relatively limited amount of instructional time is devoted to special activities. Furthermore, much of the gifted programming that exists today is more geared to students who are gifted in the linguistic and mathematical areas.

The concept of giftedness has changed over time, and the terminology used to describe it has also varied. The term *gifted* is often used to refer to the heterogeneous spectrum of students with exceptional abilities, although some professionals would restrict the use of this term to certain individuals who display high levels of intelligence. Without question, the terminology used for students generally referred to as **gifted** is confusing, as different terms are often used to convey different concepts and ideas. Other terms such as *talented* and *creative* are used to differentiate subgroups. A listing of defined various terms used to describe this population of students with exceptional abilities is provided in Table 10.1. A context for the use of this terminology is provided in the next section, where giftedness is defined. The term *gifted*, referring to a more generalized interpretation of the concept, is used most frequently in this chapter.

Much controversy and confusion surround the delivery of services to gifted students. Part of the dilemma stems from misguided beliefs that society has about this group. Other problems arise from a close examination of student needs and the ways that most schools address them. Elaboration of some of the issues follow.

The general public and many school personnel continue to hold misconceptions about students who are gifted, **talented**, or **creative.** Hallahan and Kauffman (1991) highlight some of the more general misconceptions about persons with giftedness—

TABLE 10.1 **Terms Relating to Giftedness and Creativity**

Term	Definition	Explanation
High intelligence	A composite of human traits, including a capacity for insight into complex relationships, an ability to think abstractly and solve problems, and the capacity to develop more capacity.	Children with high intelligence typically master academic tasks more quickly than their classmates. It is not unusual for them to come to kindergarten already knowing how to read, write, and calculate. These students grasp concepts presented in class faster than most other children, and they can use that knowledge to extend discussions beyond the levels of their classmates.
High IQ	High = 1.5–2 standard deviations above the mean.	IQ scores are obtained by taking tests of intelligence. Children who are gifted are often said to have a high IQ because they receive a high score on these tests. School districts and state education agencies set arbitrary cut-off scores that allow youngsters to qualify for education of the gifted. Many districts set their cut-off score at somewhere between 1.5 and 2 standard deviations above the mean. The mean or average IQ score is approximately 100. Children with an IQ score above 130, on an individually administered IQ test, are usually considered gifted.
Gifted	A term used to describe children who exhibit evidence of having high levels of intelligence.	Children who meet their state's or school district's eligibility requirements for education of the gifted. Most states require that students score above a specified IQ score (such as 130) to be considered "gifted," and also exhibit above-average academic achievement or potential. High academic achievement is often measured by the scores on an achievement test where the student scores at least two grade levels above his or her peers.
Creativity	A form of intelligence that results in advanced divergent thought, unique products, high levels of intuition, or being able to solve complex problems.	Creative individuals are able to arrive at novel solutions to problems. For example, some creative children can generate unusual stories that are either more unique, complex, or otherwise more detailed, or more humorous than those of their peers.
Convergent thinking	Taking apparently unrelated information and moving it toward a common conclusion; requires memory, classification, and reasoning abilities.	Convergent thinking abilities are useful in completing academic tasks required at school. For example, most individuals who are high academic achievers tend to be able to organize thoughts by categorizing information into meaningful groups (size, length, type). High academic achievers also have good memory skills. Good organizational skills, such as categorizing, assist in being able to remember large amounts of information and draw useful comparisons and conclusions.
Divergent thinking	Extending information in different directions from a common point; critical for creative behavior (fluency, flexibility, originality, elaboration).	Creative individuals engage in high levels of divergent thinking. They are able to act upon information by breaking it apart and extending it in an unstructured manner that results in unique and original products.

TABLE 10.1   Terms Relating to Giftedness and Creativity (Cont.)

Term	Definition	Explanation
Evaluative thinking	Thinking skills used to make decisions, and allow for comparisons and contrasts between and among items and concepts.	Another type of thinking ability that is often attributed to people who are gifted or creative and allows them to evaluate information at an advanced level. Evaluative thinking allows individuals to compare, contrast, judge, and arrive at solutions to complex problems, anticipate consequences, predict results, and analyze effects.
Talented	A term that refers to people who have superior skills or abilities in just one or a few areas.	Individuals with specific talents demonstrate specific and superior skills in fields of activities (math, or art and music, or performing arts). One way to understand the difference between giftedness and talents is to make a distinction between ability and performance.

Source: Smith, D. D., & Luckasson, R. (1992). *Introduction to special education: Teaching in the age of challenge.* Boston: Allyn & Bacon. Used with permission.

note they use the term *gifted* in the more generic sense referred to earlier. Their observations have been adapted to provide student-centered relevance.

- Gifted students are physically weak, socially inept, narrow in interests, and prone to emotional instability. *Fact:* In general, these students are quite the opposite.
- Gifted students do everything well. *Fact:* Some students show exceptional abilities in a broad range of areas; others show highly specialized abilities.
- Giftedness is a stable trait, always consistently evident in all periods of a person's life. *Fact:* Some students show indications of special abilities early on, whereas others will not demonstrate their unique and special abilities until later in life. Some individuals who show exceptional abilities at a young age will not do so later in their lives.
- Gifted students will excel without special education, needing only the incentives and instruction that are appropriate for all students. *Fact:* Most students with exceptional abilities will need a differentiated educational program to meet their needs (p. 399).

VanTassel-Baska (1989) noted some of the mistaken beliefs that educators in particular have about providing an appropriate education to students with exceptional abilities.

- A "differentiated" curriculum for the gifted means "anything that is different from what is provided for all learners." *Fact:* A "differentiated" curriculum implies a coherently planned scope and sequence of instruction that matches the needs of students and that typically does differ from the regular education curriculum.
- All experiences provided for gifted learners must be creative and focused on process. *Fact:* Core content areas are important areas of instructional focus.

◆ One curriculum package will provide what is needed for the entire gifted population. *Fact:* Students need a variety of materials, resources, and courses.

◆ **Acceleration** can be harmful because it pushes children socially and leaves gaps in their knowledge. *Fact:* This approach to meeting the needs of students with exceptional abilities is the intervention technique best supported by research (pp. 13–14).

Many professionals in the field of gifted education find the current levels and nature of services provided to this population to be unacceptable and are frustrated by the lack of specialized programming for these students. VanTassel-Baska (1989) suggests that these students cannot be served appropriately unless their learning is accelerated, they are grouped in ways that promote appropriate level activities, and they have the opportunity to socialize with other students who also possess exceptional abilities.

Basic Concepts

Teachers who have contact with students displaying exceptional abilities can benefit from knowing some basic information about giftedness. It should be noted that definitions used, assessment practices implemented, and the number of students identified and served vary greatly from state to state. Moreover, there is also an amazing amount of intrastate variation due to different practices and policies used by local school districts.

Prevalence

The number of students who display exceptional abilities is inexact. As one might surmise, this number will be influenced by how giftedness is defined and how it is measured. Figures of 3% to 5% are typically cited to reflect the extent of giftedness in the school population (National Center for Education Statistics, 1989).

The critical reader should also note the distinction between the number of students served and the number of students who might be gifted. Only certain types of gifted students may be served due to the methods used for identification. Another cautionary note about estimates of giftedness is that such figures underestimate the number of gifted students who are ethnically/culturally different, disabled, or female. These subgroups of gifted students are underrepresented in programs for students with exceptional abilities.

Definitional Perspectives

A number of prominent definitions of gifted and talented students have been developed over the years. One of the earliest cited definitions was submitted to Congress by the commissioner of education in 1972. Because this definition is referred to so often and has influenced a number of state definitions, it is presented here.

Children who are creative are included in most definitions of gifted and talented.

> The term "gifted and talented children" means children and, whenever applicable, youth, who are identified at the preschool, elementary, or secondary level as possessing demonstrated or potential abilities that give evidence of high performance capability in areas such as intellectual, creative, specific academic or leadership ability or in the performing and visual arts and who by reason thereof require services or activities not ordinarily provided by the school. (Purcell, 1978, Section 902)

A number of interesting observations can be made regarding this definition. First, there is no mention of the psychomotor domain. The reason for this omission is explained by the fact that this area is already supported substantially through other programs such as athletics. Second, the term "such as," found in the definition, suggests that the list of areas in the definition is not exhaustive. Third, the terms "demonstrated or potential abilities" are implicit in the requirement of "evidence of high performance capability."

The most important aspect of the definition for school personnel is the message that these students need "services and activities" that differ from those typically provided, if these students are to reach their potentials. This can be interpreted as providing special programs outside of general education or specialized programming within these settings.

Alternative Conceptualizations of Giftedness and Intelligence

Other useful ideas on how to define and conceptualize giftedness have been developed and espoused by professionals in the field of gifted education. Renzulli has developed a concept of giftedness that resulted from a dissatisfaction with the U.S. Department of Education definition. His primary frustrations resulted from the following factors: the omission of nonintellective considerations, the nonparallel nature of the areas highlighted in the federal definition, and the misuse of the definition on a practical level. Renzulli (1979) promotes a model depicted by three interlocking clusters of traits: above-average ability, task commitment, and creativity. He stresses that it is the "interaction among the three clusters that research has shown to be the essential ingredient for creative/productive accomplishments" (p. 9).

Sternberg (1986) elaborates on ways to conceptualize intellectual giftedness. He proposes a model that (a) consists of three subtheories that aid in understanding exceptional abilities and (b) suggests ways to measure intellectual giftedness. He describes these dimensions as follows:

> The first subtheory relates intelligence to the internal world of the individual, specifying the mental mechanisms that lead to more or less intelligent behavior. . . . The second subtheory specifies those points along the continuum of one's experience with tasks or situations that most critically involve the use of intelligence. In particular, the account emphasizes the roles of novelty and of automatization in exceptional intelligence. The third subtheory relates intelligence to the external world of the individual, specifying three classes of acts—environment adaptation, selection, and shaping—that characterize intelligent behavior in the everyday world. (p. 223)

Gardner and colleagues (Gardner, 1983; Gardner & Hatch, 1989) have developed a model that proposes the idea of **multiple intelligences.** That is, there are seven areas in which one can demonstrate specific degrees of ability. These seven areas are presented in Table 10.2, along with examples of roles that might be characteristic of a given intelligence. The table also provides a brief description of the key features of each type of intelligence.

If Gardner's ideas are to be followed closely, students would be assessed in all of the areas. If found to have strengths in an area, students would be provided opportunities to expand their interests, skills, and abilities accordingly. The attractiveness of this conceptualization is that (a) it acknowledges some ability areas that may be overlooked and (b) it tends to equally distribute the importance of different types of intelligences.

Origins of Giftedness

As for other areas of exceptionality, there has been much professional discussion as to what contributes to giftedness in a person. Most would suggest that giftedness results from some type of interaction between biology and environment.

From a biological perspective, research has shown that behavior is greatly affected by genetics. Although there have been some distortions of this notion, the main idea

TABLE 10.2   **Multiple Intelligences**

Intelligence	End-States	Core Components
Logical-mathematical	Scientist Mathematician	Sensitivity to, and capacity to discern, logical or numerical patterns; ability to handle long chains of reasoning.
Linguistic	Poet Journalist	Sensitivity to the sounds, rhythms, and meanings of words; sensitivity to the different functions of language.
Musical	Composer Violinist	Abilities to produce and appreciate rhythm, pitch, and timbre; appreciation of the forms of musical expressiveness.
Spatial	Navigator Sculptor	Capacities to perceive the visual-spatial world accurately and to perform transformations on one's initial perceptions.
Bodily-kinesthetic	Dancer Athlete	Abilities to control one's body movements and to handle objects skillfully.
Interpersonal	Therapist Salesman	Capacities to discern and respond appropriately to the moods, temperaments, motivations, and desires of other people.
Intrapersonal	Person with detailed, accurate self-knowledge	Access to one's own feelings and the ability to discriminate among them and draw upon them to guide behavior; knowledge of one's own strengths, weaknesses, desires, and intelligences.

Source: Gardner, H., & Hatch, T. (1989). Multiple intelligences go to school: Educational implications of the theory of multiple intelligences. *Educational Researcher, 18* (8), 6. Copyright © 1989 by the American Educational Research Association. Reprinted by permission of the publisher.

is that genetic factors play a role in giftedness. Other biological factors, such as the effects of nutrition, also have an impact on an individual's development.

The environment in which a child is raised also contributes to later performance and intellectual abilities. Homes in which there is much stimulation and opportunity to explore and interact with the environment, accompanied by high expectations, tend to produce children more likely to be successful scholastically and socially.

Identification and Assessment

General education teachers need to know about the assessment process that attempts to confirm the existence of exceptional abilities. We say this because teachers play a crucial role in the initial stages of the process, for it is they who typically recognize that a student might be gifted and who are likely to initiate the confirmation process.

The assessment process includes a sequence of steps, beginning with an initial referral (i.e., nomination) and culminating with the validation of any decision made. A significant amount of responsibility for identifying students who are gifted is placed on general education teachers. Although many children displaying exceptional abilities may be spotted very early (i.e., preschool years), a surprising number of them are not recognized until they are school-age. For this reason, teachers need to be aware of classroom behaviors that gifted students display. A list of such behaviors, categorized according to Clark's (1992) organization, is provided in Table 10.3.

Teachers who recognize these behaviors in their students should determine whether a student should be evaluated more comprehensively. This usually involves nominating the student for gifted services.

Teachers can be very involved in the second step in the assessment process as well. After a student has been nominated or referred, efforts are made to acquire and assemble a wide range of information that would substantiate whether a student is eligible for gifted services. The following sources of information can contribute to a better understanding of a student's demonstrated or potential ability: formal tests; informal assessments; interviews with teachers, parents, and peers; and actual student products.

A very helpful technique in many school systems to determine the performance capabilities of students is **portfolio assessment.** These portfolios contain a collection of student-generated products, reflecting the quality of a student's work. Portfolios can contain permanent products such as artwork or poetry or videotapes of student performance (e.g., theatrical production, music recital).

As VanTassel-Baska, Patton, and Prillaman (1989) point out, students who are culturally different and those who come from socially and economically disadvantaged backgrounds are typically overlooked in the process of identifying students for gifted programs. For the most part, the dilemma results from too much reliance being put on entry requirements that stress performance on standardized tests. When students obtain low test scores on instruments that may be biased against those whose background and language differ from the population on whom the tests were standardized, exclusion results. In summarizing the research on this population, VanTassel-Baska et al. provide three recommendations that should be incorporated into the identification and assessment process.

- ◆ Use nontraditional measures for identification purposes.
- ◆ Recognize cultural attributes and factors in deciding identification procedures.
- ◆ Focus on strengths in nonacademic areas, particularly in creativity and psychomotor domains (p. 3).

Characteristics

Students who are gifted and talented demonstrate a wide range of specific aptitudes, abilities, and skills. Any attempt to discuss characteristics on a general level is subject to overgeneralization. However, some distinguishable characteristics can be observed in students who are gifted or talented.

An interesting phenomenon is the paradoxical effect that certain behaviors displayed by gifted students can have. For instance, sincere, excited curiosity about a

TABLE 10.3 Classroom Behaviors of Gifted Children

Behavior Observed	Behavior Observed
In the classroom does the child: • Ask a lot of questions? • Show a lot of interest in progress? • Have lots of information on many things? • Want to know why or how something is so? • Become unusually upset at injustices? • Seem interested and concerned about social or political problems? • Often have a better reason than you do for not doing what you want done? • Refuse to drill on spelling, math facts, flash cards, or handwriting? • Criticize others for dumb ideas? • Become impatient if work is not "perfect"? • Seem to be a loner? • Seem bored and often have nothing to do? • Complete only part of an assignment or project and then take off in a new direction? • Stick to a subject long after the class has gone on to other things? • Seem restless, out of seat often? • Daydream? • Seem to understand easily? • Like solving puzzles and problems? • Have his or her own idea about how something should be done? And stay with it? • Talk a lot? • Love metaphors and abstract ideas? • Love debating issues? This child may be showing giftedness cognitively. Does the child: • Show unusual ability in some area? Maybe reading or math? • Show fascination with one field of interest? And manage to include this interest in all discussion topics? • Enjoy meeting or talking with experts in this field? • Get math answers correctly, but find it difficult to tell you how?	• Enjoy graphing everything? Seem obsessed with probabilities? • Invent new obscure systems and codes? This child may be showing giftedness academically. Does the child: • Try to do things in different, unusual, imaginative ways? • Have a really zany sense of humor? • Enjoy new routines or spontaneous activities? • Love variety and novelty? • Create problems with no apparent solutions? And enjoy asking you to solve them? • Love controversial and unusual questions? • Have a vivid imagination? • Seem never to proceed sequentially? This child may be showing giftedness creatively. Does the child: • Organize and lead group activities? Sometimes take over? • Enjoy taking risks? • Seem cocky, self-assured? • Enjoy decision making? Stay with that decision? • Synthesize ideas and information from a lot of different sources? This child may be showing giftedness through leadership ability. Does the child: • Seem to pick up skills in the arts—music, dance, drama, painting, etc.—without instruction? • Invent new techniques? Experiment? • See minute detail in products or performances? • Have high sensory sensitivity? This child may be showing giftedness through visual or performing arts ability.

Source: Reprinted with permission of Macmillan College Publishing Company from GROWING UP GIFTED, Fourth Edition, by Barbara Clark. Copyright © 1992 by Macmillan College Publishing Company, Inc.

topic being covered in class that is expressed openly and overtly can sometimes be interpreted as annoying or disruptive by a teacher or fellow students. Many behaviors that are seemingly desirable for students to demonstrate can be misperceived as problem behaviors for students who are gifted.

A comprehensive listing of characteristics is presented in Table 10.4.

An interesting characteristic that some gifted students display and that has important classroom implications is the expenditure of minimum effort while still earning high grades (Reis & Schack, 1993). This results from the fact that many gifted students are able to handle the general education curriculum with relative ease. A long-term effect of being able to accomplish good grades without working very hard is that students learn some habits that may have negative ramifications for them later when they are in challenging college programs.

Services for Students Who Are Gifted and Talented

The literature on providing effective services for students with exceptional abilities consistently stresses the need for **differentiated programming**. This means that various learning opportunities provided to these students must be different. Differentiation includes the content of what students learn, the processes used in learning situations, and the final products that students develop. Furthermore, as Lopez and MacKenzie (1993) note, "difference lies in the depth, scope, pace, and self-directedness of the expectations" (p. 288).

Many professionals in the field of gifted education argue that the preferred setting for these students is not general education; they recommend differentiated programs delivered in separate classes for the greater part, if not for all, of the school day. However, in schools today, gifted students are more likely to spend nearly all of their instructional day in general education, possibly receiving some differentiated opportunities in a pullout program.

Realities of the General Education Classroom

When students who are gifted or talented are in general education settings, they are sometimes subject to conditions that indeed hinder the possibility of maximizing their potentials. Some practices highlighted here illustrate this point.

- ◆ Their individual needs may not be met at all.
- ◆ When involved in group activities, they may end up doing all of the work (Clinkenbeard, 1991).
- ◆ They are often subjected to more stringent grading criteria (Clinkenbeard, 1991).
- ◆ They are given more of the same type of work for finishing assignments early or assigned more of the same type of tasks at the outset (Shaner, 1991).
- ◆ They are overused as co-teachers to help students who need more assistance.

TABLE 10.4 **Differentiating Characteristics of the Gifted**

I. The cognitive domain	• Extraordinary quantity of information; unusual retentiveness • Advanced comprehension • Unusually varied interests and curiosity • High level of language development • High level of verbal ability • High level of visual and spatial ability • Unusual capacity for processing information • Accelerated pace of thought processes • Flexible thought processes • Comprehensive synthesis • Early ability to delay closure • Heightened capacity for seeing unusual and diverse relationships and overall gestalts • Ability to generate original ideas and solutions • Early differential patterns for thought processing (e.g., thinking in alternatives and abstract terms, sensing consequences, making generalizations) • Early ability to use and form conceptual frameworks • An evaluative approach toward oneself and others • Persistent goal-directed behavior
II. The affective domain	• Large accumulation of information about emotions that have not been brought to awareness • Unusual sensitivity to the expectations and feelings of others • Keen sense of humor—may be gentle or hostile • Heightened self-awareness, accompanied by feelings of being "different" • Idealism and a sense of justice that appear at an early age • Earlier development of an inner locus of control and satisfaction • Advanced levels of moral judgment • High expectations of self and others, which often lead to high levels of frustration with self, others, and situations • Unusual emotional depth and intensity • Sensitivity to inconsistency between ideals and behavior
III. The physical domain	• Unusual discrepancy between physical and intellectual development • Low tolerance for the lag between their standards and their physical capacity • Cartesian split—can include neglect of physical well-being and avoidance of physical activity
IV. The intuitive domain	• Early involvement and concern for intuitive knowing, psychic and metaphysical ideas and phenomena • Open to experiences in this area; will experiment with psi and metaphysical phenomena • Creativity apparent in all areas of endeavor • Acceptance and expression of a high level of intuitive ability, especially with the highly gifted
V. The societal domain	• Strongly motivated by self-actualization needs • Advanced cognitive and affective capacity for conceptualizing and solving societal problems

Source: Reprinted with permission of Macmillan College Publishing Company from GROWING UP GIFTED, Fourth Edition, by Barbara Clark. Copyright © 1992 by Macmillan College Publishing Company, Inc.

◆ They are required to spend much time being presented content or concepts that they already know, doing repetitive drill work, and receiving instruction on new material at too slow a pace (Feldhusen, 1989).

Unfortunately, most general education teachers are not provided with the necessary understanding, skills, and resources to deal appropriately with this population. This situation is exacerbated by the fact that teachers have to deal with a wide range of abilities and needs in their classrooms. The composition of the general education classroom in many of today's public schools requires an array of accommodative knowledge and skills.

In addition, some teachers feel uncomfortable working with students who have exceptional abilities. Figure 10.1 highlights this situation by way of a personal experience. Shaner (1991) remarks that teachers who are working with gifted students can be "intimidated by him or her, paralyzed with a fear of not being able to keep up, or threatened by the student's challenges to authority" (pp. 14–15). Teachers are also concerned about being asked questions they are unprepared to answer or challenged on points they may not know well. All of these are reasonable fears; however, they can be minimized by using these opportunities as a way of increasing everyone's knowledge and by understanding how to address gifted students' needs within the general classroom setting.

Another reality is that when gifted programming is provided, it often focuses on the *intellectually* able and not on those who show artistic talent, leadership ability, specific academic prowess, or creativity (Reis, 1989). Although there are ways to develop the skills of students in these areas, such programs and opportunities may only be found outside of school.

Differentiated programming for students with exceptional abilities, wherever it occurs, must address individual needs and interests in the context of preparing the students for a world characterized by change and increasing complexity. Reis (1989) suggests that we reassess how we look at gifted education and move away from the content-based nature of most current curricula to an orientation that is based on a realistic view of future education.

Not long ago, I was invited to go on a "reef walk" with a class of gifted third- and fourth-graders. It was a very educational experience.

While we were wading in shallow water, we came upon a familiar marine organism commonly called a feather duster (tube worm). Forgetting that these students had vocabularies well advanced of their nongifted age peers, I was ready to say something like, "Look how that thing hangs on the rock."

Before I could get my highly descriptive statement out, Eddie, who always amazes us with his comments, offered the following: "Notice how securely anchored the organism is to the stationary coral."

All I could reply was "Yes, I did."

Figure 10.1 **A Personal Experience**
Source: Patton, Kauffman, Blackbourn, & Brown (1991).

Using an "Expert's" Technique for Independent Study

One interesting way to structure tasks for gifted students is to allow them to become *experts* on a topic. As an expert, each student can collect information on a subject that interests her, then share the information with the rest of the class. Although students can complete most of the work on the expert assignment independently, teachers will still need to help them plan and then monitor their progress. Winebrenner (1992) has developed two forms that teachers can use to help their *resident experts* research an interesting topic. One is appropriate for primary grades, and the other should work well with older students.

PRIMARY GRADES RESIDENT EXPERT PLANNER

Subject _____ Date _____

What I might want to learn about: _____
_____
_____
_____
_____
_____

How I can share one topic with the class: _____
_____
_____
_____
_____
_____
_____
_____
_____

UPPER GRADES RESIDENT EXPERT PLANNER

Student's name _____ Date _____

The subtopic I will study from the topic browsing planner:
_____

What I want to learn about: _____
_____
_____

Sources of information used in my study: _____
_____
_____

The most interesting information I discovered: _____
_____
_____

How I will share what I've learned with an audience: ____
_____
_____

Date I will be ready to share some information: _____
_____
_____

Source: Winebrenner, S. (1992). *Teaching gifted kids in the regular classroom.* Minneapolis, MN: Free Spirit Publishing. Used with permission.

Continuum of Program/Placement Options

A variety of ways exist for providing educational programs to students who are **gifted** and/or talented. The value of any particular programmatic option is based on the extent to which an individual's needs are met. A continuum of potential settings for providing programs to gifted students is shown in Figure 10.2. As Clark (1992) points out, all of the options have some merit; none address the needs of all students with exceptional abilities. For this reason, she feels that school systems should provide a range of programmatic alternatives.

Gifted students who are in general education classrooms for the entire instructional day can have their needs met through a variety of special provisions such as **enrichment,** acceleration, or special grouping/clustering. The challenge for teachers rests on their ability to coordinate these provisions with those required for other students in the classroom.

In many schools, students who have been identified as gifted are pulled out for a specified period of time each day to attend a special class for gifted students. When they are in the general education setting, it may be possible for them to participate in an individualized program of study, apart from the regular curriculum.

Gifted students may also participate in various adjunct programs such as mentorships, internships, special tutorials, independent study, and resource rooms—many of which will occur outside of the confines of the classroom. For students at the secondary level, spending time in classes where special programming occurs for part of the day, in addition to attending heterogeneous classes, is another possibility.

The implications of any of these programmatic options for the role and responsibilities of the general education teacher varies greatly. In some situations, the general education teacher will be the primary source of instruction for these students. In other situations, the general education teacher may serve more like a manager, coordinat-

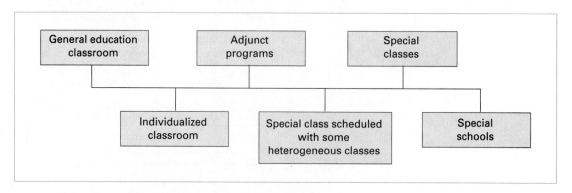

Figure 10.2   **Options for Providing Services to Gifted Students**
Source: Reprinted with permission of Macmillan College Publishing Company from GROWING UP GIFTED, Fourth Edition by Barbara Clark. Copyright © 1992 by Macmillan College Publishing Company, Inc.

ing the delivery of services provided by others. However, it is probable that teachers will be responsible for providing some level of instruction to most gifted students during the school day.

Approaches

Three general practices are frequently used in designing programs for students who have exceptional abilities: acceleration, enrichment, and special grouping. All three have merit and can be used in some fashion in general education settings.

Acceleration refers to practices that introduce content, concepts, and educational experiences to students sooner than is done with other students. It allows students to deal sooner with materials that are at more advanced levels and that are appropriate to their ability and interests. There are many types of accelerative practices, as reflected in the extensive array of options provided in Table 10.5.

All of the accelerative options described by Southern and Jones (1991) have relevance for gifted students who are in general education classrooms. The alternatives that have the most direct impact on the role of the general education teacher are **continuous progress, self-paced instruction, subject-matter acceleration,** combined classes, **curriculum compacting,** and **curriculum telescoping.** If these practices are used, they will require teachers to plan and implement ongoing instructional activities.

Other accelerative practices have a more indirect impact on ongoing activities in the general education classroom. Nevertheless, teachers should be aware of them. These other options are early entrance to school, grade skipping, mentorships, extracurricular programs, concurrent enrollment, advanced placement, and credit by examination.

Enrichment refers to techniques that provide topics, skill development, materials, or experiences that extend the depth of coverage beyond that typically addressed in the existing curriculum. This practice is commonly used in general education classes to address the needs of students who move through the existing content quickly. Many teachers' manuals/guides contain sections that provide ideas on how to deliver additional enriching activities to students who finish their work early.

As Southern and Jones (1991) note, some of what is referred to as enrichment ultimately involves acceleration. For instance, whenever topics of an advanced nature are introduced, a form of acceleration is actually being employed. The distinction used herein is based on the distinction between materials or activities that are accelerated along some dimension of difficulty or conceptual complexity and materials or activities that provide variety but do not require advanced skills or understanding.

Special grouping refers to the practice whereby gifted students of proximate ability levels or interests are grouped together for at least part of the instructional day (VanTassel-Baska, 1989). One commonly cited technique is the use of cluster grouping. This practice allows for important interaction with peers who share a similar enthusiasm, bring different perspectives to topics, and stimulate the cognitive and creative thinking of others in the group.

TABLE 10.5 Range and Types of Accelerative Options

1. Early entrance to kindergarten or first grade	The student is admitted to school prior to the age specified by the district for normal entry to first grade.
2. Grade skipping	The student is moved ahead of normal grade placement. This may be done during an academic year (placing a third-grader directly into fourth grade), or at year end (promoting a third-grader to fifth grade).
3. Continuous progress	The student is given material deemed appropriate for current achievement as the student becomes ready.
4. Self-paced instruction	The student is presented with materials that allow him or her to proceed at a self-selected pace. Responsibility for selection of pacing is the student's.
5. Subject-matter acceleration	The student is placed for a part of a day with students at more advanced grade levels for one or more subjects without being assigned to a higher grade (e.g., a fifth-grader going to sixth grade for science instruction).
6. Combined classes	The student is placed in classes where two or more grade levels are combined (e.g., third- and fourth-grade split rooms). The arrangement can be used to allow younger children to interact with older ones academically and socially.
7. Curriculum compacting	The student is given reduced amounts of introductory activities, drill review, and so on. The time saved may be used to move faster through the curriculum.
8. Telescoping curriculum	The student spends less time than normal in a course of study (e.g., completing a 1-year course in one semester, or finishing junior high school in two years rather than three).
9. Mentorships	The student is exposed to a mentor who provides advanced training and experiences in a content area.
10. Extracurricular programs	The student is enrolled in course work or summer programs that confer advanced instruction and/or credit for study (e.g., fast-paced language or math courses offered by universities).
11. Concurrent enrollment	The student is taking a course at one level and receiving credit for successful completion of a parallel course at a higher level (e.g., taking algebra at the junior high level and receiving credit for high school algebra as well as junior high math credits upon successful completion).
12. Advanced placement	The student takes a course in high school that prepares him or her for taking an examination that can confer college credit for satisfactory performances.
13. Credit by examination	The student receives credit (at high school or college level) upon successful completion of an examination.
14. Correspondence courses	The student takes high school or college courses by mail (or, in more recent incarnations, through video and audio presentations).
15. Early entrance into junior high, high school, or college	The student is admitted with full standing to an advanced level of instruction (at least one year early).

Gifted/Talented Individuals and Computer Applications

Individual	Computer Applications
Academically gifted	Programming (e.g., BASIC, LOGO, Pascal) Computer-assisted instruction Word processing data bases, spreadsheets, and graphics Telecommunications
Creative/talented	Computer-assisted design (CAD) and other art activities (e.g., using color graphics with the Amiga system) Music synthesis and Musical Instrument Digital Interface (MIDI) Analysis and cataloging of athletics, dance, acting, and other physical activities

Note: Many gifted and talented individuals are academically and creatively strong, and would therefore use computer applications from both areas.
Source: Dale, E. J. (1993). Computers and gifted/talented individuals. In Lindsey, J. D. (Ed.), *Computers and exceptional individuals* (p. 203). Austin, TX: Pro-Ed. Used with permission.

Accommodative Recommendations

This section of the chapter highlights techniques that can be useful to general classroom teachers for addressing the needs of students with exceptional abilities in their classrooms. Teachers who will be working closely with students with exceptional abilities are encouraged to consult resources that thoroughly discuss the issues associated with teaching gifted students in general education settings—see Maker (1993b), Parke (1989), or Winebrenner (1992).

Guiding Principles

First and foremost, teachers should strive to create classroom settings that foster conditions where gifted students feel comfortable and are able to realize their potentials (Sisk, 1993). To accomplish this goal, gifted students need a comprehensive long-term plan of education and must enjoy learning experiences that reflect this plan (Kitano, 1993).

Using school-based supports such as teacher assistance teams (Chalfant & Van Dusen Pysh, 1993) can also assist with addressing the needs of gifted students. When staffed properly, these teams become a rich resource of experience and ideas for dealing with a myriad of student needs.

Although special opportunities for enrichment, acceleration, and the use of higher-level skills are beneficial to gifted students, these opportunities can also be extended to other students when appropriate (Roberts, Ingram, & Harris, 1992). Many students in general education settings will find practices such as integrated programming to be exciting, motivating, and meaningful.

Organizational/Management Recommendations

To create conditions of learning that students need, it is essential to organize and manage systematically the classroom enivronment. Teachers must create a psychosocial classroom climate that is open to a "variety of ideas, materials, problems, people, viewpoints, and resources" (Schiever, 1993, p. 209). Along with this suggestion is the need to assure that the learning environment is safe, accepting, and supportive.

Grouping students raises a number of questions related to recommended practice. It is useful to group gifted students in a variety of ways. This might include cooperative cluster grouping on the basis of proximate abilities or interests or using other arrangements, such as dyads or seminar-type formats. The important recommendation is that they are afforded an opportunity to spend time with other gifted students. For instance, competitive tennis players must play persons who have similar or more advanced ability to maintain their skills.

Debate surrounds the issue of cooperative learning situations. Even though the merits of cooperative learning in classroom settings have been established, the use of heterogeneous cooperative learning arrangements with gifted students must be done cautiously. Essentially, teachers must guarantee that most of the work of the group does not always fall on gifted students who are in such arrangements. The use of cooperative learning arrangements should be encouraged but continually monitored to assure its effectiveness.

Teachers should develop comprehensive record-keeping systems that monitor the progress of all students, including gifted students who may be involved in a mix of enrichment and accelerated activities. Along these lines, a differentiated report card may be useful for conveying to parents more information about a gifted student's performance.

The following are some specific suggestions on dealing with gifted students:

- Require gifted students to follow identified classroom rules and procedures while allowing for their needs to explore and pursue their curiosity when appropriate (Feldhusen, 1993).
- Include gifted students in the development of needed procedures that emerge during the course of a school year (e.g., introduction of animals in the room).
- Explain the logic and rationale for certain rules and procedures.
- Use cluster seating arrangements rather than strict rows (Feldhusen, 1993).
- Identify a portion of the room where special events and activities take place and where stimulating materials are kept.
- Develop lesson plan formats that include instructional ideas for gifted students.
- Consult teacher guides of textbook series for ideas for enrichment activities.
- Let students who are working in independent arrangements plan their own learning activities (Feldhusen, 1993).

◆ Use contracts with students who are involved in elaborate projects to maximize communication between teacher and students (Rosselli, 1993).

◆ Involve students in their own record keeping, thus assisting the teacher and developing responsibility.

◆ Use periodic progress reports, daily logs, and teacher conferences to monitor/evaluate students who are in independent study arrangements (Conroy, 1993).

Academic Recommendations

Many professionals interested in gifted education promote the use of differentiated programming. With this in mind, general education teachers should develop instructional lessons that consider a range of abilities and interests. For gifted students, instructional activities should be qualitatively different from those assigned to the class in general—or completely different if certain accelerative options are being used.

When designing instructional activities, teachers can use the following series of questions offered by Kitano (1993) to guide this task:

◆ Do the activities include provisions for several ability levels?
◆ Do the activities include ways to accommodate a variety of interest areas?
◆ Does the design of activities encourage development of sophisticated products?
◆ Do the activities provide for the integration of thinking processes with concept development?
◆ Are the concepts consistent with the comprehensive curriculum plan? (p. 280)

Another technique that can be used effectively with gifted students in general education classes is curriculum compacting. This practice allows students to cover assigned material in ways that are faster or different. As Renzulli, Reis, and Smith (1981) point out, this process involves three phases, including the assessment of what students know and the skills they possess, identification of ways of covering the curriculum, and suggestions for enrichment/accelerative options. Renzulli and colleagues have developed a form to be used to assist teachers in compacting their curriculum. This form is presented in Figure 10.3.

As emphasized in the previous section of the chapter, acceleration and enrichment are viable ways to address the needs of gifted students within the context of a general education lesson. Two examples of these practices are provided next.

Situation 1: *Romeo and Juliet*. Figure 10.4 illustrates how *Romeo and Juliet* can be taught, keeping in mind the needs of the regular and gifted students. This literature example developed by Shanley (1993) shows how the content of the play and the activities used by the teacher can be adapted for gifted students.

Situation 2: Mathematics. Conroy (1993) offers an example of one week's schedule of activities related to the topic of two-digit multiplication (see Figure 10.5). She recommends that cluster grouping of gifted students be used to accomplish the instructional goals.

Games for Vocabulary Development

Game	Description
Trivia games	• Use teacher-made cards as question cards for use with commercial trivia board. • Relabel categories to correspond with study topics. • Use cloze technique.
Tic-tac-toe gameboards	• Put flashcards in plastic containers. • If student gets vocabulary correct, place an X or O on gameboard.
Football field	• Place cards of vocabulary words on sidelines of board laid out as football field. • Move 5 or 10 yards each time a word is correct.
"Jeopardy"	• Arrange terms in categories. • Divide students into two teams • Write questions for each term to earn points.
Checkers gameboard	• Give each student a set of flashcards. • Before checker moves, student must define opponent's word.

Source: Squires, E. L., & Reetz, L. J. (1989). Vocabulary acquisition activities. *Academic Therapy, 24,* 589–592. Copyright 1989 by Pro-Ed, Inc. Reprinted by permission.

Other more specific suggestions related to important areas such as questioning strategies and product differentiation are presented next.

- ◆ Balance coverage of basic disciplines and the arts (Feldhusen, 1993).
- ◆ Acquire an array of different learning-related materials for use with gifted students—these can include textbooks, magazines, artifacts, software, CD-ROM disks, and other media.
- ◆ Include time for independent study.
- ◆ Teach research skills (data-gathering and investigative techniques) to gifted students to facilitate their independent study abilities (Reis & Schack, 1993).
- ◆ Use integrated themes for interrelating ideas within and across domains of inquiry (VanTassel-Baska, 1989). This type of curricular orientation can be used for all students in the general education setting, with special activities designed for gifted students.
- ◆ Include higher-order thinking skills in lessons.
- ◆ Allocate time for students to have contact with adults who can provide special experiences and information to gifted students (e.g., mentors).
- ◆ Avoid assigning work missed when gifted students spend time in special programs.

Individual Educational Programming Guide

The Compactor

Name _____   Age _____   Teacher(s) _____   Individual conference
dates and persons
participating in
planning of IEP

School _____   Grade _____   Parent(s) _____

Curriculum areas to be considered for compacting. Provide a brief description of basic material to be covered during this marking period and the assessment information or evidence that suggests the need for compacting.	*Procedures for compacting basic material.* Describe activities that will be used to guarantee proficiency in basic curricular areas.	*Acceleration and/or enrichment activities.* Describe activities that will be used to provide advanced-level learning experiences in each of the regular curricula.

Figure 10.3 Curriculum Compacting Form
Source: Renzulli, J., Reis, S., & Smith, L. (1981). *The Revolving Door Identification Model.* Mansfield Center, CT: Creative Learning Press, p. 79. Reprinted with permission from Creative Learning Press, copyright © 1981.

- ◆ Manage classroom discussions so that all students have an equal opportunity to contribute, feel comfortable doing so, and understand the nature of the discussion.
- ◆ Use standard textbooks carefully, as gifted students will typically be able to move through them rapidly and may find them boring.
- ◆ Include questions that are open-ended and of varying conceptual levels in class discussions.
- ◆ Make sure gifted students have access to the latest developments in microcomputers, including simulation software, interactive technologies, CD-ROM data bases, and telecommunications.

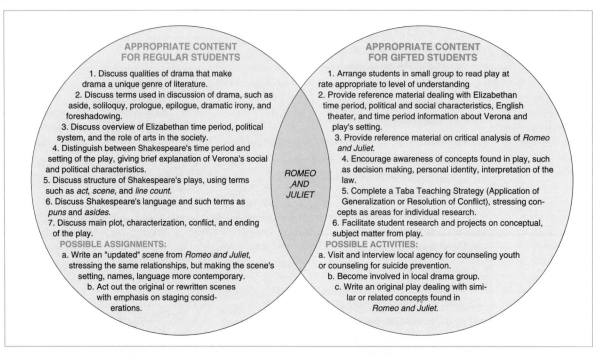

**APPROPRIATE CONTENT
FOR REGULAR STUDENTS**

1. Discuss qualities of drama that make drama a unique genre of literature.
2. Discuss terms used in discussion of drama, such as aside, soliloquy, prologue, epilogue, dramatic irony, and foreshadowing.
3. Discuss overview of Elizabethan time period, political system, and the role of arts in the society.
4. Distinguish between Shakespeare's time period and setting of the play, giving brief explanation of Verona's social and political characteristics.
5. Discuss structure of Shakespeare's plays, using terms such as *act*, *scene*, and *line count*.
6. Discuss Shakespeare's language and such terms as *puns* and *asides*.
7. Discuss main plot, characterization, conflict, and ending of the play.

POSSIBLE ASSIGNMENTS:

a. Write an "updated" scene from *Romeo and Juliet*, stressing the same relationships, but making the scene's setting, names, language more contemporary.
b. Act out the original or rewritten scenes with emphasis on staging considerations.

ROMEO AND JULIET

**APPROPRIATE CONTENT
FOR GIFTED STUDENTS**

1. Arrange students in small group to read play at rate appropriate to level of understanding
2. Provide reference material dealing with Elizabethan time period, political and social characteristics, English theater, and time period information about Verona and play's setting.
3. Provide reference material on critical analysis of *Romeo and Juliet*.
4. Encourage awareness of concepts found in play, such as decision making, personal identity, interpretation of the law.
5. Complete a Taba Teaching Strategy (Application of Generalization or Resolution of Conflict), stressing concepts as areas for individual research.
6. Facilitate student research and projects on conceptual, subject matter from play.

POSSIBLE ACTIVITIES:

a. Visit and interview local agency for counseling youth or counseling for suicide prevention.
b. Become involved in local drama group.
c. Write an original play dealing with similar or related concepts found in *Romeo and Juliet*.

Figure 10.4   **Adapting Curricular Content for Teaching** *Romeo and Juliet*
Source: Shanley, R. (1993). Becoming content with content. In C. J. Maker (Ed.), *Critical issues in gifted education: Defensible programs for the gifted* (Vol. 1, pp. 43–89). Austin, TX: Pro-Ed. Used with permission.

◆ Encourage the involvement of volunteers (e.g., parents, college/university practicum students) to assist in addressing the needs of gifted students (Feldhusen, 1993).
◆ Provide options for developing differentiated products as outcomes of various projects or lessons.
◆ Have students consider intended audiences when selecting potential final products of their endeavors.
◆ Maintain regular, on-going communication with the families of gifted students, notifying them of the goals, activities, products, and expectations you have for their children.

Social-Emotional Recommendations

Gifted students have the same physiological and psychological needs as their peers. However, they may also be dealing with perplexing concepts that are well ahead of their peers. For instance, a gifted fourth-grade female asked her teacher questions related to abortion—a topic with which she was already dealing conceptually.

Perhaps the most important recommendation that can be mentioned is for teachers to develop relationships with students so that they feel comfortable discussing

Monday: Regular students—introduce two-digit multiplication. Gifted students—same. Teacher gives all members of class an outline of the entire week of math seatwork and homework assignments ending with a test on Friday.

Tuesday: Regular students—review concepts presented Monday, guided practice. Gifted students—introduce some enrichment material, including math logic problems. Gifted students work on these as soon as they have mastered the concepts of the other problems. Teacher assigns their group to come up with some story problems and logic problems related to the week's concepts. Teacher then assists regular students in doing seatwork. Although gifted students are responsible for the test Friday and for specific portions of the homework throughout the week, such as every third problem, they choose to use class working on the enrichment or a group project.

Wednesday: Regular students—introduce three-digit multiplication. Gifted students—listen to explanation of concepts, demonstrate that they can do three problems correctly, and continue with enrichment project. Teacher moves between both groups.

Thursday: Regular students—review and guided practice in seatwork, with introduction of story problems. Gifted students—do three of six story problems and continue enrichment activities.

Friday: Regular and gifted students—take unit test on two- and three-digit multiplication. Test has application story problems. One challenge problem is more difficult. It is designed for the gifted students, but others may try it.

Figure 10.5   Schedule of Activities to Teach Two-Digit Multiplication
Source: Conroy, J. (1993). Classroom management: An expected view. In C. J. Maker (Ed.), *Critical issues in gifted education: Programs for the gifted in regular classrooms* (Vol. 3, pp. 227–257). Austin, TX: Pro-Ed. Used with permission.

their concerns and questions. Teachers can become important resources to gifted students, not only for advice, but also for information they are seeking. Creating a time when students can have individual time with a teacher can have important paybacks for both.

Teachers may also find it beneficial to schedule weekly room meetings (Feldhusen, 1993) or class councils (Kataoka, 1987) to identify and address social, procedural, or learning-related problems that arise in the classroom. The process involves group discussion and includes the following components: articulation of the problem, brainstorming and discussion of possible solutions, selection of a plan of action, implementation, evaluation, and reintroduction of the problem if the plan of action is not effective.

Some specific suggestions in dealing with gifted students in a social-emotional context are as follows:

◆ Know when to refer students to professionals trained to deal with certain types of emotional problems.

◆ Create a classroom atmosphere that encourages students to take academic risks and allows them to make mistakes without fear of ridicule or harsh negative critique.

◆ Provide time on a weekly basis, if at all possible, for individual sessions with students so that they can share their interests, ongoing events in their lives, or concerns.

◆ Require, and teach if necessary, appropriate social skills (e.g., appropriate inter-actions) to students who display problems in these areas.

◆ Work with parents on the personal development of students.

◆ Use different types of activities (e.g., social issues) to develop self-understand-ing, decision-making, and problem-solving skills. Rosselli (1993) recommends the use of bibliotherapy.

Special Areas of Concern

Underserved Groups

Four underidentified and underserved groups of gifted students exist in schools today: students who are female, culturally and ethnically different, economically disadvan-taged, or disabled.

For a variety of reasons, these groups have been underrepresented in programs serving gifted and talented students. Two related factors that have contributed to this situation are (a) the ineffectiveness of traditional assessment procedures for iden-tifying these types of students and (b) restrictive entry criteria that students must meet to qualify for gifted programs.

Excellent resources exist that comprehensively cover these important topics. Teachers are particularly encouraged to consult the first two volumes in the series *Critical Issues in Gifted Education* (Maker, 1986; Maker & Schiever, 1989) for valu-able information on these groups. Suggestions on how teachers can nurture giftedness in these different groups can be found in these and other resources (e.g., VanTassel-Baska, Patton, & Prillaman, 1989).

General education teachers should be trained to be aware of the complexities of these issues and to be responsive to situations where they believe these students may have been overlooked. This is extremely important because general education teach-ers are key players in identifying giftedness or in recognizing potential talent in these underidentified groups.

Career and Life Skills Development

Another important area that must be addressed in comprehensive programs for gifted students is career and life skills development.

Career Development. Gifted and talented students need to learn about possible career choices that await them. Doing this at an earlier time than might be done with other students is critical because some of these students will already be in accelerated programs that may necessitate early decisions about career directions. Students should learn about the nature of various career options, the specific dynamics of different disciplines, and the types of training required to work in a given discipline.

Teachers can select different ways to address the career needs of students. One way is to ensure that gifted students have access to mentoring programs where they have extensive opportunities to spend time with adults who are engaged in profes-

Developing Culturally Appropriate Materials

1. Get community input when developing new educational materials.
2. Remember cultural values, beliefs, and practices.
3. Use the language spoken by the target population; avoid direct translations of previously existing materials.
4. Use words and phrases that are used by the target population.
5. Give a direct and nonjudgmental message that is locally and regionally relevant.
6. Ascertain the reading level of the target population and design materials accordingly.
7. Use pictures, cartoons, and other visuals for groups with limited reading skills.
8. Keep written materials brief and to the point.
9. Use cultural heroes as spokespersons or endorsers, such as athletes and religious leaders, and political leaders.

Source: Randall-David, E. (1989). Strategies for working with culturally diverse communities and clients (pp. 22–23). Office of Maternal and Child Health. U.S. Department of Health and Human Services.

sional activities that interest students. Another method is to infuse the study of careers into the existing curriculum by discussing various careers when appropriate and by requiring students to engage in some of the activities associated with different careers. For instance, it is possible to acquaint students with a number of different career-relevant experiences while covering traditional subject areas.

Career counseling and guidance is also recommended. As Hardman, Drew, Egan, and Wolf (1993) point out, because of their multiple exceptional abilities and wide range of interests, some gifted students have a difficult time making career choices or narrowing down mentorship possibilities. It is extremely important that these students spend some time with counselors and/or teachers who can help them make these choices and who can help them make important postsecondary decisions.

Life Skills Preparation. All students need to be prepared for the demands and challenges of adulthood (Cronin & Patton, 1993). For the most part, due to their advanced problem-solving abilities and breadth of knowledge, students who are gifted make the transition to adulthood without too much difficulty and are able to deal successfully with most of the major life demands they will face. However, proficiency will be needed in the following areas: employment/education, home and family, leisure pursuits, physical and emotional health, community involvement, and personal responsibility and relationships.

It has been our experience that some areas of adult functioning will need attention, as the complexities of adulthood cannot be underestimated. For instance, some demands of adulthood (e.g., getting along with one's spouse) can be overwhelming for even the most gifted persons. Assurance that gifted students have a working knowledge of adulthood demands is warranted.

Summary

◆ Most gifted, talented, or creative students spend the significant part of their school careers in general education settings and require program modifications in order to maximize their learning potential.

◆ The term *gifted* has been used to refer to a broad spectrum of students with exceptional abilities in areas such as intellectual, creative, academic skills, leadership ability, or performing or visual arts.

◆ A number of myths surround the concept of giftedness (e.g., physically weak, narrow in interests, socially inept), but most common myths about gifted children are not consistent with empirical data.

◆ Prevalence figures of 3% to 5% are often cited to reflect the extent of giftedness in the general school population.

◆ The Renzulli model of giftedness includes three interlocking clusters: above-average ability, task commitment, and creativity.

◆ In order to assist in the identification of students who are gifted, classroom teachers should be aware of specific behaviors that can assist in determining whether a student should be evaluated in a comprehensive fashion.

◆ A key element of education for gifted children is differentiated programming, which refers to various learning opportunities provided to gifted students that are different from those provided to students in general. In the majority of schools, gifted students spend most of their time in the general education classroom.

◆ Reis (1989) stresses that educational programming should move away from content-based curricula and toward emphasis on the skills of knowledge acquisition and data analysis.

◆ Three general approaches have been used for programming for students who are gifted: acceleration, enrichment, and special grouping.

◆ Acceleration refers to practices that introduce content, concepts, and educational experiences at a rate faster than might be done with average students.

◆ Enrichment refers to techniques that provide topics, skill development, materials, or experiences that extend the depth of coverage beyond the existing curriculum.

◆ Special grouping refers to the homogeneous grouping of gifted students for at least part of the instructional day.

◆ Educational programs for gifted students should address possible modifications in the areas of organization and management, academic instruction, social-emotional development, and preparation for life.

◆ Comprehensive gifted programs must provide for a commitment to identification and service for underrepresented groups of gifted students. These include students who are female, culturally and ethnically different, economically disadvantaged, or disabled.

References

Chalfant, J. C., & Van Dusen Pysh, R. L. (1993). Teacher assistance teams: Implications for the gifted. In C. J. Maker (Ed.), *Critical issues in gifted education: Vol 3. Programs for the gifted in regular classrooms* (pp. 32–48). Austin, TX: Pro-Ed.

Clark, B. (1992). *Growing up gifted: Developing the potential of children at home and at school* (4th ed.). New York: Merrill.

Clinkenbeard, P. R. (1991). Unfair expectations: A pilot study of middle school students' comparisons of gifted and regular classes. *Journal for the Education of the Gifted, 15,* 56–63.

Conroy, J. (1993). Classroom management: An expected view. In C. J. Maker (Ed.), *Critical issues in gifted education: Programs for the gifted in regular classrooms* (*Vol. 3,* pp. 227–257). Austin, TX: Pro-Ed.

Cronin, M. E., & Patton, J. R. (1993). *Life skills instruction for all students with special needs: A practical guide for integrating real-life content into the curriculum.* Austin, TX: Pro-Ed.

Dale, E. J. (1993). Computers and gifted/talented individuals. In J. D. Lindsey (Ed.), *Computers and exceptional individuals* (pp. 194–211). Austin, TX: Pro-Ed.

Feldhusen, H. J. (1993). Individualized teaching of the gifted in regular classrooms. In C. J. Maker (Ed.), *Critical issues in gifted education: Vol. 3. Programs for the gifted in regular classrooms* (pp. 263–273). Austin: TX, Pro-Ed.

Feldhusen, H. J. (1993). Synthesis of research on gifted youth. *Educational Leadership, 22,* 6–11.

Gallagher, J. J. (1985). *Teaching the gifted child.* Boston: Allyn & Bacon.

Gardner, H. (1983). *Frames of mind: The theory of multiple intelligences.* New York: Basic Books.

Gardner, H., & Hatch, T. (1989). Multiple intelligences go to school: Educational implications of the theory of multiple intelligences. *Educational Researcher, 18*(8), 4–9.

Hallahan, D. P., & Kauffman, J. M. (1991). *Exceptional children: Introduction to special education* (5th ed.). Boston: Allyn & Bacon.

Hardman, M. L., Drew, C. J., Egan, M. W., & Wolf, B. (1993). *Human exceptionality: Society, school, and family* (4th ed.). Boston: Allyn & Bacon.

Kataoka, J. C. (1987). *An example of integrating literature.* Unpublished manuscript.

Kerry, T. (1980). Teaching strategies for bright pupils. In D. Jackson (Ed.), *Curriculum development for the gifted* (pp. 160–169). Guilford, CT: Special Learning Corporation.

Kitano, M. K. (1993). Critique of Feldhusen's "individualized teaching of the gifted in regular classrooms." In C. J. Maker (Ed.), *Critical issues in gifted education: Vol. 3. Programs for the gifted in regular classrooms* (pp. 274–281). Austin, TX: Pro-Ed.

Lopez, R., & MacKenzie, J. (1993). A learning center approach to individualized instruction for gifted students. In C. J. Maker (Ed.), *Critical issues in gifted education: Vol. 3. Programs for the gifted in regular classrooms* (pp. 282–295). Austin, TX: Pro-Ed.

Maker, C. J. (1986). *Critical issues in gifted education: Vol. 1. Defensible programs for the gifted.* Austin, TX: Pro-Ed.

Maker, C. J. (Ed.). (1993a). *Critical issues in gifted education: Vol. 3. Programs for the gifted in regular classrooms.* Austin, TX: Pro-Ed.

Maker, C. J. (1993b). Gifted students in the regular education classroom: What practices are defensible and feasible? In C. J. Maker (Ed.), *Critical issues in gifted education: Vol. 3. Programs for the gifted in regular classrooms* (pp. 413–436). Austin, TX: Pro-Ed.

Maker, C. J., & Schiever, S. W. (1989). *Critical issues in gifted education: Vol. 2. Defensible programs for cultural and ethnic minorities.* Austin, TX: Pro-Ed.

Mirman, N. J. (1991). Reflections on educating the gifted child. *G/C/T, 14,* 57–60.

National Center for Education Statistics. (1989). *Digest of educational statistics, 1989.* Washington, DC: U.S. Department of Education, Office of Research and Improvement.

Parke, B. N. (1989). *Gifted students in regular classrooms.* Boston: Allyn & Bacon.

Purcell, C. (1978). *Gifted and Talented Children's Education Act of 1978.* Washington, DC: U.S. Government Printing Office.

Randall-David, E. (1989). *Strategies for working with culturally diverse communities and clients.* Office of Maternal and Child Health. U.S. Department of Health and Human Services.

Reis, S. M. (1989). Reflections on policy affecting the education of gifted and talented students. *American Psychologist, 44,* 399–408.

Reis, S. M., & Schack, G. D. (1993). Differentiating products for the gifted and talented: The encouragement of independent learning. In C. J. Maker (Ed.), *Critical issues in gifted education: Vol. 3. Programs for the gifted in regular classrooms* (pp. 161–186). Austin, TX: Pro-Ed.

Renzulli, J. S. (1979). *What makes giftedness: A reexamination of the definition of the gifted and talented.* Ventura, CA: Ventura County Superintendent of Schools Office.

Renzulli, J. S., Reis, S. M., & Smith, L. M. (1981). *The revolving door identification model.* Wethersfield, CT: Creative Learning Press.

Roberts, C., Ingram, C., & Harris, C. (1992). The effect of special versus regular clasroom programming on higher cognitive processes of intermediate elementary aged gifted and average ability students. *Journal of the Education of the Gifted, 15,* 332–343.

Rosselli, H. (1993). Process differentiation for gifted learners in the regular classroom: Teaching to everyone's needs. In C. J. Maker (Ed.), *Critical issues in gifted education: Vol. 3. Programs for the gifted in regular classrooms* (pp. 139–155). Austin, TX: Pro-Ed.

Schiever, S. W. (1993). Differentiating the learning environment for gifted students. In C. J. Maker (Ed.,), *Critical issues in gifted education: Programs for the gifted in regular classrooms* (pp. 201–214). Austin, TX: Pro-Ed.

Shaner, M. Y. (1991). Talented teachers for talented students. *G/C/T, 22,* 14–15.

Shanley, R. (1993). Becoming content with content. In C. J. Maker (Ed.), *Critical issues in gifted education: Vol. 3. Programs for the gifted in regular classrooms* (pp. 116–134). Austin, TX: Pro-Ed.

Silverman, L. K. (1986). What happens to the gifted girl? In C. J. Maker (Ed.), *Critical issues in gifted education: Defensible programs for the gifted* (*Vol. 1,* pp. 43–89). Austin, TX: Pro-Ed.

Sisk, D. A. (1993). Creating and maintaining a responsive environment for gifted students. In C. J. Maker (Ed.), *Critical issues in gifted education: Vol. 3. Programs for the gifted in regular classrooms* (pp. 215–222). Austin, TX: Pro-Ed.

Smith, D. D., & Luckasson, R. (1992). *Introduction to special education: Teaching in the age of challenge.* Boston: Allyn & Bacon.

Southern, W. T., & Jones, E. D. (1991). Academic acceleration: Background and issues. In W. T. Southern & E. D. Jones (Eds.), *Academic acceleration of gifted children* (pp. 1–17). New York: Teachers College Press.

Squires, E. C., & Reetz, L. J. (1989). Vocabulary acquisition activities. *Academic Therapy, 14,* 589–592.

Sternberg, R. J. (1986). A triarchic theory of intellectual giftedness. In R. J. Sternberg & J. E. Davidson (Eds.), *Conceptions of giftedness* (pp. 223–243).

VanTassel-Baska, J. (1989). Appropriate curriculum for gifted learners. *Educational Leadership,* 13–15.

VanTassel-Baska, J., Patton, J., & Prillaman, D. (1989). Disadvantaged gifted learners at-risk for educational attention. *Focus on Exceptional Children, 22*(3), 1–16.

Winebrenner, S. (1992). *Teaching gifted kids in the regular classroom.* Minneapolis, MN: Free Spirit Publishing.

CHAPTER 11

Teaching Students at Risk

SHARON R. MORGAN

Mary is a thin, eight-year-old girl with blond hair and blue eyes. She is finishing the first grade; she was retained once in kindergarten. Ms. Skates, her teacher, does not know what to do with her. She referred Mary for special education, but the assessment revealed that she was not eligible. Although her intelligence is in the low average range, she does not have mental retardation or any other qualifying disability. Mary is shy and very insecure. She frequently cries if Ms. Skates leaves the classroom; she is very dependent on her teacher. Mary does not have any close friends, but a few of the other girls in the classroom will play with her from time to time. Mary is reading at the preprimer level and does not recognize all of her letters and sounds. She can count to 10, but does not understand any math facts.

Mary lives with her mother and three younger brothers in a three-room apartment. Her mother has been divorced twice and works as a waitress at a local coffee shop. Her mother's income barely pays the rent, buys groceries, and provides day-care for her brothers. Occasionally, when Mary's mother gets the chance to work extra at nights, when tips are better, she leaves all four children with Mary in charge. Although Mary's mother appears interested in her schoolwork, Ms. Skates has been unable to get her to a teacher's meeting, even though several have been scheduled. Ms. Skates is not sure if she should refer Mary for special education and, once again, retain her in the first grade, or promote her so that she does not fall further behind her age peers.

Mary is a good example of a child who is at risk for developing major academic and behavior problems. In the current system, children like Mary cannot be provided with special education and related services from federal programs. The result, too often, is that Mary and children like her end up dropping out of school and experience major problems as adults.

Introduction

The movement to include students with disabilities in general education has made substantial progress over the past several years. Beginning with the movement to mainstream students with disabilities part-time while providing specialized services in resource rooms, students with disabilities have become an ever-increasing part of our general educational system. More recently, the full inclusion movement has resulted in more full-time inclusion of students with disabilities into general educational programs.

Whether the inclusion movement will ever be totally adopted by all schools remains to be seen. However, one definite benefit that has resulted from the inclusion movement is the recognition that many students who are not eligible for special education services are still in need of them. Although they do not manifest problems severe enough to result in a disability classification, these students are **at risk** for developing achievement and behavior problems that could limit their success in school and as young adults.

Students at risk can be defined in many different ways. They can be defined as the overall group of students, K–12, who are at risk for developing significant academic or behavior problems, or they can be a narrowly defined group of preschool students who are at risk of failing early in their school years. For the purposes of this chapter, students who are at risk are those who face potential failure during their school years and in society as young adults.

Unlike students with disabilities, who have historically been segregated full-time and part-time from their chronological age peers, students who are considered at risk have been fully included in educational programs. Unfortunately, this inclusion has not been the result of a method of providing appropriate interventions. Rather, it has primarily been a system of neglect that too often resulted in students going from at risk to failure. Although not eligible for special education and related services, students who are at risk need specialized interventions. Without these interventions, many will be retained year after year, become behavior problems, develop drug and alcohol abuse problems, drop out of school, and fail as adults. School personnel need to recognize students who are at risk for failure and develop appropriate programs to facilitate their success in school and in society. Not doing so will result in losing many of these children, and "to lose today's at-risk students implies a society that is more than a little out of control itself" (Greer, 1991, p. 390).

Types of Students Who Are at Risk

Many students are at risk for failure. Although there is no way to identify all students who are at risk, failure is significantly more likely for certain categories of students. These include students who grow up in poverty, those who grow up without homes, those who grow up in single-parent homes, those who have abusive parents, those who abuse substances, and those who become delinquents. Although children who are in these types of situations are more likely to experience failure than others, it must be kept in mind that "to label at risk every poor child or everyone in a single-parent household is unfair and demeaning and, as research indicates, not accurate either" (Greer, 1991, p. 391).

Students Who Grow Up in Poverty

Poverty is a social condition that is associated with many different kinds of problems. Poverty has been related to crime, physical abuse, learning problems, behavior problems, and emotional problems. Of all the factors that place students at risk for academic failure, poverty is number one (Davis, 1993). Poverty is one of the underlying problems of our society. In 1991, nearly 22% of all children in the United States lived in poverty. After a steady decline in the number of children growing up in poverty during the 1960s and 1970 (The Condition of Education, 1990), the numbers have recently begun to increase. Between 1979 and 1989, the number of children growing up in poverty increased by 14.1% for African-American children, 22.7% for white children, and 69.6% for Latino children (Davis, 1993).

The largest group of children in poverty are those from minority racial groups. In 1989, nearly 44% of African-American children, 36.2% of Latino children, and

14.8% of white children were in poverty (Davis, 1993). Table 11.1 summarizes poverty rates for children in the United States and changes from 1990 to 1991. Poverty is associated with many factors that create difficulties for students. These include different kinds of disabilities (Smith & Luckasson, 1992), including mental retardation (Beirne-Smith, Patton & Ittenbach, 1994), learning disabilities (Mercer, 1991), and various health problems. Poverty is also associated with poor prenatal care, poor parenting, and numerous other factors, including hunger, limited health care, single-parent households, and poor housing conditions.

Hunger. Although many people in this country have a difficult time believing it, thousands of children go to bed hungry every night. "It is estimated that at least 5.5 million children (1 in 8 children today in the U.S.) are regularly hungry, while another 6 million other children younger than age 12 are in families living on the edge of poverty and face chronic food shortages" (Davis, 1993, p. 11). Children who are hungry have a difficult time concentrating on schoolwork and frequently display behavior problems in the classroom. Although free school lunch and breakfast programs have been expanded over the past years, hunger among school children in this country still remains a significant problem.

Health Care. Children who grow up in poverty are unlikely to receive adequate health care. Although significant progress with childhood diseases such as polio and whooping cough has been made over the past forty years, the health status of many children today is below that of children in other countries. Currently, the United States ranks twenty-second among developed nations in the area of infant mortality

TABLE 11.1 **Poverty Rates for Children in the United States**

	1990	1991
Total	20.6%	21.8%
White	15.6	16.8
Black	44.8	45.9
Latino	38.4	40.4
City	30.5	32.5
Suburb	13.3	14.7
Rural	22.9	22.5
Northeast	18.4	19.7
Midwest	18.8	19.8
South	23.8	24.0
West	19.8	22.2
Married parents	10.2	10.6
Mother only	53.4	55.4
Father only	20.7	22.3

Source: U.S. Bureau of the Census (1992). *Poverty income in the United States: 1991,* P–60, No. 180. Washington, DC: U.S. Government Printing Office.

(Davis, 1993). Poverty appears to be directly associated with many of the health problems experienced by children today (*Healthy People 2000,* 1992). Just as children who are hungry have difficulties concentrating, children who are unhealthy may miss school and fall behind academically.

School Personnel and Poverty.   Unfortunately, there is not a great deal teachers and other school personnel can do to alleviate the poverty experienced by students. However, teachers can do some things in classrooms that can reduce the impact of poverty on achievement and behaviors:

1. Recognize the impact that poverty has on students.
2. Make all students in the classroom feel important.
3. Avoid placing students in situations where limited family finances become obvious to other students.
4. Coordinate with school social workers or other school personnel whose jobs are to work with family members to secure social services.
5. Realize that students may not have supplies and other equipment that may be required for certain class activities. Contingency funds or other means to help pay for these items should be available.

Homeless Students

A tragedy of the 1980s and 1990s is the growing number of homeless people in the United States. The number of individuals who do not have homes has risen to epidemic proportions. The problems of homeless people have only recently become known for most of our society. Whereas the "homeless" historically were aging adults, often with mental illness or alcohol abuse, today as many as 25% of all homeless persons are children. "On any given night, it is estimated that between 50,000 and 200,000 children are homeless in the United States" (Davis, 1993, p. 16).

Poverty is directly associated with homelessness, so the problems of poverty are present with this group of children. The added impact of not having a home greatly compounds problems of poverty. Children who are homeless are usually very embarrassed by the fact that they do not have a place to live. Although some are lucky enough to be in a shelter, many live on the streets or in cars with their parents.

Trying to provide educational programs to homeless children is made more difficult by the transient nature of these families. Homeless families frequently move from one part of town to another, or from one community to another. Without a home, and frequently without a job to hold them to a particular area, many simply move to different locations without any communication with school personnel.

Just as school personnel are limited in the interventions they can use for children in poverty, they are also limited in regard to interventions for children without homes. Probably the best advice for school personnel is to avoid putting students in situations where their homelessness will result in an embarrassment. For example, going around the room after Christmas and having everyone tell, in graphic detail, everything Santa Claus brought them may be very uncomfortable for students who do not even have a home to go to after school. Also, insisting on a home visit may result in families avoiding any interaction with the school.

In order to work with parents who are in homeless situations, teachers and other school personnel should consider the following:

1. Arrange to meet parents at their place of work or at school.
2. Offer to assist family members in securing services from available social agencies.
3. Do not require excessive school supplies that many families cannot afford.
4. Do not expect homework of the same quality as that of children who have homes.

Schools alone cannot adequately meet the needs of homeless children. A more positive approach than simply attempting to develop school programs would be to provide the impetus to develop a school-community partnership. In a program described by Gonzalez (1991), local churches, local business groups, and individual volunteers worked with homeless shelters to provide interventions that went well beyond what the school alone could provide. The result was a program that offered very positive programs for the many students who not only were poor but did not have homes to go to after school.

Students in Single-Parent Homes

The nature of the American family has changed dramatically over the past 25 years. "During the 1980s, only six percent of all U.S. families fit the mold of the 1950s 'Ozzie and Harriet family': a working father, a housewife mother, and two children of public school age" (Davis, 1993, p. 14). The following facts describe the families of the 1990s (Davis, 1993):

- Approximately one in four children lives in a single-parent home.
- Fifty to sixty percent of all of today's children will live with only one parent during their childhood.
- The number of single-parent families in which only the mother is present increased by 19% during the 1980s.
- One in three Americans are members of a step or "blended" family.
- The number of men raising children by themselves increased by 68% between 1980 and 1990.
- Nearly 70% of all children have working mothers.
- Blended and single-parent families are very common family models.

Many things result in children being reared in single-parent homes, including divorce, death of a parent, or significant illness of a parent.

Children from Divorce.   Nationally, divorce is on an upward trend that shows no signs of decreasing. Divorce has increased to such a level that it is estimated that half of all new marriages will end in divorce. Although the birth rate in the United States

Approximately 1 in 4 children live in a single-parent home.

is declining, the number of divorces in which children are involved is increasing (Chiriboga & Catron, 1991). Currently, 44% of all children live in a nontraditional family unit, most often headed by a single, working mother (Austin, 1992). Divorce is a disorganizing and reorganizing process, particularly when children are involved, and the process often extends over several years (Morgan, 1985). Although divorce has the potential for growth and new integrations, too often it only creates problems for children, and although some children cope very well with the trauma surrounding divorce, many react with major problems (Munger & Morse, 1992). The central dilemma in many divorces is the conflict of interest between the child's need for continuity of the family unit and the parents' decision to break up the family that has provided the child's main supports (Wallerstein & Kelly, 1977; Walczak & Burns, 1984).

Divorce can affect children in many different ways. Although for long periods of time experts seemed to suggest that children usually resisted most negative effects of divorce, more recent studies indicate a variety of negative consequences associated with divorce (Morgan, 1985). These include anxiety, denial, guilt, academic problems, behavior problems, and regression (Anderson & Anderson, 1981; Beck, 1988; Chiriboga & Catron, 1991; Peterson, 1989; Sorosky, 1977).

Divorce can affect children differently at different ages. It has been shown to have a significant impact on preschool children. Some specific initial behavioral reactions include shock, depression, and regressive phenomena such as bedwetting, eating problems, and sleeping problems. In addition, anxiety and confusion are frequently present because parents do not fully explain to their children what is happening. This incomplete understanding may cause many children to feel blame for the breakup, especially if being "good" was related to being loved by the parents (Ellison, 1983; Henning, & Oldham, 1977; Wallerstein, 1983).

Children who are older frequently react differently to divorce (Morgan, 1985). For middle-school children, guilt, anxiety, fantasies, and social problems with peers are common reactions. Guilt is often the result of the child at one time wishing that the parent had gone away. The anxiety comes from trying to decide which parent to live with and then fearing rejection from the other parent. Worrying about who will take care of them if the custodial parent cannot provide the care is another fantasy that often surfaces with this age group (Chiriboga & Catron, 1991; Peterson, 1989; Sugar, 1970).

Adolescents react in other ways to divorce. Anger, hostility, and depression are common reactions among members of this age group. Other reactions include grief, shame, resentment, and sleep problems—all concomitant with academic problems (Beck, 1988; Roy & Fuqua, 1983). The actual impact of divorce on adolescents appears to be affected by several factors (Beck, 1988; Fry & Trifiletti, 1983):

♦ The dynamics of the family relationships prior to the divorce
♦ The nature of the marital breakup
♦ The relationship between the parents after the divorce
♦ The developmental status of the child at the time of the divorce
♦ The strength of personality and coping skills of the adolescent

Children in Homes Headed by Single Mothers.   Most single-parent homes are headed by mothers. In these situations, the absence of a father generally has a more negative impact on boys than on girls. The academic achievement of both boys and girls has been shown to be affected, with lower achievement being found in situations where the presence of the father was more limited.

Children in Homes Headed by Single Fathers.   Although not nearly as prevalent as single-parent homes headed by mothers, the number of single-parent homes headed by fathers has increased significantly over the past decade. The effects of growing up in a single-parent home headed by a father varies a great deal from child to child. Some of the findings of studies indicate that single-parent fathers are more likely to use other adults in their support networks than single-parent mothers, and children seem to do better when there is a large adult support network than when this network is limited (Santrock & Warshak, 1979).

Children in Homosexual-Couple Homes.   Although very rare a few years ago, the number of homes with homosexual couples and children has increased over the past several years. It is estimated that approximately 1.5 million lesbian mothers currently reside in a family unit with their children (Hoeffer, 1981). In situations like this, school personnel should respond to these parents and children with the same respect that they show other children's families (Clay, 1991). Personal feelings about homosexuality by school personnel cannot be allowed to result in any hostility toward families with homosexual parents (Stover, 1992).

Organizations Serving Culturally Diverse Communities

Alianza
3020 14th Street, N.W.
Fourth Floor
Washington, DC 20009
(202) 223-9600

Asian American Psychological Association
16591 Melville Circle
Huntington Beach, CA 92649
(213) 592-3227

Asian American Community Mental Health
Training Center
1300 W. Olympic Boulevard, #303
Los Angeles, CA
(213) 385-1474

Association of American Indian Affairs, Inc.
432 Park Avenue South
New York, NY 10016
(212) 689-8720

Association of Asian/Pacific Community
Health Organizations
310 8th Street, Suite 210
Oakland, CA 94607
(415) 272-9536

Bebashi (Blacks Educating Blacks
About Sexual Health Issues)
1319 Locust Street
Philadelphia, PA 19107
(215) 546-4140

Community Outreach Risk Reduction
Education Program (CORE)
6570 Santa Monica Boulevard
Los Angeles, CA 90038
(213) 460-4444

COSSMHO
Coalition of Hispanic Health and Human
Service Organizations
1030 15th Street, N.W.
Washington, DC 20005
(202) 371-2100

Health Education Resource Organization
(HERO)
101 West Read Street, Suite 812
Baltimore, MD 21201
(301) 685-1180

Japanese American Citizens League
National Headquarters
1765 Sutter Street
San Francisco, CA 94115
(415) 921-5225

1730 Rhode Island Avenue, N.W., #204
Washington, DC 20036
(202) 223-1240

The Kupona Network
4611 South Ellis Avenue
Chicago, IL 60653
(312) 536-3000

Multicultural Prevention Resource
Center (MPRC)
1540 Market Street, Suite 320
San Francisco, CA 94102
(415) 861-2142

National Association for the Advancement of
Colored People (NAACP)
1790 Broadway
New York, NY 10019
(212) 245-2100

National Association for Black Psychologists
1125 Spring Road, N.W.
Washington, DC 20010
(202) 576-7184

National Association of Black Social Workers
(NABSW)
2008 Madison Avenue
New York, NY 10035
(212) 369-0639

▼

National Black Women's Health Project
1217 Gordon Street, S.W.
Atlanta, GA 30810
(404) 753-0916

National Center for Urban Ethnic Affairs
1521 16th Street, N.W.
Washington, DC 20036
(202) 232-3600

National Conference of Puerto Rican Women
P.O. Box 4804
Washington, DC 20012

National Congress on American
Indians/NCAI Fund
1430 K Street, N.W., Suite 700
Washington, DC 20005
(202) 347-9520

National Council of La Raza
810 First Street, N.E., Suite 300
Washington, DC 20002
(202) 289-1380

National Institute of Mental Health
5600 Fishers Lane
Rockville, MD 20857
(301) 443-3533

National Urban League
500 E. 62 Street
New York, NY 10021
(212) 310-9000

Research Department, NUL
733 15th Street, N.W.
Washington, DC 20005
(202) 783-0220

Office of Latino Affairs
2000 14th Street, N.W., 2nd Floor
Washington, DC 20009
(202) 939-8765

Office of Minority Affairs
1012 14th Street, N.W., Suite 601
Washington, DC 20005
(202) 347-0390

Office of Minority Health
Dept. of Health & Human Services
200 Independence Avenue, S.W.,
Room 118F
Washington, DC 20201
(202) 245-0020

Office of Minority Health—Resource Center
P.O. Box 37337
Washington, DC 20013-7337
(301) 587-1938

- Maintains a computerized data base of minority health-related resources at local, state, and national levels.
- Coordinates resource persons network to provide technical assistance.

Source: Randall-David, E. (1989). *Strategies for working with culturally diverse communities and clients* (pp. 95–96). Office of Maternal and Child Health. U.S. Department of Health and Human Services.

Although there is a great deal of misinformation about the effects of homosexuality on children, most research suggests that there is no apparent harm for children who grow up with homosexual parents (Clay, 1991; Hare & Koepke, 1990; Wyers, 1987). Also, there appears to be no relationship between the parent's sexual and affectional orientation and the sexual identity of the child. (Clay, 1991; Stover, 1992).

Teachers and other school personnel can do several things to help children with homosexual parents achieve success in school activities:

1. Assist other school personnel in the awareness that gay and lesbian parents exist and need the same respect shown other parents.

2. Use contemporary terminology (e.g., gay/lesbian) the same as would be done for other minority groups (e.g., Native American, African-American).
3. Utilize classroom activities about family diversity to ensure a healthy self-identity.
4. Mention gay and lesbian groups in a positive manner; do not deal with morality issues.
5. Alert gay and lesbian parents if their children are being harassed for being from a different type of family and help the parents develop strategies for preparing their children to cope with these actions.
6. Respect secrecy in families when that is desired.
7. Provide any needed extra encouragement for students to attend school and participate in social activities.
8. Examine their own values for bias and negative stereotypes that might be projected onto the child.
9. Normalize the child's experience by pointing out that a family is two or more people who love and take care of each other. Be prepared to discuss different family structures with the entire class in a positive manner.

Students Who Experience Significant Losses

Although the continued absence of one or both parents through separation or divorce is considered a loss, the loss created by the death of a parent can result in significantly more problems for children. Unlike children living in the early part of this century, when extended families often lived together and children actually experienced death, often in the home environment with grandparents, children of today are generally insulated from death. Therefore, when death does occur, especially that of a significant person in a child's life, the result can be very devastating, often resulting in major problems in school.

Death of a Parent.　When a child's parent dies, external events impinge on the child's personality in three main ways (Feinter et al., 1981; Moriarty, 1967; Tennant, Bebbington, & Hurry, 1980):

1. The child must deal with the reality of the death itself.
2. The child must adapt to the resulting changes in the family.
3. The child must contend with the perpetual absence of the lost parent.

Children respond in many different ways to a parent's death. Some responses are guilt, regression, denial, bodily distress, hostile reactions to the deceased, eating disorders, enuresis, sleep disturbances, withdrawal, anxiety, panic, learning difficulties, and aggression (Anthony, 1972; Elizer & Kauffman, 1983; Van Eerdewegh, Bieri, Parrilla, & Clayton, 1982). It is also not unusual for sibling rivalry to become very intense and disruptive. Often, extreme family turmoil results from the death of a parent, especially when the parent who dies was the controlling person in the family (Van Eerdewegh et al., 1982).

Sibling Death.   A sibling plays an important and significant part in the family dynamics, so the death of a sibling can initiate a psychological crisis for a child. It can result in modification of a child's life situation if the grief of the parents renders them unable to maintain a healthy parental relationship with the remaining child or children.

If they experience the death of a sibling, children frequently fear that they will die. When an older sibling dies, the younger child may revert to childish behaviors in hopes of not getting older, thereby averting dying. Older children often react with extreme fear and anxiety if they are ignored by parents during the grieving period. Often these children become preoccupied with the horrifying question about their own future: "Will it happen to me tomorrow, or next week, or next year?" (McKeever, 1983). Often children react with severe depression when a sibling dies (McKeever, 1983).

Actions of School Personnel in Cases of Death.   There are no magical interventions that school personnel can implement to help children recover from the death of a parent, sibling, or friend. However, an overriding consideration must be to allow the child to grieve and to provide emotional support for the child during the grieving process. Some suggestions that educators can consider include the following (Furman, 1974):

1. Allow the child to remain with a close, loving person rather than being left with a stranger. This may require extensive absence from school. During this period, school personnel should provide homebound services to help the child keep up with schoolwork.
2. Keep daily living routines as normal as possible. School personnel should encourage family members to keep the child in the same school to prevent further disruptions from the child's regular routines.
3. Physical closeness and empathy must be provided. School counselors, social workers, and teachers must provide emotional support for the child when school attendance is resumed.
4. Help children understand the reality of death. Death education should be a part of the curriculum to assist children in understanding their personal loss. School counselors may be available to provide this intervention.
5. Children should be allowed to keep pictures and other objects of the dead individual with them in their environment. This may help by providing reminders for children of their love for the parent or friend who has died.
6. Support must be provided for children throughout the mourning period, especially toward the end of the period. Often children feel guilty when they begin to get over the death of a significant person, and they need to be provided with support during this period.

In general, children should not be prevented from crying and displaying grief, nor should they be pressured to display unfelt sorrow (Greenberg, 1975). It should be remembered that just because children quickly return to playing and activities does not mean that they are not grieving. Children are simply more active than adults and need more motor activities to help in the mourning process.

Role of Schools with Children in Single-Parent Families.   Children who find themselves in single-parent families, due to divorce or death, require a great deal of support. For many of these children, the school may be their most stable environment. School personnel must develop methods for providing the necessary supports in order to prevent negative outcomes, such as school failure, manifestation of emotional problems, or the development of behavior problems. Based on an interview conducted with children residing in single-parent homes, the following conclusions concerning the positive role schools can play were developed (Lewis, 1992):

1. Schools are a place of security and safety for students from single-parent homes.
2. Students who lose parents due to death are often treated differently by school personnel than when the loss is from divorce. Unfortunately, the child's needs are similar in both situations.
3. Teachers are the most important people in the school for children who are in single-parent homes because of their tremendous influence on self-esteem.
4. Students want to be considered just as they were before they were from a single-parent home.
5. Trust with peers and teachers is the most important factor for students from single-parent homes.
6. School personnnel often seem oblivious to the new financial situation of families with only one parent.
7. Keeping a log or diary is considered an excellent method to explore feelings and create opportunities for meaningful discussions.

There are many things schools should and should not do when dealing with students who are from single-parent homes (Wanat, 1992). Table 11.2 summarizes some of these "dos" and "don'ts."

For children who are products of divorce, schools must consider the involvement of the noncustodial parent. Unfortunately, many schools do not even include spaces for information on forms for students' noncustodial parents (Austin, 1992). In order to ensure that noncustodial parents are afforded their rights regarding their children, and to actively solicit the involvement of the noncustodial parent, school personnel should

1. Establish policies that encourage the involvement of noncustodial parents
2. Maintain records of information about the noncustodial parent
3. Distribute information about school activities to noncustodial parents
4. Insist that noncustodial parents be involved in teacher conferences
5. Structure parent conferences to facilitate the development of a shared relationship between the custodial and noncustodial parent
6. Conduct surveys to determine the level of involvement desired by noncustodial parents (Austin, 1992)

TABLE 11.2 **Some Dos and Don'ts When Working with Children with Single Parents**

Some Dos

- Collect information about students' families.
- Analyze information about students' families to determine specific needs.
- Create programs and practices that address areas of need unique to particular schools.
- Include curricular areas that help students achieve success, such as study skills.
- Provide nonacademic programs such as child care and family counseling.
- Involve parents in determining appropriate roles for school and family.
- Take the initiative early in the year to establish a communication link with parents.
- Enlist the support of both parents, when possible.
- Provide a stable, consistent environment for children during the school day.

Some Don'ts

- Don't treat single parents differently than other parents.
- Don't call attention to the fact that a child lives with only one parent.
- Limit activities such as "father/son" night or other events that highlight the differences in a single-parent home.
- Don't have "room mothers," have "room parents."
- Don't overlook the limitations of single-parent homes in such areas as helping with projects, helping with homework, and so forth.

Source: Wanat., C. L. (1992). Meeting the needs of single-parent children: School and parent views differ. *NAASP Bulletin, 76,* 43–48. Used with permission.

Students with Abusive Parents

Growing up in an abusive family places children at significant risk for problems. Abuse can be emotional or physical. Child abuse occurs in families that mirror the characteristics of society with regard to socioeconomic status, race, religion, and ethnic background. Although no one factor causes abuse, several things have been shown to be related to child abuse:

- Experience of abuse as a child
- Adolescent parents (Buchholz & Korn-Bursztyn, 1993)
- Poverty
- Low self-esteem in parents (Goldman & Gargiulo, 1990)
- Substance abuse (Goldman & Gargiulo, 1990)
- Emotional problems (Goldman & Gargiulo, 1990)

Emotional Abuse. The National Committee for Prevention of Child Abuse (1983) defines emotional abuse as

> excessive, aggressive, or unreasonable parental demands that place expectations on a child beyond his or her capabilities. Emotional abuse can show itself in constant persistent teasing, belittling, or verbal attacks. Emotional abuses also include failures to provide the psychological nurturance necessary for a child's psychological growth and development—no love, no care, no support, no guidance. (p. 5)

Although fairly difficult to identify, several characteristics are frequently displayed by children who are being emotionally abused (Gargiulo, 1990, p. 22):

- Absence of a positive self-image
- Behavioral extremes
- Depression
- Psychosomatic complaints
- Attempted suicide
- Impulsive, defiant, and antisocial behavior
- Age-inappropriate behaviors
- Inappropriate habits and tics
- Enuresis
- Inhibited intellectual or emotional development
- Difficulty in establishing and maintaining peer relationships
- Extreme fear, vigilance
- Sleep and eating disorders
- Self-destructive tendencies
- Rigidly compulsive behaviors

Physical Abuse. **Physical abuse** is more easily identified than **emotional abuse.** Physical abuse includes beating, strangulation, burns to the body, and other forms of physical brutalization. It is defined as "any physical injury that has been caused by other than accidental means, including any injury which appears to be at variance with the explanation of the injury" (*At Risk Youth in Crisis,* 1991, p. 9). The rate of child abuse in this country is staggering. In 1991 there were more than 2.7 million cases of reported child abuse; 1,400 children were abused every day; and more than 1,300 reported cases of child abuse and neglect resulted in death (Davis, 1993). Most authorities believe that only one in five cases are actually reported, meaning that the actual numbers are significantly greater. Between 1976 and 1985, the number of reported cases of child abuse increased from 669,000 to 1.9 million (National Center on Child Abuse and Neglect, 1986).

Children who are physically abused are two to three times more likely than nonabused children to experience failing grades and become discipline problems. They have difficulty with peer relationships, show physically aggressive behaviors, and are frequent substance abusers (Emery, 1989). Studies also show that children who suffer from physical abuse are likely to exhibit social skill deficits, including shyness, inhibited social interactions, and limited problem-solving skills. Deficits in cognitive functioning are also found in greater numbers in students who are abused than their nonabused peers (Weston, Ludolph, Misle, Ruffins, & Block, 1990).

Sexual abuse is another form of physical abuse that results in children who are at risk for school failure. Children may be sexually abused by their own families as well as by strangers. Sexual abuse can include actual physical activities, such as touching a child's genital areas, attempted and completed sexual intercourse, and the use of children in pornography. Exposing children to sexual acts by adults with the intention of shocking or arousing them is another form of sexual abuse (Jones, 1982; Williamson, Borduin, & Howe, 1991).

Typical Responses to Sexual Abuse in Preschoolers

Emotional

1. Fear, insecurity
2. Guilt, shame, embarrassment
3. Uncertainty about how to feel
4. Feelings of being dirty, soiled, disgraced
5. Fear of consequences from abuser, parents, system
6. Guilt because some things may have been pleasurable
7. Anger, hostility, blame
8. Acute anxiety
9. Self-doubt
10. Fear of internal damage
11. Betrayal—by abuser or by parent protector
12. Confusion about what happened that was wrong

Medical

1. Pain in the genital or anal areas, including pain or tears while going to the bathroom or when held or picked up
2. Redness, rash, swelling in genital or anal areas
3. Blood, discharge, or unusual odor from vagina or anus
4. Unusual anxiety, embarrassment, or distress from any medications applied to treat the above conditions
5. Other medical problems that could be associated with anxiety or possible sexual abuse, such as stomach pains, headaches, leg pains, throat infections, asthma

Behavioral

1. Sleep disturbances, nightmares, fear of "monsters," bedwetting
2. Loss of appetite, problems with eating or swallowing
3. Fear of certain people or places
4. School phobia: sudden dislike, refusal to attend, fear of teacher
5. Social withdrawal, stranger anxiety
6. Wetting pants, thumb sucking, rocking
7. Unprovoked crying
8. Unexplained anger, irritability, or crankiness
9. Clinginess, fear of separation, fear of other caretakers
10. Sexualized behavior, excessive masturbation, new terms for genitals, pseudo-maturity
11. Secretive behavior, having a secret, questions about them, replying "I can't tell you"

12. Re-enactment of abuse using dolls, drawings, or friends
13. Regression, infantile behavior
14. Sudden talk of an adult, imaginary, or secret friend
15. Threatened behavior: fear of violence, games with threats
16. Anxiety-related illness

Source: MacFarlane, J. T., Franks, M. T., & Jasper, E. (1986). *Sexual abuse of young children.* New York: Guilford Press. Used with permission.

School personnel should be aware of a number of physical and behavioral symptoms of sexual abuse:

- Physical injuries to the genital area
- Sexually transmitted diseases
- Difficulty in urinating
- Discharges from the penis or vagina
- Pregnancy
- Fear of aggressive behavior toward adults, especially a child's own parents
- Sexual self-consciousness
- Sexual promiscuity and acting out
- Inability to establish appropriate relationships with peers
- Running away, stealing, and abusing substances
- Using the school as a sanctuary, coming early, and not wanting to go home

The first thing that school personnel should be prepared to do when dealing with children who are abused is to report the incident to the appropriate agencies. School personnel have a moral and legal obligation to report suspected child abuse. The **suspected child abuse network (SCAN)** provides a reporting network for referral purposes. School personnel need to understand their responsibility in reporting suspected abuse and know the specific procedures to follow when making such a report. In addition to reporting suspected cases of abuse, school personnel can do the following (Gargiulo, 1990):

1. Work with local government officials to establish child abuse and neglect as a priority in the community.
2. Organize a telephone "hotline" service where parents or other caregivers can call for support when they believe a crisis is impending in their families.
3. Offer parent education programs that focus on parenting skills, behavior management techniques, child care suggestions, and communication strategies.
4. Establish a local chapter of **Parents Anonymous,** a volunteer group for individuals who have a history of abusing their children.
5. Develop workshops on child abuse for concerned individuals and disseminate literature on the topic.
6. Arrange visits by public health nurses to help families at risk for abuse after the birth of their first child.

7. Provide short-term respite day care through a Mother's Day Out program.
8. Encourage individuals to serve as foster parents in the community.
9. Institute a parent aide program in which parent volunteers assist single-parent homes by providing support.

Students Who Abuse Substances

Substance abuse among children and adolescents results in major problems and places students significantly more at risk for school failure. Students who are abusing substances have a much more difficult time succeeding in school than their peers.

Although there were indicators that drug use among youth was declining (The Condition of Education, 1990), recent data suggest that substance abuse among children and adolescents is once again on the increase. A recent survey of more than 200,000 students in junior high and high schools in 34 states revealed that drug use was higher in all categories, including alcohol, cocaine, marijuana, and hallucinogens. Hallucinogens and **inhalants** represented the largest increases (Drug use increasing, 1992). The average age at which boys first try drugs is 11; for girls, it is 13 (Greenbaum, Garrison, James, & Stephens, 1989). Unfortunately, these data support the overall fact that illicit drug use in the United States is significantly higher than in any other industrialized country (Blinn-Pike, Bell, Devereaux, Doyle, Tittsworth, & Von Bargen, 1993).

There are no specific factors that cause children and adolescents to abuse drugs and alcohol. Some evidence suggests that children who grow up with substance abusing parents are more likely to abuse substances themselves (Greer, 1990). Unfortunately, it is estimated that there are at least 15 million school-aged children who have at least one parent who is a substance abuser (Towers, 1989). Living with a parent who abuses drugs and alcohol only provides a negative role model for young children. Research also shows that students who are at greater risk for dropping out of school are significantly more likely than their chronological age peers to abuse substances (Eggert & Herting, 1993).

Although a great deal of attention has been paid to the impact of marijuana, cocaine, and alcohol abuse on children and youth, only recently has attention been focused on inhalants. Inhalant use increased for every grade level from the 1990–1991 school year to the 1991–1992 school year (Drug use increasing, 1992). One of the problems with inhalants is the wide number of substances that can be used by students, many of which are very available. Examples include cleaning solvents, gasoline, room deodorizers, glue, perfume, wax, and spray paint.

School personnel must be alert to the symptoms of substance abuse, whether the substance is alcohol, marijuana, inhalants, or something else. The following characteristics might indicate possible substance abuse:

◆ Inability to concentrate
◆ Chronic absenteeism
◆ Poor grades and/or neglect of homework
◆ Poor scores on standardized tests not related to IQ or learning disabilities

Procedures for Dealing with Missing and Runaway Students

- ◆ Always notify the school office. They may send someone to find the student.

- ◆ If you have a paraprofessional or another responsible adult in your room, you may follow—not chase—the student. When you catch up, bring him or her back to your room.

- ◆ If you are the only one to manage the rest of the students, stay with them. Let someone from the office make the pursuit or wait until someone comes to watch your students before you go.

- ◆ Send a trustworthy student out to see if the missing student is in the nearby vicinity. If so, have him or her summoned back to the classroom.

- ◆ If you have a teaching aide or assistant, send that person out to look.

- ◆ If neither a paraprofessional nor a student can assist, get help from a neighboring teacher.

- ◆ If the student goes too far, is not close enough for you or others to catch up with, or does not respond to requests to return, the only choice is to call the local authorities and the student's parents. Actually, this will be done by an administrator.

Source: Westling, D. L., & Koorland, M. A. (1989). *The special educator's handbook* (p. 151). Boston: Allyn & Bacon. Used with permission.

- ◆ Uncooperative and quarrelsome behavior
- ◆ Sudden behavior changes
- ◆ Shy and withdrawn behavior
- ◆ Compulsive behaviors
- ◆ Chronic health problems
- ◆ Signs of neglect and abuse
- ◆ Low self-esteem
- ◆ Anger, anxiety, and depression
- ◆ Poor coping skills
- ◆ Unreasonable fears
- ◆ Difficulty adjusting to changes

Once a student is identified as having a substance abuse problem, a supportive classroom environment must be provided. This includes a structured program that focuses on building positive self-esteem and creating opportunities for students to be successful.

Students Who Get Pregnant

Teenage pregnancy in this country continues at an extremely high rate. There are many unfortunate outcomes from teenage pregnancies, and one of the most significant is the increased risk that young girls, and boys, who find themselves involved in a teenage pregnancy will drop out of school. In an era of extensive sex education and fear of AIDS, the continued high levels of teenage pregnancy are surprising. Despite all of the information available for adolescents about sex and AIDS, it appears that many adolescents continue to engage in unprotected sexual activity (Arnett, 1990).

School personnel should get involved in teenage pregnancy issues before the pregnancy occurs. Sex education, information about AIDS, and the consequences of unprotected sex should be a focus of schools. Unfortunately, sex education and practices such as distributing free condoms are very controversial, with many schools refusing to get too involved in such emotional issues.

In addition to having a pregnancy prevention program, school personnel can do the following to intervene in teenage pregnancy situations:

1. Have available counseling for girls who become pregnant.
2. Develop programs that encourage girls who are pregnant to remain in school.
3. Provide parenting classes for all students.
4. Do not discriminate against girls who get pregnant, or boys who are married, in extracurricular activities.
5. Consider establishing a school-based child care program for girls who have babies and wish to remain in school.
6. Work with families of girls who are pregnant to ensure that family support is present.

Students Who Are Delinquents

Students who get into trouble with legal authorities are frequently labeled *juvenile delinquents.* **Juvenile delinquency** often results in school failure; students who are involved in illegal activities are often unfocused on school activities. It is very difficult to separate juvenile delinquency from other factors related to at-risk students. Juvenile delinquency is highly correlated with substance abuse and may be found in higher rates among poor children than among children who are raised in adequate income environments.

Juvenile delinquency is frequently related to gang activity. Although gangs are relatively new, they currently represent a major problem for adolescents, especially in large urban areas. Cantrell (1992) reported that in 1991 there were an estimated 800 gangs with nearly 100,000 members. Whether as part of a gang, in a small group, or individually, delinquent behaviors often disrupt school success. School personnel need to work with legal and social agencies in an attempt to reduce the level of delinquency that results in academic failure. Some of the characteristics of students that might suggest susceptibility to delinquent activities include the following:

1. Power tactics such as acting out anger with threats and assaults.
2. Lack of excitement over normal activities.

3. Inability to empathize with other students.
4. Lethargic behaviors when asked to do routine activities.
5. Forgetfulness about obligations.
6. Limited concept of ownership.
7. Lack of trust, especially of authority figures.
8. Expectation that all wishes and dreams will come true.
9. Poor decision-making skills.
10. Refusal to acknowledge own mistakes or take responsibility for mistakes.
11. A need to always be first or the best.
12. Denial of fear of anything.

Some efforts to control delinquency and gang activity have been proven successful. These include increasing awareness of the outcomes of gang or delinquent lifestyles, presenting alternatives to delinquent behaviors, encouraging activities that build self-esteem, drug education, teaching alternatives to violence, and providing career opportunities.

One critical thing schools can do to fight school violence is to make schools safer. Currently, the risk for violence is actually greater in schools than in the community (Smith, 1984). Increasing the number of security guards and taking similar actions have proven somewhat successful at accomplishing this. Other school actions that increase security include unannounced security checks, dog drug checks, and metal detectors.

Outcomes for Students Who Are at Risk

There are numerous possible outcomes for students who are at risk for school and community failure. Most desired is that at-risk programs will meet the needs of these children and prevent them from manifesting any negative outcomes. As more and more programs are developed for students considered at risk, it is hoped that the success rates will increase to the point that this positive outcome is the one most likely to occur.

Unfortunately, some outcomes for at-risk students that are not positive but nevertheless often occur. These include dropping out of school, becoming permanently incarcerated, and committing suicide. All at-risk programs are aimed at preventing these from occurring.

High School Dropouts

The rate of school dropouts in this country has actually declined somewhat over the past several years. Still, this outcome affects approximately 15% of all students annually, a figure way too high for a society that places so much emphasis on education. Although no one reason results in dropping out of school, most of the at-risk problems previously described can lead to this (Nevares, 1992). Poverty, growing up in single-parent homes, homelessness, and youth violence are associated with school dropouts.

Schools have developed and implemented numerous programs to reduce the dropout rate. Examples of these programs include working with students to set realistic, long-term goals for themselves (Martino, 1993), increasing expectations for students at risk (Taylor & Reeves, 1993), and developing community-based programs (Nebgen, 1992).

Many students who are at risk for school and social failure feel very much out of control of their lives. They often believe that they have very little to do with their own destiny (Greer, 1991). In order to help these students develop better feelings of self-worth, Martino (1993) suggests a goal-setting model that involves students in setting their own long-term goals. This particular program requires students to establish goals that are (1) specific and measurable, (2) attainable, (3) desired by the student, (4) specified as having starting and ending dates, (5) in written form, (6) stated in terms of expected levels of attainment, and (7) displayed on a scoresheet. By having students develop goals, monitoring their attainment, and analyzing them after a certain period, school personnel can help students develop a sense that they have some control over their own lives, something many do not feel they have (Greer, 1991).

Another example of a program to prevent dropouts involves a collaborative effort of community support. This program includes (Nebgen, 1992)

1. Mentoring that pairs adult volunteers with students
2. "Chums"—mentors for elementary-age students
3. Programs for latchkey students
4. Self-esteem training
5. Providing support for the entire family of the student

School personnel cannot provide such a program without significant community support, so a first task is to convince community leaders that such a program is needed and will benefit the entire community.

Students Who Commit Suicide

Although difficult to understand, suicide among children and youth in this country has become a major problem (Smith, 1990). It is the least-desired outcome for at-risk children, but has become the second leading cause of death among this age group. Ritter (1990) even stated that "suicide and self harm have reached epidemic proportions among adolescents" (p. 83). Although adolescents should be enjoying their life to the fullest with friends, school, and family members, too many are depressed, despondent, and decide to end their life rather than continue coping.

School personnel have a major responsibility to prevent suicides. Many schools have developed suicide education programs to help combat this tragic ending for students (Norton, Duriak, & Richards, 1989). For teachers and other school personnel, being alert to signs of depression and significant changes in individual students should be a major activity. Teachers who suspect students of contemplating suicide should contact the school counselor at once and work with family members to secure adequate interventions for the student.

Teachers in programs designed to prevent school dropouts must want to be part of the program.

General Considerations for Intervention

Specific suggestions for interventions have been provided as they relate to specific subcategories of at-risk children. However, there are some general considerations that could be applicable for most at-risk students. These include ideas that are intended to get students to like school and to be motivated to stay in school (Scales, 1992). Table 11.3 describes five principles that should be applicable for all students who are at risk for developing academic and behavior problems.

Several interventions have been found to be effective with students who are at risk (VanTassel-Baska, Patton, & Prillaman, 1989):

1. Early and systematic addressing of the needs of these children
2. Parental involvement in the educational program model
3. Effective school strategies (e.g., time on task, school leadership)
4. Use of experiential and "hands on" learning approaches.
5. Use of activities that allow for student self-expression
6. Use of mentors and role models
7. Involvement of the community
8. Counseling efforts that address the issue of "cultural values" in facilitating talent development (p. 3)

TABLE 11.3   **Five Principles Applicable for Students Who Are at Risk**

Once tracked, always stuck. Placing students in lower academic classes too often results in permanent placement.

Use the developmental power of peer relationships through teams and cooperative learning.

Use broad subject themes, interdisciplinary teaming, and flexible scheduling extensively.

Get to the good parts quickly. Provide real-life problems for students to solve that add some relevance to lessons.

Use and encourage students to use a variety of personal talents and instructional media, from reading to viewing videotapes, from building things to using computers, from music to novels and oral storytelling picked up from grandparents.

Source: Scales, P. C. (1992). From risks to resources: Disadvantaged learners and middle grades teaching. *Middle School Journal, 23,* 7–8. Used with permission.

"Probably more than any other group of students, those who are at-risk need the benefits and high support that carefully planned technology programs can provide them" (Hancock, 1993, p. 85).

A critical component for any program designed to address the needs of students who are considered at risk is a school staff who are dedicated and willing to work with these students (Ruff, 1993; Slicker & Palmer, 1993). When developing such programs, school administrators should never simply assign teachers who may not be interested in preventing at-risk students from achieving negative outcomes. When searching for school staff, administrators should seek teachers, teacher aides, and other program personnel who choose to be a part of such a program. Table 11.4 describes some of the characteristics of teachers that administrators should consider when staffing an at-risk program.

TABLE 11.4   **Characteristics of Teachers for at-Risk Programs**

- Teachers who desire to work with unsuccessful students
- Teachers who have creative ideas for teaching and learning
- Teachers who agree not to use worksheets, but use manipulatives and other activities that lead to involvement
- Teachers who are interested in implementing a reward system
- Teachers who are interested in receiving training
- Teachers who are willing to have outside observers in their classrooms
- Teachers who are interested in participating in research on the achievement, attendance, and discipline of their students
- Teachers who will document their strategies, successes, and failures
- Teachers who believe in the philosophy of the team

Source: Taylor, R. & Reeves, J. (1993). More is better: Raising expectations for students at risk. *Middle School Journal, 24,* 13–18. Used with permission.

Suicide: Risk Factors and Responsibilities

◆ *What are the risk factors?*
Although there are many factors related to suicide among young people, these are the most closely related:

- Previous psychiatric disorders, especially depression
- Loss of a parent or another family disruption
- Familial characteristics, such as being the relative of a suicide victim
- Biological factors such as low concentrations of some chemical substances
- Particular personality traits like impulsivity, aggression, perfectionism, or hopelessness
- Other factors, such as homosexuality, access to weapons, friendship with a suicide victim, or previous suicidal behavior (Kupfer, 1991)

◆ *Responsibilities of educators*
Guetzloe (1989) presented a list of responsibilities for school district officials that relate to youth suicide. They include:

- Being aware of risk factors for suicide
- Detecting signs of potential suicide, including threats and ideation
- Reporting suicidal behavior to the contact person or crisis team designated on the campus
- Getting emergency medical services if they are necessary
- Making immediate referral to child-study teams for further assessment
- Providing immediate and continuing emotional support for and supervision of suicidal youngsters
- Guiding parents in obtaining assistance
- Providing long-term follow-up services

Summary

◆ Students who are at risk may not be eligible for special education programs.

◆ At-risk students include those who are in danger of developing significant learning and behavior problems.

◆ Poverty is a leading cause of academic failure.

◆ Poverty among children is increasing in this country.

◆ Poverty is associated with homelessness, poor health care, hunger, and single-parent households.

◆ Hunger is a major problem in our country.

◆ The United States ranks only twenty-second among developed nations in the area of infant mortality.

◆ As many as 25% of all homeless people are children.

◆ Students in single-parent homes face major problems in school.

◆ About 25% of all children live in single-parent homes.

◆ Divorce is the leading cause of children living in single-parent homes.

◆ Children react in many different ways to divorce.

◆ Schools must take into consideration the rights of the noncustodial parent.

◆ More and more children are growing up in homes with homosexual parents.

◆ The death of a parent, sibling, or friend can have a major impact on a child and his school success.

◆ Child abuse is a major problem in this country and causes children to experience major emotional trauma.

◆ School personnel are required by law to report suspected child abuse.

◆ Drug use among students is on the increase after several years of decline.

◆ Teenage pregnancy continues to be a problem, even with the fear of AIDS and sex education.

◆ Numerous programs and interventions have been proven to be effective in working with at-risk students.

References

Anderson, H. W., & Anderson, G. S. (1981). *Mom and dad are divorced, but I'm not.* Chicago: Nelson Hall.

Anthony, S. (1972). *The discovery of death in childhood and after.* New York: Basic Books.

Arnett, J. (1990). Contraceptive use, sensation seeking, and adolescent egocentrism. *Journal of Youth and Adolescence, 19,* 171–180.

At risk youth in crisis: A handbook for collaboration between schools and social services. (1991). Albany, OR: Linn-Benton Education Service Digest.

Austin, J. F. (1992). Involving noncustodial parents in their student's education. *NASSP Bulletin, 76,* 49–54.

Beck, I. (1988, September 12). Help teen-agers keep ties with divorced parents. *El Paso Times,* 3D.

Blinn-Pike, L. M., Bell, T., Devereaux, M., Doyle, H., Tittsworth, S., & Von Bargen, J. (1993). Assessing what high risk young children know about drugs: Verbal versus pictorial methods. *Journal of Drug Education, 23,* 151–169.

Buchholz, E. S., & Korn-Bursztyn, C. (1993). Children of adolescent mothers: Are they at risk for abuse? *Adolescence, 28,* 361–382.

Cantrell, M. L. (1992). Guest editorial. *Journal of Emotional and Behavioral Problems, 1,* 4.

Chiriboga, D. A., & Catron, L. S. (1991). *Divorce.* New York: University Press.

Clay, J. W. (1991). Respecting and supporting gay and lesbian parents. *Young Children,* March, 51–57.

Condition of Education. (1990). Washington, DC: Office of Educational Research and Improvement.

Davis, W. E. (1993). *At-risk children and educational reform: Implications for educators and schools in the year 2000 and beyond.* Orono, ME: College of Education, University of Maine.

Drug use increasing. (1992). *Youth Today, 1,* 27–29.

Eggert, L. L., & Herting, J. R. (1993). Drug involvement among potential dropouts and "typical" youth. *Journal of Drug Education, 23,* 31–55.

Elizer, E., & Kauffman, M. (1983). Factors influencing the severity of childhood bereavement reactions. *American Journal of Orthopsychiatry, 53,* 393–415.

Ellison, E. (1983). Issues concerning parental harmony and children's psychosocial adjustment. *American Journal of Orthopsychiatry, 53,* 304–309.

Emery, R. E. (1989). Family violence. *American Psychologist, 44,* 321–327.

Felner, R., Ginter, M., Boike, M., & Cowan, E. (1981). Parental death or divorce and the school adjustment of young children. *American Journal of Community Psychology, 9,* 181–191.

Fry, P., & Trifiletti, R. (1983). An exploration of the adolescent's perspective: Perceptions of major stress dimensions in the single parent family. *Journal of Psychiatric Treatment and Evaluation, 5,* 324–333.

Furman, E. (1974). *A child's parent dies.* New Haven, CT: Yale University Press.

Gargiulo, R. M. (1990). Child abuse and neglect: An overview. In R. L. Goldman & R. M. Gagiulo (Eds.), *Children at risk* (pp. 1–35). Austin, TX: Pro-Ed.

Goldman, R. L., & Gargiulo, R. M. (1990). Child abuse. In R. L. Goldman & R. M. Gargiulo (Eds.), *Children at risk* (pp. 37–49). Austin, TX: Pro-Ed.

Gonzales, M. L. (1991). School-community partnerships and the homeless. *Educational Leadership, 49,* 23–24.

Greenbaum, S., Garrison, R., James, B., & Stephens, R. (1989). *School bullying and victimization.* National School Safety Center Resource Paper. Malibu, CA: Pepperdine University.

Greenberg, L. I. (1975). Therapeutic grief work with children. *Social Casework, 56,* 396–403.

Greer, J. V. (1990). The drug babies. *Exceptional Children, 56,* 383.

Greer, J. V. (1991). At-risk students in the fast lanes: Let them through. *Exceptional Children, 57,* 390–391.

Guetzloe, E. C. (1989). *Youth suicide: What the educator should know.* Reston, VA: CEC.

Guetzloe, E. C. (1993). Answering the cry for help—Suicidal thoughts and actions. *Journal of Emotional and Behavioral Problems, 2*(2), 34–38.

Hancock, V. E. (1993). The at-risk student. *Educational Leadership, 50,* 84–85.

Hare, J., & Koepke, L. A. (1990). Susanne and her two mothers. *Day Care and Education, 18,* 20–21.

Healthy People 2000. (1992). Washington, DC: U.S. Government Printing Office.

Henning, J., & Oldham, J. (1977). Children of divorce: Legal and psychological crises. *Journal of Clinical Child Psychology, 6,* 55–59.

Hoeffer, T. D. (1981). *Alternative family styles.* St. Louis: Mosby.

Jones, J. G. (1982). Sexual abuse of children: Current concepts. *American Journal of Diseases of Children, 136,* 142–146.

Kupfer, D. J. (1991). Summary of the national conference on risk factors for youth suicide. In

L. Davidson & M. Linnoila (Eds.), *Risk factors for youth suicide* (pp. xv–xxii). New York: Hemisphere Publishing.

Lewis, J. K. (1992). Death and divorce—Helping students cope in single-parent families. *NAASP Bulletin, 76,* 49–54.

MacFarlane, J. T., Franks, M. T., & Jasper, E. (1986). *Sexual abuse of young children.* New York: Guilford Press.

McKeever, P. (1983). Siblings of chronically ill children: A literature review with implications for research and practice. *American Journal of Orthopsychiatry, 53,* 209–217.

Martino, L. R. (1993). A goal-setting model for young adolescent at risk students. *Middle School Journal, 24,* 19–22.

Mercer, C. D. (1991). *Students with learning disabilities* (5th ed.). New York: Merrill.

Morgan, S. R. (1985). *Children in crises: A team approach in the schools.* Austin, TX: Pro-Ed.

Moriarty, D. (1967). *The loss of loved ones.* Springfield, IL: Charles C. Thomas.

Munger, R., & Morse, W. C. (1992). When divorce rocks a child's world. *The Educational Forum, 43,* 100–103.

National Committee for Prevention of Child Abuse. (1983). *It shouldn't hurt to be a child.* Chicago: NCPCA.

Nebgen, M. (1992). A community of caring. *The Executive Educator, 14,* 38–39.

Nevares, L. (1992). Credit where credit is due. *The Executive Educator, 14,* 50–53.

Norton, E. M., Duriak, T. D., & Richards, M. (1989). Peer knowledge of and reaction to adolescent suicide. *Journal of Youth and Adolescence, 18,* 427–437.

Peterson, K. D. (1989, February 12). Does a split have lasting effects? *USA Today,* 9.

Peterson, K. S. (1991, April 24). Suicide by older teens on upswing. *USA Today,* 1.

Randall-David, E. (1989). *Strategies for working with culturally diverse communities and clients.* Washington, DC: Office of Maternal and Child Health. U.S. Department of Health and Human Services.

Ritter, D. R. (1990). Adolescent suicide. *School Psychology Review, 19,* 83–95.

Roy, C., & Fuqua, D. (1983). Social support systems and academic performance of single-parent students. *The School Counselor, 30,* 183–192.

Ruff, T. P. (1993). Middle school students at risk: What do we do with the most vulnerable children in American education? *Middle School Journal, 24,* 10–12.

Santrock, J. W., & Warshak, R. A. (1979). Father custody and social development in boys and girls. *Journal of Social Issues, 35,* 112–125.

Scales, P. C. (1992). From risks to resources: Disadvantaged learners and middle grades teaching. *Middle School Journal, 23,* 3–9.

Slicker, E. K., & Palmer, D. J. (1993). Mentoring at-risk high school students: Evaluation of a school-based program. *The School Counselor, 40,* 327–334.

Smith, D. D., & Luckasson, R. (1992). *Introduction to special education.* Boston: Allyn & Bacon.

Smith, T. E. C. (1990). *Introduction to education* (2nd ed.). St. Paul: West Publishing.

Smith, V. (1984). Tracking school crime. *American School and University, 57,* 54.

Sorosky, A. D. (1977). The psychological effects of divorce on adolescents. *Adolescence, 50,* 71–74.

Stover, D. (1992, May). The at-risk students schools continue to ignore. *The Education Digest,* 37–40.

Sugar, M. (1970). Children of divorce. *Pediatrics, 46,* 82–88.

Taylor, R., & Reeves, J. (1993). More is better: Raising expectations for students at risk. *Middle School Journal, 24,* 13–18.

Tennant, C., Bebbington, P. R., & Hurry, J. (1980). Parental death in childhood and risk of adult depressive disorders: A review. *Psychological Medicine, 10,* 289–299.

Towers, R. L. (1989). *Children of alcoholics/addicts.* Washington, DC: National Education Association.

U.S. Bureau of Census. (1992). *Poverty income in the United States: 1991,* P-60, No. 180. Washington, DC: U.S. Government Printing Office.

Van Eerdewegh, M. M., Bieri, M. D., Parrilla, R. H., & Clayton, P. J. (1982). The bereaved child. *British Journal of Psychiatry, 140,* 23–29.

Van Tassel-Baska, J., Patton, J. R. & Prillaman, D. (1989). Disadvantaged gifted learners at-risk for educational attention. *Focus on Exceptional Children, 22,* 1–16.

Walczak, Y., & Burns, S. (1984). *Divorce: The child's point of view.* New York: Harper & Row.

Wallerstein, J. S., & Kelly, J. (1976). The effects of parental divorce: Experiences of the child in later latency. *American Journal of Orthopsychiatry, 46,* 256–269.

Wanat, C. L. (1992). Meeting the needs of single-parent children: School and parent views differ. *NASSP Bulletin, 76,* 43–48.

Westling, D. L., & Koorland, M. A. (1989). *The special educator's handbook.* Boston: Allyn & Bacon.

Weston, D., Ludolph, P., Misle, B., Ruffins, S., & Block, J. (1990). Physical and sexual abuse in adolescent girls with borderline personality disorder. *American Journal of Orthopsychiatry, 60,* 55–66.

Williamson, J. M., Borduin, C. M., & Howe, B. A. (1991). The ecology of adolescent maltreatment: A multilevel examination of adolescent physical abuse, sexual abuse, and neglect. *Journal of Consulting and Clinical Psychology, 59,* 449–457.

Wyers, N. L. (1987). Homosexuality in the family: Lesbian and gay spouses. *Social Work, 32,* 143–148.

CHAPTER 12

Classroom Organization and Management

The ability to manage the classroom environment effectively and efficiently can greatly enhance the quality of the educational experience for students with disabilities. Well-organized and well-managed classrooms allow for more time to be devoted to productive instructional endeavors. As Smith, Finn, and Dowdy (1993) point out, students with disabilities must be able to "exhibit appropriate behaviors and follow classroom rules to facilitate their success in regular classrooms" (p. 319). However, in addition to the benefits to students, well-designed and well-managed classrooms help teachers as well.

The purpose of this chapter is to present a model for conceptualizing the major components of **classroom management,** to discuss these dimensions, and to provide specific suggested practices. Although sound organizational and management tactics are useful for all students in education settings, the orientation of this chapter is to underscore those practices that are particularly relevant to students with disabilities.

Fundamentals of Classroom Organization and Management

The importance of good classroom organization and management techniques has been affirmed by many professionals in the field of education (Charles, 1983; Doyle, 1986; Evertson, Emmer, Clements, Sanford, & Worsham, 1989). Although much attention is given to curricular and instructional aspects of students' educational programs, organizational and management dimensions are typically envisioned as less important prerequisites to instruction. Doyle (1986) points out that more professionals are placing management "at the center of the task of teaching" (p. 394). Unquestionably, it is the one area that first-year teachers consistently identify as most problematic.

Definitional Perspective

A generally recognized definition of **classroom organization** and management does not exist. The concept of classroom organization and management used in this chapter reflects a liberal application and interpretation of the term. It is defined here as *all teacher-directed activities that support the efficient operations of the classroom that lead to the establishment of optimal conditions of learning and order.* Although it does include proactive methods of **behavior management,** it also covers many other facets of the instructional environment.

Without question, other definitions of classroom management and organization exist. Most definitions relate classroom management to the systematic structuring and control of the classroom environment that leads to conditions where teaching and learning can occur.

Model of Classroom Management

The nature of every classroom environment involves a number of elements that have a profound effect on the effectiveness of instruction and learning (Doyle, 1986). Six of these are described briefly below:

- *Multidimensionality* refers to the vast number of activities that occur in a classroom within the course of an instructional day.
- *Simultaneity* refers to the fact that many different events occur at the same given time.
- *Immediacy* refers to the rapid pace at which events occur in classrooms.
- *Unpredictability* refers to the reality that some events occur unexpectedly, cannot be anticipated, but require attention nonetheless.
- *Publicness* refers to the fact that classroom events are witnessed by a significant number of students who are very likely to process how teachers deal with these ongoing events.
- *History* refers to the reality that, over the course of the school year, various events (experiences, routines, rules) shape how the dynamics of classroom behavior will be conducted.

Considering these elements reaffirms the complexity of teaching large numbers of students. To address these important aspects of classroom dynamics, teachers need to identify ways to organize and manage their classrooms to maximize the potential opportunities for learning to occur. With this in mind, a model that graphically depicts the multifaceted dimensions of classroom organization and management is presented in Figure 12.1. This model of organization and management evolved from a model on the components of effective instruction designed by Polloway and Patton (1993). It reflects an adaptation of what Polloway and Patton identify as "precursors to teaching."

Many teachers believe that behavior management/discipline embodies what classroom management is all about. However, the effective and efficient management of a classroom must include other components. To create an orderly environment conducive to learning, teachers must pay attention to psychosocial, procedural, physical, behavioral, instructional, personnel, and time management variables that have a critical impact on learning and behavior. Much of what is contained in Figure 12.1 and discussed in this chapter needs to be considered before the beginning of the school year. As will be seen, the emphasis throughout this chapter is on preventing management-related problems by addressing the issues head-on beforehand.

Guiding Principles

A number of overriding principles guide efforts to develop and implement appropriate classroom organization/management procedures. These principles apply to all the dimensions of the model depicted in Figure 12.1.

- Good classroom organization/management must be planned, it does not just happen (Evertson et al., 1989).

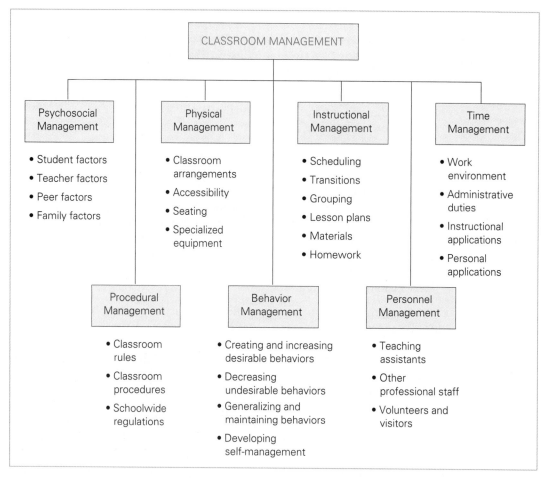

Figure 12.1   Dimensions of Classroom Organization and Management

◆ Proactive classroom managers fare better than reactive ones (Cummings, 1983).

◆ Consistency is the key to establishing an effective management program (Polloway & Patton, 1993).

◆ Two select teacher characteristics enhance one's ability to manage classrooms effectively (Kounin, 1970):

1. *With-it-ness:* overall awareness of what is happening in the classroom,
2. *Overlapping:* the ability to deal with more than one event simultaneously.

Although sound classroom management practices are useful with all students, the suggestions provided in this chapter are particularly helpful for students with disabilities who have special needs and require individualized consideration.

Components of Effective Classroom Organization and Management

This section of the chapter discusses the major elements and subcomponents of classroom management highlighted in Figure 12.1. The format that is used includes a short description of each element and, where appropriate, specific samples of these recommendations. Specific suggestions that relate to each of the topics covered are provided at the end of each section.

Psychosocial Management

This dimension refers to the psychological and social dynamics of the classroom. It includes consideration of **classroom climate.** This element is important because it relates to qualitative aspects of the classroom atmosphere in which students must function.

The dynamics of classrooms are influenced by certain *student factors.* Their attitudes about school, authority figures, and other classmates can have a remarkable impact on how they behave and react to various organizational and management demands. Other factors that need to be taken into consideration include the nature of previous educational experiences, how they feel about themselves, and their own expectations (i.e., potential for success or failure).

The psychological atmosphere of any classroom depends in great part on certain *teacher factors,* including disposition, competencies/skills, and actions. A teacher's attitudes toward students with special needs can dramatically affect the quality of education that a student will receive during the time he or she is in the classroom. Personal philosophies about education, discipline, and curriculum weigh heavily. The type of expectations a teacher holds about students have been found to influence outcomes.

Peers are also key players related to the psychological and social atmosphere of a classroom, especially for older students. Factors such as values and pressures must be understood by teachers.

The final component involves a variety of *family-generated factors.* Polloway and Patton (1993) have identified three major issues related to parents that can have an effect on students: attitudes toward education, level of personal support and involvement, and amount of pressure placed on children. The last two factors can be problematic in either extreme.

The recommendations provided here should help create a positive, nurturing environment that contributes to more positive outcomes for all students:

- Let students know that they are valued (DeLuke & Knoblock, 1987).
- Let students know that you are sensitive to their needs and concerns.
- Convey enthusiasm about learning and the schooling experience—it has a contagious effect.
- Create a supportive, safe setting in which students can learn without fear of being ridiculed or threatened by physical violence or verbal abuse.

Peers are critical to the psychological and social atmosphere of a classroom.

- Treat all students with fairness—students react favorably to reasonable expectations and even-handed enforcement of them (Charles, 1983).
- Try to acknowledge each student in some personal way each day.
- Create a learning environment that is built on success and self-worth.
- Understand the family and cultural contexts from which students come.
- Communicate the expectation that students will be successful academically and that appropriate academic behaviors will be required.
- Make yourself available both physically and personally to students if they need to talk.
- Listen to the news of a student's personal world with interest and nonjudgment (O'Melia & Rosenberg, 1989).
- Establish that each student in the classroom has rights (e.g., not to be interrupted when working or responding to a teacher inquiry) and that you expect everyone to respect those rights.
- Instill in students that you expect them to understand that they are responsible for their own behavior.
- Convey to students that every student's thoughts and ideas are important.
- Encourage risk taking and nurture students to take on scholastic challenges.

Procedural Management

This dimension refers to the rules, procedures, and regulations that are part of the standard operating procedures of a classroom. The guidelines discussed here are intended to provide direction to school staff and students as to what is expected of all parties. It is extremely important that all rules, procedures, and regulations be identified before the school year begins and that plans be developed to teach them to students during the first days of the school year.

Equally important is preparation for dealing with violations of rules that will occur. Immediate and consistent consequences are needed. Various disciplinary techniques can be implemented to ensure that inappropriate behavior is handled effectively. These will be covered in a subsequent section of the chapter.

Students with exceptional needs will benefit from being taught the appropriate operating procedures. They benefit greatly from being taught systematically the administrative and social rules operative in a classroom. The suggestions provided in this section are organized around three major elements: classroom rules, in-class procedures, and schoolwide regulations.

Most individuals respond best in situations where they know what is expected. *Classroom rules* provide a general sense of what is expected of students. The rules that are chosen should be essential to classroom functioning and help create a positive learning environment (Christenson, Ysseldyke, & Thurlow, 1989; Salend, 1990). The implementation of reasonable classroom rules that are presented appropriately can be very beneficial to students with special needs who are in general education settings. Some specific suggestions for this are as follows:

- ◆ Develop no more than seven rules for the classroom.
- ◆ Keep the rules brief and state them clearly.
- ◆ Explain the rules thoroughly and discuss the specific consequences if they are violated.
- ◆ State the rules in a positive way—avoid statements that are stated in a negative way such as "not allowed."
- ◆ Post the rules in a location that all students can see.
- ◆ Discuss exceptions to the rules in advance so that students are aware (Salend, 1990).
- ◆ Teach the rules through modeling and practice.
- ◆ Review the rules on a regular basis and when new students are placed in the class.
- ◆ Involve students in rule setting when appropriate (Evertson et al., 1989).

Perhaps one of the most overlooked areas of classroom management is the development of logical *classroom procedures*. Classroom procedures refer to the specific way certain activities or situations will be performed. For example, procedures need to be established for using the pencil sharpener, using the rest room, and entering and leaving the classroom.

This area can cause much distress for teachers if not attended to prior to the arrival of students at the beginning of the school year. Teachers are surprised by the complexity and detail associated with the many seemingly trivial areas that need to be considered (Evertson et al., 1989). Many of these procedural areas combine to form the mosaic of one's management system. Some specific suggestions for this are as follows:

◆ Identify all situations for which a procedure will need to be developed.
◆ Explain each procedure thoroughly.
◆ Teach each procedure through modeling, guided practice, and independent practice, letting every student have an opportunity to practice the procedure.
◆ Introduce classroom procedures during the first week of school, scheduling priority procedures for the first day, and covering other ones on subsequent days.
◆ Avoid information overload for students by not introducing too many procedures at once (Doyle, 1986).
◆ Incorporate any school regulation of importance and relevance into classroom procedures (e.g., using the rest rooms).

Most schools have *schoolwide regulations* that apply to everyone in the school building. These include nonclassroom (e.g., procedures for being absent) as well as classroom requirements (e.g, a hall pass system). From a classroom organization/management perspective, it is important to know how schoolwide regulations affect the rules and procedures developed for a classroom.

Physical Management

This dimension includes the various aspects of the physical environment that teachers can manipulate to enhance the conditions of learning. For students with disabilities, it may become particularly important to address features of the physical setting to ensure that their individual needs are met.

Classroom arrangements refers to many different facets of the classroom, including the layout, storage, wall space, and signage. Certain aspects of these areas have special meaning for students with special needs.

Listed below are specific suggestions for physically managing the classroom environment:

◆ Consider establishing areas of the classroom that are designated for certain types of activities (e.g., discovery, independent reading, etc.).
◆ Clearly establish which areas of the classroom, such as the teacher's desk, are off limits.
◆ Begin the school year with a structured environment, moving to more flexibility after rules/procedures have been established.
◆ Notify students with visual impairments of changes made to the physical environment.
◆ Furniture should be arranged so that the teacher and students can move easily around the classroom.
◆ Consider alternative desk arrangements (e.g., clusters of five to six students) in addition to the traditional yet effective row configuration (Charles, 1983).
◆ Direct students' attention to the information to be learned from bulletin boards, if they are used for instructional purposes.
◆ Establish traffic patterns that students can use that minimize congestion and disruption to other students (Charles, 1983).

Ways to Involve Other Personnel in Managing Disruptive Behavior

- ◆ The school principal or administrator can
  Supply any necessary equipment or materials
  Provide flexibility in staffing patterns
  Show support for the teacher's actions

- ◆ The school guidance counselor can
  Provide individual counseling sessions
  Work with other students who may be reinforcing the inappropriate behavior
    of the disruptive student
  Offer the teacher information about what may be upsetting to the student

- ◆ The school nurse can
  Review the student's medical history for possible causes
  Recommend the possibility and practicality of medical or dietary intervention
  Explain the effects and side effects of any medication the student is taking or
    may take in the future

- ◆ The school psychologist can
  Review the teacher's behavior management plan and make recommendations
    for changes
  Observe the student in the classroom and in other settings to collect behavioral
    data and note possible environmental instigators
  Provide any useful data on the student that may have been recently collected,
    e.g., test scores, behavioral observations, etc.

- ◆ The student's parents can
  Provide information about the student's behavior at home
  Convey their feelings about the student's learning and social behavior needs
  Suggest suitable consequences
  Provide a home and community management plan that is coordinated with the
    school's plan

- ◆ The social worker can
  Provide additional information about the home environment
  Schedule regular visits to the home
  Identify other public agencies that may be of assistance

- ◆ Other teachers can
  Provide curricular and behavior management suggestions that work for them
  Offer material resources
  Provide carryover and consistency for the tactics used

Source: Westling, D. L., & Koorland, M. A. (1989). *The special educator's handbook* (p. 119). Boston: Allyn & Bacon. Used with permission.

- Secure materials and equipment that are potentially harmful to students if used without proper supervision such as certain art supplies, chemicals, and science equipment.
- Avoid creating open spaces that do not have any clear purpose, as they often can lead to staging areas from which problems can arise (Rosenberg et al., 1991).
- Provide labels and signs for areas of the room to assist students in better understanding what and where things are; it is particularly critical to identify areas that are off-limits.

Although *accessibility* is very much related to the general layout considerations, it warrants special attention due to legal mandates. The concept of **accessibility** actually means more than physical accessibility, including other issues such as program accessibility.

The primary concern related to accessibility is to ensure that students with disabilities can utilize the classroom like other students and that the room is free of any potential hazards. Specific suggestions are provided below:

- Ensure that the classroom is accessible to students who use wheelchairs, braces, crutches, or other forms of mobility assistance—this involves doorways, space to move within the classroom, floor coverings, learning centers, microcomputers, chalkboards/dry erase boards, bookshelves, sinks, tables, desks, and any other areas that students use.
- Guarantee that the classroom is free of hazards (e.g., low hanging mobiles or plants) that could be injurious to students who have a visual impairment.
- Label storage areas and other parts of the classroom for students with visual impairments using raised lettering or braille.

Even though *seating* is technically a subcomponent of classroom arrangements, it warrants a separate discussion due to its importance for students with special needs. Considering where to seat students can prevent a host of problems that are likely to arise if neglected. Below are some specific suggestions:

- Seat students with behavior problems first so that they are in close proximity to the teacher for as much of the time as possible; later, after these students are under control and more self-control is demonstrated, more distant seating arrangements are possible and desirable.
- Locate students for whom visual distractions can interfere with attention to tasks (e.g., attentional problems, hearing impairments, behavior problems) so that these distractions affect them minimally.
- Establish clear lines of vision (a) for students so that they can attend to instruction and (b) for the teacher so that students can be monitored throughout the class period (Rosenberg, O'Shea, & O'Shea, 1991).
- Ensure that students with sensory impairments are seated so that they can maximize any residual vision and hearing.

Teachers are encouraged to think carefully about where to seat students who have problems with controlling their behaviors and students with various sensory impairments. The judicious use of planned seating arrangements can minimize problems as well as create better opportunities for students to benefit from ongoing class activities.

Some students with disabilities will require the use of *specialized equipment*. This might include items that were discussed in other chapters such as wheelchairs, hearing aids, other types of amplification systems, communication devices, adaptive desks and trays, prone standers (i.e., stand-up desks), and certain medically related items.

Teachers need to understand how this equipment works, how it should be used, and what adaptations will need to be made to the classroom environment to accommodate the student who will be using specialized equipment. The other students in the classroom should be prepared and introduced to the novel equipment as well.

Behavior Management

Some teachers feel that the most important component of classroom management involves the management of behaviors that disrupt the learning environment in any way. Certainly, the ability to control inappropriate behaviors is extremely useful, but it only represents part of a comprehensive behavior management program. Also included in such a plan are techniques for creating new behaviors or increasing desirable behaviors that are minimally existent. Moreover, a sound program of behavior management must assure that behaviors learned or changed are maintained over time and demonstrated in different contexts.

It is not possible to cover in sufficient detail all of the complexities of the various facets of behavior management. One should refer to other resources for this purpose (see Alberto & Troutman, 1990; Kaplan, 1990). However, this section will provide teachers with recommendations that should guide behavior management practice in the following areas: creating and increasing desirable behaviors, decreasing undesirable behaviors, generalizing behavior to new situations, maintaining behaviors over time, and establishing self-regulatory behavior.

Creating and Increasing Desirable Behaviors. What should happen in classrooms is the acquisition of desired new behaviors whether they be scholastic, personal/social, or vocational. With this in mind, it is important to understand that a **reinforcer** is any event that increases the strength of the behavior it follows. *Positive reinforcement* can best be described as presenting a pleasant consequence after performance of an appropriate behavior. **Positive reinforcers** can take different forms; ultimately the true manifestation of what is considered reinforcing depends on the individual. Reinforcers can be praise, physical contact, tangible items, activities, or privileges. *Negative reinforcement* involves the removal of something unpleasant after performance of a desired behavior. Both reinforcement operations are used in classroom situations. The use of reinforcement is the most socially acceptable and instructionally sound tactic of providing consequences to increase desired behaviors (Polloway & Patton, 1993).

Three basic principles must be followed for positive reinforcement to be effective. It must be meaningful to the student, contingent upon the proper performance

Treatment of Children with Stimulant Medication

What Should Be Expected

1. Temporary management of diagnostic symptoms:
   a. Overactivity (improved ability to modulate motor behavior)
   b. Inattention (increased concentration or effort on tasks)
   c. Impulsivity (improved self-regulation)
2. Temporary improvement of associated features:
   a. Deportment (increased compliance and effort)
   b. Aggression (decrease in physical and verbal hostility)
   c. Social interactions (decreased negative behaviors)
   d. Academic productivity (increased amount and accuracy of work)

What Should Not be Expected

1. Paradoxical response
   a. Responses of normal children are in same directions
   b. Responses of normal adults are in same directions
   c. Responses of affected adults and children are similar
2. Prediction of response
   a. Not by neurological signs
   b. Not by physiological measures
   c. Not by biochemical markers
3. Absence of side effects
   a. Infrequent appearance or increase in tics
   b. Frequent problems with eating and sleeping
   c. Possible psychological effects on cognition and attribution
4. Large effects on skills or higher-order processes
   a. No significant improvement of reading skills
   b. No significant improvement of athletic or game skills
   c. No significant improvement of positive social skills
   d. Improvement in learning/achievement less than improvement in behavior/attention
5. Improvement in long-term adjustment
   a. No improvement in academic achievement
   b. No reduction in antisocial behavior or arrest rate

Source: Swanson, J. M., McBurnett, K., Wigal, T., Pfiffner, L. J., Lerner, M. A., Williams, L., Christian, D. L., Tann, L., Wilcutt, E., Crowley, K., Clevenger, W., Khouzam, N., Woo, C., Crinella, F. M., & Fisher, T. D. (1993). Effect of stimulant medication on children with attention deficit disorder: A "review of reviews." *Exceptional Children, 60,* 159. Used with permission.

of a desired behavior, and presented immediately. In other words, for positive reinforcement to increase levels of desirable behavior, students must find the reinforcement pleasurable in some fashion, understand that it is being given as a result of the behavior demonstrated, and receive it soon after they do what was asked.

An illustrative application of the principle of positive reinforcement is **contingency contracting.** This is a technique that works very well with older students. With this methodology, the teacher develops contracts with students that state (a) what behaviors (e.g., academic work, social behaviors) students are to complete or perform and (b) what consequences (i.e., reinforcement) the instructor will provide. These contracts are presented as binding agreements between student and teacher. Figure 12.2 is an example of a contract for a secondary-level student.

CONTRACT

_____ will demonstrate the following appropriate behaviors in the classroom:
(Student's name)

1. Come to school on time.
2. Come to school with homework completed.
3. Complete all assigned work in school without prompting.
4. Ask for help when necessary by raising hand and getting teacher's attention.

_____ will provide the following reinforcement:
(Teacher's name)

1. Ten tokens for the completion of each of the above four objectives. Tokens for the first two objectives will be provided at the beginning of class after all homework assignments have been checked. Tokens for objectives 3 and 4 will be provided at the end of the school day.
2. Tokens may be exchanged for activities on the Classroom Reinforcement Menu at noon on Fridays.

_____   _____
Student's signature   Teacher's signature

                                   _____
                                   Date

Figure 12.2   **Sample Contract Between Student and Teacher**
Source: Zirpoli & Melloy (1993). *Behavior management: Applications for teachers and parents* (p. 189). Columbus, OH: Merrill. Used with permission.

The way students are grouped will impact on their behaviors.

Specific suggestions for reinforcement techniques are as follows:

◆ Determine what is reinforcing to students by (a) casually talking to them or (b) through the administration of a general interest inventory or specifically designed reinforcement survey that uses student language and provides a range of potential reinforcers.
◆ Select meaningful reinforcers that are easy and practical to deliver in classroom settings (Idol, 1993).
◆ Catch students behaving appropriately and provide them with the subsequent appropriate reinforcement. This is particularly important early on so that students experience the effects of positive reinforcement.
◆ Use the Premack Principle regularly (this refers to having more desirable activities available, contingent upon the performance of less desirable ones).
◆ Use reinforcement techniques to gradually approximate a desired behavior that requires the mastery of numerous substeps (i.e., reinforcing successive approximations of a target behavior).
◆ Reinforce proximate peers to demonstrate to a student that certain behaviors will result in positive outcomes.

Decreasing Undesirable Behaviors.   Every teacher will face situations where undesirable behaviors are present, resulting in the need to invoke behavior reduction techniques. Teachers can select from a range of techniques; however, it is recommended that teachers choose approaches according to a sequence of options, beginning with less intrusive interventions. A recommended sequence of reduction strategies is depicted in Figure 12.3. Alternative hierarchical arrangements have been suggested by other professionals (Nelson & Rutherford, 1983; Polloway & Patton, 1993; Smith & Rivera, 1993).

The use of *natural and logical consequences* can lead to children and adolescents learning to be more responsible for their behaviors (West, 1986). The essential characteristic of **natural consequences** is that the situation itself provides the contingencies for a certain behavior. For example, if a student forgets to return a permission slip to attend an off-campus event, the natural consequence is that the student is not allowed to go and must remain at school.

Logical consequences are used in situations where there is a logic between an inappropriate behavior and the consequences that follow. If a student forgets lunch

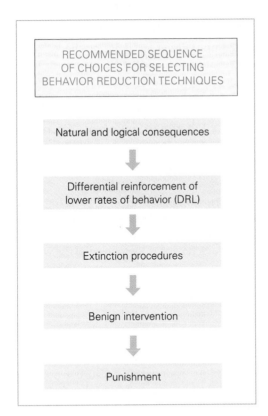

Figure 12.3   **Recommended Sequence of Choices for Selecting Behavior Reduction Techniques**

money, a logical consequence might be that money must be borrowed from someone else. The uncomfortable consequence is the hassle and/or embarrassment of requesting financial assistance. The attraction of these tactics is that students should recognize that it is their behavior that has created the discomfort and not something the teacher has done to them. When using this approach, teachers should clarify to students that they are responsible for their own behaviors.

The second option on the continuum is the use of ***differential reinforcement of lower (DRL) rates of behavior.*** The attraction of this technique is that it involves the use of positive reinforcement strategies as a behavior reduction tool. A teacher using this procedure provides appropriate reinforcement to students for meeting criterion levels that specify lower rates of a certain behavior, even though the behavior is an undesirable one. For this reason, it is important to remember that the unwanted behavior should be decreasing in frequency and/or duration.

An example of this technique that is used with groups of students is the good-behavior game (Barrish, Saunders, & Wolf, 1969), in which student teams receive some type of reinforcement if the number of occurrences of inappropriate behavior remain under a preset criterion. Listed below are some specific suggestions:

◆ Understand that undesirable behaviors will still be evidenced with this strategy and must be tolerated until target levels are reached.
◆ Reduce the criterion level after the student has demonstrated stability at the present level.
◆ Avoid making too great a jump between criterion levels to ensure that students are able to meet the new demands—readjust levels if this does happen.
◆ Explain to students involved in group contingency interventions, who typically behave appropriately and who feel they are being penalized for the actions of others, that ultimately better classroom control will be of benefit to them.

The next option involves ***extinction*** procedures. This technique simply requires the teacher to withhold reinforcement of a behavior. Over time, such action, in combination with the positive reinforcement of related desirable behaviors, should result in extinguishing the inappropriate behavior. One behavior for which this technique is useful is giving teacher attention (i.e., reinforcement) to student misbehavior. For some situations, it will be necessary to involve a student's peers in the extinction process to eliminate a behavior that may be reinforced by their actions. Below are some specific suggestions:

◆ Be sure to analyze what is reinforcing the undesirable behavior and isolate the reinforcer(s) before initiating this procedure.
◆ Understand that this technique is desirable because it does not involve punishment, but it will take time to be effective.
◆ Do not use this technique with behaviors that require immediate intervention (e.g., fighting).
◆ Recognize that the withholding of reinforcement (a) is likely to induce a spiking effect in the occurrence of the undesirable behavior, as students intensify

their efforts to receive the reinforcement they are used to getting, and (b) may produce an aggressive response.

◆ Provide reinforcement to students who demonstrate appropriate incompatible behaviors.

The fourth option in the sequence is the use of techniques that border on being **punishment** but are so unobtrusive that they can be considered *benign tactics*. Most of the suggestions come from a concept developed by Cummings (1983) called the "law of least intervention." Her idea is to eliminate disruptive behaviors quickly with a minimum of disruption to the classroom/instructional routine. The following suggestions can be organized into physical, gestural, visual, and verbal prompts:

◆ Position one's physical presence near students who are likely to create problems.
◆ Touch a student's shoulder gently to convey your awareness that the student is behaving in some inappropriate way.
◆ Use subtle and not-so-subtle gestures to stop undesirable behaviors (e.g., pointing, head-shaking, or other signals).
◆ Establish eye contact and maintain it for a while with a student who is behaving inappropriately. This results in no disruption to the instructional routine.
◆ Stop talking for a pronounced length of time to redirect student attention.
◆ Call on students who are not attending, but ask them questions that they can answer successfully, or use students' names in the course of the presentation.
◆ Use humor to redirect inappropriate behavior.

The last option in this hierarchy and the one that is most intrusive is the use of some form of *punishment*. It is the least preferable option because it involves the presentation of something unpleasant or the removal of something pleasant as a consequence of the performance of an undesirable behavior, and neither situation is attractive. However, situations arise when it becomes the option of choice, as the various types of punishers do provide a more immediate cessation of undesirable behaviors.

Three punishment techniques represent approaches more commonly used in classrooms. These include reprimands, **time out,** and **response costs**/penalties. For these forms of punishment to work, it is critical that they be applied immediately after the occurrence of the undesirable behavior and that students understand why they are being applied. A useful overview of these techniques is provided in Table 12.1.

A reprimand represents a type of punisher where an unpleasant condition (verbal reprimand from the teacher) is presented to the student. Below are some specific suggestions:

◆ Do not let this type of interchange dominate the type of interactions with students.
◆ Look at the student and talk in a composed way.
◆ Do not verbally reprimand a student from across the room. Get close to the student and maintain a degree of privacy.

TABLE 12.1   **Three Commonly Used Punishment Techniques**

Type	Definition	Advantages	Disadvantages

Reprimand	A verbal statement or non-verbal gesture that expresses disapproval.	Easily applied with little or no preparation required.
		  No physical discomfort to students.
			Sometimes not effective.
			  Can serve as positive reinforcement if this is a major source of attention.

Response cost	A formal system of penalties in which a reinforcer is removed contingent upon the occurrence of an inappropriate behavior.	Easily applied with quick results.
		  Does not disrupt class activities
		  No physical discomfort to students.
			Not effective once student has "lost" all reinforcers.
			  Can initially result in some students being more disruptive.

Time out	Limited or complete loss of access to positive reinforcers for a set amount of time.	Fast-acting and powerful.
		  No physical discomfort to students.
			Difficult to find secluded areas where students would not be reinforced inadvertently.
			  May require physical assistance to the time-out area.
			  Overuse can interfere with educational and prosocial efforts.

Source: Reprinted with permission of Macmillan College Publishing Company from STUDENT TEACHER TO MASTER TEACHER by Michael S. Rosenberg, Lawrence O'Shea, and Dorothy J. O'Shea. Copyright © 1991 by Macmillan College Publishing Company, Inc.

♦ Let the student know exactly why you are concerned.
♦ Convey to the student that it is the behavior that is the problem and not the person.

Time out is a technique whereby a student is removed from a situation in which the student typically receives some type of positive reinforcement, thus being prevented from enjoying something pleasurable. There are different versions of removing a student from a reinforcing setting: (a) Students are allowed to observe the situation from which they have been removed (contingent observation); (b) students are excluded from the ongoing proceedings entirely; and (c) students are secluded in a separate room. The first two versions are most likely to be used in general education classrooms. The following suggestions are extremely important if this approach is used:

♦ Confirm that the ongoing situation from which a student is going to be removed is indeed reinforcing; if not, this technique does not serve as a punisher and may be a form of positive reinforcement.
♦ Ensure that the time-out area is devoid of reinforcing elements. If it is not a neutral setting, this procedure will also fail.
♦ Do not keep students in time out for long periods of time or use it frequently, as students will miss significant amounts of instructional time.

♦ Incorporate this procedure as one of the classroom procedures explained and taught at the beginning of the school year.

♦ Consider using a time-out system where students are given one warning before being removed.

♦ Signal to the student when it is appropriate to return.

♦ As they return to the ongoing activities, ask students if they know why they were removed. If they do not know, explain the reasons to them at a time when instructional routine will not be interrupted.

♦ Do not use this technique with certain sensitive students.

♦ Inform the school administration and obtain permission if seclusion is used.

♦ Keep records on frequency, reason for using, and amount of time spent in time out, if seclusion is used.

Response cost involves the loss of something the student values such as privileges or points. It is a system where a penalty/fine is invoked for occurrences of inappropriate behavior. Below are some specific suggestions:

♦ Explain very clearly to students how the system works and how much one will be fined for a given offense.

♦ Tie this procedure in with some type of reinforcement system.

♦ Make sure all penalties are presented in a nonpersonal manner.

♦ Confirm that privileges lost are indeed reinforcing to students.

♦ Make sure that all privileges are not lost quickly, resulting in a situation in which a student may have little or no incentive to behave appropriately.

Developing Self-Management Behaviors

Ultimately, we want students to be able to manage their own behaviors without any external assistance, as this will be required to function independently in life. This self-regulation should be the goal of all programs designed to change behaviors, and, as a result, efforts should be directed at achieving this goal with students. Special attention may need to be given to a host of students in general education who do not display this type of independent behavioral control.

Self-management includes a number of subcomponents. Although variations exist, the subcomponents listed in Figure 12.4 represent often-cited aspects of self-management. Below are some specific suggestions:

♦ Allocate instructional time to teach these elements of self-management to some students.

♦ Provide strategies and assistive materials (e.g., self-recording forms) for students.

♦ Model how effective self-managers operate. Point out actual applications of the essential elements highlighted in Figure 12.4, and follow this with opportunities for students to practice these techniques with guidance from the teacher.

Teaching Students to Manage Their Own Behaviors

◆ Make students aware of how certain events, people, places, or conditions influence their behavior. Let them know how these might be changed. Suggest alternatives.

◆ Teach students how to observe and record their own behavior. Help them pinpoint the inappropriate actions they want to decrease and the appropriate ones to increase. Show them how to record incidences of inappropriate behavior.

◆ Allow students to set their own goals for increasing or decreasing certain behaviors.

◆ Teach students how to "remind" themselves to act appropriately. Have them practice saying to themselves such phrases as "No hitting," "We don't cheat," "Leave Maria alone," "Try harder," etc.

◆ Show students how to self-impose a relaxation or time-out period when they feel frustrated or angry.

◆ Offer a variety of reinforcers from which students can choose the one they like the most when they have behaved appropriately.

Source: Westling, D. L., & Koorland, M. A. (1989). *The special educator's handbook* (p. 106). Boston: Allyn & Bacon. Used with permission.

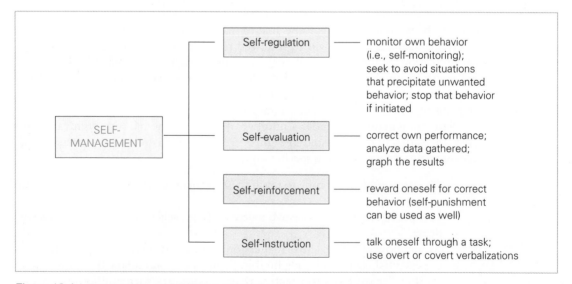

Figure 12.4 **Components of Self-Management**
Source: Dowdy, Patton, Polloway, & Smith. (in press). *Guide to attention deficits in the classroom.* Austin, TX: Pro-Ed. Used with permission.

◆ Help students identify natural reinforcers that are available to them and that will be useful in implementing self-management tactics.

Instructional Management

All of the dimensions discussed in this chapter relate in some way to instructional outcomes. However, certain aspects of the instructional process per se are eminently associated with sound organizational/management practice. For this reason, selected topics have been chosen for discussion and for which specific suggestions are offered in this section. These selected topics include scheduling, transitions, grouping, lesson planning, material management, record keeping, and homework.

Scheduling involves the general temporal arrangement of events for either (a) the entire day (i.e., master schedule) or (b) a specific class period. The focus of this section is on the latter. Polloway and Patton (1993) stress that "the importance of a carefully planned schedule within the context of an organized classroom cannot be overemphasized" (p. 66). This is particularly true in classrooms in which students with disabilities have been placed.

The thoughtful scheduling of a class period can contribute greatly to the amount of time that students can spend engaged in learning. It can also add to the quality of what is learned. For instance, a science lesson might include the following components:

◆ Transitional activities
◆ Attention-getting/motivating techniques
◆ Data-gathering techniques
◆ Data-processing techniques
◆ Closure activities
◆ Transitional activities

All components lend themselves to a sequence of activities that supports whatever the instructional goal might be for the day. Various reminders or cues from the teacher augment such a system. Below are some specific suggestions:

◆ Provide time reminders (visual and audible) for students during the class period so that they know how much time is available.
◆ Plan for transitions (see next section).
◆ Require students to complete one activity or task before moving on to the next (Gallagher, 1988).
◆ Vary the nature of class activities to keep students engaged and to maintain instructional tempo and pace.

An adjunct to scheduling is planning for *transitions*. Throughout the school day, students deal with many **transitions**: arrival at school, movement in and out of classes, changing activities within a given class period, movement to and from recess and lunch, and dismissal from school. The general idea of transitions was covered earlier; the focus of this discussion is on the transitions that occur within a class period. Adequate attention to establishing efficient transitions can minimize disruptions, maximize the amount of time allocated to instructional tasks, and maintain desired conditions of learning. A list of ways to ease transition times follows:

- Model appropriate ways to transition between activities (Rosenberg et al., 1991).
- Let students practice the appropriate transition skills.
- Use any number of cues and associated activities to signal to students that it is time to change instructional routine. Rosenkoetter and Fowler (1986) offer many specific recommendations for dismissing students from one setting and moving to another.

Grouping refers to how students are organized for instructional purposes. The need to place students into smaller group arrangements depends to a great extent on the nature of the curricular area or the goal of a specific lesson. For students with special needs, the overriding concern within a group setting is attention to individual needs. The use of innovative grouping arrangements and different cooperative learning opportunities allows for variety in the instructional routine for students with special needs. Some specific suggestions follow:

- Give serious consideration to the makeup of groups.
- Make sure that group composition is not constant. Vary membership as a function of having different reasons for grouping students.
- Use different grouping arrangements that are based on interest or for research purposes (Wood, 1992).
- Use cooperative learning arrangements on a regular basis, as this approach, if structured properly, facilitates successful learning and socialization.
- Determine the size of groups based on ability levels: the lower the ability, the smaller the size of the group (Rosenberg et al., 1991).

The purpose of *lesson plans* is to help teachers prepare for instruction. More precisely, the plans serve as "blueprints that describe and guide the teacher's activities in presenting the lesson" (Charles, 1983, p. 97). The reality is that many teachers start out writing very detailed lesson plans and eventually move to less comprehensive formats. However, it should be noted that many teachers continue to use detailed plans throughout their teaching careers, as they find the detail helpful in providing effective instruction. Some specific suggestions in developing lesson plans follow:

- Create interest in and clarify the purpose of lessons. This is particularly important for students with special needs.
- Consider providing direct instruction on some topics to help students acquire an initial grasp of new material.
- Assign independent practice, some of which can be accomplished in class and some of which should be done as homework.
- Plan activities for students to finish early. This might be particularly true for gifted students.
- Anticipate problems that might arise during the course of the lesson. By doing so, you can identify techniques for dealing with potential problems.

Name Calling!

Show your students some representative works of famous artists. Make certain that you have examples from different countries, time frames, and styles. Tell the students something about the artist and the style but not the titles of the works. Encourage them to choose the ones they like best and talk about how differently a single piece of art can appeal to people. Ask the students to give each of the paintings a title reflecting what they think each painting is all about. When they are through, let them share their titles with the entire class. Ask them to consider the following questions:

- ◆ Which titles expressed similar feelings about each painting?

- ◆ Which titles were very different from the others suggested?

- ◆ Were they surprised to find someone very different from themselves express the same feeling about a painting?

- ◆ Did they expect certain classmates or groups of students to respond to the artwork in a certain way because of a stereotype based on cultural or racial bias?

- ◆ Did anyone look at a painting differently as a result of listening to someone else's point of view?

This activity will not only encourage students to appreciate differences among people but also help develop creative thinking skills. Variations of this activity could use: short stories, essays, instrumental music, poetry, vocal music, or pictures/photographs.

Remember to provide time to relate the works of art to their cultural backgrounds. Explore the cultural differences represented. The students will want to know why the artists did what they did. That's the best moment to get into the people, places, times, and how they relate to today!

Adapted from an exercise by Katie Williams, Lois Jones, and Karen Catignani, teachers, McKissack Elementary, and Linda Walker, community participant.
Source: Pasternak, M. G. (1979). *Helping kids learn multi-cultural concepts: A handbook of strategies* (p. 115). Champaign, IL: Research Press. Used with permission.

Most curricular areas include the use of various instructional *materials*—either commercially available or teacher-produced. Since materials are so important to ongoing instructional routines, it is important to consider ways to select, obtain, manage, and organize them.

- Obtain adaptive materials that might be needed for certain students (e.g., large-print materials, books on tape).
- Select materials that can be used with students displaying a range of learning-related challenges.
- Make sure that catalogs from which materials will be ordered are current.
- Consult with special education personnel about the availability of adaptive materials.
- Develop classroom procedures for material distribution and collection.
- Create storage areas for materials that are easy to access by any student.

As mentioned earlier, *homework* is a form of independent practice that can help students with special needs become more proficient with newly learned material. Some important recommendations that can enhance the use of homework with these students are listed at the end of this section.

A useful idea that is worth considering is an assignment book. This is recommended with students who have difficulty with this instructional demand. Teachers can check to see if the appropriate assignment has been written down correctly.

Below are listed some specific suggestions in assigning homework:

- Take time to set the purpose for a given homework assignment.
- Do not assign homework that is too complex or too novel.
- Assign activities that students have a reasonable chance of completing.
- Present homework assignments clearly, write them on the chalkboard, and determine that students understand what they are to do.
- Inform students what format and standards of neatness are expected (Evertson et al., 1989).
- Establish classroom procedures that will govern how homework is assigned and collected.
- Determine where problems in completing homework assignments might occur by administering a checklist such as the *Homework Problem Checklist* (Anesko, Shoiock, Ramirez, & Levine, 1987).

Personnel Management

A comprehensive model of classroom management must address the fact that teachers are very likely to have regular contact with other personnel. The nature of the contact may be brief (i.e., a meeting) or extended (a full-time assistant in the classroom). The types of people that classroom teachers may encounter include other teachers, professional support staff (e.g., speech/language pathologists, psychologists), paraprofessionals, teacher trainees, volunteers, peer tutors, and substitute teachers.

The probability of working with other personnel is increased when students with various types of special needs are in a classroom. For this reason, a number of recommendations are provided here.

◆ Establish good working relationships with support personnel.
◆ Attempt to understand what services professional support personnel are providing to students in your class.
◆ Establish unequivocally the roles and responsibilities of aides, volunteers, and trainees.
◆ Consider delegating noninstructional duties to aides when they are available.
◆ Train students to be effective peer tutors.
◆ Supply substitute teachers with detailed information about the organization and management of the classroom (Cummings, 1983).

Time Management

All of the preceding dimensions of the model of classroom management relate to the management of teacher time. However, there are some additional suggestions that can be given that will further enhance your efforts to be more efficient. The areas that will be discussed are the work environment, administrative duties, instructional applications, and personal applications.

The *work environment* refers to the immediate work area used by teachers—usually the desk and files. The primary focus is on organization. Consideration must be given to how teachers want to utilize their immediate work areas and how well they organize these areas. A decision needs to be made, for instance, as to how a teacher's desk will be used. Some teachers make this area off-limits to all students; other teachers use it for storage only or for a work area. Presented are some specific suggestions in establishing a work environment:

◆ Keep the teacher's desk organized and clear of stacks of papers.
◆ Organize files so that documents and information can be retrieved easily and quickly. Use color-coded systems if possible.
◆ Handle most paperwork only once.

The nature of teaching implies that, along with the instructional duties, there are numerous *administrative duties* to perform. Two of the most time-demanding activities are participating in meetings and handling paperwork, including various forms of correspondence (Collins, 1987). Below are some strategies for handling paperwork:

◆ Prepare form letters for all necessary events (e.g., permissions, notifications, status reports, memo formats, reimbursement requests).
◆ Prepare master copies of various forms that are used regularly (e.g., certificates/awards, record sheets, phone conversation sheets).
◆ Keep notes of all school-related phone conversations with parents, teachers, support staff, administrators, or any other person.
◆ Make the most of meetings—request an agenda and ask that meetings be scheduled at times that are convenient.

Some additional *instructional applications* of time-management techniques not covered in the section on instructional management are provided here. For the most

Microcomputers provide an excellent opportunity for teachers to manage the instructional environment.

part, these suggestions focus on the use of materials and technology that make the job of teaching easier. The most attractive piece of equipment now available to teachers to facilitate instructionally related tasks is the microcomputer. With the appropriate software, teachers can use this tool to greatly reduce the amount of time spent on certain instructionally related tasks (e.g., test generation, graphic organizers, IEP development). Below are some specific suggestions:

◆ Use self-correcting materials with students to reduce the amount of time required to correct student work.
◆ Use software programs for recording student scores and determining grades.
◆ Use computers to generate a variety of instructionally related materials (tests, graphic organizers, puzzles).
◆ Give students computer-generated calendars that include important dates.

It is impossible to completely divorce the management of one's personal and professional time. With that in mind, it is worthwhile considering various time management tactics that have a more *personal application* but can affect one's efficiency and effectiveness in the classroom as well. A listing of some of the most common recommendations is provided below.

◆ Use a daily to-do list.
◆ Break down major tasks into smaller pieces and work on them.

◆ Avoid getting overcommitted.

◆ Work during work time. This might mean avoiding situations at school where long social conversations will cut into on-task time.

◆ Avoid dealing with trivial activities if important ones must be addressed.

◆ Use idle time (e.g., waiting in lines) well. Always be prepared for these situations by having reading material or other materials available.

The efficient management of one's professional and personal time can pay off in making the day-to-day demands less overwhelming. Thus, it is time well spent to become a better time manager. Teachers interested in more in-depth coverage of how to apply time-management concepts to the classroom are referred to Collins (1987).

Summary

◆ Organizational and management dimensions are critical elements of classroom management often overlooked in the design of educational programs.

◆ Classroom management includes all teacher-directed activities that support the efficient operations of the classroom and that lead to the establishment of optimal conditions of learning and order.

◆ Key elements that have a significant effect on instruction and learning are multidimensionality, simultaneity, immediacy, unpredictability, publicness, and history.

◆ Key principles of successful classroom management are careful planning, proactive strategies, consistency, awareness, and overlapping.

◆ A significant aspect of successful management is a teacher's attitude toward students with special needs.

◆ Classroom rules provide a general sense of what is expected of students. The rules chosen should be ones essential for classroom functioning and for the development of a positive learning environment.

◆ Classroom procedures are also key aspects of successful management. They include the specific ways in which certain activities or situations will be performed.

◆ Key aspects of physical management include classroom arrangement, accessibility, seating, and the use of specialized equipment.

◆ Desirable behaviors are increased through the use of positive reinforcement.

◆ Undesirable behaviors can be reduced through a variety of reduction strategies. A hierarchy of options would include (from least to most restrictive) natural and logical consequences, differential reinforcement, extinction, benign tactics, reprimands, response costs/penalties, and time out. Successful behavior management programs include attention to the importance of generalization and the development of self-management.

◆ Scheduling involves the general temporal arrangement of events for a day or a specific class.

◆ Successful teachers engage in the careful management of time. Organizational strategies related to the work environment, administrative duties, and efficient instructional applications promote successful time management.

References

Alberto, P. A., & Troutman, A. C. (1990). *Applied behavior analysis for teachers: Influencing student performance* (3rd ed.). New York: Macmillan.

Anesko, K. M., Shoiock, G., Ramirez, R., & Levine, F. M. (1987). The homework problem checklist: Assessing children's homework difficulties. *Behavioral Assessment, 9,* 179–185.

Barrish, H. H., Saunders, M., & Wolf, M. M. (1969). Good-behavior game: Effects of individual contingencies for group consequences on disruptive behavior in a classroom. *Journal of Applied Behavior Analysis, 2,* 119–124.

Charles, C. M. (1983). *Elementary classroom management.* New York: Longman.

Christenson, S. L., Ysseldyke, J. E., & Thurlow, M. L. (1989). Critical instructional factors for students with mild handicaps: An integrative review. *Remedial and Special Education, 10*(5), 21–31.

Collins, C. (1987). *Time management for teachers: Practical techniques and skills that give you more time to teach.* West Nyack, NY: Parker Publishing.

Cummings, C. (1983). *Managing to teach.* Edmonds, WA: Teaching Inc.

DeLuke, S. V., & Knoblock, P. (1987). Teacher behavior as preventive discipline. *Teaching Exceptional Children, 20,* 18–24.

Doyle, W. (1986). Classroom organization and management. In M. C. Wittrock (Ed.), *Handbook of research and teaching* (3rd ed., pp. 392–431). New York: Macmillan.

Emmer, E. T., Evertson, C. M., Sanford, J. P., Clements, B. S., & Worsham, M. E. (1989). *Classroom management for secondary teachers* (2nd ed.). Englewood Cliffs, NJ: Prentice-Hall.

Gallagher, P. A. (1988). *Teaching students with behavior disorders: Techniques for classroom instruction* (2nd ed.). Denver, CO: Love Publishing.

Idol, L. (1993). *Special educator's consultation handbook* (2nd ed.). Austin, TX: Pro-Ed.

Kaplan, J. S. (1990). *Beyond behavior modification: A cognitive-behavioral approach to behavior management in the school.* Austin, TX: Pro-Ed.

Kounin, J. (1970). *Discipline and group management in classrooms.* New York: Holt, Rinehart & Winston.

Nelson, C. M., & Rutherford, R. B. (1983). Time-out revisited: Guidelines for its use in special education. *Exceptional Education Quarterly, 3*(4), 56–67.

O'Melia, M. C., & Rosenberg, M. S. (1989). Classroom management: Preventing behavior problems in classrooms for students with learning disabilities. *LD Forum, 15*(1), 23–26.

Pasternak, M. G. (1979). *Helping kids learn multi-cultural concepts: a handbook of strategies.* Champaign, IL: Research Press.

Polloway, E. A., & Patton, J. R. (1993). *Strategies for teaching learners with special needs* (5th ed.). New York: Macmillan.

Rosenberg, M. S., O'Shea, L., & O'Shea, D. J. (1991). *Student teacher to master teacher: A handbook for preservice and beginning teachers of students with mild and moderate handicaps.* New York: Macmillan.

Rosenkoetter, S. E., & Fowler, S. A. (1986). Teaching mainstreamed children to manage daily transitions. *Teaching Exceptional Children, 19,* 20–23.

Salend, S. J. (1990). *Effective mainstreaming.* New York: Macmillan.

Smith, D. D. & Rivera, D. (1993). *Effective discipline* (2nd ed.). Austin, TX: Pro-Ed.

Smith, T. E. C., Finn, D. M., & Dowdy, C. A. (1993). *Teaching students with mild disabilities.* Fort Worth, TX: Harcourt Brace Jovanovich.

Swanson, J. M., McBurnett, K., Wigal, T., Pfiffner, L. J., Lerner, M. A., Williams, L., Christian, D. L., Tann, L., Wilcutt, E., Crowley, K., Clevenger, W., Khouzam, N., Woo, C., Crinella, F. M., & Fisher, T. D. (1993). Effect of stimulant medication on children with attention deficit disorder. *Exceptional Children, 60,* 154–162.

Turla, P., & Hawkins, K. L. (1983). *Time management made easy.* New York: E. P. Dutton.

West, G. K. (1986). *Parenting without guilt.* Springfield, IL: Charles C. Thomas.

Westling, D. L., & Koorland, M. A. (1989). *The special educator's handbook.* Boston: Allyn & Bacon.

Wood, J. W. (1992). *Adapting instruction for mainstreamed and at-risk students* (2nd ed.). New York: Macmillan.

Zirpoli & Melloy. (1993). *Behavior management: Applications for teachers and parents* (p. 189). Columbus, OH: Merrill.

CHAPTER 13

Curricular and Instructional Accommodations: Elementary Level

Elementary school presents a unique opportunity for the inclusion of young students with disabilities and other special needs into general education. At this level, the degree of curricular differentiation tends to be most limited, so it is a time when quality of educational needs for all students will be at its greatest.

Elementary school also offers an important beginning point for students with disabilities to profit from interaction with their nondisabled peers. There remains little question that preparation for successful lives beyond the school setting requires the ability to work with a diversity of individuals, thus, a clear benefit from inclusion can be obtained both for students who are disabled and for their peers. There is clearly no better time for this to take place than in early childhood and throughout the primary and elementary grades.

The advent of the inclusion movement (REI) (e.g., Reynolds, Wang, & Walberg, 1987; Wang, Reynolds, & Walberg, 1986; Will, 1986) as discussed in Chapter 1 has increased the likelihood that many students with disabilities will receive a significant portion, or all, of their instruction in the general education classroom. According to the 15th Annual Report to Congress, 78% of all students with disabilities (aged 6–18) served in general education–based programs (i.e., general education classes and/or resource rooms) during 1990–1991 (U.S. Department of Education, 1993). The effects of the increased commitment to inclusion will more likely be seen in recently emerging data from the early 1990s. Thus it becomes important that, beginning at the elementary level, careful attention be given to these students' educational needs.

The purpose of this chapter is to provide an overview of curricular and instructional accommodations relative to the inclusion of elementary-aged students with special needs into mainstream settings. The discussion that follows emphasizes instructional accommodations and modifications that provide the means for achieving curricular goals.

Curricular Considerations

Curriculum has been defined in varied ways. Hoover (1988) describes **curriculum** as the planned learning experiences that have intended educational outcomes. Comfort (1990) indicates that it is a "set of learnings . . .[of] what students are intended to learn" (p. 398). Armstrong (1990) refers to it as a "master plan for selecting content and organizing learning experiences for the purpose of changing and developing learners' behaviors and insights" (p. 4). For students with disabilities, and truly for students in general, any consideration of curriculum should include an outcomes orientation so that our definition embraces the preparation of students for life after school.

Although curriculum design often is preordained in some general education programs, it is nevertheless worth considering the concept of *comprehensive curriculum,* proposed by Polloway, Patton, Payne, and Payne (1989). This refers to a program guided by the reality that students are enrolled in school on only a time-limited basis. Thus, the true evaluation of the curriculum is how much it contributes to the quality of students' lives once they leave school. Educators must consider what will happen in the future, and that requires a perspective that is sensitive to the environments to which students will need to adapt in order to function successfully. An acceptance of this premise results in curriculum design being governed by a "subsequent environments as an attitude" approach (Polloway, Patton, Smith, & Roderique, 1992).

The central attributes of a comprehensive curriculum (as adapted from Polloway, Patton, Epstein, & Smith, 1989) include the following features, which have relevance for students at the elementary level:

- Responsive to the needs of the individual at the current time
- Reflective of the need to balance maximum interaction with peers who are not disabled against critical curricular needs
- Derived from a realistic appraisal of potential long-term outcomes of individual students
- Consistent with relevant, forthcoming transitional needs (e.g., from elementary to middle school)

The advantage of program design efforts for students with disabilities who are included in general education classes at the elementary level is that the curricular needs of the vast majority of the students are quite consistent with those of their peers. Thus, with appropriate modifications in instruction and with collaborative arrangements, most students' needs can largely be met in the general education classroom.

Academic Instruction

Elementary students in general, and certainly most students with disabilities, need a primary emphasis on instruction in reading, writing, and mathematics to maximize academic achievement. These needs can typically be met by a developmental approach to instruction supplemented as needed by a remedial focus. Some research support exists to suggest that typical reading instruction, for example, in resource rooms and general education classrooms, tends to be very similar (Wesson & Deno, 1989).

To select reading as an example, an initial concern is to consider the common approaches of **basal series, direct instruction,** and **whole language.** *Basal series* are the typical means that many instructors use to teach reading—and, for that matter, other curricular domains, including spelling and math—in the elementary school. Most reading basals are intended to meet developmental needs in reading. Although they are routinely criticized, they remain by far the most common approach to reading instruction (Wesson, 1989). Issues to consider relative to students with disabilities have been addressed by Polloway and Smith (1992), who indicated that such series have both advantages and disadvantages. In particular, they stated (pp. 307–308):

> On the positive side, they contain inherent structure and sequence, controlled vocabulary, a wide variety of teaching activities, and preparation for the teacher. Weaknesses, on the other hand, include inappropriate pacing for an individual child, overconcern for certain skills to the exclusion of others, and encouragement of group instructional orientation.

Direct instruction has often been associated with a remedial perspective, although it clearly has often played a significant role as a preventative approach as well. Often this orientation has been tied to a focus on basic skills, which has constituted the typical orientation core for most elementary special education curricula. In the area of reading, direct instruction programs have mostly been associated with an emphasis on skills-based, decoding orientations.

Basic skills programs typically have a long-term orientation in the sense that they are based on the presumption that instruction in such skills ultimately will increase students' academic achievement levels and may enable them to reach a minimal level of functional literacy. Not all basic skill programs have equal effectiveness; rather those that incorporate the tenets of effective instructional practice (Stevens & Rosenshine, 1981) have most often empirically demonstrated substantial gains in achievement. These concepts are quite consistent with the basic tenets of direct instruction and include characteristic features such as high levels of academic engaged time, signals for attention, ongoing feedback to learners, group-based instruction, fast pacing, and error-free learning. In evaluating direct instruction programs, finally, it is important to differentiate these teaching methods from the overall curriculum such as might be provided with a commercial program such as *DISTAR* or *Reading Mastery*.

Whole language approaches to academic instruction at the primary and elementary level are currently increasing in popularity and usage. Such approaches embrace a more holistic view of learning than direct instruction, which tends to be more oriented to specific skills. As such, whole language programs tend to break down artificial barriers between reading, writing, and speaking, and tend to be more literature-based. Some recent research (see Mather, 1992, for a review) tends to support the efficacy of such approaches with learners of diverse abilities.

Schewel (1993), drawing on the work of Chiang and Ford (1990), provides a clear picture of whole language "in action" when she describes its implementation:

> Core activities that characterize the whole language approach include orally sharing stories by the teacher; sharing book experiences through material such as "Big Books"; sustained silent reading; silent reading time segments in which students write responses to what they are reading and share this with other students or with the teacher in individual conferences; language experience activities in which children write stories in a group or individually to be used for future reading experiences; time set aside for large group writing instruction followed by students' writing, revising, editing, and sharing their own writing; and finally reading and writing activities that involve a content area theme such as science or social studies.

Each of these three methods presents possible benefits to the inclusion of students with disabilities in general academic programs. However, teachers must review progress on a regular basis and make necessary modifications because it is unlikely that any one program can meet each student's entire realm of needs. Mather (1992) presents an excellent review on the issues surrounding whole-language and code-emphasis approaches to reading (such as is common with direct instruction programs). Her review of the literature argues persuasively for the fact that for students who are not good readers, skill instruction is necessary for their progress to be satisfactory. The challenge for classroom teachers is to balance the needs of able readers, for whom explicit instruction in phonics may prove unnecessary and for whom meaning-based instruction is clearly most appropriate, with the needs of those students who may require systematic instruction to provide them assistance in unlocking the alphabetic relationships of our written language.

Although the focus of this discussion was, for illustrative purposes, on reading and language arts, obviously other curricular areas are of significance to students with special needs as they are for students in general. In math, students need to have a focus on the development of both computational skills and problem-solving abilities. Within the area of computation, teachers should focus first on the students' conceptualization of the particular skill and then on the achievement of automaticity with skills. Cawley's (1984) interactive unit and Miller, Mercer, and Dillon's (1992) concrete/semi-concrete/abstract systems afford excellent options to the teacher. Problem solving can be particularly difficult for students with disabilities, and thus warrants special attention. Systematic steps should be taught and followed so that students learn to understand and implement strategies to reason through problems.

In addition to the potential benefits of inclusion in core academic areas (i.e., basic skills), there are also important reasons to promote general class placement in other academic areas. This can be particularly important in subject areas such as science, social studies, health/family life, and the arts because these subjects present unique problems to teachers in special settings if the special teacher would have to endeavor to create a curriculum for each area. The use of **cooperative teaching** (discussed later in the chapter) presents an excellent alternative for the delivery of instruction in these areas. These areas also lend themselves well to integrated curricular approaches, which are discussed later in the chapter.

Social Skills

Another area of curricular concern for elementary students with disabilities is **social skills.** Virtually all students identified as having mental retardation or behavior disorders, and many students identified as having learning disabilities, need attention to social skills acquisition (Cullinan & Epstein, 1985; Polloway, Epstein, & Cullinan, 1985). The challenge for classroom teachers will be to find ways to incorporate such a focus within their classes. This area may be a particularly apt one for seeking assistance from a special education teacher or a counselor. A key concern here is that the social domain will often be predictive of success or failure in inclusive settings. For example, Gresham (1982, 1984) has stressed that students with disabilities interact infrequently and, to a large extent, negatively with their peers. He argued that many pupils have been placed in inclusive settings without the necessary social skills to succeed in these environments and gain acceptance by their peers.

Polloway, Patton, Epstein, and Smith (1989) identified four approaches that have been associated with the social domain: social skills acquisition, behavioral change, **affective education,** and cognitive interventions. Efforts focused on *direct social skills training* are concerned with the attainment of skills necessary for students to overcome situations in classrooms, on the job, and in other areas that prevent assimilation (Masters & Mori, 1986). A *behavioral change* strategy typically focuses on identifying a target behavior and implementing a reinforcement system that will lead to modification in a behavior. Steps in such programs typically include (1) selecting the target behavior, (2) collecting baseline data, (3) identifying reinforcers, (4) implementing a procedure for reinforcing appropriate behaviors; and (5) evaluating the intervention. *Affective education* typically emphasizes self-control and the relationship between self and others in the environment (Shea & Bauer, 1987). A primary emphasis frequently is placed on the emotional, rather than just the behavioral, aspects of social adjustment. Finally, a fruitful direction has been the use of *cognitive approaches* to behavioral change and social skills acquisition (in which students are, for example, taught to monitor their own behavior, engage in self-instruction, or design, and/or implement their own reinforcement program). To the degree to which they can demonstrate meaningful and long-lasting behavior change, such programs offer significant promise for social adjustment programming in the future.

Korinek and Polloway (1993) provided a general context for viewing instruction in the social domain for students who have difficulties in this area. They indicated that the instructional priority should be for skills most needed by students in their immediate interactions in the classroom, thus enhancing the likelihood of successful inclusion. Teachers can begin by teaching students behaviors that will "naturally elicit desired responses from peers and adults" (Nelson, 1988, p. 21) such as sharing, smiling, asking for help, attending, turn taking, following directions, and problem solving (McConnell, 1987; Cartledge & Milburn, 1980). These skills are important for students to gain social acceptance. Additionally, they have applicability across multiple settings.

A second key consideration (as identified by Korinek & Polloway, 1993) in designing or selecting a social adjustment program is the degree to which it promotes both **social competence** and social skills. Whereas social skills facilitate interpersonal interactions and maintain a degree of independence in daily functioning, social competence involves the use of the skills at the right times and places, showing social perception, cognition, and judgment of how to act in different situations (Haring, 1988; Sargent, 1991). A limited focus on the skill training without considering social competence may decrease the likelihood that the child will maintain the specific social skills or transfer them to other settings.

Transitional Needs

In addition to the academic and social components of the curriculum, a third general area concerns career education and transition. Included herein are an emphasis on career awareness and a focus on transitional variables as related to movement to middle and secondary school settings (i.e., a vertical transition) that have been identified as crucial to students with disabilities (Jaquish & Stella, 1986; Polloway, 1984; Robinson, Braxdale, & Colson, 1988).

Career education in general, and **life skills** in particular, have become major emphases of the efforts of many secondary school teachers, especially those who are

Cultural Diversity Awareness Activities

The following activities can be used to help develop cultural awareness among students.

- Introduce the concept of cultural diversity by asking students to identify three ways they are alike and different.
- Have students role-play a politician who addresses an audience and talks about cultural diversity in this country.
- Display posters and pictures in the classroom that depict various cultures.
- Have students share information about their own cultural heritage.
- Invite speakers to tell about their own particular heritage.
- Assign independent studies or group projects that focus on various cultural groups.
- Collect and discuss newspapers and magazines developed for various cultural groups.

For African-American Awareness:

- Have students make "dream T-shirts" to be worn on January 19th, Martin Luther King, Jr. Day; discuss Martin Luther King, Jr. and his role in the civil rights movement.
- Have students make musical instruments used in African chants, such as drums, rattles, sticks, and so forth.
- Have students make African jewelry.

For Hispanic Awareness:

- Display Aztec calendars; discuss the calendar's development and meaning.
- Have students make maps of the lower United States, and Central and South America.
- Discuss various aspects of Spanish heritage.

For Asian-American Awareness:

- Celebrate the lunar New Year (February 6) and discuss the various symbols of the calendar (e.g., serpent, dog, pig, and so forth).
- Have students make pleated fans.
- Display a map of the various Asian countries.

For American Indian Awareness:

- Discuss how American Indian tribes identify months of the year.
- Have students make and wear Native American clothing.
- Discuss a map of the numerous Indian tribes across the country.

Source: Mack, C. (1988). Celebrate cultural diversity. *Teaching Exceptional Children, 21,* 40–43. Used with permission.

working with students who have disabilities. However, life skills concepts should also be incorporated into elementary and middle school programs. For illustrative purposes, it is useful to consider the Adult Performance Level (APL) model of functional competency (APL Project, 1975; Daniels & Wiederholt, 1986; LaQuey, 1981). The APL model was based on an adult education program, but it since has been used as a model for developing a secondary-level special education curriculum. This model has been adapted to provide a contribution to elementary school curriculum design as well (Cronin, 1988; Patton, Cronin, Polloway, Hutchison, & Robinson, 1989). The APL model provides an illustration of functional content derived from career/life skills education that focuses on consideration for subsequent environments. Figure 13.1 provides an outline of a matrix to illustrate topics that may be incorporated into an elementary curriculum. The essential point is that even programs for young children should be designed with consideration given to positive long-term outcomes for all students.

Concepts and topics related to life skills should be integrated into existing subject areas, thus broadening the curriculum without creating a "new subject." Patton (1986) suggested three ways to add career relevance to the extant curriculum. The first is *augmentation,* using other career education–oriented materials to supplement the existing curriculum. The second approach is to retain the existing curriculum and to *infuse* relevant career education topics into regularly assigned lessons. A third approach is through the use of an *integrated curriculum,* similar to the unit approach traditionally used in many education programs (Kataoka & Patton, 1989). An integrated curriculum draws together content from variant academic areas and enables students to apply the academic skills they have been learning across these areas. Furthermore, this type of programming can link academic skills and life skills. Using a matrix format for organizing the curriculum (see Figure 13.2), the interrelationships can be developed by tying together reading, math, and language skills, as well as other subject/skill areas. Integrated curricula are particularly effective in teaching primary- and elementary-aged students important cross-subject linkages.

A related transitional concern for students with disabilities in the elementary school is to provide for their movement to the middle school or junior high level. Smith, Robinson, and Voress (1982) suggested that this transition is particularly critical.

Teachers should consider a number of concerns in their efforts to effect this successful vertical transition. Some particular areas of emphasis include organization, time management and study skills, note-taking strategies, strategies for completing homework, and the successful use of lockers (Polloway, 1984; Polloway et al., 1992). Robinson et al. (1988) grouped the major changes in demands on behavior faced by students in junior high as academic, self-management/study skills, and social/adaptive. They stressed that behaviors in each of these three areas may interact in causing difficulties for students.

A variety of instructional strategies may assist in this transition process: having middle school faculty visit elementary classes to discuss programs and expectations, videotaping middle school classes, and taking field trips to the middle school to get a

APL Model of Functional Competency: Examples of Tasks				
Elementary School				
	Consumer Economics	Occupational Knowledge	Health	Community Resources	Government and Law
Reading	Look for ads in the newspaper for toys.	Read books from library on various occupations.	Read the school lunch menu.	Find television listing in the *TV Guide*.	Read road signs and understand what they mean.
Writing	Write prices of items to be purchased.	Write the specific tasks involved in performing one of the classroom jobs.	Keep a diary of food you eat in each food group each day.	Complete an application to play on a little league team.	Write a letter to the mayor inviting him/her to visit your school.
Speaking, Writing, Viewing	Listen to bank official talk about savings accounts.	Call newspaper in town to inquire about delivering papers in your neighborhood.	View a film on brushing teeth.	Practice the use of the 911 emergency number.	Discuss park playground improvements with the mayor.
Problem Solving	Decide if you have enough coins to make a purchase from a vending machine.	Decide which job in the classroom you do best.	Role-play what you should do if you have a stomachache.	Role-play the times you would use the 911 emergency number.	Find the city hall on the map. Decide whether you will walk or drive.
Interpersonal Relations	Ask for help finding items in a grocery store.	Ask a student in the class to assist you with a classroom job.	Ask the school nurse how to take care of mosquito bites.	Call the movie theater and ask the show times of a movie.	Role-play asking a policeman for help if lost.
Computation	Compute the cost of a box of cereal using a coupon.	Calculate how much you would make on a paper route at $3 per hour for 5 hours per week.	Compute the price of one tube of toothpaste if they are on sale at 3 for $1.	Compute the complete cost of going to the movie (adm., food, transp.).	Compute tax on a candy bar.

Figure 13.1   **Life Skills in the Elementary School Curriculum**
Source: Patton, J. R., Cronin, M. E., Polloway, E. A., Hutchison, D. R., & Robinson, G. A. (1989). Curricular considerations: A life skills orientation. In G. A. Robinson, J. R. Patton, E. A. Polloway, & L. Sargent (Eds.), *Best practices in mild mental retardation* (p. 31). Reston, VA: CEC-MR. Used with permission.

sense of the physical layout, the changing of classes, and specific environmental and pedagogical factors (Jaquish & Stella, 1986). Additionally, there is clearly a need for cooperative planning and follow-up.

| Science Sub-topics | Science Activities | Related Subject/Skill Areas | | | | | |
		Math	Social Studies	Arts	Computer Application	Life Skills	Language Arts
Introductory Lesson	• Attraction of ants • Collection • Observation • Research ant anatomy	• Measurement of distance traveled as a function of time	• Relationship of population demographics for ants and humans	• Drawings of ant anatomy • Ant mobiles • Creative exploration	• Graphic drawings of ants	• Picnic planning • Food storage protection	• Oral sharing of observations
Ant Farms	• Individual set-ups • Daily observation • Development of collection procedures	• Linear measurement • Frequency counts	• Roles in the community • Relationship to human situations	• Diagram of farm • Diorama • Ant models • Role-playing of ant behavior	• Spreadsheets for calculations • Graphing • Data base storing observations	• Relate to engineers, architects, sociologists, geographers	• Library skills • Creative writing • Spelling • Research involving notetaking, outlining, and reading • Vocabulary development • Oral reports
Food Preferences Chart	• Research and predict • Construct apparatus for determining preference • Design data collection procedures • Collect/record data • Experiment with food substance positions	• Frequency counts • Graphs of daily results	• Discussion of human food preferences • Cultural differences	• Design data collection forms • Role-play ant eating behavior		• Graphic designer • Food services • Researchers	
Ant Races	• Conduct races with and without food • Data collection • Predictive activities	• Temporal measurement • Averages	• History of racing • Sports and competition	• Film making • Rewrite lyrics to "The Ants Go Marching In" based on activities	• Graphic animation	• Athletics • Coaches	
Closing	• Analyze information	• Tabulate data		• Finalize visual aids	• Print out	• Guest speakers	• Presentation

Figure 13.2 **Integrated Curriculum**

Source: Kataoka, J. C., & Patton, J. R. (1989). Integrated curriculum. *Science and Children, 16,* 52-58. Reprinted with permission from NSTA Publications, copyright 1989 from *Science and Children,* National Science Teachers Association, 1840 Wilson Boulevard, Arlington, VA 22201-3000. Used with permission.

Cooperative/Collaborative Teaching

Cooperative, or collaborative, teaching can be defined as "an educational approach in which general and special educators work in a coactive and coordinated fashion to jointly teach academically and behaviorally heterogeneous groups of students in educationally integrated settings" (Bauwens, Hourcade, & Friend, 1989, p. 18). It represents a logical outgrowth of collaborative efforts between teachers that has its roots in consultative arrangements, additional help given by special education teachers to nonidentified children, and the sharing of teaching assistants, especially to accompany students who are disabled in the general education classroom. It has particular relevance at the primary and elementary levels because curricular needs for students with and without disabilities tend to be most congruent at these levels.

Cooperative teaching involves a team approach to supporting students within the general classroom by offering the content expertise of the classroom/subject teacher combined with certain pedagogical skills of the special education teachers.

In many ways, cooperative teaching can be considered the essence of the movement toward prereferral interventions discussed in Chapter 2 because it establishes a vehicle for prevention and correction of learning problems in addition to an alterna-

Collaborative teaching with special and general educators works well in elementary classrooms.

Effective Teachers Integrate Subject Matter

When a topic is introduced in reading, it can be extended by integrating it into the other areas of the curriculum. With a little imagination, a topic could be the feature of the day, week, or even month. Some suggestions to extend the topic of "bears" are:

Listening.   After asking the students to listen for specific information, the teacher could read a story about bears. The students would then give the information they had learned.

Speaking.   While students look at the wordless picture book *Deep in the Forest* (Turkle, 1976), they could tell the story of the little bear who finds himself in Goldilocks's place. Talk about the meaning of terms such as "bear hug" or "hungry as a bear."

Writing.   Have students write the story of "Goldilocks and the Three Bears" in their own words or write a new ending to the same story. Other students could write a report about different kinds of bears.

Study Skills.   Students could use the card catalog in the library to look up other books about bears or make a bibliography of books in the classroom that are about bears.

Mathematics.   Have students answer story problems about bears.

Social Studies.   Students could study how the expansion of man has affected the bear population and in what areas of the world bears live today.

Science.   What hibernation is, how bears prepare to hibernate, and other animals that hibernate could be studied.

Art.   Bear puppets could be constructed. Bears could be drawn or painted using a wide variety of materials.

Music.   Songs about bears could be sung. Students could make up their own songs about bears.

Physical Education.   Bears could be utilized in any number of activities, such as tossing a ball or bean bag at a bear or running a relay race in which students pass a bear, instead of a baton, to the next runner.

Source: Mandlebaum, L. H. (1989). Reading. In J. R. Patton, E. A. Polloway, & L. R. Sargent, (Eds.), *Best practices in mild mental retardation*. Reston, VA: CEC-DMR (pp. 102–103). Used with permission.

tive vehicle for the remediation of identified deficits. It can be an excellent vehicle for providing general classroom support for students with disabilities as well as other students experiencing learning difficulties.

Although cooperative teaching can be implemented in varied forms, it basically involves special education teachers joining their colleagues in general education classes, typically for several periods per day. Given the curricular congruence for elementary-aged students with and without disabilities, it holds great promise for implementation at this level. Bauwens et al. (1989) discussed three somewhat distinct but nevertheless related forms of cooperative teaching: complementary instruction, **team teaching,** and supportive learning activities.

Team teaching involves the general and special education teacher planning one lesson jointly and teaching it to students with and without disabilities. Sometimes each teacher may be responsible for one aspect of the teaching.

In *supportive learning activities* the general and special educator plan and teach the lesson to the whole class. The general educator's responsibility is to deliver the main content; the special educator plans and implements activities that reinforce the learning of the content material.

Wiedemeyer and Lehman (1991, pp. 7–8) outlined key features of a collaborative instructional model, inclusive of cooperative teaching, which (as adapted) include the following functions to be shared by general and special education teachers:

1. Collaborative teaching
    a. Sharing in planning, presenting, and checking assignments
    b. Curriculum adaptation to meet needs of those with unique learning needs
    c. Incorporation of joint input into IEPs for shared students
    d. Participation in parent conferences
2. Monitoring of students
    a. Checking for attending behaviors
    b. Checking for note taking and writing down of assignments
    c. In-class individual or small-group tutoring
    d. Supplementary note taking
    e. Checking for appropriate use of in-class study time
3. Developing units in social, problem-solving, or study skills, especially as required by students experiencing difficulty
4. Sharing of materials and expertise in programming
5. Developing materials at a lower level
6. Providing generalization opportunities and activities
7. Sharing special instructional techniques and strategies

Although it is most often discussed regarding students with mild disabilities, cooperative teaching, or **"supported education"** (a school-based equivalent of "supported employment") as it is referred to in some circles, has also been recommended for students with more severe disabilities as a component of a program of full inclusion. Hamre-Nietupski, McDonald, and Nietupski (1992) provide a detailed discussion of how to modify programs to respond to four key challenges to the success of such a program: providing a functional curriculum in the general education class, providing community-based learning opportunities, scheduling staff coverage, and promoting social integration.

Community-based instruction is needed because of generalization problems. Curriculum guides that emphasize or include community-based instruction should be used. Teachers can bring resources from the community to the classroom or let students with disabilities visit community resources with groups of their peers who are not disabled. At the elementary level, such opportunities promote career awareness and help overcome problems that students have with generalization.

To promote *social integration,* emphasis must be placed on developing friendships between peers with and without disabilities. Teachers can pair different students for different activities, modeling and encouraging socialization. Support teachers and special education teachers can also model interactions. Formal lessons can be developed that encourage students to talk about their similarities and differences.

Social skills of students with severe disabilities will not develop by just placing them in the inclusive settings. McEnvoy, Shores, Wehby, Johnson, and Fox's (1990) review of the literature on inclusion revealed three main factors influencing successful inclusion: attitudes of peers, organization of the classroom environment, and the use of specific teacher prompts for interaction and contingent teacher praise. McEnvoy et al. (1990) reported that the more instruction, physical prompts, modeling, and praise provided by teachers, the more social interaction skills students were able to develop.

Listening skills can be taught to students with attention problems.

Cooperative teaching is clearly not a simple panacea for the successful accommodation of students with disabilities in the general education classroom, and obviously the challenges that it creates are magnified as the diversity of the students within the elementary classroom increases. As Bauwens et al. (1989) reported, three obstacles or barriers in particular have been identified as critical to successful implementation: time, cooperation with others, and workload. *Time* problems must be alleviated through careful planning of scheduled discussions on teaching and/or through released time support from administrators. The issue of *cooperation* is best addressed through training in the use of cooperative teaching, experience with the process, and the development of guidelines specific to the program. Finally, the concern for *workload* is addressed as the team relationship develops to incorporate each individual's area of expertise as well as interests. Finally, a fourth critical issue, not addressed by Bauwens et al., is the *voluntary nature* of the program. There is little question that decrees of team teaching arrangements without regard to key input from the teachers themselves will secure no positive purpose for the teachers or ultimately for the students.

Instructional Considerations

The keys to successful inclusion are the modifications and accommodations that can be made to instructional programs in the general education classroom. As the traditional adage goes, "Special education is not necessarily special, it is just *good teaching.*" For successful achievement by students with disabilities in inclusive settings, "good teaching" often means appropriate modifications and accommodations. Assuming the curricular content is appropriate for individual students who are disabled, the challenge is to adapt it as necessary to facilitate learning.

Cheney (1989) suggested that modifications should address three general matches: the level of achievement of the student and the level of the instructional material, the characteristics of the learner and the response modes required by the material or technique, and the motivational aspects of the learner and of the material. To address the issue of "making the match," teachers should informally assess their instructional program to ensure that students in general, and those with disabilities in particular, are learning at a satisfactory level.

In a related vein, Cohen (1990) conceptualized modifications as consisting of attention to content, environment, and instruction through approaches that may be seen as teacher-, peer-, and self-mediated (see Figure 13.3). That is, adaptations can be considered at least these nine ways, and the teacher should consider varied options in designing programs. For example, a *self-mediated-instruction* adaptation would be the use of self-monitoring procedures for increasing attention, which are discussed later in the chapter.

Hoover (1990) provided a useful procedural model for curriculum modification. His five-step process for the adaptation process is presented in Figure 13.4. This model outlines the specific steps through which a teacher can systematically ascertain the need for changes and the specific areas that will be effective in a given situation. These models should be kept in mind when considering possible modifications to be made.

Principles for Individualized Teaching

- Teach individually during the acquisition stage of learning.

- Group students together who need to acquire the skill. Others students should be working on proficiency or maintenance of previously acquired skills.

- Keep the acquisition group flexible. Move students in who are ready to acquire the skill and move students out who are ready to develop proficiency.

- Divide acquisition teaching time equally among all students in order to ensure equity.

- Keep "problem" students close to you to better ensure contact.

- Use simple and consistent verbal directions.

- Use plenty of demonstration and provide models.

- Don't just show and tell; have students demonstrate the skill being learned.

- Make sure every student is actively involved during practice of the skill being acquired.

- Make sure all students are attentive. You might ask students what you just said or ask them what other students just said or did.

- Make sure students can demonstrate the skill consistently before moving them to the proficiency learning activities.

Source: Westling, D. L., & Koorland, M. A. (1989). *The special educator's handbook* (p. 27). Boston: Allyn & Bacon. Used with permission.

Following is a discussion of modifications and accommodations to be made for students with disabilities in elementary classes. These vary significantly in terms of their nature and particularly in terms of their "treatment acceptability"—that is, the ease with which they can be implemented (Reynolds & Salend, 1990). The authors do not intend to suggest that all of these suggestions may be appropriate or even desirable in a given situation. Teachers will need to determine how far they wish to go in making specific adaptations. However, it is worth noting that many of the suggested modifications will prove beneficial to far more students than just those for whom they may have been initially intended (i.e., those with disabilities).

Enhancing Content Learning Through Listening

Wallace, Cohen, and Polloway (1987) argued that children will not necessarily listen simply because they are told to do so. Rather, they often will need to have oral pre-

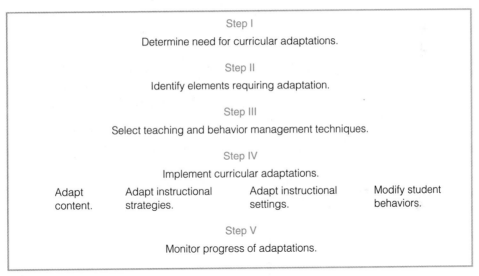

	Content	Environment	Instruction
Teacher-Mediated			
Peer-Mediated			
Self-Mediated			

Figure 13.3   **Curricular Modification: Teacher Decision Making**
Source: Cohen, S. B. (1990). A modification perspective of special education curriculum: Introduction. *Academic Therapy, 25,* 393. Used with permission.

Step I

Determine need for curricular adaptations.

Step II

Identify elements requiring adaptation.

Step III

Select teaching and behavior management techniques.

Step IV

Implement curricular adaptations.

| Adapt content. | Adapt instructional strategies. | Adapt instructional settings. | Modify student behaviors. |

Step V

Monitor progress of adaptations.

Figure 13.4   **Curriculum Adaptation Process**
Source: Hoover, J. J. (1990). Curriculum adaptation: A five step process for classroom implementation. *Academic Therapy, 25,* 409. Used with permission.

sentations provided in ways that promote successful listening. For students who struggle with *selective attention* (i.e., focus) and/or *sustained attention* (i.e., maintained over a period of time), it becomes increasingly important that teachers consider those elements of speaking which support the listener. Wallace, Cohen, and Polloway (1987, p. 75) indicated that listeners attend more when

  ◆ The salience of elements is increased such as through repetition, vocal emphasis, and so forth

- The oral message is meaningful, logical, and organized
- Messages are given in short units
- The speaker can be clearly heard and understood
- The speaker allows for listener participation in the form of clarification, feedback, responding, or other active strategies
- The speaker has focused attention by telling the child to listen or by stating how the message will be of importance to the listener
- Reinforcement for attending is given in the form of participation, praise, or increased ability to perform a task
- Oral presentations are accompanied by visual aids that emphasize important points
- The listener feels comfortable within the environment and has a positive attitude toward the speaker and the subsequent interaction
- The listener knows there will be an opportunity to reflect upon and integrate the message before having to formulate a response

A complement to these considerations is to develop strategies to build listening skills. A variety of techniques can be effective in enhancing listening. Mandlebaum and Wilson (1989, pp. 451–452), reviewing the literature on this topic, suggested that teachers select from the following techniques:

1. Provide students with direct instruction in listening strategies.
2. Establish a goal for the lesson so that students will know what is expected.
3. Plan listening lessons so that students are actively involved with the information they have learned.
4. Plan purposeful listening activities that relate to other curriculum areas.
5. Make messages logical and well organized, repeating important information.
6. Give information in short segments.
7. Following a listening activity, ask questions that require more than simply recalling facts.
8. Act as a model of listening behavior, use peer models, and have students self-monitor their listening behavior.
9. Involve students in rehearsing, summarizing, and taking notes of the information to be learned.
10. Practice nonverbal messages that speakers give and engage students in role-playing activities.
11. Use verbal, pictorial, or written advance organizers before lessons begin to cue students when to listen for important information.
12. Provide prompts that notify students that the information about to be presented is important enough to remember or write down.
13. Teach students to attend to teacher cues that denote important information.
14. Before beginning a listening activity, review the rules for good listening behavior (e.g., sitting quietly, not getting up and moving around, paying close attention to the story).

15. Involve students in a wide variety of listening activities that relate to the skills that they will need outside the school environment.
16. Use teacher questions and prompts to cue students to respond (e.g., "Tell me more").
17. Teach students to use a self-questioning technique while listening.
18. Teach students to use visual imagery while listening.

One way to develop good listening skills that is worthy of further elaboration is through the use of *guided listening*. As Wallace et al. (1987) noted, this procedure has as its goal an increase in long-term retention. It can be appropriately used every few weeks. After a 10- to 15-minute speech is presented (by tape or lecture), the teacher leads the class through the following steps:

1. The teacher sets the major purpose (e.g., "Listen to remember everything").
2. The teacher lectures, reads, or plays a recorded selection. If the teacher is lecturing, she records her lecture.
3. The teacher reminds the students that she asked them to listen to remember everything and lists what they remember on the board. (She may have two students perform this task.) During this stage, the teacher accepts and writes everything the students contribute. She makes no corrections and asks no questions.
4. The teacher reads everything listed on the board, directing the students to look for incorrect or missing information.
5. The students listen again to the tape, record, or reading to correct wrong information and obtain missing information.
6. The information on the board is amended and added to as needed.
7. The teacher asks the students which ideas on the board seem to be the main ideas, the most important ideas, the ones they think they should remember for a long time. She marks these items.
8. Now that the students have mastered the literal level of the selections, the teacher raises any inferential questions she feels are vital for complete understanding.
9. The teacher erases the board and tests short-term memory with a test that is not dependent on reading or writing skills. (Oral true-false or multiple-choice items will do.)
10. Long-term memory should then be assessed with a similar test containing different items several weeks later (Manzo, 1975, pp. 302–303).

Modifying Oral Presentations

A key accommodation to facilitate the success of students with disabilities is for teachers to consider effective vehicles for the presentation of content. As with any accommodations, such changes often will prove to be of benefit to students in general. Some specific considerations are as follows (adapted from Chalmers, 1991; Cheney, 1989; Dowdy, 1990; McDevitt, 1990):

- When mastery of prior content is not assured, use concrete concepts before teaching abstractions.
- Relate information to be presented to the students' experiential base.
- Provide students with an overview before beginning the lesson.
- Reduce the number of concepts introduced at a given time.
- Encourage children to detect errors in messages and report what they could not understand.
- Monitor the language level used to ensure that vocabulary and complex sentence structures are understood. Avoid puns, idioms, and metaphors unless clear explanations are provided.
- Provide consistent review of lessons before subsequent content is introduced.
- Lessen distractions within the learning environment.
- Adjust pace as needed.
- Keep oral directions short and direct and supplement with written directions as needed.
- Provide follow-up presentations, which may include repetition, review, more complete explanations, additional examples, or the modeling of skills in varied ways.
- Provide further guided practice by requiring more responses, lengthening practice sessions, or scheduling extra practice sessions.
- Clarify directions for homework and other follow-up activities so that they are understood and tasks can successfully be completed.

Learning from classroom presentations is obviously critical to academic achievement. For students in the primary grades, instruction is generally not focused primarily on teacher oral presentation of content at length. However, as lecturing begins to become more common in the upper elementary grades, and particularly in the middle school, students will need to develop note-taking skills. Although the teaching of note-taking skills as a learning strategy is a task frequently undertaken as part of a general education support program initiated by resource teachers, often the critical element is how that content is presented by the teacher. The following pointers on ways to facilitate both note taking and learning are adapted from Beirne-Smith (1989). Since they coincide to some degree with the themes of listening and modifying presentations discussed earlier, there are naturally areas of overlap.

1. *Organize your lecture.*
2. *Use key words and phrases,* such as "first," or "the main theme."
3. *Summarize ideas.*
4. *Repeat important statements* to cue the importance of the statement.
5. *Pause occasionally* to allow students time to fill in blank spaces or catch up to the previous statement.
6. *Provide advance organizers* (e.g., topic outlines or partially completed notes) to assist the student in organizing and recording information.
7. *Write important points on the board.*

8. *Simplify transparencies* because too much information is confusing and less likely to be recorded.
9. *Encourage students to record all visually presented material* exactly as displayed and to leave space between main sections for questions to be made on the material.
10. *Use humor or anecdotes* to illustrate important points.
11. *Model note-taking skills* (e.g., with the overhead projector).
12. *Observe students* during note taking and adjust the pace of your lecture.

Adapting Reading Tasks

In many instances, instructional tasks, assignments, or materials being used in the classroom may be relevant and quite appropriate for students with disabilities but may be problematic because of reading demands that hinder appropriate student responding. Teachers should therefore consider some options that can be helpful in accommodating particular learner difficulties through the modification of the task or the materials. The following suggestions (adapted from Chalmers, 1991; Cheney, 1989; Dowdy, 1990; Hoover, 1990; Reynolds & Salend, 1990; Schumm & Strickler, 1991) address problems that may arise in processing reading content.

◆ Establish a purpose for all reading assignments.
◆ When discussing stories, paraphrase material to clarify content.
◆ Highlight key words and phrases (e.g., color coding) and concepts (e.g., outlines, study guides).
◆ Encourage feedback from students to check for understanding.
◆ Preview reading material to assist students in establishing purpose, activating prior knowledge, budgeting time, and focusing attention.
◆ Create vocabulary lists and preteach these words before the lesson to ensure that students can use this vocabulary rather than just recognize it.
◆ Provide page numbers where specific answers can be found in a reading comprehension/content assignment.
◆ Use brief individual conferences with students to verify comprehension.
◆ Reduce extraneous noise.
◆ Ensure that the readability levels of the textbooks and trade books used in class are commensurate with the student's language level.
◆ Locate lower-level supplements in the same topic so that tasks can be adapted to be multilevel, and multimaterial.
◆ Tape text reading or have it read orally to a student. Consider the use of peers, volunteers, and/or paraprofessionals in this process.
◆ Rewrite (or solicit staff or volunteers to do so) material to simplify its reading level, or provide chapter outlines or summaries.
◆ Utilize visual aids (e.g., charts, graphs) to supplement reading tasks.
◆ Demonstrate how new content to be learned relates to content previously learned.

Enhancing Written Responding

The modifications noted here (adapted from Chalmers, 1991; Cheney, 1989; and Dowdy, 1990), may assist students who may have difficulty with responding in written form. In this case, the task adaptations are related not to the presentation of the stimulus but rather to the required responses implicit in the task or assignment.

- ◆ Avoid large amounts of written work (both in class and homework).
- ◆ When appropriate, allow children to select the most comfortable method of writing (i.e., cursive or manuscript).
- ◆ Change the response mode to oral as appropriate.
- ◆ Set realistic, mutually agreed upon expectations for neatness.
- ◆ Allow children to circle or underline responses rather than writing them.
- ◆ Let students type or tape record answers instead of giving them in writing.
- ◆ Fasten materials to the desk to alleviate coordination problems.
- ◆ Provide the student with a copy of lecture notes produced by the teacher or a peer.
- ◆ Reduce amounts of board copying and/or text copying; provide children with the written information itself or with an outline of key content.
- ◆ Allow sufficient space for answering problems.
- ◆ Allow group written responding (via projects or reports; see "Cooperative Learning" below).

Involving Peers: Cooperative Learning

An increasingly popular intervention in the classroom is cooperative learning. This approach has been promoted as a means of facilitating the inclusion of students with disabilities into general education classrooms. It can be defined as classroom techniques that involve students in group learning activities with recognition and reinforcement based on group performance (Johnson & Johnson, 1981; Slavin, 1987). The key feature is that the individual student's success directly affects the success of other students (Slavin, 1987).

A number of specific strategies have been identified with cooperative learning. According to Slavin (1987) and Schniedewind and Salend (1987), a variety of formats can be used to implement cooperative learning. These include **peer teaching,** group projects, the **jigsaw technique,** and student-teams achievement division.

Peer teaching or peer tutoring is a relatively easy system of cooperative learning to manage. It is an approach that can benefit both the student being tutored and the individual providing the tutoring. Cooke, Heron, and Heward (1983) developed an excellent guide for peer tutoring in the primary grades that involves a reciprocal relationship so that all students can be both tutor and tutee. Their book should be consulted for detailed information on implementation.

A variety of specific activities fall under the concept of peer tutoring. Some examples to consider are reviewing task directions, drill and practice, recording material dictated by a peer, modeling of acceptable or appropriate responses, and providing pretest practice (such as in spelling). Cooke et al. (1983) summarize the advantages of such peer tutoring (beyond peer availability) as follows:

> First, they can be highly effective tutors. Research clearly indicates that children can effectively teach each other skills. These gains are optimized when the peer tutoring program is highly structured, when there is an emphasis on repetition, when learning reaches mastery levels before the tutee advances, when a review system is incorporated, and when tutors are trained. Second, tutors benefit academically from teaching skills to a peer. Third, with a peer tutoring program, both the content and pairs can be individualized to meet each student's needs. Fourth, peer tutoring allows for intensive one-to-one instruction without requiring the rest of the class to work on "independent seat work." Fifth, one-to-one instruction can substantially increase the number of opportunities a child has to give correct responses and receive immediate feedback on those responses. Sixth, peer tutoring is an excellent tool for successfully mainstreaming handicapped students into the regular classroom for academic instruction. Finally, both handicapped and regular education students can be taught valuable social skills through a structured and positive peer tutoring program. (p. 2)

Group projects are intended to provide an opportunity for students to pool their knowledge and skills to complete an assignment. The task is assigned to the entire group, with the goal being to develop a single product reflecting the contributions shared by all members of the group. For example, in art, a collage is a good example of what could be completed as a group project. In social studies, a report on one of the fifty states might involve individual students responsible respectively for drawing a map, sketching the history, collecting photos of scenic attractions, and developing a display of products from that state. With group projects, as with other cooperative groups, the establishment of groups by matching high, average, and low achievers and perhaps through the use of a sociogram can be effective (Peck, 1989).

The *jigsaw* format involves giving all students in a group individual tasks to be completed before the group can reach its goal. For example, Salend (1990) discussed an assignment related to the life of Dr. Martin Luther King, Jr. in which each student was given a segment of his life to research. The students then had to teach others in their group the information from the segment on which they had become experts.

The concept of *student-team achievement divisions* (STAD) is to assign students to diversely constituted teams (typically four persons to a group), which then meet together to review specific teacher-generated lessons. The teams work together toward content mastery, at which time all students take quizzes individually without assisting each other. As Slavin (1987) noted, STAD embraces three concepts central to successful team learning methods: team rewards, individual accountability, and equal opportunities for success. *Team rewards* derive from content learning by members, who are then assessed by team scores across individual scores. *Individual accountability* comes from commitment to tutoring and learning, since all must learn the content for the team to be successful. *Equal opportunities for success* come by focusing on degree of improvement in scores on the individual's own paper.

In addition to these formats, other formats that promote cooperative learning are also available. According to Slavin (1987), these include *Teams-Games-Tourna-*

Computer Applications Facilitating Special Education Teachers' Instructional Productivity

Stage	Description	Related Topics and Strategies
Planning	Using microcomputers to assist in the outlining of instructional intervention and strategies	Assessing student abilities and learning difficulties; identifying software sources that enhance instructional objectives; using computer lesson plans
Preparing	Using microcomputers to facilitate the production of print and electronic instructional materials	Utilities that create worksheets, certificates, flashcards, etc.; using authoring systems to create on-line lessons
Managing	Ways to consider using microcomputers to conduct and manage instruction; strategies that facilitate and manage student behavior and interests during computer-based learning activities	Time management of classroom-based and lab-based computers; monitoring students' computer performance; effective feedback and praise relative to computer work
Extending	Using existing technology and software creatively and effectively for additional instructional impact	Review and maintenance of skills; repurposing software; remaining current with teaching/practice-oriented literature on technology; using learner-centered software

Source: Gardner, J. E., & Edyburn, D. L. (1993). Teaching applications with exceptional individuals. In Lindsey, J. D. (Ed.), *Computers and exceptional individuals* (p. 274). Austin, TX: Pro-Ed. Used with permission.

ments (similar to STAD with weekly tournaments versus quizzes), *Team Assisted Individualization* (which combines cooperative learning with individualized instruction in the area of mathematics), and *Cooperative Reading and Composition* (which establishes teams to promote reading activities and development of team composition books; see Slavin, Stevens, & Madden, 1988).

Modifying the Temporal Environment

Time is frequently a critical element that must be addressed in terms of classroom modifications. For many students with disabilities, modifications in time constraints can be of great assistance in promoting success. At the same time, when handled properly, these modifications need not impinge on the integrity of the assignments nor present undue burdens to the teacher. Some suggestions (from Chalmers, 1991; Dowdy, 1990; Guernsey, 1989; Polloway, Patton, Epstein, & Smith, 1989) follow:

- ◆ Develop schedules that balance routines with novelty to establish predictability and to sustain excitement, respectively.

◆ Review class schedules with students to establish routines.

◆ Provide individual students with a copy of the schedule.

◆ Increase the amount of time allowed to complete assignments/tests.

◆ Contract with students concerning time allotment and tie reinforcement to a reasonable schedule of completion.

◆ Consider reducing the amount of work or the length of tests as opposed to simply allowing more time for completion (e.g., complete every other math problem).

◆ Allow extra time for practice for students who understand content but need additional time to achieve mastery.

◆ Adjust homework assignments (e.g., the number of math problems or the total length of a reading assignment) to produce equity in time engaged.

◆ Teach time-management skills (use of timeline, checklists, and prioritizing time and assignments).

◆ Space short work periods with breaks or change of task (thus using the Premack principle for scheduling—making high-probability, desired events contingent on completion of low-probability, less desired events).

Modifying the Classroom Arrangement

Changes in the classroom arrangement can also be helpful in accommodating students with special needs. Some specific examples (from Cheney, 1989; Dowdy, 1990; Guernsey, 1989; Hoover, 1990; and Minner & Pater, 1989) are listed next.

◆ Establish a climate which fosters positive social interactions between students.

◆ Develop a schedule and routine that maximizes time on-task.

◆ Balance structure, organization, and regimentation with (as appropriate) freedom, exploration, and permissiveness.

◆ Use study carrels.

◆ Locate student seats and learning activities free from distractions.

◆ Allow students to select their own seat in a place that is best for them to work and study and be near friends (as long as work is subsequently completed).

◆ Help students keep their work spaces free of unnecessary materials.

◆ Arrange materials in the class based on frequency of use.

◆ Provide opportunities for approved movement within the class.

◆ Arrange furniture to facilitate proximity.

◆ Establish high-frequency and low-frequency areas for class work (thus using the Premack principle for class arrangement). Space can be set aside for group work, individual seatwork, and free-time activities.

Enhancing Motivation

For many students, school activities may appear irrelevant or uninteresting. Although this concern becomes more problematic at the secondary level, it is critical that young students be taught in a way that prevents subsequent motivational problems. Motivation can be enhanced through attention to both the motivational qualities of the material and the characteristics of the student (Cheney, 1989). Techniques for enhancing motivation (adapted from Cheney, 1989, p. 29) include the following:

- Have students set personal goals and graph progress.
- Use timed tests and encourage students to "beat the clock."
- Use contingency contracts so that a given amount of work at an agreed degree of accuracy earns students a desired activity or privilege.
- Allow students to choose where to work, what tools to use, what to do first, and who to sit by, as long as academic work is being completed.
- Incorporate drill-and-practice into a game format.
- Provide immediate feedback (e.g., through teacher monitoring or self-correcting materials) on the correctness of work.
- Allow extra credit for bonus work.
- Camouflage instructional materials that may be at a lower instructional level (using folders, covers).
- Use high-status materials for instructional activities (magazines, catalogues, newspapers, checkbooks, drivers' manuals).
- Allow students to earn points or tokens to exchange for a valued activity or privilege.
- Provide experiences that ensure success and provide feedback when students are successful.

Promoting Self-Management

An obvious challenge that ensues from any inclusion efforts is to maintain classroom discipline and ensure student motivation. As the diversity within a class increases, the task of management can also increase significantly. Although the full topic of classroom and behavior management is well beyond the scope of this chapter, we focus specifically on the area of self-regulation as a tool for enhancing classroom management. As Markel (1981) noted, self-management programs provide promise for successfully including students with disabilities into the classroom, particularly because research supports the fact that such "strategies have been effective in increasing various task behaviors in special and regular classrooms, [and] they appear to be as effective as similar externally imposed procedures and hold the promise of generalizing across settings" (p. 165). She listed the following examples of self-management strategies: self-instruction, problem solving, self-selection of objectives, self-determination of criteria, self-observation, self-monitoring/recording and evaluation, self-reinforcement and contracting, and self-punishment.

Developing Responsive Grading Practices

The assignment of grades is an integral and somewhat controversial aspect of education. As Hess, Miller, Reese, and Robinson (1987) indicated, "Grading is an important aspect of documenting the educational experience of students [and thus] assignment of grades has created and will continue to create debate within the educational community" (p. 1). Thus, grading practices have been subjected to frequent evaluation and review. Issues that arise from the grading of students with special needs can be particularly problematic.

Grading issues received relatively scant attention prior to the advent of the reform movement and the increased inclusion of students with disabilities in general education classes (Lindsey, Burns, & Guthrie, 1984). More recently, a series of research papers has addressed some aspects of grading (e.g., Donohue & Zigmond, 1990; Zigmond, Levin, & Laurie, 1985; Valdes et al., 1990). However, these studies have primarily focused on secondary school practices. The suggestions that follow derive more from best judgments about grading than from empirically validated practices. Polloway and Patton (1993) suggested a series of considerations from which the following are adapted:

◆ Keep the lines of communication open so that special and general education teachers meet on a regular basis to discuss student progress.
◆ Consider effort as a basic criterion central to grade assignment.
◆ Emphasize the acquisition of new skills as a basis for grades assigned, thus providing a perspective on the student's relative gains. Charting progress may help illustrate these gains.
◆ Investigate alternative procedures for evaluating content taught (e.g., evaluation via oral examinations for poor readers in a science class).
◆ Whenever possible, engage in cooperative grading agreements (e.g., grades for language arts might reflect both classroom and reading performance in the resource room).
◆ Consider the use of narrative reports as a key portion of the report card, especially for younger children. These reports can be complemented by comments on specific target behaviors related to a student's IEP.

Adaptive Instruction

We conclude with mention of a comprehensive program that seeks to provide instructional modifications and support to students with disabilities in integrated settings. The Adaptive Learning Environments Model (ALEM) (Wang & Zollers, 1990) is an example of adaptive instruction for teaching students with and without disabilities in the general education classroom. ALEM provides a structure for an inclusion program for students with mild or moderate disabilities. One of its main objectives is to provide direct teaching and related services to help students acquire basic academic skills while developing a positive self-image, social and intellectual competence, a sense of responsibility for their education, and practical competence for dealing with academic and social requirements in school. ALEM provides a highly structured basic skills mastery progress plan for each student, while the social skills, personal development, and basic skills enrichment components are exploratory. The program uses diagnostic-prescriptive assessments that use both curriculum-based and criterion-referenced measurements to monitor progress. The interested reader may wish to review the program further by referring to the reports by Wang and colleagues (e.g., Wang & Zollers, 1990).

Summary

◆ The curriculum for elementary students who have disabilities should meet their current and long-term needs, facilitate their interaction with nondisabled peers, and be related to the transition into middle school.

◆ Reading instruction for young students should draw elements from both direct instruction and whole-language approaches to provide a comprehensive, balanced program.

◆ Math instruction should provide students with concrete and abstract learning opportunities and should stress the development of problem-solving skills.

◆ A variety of approaches has been advanced for developing social competence. Teachers should select programs and strategies that focus on skills most needed by students in their classrooms.

◆ Life skills instruction should be a part of the elementary curriculum through the use of augmentation, infusion, and/or integrated curricula.

◆ Cooperative teaching involves a team approach where general and special education teachers share their talents in providing class instruction along with supports to students with disabilities.

◆ Cooperative teaching requires a commitment to planning, time, and administrative support to reach its potential for success.

◆ Instructional modifications should be evaluated against their "treatment acceptability"—that is, the ease with which they can be implemented (Reynolds & Salend, 1990).

◆ Listening is a skill that requires of many students conscious effort and, of teachers, planned intervention strategies.

◆ Reading tasks can be adapted by a variety of instructional strategies such as clarifying intent, highlighting content, modifying difficulty level, and using visual aids.

◆ Written responding can be facilitated through modifications in the nature of the task response requirements.

◆ Cooperative learning affords teachers a unique opportunity to involve students with disabilities in classroom activities. Options include peer teaching, group projects, and the jigsaw format.

◆ Modifications in class schedules and/or classroom arrangements should be considered as a basis for enhancing the learning of students with disabilities.

◆ Motivational aspects of learning cannot be taken for granted and should be programmed for.

◆ Classroom grading practices should be flexible enough to facilitate, rather than doom, integration efforts.

References

Adult Performance Level (APL) Project (1975). *Adult functional competency.* Austin: University of Texas, Office of Continuing Education.

Armstrong, D. G. (1990). *Developing and documenting the curriculum.* Boston: Allyn & Bacon.

Bauwens, J. (1991, March). *Cooperative teaching.* Presentation made at annual Iowa Best Practices in Special Education Conference in Cedar Rapids, IA.

Bauwens, J., Hourcade, J., & Friend, M. (1989). Cooperative teaching: A model for general and special education integration. *Remedial and Special Education, 10*(2), 17–22.

Beirne-Smith, M. (1989). A systematic approach for teaching notetaking skills to students with mild learning handicaps. *Academic Therapy, 24,* 425–437.

Cartledge, G., & Milburn, J. F. (1980). *Teaching skills to children: Innovative approaches.* New York: Pergamon Press.

Cawley, J. (1984). *Developmental teaching of mathematics for the learning disabled.* Austin, TX: Pro-Ed.

Chalmers, L. (1991). Classroom modifications for the mainstreamed student with mild handicaps. *Intervention in School and Clinic, 27,* 40–42.

Chiang, B., & Ford, M. (1990). Whole language alternatives for students with learning disabilities. *LD Forum, 16,* 31–33.

Cheney, C. O. (1989). The systematic adaptation of instructional materials and techniques for problem learners. *Academic Therapy, 25,* 25–30.

Cohen, S. B. (1990). A modification perspective of special education curriculum: Introduction. *Academic Therapy, 25*(4), 391–394.

Comfort, R. (1990). On the idea of curriculum modification by teachers. *Academic Therapy, 25,* 397-405.

Cooke, N. L., Heron, T. E., & Heward, W. L. (1983). *Peer tutoring: Implementing classroom wide programs.* Columbus, OH: Special Press.

Cronin, M. E. (1988). Adult performance outcomes/life skills. In G. Robinson, J. R. Patton, E. A. Polloway, & L. Sargent (Eds.), *Best practices in mental disabilities* (Vol. 2), pp. 39–52). Des Moines: Iowa State Department of Education.

Cullinan, D., & Epstein, M. (1985). Teacher related adjustment problems. *Remedial and Special Education, 6,* 5–11.

Daniels, J. L., & Wiederholt, J. L. (1986). Preparing problem learners for independent living. In D. D. Hammill & N. R. Bartel (Eds.), *Teaching students with learning and behavior problems* (4th ed., pp. 294–345). Austin: Pro-Ed.

Donohue, K., & Zigmond, N. (1990). Academic grades of ninth-grade students. *Exceptionality, 1,* 17–27.

Dowdy, C. (1990). *Modifications for regular classes.* Unpublished manuscript, Alabama Program for Exceptional Children.

Dunlap, L. K., Dunlap, G., Koegel, L., & Koegel, R. L. (1991). Using self-monitoring to increase independence. *Teaching Exceptional Children, 23*(3), 17–26.

Gardner, J. E., & Edyburn, D. L. (1993). Teaching applications with exceptional individuals. In J. D. Lindsey (Ed.), *Computers and exceptional individuals* (pp. 269–284). Austin, TX: Pro-Ed.

Gresham, F. M. (1982). Misguided mainstreaming: The case for social skills training with handicapped children. *Exceptional Children, 48,* 420–433.

Gresham, F. M. (1984). Social skills and self-efficacy for exceptional children. *Exceptional Children, 51,* 253–261.

Guernsey, M. A. (1989). Classroom organization: A key to successful management. *Academic Therapy, 25,* 55–58.

Hamre-Nietupski, S., McDonald, J., & Nietupski, J. (1992). Integrating elementary students with multiple disabilities into supported regular classes: Challenges and solutions. *Teaching Exceptional Children, 24,* 6–9.

Haring, N. G. (1988). Overview of special education. In N. G. Haring & L. McCormick (Eds.), *Exceptional children and youth* (4th ed.). Columbus, OH: Merrill.

Hess, R., Miller, A., Reese, J., & Robinson, G. (1987). *Grading-credit-diploma: Accomodation practices.* Des Moines, IA: Department of Education.

Hoover, J. J. (1988). *Curriculum adaptation for students with learning and behavior problems: Principles and practices.* Lindale, TX: Hamilton Publications.

Hoover, J. J. (1990). Curriculum adaptations: A five-step process for classroom implementation. *Academic Therapy, 25,* 407–416.

Jaquish, C., & Stella, M. A. (1986). Helping special students move from elementary to secondary school. *Counterpoint, 7*(1), 1.

Johnson, D. W., & Johnson, R. T. (1981). Organizing the school's social structure for mainstreaming. In P. Bates (Ed.), *Mainstreaming: Our current knowledge base* (pp. 141–160). Minneapolis: Minnesota University.

Journal for the Education of the Gifted [Special issue], 1990, *14*(1).

Kataoka, J. C., & Patton, J. R. (1989). Integrated curriculum. *Science and Children, 16,* 52–58.

Korinek, L., & Polloway, E. A. (1993). Social skills: Review and implications for instruction for students with mild mental retardation. In R. A. Gable & S. F. Warren (Eds.), *Advances in mental retardation and developmental disabilities* (Vol. 5, pp. 71–97). London: Jessica Kingsley Publishers.

LaQuey, A. (1981). *Adult performance level adaptation and modification project.* Austin, TX: Educational Service Center, Region XIII.

Lindsey, J. Burns, J., & Guthrie, T. D. (1984). Intervention grading and secondary students. *The High School Journal, 67,* 150–157.

McConnell, J. (1987). Entrapment effects and generalization. *Teaching Exceptional Children, 17,* 267–273.

McDevitt, T. M. (1990). Encouraging young children's listening. *Academic Therapy, 25,* 569–577.

McEnvoy, M. A., Shores, R. E., Wehby, J. H., Johnson, S. M., & Fox J. J. (1990). Special education teachers' implementation of procedures to promote social interaction among children in integrated settings. *Education and Training in Mental Retardation, 25,* 267–276.

Mack, C. (1988). Celebrate cultural diversity. *Teaching Exceptional Children, 21,* 40–43.

Mandlebaum, L. H. (1989). Reading. In J. R. Patton, E. A. Polloway, & L. R. Sargent (Eds.), *Best practices in mild retardation.* Reston, VA: CEC-MR.

Mandlebaum, L. H., & Wilson, R. (1989). Teaching listening skills in the special education classroom. *Academic Therapy, 24,* 449–459.

Manzo, A. V. (1975). Expansion modules for the ReQuest, CAT, GRP, and REAP reading study procedures. *Journal of Reading, 42,* 498–502.

Markel, G. (1981). Self-management in the classroom: Implications for mainstreaming. In P. Bates (Ed.), *Mainstreaming: Our current knowledge base* (pp. 161–183). Minneapolis: Minnesota University.

Masters, L. F., & Mori, A. A. (1986). *Teaching secondary students with mild learning and behavior problems.* Rockville, MD: Aspen.

Mather, N. (1992). Whole language reading instruction for students with learning disabilities: Caught in the crossfire. *Learning Disabilities Research and Practice, 7,* 87–95.

Miller, S. P., Mercer, C. D., & Dillon, A. S. (1992). CSA: Acquiring and retaining math skills. *Intervention in School and Clinic, 28,* 105–110.

Minner, S., & Prater, G. (1989). Arranging the physical environment of special education classrooms. *Academic Therapy, 25,* 91–96.

Nelson, N. W. (1988). Curriculum-based language assessment and intervention. *Language, Speech and Hearing Services in School, 20,* 170–183.

Patton, J. R. (1986). *Transition: Curricular implications.* Honolulu: Project Ho-ho-ko, University of Hawaii.

Patton, J. R., Cronin, M. E., Polloway, E. A., Hutchinson, D. R., & Robinson, G. A. (1989). Curricular considerations: A life skills orientation. In G. A. Robinson, J. R. Patton, E. A. Polloway, & L. Sargent (Eds.), *Best practices in mild mental retardation* (pp. 21–37). Reston, VA: CEC-MR.

Peck, G. (1989). Facilitating cooperative learning: A forgotten tool gets it started. *Academic Therapy, 25,* 145–150.

Polloway, E. A. (1984). Transition services for early age individuals with mild mental retardation. In R. Ianacone & R. Stodden (Eds.), *Transition issues and directions* (pp. 11–24). Reston, VA: CEC-MR.

Polloway, E. A., Epstein, M. H., & Cullinan, D. (1985). Prevalence of behavior problems among educable mentally retarded students. *Education and Training in Mental Retardation, 20,* 3–13.

Polloway, E. A., & Patton, J. R. (1993). *Strategies for teaching students with special needs* (5th ed.). Columbus, OH: Merrill.

Polloway, E. A., Patton, J. R., Epstein, M. H., & Smith, T. E. C. (1989). Comprehensive curriculum: Program design for students with mild handicaps. *Focus on Exceptional Children, 21*(8), 1–12.

Polloway, E. A., Patton, J. R., Payne, J. S., & Payne, R. A. (1989). *Strategies for teaching learners with special needs* (4th ed.). Columbus, OH: Merrill.

Polloway, E. A., Patton, J. R., Smith, J. D., & Roderique, T. W. (1992). Issues in program design for elementary students with mild retardation: Emphasis on curriculum development. *Education and Training in Mental Retardation, 27,* 142–150.

Polloway, E. A., & Smith, T. E. C. (1992). *Language instruction for students with disabilities.* Denver, CO: Love Publishing.

Reynolds, C. T., & Salend, S. J. (1990). Teacher-directed and student-mediated textbook comprehension strategies. *Academic Therapy, 25,* 417–427.

Reynolds, C. T., Salend, S. J., & Beachan, C. L. (1989). Motivating secondary students: Bringing in the reinforcements. *Academic Therapy, 25,* 81–90.

Reynolds, M. C., Wang, M. C., & Walberg, H. J. (1987). The necessary resturcturing of regular and special education. *Exceptional Children, 53,* 391–398.

Robinson, S. M., Braxdale, C. T., & Colson, S. E. (1988). Preparing dysfunctional learners to enter junior high school: A transitional curriculum. *Focus on Exceptional Children, 18*(4), 1–12.

Salend, S. J. (1990). *Effective mainstreaming.* New York: Macmillan.

Sargent, L. (1989). Social skills. In G. Robinson, J. R. Patton, E. A. Polloway, & L. Sargent (Eds.), *Best practices in mild mental retardation.* Reston, VA: CEC-MR.

Sargent, L. (1991). *Social skills for school and community.* Reston, VA: CEC-MR.

Schewel, R. (1993). Reading. In E. A. Polloway & J. R. Patton (Eds.), *Strategies for teaching learners with special needs.* Columbus, OH: Merrill/Macmillan.

Schniedewind, N., & Saland, S. (1987). Cooperative learning works. *Teaching Exceptional Children, 19,* 22–25.

Schumm, S. J., & Strickler, K. (1991). Guidelines for adapting content area textbooks: Keeping teachers and students content. *Intervention in School and Clinic, 27,* 79–84.

Shea, T. M., & Bauer, A. M. (1987). *Teaching children and youth with behavior disorders* (2nd ed.). Englewood Cliffs, NJ: Prentice-Hall.

Slade, D. L. (1986). Developing foundations for organizational skills. *Academic Therapy, 21,* 261–266.

Slavin, R. E. (1987). *What research says to the teacher on cooperative learning: Student teams* (2nd ed.). Washington, DC: National Education Association.

Slavin, R. E., Stevens, R. J., & Madden, N. A. (1988). Accommodating student diversity in reading and writing instruction: A cooperative learning approach. *Remedial and Special Education, 9*(1), 60–66.

Smith, D. D., Robinson, S., & Voress, J. (1982). The learning disabled: The transition from dependence to independence. *Topics in Learning and Learning Disabilities, 2*(3), 27–39.

Stevens, R., & Rosenshine, B. (1981). Advances in research on teaching. *Exceptional Education Quarterly, 2,* 1–9.

Turkle, B. (1976). *Deep in the forest.* New York: E. P. Dutton.

U.S. Department of Education. (1992). *14th annual report to Congress on the implementation of the Education of All Handicapped Children Act.* Washington, DC: Government Printing Office.

Valdes, K. A., Williamson, C. L., & Wagner, M. M. (1990). *The national longitudinal transition study of special education students.* Menlo Park, CA: SRI International.

Wallace, G., Cohen, S., & Polloway, E. A. (1987). *Language arts: Teaching exceptional children.* Austin, TX: Pro-Ed.

Wang, M. C., Reynolds, M. C., & Walberg, H. J. (1986). Rethinking special education. *Educational Leadership, 44,* 26–32.

Wang, M. C., & Zollers, N. J. (1990). Adaptive instruction: An alternative service delivery approach. *Remedial and Special Education, 11*(1), 7–21.

Wesson, C. L. (1989). A continuum of options for developing instructional plans in reading for elementary mildly and moderately handicapped students. *Academic Therapy, 24,* 593–606.

Wesson, C. L., & Deno, S. L. (1989). An analysis of long-term instructional plans in reading for elementary resource room students. *Remedial and Special Education, 10*(1), 21–28.

Westling, D. L., & Koorland, M. A. (1989). *The special educator's handbook.* Boston: Allyn & Bacon.

White, A. E., & White, L. L. (1992). A collaborative model for students with mild disabilities in middle schools. *Focus on Exceptional Children, 24*(9), 1–10.

Wiedmeyer, D., & Lehman, J. (1991). House plan: Approach to collaborative teaching and consultation. *Teaching Exceptional Children, 23*(3), 6–10.

Will, M. (1986). Educating children with learning problems: A shared responsibility. *Exceptional Children, 52,* 411–415.

Zigmond, N., Levine, E., & Laurie, T. (1985). Managing the mainstream: An analysis for teacher attitudes and student performance in mainstream high school programs. *Journal of Learning Disabilities, 18,* 535–541.

CHAPTER 14

Curricular and Instructional Accommodations: Secondary Level

Introduction

Unique differences exist between elementary and secondary settings in terms of organizational structure, curricula, and learner variables. One difference is the wider gap found between the demands of the classroom setting and the ability of many students with disabilities. Academically, the gap widens, as many students with disabilities exhibit limited achievement in basic skills and lack the ability to perform higher cognitive tasks (Polloway & Smith, 1992; Smith, Finn, & Dowdy, 1993). These skills include gaining information from textbooks, memorizing large amounts of information, paraphrasing, discriminating important information from less important, notetaking, theme writing, proofing papers, and test-taking skills (Schumaker & Deshler, 1988).

Including students with disabilities in general education programs is more difficult at the secondary level than in the elementary grades. There are numerous reasons for this increased difficulty. First, teachers, trained primarily as content specialists, are expected to present complex material in such a way that a diverse group of students can master the information and be successful at performing the tasks associated with mastery (National Joint Committee on Learning Disabilities, 1988). Secondary teachers are more likely to focus on teaching the content than individualizing instruction to meet the unique needs of individual students. Their goals revolve around "teaching history"; "teaching science"; or "teaching English"—not teaching Jake, Alex, and Bonnie. These teachers may be reluctant to change their grading system or make other accommodations, thus making it very difficult for students with disabilities to experience success in general education settings. This may also lead to students not graduating from high school, something that can have a lifelong impact.

A second reason that makes including students with disabilities at the secondary level difficult is the general nature of adolescence. Adolescence is a difficult and trying time for all young people. For students with disabilities, the developmental period is even more difficult (Smith, Price, & Marsh, 1986). Problems associated with adolescence are only exacerbated by the presence of a disability (Polloway & Smith, 1992; Smith et al., 1993). A third problem in integrating students with disabilities at the secondary level is the current movement to reform schools. Unfortunately, the reform movement has often resulted in problems for students with disabilities. Having to take more math and science courses, and achieving a passing grade on a minimum competency test, may prove too difficult for many students who experience learning and behavior problems.

Many problems are associated with the inclusion of students with disabilities into general education classes in secondary schools. Although the system requires classroom teachers to provide appropriate education for these students, they often do not have the skills or inclination required to do so. These teachers may also become very frustrated with the lack of progress made by some students, and the seemingly endless efforts that too often result in limited success (Chalmers, 1991). Regardless of the difficulties associated with placing students with problems in general education programs, the trend to do so is apparent. Although the inclusion movement may not be totally adopted, more and more students with disabilities are going to depend on classroom teachers to provide appropriate educational programs. Therefore, classroom teachers in secondary schools must be better prepared to deal with students who require some special forms of instruction.

Secondary School Curricula

More curricular differentiation is present at the secondary level to accommodate the individual needs and interests of the wide variety of students attending America's comprehensive high schools than is found in elementary schools (Smith, 1990). Most high schools have a general curriculum that all students must complete. This curriculum, generally prescribed by the state education agency, includes science, math, social studies, and English/literature. Often, states and local education agencies add to the required general curriculum areas such as sexuality education, drug education, and foreign languages (Smith, 1990).

There are numerous opportunities for students to choose curricular alternatives, which are usually related to postschool goals. For example, students planning to go to college choose a college-preparatory track, which builds on the general curriculum with higher-level academic courses. This college-preparatory track helps prepare students for rigorous courses found on college campuses. Other students choose a vocational track, which is designed to help prepare them for specific job opportunities after high school, and still other students choose the basic track. The basic curricular track is the general curriculum, with some course choices for students who do not plan to go to college and who are not interested in a specific vocational choice (Smith, 1990).

Although the specific curricula offered in different secondary schools vary, they generally follow state guidelines. Individual schools, however, do offer unique curricular options that appeal to particular students. The curricular track that students choose should be an important consideration, because the decision could have long-term implications after the student exits the school.

The educational reform movements of the 1980s have had a direct impact on the secondary curriculum. As noted, schools have begun to offer, and in some cases require, more science and math courses. Also, in many states and districts, students must successfully complete high school competency examinations before they are eligible for graduation. More stringent rules related to the number of electives students can take have resulted in many students not getting to take the courses they want. One result of this could be more school dropouts (Smith et al., 1986).

Special Education Curriculum in Secondary Schools

The curriculum for students with disabilities is the most critical programming consideration in secondary schools. Students can have excellent teachers, but if the curriculum is inappropriate to meet their needs, then the teaching may be inconsequential. The high school special education curriculum must be comprehensive and include opportunities for socialization; it must (Polloway & Patton, 1993)

- ◆ Be responsive to the needs of individual students
- ◆ Facilitate maximum integration with nondisabled peers
- ◆ Be related to the type of classroom model used to deliver services (general classroom, resource room, self-contained special classroom)

In 1979, Alley and Deshler identified five curricular approaches commonly used with secondary special education students: (1) basic skills remediation, (2) tutorial approach, (3) learning strategies model, (4) functional curriculum, and (5) work-study model. A more recent article identified six major curricular options (Polloway, Patton, Epstein, & Smith 1989):

- ◆ Basic skills
- ◆ Social skills
- ◆ Tutorial
- ◆ Learning strategies
- ◆ Vocational
- ◆ Adult outcomes

Regardless of the specific curriculum used, schools also need to focus on the transition needs of students from high school to post–public school settings.

Determining Curricular Needs of Students

As noted in Chapter 13, the adoption of a curriculum for any student should be based on an appraisal of desired long-term outcomes and an assessment of current needs (Polloway et al., 1989). At the elementary level, consideration of the future demands of middle and high school suggests a primary focus on the development and refinement of basic academic and social skills, as well as a beginning emphasis on career awareness and lifelong skills of independence. Although many different components could be included in the elementary curriculum, a focus on basic academic skills and preparation for middle and high school is an obvious choice.

Polloway and Patton (1993) suggest that elementary students also be taught specific transitional skills that will facilitate success in middle and high schools, such as self-management, study skills, note taking, and homework skills. Still other nonacademic needs, such as resisting peer pressure, negotiating, accepting negative feedback, and asking questions are critical learning needs that should be addressed in the elementary curriculum to facilitate the success of students in secondary settings (Hazel, Schumaker, Shelon, & Sherman, 1982). Although some schools involved in restructuring are providing learning opportunities in these areas, many schools continue to focus almost strictly on academics.

Regardless of the seemingly "common" areas that should be included in an elementary curriculum, curricular variation is common. The result is that students arrive in secondary settings with a wide range of academic preparation and varying, often limited, degrees of exposure to transitional subjects such as life skills, career awareness, study skills, and self-management. Since high schools represent a final chance for personnel in public education to prepare students for their futures outside of school, curricular considerations and decisions are critically important. Data that have been collected in follow-up studies of students with disabilities have, for the most part, suggested that schools are doing a poor job of preparing students with disabilities for life after high school.

To limit the number of young adults with disabilities who are unemployed, underemployed, and having difficulties living independently, school personnel need to determine the skills necessary for students to experience success in postschool environments and focus interventions to help students develop those skills (Dowdy & Smith, 1991; Smith & Dowdy, 1992). A seven-step model for curricular decision making for students with disabilities has been developed that will enable school personnel, parents, and students to better plan for life after high school. The future-based assessment and intervention model can also be used for students in elementary grades; however, its application is more appropriate at the secondary level. Figure 14.1 reveals the future-based assessment and intervention model.

The first step of the future-based assessment and intervention model is when parents and student have a conference with school personnel to identify the student's interests and goals in terms of postsecondary training, employment, and independent living. During this step, all parties involved in the planning identify the desired future for the student. The appropriateness of these goals is tested in the second step of the

Step	
Student/parent interview: Identify interests and goals for post-secondary training, employment, and independent living.	1
Conduct comprehensive assessment including academic, vocational, and independent living skills.	2
Interdisciplinary team meeting: Analyze assessment data and refine future goals.	3
Determine the characteristics/skills necessary for individuals to be successful in future vocational, academic, and independent living situations.	4
Identify discrepancies between the characteristics/skills of the student and the skills necessary for success in designated future academic, employment, and independent living situations.	5
Develop and implement intervention plans (IEPs and Transition plans) to address discrepancies identified in step 5.	6
Ongoing analysis of student characteristics and future vocational, academic, and social situations to determine if adjustments regarding future needs are to be made (must be done on an annual basis).	7

Figure 14.1 **Future-Based Assessment and Intervention Model**
Source: Smith, T. E. C., & Dowdy, C. A. (1992). Future-based assessment and intervention for students with mental retardation. *Education and Training in Mental Retardation, 27,* 258. Used with permission.

model through administration of a comprehensive assessment battery. The assessment process collects information regarding the student's future in areas such as academic potential, vocational potential and interests, and social skills. In step 3, the original team is reconvened to consider the impact of the assessment data on the goals developed during step one. It is possible that goals will be revised at this time to more accurately reflect the student's ability levels.

In step 4, the skills needed to succeed in the designated goals are identified. These skills are then compared to the current skill levels of the student, and the discrepancies are identified (step 5). After this analysis, in step 6, curricular choices are made that provide the training and education necessary to facilitate the student's success in each area. For students with disabilities, these goals should be delineated in the IEP.

The final step of the future-based model, step 7, reflects the constant need for monitoring and affirming that the curricular choices are appropriate. This review should be ongoing and may be part of the required annual IEP review. This ongoing review and analysis allows teachers, parents, and the students themselves to know what progress is being made toward the future goals for the student. If progress is insufficient, then the future goals may need to be adjusted. Likewise, if progress is more rapid than anticipated, then the future goals may be revised upward.

Although students with disabilities have individualized education programs (IEPs) that detail specific goals, objectives, and services, the programs must be related to a particular curricular model. As previously noted, without an appropriate curriculum, the greatest teaching efforts may go unrewarded. Numerous variables should be considered before making the important curricular decision. Examples include

- The intellectual level of the student
- What parents want for their child
- How classroom teachers accept students with disabilities
- What kind of special education support services are available (Polloway & Patton, 1993)

Table 14.1 summarizes several factors related to making curricular decisions for students with disabilities.

Programs for Students in Secondary Schools

High school programs for students with disabilities need significant reform if the outlook for the future of these young people is to change. The 15th Annual Report to Congress on the Implementation of the Individuals with Disabilities Education Act (U.S. Department of Education, 1993) reported that only 45.7% of students with disabilities graduated from high school with a diploma during the 1990–1991 school year. The report also showed that 23.3% of all students with disabilities actually dropped out of school. This is a significantly higher dropout rate than is found in the general student population. Figure 14.2 reveals the basis for students exiting school during the 1990–1991 school year.

TABLE 14.1 **Factors Related to Curricular Decisions**

1. Student Variables

- Cognitive-intellectual level
- Academic skills preparedness
- Academic achievement as determined by tests
- Academic achievement as determined by class grades
- Grade placement
- Motivation and responsibility
- Social interactions with peers and adults
- Behavioral self-control

2. Parent Variables

- Short- and long-term parental expectation
- Degree of support provided (e.g., financial, emotional, academic)
- Parental values toward education
- Cultural influence (e.g., language, values)

3. Regular Class Variables

- Teacher and nonhandicapped student acceptance of diversity (classroom climate)
- Administrative support to integrated education
- Availability of curricular variance
- Accommodative capacity of the classroom
- Flexibility of daily class schedules and units earned toward graduation
- Options for vocational programs

4. Special Education Variables

- Size of caseload
- Availability of paraprofessionals or tutors in the classroom
- Access to curricular materials
- Focus of teacher's training
- Consultative and materials support available
- Related services available to students

Source: Polloway, E. A., Patton, J. R., Epstein, M. H., & Smith, T. E. C. (1989). Comprehensive curriculum for students with mild handicaps. *Focus on Exceptional Children, 21*(8), p. 8. Used with permission.

In addition to students with disabilities exiting schools for other than optimal reasons, several follow-up studies have shown that adults with disabilities are likely to be employed part-time, underemployed, or unemployed to a significantly greater degree than their nondisabled peers (Smith et al., 1986; Wehman, Kregel, & Barcus, 1985; Edgar, 1988). Therefore, regardless of the efforts made in secondary schools to meet the individual needs of students with disabilities, available information suggests that many of these students are still unprepared to achieve success as young adults.

Students themselves are aware that they are not being adequately prepared for post–high school demands (Dowdy, Carter, & Smith, 1990). In comparing the transitional needs of high school students with learning disabilities to their nondisabled

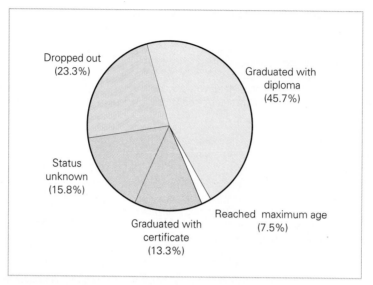

Figure 14.2   Basis of Exit for Students with Disabilities Aged 14 and Older: School Year 1990–1991
Source: U.S. Department of Education, Office of Special Education Programs, Data Analysis·System (DANS).

peers, Dowdy et al. (1990) found that, although both groups expressed an interest in help with career decisions, significant differences were noted in several areas. For example, students with learning disabilities were far more interested in learning how to find a job, how to keep a job, and how to live independently than their nondisabled peers. As a group, students with disabilities expressed an insecurity about their futures when compared to students without disabilities.

Most secondary students with disabilities are currently included in general education classrooms for at least a portion of each school day. Therefore, the responsibility for these students becomes a joint effort between general education classroom teachers and special education personnel (Smith, Price, & Marsh, 1986). Unfortunately, many of these students do not experience success in the general classroom setting. They frequently fail classes, become frustrated and act out, and may even drop out of school because they are not prepared to meet the demands placed on them by secondary teachers. There are numerous reasons why many students with disabilities fail in secondary classes:

◆ Lack of communication between special education personnel and classroom teachers
◆ Discrepancies between the expectations of classroom teachers and the abilities of students
◆ Lack of understanding by the students about the demands of the classroom
◆ Lack of understanding and knowledge by classroom teachers about students with disabilities

◆ Lack of knowledge by special education personnel in working with classroom teachers

Regardless of the reasons why some students with disabilities do not achieve success in general education settings, the fact remains that the current trend is toward inclusion. Therefore, educators, both classroom teachers and special education personnel, must work together to increase the chances that these students will be successful.

Roles of Personnel

As noted, the responsibility for educating students with disabilities in public schools is shared by general classroom teachers and special education personnel. Therefore, educators must improve their skills at working together to help students who are experiencing various learning and behavior problems.

General Classroom Teachers. The primary role of general classroom teachers is to assume the responsibility for students with disabilities in particular classes or subject areas. Most classroom teachers present information using one general technique, but they are likely to have to expand their instructional activities when dealing with students with disabilities to facilitate the success of all students. This could include making various accommodations or modifications in instructional techniques and materials, which will be discussed later in the chapter.

Classroom teachers have five general responsibilities for all of the students in their classes, including those with disabilities (Jenkins, Pious, & Jewell, 1990):

1. Educating and managing behavior
2. Making major instructional decisions, determining the pace, and monitoring progress
3. Following a curriculum that reflects normal development and identifying any child whose progress is discrepant
4. Managing instruction for a heterogeneous, diverse population through grouping and individualization
5. Seeking, using, and managing assistance for students with educational needs that differ significantly from those of their peers

In addition to these five areas, Rosenshine and Stevens (1986) suggest that classroom teachers focus on equalizing opportunities for students with disabilities in their classes. They suggest that teachers ensure that all students have an opportunity to answer teacher questions and a good chance for achieving at least moderate success in classroom activities. This is not a call for teachers to "give" students with disabilities passing grades, only a request that students with disabilities have an equal chance at being successful.

Classroom teachers should also do all they can to work effectively with special education professionals. They should openly communicate with these professionals about their concerns and needs in working with specific students in their classroom. Open communication and dialogue between classroom teachers and special education

Checklist for Selecting and Evaluating Materials

◆ Are perspectives and contributions of people from diverse cultural and linguistic groups—both men and women, as well as people with disabilities—included in the curriculum?

◆ Are there activities in the curriculum that will assist students in analyzing the various forms of the mass media for ethnocentrism, sexism, "handicapism," and stereotyping?

◆ Are men and women, diverse cultural/racial groups, and people with varying abilities shown in both active and passive roles?

◆ Are men and women, diverse cultural/racial groups, and people with disabilities shown in positions of power (i.e., the materials do not rely on the mainstream culture's character to achieve goals)?

◆ Do the materials identify strengths possessed by so-called "underachieving" diverse populations? Do they diminish the attention given to deficits, to reinforce positive behaviors that are desired and valued?

◆ Are members of diverse racial/cultural groups, men and women, and people with disabilities shown engaged in a broad range of social and professional activities?

◆ Are members of a particular culture or group depicted as having a range of physical features (e.g., hair color, hair texture, variations in facial characteristics and body build)?

◆ Do the materials represent historical events from the perspective of the various groups involved or solely from the male, middle-class, and/or Western European perspective?

◆ Are the materials free of ethnocentric or sexist language patterns that may make implications about persons or groups based solely on their culture, race, gender, or disability?

◆ Will students from different ethnic and cultural backgrounds find the materials personally meaningful to their life experiences?

◆ Is a wide variety of culturally different examples, situations, scenarios, and anecdotes used throughout the curriculum design to illustrate major intellectual concepts and principles?

◆ Are culturally diverse content, examples, and experiences comparable in kind, significance, magnitude, and function to those selected from mainstream culture?

Source: Garcia, S. B., & Malkin, D. H. (1993). Toward defining programs and services for culturally and linguistically diverse learners in special education. *Teaching Exceptional Children, 26,* 52–58. Used with permission.

personnel is crucial if inclusion is to be successful (Mims, Harper, Armstrong, & Savage, 1991). Communication among all individuals providing services to students with disabilities is the most important factor related to the success of the inclusion movement.

When working with students who are disabled, classroom teachers must realize that there is no one particular method that always works with these students; they have to individualize their efforts. There are, however, some general methods that can be effective with students with disabilities. Christenson, Ysseldyke, and Thurlow (1989) describe the following areas.

1. *Classroom Management.* Research has demonstrated that classes where teachers have effective behavior management procedures in place have more time for student involvement and instruction. The key is to be proactive, having a well-established routine and a few clearly stated classroom rules and procedures. Classroom rules should always be stated in positive terms and should be very explicit. Teachers cannot assume that students will know how to act if the rule only tells them how *not* to act. For example, instead of posting a rule that students may not sit on the tops of desks, state that students should sit in their desks, with feet on the floor.

2. *Positive School Environment.* Students learn more effectively in a classroom where a humanistic focus is present in combination with an academic orientation (Samuels, 1986). When planning each day's activities, teachers should build in tasks or accommodations that will offer each student a measure of success. All students need to be successful from time to time to maintain their attention and motivation. Using cooperative learning activities, such as those described in Chapter 13, is another way to develop a positive atmosphere in a class.

   Teachers should always set high goals for students. This should always be accompanied by a classroom environment where students feel they have the confidence of the teacher to achieve the goals. Students need to believe that their teachers care about them and will support them in their efforts to achieve goals.

3. *Appropriate Instructional Match.* The degree to which there is an instructional match depends on a discrepancy analysis between the characteristics of the student and the demands of the task. The student analysis is often difficult due to the hidden nature of many mild cognitive disabilities. Teachers have been observed telling students with a learning disability to "try harder" to read. That same teacher would never ask a student with a visual impairment to try harder to see or ask a student with a hearing impairment to listen "more carefully."

   It is important for teachers to know the unique characteristics of their students, especially those with disabilities or who are at risk for developing disabilities, such as behavior problems and emotional problems. Achievement levels of students are frequently only the tip of the iceberg when it comes to functioning successfully in class. Less obvious characteristics, such as inattention, distractibility, slow work rate, and difficulty processing multiple directions can be the major culprits in successful learning. Therefore, accommodations or modifications used by teachers must address specific characteristics that can have a very negative effect on successful learning (see Figure 14.3).

Several guides have been developed to help teachers match instructional techniques to students who are having difficulties in the classroom. Dowdy, Smith, Patton, and Polloway (in press) developed a *Guide to Attention Deficits in the Classroom* that includes a rating scale of 76 characteristics that may describe students with attention deficits and learning disorders. This rating scale may be used to identify a student's profile of limitations that may cause learning challenges in the classroom. A series of teacher modifications are included for each specific characteristic, thus giving teachers some direct activities related to specific characteristics.

Difficulty completing assignments	• List and/or post (and say) all steps necessary to complete each assignment. • Reduce the assignment into manageable sections with specific due dates. • Make frequent checks for work/assignment completion. • Arrange for the student to have a "study buddy" with phone number in each subject area.
Difficulty with any task that requires memory	• Combine seeing, saying, writing, and doing; student may need to subvocalize to remember. • Teach memory techniques as a study strategy (e.g., mnemonics, visualization, oral rehearsal, numerous repetitions).
Difficulty with test taking	• Allow extra time for testing; teach test-taking skills and strategies; allow student to be tested orally. • Use clear, readable, and uncluttered test forms. Use test format that the student is most comfortable with. Allow ample space for student response. Consider having lined answer spaces for essay and short-answer tests.
Confusion from nonverbal cues (misreads body language, etc.)	• Directly teach (tell the student) what nonverbal cues mean. Model and have student practice reading cues in a safe setting.
Confusion from written material (difficulty finding main idea from a paragraph; attributes greater importance to minor details)	• Provide student with copy of reading material with main ideas underlined or highlighted. • Provide an outline of important points from reading material. • Teach outlining, main idea/details, concepts. • Provide tape or text/chapter.
Confusion from spoken material, lectures, and A.V. material (difficulty finding main idea from presentation, attributes greater importance to minor details)	• Provide student with a copy of presentation notes. • Allow peers to share carbon-copy notes from presentation (have student compare own notes with copy of peer's notes). • Provide framed outlines of presentations (introducing visual and auditory cues to important information). • Encourage use of tape recorder. • Teach and emphasize keywords (*the following. . ., the most important. . .,* etc.).

Figure 14.3   **Examples of Specific Accommodations and Modifications Associated with Characteristics**

4. *Clear Teaching Goals and Expectations.* Effective teachers have a carefully developed master plan that includes teaching goals for each specific lesson taught. These goals are important for the teachers, to focus their instruction, but it is also important that teachers communicate these goals to the students frequently and explicitly. Students have a tendency to perform better when they know the goals of the instruction, as specifically as possible. It is better for teachers to say, "Today you are going to learn to name the reasons for the civil war" than to say "Today we are going to study the civil war." Teachers should set high expectations, monitor achievement continuously, and give frequent, task-specific feedback.

5. *Quality of Instruction.* Obviously, one of the primary roles for all teachers is to provide quality instruction. In order to do this, teachers need to explain lessons clearly, use modeling and demonstration techniques, and monitor whether the concepts are understood by students (Carroll, 1985; Rosenshine & Stevens, 1986). Following is an outline of the steps used in an effective lesson, which has been adapted from the work of Deshler, Schumaker, Lenz, and Ellis (1984). Figure 14.4 contains a list of these steps with questions that can be used by teachers for self-evaluation following a lesson.

   ◆ Review the previous lesson.
   ◆ Use an advance organizer or graphic organizer to introduce the lesson.
   ◆ Obtain student attention and commitment to learn.
   ◆ Provide direct instruction (include modeling, demonstration, examples, manipulatives).
   ◆ Use a variety of tasks/activities/questions to maintain interest and generate student response.
   ◆ Provide guided practice (monitor boardwork, simple worksheets, small group games with teacher).
   ◆ Provide independent practice for generalization (homework, workbooks, regular textbooks, computer, games).
   ◆ Ask students to evaluate learning/use informal tests (rapid-fire questioning, brief written assessment).
   ◆ Close with a summary and transition to next lesson. Provide student feedback as appropriate. Document observations: student and self-evaluation.

   Before any lesson, a teacher should establish clear goals and objectives and pretest students to determine their level of knowledge on the topic.

6. *Instructional Support for Individual Students.* Instruction is made more effective when teachers monitor students' work frequently and adjust or adapt instruction to meet individual needs of students. Some students require more guided practice, more drill, and more practice to reach automaticity. When students are moved too quickly through the curriculum, they often do not obtain sufficient

(1) Reviews previous lesson	Was my transition smooth and meaningful?
(2) Uses advanced organizer to introduce new lesson	Were my objectives clear? Did I have the right number of objectives?
(3) Obtains student attention and commitment to learn	Was my motivation/attention technique effective? Did I make the lesson relevant to the student?
(4) Provides direct instruction (includes modeling/demonstration/ manipulatives)	Was my subject matter background okay? Did I use overhead, chalkboard, graphics, models, etc? Was there a balance between student/teacher talk?
(5) Uses a variety of tasks/ activities/questions to maintain interest and generate student responses	Were my questions effective? Did my class ask questions? Did I wait for replies to my questions? Did I involve all students?
(6) Provides guided practice (boardwork, simple work-sheets, small group games with teacher)	Did I transform students from "passive listeners" to "active participants"? Was teacher activity balanced with student activity? Did I provide timely feedback?
(7) Provides independent practice for generalization (workbooks, textbooks, computer, games)	Did I include appropriate homework? Did I use materials that require generalization?
(8) Asks students to evaluate learning/use informal tests (rapid-fire questioning, brief written assessment)	If I didn't know something, did I promise to look it up? Did I ask them what they had learned to teach self-evaluation? Was my assessment directly related to my objective?
(9) Closes with summary and transition to next lesson	Did I have a smooth closing and transition to the next activity?
(10) Provides student feedback as appropriate	Did I identify students who needed an individual behavior change plan?
(11) Documents observations: students and self	Was my behavior management technique effective? Was learning effective and fun?

Figure 14.4   **Steps in an Effective Lesson and Corresponding Questions**

practice to maintain and then generalize instruction. Waiting until evaluation time may result in several days of wasted instruction. By providing ongoing monitoring and instructional support, teachers can prevent students from sitting in classes without realizing success.

7. *Efficient Use of Time.*   One of the most important roles of classroom teachers is to maximize their available time with students. Many studies have reported that actual instruction time during school hours is very low (Smith, 1990). The amount of time teachers allocate to instruction, the amount of time students

Guidelines for Directing Independent Student Activities

◆ Don't introduce new tasks or concepts when students are working independently. Work on proficiency or maintenance of skills or objectives already acquired.

◆ Use tasks intended to help the student achieve the objective, either equivalent tasks or support tasks.

◆ Use a standard format; don't continuously change the nature of the materials. Use clear, simple directions.

◆ Be able to hold the learner accountable. Require a written product when appropriate.

◆ Physically separate the students unless good pairs can be arranged.

◆ Make use of audiovisual materials, self-correcting learning materials, programmed materials, computer programs, and other materials that support the objective.

◆ Provide a sufficient amount of work for each student.

◆ Provide a "cushion activity" for each student. (A cushion activity is a high-interest activity the student likes to do that may or may not be related to the objective.)

Source: Westling, D. L., & Koorland, M. A. (1989). *The special educator's handbook* (p. 27). Boston: Allyn & Bacon. Used with permission.

actually spend engaged in academic tasks, and the amount of time students spend in active academic responding are critical in determining a student's opportunity to learn. For students with disabilities, efficient use of time is even more important.

Although the amount of time allotted for instruction is important, the quality of instruction is also critical. Simply having students spend large amounts of time in some activities does not guarantee learning. An example is having students complete worksheets when they may not understand the concepts or have already learned the concept. Teachers must consider the amount of time, as well as the quality of activities that occur during that instructional time.

8. *Substantive Student Interaction.*   Teachers need to facilitate student interaction. Research has shown that the opportunity to engage in active academic responses is positively correlated with academic achievement (Reid, 1986). Effective teachers give cues and prompts that have the potential of increasing students' ability to deliver the correct response and thus increase the amount of positive feedback they receive. It is important for all students to have an oppor-

tunity to actively participate. As a result of many students with disabilities having slow processing abilities and oral language difficulties, teachers may need to develop strategies to facilitate their interactions. Peer tutoring, choral responding, and cooperative learning offer alternative modes of providing opportunities for active responding which may prove beneficial for students with problems.

9. *Monitoring of Student Understanding and Progress.*   Active and frequent monitoring is considered the key to keeping the total instructional cycle effective (Good & Brophy, 1987). Although teachers plan for instruction for groups of students, the process of frequent monitoring and adapting is the key to maintaining the match between the individual and the instruction. Effective monitoring should require the student to demonstrate the learned skill, not simply state that there are no questions. The first items of a task being completed for practice should be checked by the teacher. Students should also be asked to explain what they are doing to ensure that an efficient strategy has been selected.

   If teachers wait until a grade-reporting period to evaluate a student's progress, significant amounts of time may be lost. Therefore, constant, ongoing monitoring becomes a very important role for teachers with students who have disabilities.

10. *Evaluation of Student Performance.*   Direct assessment of student knowledge is essential for determining whether the instructional goals and objectives have been reached. Effective assessment requires frequent evaluation that is designed to measure exactly what has been taught. Feedback should be explicit regarding the inaccuracy or accuracy of the response and it should be directly related to the task being completed by the student. For example, "You have really learned your multiplication facts" is preferable to "You have really worked hard on this." Through frequent testing, teachers can make better, data-based decisions to determine future goals.

Probably the most important role of classroom teachers when dealing with students who have disabilities is teaching content courses (Deshler & Schumaker, 1988). When teaching content courses, such as history and science, they should treat students with disabilities as they treat all other students, remembering that the students with special needs would not be placed in the general classroom setting if an interdisciplinary team had not determined that they could benefit from instruction in that environment.

Within the classroom, teachers can do several things that will facilitate the success of students with disabilities. They can modify the environment, alter the task presentation, vary the student requirements, and make the grading procedures more flexible. However, the realities of the classroom at the secondary level may not permit full individualized instruction and the presentation of tasks outside a limited range (Bryan, Bay, & Donahue, 1988).

In addition to the specific roles noted earlier, classroom teachers are also very involved in many of the activities completed by special education teachers. The following section describes the primary activities of special education personnel. Please keep in mind that classroom teachers perform many of these roles as well as those previously described.

Collaborative Role of the Special Education Teacher

The special education teacher plays an important role in the successful inclusion of students with disabilities in secondary schools. In addition to the responsibilities for collaborating with general educators, the special education teacher must focus significant efforts on preparing students for the variety of challenges that occur daily in the general education environment, as well as preparing them for their future challenges in independent living and employment. Above all, special education teachers play a major support role for general classroom teachers. They should communicate regularly with classroom teachers and always be available to provide any assistance, either consultative in nature or through direct instruction.

The specific roles of the special education teacher include counseling students for the personal crises that may occur daily and preparing students for content classes, the high school graduation exam, postsecondary training, independent living, and, ultimately, employment (Smith, Finn, & Dowdy, 1993). In actuality, for most students with disabilities included in general classes, special education teachers and general teachers collaborate in performing all of these roles.

Adolescents often need counseling to help them deal with the changes they are undergoing.

Counseling for Today's Crises.   Adolescence is a difficult time of change for all children; for children with disabilities, the period is even more challenging. In our evolving society, students are constantly trying to grasp the subtle changes in roles for males and females. They experience more exposure to drugs and alcohol, and pregnancy and AIDS are common issues. The increased tension, frustration, and depression can lead to suicide, the second leading cause of death among adolescents (Guetzloe, 1988; Spirito, Hart, Overholser, & Halverson, 1990; Smith, Finn, & Dowdy, 1993), or a variety of behavior and emotional problems. Special education teachers need to collaborate with general educators to help students deal with these problems.

Preparing for High School Content Classes.   The special education teacher should be aware of factors such as classroom teacher expectations, teaching styles, and the demands of the learning environment (Welch & Link, 1991). One way special education teachers can help students deal with the "general education world" is to teach them how to self-advocate. In order to do this, students need to understand their learning or behavior problems. Therefore, special education teachers may need to have a discussion with their students about the nature of specific disabilities.

Deshler & Schumaker (1988) propose that the primary role of special education teachers should be to teach their students effective strategies for generalization to compensate for their learning deficits and therefore increase the likelihood for success in mainstream classes. They suggest teaching numerous strategies including those for memory, test taking, listening, note taking, proofing, time management, and organization. Specific techniques for these will be discussed later in the chapter. If students with learning problems know how to use these kinds of strategies, they will have a better chance of achieving success in general classrooms.

When working with students with disabilities in general education classrooms, the role of the special educator expands to include informing the general educator as to the unique abilities and challenges presented by each special student, providing ongoing support and collaboration for the student and teacher, and frequent monitoring to ensure that the arrangement is satisfactory for both the student and the teacher. These activities are common for special education teachers in today's public schools, where the majority of students with disabilities are included in general classes for at least a portion of each school day.

Preparing for the High School Graduation Exam.   Passing the high school graduation exam as a requirement for receiving a regular diploma, begun in the 1980s as part of the national reform movements in education, is a relatively new phenomenon. Students with disabilities may or may not be required to take the exam, depending on state regulations and local school district policies. In some states, students with disabilities are granted a regular high school diploma without having to complete the examination; in others, students with disabilities who do not pass the graduation exam are given a certification of attendance.

Special education teachers, in conjunction with classroom teachers, have two roles regarding the high school graduation exam. On one hand, they are obligated to help the student prepare for the exam if it is the decision of the IEP team that the student should be prepared to take the exam. On the other hand, the special education teacher and classroom teachers may feel the need to focus on convincing the student and parents that time could more appropriately be spent on developing functional skills rather than preparing for the graduation exam.

Preparing for Postsecondary Training.   It is more important than ever for students with disabilities to attempt postsecondary education if they have the ability and motivation. This is one component of a transition program for students. Postsecondary education does not have to be a regular college (Vogel, 1990); it could be a community college, vocational-technical school, trade school, or some other form of education and training. Teachers, both general and special education, need to inform students about future employment trends and help them select a realistic career with employment potential. The following facts, noted in the report from the Hudson Institute, *Workforce 2000: Work and Workers for the 21st Century* (1987), have several implications for students with disabilities:

1. Higher levels of academic achievement will be required, and very few jobs will be appropriate for individuals deficient in reading, writing, and math.
2. There will be an increase in service industry jobs and a decrease in manufacturing jobs.
3. More than half of the new jobs created in the 1990s will require education beyond high school, and more than a third will be filled with college graduates.

Preparing for Independent Living.   Independent living is a realistic goal for most individuals with disabilities; however, to live successfully in today's complex, automated world, direct instruction in certain independent living skills may be required. This is also important in a student's transition program. Following are some of the areas that have been specifically cited as problematic for persons with mild disabilities (Chesler, 1982; Cullinan, Epstein, & Lloyd, 1983; Halpern, Close, & Nelson, (1986):

- Sexuality
- Drug abuse education
- Managing personal finances
- Developing and maintaining social networks
- Maintaining a home
- Managing food
- Career counseling and employment
- Transportation
- Handling and avoiding problems
- Self-confidence and self-esteem
- Dependency
- Organization

Special education teachers must help students with disabilities achieve competence in these areas. Several excellent curricular guides are available to structure intervention

Demands of Adulthood

Adult Domains	Knowles's Domains	Examples
Vocational/education	Vocation and career	Being interviewed Getting along at work Changing jobs
Home and family	Home and family living	Dating Family planning Raising children Solving marital problems Financial planning
Recreation and leisure	Enjoyment of leisure	Choosing hobbies Buying equipment Planning recreational outings
Community involvement	Community living	Using community resources Voting Getting assistance
Emotional/physical health	Health	Exercising Treating medical emergencies Understanding children's diseases
Personal development	Personal development	Making decisions Dealing with conflict Establishing intimate relationships Understanding oneself

Source: Patton, J. R., Cronin, M. E., Polloway, E. A., Hutchinson, D., & Robinson, G. A. (1989). In J. R. Robinson, E. A. Polloway, & L. R. Sargent (Eds.), *Best Practices in Mild Mental Retardation* (p. 27). Reston, VA: CEC-MR. Used with permission.

in these areas; however, creative teachers can go into the community and gather the real materials from banks, restaurants, the local court house, and so forth, for developing their own program. Patton, Cronin, Polloway, Hutchinson, and Robinson (1989) suggest the infusion of life skills into existing curricula and constantly updating material as new technological advances are introduced.

Preparing for Employment. The ultimate goal of all education is the employment of graduates at their maximum vocational potential. The passage of the Americans with Disabilities Act (ADA) in 1990 should make that dream a reality for millions of people with disabilities. The law encompasses areas of employment, transportation, public accommodations, and telecommunications, and prohibits discrimination against individuals with disabilities. ADA requires employers to make "reasonable accommodations" that would assist persons with disabilities in performing their jobs. Teachers need to help students prepare for employment by teaching them the necessary skills for vocational success.

In addition to making accommodations in their own classes, teachers must be sure that students with disabilities can communicate their strengths and limitations to persons in postsecondary and future employment settings. Therefore, a key role for teachers is to teach self-advocacy. These self-advocacy skills will empower individuals and allow them to seek employment and independent living opportunities on their own.

Role of the Parent

Parents, like general classroom teachers and special education teachers, are involved in educational programs for students with disabilities at the secondary level; they should be involved in program development and implementation. Chapter 15 focuses entirely on the role of parents and other family members in educating students with disabilities. The important thing to remember is that parents and other family members are critical in the educational process. Without the involvement of this important group of individuals, students are less likely to achieve the level of success they need.

Methods for Facilitating Students' Success in General Education Classes

Students with disabilities are currently placed in general education classrooms for instruction when they are determined to have the academic ability necessary for success. If the inclusion movement is ever fully implemented, students with disabilities will be placed in general education classes, without a great deal of attention to their academic abilities. For most of these students, there is no need to dilute the curriculum; however, in order for them to benefit from instruction, accommodations by the teacher or strategies used by students may be essential. Students with disabilities in secondary classes need to have a fair opportunity to achieve success; they do not need teachers to *give* them grades.

Accommodations

Accommodations can be described as "efforts by the teacher to modify the environment and curriculum in such a way that students with disabilities can achieve success" (Polloway & Smith, 1992, p. 439). Accommodations are usually simple actions that can be taken by teachers that make success for some students much more likely. Allowing blind students to read using an alternative information source, braille, is universally accepted. Altering teaching methods or materials for students with other problems is a similar process. A study by Ysseldyke, Thurlow, Wotruba, and Nania (1990) found that "altering instruction so that the student can experience success, modifying the curriculum in a number of ways, adjusting the lesson pace to meet a student's individual rate of mastery, and informing students frequently of their instructional needs were viewed as equally desirable by elementary and secondary teachers" (p. 6). These are examples of accommodations.

Accommodations should be designed to offer the *least* amount of alteration from regular programming and still allow the student to benefit from instruction. This approach is fair to nondisabled students and provides the students with disabilities a more realistic representation of their abilities and limitations. If too many accommodations are made, some students develop an inflated view of their abilities, focusing on their achievements and disregarding the presence of the modifications. For example, students in remedial classes with high grades may begin to feel that they would be equally successful in college because of their high class standing. Failure to recognize the basic nature of the classes may set them up for failure in a college or other academically demanding environment. Students with too many accommodations may also begin to feel that they bring very little to the class; this can further damage an already fragile self-concept. It is important that modifications used in settings or classes designed to prepare an individual for a future job or postsecondary training program reflect realistic changes that can be replicated in these future environments.

There are many different accommodations that can be used effectively with students with disabilities. These include altering the way information is presented, the materials used, and the physical environment. Table 14.2 describes several accommodative strategies.

In addition to the accommodations noted above, there are numerous additional actions that teachers can take that will *accommodate* for a student's learning difficulties. Some include using vocabulary guides for students, cued text, advance organizers, and providing a structured overview for students (Leverett & Diefendorf, 1992). One accommodation that can greatly facilitate success is in the area of assignments. Often, a great deal of a student's grade may be determined by the quality of work on assignments. Some students with disabilities do not understand an assignment, or do not have the ability or time to complete the assignment. Therefore, teachers may need to make some accommodations in the area of assignments. Chalmers (1991) suggests the following:

1. *Preteach vocabulary and preview major concepts.* Students must have the vocabulary necessary to complete an assignment. If they do not know a particular word, they may not know how to find its definition causing them to possibly fail the assignment. Similarly, students need to understand the major concepts required to complete the assignment.
2. *State a purpose for reading.* Students need to know *why* they have to do things. Helping them understand the context of the assignment may aid in their motivation.
3. *Provide for repetition of instruction.* Choral responding, group work, and hands-on activities are examples of providing students with disabilities with the opportunities necessary for learning. One instance may simply not be sufficient for learning to occur.

TABLE 14.2 **Accomodative Strategies**

Strategy	Description
Outlines	Simple course outlines assist pupils in organizing notes and information.
Story guides	Expanded outlines. Provide specific information such as assignments and evaluation criteria.
Advance organizers	A set of questions or other guides indicating the most important parts of reading assignments.
Audiovisual aids	Overhead projectors, films, film strips, and chalkboard are examples. Reinforce auditory information and enable students with auditory deficits to access information.
Varying instructional strategies	Alternative teaching strategies enable students to utilize their most efficient learning style.
Seating arrangement	Place students in locations that minimize problems. Examples: close to front of class for children with auditory and visual problems; away from other children for students with behavior problems; away from windows and doors for those with distractibility problems.
Tape recorders	Using tape recorders can greatly benefit children with visual problems, memory problems, reading problems, etc. Taped textbooks, tests, and lectures can facilitate learning.

Source: Polloway, E. A., & Smith, T. E. C. (1992). *Language instruction for students with disabilities* (p. 440). Denver, CO: Love Publishing. Used with permission.

4. *Provide clear directions and examples.* "I didn't understand" is a common response from students when they fail. For many students, this response may simply be an effort to evade negative consequences. For many students with disabilities, however, the statement may reflect a true misunderstanding of the assignment. Therefore, teachers need to make every effort to explain all assignments in such a way that they are understandable by all students.

5. *Make time adjustments.* Teachers should individualize the time requirements associated with assignments. Some students may be capable of performing the work successfully, only to become frustrated with time restraints. Teachers should make adjustments for students who simply need more time or who may become overwhelmed by the volume of work required in a particular time period.

6. *Provide feedback.* All individuals need feedback; they need to know how they are doing. For students with disabilities and a history of failure, the feedback, especially positive feedback, is even more critical. Teachers should provide feedback for every assignment as soon as possible after the assignment is completed.

7. *Have students keep an assignment notebook.* Often, students with disabilities are disorganized; they may need some organization imposed upon them

externally. Requiring students to keep an assignment notebook is an example. The assignment notebook not only negates the excuse "I did not have my assignment" or "I lost my assignment," but it also helps some students maintain a semblance of order in their assignments and facilitates their completion of all required work.

8. *Provide an alternate assignment.* Provide opportunities for students to complete an assignment differently. For example, if a student has difficulty with oral language, the teacher could accept a written book report rather than an oral one. Videotaped, tape-recorded, and oral presentations can be used in conjunction with written presentations.

9. *Allow manipulatives.* Cue cards, charts, and number lines are examples of manipulatives that can help some students comprehend information. Some students prefer to learn visually, whereas others prefer the auditory mode. Manipulatives can facilitate the learning of all students.

10. *Highlight textbooks.* Highlight the important facts in textbooks. These books can be passed on to other students with similar reading problems next year. Highlighting material enables students to focus on the important content and discard other information.

Another accommodation that is critical for students with disabilities is test modification. Some students, for example, are very poor readers. When these students are required to take a test, reading the questions themselves, the result may be that the teacher is assessing the student's poor reading skills rather than knowledge in a particular content area. Ways in which teachers can accommodate for this situation include

- ◆ Having another student read the test to the student
- ◆ Having the special education teacher or aide read the test to the student
- ◆ Giving the student additional time to complete the test
- ◆ Rewording the test to include only words that are within the student's reading vocabulary

Smith, Finn, and Dowdy (1993) list other areas where teachers can accommodate for students during testing:

1. Spacing of items on the pages
2. Space allowed for responses
3. Margins
4. Readability of the test
5. Test length
6. Test organization
7. Test instructions
8. Item type (p. 309)

These accommodations do not give the student an unfair advantage; they simply make it possible for the student to be successful if the information necessary for the test is available.

Tape Recorder as an Instructional Aid

Taped Lecture

1. Use only if the student is unable to attend the lecture or if listening to the lecture again would be beneficial.
2. Try using taped lectures in the resource room on a trial basis to determine if they will be effective.
3. Coordinate with all teachers involved with the student when using taped lectures.
4. Tape lectures and other activities that are considered the most difficult.

Lecture Summaries

1. Keep lecture summaries to a length of approximately 15 to 25 minutes.
2. Emphasize the primary points; do not include extraneous materials.
3. Present information on the tapes in an ordered, well-organized format.
4. Attach a written outline with the tape to help students follow along with the oral summary.

Taped Textbooks

1. Tape material as it will be assigned, such as by chapter or unit.
2. Use only readers with a pleasant, easily understood voice.
3. Include printed material so that the student can follow along with the taped material.

Source: Price, B. J. (1984). The tape recorder as an instructional aid in special education. *Educational Technology, 24,* 42–46. Used with permission.

Another important accommodation that teachers can make to help students with disabilities is the alteration of materials. Ellis and Lenz (1990) describe a way to reduce the content in textbooks as an accommodation. Often, students are capable of reading and understanding, but their reading skills are such that it takes them significantly longer to read than their peers. Therefore, teachers may wish to reduce the amount of content without altering the nature of the content.

Teachers also have some control over how they implement the school curriculum (Carnine, 1991; Simmons, Fuchs, & Fuchs, 1991; Smith, Finn, & Dowdy, 1993). They can alter their speed of presentation of the materials, develop ways to inform students that certain information is important, and quickly cover information that is required to be included, but that has limited importance to students. The only limitation in modifying the curriculum is the teacher's creativity. For example, there are numerous ways that teachers can convey the importance of specific information to students:

- Repeating important information several times
- Writing important facts on the board
- Repeating the same information about a particular topic over several days
- Distributing handouts that contain only the most important information about a particular topic

Study Skills

Often, accommodations made by teachers are insufficient to guarantee that students with problems will be successful. In addition to the teacher's actions, students must develop some skills or strategies that will help them overcome their disability (Smith & Dowdy, 1989). Some classroom teachers make every effort to provide all of the accommodations that are needed by students. However, there are some teachers who do not have such a positive attitude. For many of these teachers, students have to rely on their own means to help them achieve success. Whether students have teachers who make accommodations, understanding how to use study skills will greatly enhance their chances for being successful in future activities, academic, vocational, or social. Classroom teachers can help students by ensuring that they have an understanding and ability to use a repertoire of study skills.

Study skills are different skills that students can use to help them achieve success, either in academic, vocational, or social settings (Smith et al., 1993). Study skills can be defined as the "tools used to acquire, record, locate, organize, synthesize, and remember information effectively and efficiently" (Hoover, 1988, p. 10). Examples of study skills include:

- Note taking and studying for tests
- Understanding reading material
- Reading rate
- Remembering information
- Listening
- Managing behavior and time

Many students have an innate ability in these areas. For example, some students are good readers, with reading comprehension being a part of this ability; other students have an easy time memorizing facts. These students may not need teachers to provide instruction in study skills. For other students, however, study skills need to be taught. Therefore, to facilitate students' success in general education classrooms, classroom teachers may want to teach students study skills.

Hoover (1988) listed a series of study skills and their significance for learning. For example, the study skill listening is critical in most educational settings because teachers provide so much information verbally. If students are not able to attend to auditory information, they will miss a great deal of the information provided by the teacher. Table 14.3 summarizes study skills and their significance for learning.

TABLE 14.3   **Study Skills and Their Significance for Learning**

Study Skill	Significance for Learning
Reading rate	Rates vary with type and length of reading materials.
Listening	Ability to listen is critical in most educational activities.
Note taking/outlining	Ability to take notes and develop outlines is critical in content courses.
Report writing	Written reports are frequently required in content courses.
Oral presentations	Some teachers require extensive oral reporting.
Graphic aids	Visual aids can help students who have reading deficits.
Test taking	Students must be able to do well on tests if they are to succeed in content courses.
Library usage	Ability to find and use resource information from the library is critical in content courses.
Reference material/ dictionary usage	Using reference materials makes learners more independent.
Time management	Ability to manage and allocate time is critical for success in secondary settings.
Self-management of behavior	Leads to independence.

Source: Hoover, J. J. (1988). *Teaching handicapped students study skills.* (2nd ed). Lindale, TX: Hamilton Publications. Used with permission.

There are many different ways that teachers can teach study skills. For example, in working with students and their reading comprehension, teachers might teach students to underline facts that are important, pay attention to margin notes and use the SQ3R reading method or some other method that focuses on asking questions and trying to answer them during the reading process (Smith et al., 1993). When teaching students organizational skills, teachers can use logs and charts, work stations, and color coding of materials, times, and guided notes (Shields & Heron, 1989).

Regardless of how a particular study skill is taught, there is a sequence that can generally be followed. This includes (Beirne-Smith, 1989):

1. Determining how the skill is currently being used.
2. Teaching any preskills that are necessary.
3. Teaching the specific study skill.
4. Providing students the opportunity for practice.
5. Helping students generalize the skill to other situations.

Summary

◆ Unique differences exist between elementary and secondary settings in terms of organizational structure, curricula, and learner variables.

◆ Integrating students with disabilities into general classes is more difficult at the secondary level than in the elementary grades.

◆ Secondary teachers focus more on content than do elementary teachers.

◆ The period of adolescence adds to problems experienced by students with disabilities.

◆ Natural curricular differentiation is present in secondary schools, accommodating for individual needs and interests, to a degree.

◆ Secondary curricula generally follow state guidelines.

◆ There are six major curricular options for students with disabilities at the secondary level: (1) basic skills, (2) social skills, (3) tutorial, (4) learning strategies, (5) vocational, and (6) adult outcomes.

◆ Future-based assessment offers one method for developing programs for adolescents with disabilities.

◆ Students with disabilities need to be taught how to self-advocate.

◆ Classroom teachers and special education teachers must work closely together at the secondary level.

◆ Special education teachers must help prepare students for content classes.

◆ Transition is a major endeavor at the secondary level for students with disabilities.

◆ Accommodations are changes that teachers can make that facilitate the success of students with disabilities.

◆ Study skills are skills that students with disabilities can use to help them achieve success in general and special education classes.

References

Aaron, A. (Ed.). (1988). *Reasonable accommodations: A faculty guide to teaching college students with disabilities.* New York: Professional Staff Congress/CUNY.

Alley, G. R., & Deshler, D. D. (1979). *Teaching the learning disabled adolescent: Strategies and methods.* Denver, CO: Love Publishing.

Baker, J., & Zigmond, N. (1990). Are regular education classes equipped to accommodate students with learning disabilities? *Exceptional Children, 56,* 515–526.

Beirne-Smith, M. (1989). Teaching note-taking skills. *Academic Therapy, 24,* 452-458.

Brophy, J., & Good, T. L. (1986). Teacher behavior and student achievement. In M. Wittrock (Ed.), *Handbook of research on teaching* (3rd ed., pp. 328–375). New York: Macmillan.

Bryan, T., Bay, M., & Donahue, M. (1988). Implications of the learning disabilities definition for the regular education initiative. *Journal of Learning Disabilities, 21*(1), 23–27.

Carnine, D. (1991). Curricular interventions for teaching higher order thinking to all students: Introduction to special series. *Journal of Learning Disabilities, 24,* 261–269.

Carroll, J. B. (1985). The model of school learning: Progress of an idea. In L. W. Anderson (Ed.), *Perspectives on school learning: Selected writings of John B. Carroll* (pp. 82–108).

Chalmers, L. (1991). Classroom modifications for the mainstreamed student with mild handicaps. *Intervention in School and Clinic, 27,* 40–42.

Chesler, B. (1982). ACLD committee survey on LD adults. *ACLD Newsbrief, 145,* 1–5.

Christenson, S. L., Ysseldyke, J. E., & Thurlow, M. L. (1989). Critical instructional factors for students with mild handicaps: An integrative review. *Remedial and Special Education, 10*(5), 21–31.

Cullinan, D., Epstein, M. H., & Lloyd, J. W. (1983). *Behavior disorders of children and adolescents.* Englewood Cliffs, NJ: Prentice-Hall.

Deshler, D., & Schumaker, J. B. (1988). Learning strategies: An instructional alternative for low-achieving adolescents. *Exceptional Children, 52,* 83–89.

Deshler, D., Schumaker, J. B., Lenz, B. K., & Ellis, E. S. (1984). Academic and cognitive interventions for LD adolescents (Part II). *Journal of Learning Disabilities, 17*(3), 170–179.

Dowdy, C. A., Carter, J., & Smith, T. E. C. (1990). Differences in transitional needs of high school students with and without learning disabilities. *Journal of Learning Disabilities, 23*(6), 343–348.

Dowdy, C. A., Patton, J. R., & Polloway, E. A. (in press). *Guide to attention deficits in the classroom.* Austin, TX: Pro-Ed.

Dowdy, C. A., & Smith, T. E. C. (1991). Future-based assessment and intervention. *Intervention in School and Clinic, 27*(3), 101–106.

Edgar, E. (1988). Employment as an outcome for mildly handicapped students: Current status and future directions. *Focus on Exceptional Children, 2*(1), 2–8.

Ellis, E. S., & Lenz, B. K. (1990). Techniques for mediating content-area learning: Issues and research. *Focus on Exceptional Children, 22,* 1–16.

Garcia, S. B., & Malkin, D. H. (1993). Toward defining programs and services for culturally and linguistically diverse learners in special education. *Teaching Exceptional Children, 26,* 52–58.

Good, T. L., & Brophy, J. E. (1987). *Educational psychology* (3rd ed.). New York: Longman Press.

Guetzloe, E. (1988). Suicide and depression: Special education's responsibility. *Teaching Exceptional Children, 20,* 25–28.

Halpern, A. S., Close, D. W., & Nelson, D. J. (1986). *On my own: The impact of semi-independent living programs for adults with mental retardation.* Baltimore: Paul H. Brookes.

Hazel, J. S., Schumaker, J. B., Shelon, J., & Sherman, J. A. (1982). Application of a group training program in social skills to learning disabled and non-learning disabled youth. *Learning Disability Quarterly, 5,* 398–408.

Hoover, J. J. (1988). Implementing a study skills program in the classroom. *Academic Therapy, 24,* 471–476.

Hudson Institute. (1987). *Workforce 2000: Work and workers for the 21st century.* Indianapolis, IN: Author.

Jenkins, J. R., Pious, C. G., & Jewell, M. (1990). Special education and the regular education initiative: Basic assumptions. *Exceptional Children, 56*(6), 479–491.

Leverett, R. G., & Diefendorf, A. O. (1992). Suggestions for frustrated teachers. *Teaching Exceptional Children, 24,* 30–35.

Mims, A., Harper, C., Armstrong, S. W., & Savage, S. (1991). Effective instruction in homework for students with disabilities. *Teaching Exceptional Children, 23,* 42–44.

National Joint Committee on Learning Disabilities. (1988). Letter to NJCLD member organizations.

Patton, J. R., Cronin, M. E., Polloway, E. A., Hutchinson, D., & Robinson, G. A. (1989). Curricular considerations: A life skills orientation. In G. A. Robinson, J. R. Patton, E. A. Polloway, & L. R. Sargent (Eds.), *Best practices in mild mental disabilities.* Reston, VA: CEC-MR.

Polloway, E. A., Patton, J. R., Epstein, J. H., & Smith, T. E. C. (1989). Comprehensive curriculum for students with mild handicaps. *Focus on Exceptional Children, 21,*(8), 1–12.

Polloway, E. A., & Smith, T. E. C. (1992). *Language instruction for students with disabilities.* Denver, CO: Love Publishing.

Price, B. J. (1984). The tape recorder as an instructional aid in special education. *Educational Technology, 24,* 42–46.

Reid, E. R. (1986). Practicing effective instruction: The exemplary center for reading. *Exceptional Children, 52,* 510–519.

Rosenshine, B., & Stevens, R. (1986). Teaching functions. In M. Wittrock (Ed.), *Handbook of research on teaching* (3rd ed., pp. 376–391). New York: Macmillan.

Samuels, S. J. (1986). Why children fail to learn and what to do about it. *Exceptional Children, 53,* 7–16.

Schumaker, J. B., & Deshler, D. D. (1988). Implementing the regular education initiative in secondary schools: A different ball game. *Journal of Learning Disabilities, 21*(1), 36–42.

Shields, J. M., & Heron, T. E. (1989). Teaching organizational skills to students with learning disabilities. *Teaching Exceptional Children, 20,* 8–13.

Simmons, D. C., Fuchs, D., & Fuchs, L. S. (1991). Instructional and curricular requisites of mainstreamed students with learning disabilities. *Journal of Learning Disabilities, 24,* 354–359.

Smith, T. E. C. (1990). *Introduction to education* (2nd ed.). St. Paul, MN: West Publishing.

Smith, T. E. C., & Dowdy, C. A. (1992). The role of study skills in the secondary curriculum. *Academic Therapy, 24,* 479–490.

Smith, T. E. C., Finn, D. M., & Dowdy, C. A. (1993). *Teaching students with mild disabilities.* Ft. Worth, TX: Holt, Rinehart, & Winston.

Smith, T. E. C., Price, B. J., & Marsh, G. E. (1986). *Mildly handicapped children and adults.* St. Paul, MN: West Publishing.

Spirito, A., Hart, K. I., Overholser, J., & Halverson, J. (1990). Social skills and depression in adolescent suicide attempters. *Adolescence, 25,* 543–552.

U.S. Department of Education. (1991). *13th annual report to Congress on the Implementation of the Individuals with Disabilities Education Act.* Washington, DC: U.S. Government Printing Office.

Vogel, S. A. (1990). Postsecondary counseling for adults with learning disabilities. In C. A. Dowdy & B. D. Perry (Eds.), *Bridge to success for adults with learning disabilities: A training series* (pp. 7–8). Birmingham, AL: University of Alabama at Birmingham.

Walberg, H. J. (1984). Improving the productivity of America's schools. *Educational Leadership, 41,* 19–30.

Welch, M., & Link, D. P. (1991). The instructional priority system: A method for assessing the educational environment. *Intervention in the School and Clinic, 27*(2), 91–96.

Wehman, P., Kregel, J. K., & Barcus, J. M. (1985). From school to work: A vocational transition model for handicapped students. *Exceptional Children, 52,* 25–37.

Westling, D. L., & Koorland, M. A. (1989). *The special educator's handbook*. Boston: Allyn & Bacon.

Ysseldyke, J. E., Thurlow, M. L., Wotruba, J. W., & Nania, P. A. (1990). Instructional arrangements; Perceptions from general education. *Teaching Exceptional Children, 22,* 4–8.

CHAPTER 15

Working with Families
of Students
with Disabilities

Introduction

Students with disabilities require the educational system to make accommodations and provide specialized interventions in order to meet their unique learning challenges. As has previously been described, schools are legally responsible to provide appropriate educational programs for these students. No longer can they use as an excuse the notion that they do not have trained staff, that there are limited funds, or that educational programs in general school environments are inappropriate for students with disabilities. Significant changes have occurred in the provision of services to this group of students. Currently, they are educated with their nondisabled peers as much as possible, and their educational programs are determined by an individual planning process.

Another major change in the provision of educational services to students with disabilities is the involvement of parents. Prior to PL 94–142, which mandated current educational services for students with disabilities, schools frequently did not encourage parents to participate in the educational process of their children. The result was that parents were often left out of the decision-making activities that resulted in specific interventions for their children. Often, parents were not only left out of the decision-making process, they were not even informed of the programs the school was implementing for their children. Some school personnel did make significant efforts to keep parents involved in the education of their children. Unfortunately, others did little or nothing to secure parental involvement. This attitude about parental involvement has changed dramatically in the last decade.

Legislation and parental advocacy have resulted in the current level of parental involvement in the education of students with disabilities. Not only have legal mandates resulted in parental involvement, but most school personnel now see the merit in having parents participate in the educational process. This has brought about a stronger effort on behalf of school personnel to include parents in all aspects of a student's individualized educational program (IEP) process, including identification, referral, assessment, program planning, and program implementation.

Although schools are more interested in involving families in the educational programs of their children, getting parents to be active participants in the process may prove difficult. Parents are so used to schools doing what they want with children at both elementary and secondary levels, without asking for parental input, that they have become accustomed to nonparticipation. There are several ways to involve families in the education of children with disabilities. Dunst, Johanson, Trivette, and Hamby (1991) described six different methods for involving families:

- Enhancing a sense of community among the families
- Mobilizing resources and supports
- Shared responsibility and collaboration
- Protecting family integrity
- Strengthening family functioning
- Proactive human service practices

Table 15.1 describes each category and gives examples of **family support** principles associated with each. In addition to these suggestions, simple ideas such as arranging meeting times around the schedules of parents are also effective.

TABLE 15.1 **Major Categories and Examples of Family Support Principles**

Category/Characteristic	Examples of Principles
1. *Enhancing a sense of community.* Promoting the coming together of people around shared values and common needs in ways that create mutually beneficial interdependencies	• Interventions should focus on the building of interdependencies between members of the community and the family unit. • Interventions should emphasize the common needs and supports of all people and base intervention actions on those commonalities.
2. *Mobilizing resources and supports.* Building support systems that enhance the flow of resources in ways that assist families with parenting responsibilities	• Interventions should focus on building and strengthening informal support networks for families rather than depending solely on professionals' support systems. • Resources and supports should be made available to families in ways that are flexible, individualized, and responsive to the needs of the entire family unit.
3. *Shared responsibility and collaboration.* Sharing of ideas and skills by parents and professionals in ways that build and strengthen collaborative arrangements	• Interventions should employ partnerships between parents and professionals as a primary mechanism for supporting and strengthening family functioning. • Resources and support mobilization interactions between families and service providers should be based on mutual respect and sharing of unbiased information.
4. *Protecting family integrity.* Respecting the family's beliefs and values and protecting the family from intrusion upon its beliefs by outsiders	• Resources and supports should be provided to families in ways that encourage, develop, and maintain healthy, stable relationships among all family members. • Interventions should be conducted in ways that accept, value, and protect a family's personal and cultural values and beliefs.
5. *Strengthening family functioning.* Promoting the capabilities and competencies of families necessary to mobilize resources and perform parenting responsibilities in ways that have empowering consequences	• Interventions should build on family strengths rather than correct weaknesses or deficits as a primary way of supporting and strengthening family functioning. • Resources and supports should be made available to families in ways that maximize the family's control over and decision-making power regarding services they receive.
6. *Proactive human service practices.* Adoption of consumer-driven human service-delivery models and practices that support and strengthen family functioning	• Service-delivery programs should employ promotion rather than treatment approaches as the framework for strengthening family functioning. • Resource and support mobilization should be consumer-driven rather than service provider–driven or professionally prescribed.

Source: From "Family-oriented early intervention policies and practices: Family-centered or not?" by C. J. Dunst, C. Johanson, C. M. Trivette, and D. Hamby, *Exceptional Children, 58,* 1991, p. 117. Copyright 1991 by the Council for Exceptional Children. Reprinted with permission.

Some families will become more involved with the education of their child than others. One study reported that 23% of the respondents said they had no involvement in the education of their children in public school special education programs, 43% said they were somewhat involved, and only 34% said they were actively involved in their child's special education programs (Haring, Lovett, & Saren, 1991). Parents from rural areas are more likely than parents from urban centers to be engaged in their child's educational program. School personnel need to encourage those parents who are active in their child's education to maintain their commitment while developing strategies that will increase the involvement of parents who are less likely to be interested in their children's educational program.

Obviously many different variables are associated with level of parental involvement. In one study, Cone, Delawyer, and Wolfe (1985) concluded that four primary variables are positively correlated with parental involvement in educational programs:

1. Family income
2. Educational level of the mother
3. Educational level of the father
4. Amount of time the student spends in special education

In other words, more educated parents and parents with higher incomes are more likely to be involved in their child's educational program than those with lower incomes and lower educational levels. Also, the time a child spends in special education programs correlates with more involvement from parents. Parents from smaller communities are also more likely to be involved in the educational program for their son or daughter.

The primary negative correlation with participation in the special education process was the student's grade level. Parents of children in lower grades were more likely to be involved than parents with older children. In some cases, this may be due to older students being embarrassed by their parents' involvement. In another study, researchers found that the ethnicity of the families was correlated to participation in the individualized educational program (IEP) process. This study found that Anglo parents participate most, followed by African-American families and Hispanic families (Lynch & Stein, 1987).

There are many different areas in special education where family participation can and should occur. This includes involvement with the student's assessment and IEP development, involvement with parent groups, observing the student in the school setting, and communicating with parents. Of these major areas, participation in developing the IEP process occurs the most frequently. In a study of 99 families with children with disabilities, 85 families reported that their level of participation in their child's IEP development was either very high or somewhat high. Only 10 families indicated little participation. Sixty-seven of the families said they had some level or high levels of participation in the assessment process, and 52 families indicated they participated in parent groups at some or high levels (Meyers & Blacher, 1987).

The general conclusions that can be drawn from the research suggest that some families are very involved in their child's special educational program, whereas others have limited or no involvement. Schools meet the letter of the law by simply inviting

Relevant Information on Specific Cultural Groups

Asian-Americans

Important Cultural Values and Behaviors	Clinical Application
Nonverbal Communication Styles	
Greetings: Women do not shake hands with each other or with men.	Be cautious about offering your hand first with a woman client or family member.
Traditional greeting is a "wai"—a joining of hands, raised up to the chest, and head bowed slightly.	Greet clients in their cultural style to communicate an understanding of, and respect for, their culture.
Touching of strangers is inappropriate.	Be cautious about touching client. Communicate concern in other ways; offer tea, a symbol of friendship and goodwill.
Touching of head may be construed as an attempt to rid the spirit in some Asian groups. Indo-Chinese believe that the soul or spirit resides in the head.	Be cautious about touching the head of any member of the Asian culture.
Eye-to-eye contact between strangers is considered shameful.	Don't gaze steadily if the client appears to be uncomfortable. Asians are more comfortable with fleeting eye contact.

African-Americans

Important Cultural Values and Behaviors	Clinical Application
Nonverbal Communication Styles	
Listening behavior—tend to look at someone when they are talking, and look away while listening. Prolonged eye contact is considered to be staring. May perform other activities; likely to nod their heads and make responses to indicate they are listening.	Understand these cultural differences so you do not misinterpret these behaviors as indifference. Avoid prolonged eye contact.
Body space—blacks move in closer than whites when talking.	Understand these differences and allow client to define parameters of contact.

Hispanics/Latinos

Important Cultural Values and Behaviors	Clinical Application
Nonverbal Communication Styles	

Hispanics tend to
• Touch people with whom they are speaking

▼

Hispanics/Latinos (Cont.)	
Important Cultural Values and Behaviors	Clinical Application
Nonverbal Communication Styles	
• Sit and stand closer than Anglos	Allow client to define body space parameters.
• Shake hands or engage in an introductory embrace, kissing on the cheek, back slapping	Shake hands in greeting.
• Interpret prolonged eye contact as disrespectful	Avoid prolonged eye contact.
• Expect elderly to be treated with respect	Address elderly more formally than younger clients.

Source: Randall-David, E. (1989). *Strategies for working with culturally diverse communities and clients.* Washington, DC: Office of Maternal and Child Health, U.S. Department of Health and Human Services.

parental participation. However, school personnel should do more. They need to develop different strategies that will facilitate parental involvement. Although some parents create problems for the school because of their level of involvement, for the most part educational programs are greatly strengthened with parental support. Some strategies are discussed later in the chapter.

The Family

The viewpoint of what constitutes a family has changed dramatically over the past decade. Traditionally, a **family** has been described as a group of individuals who live together that includes a mother, father, and one or more children. However, this stereotypical picture of a family has been challenged. "The idealized **nuclear family** of yesteryear with the stay-at-home, take-care-of-the-children mother and the outside-the-home breadwinner father no longer represents the typical American family" (Allen, 1992, p. 319). This rather traditional view of family has been changed by the reality that many families do not resemble this model.

Currently, there are many different family compositions. For example, a large number of families are single-parent families, most frequently with a mother. "Ninety percent of the families receiving AFDC (Aid to Families with Dependent Children) are headed by single mothers with living but absent fathers" (Allen, 1992, p. 312). Some single-parent families are headed by a father, and, in some cases, children live with one or more of their grandparents, without either mother or father present. Other families consist of a husband and wife without children. And, although not as common as they once were, some families are extended family units, with grandmother or grandfather living with the parents and child. Children also live in foster homes, where the foster parents serve all legal roles as birth parents.

There is also a question about family units composed of homosexual individuals. Do these "gay" unions form a family? Regardless of individual opinions on this issue, there are gay adults who have children. In these situations, schools must interact with the parent-child unit as a family. Whether school personnel consider this structure a family or not, they must deal with the situation as a family unit. Obviously, the nature of families varies significantly. The key idea for school personnel to remember is that students' parents, or grandparents when they are in the role of parents, should be involved in educational programs regardless of the specific composition of the family. School personnel must put aside any personal feelings they may have about various types of lifestyles and work with students' families to develop and implement the best possible programs for the students.

Although undergoing major changes in structure, the family remains the basic unit in our society. It is a dynamic, evolving social force. The family has always been the foundation for our society, and although there is debate about the current role of families and their composition, the family remains the key ingredient in a child's life. School personnel must include the family in all key decisions affecting children, those with special needs and those without.

Families and Children with Disabilities

The birth of any child results in changes in the family structure and dynamics. Obviously, a first child changes the lives of the mother and father, but subsequent births also affect the dynamics of the family unit. Areas affected include finances, amount and quality of time parents can devote to specific children, relationship between the husband and wife, and future family goals. The birth of a child with a disability only exacerbates these changes. The almost immediate financial and emotional impact can create major problems for all family members, including parents and siblings (Creekmore, 1988).

When a child with a disability becomes a member of the family, whether through birth, adoption, or later onset of the disability, the entire family must make adjustments. Important decisions and the solutions to many problems must be made. Some of the problems facing families are (Allen, 1992)

- Expensive (and perhaps painful or life-threatening) medical treatment, surgery, hospitalization that may occur repeatedly and for extended periods
- Heavy expenses and financial burdens other than medical, such as special foods and equipment
- Frightening and energy-draining crises, often recurring, as when the child stops breathing, turns blue, or has a major convulsion
- Transportation problems, baby-sitting needs for the other children, time away from jobs to get the disabled child to consultation and treatment appointments
- Lack of affordable child care for families with children who are developmentally disabled
- Continuous day and night demands on parents to provide what are routine but difficult caregiving tasks (for example, it may take an hour or more, five to

six times during a single day and night, to feed a child with a severe cleft palate condition)

◆ Constant fatigue, lack of sleep, little or no time to meet the needs of other family members

◆ Little or no opportunity for recreational or leisure activities; difficulty (and additional expense) of locating babysitters who are both qualified and willing to care for a disabled child, especially if the child has severe medical or behavioral problems

◆ Lack of respite care facilities

◆ Jealousy or feelings of rejection among brothers and sisters, who may feel the special child gets *all* the family's attention and resources

◆ Marital problems arising from finances, fatigue, differences about management of the child's disability, or feelings of rejection by husband (or wife) that he or she is being passed over in favor of the child (p. 321)

Regardless of the many problems that must be dealt with, a primary difficulty that must be confronted is the acceptance and understanding of the child and the disability. Understanding a diagnosis and the implications of that diagnosis are critical in a family accepting a child with a disability. Parents with a low level of understanding of a diagnosis will likely not clearly understand what expectations for the child are realistic. This could result in major problems between the child and other family members (Switzer, 1985). For example, parents might not understand the nature of a learning disability and therefore accuse the child of being lazy and not trying. Parents who do not understand the potential for students with mental retardation might also have unrealistic expectations, or even have expectations that will extremely limit the child's success. For example, parents of adolescents with mental retardation might not support a school work program for their son or daughter because of their belief that adults with mental retardation are not capable of holding a job.

Families who experience the entry of a child with a disability into the family unit experience a variety of reactions (Cook, Tessier, & Klein, 1992):

◆ Shock, disbelief, and denial
◆ Anger and resentment
◆ Bargaining
◆ Depression and discouragement
◆ Acceptance

Although not all parents go through these stages, many do. School personnel, including teachers, counselors, and administrators, need to be aware of these reactions and be prepared to deal with family members who are experiencing various feelings related to their discovery that their child has a disability. For example, when parents feel guilt after learning that their child has a disability, school personnel should listen with acceptance to the parents and help them understand the nature of the disability and their lack of responsibility. Figure 15.1 depicts possible parental reactions and various interventions that schools can utilize to help family members.

Switzer (1985) described a model to help parents accept the fact that their child has a disability. The model, termed the cognitive problem-solving model, consists of

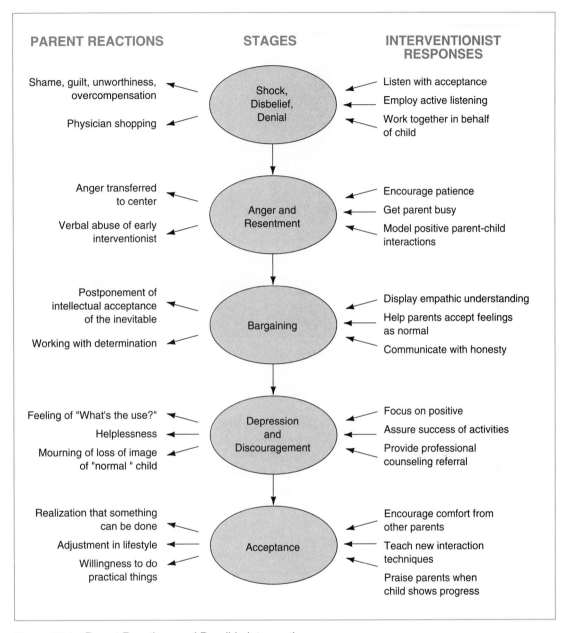

Figure 15.1 **Parent Reactions and Possible Interventions**

Source: Reprinted with permission of Macmillan Publishing Company from ADAPTING EARLY CHILDHOOD CURRICULA FOR CHILDREN WITH SPECIAL NEEDS, Third Edition, by Ruth E. Cook, Annette Tessier, and Diane Klein. Copyright © 1992 by Macmillan Publishing Company.

Parents react in many different ways when they discover they have a child with a disability.

five different seminars. The focus in the first two seminars is on definitions. During these sessions, information is provided to help parents understand different disabilities and the impact of different disabilities on their children. Session three focuses on life at home and how parents can become involved in the child's educational programs. In session four, similar issues are discussed as they relate to the child in school. Finally, session five targets the future. These seminars, scheduled weekly for 90 minutes, are intended to provide parents with factual information that should dispell some myths they may have encountered and help them identify and implement "more responsive treatment options" for their children.

School personnel need to be aware of family members' acceptance level of children with disabilities and make efforts to improve this acceptance. If parents and other family members do not accept the child with a disability, educational efforts will be significantly less than optimal.

Siblings of Students with Disabilities

Just as the adults in a family are important in developing and implementing appropriate educational programs, so too are siblings of children with disabilities. With approximately 10% of the school population identified as disabled, the number of children with disabled siblings can only be estimated to be significant. Although not all nondisabled siblings experience problems (Gargiulo, O'Sullivan, Stephens, & Gold-

Ethical and Legal Rights of Parents

- ◆ Right to be informed regarding educational changes concerning their child
- ◆ Right to be asked for information when evaluating the child's need and right to a special education program
- ◆ Right to be involved in educational decision making about their child
- ◆ Right to be kept informed about the educational progress of their child
- ◆ Right to be asked for their legitimate opinion regarding their child's educational needs
- ◆ Right to be involved in determining appropriate future directions for their child's educational program
- ◆ Assumption that parents desire to be involved in their child's educational program
- ◆ Assumption that parents care about their child's educational program
- ◆ Assumption that parents will make every attempt to support their child and the school's efforts to provide an appropriate education for their child

man, 1989–1990), research suggests that many children who have siblings with disabilities have significant problems related to the disability. The mere presence of a child with a disability can have "a profound impact on family structure and dynamics" (Gargiulo, et al., 1989–1990, p. 21). This, plus the movement to focus more on family interventions for students with disabilities, results in a reason to consider the needs of nondisabled siblings (Summers, Bridge, & Summers, 1991).

A child with a disability has an impact on siblings in two primary ways: economic and emotional. As a result of the financial impact the child with a disability has on the family, nondisabled siblings may feel that they are being deprived of having certain things. This may be factual, or simply a perception. Regardless, nondisabled siblings may feel resentment if they think that their sibling with a disability is draining the economic base from the family.

Siblings of children with disabilities may also feel they are emotionally deprived. Their parents may spend a great deal more time with the child with the disability than with them. Although this may be a necessity because of the disability, the nondisabled brother or sister may not be mature enough to understand this reality. Parents must convey to the nondisabled siblings that they are loved just as much as the child with the disability, even though more money and time may be spent on that child (Creekmore, 1988).

There are many ways parents and school personnel can help siblings who may be experiencing feelings of being deprived emotionally or financially. One good way is to involve siblings in intervention programs. Even young children feel as if they are more a part of the family if they are involved in the intervention program. Although involving siblings in the intervention program is usually very positive, parents need to be aware that too much responsibility for the sibling can result in negative attitudes. The siblings of the child with a disability do not need to feel that they are burdened by the brother or sister (Gargiulo, 1985).

Other ways siblings can become involved and made to understand the disability include the following:

1. *Inform siblings of the nature and cause of the disability.* Often, siblings are concerned that they might become disabled like their brother or sister and let fear limit their interactions. In most situations, this is far from likely, and siblings need to understand that fact.
2. *Allow siblings to attend conferences with school personnel.* When they are mature enough to understand the process, siblings are in a better position to help when they are aware of the program and their role in the program. Siblings may also have some good suggestions that can be used by school personnel or other family members.
3. *Openly discuss the disability with all family members.* Trying to be secretive about a family member's disability can only encourage inaccurate conclusions and unwarranted fears. Parents need to be open with information about a child when siblings are capable of understanding the disability.

Obviously, when dealing with siblings of children with disabilities, parents and school personnel must take into consideration the maturity and ability to understand of the nondisabled child. When this is done, the siblings of children with disabilities can become a great asset to the family and school in attempting to provide appropriate educational programming. They can be supportive of the child at home, and possibly even provide assistance.

One way some schools are involving siblings of children with disabilities is through **sibling support groups.** "The primary purpose of most sibling support groups is to provide information" (Summers et al., 1991, p. 20). Often, children who have siblings with disabilities are not provided information about their brother or sister. This can result in misinformation, fear, and other emotions that are often without a foundation. Providing accurate information to siblings in a clear, understandable manner can help them understand the nature of the disability of their brother or sister.

In addition to providing information, sibling support groups can also provide a forum for children to share experiences and support with other children who have siblings with disabilities. Just as parent support groups can help parents cope with the problems associated with having a child with a disability, sibling support groups can help children cope with a disabled brother or sister. It might prove helpful for a child to know that other children experience similar problems as a result of a sibling with a disability. Understanding that similar problems exist and possibly learning new ways to deal with the problems can be very helpful. Although a great deal of research has not been done on the effects of sibling support groups, most data suggest that these groups can be very beneficial (Summers et al., 1991).

Teachers, school counselors, and administrators should work together to provide leadership in developing and maintaining sibling support groups. Although special education teachers may be very active in this process, classroom teachers, by virtue of their having many of these nondisabled siblings in their classes, should be heavily involved. School counselors, often overlooked for activities other than scheduling, can be key individuals in developing sibling support groups. When working with sibling support groups, teachers and other school personnel should keep the following in mind:

1. Recognize that different disabilities produce different effects in sibling relations. Do not treat all siblings of children with disabilities as if they were experiencing the same thing.
2. Make sure that children feel comfortable in the group, since sharing feelings and changing behavior can be difficult.
3. Emphasize the importance of prosocial behavior, and encourage children to share prosocial experiences.
4. Make the group an enjoyable experience as well as an informative one (Summers et al., 1991, p. 21).

In addition to these reminders, school personnel should also be aware that different cultural groups may react differently to family members with disabilities. This awareness is important in developing programs that are germane for all students. There are numerous activities that teachers can use with sibling support groups. Table 15.2 describes a series of six sessions that could be used to get a support group started.

TABLE 15.2 Examples of Sessions in Sibling Support Groups

Session 1	*Ice breaker.* Involve siblings in varous activities to enable them to get to know each other and to feel comfortable in the group.
Session 2	*What it's like to have a disability.* Students go through a series of simulations to better understand what it is like to have a disability.
Session 3	*Learn about the sibling's disability.* Students learn about their sibling's specific disability through role-playing, information sharing, and other activities.
Session 4	*Exploring feelings.* The purpose of this session is to allow students to explore their own feelings about having a sibling with a disability. Story sharing, role-playing, and impromptu stories are examples of activities.
Session 5	*Sibling observation.* During Session 5, students get together to observe their sibling in an intervention setting. This enables them to better understand the special programs their siblings are involved in.
Session 6	*Summary session.* This final session is used to remind participants what they have learned. Children may be asked to summarize their new knowledge and feelings.

Source: Summers, M., Bridge, J., & Summers, C. R. (1991). Sibling support groups. *Teaching Exceptional Children, 23,* 20–23. Used with permission.

Family and School Collaboration

School personnel and families of students with problems need to collaborate with each other in order to maximize educational efforts. Although parents were once thought to be unimportant in educational programs, they are now considered to be critical for achieving maximum success. All school personnel, classroom teachers, special education teachers, administrators, and support personnel, need to be actively involved with families to improve educational opportunities.

Need for Family and School Collaboration

Parents of children with disabilities and school personnel are partners in providing appropriate educational services. However, parents are actually the "senior partners" because they are responsible for the children 24 hours each day, 365 days each year, for their entire lives (Allen, 1992). Often, school personnel do not acknowledge this role for parents, opting instead to consider themselves as the "senior" members of the team. They may feel that they know more about a particular type of problem than the parents do, and should therefore make most of the decisions regarding the child.

As previously noted, some parents are active participants with school personnel, whereas others tend to limit their involvement. Although some school personnel may feel that "life without parent involvement" is easier, there are numerous reasons why parents of children with disabilities need to be encouraged to participate in the educational process (Allen, 1992):

1. Parents are the key individuals in the socialization of their children.
2. Parents know their children better than school personnel do.
3. Members of the child's family can facilitate the transfer of knowledge learned at school to community settings.
4. Children have a much greater chance for success if their parents and school personnel maintain consistent expectations.
5. Parents provide a significant amount of reinforcement to their children for appropriate actions.
6. Children with disabilities make greater developmental gains when parents provide home teaching (Shearer & Shearer, 1977).
7. Parents participating in programs for their children are in a position to interact and benefit from other parents with children with disabilities.

School personnel should facilitate parental involvement. Such involvement can only enhance educational programs.

Legal Requirements for Collaboration

Although the role of families in all aspects of child growth and development has been acknowledged for a long time, public schools have traditionally not included families in many decisions regarding the education of children (Krauss, 1990). Public Law 94–142 requires schools to involve families in the education of their children much more than previously done (Haring, Lovett, & Saren, 1991; Lusthaus, Lusthaus, & Gibbs, 1981; Smith, Price, & Marsh, 1986). The law, and its subsequent amendments including the Individuals with Disabilities Education Act (IDEA), requires schools to

- ◆ Involve parents in all decision-making activities regarding the education of their child
- ◆ Inform parents of impending actions regarding their child
- ◆ Make available due process rights for parents and their child
- ◆ Enable parents to request a due process hearing if the disagreement with school personnel cannot be resolved

Although not required by law, many states and local education agencies attempt to resolve disputes between parents and school personnel through **mediation.** Mediation can be a commonsense method of working through conflicts. It creates an environment where parents and school personnel can interact in an attempt to develop a consensus regarding a child's educational program (Dobbs, Primm, & Primm, 1991).

Public Law 99–457, the 1986 amendments to PL 94–142, significantly altered the relationship between families and agencies serving children with disabilities. The law, which mandated that schools serve children with disabilities ages 3 to 5, provided financial incentives to states for serving children ages birth through 2 years of age. It requires agencies that serve children ages birth through 2 years to develop an **Individual Family Service Plan (IFSP)** for each child and the child's family. "The IFSP effectively redefines the service recipient as being the family (rather than the child alone), requires explicit judgments about the family's service needs, and reconstitutes the decision-making team by mandating family representation" (Krauss, 1991, p. 388).

The IFSP requirement acknowledges the role of the family in the education of children with disabilities. It makes the assumption that families cannot be instrumental in a child's intervention program if their own needs are not being met. For example, if a family is living in public housing that is about to be closed, a primary need of theirs is safe, affordable housing. This concern may be so overwhelming that the needs of a toddler with a disability get pushed aside until the housing crisis can be solved. The IFSP takes these kinds of family needs into consideration and attempts to provide interventions that can help solve some of the family's problems and provides services to children with disabilities.

Regardless of the legal requirements for parental involvement, some schools continue to limit the influence of parents. In one study, conducted four years after PL 94–142 was implemented, Halpern (1982) found that parents' perspectives of their child's educational program were rarely sought by schools. Parents had to take the initiative and interject themselves in the educational process. In addition to some schools not soliciting parental involvement, many parents simply choose not to participate in their child's educational program. On the other hand, some parents take full advantage of the law and get extremely involved in all school activities related to their children.

Assessing Family Needs

In order to optimally involve families in the education of students with disabilities, an assessment needs to be completed to determine family needs (Shea & Bauer, 1991). It is simply insufficient to determine only the needs of the child when attempting to involve the entire family in the child's educational program. Assessment of the family will facilitate efforts by schools to design an intervention program that takes advantages of family strengths and helps alleviate family weaknesses.

Finn and Valdasy (1990) have developed a **family needs assessment** scale around Maslow's hierarchy of needs. This family needs scale is completed through an interview process with one or more family members and enables the interviewer to collect information that is pertinent to the family's ability to function as a family unit. Basic needs, such as financial and housing, are assessed along with other areas that will help service providers understand the family and their child with a disability. This scale, and others that are similar (Shea & Bauer, 1991), are intended to enable agencies providing services to have a better understanding of the needs of the family as well as the individual needs of a child with a disability.

Specific Collaboration Activities

Following the determination of family needs, school personnel are better prepared to develop programs that will be beneficial to students with disabilities. Based on the results from this determination, school personnel will also have a better idea about how to include the family in the plan. There are many different ways parents and other family members can become involved with the education of a child with a disability or one who is at risk for developing problems. This includes involvement in planning, implementing, and evaluating programs. A first priority is effective communication among school personnel, parents, and other family members. Without effective communication, successful collaboration will be difficult, if not impossible, to achieve.

Communicating with Parents

A critical element in any collaboration between school personnel and parents is communication (Creekmore, 1988). Many parents complain that there is simply too little communication between themselves and the school. Often, problems that may arise between parents and school personnel can be avoided with proper communication. Effective communication must be regular as well as useful. Communicating with parents only once or twice per year, or communicating with parents regularly but with information that is not useful, does not serve the purpose of facilitating educational services to children.

Meyers and Blacher (1987) studied 99 families who had children with disabilities and found that only 11 of the 99 indicated that they had frequent communication with school personnel. Another 36 said they had regular communication. On the negative side, 18 families responded that they had occasional communication, and 34 families said they had rare or no communication with school personnel. These results mean that approximately one-third of the families in the study had rare or no communication with school personnel. With collaboration between school personnel and families of children with disabilities being so critical, these data suggest a major effort is needed to improve communication between these two entities.

Communication between school personnel and parents can take many forms. It does not have to be formal, written communication. Effective communication can be informal, by telephone calls, written notes, newsletters, or in a number of other ways that communication occurs. When communicating with parents, school personnel should be aware of how they convey various messages. For example, school personnel should never "talk down" to parents. Although some parents may be less educated than the school personnel, they are still able to understand information and they should be considered the "senior partners" in the educational process of the student. School personnel should also choose their words thoughtfully. Some words convey very negative meanings, whereas other words are just as useful in transmitting the message and are more positive. Table 15.3 provides a sample of words that should be avoided and their better alternatives. When communicating with parents, school personnel should always be aware of cultural and language differences that may exist. Taking these factors into consideration will only enhance the quality of communication that occurs with family members.

TABLE 15.3 **Sample Word Choices**

Avoid	Use Instead
Must	Should
Lazy	Can do more with effort
Culturally deprived	Culturally different, diverse
Troublemaker	Disturbs class
Uncooperative	Should learn to work with others
Cheats	Lets others do his or her work
Below average	Works at his (her) own level
Truant	Absent without permission
Impertinent	Discourteous
Steals	Takes things without permission
Dirty	Has poor grooming habits
Disinterested	Complacent, not challenged
Stubborn	Insists on having his (her) own way
Insolent	Outspoken
Wastes time	Could make better use of time
Sloppy	Could be neater
Mean	Has difficulty getting along with others
Time and time again	Usually, repeatedly
Dubious	Uncertain
Poor grade or work	Work below his (her) usual standard
Will flunk	Has a chance of passing if...

Source: Shea, T. M., & Bauer, A. M. (1991). *Parents and teachers of children with exceptionalities: A handbook for collaboration* (2nd ed., p. 82). Boston: Allyn & Bacon. Used with permission.

Informal Exchanges. Informal exchanges take place without preparation. Teachers may see a parent in the community and stop and talk momentarily about the parent's child. Teachers should always be prepared to talk to parents about their children, regardless of the setting. The only consideration that should be made is that teachers should not talk about confidential information in a setting where individuals who do not have a need to know are present. If the conversation becomes too involved, the teacher should request that it be continued later, in a more appropriate setting. If this recommendation is made, the teacher must follow through and schedule a meeting that is convenient for the parents.

Parent Observations. Parents should always be encouraged to come to the school and observe their child in the educational setting, so long as their observation is not an embarrassment to the student. Older students may not want their parents observing them. If this is the case, school personnel should try to explain to parents the potential embarrassment; however, the ultimate decision still rests with the parents. Often, parents feel that they are not welcome in a particular classroom. Although the parent's presence could cause some disruption from the daily routine, school personnel need to keep in mind that parents have a critical stake in the success of the educational efforts. Therefore, parents should always feel welcome to observe the student in the educational setting. If the teacher feels that one time would be better than others, this should be conveyed to the parent; however, the parent should be able to come to the school and observe the child at any time.

Telephone Calls. Many teachers use telephone calls a great deal and very effectively to communicate with parents. Parents feel that teachers are interested in their child if the teacher takes the time to call and discuss the child's progress with the parent. When using the telephone for communication purposes, teachers should remember to call when there is good news about the child as well as to report problems the child is experiencing. It makes parents feel very good to get a call from a teacher who says that the child is doing well and having no problems. Again, understanding the language and culture of the home is important when making telephone calls.

Teachers should give parents their home telephone numbers. Often parents, especially those who work during the day, have a difficult time contacting the teacher. Teachers should be available to parents at the parents' convenience, even if it is at night or on weekends. Giving parents a telephone number is reassuring to parents.

Written Notes. Written communication to parents is also an effective method of communicating about a child's progress. When using written communication, teachers need to be aware of the literacy level of the parents and use words and phrases that are readily understandable by the parents. They should also be aware of the primary language of the home. Written communications that are not understood can be very intimidating for parents. When using written communication, teachers should provide an opportunity for parents to respond, either in writing or with a telephone call.

Other Forms of Communication.   In addition to the methods of communication just discussed, school personnel can convey information to parents in other ways:

- Newsletters
- Parent/family support groups
- Brown-bag seminars
- Open houses

School personnel should use every available means to communicate with parents. This is a responsibility of both classroom teachers and special education teachers. Teachers should never assume that other school personnel will be communicating with parents, and therefore that they do not have to. Effective communication between school personnel and parents can involve many different people.

Parent–Teacher Conferences

One excellent method for school personnel and parents to communicate with each other is through parent–teacher conferences. These can be formal, such as IEP and IFSP meetings, or informal, when parents call a teacher and request a meeting with one or more teachers about a particular problem. Regardless of the purpose or formality of the meeting, school personnel should consider several actions that will help focus attention on specific topics. School personnel should send advance information home to parents and make the parents feel at ease about participating in the meeting.

When preparing to meet with parents and discuss children who are experiencing problems, school personnel need to anticipate various components of the discussion. This includes having an idea about the questions that parents may want to ask, as well as knowing what questions should be addressed to the parents. These questions will be different for each family. For example, a family with an elementary student who is having difficulty learning to read will have significantly different questions than will the family with an adolescent who is frustrated about future academic directions. Tables 15.4 and 15.5 provide examples of the kinds of questions that should be anticipated by school personnel. By anticipating the questions in advance, school personnel are in a better position to have a successful meeting than if they approach the meeting without any planning.

IEP Meetings.   Parents should be involved in the development of students' individualized educational programs (IEPs) for two reasons. First, there is a legal requirement for parental participation. Public Law 94–142 and IDEA require that parents be invited to participate in the development of the child's IEP. Parents are supposed to "sign off" on the completed IEP.

Although the legal requirement to have parents participate in the IEP development is important, the more important reason is to gain the input of parents. In most instances, parents know more about their children than school personnel. They have been involved with the child longer and are involved more than the hours of a school

Sample Letter Written to a Student's Parents to Reiterate a Home Instructional Program That Was Agreed upon by His Parents and the Resource/Consultant

Letter to Parents

February 20, 19____

Dear Mr. and Mrs. _____,

I was glad that we had the chance to talk yesterday concerning R.'s progress. I feel that structured home reading will really be a benefit, and I'm glad you agree.

As we discussed R. will use one copy of the book, and you will use another. Your copy is marked with an → at the beginning of the 100-word passage and with /100 where the passage ends. There is a marked time sample like this for every section in the book.

R. is to be corrected for reading errors before and after this 100-word passage. He is not to be corrected when reading the 100 words. During this time, you will count the number of errors he makes. Please use the error correction procedure I sent you last semester. If R. corrects himself within five seconds, a word is counted as correct. Things that are counted as wrong include:

1) calling out the wrong word (i.e., *bat* for *bath*)
2) skipping a word or line
3) losing the place (if this happens, show him the place)
4) leaving off or putting on endings to words (i.e., *call* for *called*)

On the assignment card is a place to record pages read and errors. Either write the number of errors or record tally marks for errors in the space provided for errors.

Example:	*Pages*	*Errors*
	pp. 3–5	5

Please have R. bring the card to me each Monday. I will record his scores for the week.

If you have any questions or problems, please feel free to call me at 217–4963. Thank you so much for your help.

Sincerely,

Ms. Bedford
Resource/Consulting Teacher

P.S. If R. makes more than six errors, have him read the same story the next day.

Source: Idol, L. (1983). *Special educator's consultation handbook* (p. 280). Austin, TX: Pro-Ed. Used with permission.

TABLE 15.4   Questions Parents May Ask Teachers

- What is normal for a child this age?
- What is the most important subject or area for my child to learn?
- What can I work on at home?
- How can I manage her behavior?
- Should I spank?
- When will my child be ready for community living?
- Should I plan on her learning to drive?
- Will you just listen to what my child did the other day and tell me what you think?
- What is a learning disability?
- What is a moderate mental handicap?
- Can IQ be improved?
- My child is emotionally handicapped; is it my fault?
- The doctor said my child will grow out of this. What do you think?
- Will physical therapy make a big difference in my child's control of his hands and arms?
- Have you become harder on our child? Her behavior has changed at home.
- Can I call you at home if I have a question?
- What is all this fuss about putting our child in special education? We have no handicapped people in our family.
- What is the difference between delayed, retarded, mentally handicapped, and learning disabled?
- What kind of after-school activities can I get my child involved in?
- Can my child live on his own?
- What should I do about sexual activity?
- My child missed the bus; whom do I talk to?
- What's he going to be like in five years?
- Will she have a job?
- Who takes care of him when I die?
- What happens if she doesn't make her IEP goals?
- When can my child get out of special education?

Source: Westling, D. L., & Koorland, M. A. (1988). *The special educator's handbook* (p. 208). Boston: Allyn & Bacon. Used with permission.

day. Schools need to take advantage of this knowledge about a child in the development of the IEP (Dowdy & Smith, 1991; Smith & Dowdy, 1992; Smith, Finn, & Dowdy, 1993).

An example of how parents should be involved in the development of IEPs is described in the future-based assessment and intervention model (Dowdy & Smith, 1991; Smith & Dowdy, 1992). In this model, school personnel, parents, and the student discuss likely "futures" for the student and the necessary interventions that will help the student achieve those futures. These agreed futures then guide the development and implementation of educational programs for the student. As students get nearer to exiting the public school system, the future-based model can better meet the individual, unique future needs of each student.

Although there have been various reports regarding the involvement of parents in IEP meetings, overall attendance appears to be good. In one study of 168 parents, it was determined that the students' mothers attended the vast majority of IEP meet-

TABLE 15.5 **Questions Teachers Should Ask Parents**

- What are activities at home that you could provide as a reward?
- What are particular skill areas that concern you most for inclusion on the Individualized Educational Plan?
- What behavior at home do you feel needs to improve?
- Would you be interested in coming to a parent group with other parents of my students?
- When is a good time to call at home?
- Can I call you at work? What is the best time?
- Is there someone at home who can pick the child up during the day if necessary?
- Is there a friend who can come to meetings with you, if you don't like coming alone?
- Is there a place in your neighborhood where meetings could take place?
- Would you be interested in volunteering in our school?
- Could you help on an occasional field trip?
- What is the most difficult problem you face in rearing your child?
- What are your expectations for your child?
- How can I help you the most?
- What is your home routine in the evenings? Is there a quiet place for your child to study?
- Can you or your spouse do some special activity with your child if he or she earns it at school?
- Can you spend some time tutoring your child in the evening?
- Would you like to have a conference with your child participating?
- When is the best time to meet?

Source: Westling, D. L., & Koorland, M. A. (1988). *The special educator's handbook* (p. 209). Boston: Allyn & Bacon. Used with permission.

ings (Scanlon, Arick, & Phelps, 1981). Even though parents are attending IEP conferences, they may not be actively involved in the planning process. In studying the roles of participants in child study teams, Trailor (1982) found that parents spoke only about 10% of the time in conferences. A more recent study of parental participation in IEP development and other special education activities found less than favorable results. In their conclusions, Yanok and Derubertis (1989) stated that, "even though 13 years have elapsed since the passage of PL 94–142, the Act has not significantly altered the levels of school participation of parents of exceptional children" (p. 198).

In order to obtain more involvement in conferences, school personnel may need to be proactive in soliciting parental input. Simply inviting parents to attend is not sufficient. In facilitating exchange between school personnel and parents, deBettencourt (1987) suggests the following:

1. Hold conferences in a small location that is free from external distractions; hold phone calls and other forms of interruptions so that parents feel you are truly interested in them and their child.
2. Hold conferences on time and maintain the schedule; do not let conferences start late or run over because many parents may be taking off from work to attend.
3. Arrange the room so that parents and school personnel are comfortable and can look at each other without barriers, such as desks and tables, between them.
4. Present information clearly, concisely, and in a way that parents can understand; do not "talk down" to the parents.

Goldstein and Turnbull (1981) described one method that was effective in increasing parental participation in the IEP conference. The method used a parent advocate who was assigned to the parent and attended the conference with the parent. The parent advocate, a member of the school staff, facilitated parental participation by introducing the parents to the other team members, verbally reinforcing parental participation, directing questions to the parents, and summarizing the discussion at the end of the conference.

IFSP Meetings.   Schools are required to develop Individual Family Service Plans (IFSPs) for students receiving services in the birth to three-year-old program. Like the IEP, IFSPs must contain some specific information concerning the child and family. The first meeting to develop the IFSP must be held within 45 days from when the child was referred for an evaluation (Colarusso & Kana, 1991). The IFSP must minimally contain (Krauss, 1990)

◆ A statement of child's present functioning level in the following areas: physical development, cognitive development, language and speech development, psychosocial development, and self-help skills
◆ A statement of family's strengths and needs
◆ Specific goals or outcomes for the family and child
◆ Means to evaluate goals
◆ Services required to facilitate goal achievement
◆ The family's case manager

Family involvement in the development of the IFSP is a primary consideration. Public Law 99–457, which implemented the IFSP requirement, was the first federal legislation that truly focused services for individuals with disabilities on the entire family, not only the child with the disability (Colarusso & Kana, 1991). The result is that family input is not only legally mandated, but is highly sought after.

Home Visits.   There is no better way to get an understanding of the home situation than a home visit. These can provide a vast amount of information that can help teachers better understand the student, but they are often difficult to arrange. When possible, school personnel should consider making the extra effort required to arrange and make home visits. When visiting homes, school personnel need to follow certain procedures, including:

◆ Have specific information to deliver or obtain.
◆ Make an appointment and doublecheck before going to the home.
◆ If you desire to meet with parents alone, find out if it is possible to have the child elsewhere during the scheduled visit.
◆ Do not stay too long—certainly no more than an hour.
◆ Arrive at the scheduled time.
◆ Dress as a professional.
◆ Consider making visits with another school system resource person such as the school social worker.
◆ Be sure to do as much listening as talking.
◆ Leave on a positive note (Westling & Koorland, 1988).

The age of the student and cultural background of the family are considerations that should be made before scheduling a home visit.

Home-Based Intervention

One very important way families can become involved with the education of a family member with a disability is through home-based intervention. For preschool children, home-based services are fairly common; however, parents providing instruction at home for older students is not as frequent. Regardless of this reality, there have been many reports that such instruction can be very beneficial to students with disabilities (Binkard, 1985; Brown & Moore, 1992; Ehlers & Ruffin, 1990; Polloway & Smith, 1992; Schulze, Rule, & Innocenti, 1989; Smith, Finn, & Dowdy, 1993).

When children with disabilities enter public schools, the need for home-based interventions may be considered less important than when they were in a preschool program. This is an unfortunate assumption on the part of parents and school personnel. Even though most parents assume the school will provide all the educational interventions their children may need, students with disabilities need parental involvement in their educational programs.

There are numerous ways parents and other family members can get directly involved at home in the student's educational program (Binkard, 1985). These include (1) providing reinforcement, (2) providing motivation, (3) providing direct instructional support, and (4) supporting students with school personnel.

Providing Reinforcement. Parents need to reinforce their children's efforts. Most students with disabilities experience significant levels of failure and frustration. Frequently, the more they attend school, the more they fail. This failure cycle becomes very difficult to break, especially after it is established over several years. One way to help break this failure cycle is through reinforcing success. Parents need to work with school personnel to provide positive reinforcement for all levels of success. If students are not capable of achieving full success in an area, they need to be rewarded for their positive efforts in the proper direction.

Parents are in an excellent position to provide positive reinforcement. They are with the child more than school personnel and are involved in all aspects of the child's life, not just the academic/school area. As a result, parents are in a position to provide reinforcement in areas where the child desires rewards, such as time with friends, money, toys, or trips. For many students, simply allowing them to have a friend over or stay up late at night on a weekend may prove reinforcing. School personnel do not have these types of reinforcers available to them; therefore, parents should take advantage of their repertoire of rewards and reinforce positive efforts of students.

Providing Motivation. Many students have become so used to school failure that they have given up. They make limited effort in school work because they are accustomed to their hard work resulting in failure. It is human nature to quit trying after all efforts have resulted in limited success. Therefore, a key role that parents of students with disabilities can play is motivation. Just as parents are in a unique role to provide positive reinforcement, they are also able to provide motivation in ways teachers cannot.

Brown and Moore (1992) describe a method to motivate poor elementary readers at home. Their program, called the Bama Bookworm Program, requires parents to listen to their children read four nights each week for a month. The program uses stickers, which are later redeemable for pizzas, t-shirts, and a pizza party, as reinforcers. The entire program is based on positive reinforcement for students who work at home with their parents.

Parents should also help motivate their older children's efforts in school. Using a positive reinforcement system can provide incentives for adolescents who need a little extra "push" to get started. School personnel can assist parents in motivating adolescents by discussing potentially desirable reinforcers and by suggesting some home activities.

Providing Direct Instructional Support. Parents and other family members may become directly involved with instructional programs at home. In fact, for many students with disabilities, this direct involvement from family members can be critical to their success. Unfortunately, many family members provide less direct instruction as the child gets older, assuming that the student is capable of doing the work alone. Too often, the reverse is true; students may need more assistance at home as they progress through the grades. Since parents are generally with the child more than school personnel, it seems logical that they are involved in direct instruction, and with methods such as coincidental teaching, where parents teach their children various skills in real-life situations, parental involvement in teaching skills is not burdensome and can be truly effective (Schulze, Rule, & Innocenti, 1989).

Advocates for expanding the role of parents in educating their children adhere to the following assumptions (Ehlers & Ruffin, 1990):

◆ Parents are the first and most important teachers of their children.
◆ The home is the child's first schoolhouse.
◆ Children will learn more during the early years than at any other time in life.
◆ All parents want to be good parents and care about their child's development (p. 1).

The key role of parents must be exploited if students with problems are to receive the maximum interventions possible. Teachers and other school personel can do just so many things to help children with special needs.

Lombardino and Mangan (1983) studied the results of a parent training program on children with disabilities. The program focused on helping parents get involved with a language training program for their children. Results indicated that after receiving training in language programming, the parents became effective instructors for their children. Another study that investigated the effects of training

Evaluation and Information on Special Education Software Sources

Apple Foundation
20525 Mariani Avenue
Cupertino, CA 95014

Center for Special Education Technology
Information Exchange
The Council for Exceptional Children
1920 Association Drive
Reston, VA 22091

Educational Software Exchange Library (EDSEL)
c/o Stanford Avenue School
2833 Illinois Avenue
Southgate, CA 90281

EPIE Institute
Teachers' College
Columbia University
525 W. 120th Street
New York, NY 10027

International Council for Computers in Education
University of Oregon
Eugene, OR 97403

LINC Resources
4820 Indianola Avenue
Columbus, OH 43214

Microcomputer Information Coordination
139 C.R.U., K.U.M.C.
39th and Rainbow
Kansas City, KS 66103

MicroSIFT Project
Northwest Regional Educational Laboratory
710 S.W. 2nd Avenue
Portland, OR 97204

National Education Association
Educational Computer Service
4720 Montgomery Lane
Bethesda, MD 20814

Software Reports
10996 Torreyana Road
P.O. Box 85007
San Diego, CA 92138

Special Education Software Review
3807 N. Northwood
Peoria, IL 61614

Source: Taber-Brown, F. M. (1993). Software evaluation and development. In J. D. Lindsey (Ed.). *Computers and exceptional individuals* (p. 67). Austin, TX: Pro-Ed. Used with permission.

---

parents on their children with disabilities confirmed that with proper training, parents can improve their instructional skills with their children (Sandler, Coren, & Thurman, 1983).

Thurston (1989) describes a home tutoring program that is very effective for students with disabilities. In step 1, the parents and teachers discuss the areas in which home tutoring would be most helpful. Many parents will feel more comfortable helping their children "practice" skills than helping them learn new skills. Therefore, teachers should help identify topics in which practice would benefit the student.

In step 2 of the model, family members implement specific home tutoring procedures. This includes selecting the location for the tutoring, deciding on a time for tutoring, and other components necessary for an effective tutoring session. Step 3 is when the family member providing the tutoring uses proper techniques for positive reinforcement and error correction. When correcting a child's error, the family member should

Parents are the first and most important teachers of their children.

- Stop the child immediately
- Provide the correct answer/response
- Ask the child for the correct answer/response
- Provide positive reinforcement if the answer/response is correct
- Repeat the procedure if the answer/response is incorrect
- Always provide positive reinforcement when the correct answer/response is received

In step 4 of the process, family members should terminate the tutoring session and make a record of the student's accomplishments. Tutoring periods should be short, probably no more than 15 minutes, and should always end with a record of the day's activities. A visual chart, where the student can actually "see" progress, is often very reinforcing to the student (Thurston, 1989).

Too often, when people hear that families are involved in a child's educational program, the assumption is that the "family" is really the child's mother. This is unfortunate, because the involvement of the entire family is the goal for school personnel. Mother, father, and siblings should be included in planning and implementing programs designed to help students with special needs.

Hietsch (1986) described a program that aims at encouraging fathers to get involved in the educational program of their child. The program focuses on a Father's

Day when the fathers of children in the class are all invited to attend for the day. The end goal, of course, is to get fathers to be more involved in all aspects of the child's educational program, not simply have the father show up at the school one day during the school year.

In order to help make Father's Day a success, school personnel should consider several factors. The following have been suggested for a Father's Day outing at a bowling alley (Hietsch, 1986):

1. Make sure that fathers are given enough advance notice to arrange to have the day off from work. It is a good idea to announce the occasion at the beginning of the school year, for example, "Father's Day will be May 18th this year!" This also arouses interest early in the year.
2. Send a reminder letter home a week to 10 days before Father's Day to rekindle enthusiasm and ensure good attendance.
3. Know the first names of all of the fathers so that introductions are easier.
4. Common denominators help to break the ice. Bring out similar jobs or interests.
5. Ask a shy father to help keep score at the bowling alley or pass items at lunch time.
6. Have children show their fathers special items (papers, puppets, etc.) in the classroom.
7. Make trophies or awards ahead of time for categories such as Most Gracious Bowler, Best Form, or First to Arrive, and see that *everyone* gets one!
8. Display the bowling score sheets for the rest of the school to see.
9. Give individual help to the children in writing and illustrating experience stories the next day to help make Father's Day a learning experience (p. 259).

Family members can become involved in their child's educational program in many ways. The role of teachers, both classroom and special education, is to help family members understand the importance of their involvement and give them suggestions for how to get involved. Students with disabilities, and those at risk for developing problems, require the assistance from all parties in order for them to break out of the failure cycle. Family members are critical components of the educational team that must be involved with these children's efforts.

Summary

◆ A major change in the provision of educational services to students with special needs is the involvement of families.

◆ Traditionally, families have been left out of decisions regarding services for students with disabilities.

◆ Getting parents to participate in school decisions is often difficult.

◆ Schools should take proactive steps to ensure the involvement of families of students with disabilities.

◆ Parents of young students are more likely to be involved in the educational process than are parents of older students.

◆ Families are apparently involved in the IEP development for their child.

◆ Unlike families of the past, today's families vary considerably in their composition.

◆ Regardless of their own values, school personnel must involve all family members of a student with special needs, regardless of the type of family.

◆ Family members must make adjustments when a child with a disability becomes a family member, either through birth or adoption.

◆ Acceptance of the child with a disability is the ultimate problem for many families.

◆ Siblings of students with disabilities also experience problems.

◆ Siblings of children with disabilities should be involved with their disabled brother or sister.

◆ Families and schools must collaborate to ensure the appropriate educational programs for students with disabilities.

◆ IDEA requires schools to involve families in educational decisions for students with disabilities.

◆ A critical component in any collaboration between school personnel and familiy members is communication.

◆ All types of communication, formal and informal, between school and families are important.

◆ School personnel should attempt to make parents and other family members feel comfortable and encourage their participation during school conferences.

◆ Family members should be encouraged, and taught how, to become involved in the educational program implemented in the school.

References

Allen, K. E. (1992). *The exceptional child: Mainstreaming in early childhood education* (2nd ed.). Albany, NY: Delmar.

Binkard, B. (1985). A successful handicap awareness program—Run by special parents. *Teaching Exceptional Children, 18,* 12–16.

Brown, D., & Moore, L. (1992). The Bama Bookworm Program. *Teaching Exceptional Children, 24,* 17–21.

Colarusso, R. P., & Kana, T. G. (1991). Public Law 99–457, Part H, infant and toddler programs: Status and implications. *Focus on Exceptional Children, 23,* 1–12.

Cone, J. D., Delawyer, D. D., & Wolfe, V. V. (1985). Assessing parent participation: The parent/family involvement index. *Exceptional Children, 51,* 417–424.

Cook, R. E., Tessier, A., & Klein, M. D. (1992). *Adapting early childhood curricula for children with special needs.* New York: Merrill.

Creekmore, W. N., and students. (1988). Family–classroom: A critical balance. *Academic Therapy, 24,* 207–220.

deBettencourt, L. U. (1987). How to develop parent relationships. *Teaching Exceptional Children, 19,* 26–27.

Dobbs, R. F., Primm, E. B., & Primm, B. (1991). Mediation: A common sense approach for resolving conflicts in education. *Focus on Exceptional Children, 24,* 1–12.

Dowdy, C. A., & Smith, T. E. C. (1991). Future-based assessment and intervention. *Intervention, 27,* 101–106.

Dunst, C. J., Johanson, C., Trivette, C. M., & Hamby, D. (1991). Family-oriented early intervention policies and practices: Family-centered or not? *Exceptional Children, 58,* 115–126.

Ehlers, V. L., & Ruffin, M. (1990). The Missouri project—Parents as teachers. *Focus on Exceptional Children, 23,* 1–14.

Finn, D. M., & Valdasy, P. F. (1990). *Family needs scale.* Unpublished assessment instrument. University of Alabama at Birmingham. Birmingham, AL: U.A.B.

Gargiulo, R. S. (1985). *Working with parents of exceptional children.* Boston: Houghton Mifflin.

Gargiulo, R. S., O'Sullivan, P., Stephens, D. G., & Goldman, R. (1989-90). Sibling relationships in mildly handicapped children: A preliminary investigation. *National Forum of Special Education Journal, 1,* 20–28.

Goldstein, S., & Turnbull, A. P. (1981). Strategies to increase parent participation in IEP conferences. *Exceptional Children, 48,* 360–361.

Halpern, R. (1982). Impact of PL 94–142 on the handicapped child and family: Institutional responses. *Exceptional Children, 49,* 270–273.

Haring, K. A., Lovett, D. L., & Saren, D. (1991). Parent perceptions of their adult offspring with disabilities. *Teaching Exceptional Children, 23,* 6–10.

Hietsch, D. G. (1986). Father involvement: No moms allowed. *Teaching Exceptional Children, 18,* 258–260.

Idol, L. (1983). *Special educator's consultation handbook.* Austin, TX: Pro-Ed.

Krauss, M. W. (1990). New precedent in family policy: Individualized family service plan. *Exceptional Children, 56,* 388–395.

Lombardino, L., & Mangan, N. (1983). Parents as language trainers: Language programming with developmentally delayed children. *Exceptional Children, 49,* 358–361.

Lusthaus, C. S., Lusthaus, E. W., & Gibbs, H. (1981). Parents' role in the decision process. *Exceptional Children, 48,* 256–257.

Lynch, E. W., & Stein, R. C. (1987). Parent participation by ethnicity: A comparison of Hispanic, Black, and Anglo families. *Exceptional Children, 54,* 105–111.

Meyers, C. E., & Blacher, J. (1987). Parents' perceptions of schooling. *Exceptional Children, 53,* 441–450.

Polloway, E. A., & Smith, T. E. C. (1992). *Language instruction for students with disabilities.* Denver, CO: Love Publishing.

Randall-David, E. (1989). *Strategies for working with culturally diverse communities and clients.* Washington, DC: Office of Maternal and Child Health. U.S. Department of Health and Human Services.

Sandler, A., Coren, A., & Thurman, S. K. (1983). A training program for parents of handicapped preschool children: Effects upon mother, father, and child. *Exceptional Children, 49,* 355–357.

Scanlon, C. A., Arick, J., & Phelps, N. (1981). Participation in the development of the IEP: Parents' perspective. *Exceptional Children, 47,* 373–374.

Schulze, K. A., Rule, S., & Innocenti, M. S. (1989). Coincidental teaching: Parents promoting social skills at home. *Teaching Exceptional Children, 21,* 24–27.

Shea, T. M., & Bauer, A. M. (1991). *Parents and teachers of children with exceptionalities: A handbook for collaboration.* Boston: Allyn & Bacon.

Shearer, M. S., & Shearer, D. E. (1977). The portage project: A model for early childhood education. *Exceptional Children, 39,* 210–217.

Smith, T. E. C., & Dowdy, C. A. (1992). Future-based assessment and intervention and mental retardation. *Education and Training in Mental Retardation, 27,* 23–31.

Smith, T. E. C., Finn, D. F., & Dowdy, C. A. (1993). *Teaching students with mild disabilities.* Ft. Worth, TX: Holt, Rinehart & Winston.

Smith, T. E. C., Price, B. J., & Marsh, G. E. (1986). *Mildly handicapped children and adults.* St. Paul, MN: West Publishing.

Summers, M., Bridge, J., & Summers, C. R. (1991). Sibling support groups. *Teaching Exceptional Children, 23,* 20–25.

Switzer, L. S. (1985). Accepting the diagnosis: An educational intervention for parents of children with learning disabilities. *Journal of Learning Disabilities, 18,* 151–153.

Taber-Brown, F. M. (1953). Software evaluation and development. In J. D. Lindsey (Ed.), *Computers and exceptional individuals* (pp. 57–72). Austin, TX: Pro-Ed.

Trailor, C. B. (1982). Role clarification and participation in child study teams. *Exceptional Children, 48,* 529–531.

Thurston, L. P. (1989). Helping parents tutor their children: A success story. *Academic Therapy, 24,* 579–587.

Westling, D. L., & Koorland, M. A. (1988). *The special educator's handbook.* Boston: Allyn & Bacon.

Yanok, J., & Derubertis, D. (1989). Comparative study of parental participation in regular and special education programs. *Exceptional Children, 56,* 195–199.

Glossary

Acceleration. A form of programming for students who are classified as gifted and talented, where the students move through the curriculum at a more rapid pace than their chronological age peers.

Accessibility. The ability of a person with a disability to make use of a physical location or program.

Adaptive behavior. A way of conduct that meets the standards of personal independence and social responsibility expected from that cultural and chronological age group.

Additions. An expressive language problem characterized by individuals inserting words or sounds into their speech.

Affective education. Educational programs that focus on the emotional health of a child.

Allergens. Substances that individuals are allergic to, such as dust, certain foods, or animal dander.

Alternative communication. Any system of conveying ideas that is used in lieu of human speech.

American Sign Language (ASL). A particular form of sign language used by many individuals with severe hearing impairments.

American Speech-Language-Hearing Association. The major professional organization for speech-language and hearing professionals.

Americans with Disabilities Act (ADA). Major legislation passed in 1990 that guarantees equal rights for individuals with disabilities.

Annual goals. Goals for the year that are developed for each student served in special education and made a part of the student's individualized educational program (IEP).

Anxiety/withdrawal. A form of emotional/behavior disorder where children are very anxious and do not interact with their peers.

At-risk students. Students who are likely to develop learning or behavior problems because of a variety of environmental factors.

Ataxia. A form of cerebral palsy characterized by balance problems.

Athetosis. A form of cerebral palsy characterized by involuntary movements.

Attention deficit/hyperactivity disorder (ADHD). A problem associated with short attention problems and excessive motor movements.

Attention problems—immaturity. A form of behavior problems associated with attention deficits.

Augmentative communication. Methods used to facilitate communication in individuals, including communication boards, computers, and sign language.

Autism. A severe disorder that affects the language and behavior of children, caused by neurological problems.

Basal series. The type of reading programs used in most elementary schools in general education classrooms.

Behavioral approach. An intervention model based on behaviorism that is often used with children with emotional problems.

Behavioral model. An intervention approach for students with serious emotional disturbance that focuses on behaviorism.

Behavior management. Systematic use of behavioral techniques, such as behavior modification, to manage ways of conduct.

Biophysical approach. An intervention approach for students with serious emotional disturbance that includes behaviorism and the use of medication therapy.

Blind. A category of disabilities characterized by severe visual impairment that usually results in an inability to read printed material.

Career education. A curricular model that focuses on the future vocational opportunities for students.

Cerebral palsy. A disorder affecting balance and voluntary muscles that is caused by brain damage.

Child and Adolescent Service System Program (CASSP). A national model to facilitate the collaboration between education and mental health agencies.

Child study committee or team. The group of individuals, including teachers and parents, who develop an individualized education program (IEP) for a child.

Chronic health problem. A physical condition that is persistent and results in school problems for the child.

Classroom climate. The nature of the learning environment, including teacher rules, expectations, discipline standards, and openness of the teacher.

Classroom management. A combination of techniques used by teachers in classrooms to manage the environment, including behavior modification.

Classroom organization. Methods used by teachers to manage the learning environment through physical organization of the classroom, classroom rules, and use of other structure.

Cochlea. The part of the inner ear containing fluid and nerve cells that processes information to the brain.

Cochlear implant. A technological device inserted in the place of the cochlea that enables some individuals to hear sounds.

Cognitive-behavioral intervention. Instructional strategies that use internal control methods, such as self-talk and self-monitoring, in ways that help students learn how to control their own behavior.

Cognitive deficiency. A deficiency in the intelligence processes, including thinking, memory, and problem solving.

Cognitive model. An intervention approach that focuses on teaching students how to deal with their own problems; this includes self-monitoring and the use of mnemonic devices.

Collaboration. The process of interactions between teachers and special education teachers to provide instruction to an inclusive classroom.

Communication board. An augmentative communication device that includes letters or symbols that enables a person to communicate either manually or through computer technology.

Community-based instruction (CBI). A model in which instruction is provided in a community setting where skills that are learned will actually be used.

Conduct disorder. A type of behavior problem that is characterized by negative and hostile behaviors, generally toward authority figures.

Conductive hearing loss. A form of hearing impairment caused by problems with the outer or middle ear that impedes sound traveling to the inner ear.

Consultation. The process where an instructional specialist provides suggestions for other educators to use in their inclusive classrooms.

Contingency contracting. Developing behavioral contracts with students based on their completing specific tasks or behaviors in return for positive reinforcers.

Continuous progress. A form of educational programming that allows students to move through a curriculum at their own pace.

Continuum of services. A model that provides placement and programming options for students with disabilities along a continuum of least-to-most restrictiveness.

Cooperative learning. An instructional and learning process that uses teams of children to teach each other and work together on various learning activities.

Creativity. A form of intelligence characterized by advanced divergent thinking skills and the development of original ideas and responses.

Criterion-referenced tests. Tests that compare a child to a particular mastery level rather than to a normative group.

Curricular infusion. The practice of infusing various enrichment activities into the general curriculum for students who are gifted and talented.

Curriculum. A systematic grouping of content, coursework, extracurricular activities, and materials for students in an educational setting.

Curriculum compacting. An approach used with gifted and talented students where less time is spent on general curriculum activities and more time on enrichment activities.

Curriculum telescoping. An approach used with students who are achieving well academically that enables them to move through a curriculum at a more rapid pace than is typical.

Cystic fibrosis. A health disorder that is characterized by fluid and mucus buildup in the respiratory system, resulting in death.

Deaf. A severe level of hearing impairment that generally results in the inability to use residual sound for communication purposes.

Developmental period. The period of an individual's life from birth to the 18th year when most cognitive development occurs.

Diabetes. A health condition where the pancreas does not produce sufficient levels of insulin to metabolize various substances, including glucose.

Diagnostic and Statistical Manual of Mental Disorders (DSM-IV). The diagnostic manual used by medical and psychological professionals.

Diagnostic tests. Tests and other evaluation methods that are designed to result in a diagnosis of a specific problem.

Differentiated programs. An instructional approach that requires various curricula or programs for different students in the same classroom.

Differential reinforcement of lower rates of behavior (DRL). A model that provides reinforcement for behaviors that are moving the student in the desired direction.

Diplegia. Paralysis of corresponding parts on both sides of the body, commonly affecting the arms.

Direct instruction. A technique where the teacher instructs students on a particular topic.

Disability. A condition that affects a person's functioning ability, either physical, mental, or both.

Disorders in articulation. Language problems that center around word and sound pronunciation.

Distortions. Language problems characterized by altering the correct sound of letters and words.

Dual system of education. The current model in most states that supports one program for students with disabilities and another for those in general education.

Due-process safeguards. Constitutional rights of students with disabilities and their parents related to the provision of an appropriate educational program.

Ecological assessment. Evaluating individuals in the context of their environments and taking into consideration all environmental factors.

Educable mentally retarded (EMR). A term traditionally used to describe students with mental retardation with an intelligence quotient (IQ) in the 50–70 range.

Efficacy studies. Research that investigates the efficacy, or effectiveness, of various programs for individuals with disabilities.

Emotional abuse. A form of child abuse that centers around emotionally abusing a child, such as ridiculing the child in public or always making a child feel like a failure.

Emotional/behavioral disorder. The new term used by many professionals to identify children with emotional and behavioral problems.

Enrichment. A variety of methods that are used to facilitate appropriate education for students classified as gifted and talented enabling students to progress beyond the typical curriculum.

Expressive language. Language that is spoken or written; language that is expressed in some way.

Extinction. The removal of reinforcement from an individual that will result in a particular behavior being terminated.

Facilitated communication. A controversial method of dealing with children with autism in which an individual provides limited resistance to a child's arm, which then uses a communication board to communicate.

Family. A unit of individuals who are related or who are together through legal means, providing support for each other.

Family needs assessment. Evaluation that focuses on the entire family, not just a particular child in the family, to determine the needs of the family as a unit.

Family support. A model to provide services for individuals with disabilities by providing a wide array of supports for families.

Fluency. The smoothness and rapidity in various skills, such as speech, oral language, reading, and other skills associated with thinking.

Form. The rule systems of language that includes phonology, morphology, and syntax.

Full inclusion. The movement or trend to fully include all students with disabilities, regardless of the severity, into all general education programs.

Future-based assessment. An evaluation model that focuses on determining the likely future environments of individuals and proceeds to develop intervention programs around those future environments.

Gifted. A term used to describe students who perform significantly above average in a variety of areas, including academic, social, motor, and leadership.

Gifted and talented (GT). A term frequently used to describe high-achieving students as well as students who excel in other areas, such as the arts.

Hard of hearing. A disability category that refers to individuals who have a hearing loss but who can benefit from their residual hearing abilities.

Hearing-impaired. A disability that affects an individual's sense of hearing. The term includes those with residual hearing (hard of hearing) and those without residual hearing (deaf).

Hemiplegia. Paralysis of one lateral half of the body, commonly manifested in an arm and leg on the same side being impaired.

Homework. A form of individual practice that generally occurs in the home environment after school hours.

Human immunodeficiency virus (HIV). A major fatal disease that is currently impacting all areas of our society, including children in public schools.

Inclusion. The practice of integrating students with disabilities into general education settings, with support services provided in the general classroom by specialists.

Individual family service plan (IFSP). An individualized plan that is required to provide services to infants and toddlers with disabilities and their families.

Individuals with Disabilities Education Act (IDEA). Federal legislation that reauthorizes Public Law 94–142 and requires states and local schools to provide an appropriate educational program for students with disabilities.

Inhalants. A group of drugs and substances that can cause hallucinations and other reactions; examples include fingernail polish, paint thinner, and glue.

Intelligence. The term used to describe the cognitive capacity of an individual.

Intelligence quotient (IQ). A number used to express the apparent relative intelligence of a person determined by a standardized intelligence test.

Intelligence tests. Tests that are designed to determine an individual's intelligence level, which is usually reported as an intelligence quotient (IQ).

Juvenile delinquency. A legal term used to describe youth who have broken the law.

Language. A formal method of communication used by people that uses signs and symbols to represent ideas and thoughts, and the rules that apply to standardize the system.

Language disabilities. Any number of impairments that interfere with an individual's ability to communicate with others, such as voice disorders, expressive language skills, and receptive language abilities.

Learning disabilities (LD). The disability category that is characterized by students not achieving commensurate with their ability levels.

Least restrictive environment (LRE). The placement of disabled students alongside students without disabilities as much as possible.

Leukemia. A form of cancer that attacks the blood cells, frequently found in children.

Levels of support. The supports that are necessary to enable an individual with a disability to function as independently as possible in the community.

Life skills. A curricular orientation that emphasizes teaching abilities that will be required to function as an adult in a community setting.

Logical consequences. Expected repercussions after a particular behavior.

Low vision. Students who have a visual impairment but who also have functional use of some residual vision; these students can read print.

Mainstreaming. The term originally used to describe placing students with disabilities in general education classroom settings.

Mediation. The process of attempting to resolve disputes between parents and school personnel over a child with a disability before the dispute reaches a due-process hearing or court.

Mental age. A measure used in psychological testing that expresses a person's mental attainment in terms of the number of years it takes an average child to reach the same level.

Mental retardation. A disability related to deficiencies in cognitive abilities that occurs before the age of 18 and is associated with deficits in adapted behavior; this classification generally requires the individual to have an IQ score of about 70 or below.

Mild mental retardation. A level of mental retardation that usually includes those with an IQ range of about 50 to 70.

Moderate mental retardation. A level of mental retardation that usually includes those with an IQ range of about 35 to 50.

Motor excess. A level of physical activity that is above expected levels for that age and cultural group.

Multiple intelligences. The theory that there are many different types of intelligences, rather than a single, general factor common in all individuals.

Muscular dystrophy. A progressive disease that is characterized by a weakening of the muscles.

Myelomeningocele. A form of spina bifida where part of the spinal cord is included in the outpouching, which usually results in lower trunk and limb paralysis.

Negative reinforcement. The removal of an unpleasant consequence following a student's behaving or responding in the appropriate manner.

Nondiscriminatory assessment. A method of evaluating students that prevents discrimination on the basis of cultural differences.

Norm-referenced tests. Evaluation procedures that are designed to enable the comparison of a child with a normative sample.

Nuclear family. A reference to the modern family that is somewhat traditional in that there are two parents and children; however, both parents now generally work.

Ophthalmologist. A medical doctor who specializes in the treatment of vision disorders and disorders of the eye.

Optician. A professional whose primary role is to develop visual lenses for corrective purposes.

Optometrist. An individual who specializes in fitting eyeglasses to individuals with vision problems.

Other health impaired (OHI). The federal disability category that includes children with health problems that can result in eligibility for special education and related services.

Paraplegia. Paralysis of the lower half of the body with involvement of both legs.

Parents Anonymous. A support group for parents who have a history of abusing their children.

Pediatric cancer. Any form of cancer that occurs in children.

Peer tutoring. An instructional technique that uses children to teach other children a variety of skills.

Pharmacological intervention. The use of drugs to combat behavior or attention problems.

Phonation. The process of putting speech sounds together to form words and sentences.

Phonology. The rules within a language that are used to govern the formation of words and sentences from sounds.

Physical abuse. The treatment of children in inappropriate physical ways that are illegal and can lead to disabilities and even death.

Physical disabilities. A variety of impairments related to health problems, such as spina bifida, cerebral palsy, and polio.

Perinatal. A period of time that occurs during the birthing process.

Portfolio assessment. A qualitative method of evaluating children that considers their work, in addition to their performance on tests.

Positive reinforcement. Affirmative, pleasant consequences that are given an individual following an appropriate behavior or response.

Postnatal. The period of time after a child is born.

Pragmatics. The relationships among language, perception, and cognition.

Prenatal. Occuring prior to the birth of a child, during the approximately 9 months of gestation.

Prereferral interventions. A series of processes that should be attempted by general education teachers for students who are experiencing problems, prior to referring them for special education services.

Procedural management. The component of classroom management that deals with classroom procedures, such as rules, expectations, and daily routines.

Procedural safeguards. Rights of children with disabilities and their parents regarding the provision of a free, appropriate public education.

Processing problems. The primary problems experienced by students classified as having a learning disability, including thinking, memory, and organization.

Profound mental retardation. The lowest level of functioning in the traditional classification system for individuals with mental retardation, representing an IQ range below 20.

Psychodynamic approach. An intervention model for students with serious emotional disturbance that focuses on psychoanalytical methods.

Psychosocial management. An intervention model for students with serious emotional disturbance that focuses on the psychosocial elements.

Psychotic behavior. Ways of conduct indicative of a serious mental illness, such as schizophrenia.

Public Law 94–142. The key legislation that was passed in 1975 revolutionizing services for children with disabilities in public schools.

Punishment. The application of something that is unpleasant to a child after an inappropriate behavior: the least-desired behavior management method available.

Pure tone audiometry. The method used to evaluate hearing loss and hearning capabilities of individuals.

Quadriplegia. A paralysis that affects both arms and both legs.

Referral process. The process of identifying and referring a child for special education services who might be eligible under IDEA.

Regular Education Initiative (REI). The term used to describe the original movement to place students with disabilities in general education classes all day, every day.

Reinforcement. The process of providing consequences, positive or negative, following a particular behavior or response.

Related services. Facilities required by IDEA that will enable a student with a disability to benefit from special education, such as occupational therapy, physical therapy, and orientation and mobility training.

Reprimand. A statement to a student indicating that a certain behavior(s) is inappropriate.

Resource room. A special education classroom where students go from the general education classroom for brief periods during the day for specific help in problem areas.

Response cost. A behavior management technique where rewards or reinforcers are taken away from students who do not exhibit appropriate behaviors.

Restructuring. The process of making major changes in public school programs, including site-based management and co-teaching activities.

Rigidity. A form of cerebral palsy that results in extreme involuntary muscle contractions.

Self-contained classroom. A special education environment where students are segregated from their nondisabled peers for most or all of the school day.

Self-evaluation. A method that students can use to assess their own behaviors or work.

Self-instruction. Various techniques that students can use to teach themselves materials.

Self-management. A cognitive strategy that helps individuals with attention or behavior problems to manage their own problems.

Self-monitoring. A cognitive strategy where students keep track of and record information about the own behaviors.

Self-paced instruction. A model for serving students who are classified as gifted and talented in which they are able to move through a curriculum at their own pace.

Self-reinforcement. A cognitive strategy where students affirm themselves for appropriate behaviors.

Self-talk. A cognitive strategy where individuals talk themselves through various situations or problem areas.

Semantics. The system within a language that governs content, intent, and meanings of spoken and written language.

Sensorineural loss. A type of hearing loss that affects the nerves leading from the inner ear to the brain.

Severe mental retardation. A level of mental retardation with an IQ range of approximately 20 to 35.

Sibling support groups. Groups developed for the siblings of individuals with disabilities to provide ongoing supports.

Snellen chart. The chart used by schools and others to screen individuals for visual problems.

Social competence. The ability to use social skills properly in appropriate contexts.

Socialized aggression. A form of behavior disorder affecting children whose inappropriate behaviors are acceptable in a group setting.

Social skills. Any number of skills that facilitate an individual's successful participation in a group.

Sociological intervention. An intervention model for children with emotional problems based on working with the entire family.

Spasticity. A form of cerebral palsy when the muscles involuntarily contract.

Specialized instruction. Any educational activity that is not typical and that is generally utilized for children with particular needs.

Speech. The vocal production of language that is the easiest, fastest, and most efficient means of communicating.

Speech disabilities. Any number of disorders affecting an individual's ability to communicate orally.

Spina bifida. A physical disability that results in the spinal column not closing properly, leaving an exposed spinal cord.

Stuttering. A language disorder that results in a person's expressive language being difficult to understand due to breaks and repetitions in speech.

Subject matter acceleration. A system of providing accommodations for students classified as gifted and talented in which the student moves through a particular subject area at an increased rate.

Substance abuse. The practice of using illegal or inappropriate substances, such as alcohol, cocaine, or inhalants.

Substitutions. An expressive language problem characterized by the practice of substituting words or sounds in oral language activities that are not present.

Supported education. The model of teaching used when students with disabilities are included in general education classes, with the supports necessary for them to achieve success.

Suspected child abuse network (SCAN). A formalized network that responds to allegations of child abuse.

Syntax. Various rules of grammar that relate to the endings of words and the order of words in sentences.

Talented. The second component to the category of gifted and talented that includes children who excel in various arts and nonacademic areas.

Team teaching. The utilization of more than one professional or paraprofessional who actually co-teach classes of students or lessons.

Time out. A behavior management technique where the student is isolated from receiving reinforcement.

Trainable mentally retarded (TMR). A term frequently used in schools to identify students with IQ ranges of 30 to 50.

Transition. The process of moving students from one setting to another, such as preschool programs to kindergarten, elementary school to junior high school, and high school to work.

Traumatic brain injury (TBI). A disability category that results from an injury to the brain, causing a student to have significant problems in school.

Tremor. A mild form of cerebral palsy that causes trembling.

Voice disorders. Atypical expressive, oral language affecting pitch, loudness, or quality of sounds.

Whole language. A language arts curricular approach that focuses on teaching language arts as a whole, including written skills, reading, and oral language skills.

Index

Page references followed by *f* or *t* indicate figures or tables, respectively.